THE ORDEAL

OF THE

PRESIDENCY

HERBERT HOOVER

IN THE

WHITE HOUSE

CHARLES RAPPLEYE

SIMON & SCHUSTER

NEW YORK   LONDON   TORONTO   SYDNEY   NEW DELHI

Simon & Schuster
1230 Avenue of the Americas
New York, NY 10020

First Simon & Schuster hardcover edition May 2016

SIMON & SCHUSTER and colophon are
registered trademarks of Simon & Schuster, Inc.

For information about special discounts for bulk purchases,
please contact Simon & Schuster Special Sales at
1-866-506-1949 or business@simonandschuster.com.

The Simon & Schuster Speakers Bureau can bring authors to your live event.
For more information or to book an event contact the Simon & Schuster Speakers
Bureau at 1-866-248-3049 or visit our website at www.simonspeakers.com.

Interior design by Ruth Lee-Mui

Manufactured in the United States of America

10   9   8   7   6   5   4   3   2   1

Library of Congress Cataloging-in-Publication Data

Rappleye, Charles, author.
   Herbert Hoover in the White House: the ordeal of the presidency /
Charles Rappleye.—First Simon & Schuster hardcover edition.
      pages cm
   Includes bibliographical references and index.
   1. Hoover, Herbert, 1874–1964.   2. Presidents—United States—Biography.
3. United States—Politics and government—1929–1933.   I. Title.
   E802.R335   2016
   973.91'6092—dc23
   [B]   2015027333

ISBN 978-1-4516-4867-6
ISBN 978-1-4516-4869-0 (ebook)

This book is dedicated to my son Dexter and my daughter Kelly,
beloved of their father.

CONTENTS

PART III: THE BITTER END

History asks: "Did the man have integrity?"
"Did the man have unselfishness?"
"Did the man have courage?"
"Did the man have consistency?"

And if the individual under the scrutiny of the historical microscope measured up to an affirmative answer to these questions, then history has set him down as great indeed in the pages of all the years to come.

INTRODUCTION

I was a journalist before I became an author, and all my books tend to reflect the journalistic impulse to discovery. That is, I tend to avoid the beaten path, and choose instead subjects who have been overlooked. That is a rare circumstance for a person who reaches so high an office as the presidency of the United States, but that was the case with Herbert Hoover.

That is not because Hoover's presidency was insignificant. He led the country in the teeth of the most dire economic crisis in American history, a trauma that, in cause and result, might well be considered the labor pains attendant to the birth of the modern era. At the same time, all of the civilized world was wrestling with the allure and the dangers presented by the isms of the left and the right—communism, fascism, and every stripe of the spectrum in between. In this titanic struggle, Hoover found the resolve to stay off the shoals and steer by his own lights.

Still Hoover remains very much unknown to most Americans. When he is recalled at all, it is in defeat and in caricature—the clay-footed conservative who preached the old dogmas of laissez-faire while the false idols of capital came crashing down; handmaiden to the elite, scourge of the huddled masses.

Hoover himself must take some responsibility for this thin and misleading depiction, by dint of his stinting approach to public life. He disliked speeches, made few public appearances, and never formed that bond to the American people that has been the foundation for every successful presidency. More than that, Hoover's successor in office was the twentieth century's most important president, Franklin Delano Roosevelt. Inevitably, Hoover was overshadowed, his travails ignored, and his moments of success forgotten. In the version of the story written by the winners, Hoover played the foil, the stooge to the princely Squire of Hyde Park.

Certainly Roosevelt joined in this concerted effort to paint Hoover in the most unflattering tones. In the years after he first trounced Hoover, FDR used him repeatedly as the straw man to knock down again. "Back in 1932" became a campaign refrain; nor did Roosevelt confine his hostility to elections. When Democratic chieftain Bernard Baruch proposed drafting Hoover to help organize domestic production during World War II, Roosevelt dismissed the notion. "I'm not Jesus Christ," the president told Baruch. "I'm not going to raise him from the dead."

And so Hoover remained buried, condemned as a relic of the past by a forward-looking nation. He was a convenient touchstone, a benchmark by which a new generation could measure its politics and its progress, how far they had come and how much they had changed.

But that time, too, has now passed by, or at least arrived at an uncertain maturity. The confidence of the postwar era, the bland acceptance of government intervention and large-scale public spending, has been replaced by ambivalence, with doubts about the efficacy of government and perplexity over mountainous debt. With America and Europe bound together in protracted economic stagnation, the idea of some alternative strategy takes on a new urgency. With so many predictions turned sour, denizens of this modern moment might want to look back.

This book is not an effort to resurrect Hoover as a forgotten hero ready for a new turn in the sun. His was a failed presidency, and not just because of fate, or poor timing. But I do hope in this work to fill in gaps papered over by homilies and assumptions that are now wearing thin. Not all that's been discarded in the headlong rush to the future has been trash; not all that we have acquired along the way has been gold.

The passage of time has wrought another, inevitable effect that makes this book unique, and I hope useful. Until now, every portrait of Hoover has necessarily been colored by the passions and polemics of the era. His biographers were all partisans—committed either to his defense, or, more common, to showing his error, and thus burnishing the reputation and legend of Franklin Roosevelt.

That is not the case here. This is the first portrait of Hoover's presidency to be drawn at a remove, from published documents and oral histories that can be weighed in the scales of time and experience rather than partisan political belief.

Consider, for instance, the question of who started the Depression, and where it began. For those who lived through those difficult years this was a defining issue, freighted with the burden of blame. In the instant, Hoover insisted that the roots lay abroad, that the economic dislocation of the 1930s began with the Great War and the peace settlement struck at Versailles. To the opposition, it was just as obvious that the Depression was homegrown, the product of Republican policies that were implemented in large part by Hoover himself.

Both sides played this game. It seems apparent that Hoover's insistence on locating the onset of the Depression in Europe was at least in part defensive, and it is equally clear that those who blamed the Republicans—who dominated the boom years but were reviled thereafter—sought to score political points.

In the decades since, studies by a generation of economists reached a rough consensus that the Depression was a global phenomenon rooted at Versailles and exacerbated by the efforts of all the Western democracies to resurrect the prewar gold standard. This rendering certainly does not exonerate Hoover—his great error was to fight to the last in defense of gold. But nor does it condemn him the way the New Deal intellectuals would have it. In fact, adherence to the gold standard was one of the few policies to enjoy a real consensus at the time; even those who abandoned gold did so only reluctantly, and only because they saw no way to hold on. Hoover was wrong, but he was not stupid, and he was certainly not the hidebound dullard of popular myth.

Hoover is certainly not obscure. His name pops up frequently, albeit usually as the prototype of a failed president, or leading the pack in a worst-president contest. But the actual Hoover, once hailed as the exemplar of the Progressive era, elected in a landslide, embodiment of the ideal of the nonpolitician elevated to high office—that Hoover has been lost to the modern era.

I knew little of Hoover when I began this project. My previous books dealt with the nation's founding era, and with postwar crime and politics—for me the Great Depression was a blank, memorialized solely in my grandmother's pronouncements about thrift and toil. I began with just one assumption—that there was more to Hoover's story than the historical caricature marked out above.

At first pass I learned the broad outlines of Hoover's official portrait—the well-meaning Quaker overwhelmed by historical circumstance, the economic conservative who stood by as the ship of state foundered. Eminent historians vied for the most eloquent condemnation of his tenure; summarizing the consensus version, Arthur Schlesinger Jr., dean of the New Deal interpreters, wrote that Hoover "was portrayed as the embodiment of the illusions and complacencies of the New Era, a cold, self-righteous president who misconceived the problems of his age and determinedly sacrificed human beings on the altar of dogma." It was a resounding and conclusive verdict.

But as I delved into the books and plumbed contemporary sources to follow the course of his presidency a new Hoover emerged, a character and an executive who contradicts the historical Hoover in two fundamental ways. First, Hoover was not the mild Quaker soul that his friends liked to portray, simply unfortunate to have entered the White House at such an unpropitious moment.

That was a whitewash, the product of the more common arts of hagiography, and of a kind of journalistic decorum no longer practiced today. Hoover was a kindly enough man in person and to his friends, but in the capacity of his office he was surly, easily frustrated, and sometimes vindictive. He regarded enemies and often his friends with suspicion, allowed few to get close to him, and proved inconstant in his alliances. A look inside his White House sanctum found him seething with anger; his advisors counseled that he use fear as a weapon and Hoover embraced it, winning some legislative battles but losing the war for hearts and minds.

The presidency was the first elected office Hoover ever held, and it showed. His status as a political novice served him well in his race against New York governor Al Smith, who was the quintessential politician of the time, a garrulous backslapper who embodied the spirit and the pluck of Gotham's tenements. But in office Hoover's nature betrayed him. Through a curious combination of arrogance and personal pique he managed to turn much of his own party against him, and within a year, well before the Depression had fully revealed itself, Hoover had shown himself to be hapless and inept as president.

When the Depression arrived, then, Hoover was already feuding with Congress and with the press. He retained the nominal powers of his office, but not the sinews of popular and political support. The traditional first-blush honeymoon of his presidential term had already been squandered.

This set the stage for the second principal surprise of my research. That was that, contrary to so much written at the time and after, Hoover made an active and energetic response to the economic tsunami that hit the nation. No other officer in his administration was so quick to recognize the implications for employment when the stock market crashed in October, and none was more creative in fashioning a response.

That is not to say Hoover was right in the particulars of his program. And he was hamstrung in his policies by his distinctly antidemocratic tendencies, his penchant for secrecy, and his fearful, even paranoid view of those who might disagree with him. But Hoover was not the complacent, clueless stooge of the moneyed classes that his critics derided then and for a generation after.

More than that, Hoover was right about some of the most critical questions posed by the historic breakdown in the global economy. The first was the most fundamental—was this crisis a death blow to the whole idea of capitalism? Was the economic system that had raised up Western civilization, and which had reached its fullest flower in America, was that system doomed?

For peoples and nations around the globe the answer was yes. The crisis brought on a wave of revolution, and the advent of socialist and fascist alternatives to liberal capitalist democracy. Many Americans reached the same conclusion, and calls for a new order built around a central economic directorate arose from the left and the right. But in the White House Hoover never wavered, rejecting the idea of a planned economy as inimical to personal liberty and insisting that individual initiative remained the mainspring of economic progress. The passing decades have confirmed Hoover's instinct in the most graphic terms.

Beyond the watershed question of capitalism per se, Hoover made the further judgment that the primary systemic malfunction exposed by the Depression was the collapse of credit. Here again his powers of perception surpassed those of most contemporary observers in or out of government. And while he proved unable to surmount the breakdown brought on by the credit crunch—it is fair to say that, given the scale of the calamity, no single prescription could have overcome it—he did mobilize a creative, even daring institutional response.

That response was creation of the Reconstruction Finance Corporation, a multibillion-dollar agency established to thaw frozen assets and open channels of credit by supporting banks and other private institutions with public funds. It was a step that violated Hoover's closely held proscription against government action in the marketplace, and it engendered stiff opposition in Congress. But Hoover recognized the need and pushed it through.

The RFC stood for decades after as a historical anomaly, a curio from the early days of the Depression, until American policymakers faced a similar crisis in 2008. Then, with the global financial system on the verge of another massive seizure, Presidents George W. Bush and Barack Obama instituted the Troubled Asset Relief Program, a latter-day reprise of Hoover's RFC. Economists and politicians still debate whether TARP was the appropriate policy, but it should at least earn Hoover a reprieve from the early verdict that he failed to grasp the significance of the Depression, or to formulate a response.

There are other aspects of the Hoover presidency that have been lost to American political discourse by his historical eclipse, elements less critical to Hoover's reputation and legacy but still quite relevant to questions of policy and governance. Hoover was, for example, perhaps the greatest pacifist ever to occupy the White House, and his record of amity to the international community, and hostility to the arms industry at home, could stand as a beacon to later generations frustrated with the seemingly inexorable rise and application of American arms.

Similarly, Hoover carved out a subtle and useful thesis on the role of government as a facilitator but not a director in the capitalist system. His guiding principle was "cooperation," a mode that eschewed equally the antagonism of the left and the determined inaction of the right. Hoover was full of contradictions and often obtuse—he built a bureaucratic empire at the Department of Commerce while counseling against big government—but in this case his preachments fostered an ethos of comity that current-day bureaucrats would do well to emulate.

My sense of Hoover's progress from the scene of action to the pages of history does not mean I did not rely on prior works of biography and commentary in preparing this book. I did so freely, as the source notes to this volume will attest. The facts and events remain the same, after all; the difference between this version of Hoover and those that came before lie in matters of emphasis and nuance, not in outright revision.

Still, much of the material presented here is being published for the first time. When I began writing there was just a single volume in print devoted to Hoover's term in the White House, and that a fairly academic summary, rather than the sort of internal and chronological account presented here. This gave me the opportunity to offer a fresh look at a presidency marked by action, conflict, and momentous crisis.

I strove at the same time to fashion a more personal portrait of Hoover than was previously available. Hoover was an intensely private individual—an unfortunate trait in such a public man—and always careful to keep his personal thoughts and feelings out of the public record.

I was fortunate, then, both in recounting Hoover's presidency and exploring his character, to have at my disposal several texts that were either unavailable or largely overlooked in prior Hoover scholarship. They are the diaries kept by several key friends and associates, documents maintained at the Herbert Hoover Presidential Library, in West Branch, Iowa, and in the archives at the Hoover Institution, founded at Stanford in 1919 by Hoover himself.

These extensive diaries include those kept by Hoover's presidential physician, Navy Lieutenant Joel Boone; Hoover press secretary Ted Joslin, whose daily entries enhance the account he gave in his 1934 memoir *Hoover*

Off the Record; Secretary of State Henry L. Stimson, also augmenting a published memoir; the daily diary of Hoover's associate and longtime personal financial manager Edgar Rickard; and the exceptionally detailed journal maintained by James MacLafferty, a former congressman who entered into Hoover's service as a covert liaison with lawmakers and party activists.

I also had the benefit of the personal letters Hoover's wife, the former Lou Henry, wrote to her son Allan. Both Lou and Herbert Hoover agreed that they would keep all personal correspondence out of the public realm, but sometime after the death of his mother Allan Hoover decided it would serve the interest of history to place his correspondence with his mother in the collection at West Branch. Lou's reflections on her husband's feelings and motives provide the most intimate possible insights into her husband's trials in high office.

Together with an extensive historical record, these personal diaries allowed me to portray an embattled chief executive wrestling with some of the greatest challenges ever to confront any American president. It is a story that has remained hidden from view, overshadowed by the natural resentments of a people who suffered through stunning, unprecedented privation, and by the masterful performance of the far more gifted politician who followed Hoover in office.

I endeavor here to restore Hoover to a new generation as a person and as a leader, a man beset by personal contradictions that compromised his tenure in office, but who remained a person of integrity, principle, and even wisdom. He presided over the nation in a time of crisis that may feel all too familiar; in his successes and in his failures, modern readers will find much that resonates today.

PART I

THE
RISE AND FALL
OF HERBERT
HOOVER

ONE

HE DID NOT CHOOSE

Wʜᴇɴ ᴛʜᴇ ɴᴇᴡs ᴄᴀᴍᴇ, sᴛᴀʀᴛʟɪɴɢ, ᴜɴᴇxᴘᴇᴄᴛᴇᴅ, ɪᴛ ꜰᴏᴜɴᴅ Herbert Hoover in his favorite haunt, under the soaring stands of first-growth redwoods that were the distinguishing feature of the Bohemian Grove. Established as an annual frolic hosted by actors and journalists on a hillside north of San Francisco and close by the Russian River, the club had already evolved into a rustic redoubt for the elite; now it suited Hoover's sensibilities, and his self-image.

From hardscrabble beginnings on the Iowa prairie, Hoover had come far, attaining the status of globe-trotting millionaire and, for the past eight years, secretary of commerce, a key member in the cabinet of two successive presidents. A lifelong outdoorsman, Hoover valued the quiet majesty of the deep woods, and maintained his own rural retreat in southern Oregon. But he liked as well the trappings of success that marked his exceptional progress, and the companionship of the powerful and accomplished men—women were not invited—who, like Hoover, made the annual trek north into the woods.

By 1926, Hoover had graduated from esteemed guest at the Bohemian Grove to majordomo of the newest of more than a score of satellite camps tented among the roots of the towering trees. Now, Hoover and two college friends were settled into a collection of small log cabins on Kitchen Hill, close by a clearing filled with plank tables where the men shared their daily communal breakfast. Hoover and his friends named their hideaway the "Cave Man Camp."

It was all about fun and games—Hoover especially enjoyed the martinis, poured from a three-foot shaker, that were the pride of the Halcyon Camp nearby. Yet Hoover shared with the club and its members a paradox that was never far below the surface. The motto of the Bohemian Grove was "Weaving Spiders Come Not Here"—a phrase lifted from Shakespeare to suggest that these sylvan grounds were not the place for the prosaic plots of business and politics. Each year, emphasizing the same theme, the club opened its summer season with an elaborate, ritualized bonfire dubbed the "Cremation of Care." But for Hoover, even more than most of his fellow Bohemians, care was constant, and business was never truly banished.

All this was brought to bear on August 2, 1927, when a courier delivered the seminal telegram. It was telling that the message did not emanate from the man who prompted it—Hoover's boss, Calvin Coolidge—but from the Associated Press, which sought Hoover's reaction. The telegram displayed the staccato brevity of the medium: "President Coolidge issued statement as follows Quote I do not choose to run for president in 1928 Unquote Please telephone or telegraph your views of Presidents statement."

Word of the surprise telegram spread quickly through the camp, and a crowd of men made their way to Hoover's homey cabin to learn what he had to say. The AP cable was followed by hundreds more—so many that the switchboard operator at the Grove had to send out for help. Most of these missives called for Hoover to announce his candidacy for the nation's top office, but Hoover answered with caution. "I regret the suggestion" that the president might stand down, Hoover said in a statement for reporters. In case the implication was unclear, Hoover added: "President Coolidge should be renominated and re-elected."

That same day Hoover sent out a telegram of his own—this one a private communication—instructing a cohort of friends and political backers in New York to "sit tight." There might well be a campaign, but any more now would appear unseemly. There should be no demonstrations of any kind until Coolidge had clarified his cryptic utterance.

This was for show. Hoover wanted to conceal his ambition, from the public but also from President Coolidge, whose real motives remained obscure. But that same night, Hoover made a hasty exit from his summer retreat to conduct a secret, midnight meeting with Ralph Arnold, Hoover's principal political booster in California. They met at the train depot in Santa Rosa, the town closest to the Grove, then quickly retired to a booth in a nearby tavern that offered more privacy. Arnold, a Stanford friend and fellow geologist, had taken the train north on short notice to seek permission to put Hoover's network of home-state political backers into motion; that night, Hoover gave Arnold his blessing. Herbert Hoover's campaign for the presidency got under way that night.

As if to confirm the decision, the next day Hoover ordered his personal secretary to distribute to Hoover intimates around the country a secret code, a cipher that would be employed for sensitive political communications.

Hoover was being surreptitious, but not without reason. Just what did Coolidge mean by "choose," anyway? His statement was less than it seemed, some politicos held, and left the door open for a draft. "I can understand his not choosing to be a candidate," one Republican senator interpreted of Coolidge's utterance, but "I do not see how he can decline if selected." Charles Dawes, Coolidge's vice president, saw the statement as nothing more than a ploy. The president "ardently desired" another term, Dawes said.

Coolidge himself did nothing to dispel the confusion he'd instigated. For the rest of that week, and through the months of political jockeying that followed, journalists, pundits, and kingmakers all took turns pressing the president for clarification. True to his moniker, Silent Cal spurned them all.

Despite the jolt of the Coolidge announcement, Hoover stuck to the schedule of his Western sojourn. His next stop was Palo Alto, which represented as much of a home as the world-traveled Hoover could claim. He'd attended college at Stanford—was a member of its pioneer class, in fact, and later a principal benefactor—and it was there, during his last year at school, he'd met his wife, Lou. Twenty years later, in 1919, returning to the United States from more than a decade abroad, he and Lou raised a house close by the campus. It never became their primary residence—Hoover stayed there only in the summers, and rarely more than weeks at a time—but it served as a touchstone, a home that Lou designed from the ground up, one place they could truly call their own.

Hoover was accompanied on this Western swing by George Akerson, one of several personal aides who were in constant attendance on the man they affectionately referred to as "The Chief." And at Palo Alto he joined with Allan, the younger of two sons he raised with Lou. Allan was then enrolled at Stanford, following in his parents' footsteps.

Together at the Palo Alto house Hoover and Akerson composed careful communications to Hoover's friends and political supporters. Every move should be weighed carefully, they were instructed, but precincts should be quietly sounded, and political prospects assayed. This had all come as something of a shock. Hoover had entertained thoughts of the presidency in the past, but the years of government service had begun to wear on him. Had Coolidge decided to remain in office—and few believed his tenancy in jeopardy, should he run for a second full term—Hoover might well have resigned. Now Coolidge had opened the door, and Hoover's prospects had changed dramatically. He wanted to be prepared, but he did not want to be hasty.

For now, Hoover would stick to his schedule, which called for a visit to another paradisiacal California locale—Catalina, the jewel of the Channel Islands, off the coast near Los Angeles. Technically this was official business, an inspection of facilities maintained by the federal Bureau of Fisheries, a division of the Commerce Department. In truth, he was bound for a weekend of fishing, a passion of his from an early age. Fishing provided Hoover a rare respite in a life crammed with meetings, agendas, deadlines, and obligations, affording moments of solitude for thought and introspection. On this particular occasion, Hoover had much to ponder.

Hoover's base of operations on Catalina Island was the Avalon Tuna Club, thirty years old and already legendary among devotees of the still novel sport of deep-sea fishing with a rod and reel. Hollywood figures like John Barrymore and Cecil B. DeMille frequented the place; more important to Hoover, so did Theodore Roosevelt, the nation's most famous sportsman and the lodestar of Hoover's early political career. Hoover had been fascinated with the strategy and elaborate gear of the fisherman ever since the fateful afternoon in his youth when a kindly old angler found a teenaged Hoover fishing with worms and gave him a handful of used trout flies.

Hoover developed some curious habits for a fisherman; he rarely changed into outdoors gear, preferring his workaday, blue-serge suits and the high, starched shirt collars that were already fading from use even as formal wear. But he fished streams all over the country and in 1926 was elected president of the Izaak Walton League, one of the nation's first conservation organizations, named for the seventeenth-century angler and author. By the summer of 1927 Hoover was a freshwater expert, but he'd yet to snag one of the elusive Pacific sailfish, famous for leaping clear out of the water when fighting off a fisherman's strike.

Accompanied by his son Allan, Hoover trolled off Catalina for two full days. They sighted schools of tuna and swordfish but landed not a single one. Hoover loved the lore of sport fishing and could trade stories for days, but the actual business of fishing he considered a solitary pursuit, to be spent alone and in silence; that would afford him plenty of time to consider his political prospects.

Even more than with most men, to plumb the nature of Hoover's contemplation is an act of sheer speculation. Hoover was an intensely private person, resentful of intrusions on his time and his thoughts, guarded in his communications, and averse to creating diaries or other memoranda that might divulge glimpses of an inner life. But we know the circumstances he faced, and we know something of the way his mind worked.

Hoover was a geologist by training and an engineer by trade, an industrial entrepreneur who made his fortune by exploiting underutilized and sometimes abandoned mining operations. Such enterprises involved deliberation and risk, a process Lou Hoover described in a letter to one of her sons. In considering an electoral contest, Lou wrote, Hoover approached it "just as he takes everything, which means in his own particular engineering way."

Lou went on to explain: for an election or even an appointed post,

Hoover's method was to consider who might be available for the job, and whether he himself was the best fitted for the position. Should the answer be in the affirmative—and for Hoover that was often the case—then "he looked at the possibility of success." It was always a question of probability; there were no certainties, not with "ever so many perfectly indeterminable factors."

But this was just the beginning. Having made the decision to go ahead, "then, characteristically, he began to study all the points in favor of the other party, all against himself. Just as he used to study all the adverse factors in a mine that had to be developed. And always he saw all the possible ones, even the ones that never materialized, so that he could be ready to combat them if he did." Here, on the cusp where decision led to action, was where the darkness would set in. It was "the position he would get in in engineering projects about this time—of being very pessimistic. He sees all the possible advantage that may come to the other side, all the wise steps they could take, all the possible misfortunes that might befall his own cause."

To Lou this was all part of her husband's exceptional mind going through its process, working toward an ultimate resolution. To others, however, it was an element of personality, a distinguishing factor. William Allen White, the Kansas editor, Progressive spokesman, and an early Hoover booster, considered Hoover to be "constitutionally gloomy," possessed of a "perverse acerbity." Another observer remarked that Hoover carried "an unpleasant dourness about him."

Whether intrinsic to Hoover's character or an element of strategy, this phase of dark premonition could be maddening. But those close to him, like Hoover himself, simply had to ride it out. "I should begin to wonder what the prospects were myself," Lou confessed to her two sons, "were I not so accustomed to see this phase come on." Instead, she had learned that this darkness was preamble to a certain clarity. Lou came "to realize that was when he built up all possible protection against these very same possible advantages against him." Thus girded, Hoover would sally forth.

Taking Lou as our guide, we can venture out with Hoover on his fishing cruise off Catalina Island and consider with him the prospects for his ascension to the nation's highest office. The fact was, the November election, more than a year distant, was the easy part of the equation. The Republican Party had dominated American politics for a generation, controlling the White House since before the turn of the century with the sole exception of Woodrow Wilson, who reached the presidency only due to Republican strife, and whose long and tragic decline had left his Democratic Party in disarray. Since Wilson, the GOP had presided over a decade of unprecedented prosperity. Most observers expected a repeat of 1924—a Republican landslide.

The political question of the moment was who would capture the Republican nomination, and here the drama became more intriguing. Calvin Coolidge had emerged as the Republican leader largely by accident—first as a last-minute selection for vice president, and then assuming the top job after Warren Harding died in office. Coolidge had proved a surprisingly able chief executive, staid and sure-footed, a counterpoint to the heyday of America's adolescence—the Jazz Age—over which he presided. But his circumspect conservatism spoke for just one wing of the party, and sidelined the Progressive, Teddy Roosevelt Republicans. Nor had he cultivated anything like an heir; to the end, Coolidge would maintain a warm connection to the American public, but to the pretenders to his office, and particularly to Herbert Hoover, he would remain aloof.

Aside from Coolidge, the party leadership consisted primarily of a pride of senatorial lions, all longtime pols, some of them renowned orators and each of them commanding genuine allegiance in their home districts, but none with a national following. Perhaps the strongest of the Republican hopefuls was Vice President Charles Dawes, earthy and voluble, a true American hybrid businessman-diplomat. Dawes was named America's first budget director in 1921, and in 1925 he won the Nobel Prize for his work to reschedule European payments on the debts left over from the world war. But Dawes was prone to gaffes, and had managed to incur over four years the enduring enmity of his boss, Coolidge. Few accorded him a real shot at the prize.

And then there was Hoover. At fifty-three years of age he was a unique character in American public life, universally known but still a largely private figure—an unknown quantity full of promise and ineffable appeal. Unlike the career politicians that he liked to disparage, Hoover had a story outside the drawing rooms where the party hacks did their business. He'd been orphaned at an early age, worked his way through school, and made his fortune in faraway lands.

In his commercial success Hoover joined the ranks of the self-made businessmen who were the titans of the era—men like Henry Ford and Thomas Edison, masters of technology in a time when factories and mass production were changing the social landscape of America. Massive, elaborate machines, the behemoths traced by the brushes of Diego Rivera and Thomas Hart Benton, were driving bigger, richer, and more powerful business firms; machines and the engineers who made them were creating new jobs for tens of thousands of industrial workers, while displacing tens of thousands more who found their skills suddenly outdated. As a mining engineer and as an administrator, Hoover was a technocrat who allayed the fears of a future suddenly present; as a public figure he could offer a vision grounded in real-world experience.

More than that, Hoover enjoyed unrivaled moral stature at home and the world over, an enduring legacy of his exploits during the cataclysm of the world war. While the other "great men" of his generation were manufacturing munitions or commanding soldiers, Hoover was marshaling humanitarian relief projects, first providing aid to Americans stranded by the outbreak of hostilities, and then collecting foodstuffs for starving masses beggared by the clashing armies. In occupied Belgium, and later across all of Europe, Hoover directed sprawling volunteer agencies that fed literally millions of civilians. Aided by a legion of volunteers who were proud to call him their Chief, Hoover headed off impending famine and directed something akin to an ad hoc Marshall Plan for postwar Europe.

When America finally entered the war in 1917, President Wilson asked Hoover to set aside Belgian Relief and come to Washington to administer the wartime Food Administration. The fighting had devastated European farming operations, and someone had to coordinate U.S. food production with aid to Europe and the Allied armies. Hoover did so with what became his hallmark, a commitment to voluntary action as opposed to coercive enforcement. "Our conception of the problem is that we should assemble the voluntary effort of the people," Hoover declared at the outset. "We propose to mobilize the spirit of self-denial and self-sacrifice in this country."

Over the next twelve months he achieved dramatic results by exhortation under the slogan "Food Will Win the War." In the process, Hoover made himself a household name; every homemaker in the country adopted his regime of Meatless Mondays and Wheatless Wednesdays, and the term "Hooverize" entered the dictionary as a synonym for economizing on food.

His efforts then, and his service with the American mission during the peace talks at Versailles, marked him as an American leader of a different stripe. No less a sage than John Maynard Keynes, who conferred with Hoover during the Versailles caucuses, wrote soon after that, "Mr. Hoover was the only man who emerged from the ordeal of Paris with an enhanced reputation." At home in America, Hoover's wartime accomplishments were renowned as feats of vision, personal drive, and administrative mastery. A writer for *Collier's* dubbed Hoover "the supreme illustration of American character." From his more rarefied seat on the Supreme Court, Justice Louis Brandeis agreed that Hoover was "the biggest figure injected into Washington life by the war."

By the close of the war, Hoover's profile loomed so large that in 1920 he saw his name entered as a candidate in presidential primaries for both parties. It was a heady experience for a man not yet fifty years old, but the "Hoover boom" was clearly premature and easily derailed by party insiders. In the years that followed, rather than cultivate political favors or connections, Hoover had sought renown for diligent and efficient civil service. He had never made an overt bid for elected office or publicly expressed any interest in doing so.

Yet here was Hoover, distinguished as the most active, the most effective, and the highest-profile public official of his time—"Secretary of Everything," the newspapers called him, or, as one Washington wag put it, "Secretary of Commerce and Under Secretary of all the other departments." His bureaucratic claim-jumping grated on his fellow cabinet members, but his activist approach and the apparent success of his policies gave him an exclusive claim—with the possible exception of Andrew Mellon, the wealthy but colorless secretary of the treasury—as author of the unparalleled economic success of the Roaring Twenties.

His reputation as a problem solver only grew during his years at Commerce, and was burnished again in the spring of 1927, when heavy rains drenched the Midwest and the mighty Mississippi breached hundreds of levees. Flooding in six states inundated millions of acres and made hundreds of thousands refugees in their own country. Faced with devastation and prospective famine, President Coolidge granted Hoover emergency powers and dispatched him to the flood zone. For the next three months, operating from a base camp atop the Chickasaw Bluffs outside Memphis or crisscrossing the region in a private rail car, Hoover coordinated the efforts of Red Cross aid workers, National Guardsmen, and thousands of individual volunteers. This jury-rigged relief army, so akin to Hoover's wartime agencies, erected more than 150 refugee camps and laid groundwork for resurrection of the Southern economy, all the while keeping Hoover's name in national headlines. By the time Coolidge announced in August that he might step aside, Hoover backers could choose from several colloquial titles for their champion—"The Great Engineer," "The Great Humanitarian," or now, "The Master of Emergencies."

All of this was to the good. Hoover had a national reputation colored in the storybook hues of humble beginnings and charitable works. But Hoover knew this plunge into politics entailed more than just a campaign for office. With a little luck, and with few genuine rivals in the field, his personal stature might even carry him to the White House. What then? A life far more public than the one he led as a cabinet secretary. Constant press attention, constant scrutiny. It was a prospect that gave Hoover pause. He was, after all, a man whose temper boiled at the slightest affront, who disputed every nuance of interpretation through a medium—the partisan press—that added its own distinct shading to every picture. Even aside from the ordeal of public life, Hoover reviled the horse-trading, the backslapping, and the constant compromises that were intrinsic to the democratic process. "Nothing could be more abhorrent to me in the wide world than to go into politics in any shape or form," Hoover wrote in 1916.

Three years later, having actually ventured into public office as head of the wartime Food Administration under Woodrow Wilson, Hoover remained adamant in his aversion to politics. Answering a suggestion that he toss his hat in the presidential ring, Hoover insisted, "The whole idea fills my soul with complete revulsion." There was little chance he would prevail, Hoover contended, but more than that, he knew himself well enough to know that he was not suited to the job. "I do not . . . have the mental attitude or the politician's manner that is needed," he wrote.

That much was plain to anyone who met him. Hoover was profoundly shy, an inward reticence that found outward expression in eyes averted to the ground, in hands that sought in his pockets for keys or coins to jiggle for distraction, in personal manners that were so halting and so encumbered that he often came off as outright rude. While Hoover was still at Commerce Henry Pringle, an astute historian and chronicler of contemporary Washington, recognized him as "abnormally sensitive, filled with an impassioned pride in his personal integrity, and ever apprehensive that he may be made to appear ridiculous." These themes played out constantly in Hoover's subconscious; when he was confronted by rivals or disparaged in the press, Hoover simply agonized. "Above all," Hoover explained to a friend, "I am too sensitive to political mud."

There was another element that undoubtedly gave Hoover pause, as it would most any levelheaded aspirant to such an august post. Simply put, Hoover was in awe of the office. He made no secret of it; in one 1928 speech Hoover averred that, "The Presidency is more than executive responsibility. It is the inspiring symbol of all that is highest in America's purpose and ideals." Filling that role was a tall order, and there is little doubt that at times—certainly in the years to come but also in his early musings—Hoover wondered if he were up to the task.

This was the downside, the pessimistic phase of Hoover's deliberation. High office promised acclaim and real power, but it would cost him personally, even in the best of times. Hoover's first instinct was to recoil; the price was higher than he was ready to pay.

Still, the kingmakers couldn't ignore Hoover's stature, and the invitations kept coming. In 1920, Louis Wehle, like Hoover a member of Woodrow Wilson's wartime administration, approached Hoover to propose that he run for president as a Democrat on a ticket with the man who would become his nemesis, Franklin Delano Roosevelt. The idea wasn't so outlandish at the time; Hoover and Roosevelt lived in the same Washington neighborhood and traveled in the same social circles. Having posed the question, Wehle waited while Hoover gave it close consideration. There were many reasons for Hoover to hesitate, first among them that the Democrats had little chance for success that year. But when he finally declined, Hoover cited a different concern. He told Wehle, "I don't believe that I want to get into a situation where I have to deal with political bosses."

Yet throughout that same primary season of 1920, Hoover continued to entertain overtures from both political parties, countenanced the formation of Hoover for President clubs in precincts all around the country, and saw his name placed on the ballot in several key states. Hoover always disclaimed interest in these early ventures, but the direction of his inclinations was becoming clear. For all his diffidence, Hoover was drawn inexorably to the public arena.

This raises one more factor that was certainly part of Hoover's deliberation that August weekend off the California coast, though there may be a genuine question whether the prospective candidate even recognized it. That factor was Hoover's personal ambition, a latent but constant and powerful impulse that lay deep in his consciousness. Hoover always couched his public career in terms of sacrifice and service; to seek office for its own sake, he believed, would "imply entry upon a road of self-seeking," and in taking such a step, he felt, "I would not be myself." But the yen for power and place remained. It was obscured by a steely and vigilant sense of personal decorum, but some who knew Hoover considered it among his most salient personal traits.

To Eugene Meyer, a financier who was a friend in Washington and later joined Hoover's administration, "Hoover was always ambitious politically from the beginning." He did not attribute this impression to any specific instance, but he could sense Hoover's hunger for higher office. "You could smell it," Meyer told an interviewer years later. A British diplomat, surveying the political scene in America in 1922, got the same impression, informing his home office that Hoover "has his eyes firmly fixed on the White

House." Four years later, State Department official William R. Castle, later a principal bureaucratic ally of Hoover's, was more judgmental. "He seems to be insanely ambitious for personal power," Castle told a friend.

The longer he stayed in Washington, the longer he toiled in the proximity of the White House, the more the hunger grew. Hoover continued to profess his disdain for politics, but even among close friends, Hoover's desire was becoming apparent. Edgar Rickard, a longtime associate of Hoover's who handled business affairs for him and for Lou, marked the progress of Hoover's political leanings in his personal diary. As early as 1926, Rickard discerned that, "the Chief's ideas have been more and more influenced by political concern than heretofore, which I do not like to record." A year later, he found that Hoover continued his "intense" interest in politics.

Rickard discussed his apprehensions with a mutual friend. "He also senses that the Chief has a tendency to weigh his mode of life and daily activities from a political standpoint," Rickard noted. This was a disappointment to men who believed, as Hoover did himself, that his motives were uniformly altruistic, but Rickard and his friend decided that it came with the territory. "It cannot be avoided," Rickard's friend observed, "if he is to succeed to a higher place." With Coolidge bowing out, that "higher place" was vacant, there for the taking.

While Hoover may have succeeded in concealing his ambition—at least from himself—he cultivated a sense of duty that served in its place. He had already made his fortune, he told close friends; now he sought "some job of public service;" he was ready, he said, to "get into the big game somewhere." The term "service" was key: it was not acclaim Hoover was seeking, just a way to help raise up his fellow Americans.

Hoover's long and trying experience abroad provided him ample material for this internal subterfuge. Returning to America after Versailles, he was convinced that the "miasmic infections" of hate and fear, bred of "the boiling social and economic cauldron of Europe," threatened American progress and independence. "I came to believe," he wrote later, "that through public service I could contribute something to ward off the evils" he'd seen.

At the same time, Hoover's work as an engineer overseas had instilled in him the tenets of the Progressive movement that dominated American politics at the turn of the century. Along with a generation of idealistic reformers, Hoover was convinced that technology and logic, applied on a macro scale, were the only answer to the "great theories spun by dreamers"—social and political theories that could lead to "social and political havoc." Engineers especially, with all their expertise in the discipline of efficiency, were naturally suited to lead a social and economic reformation. Their training, Hoover believed, placed them in "a position of disinterested service." Among his many posts, Hoover accepted in 1919 the presidency of the American Institute of Mining Engineers; that same year he helped launch, and became head of, the new Federated American Engineering Societies. This was more than a simple trade society, Hoover emphasized: it was "created for the sole purpose of public service."

Hoover preached this gospel of progress early in his postwar period, when he found himself beset by magazines seeking stories and speaker programs seeking keynoters. This gave rise, by Hoover's own count, to thirty-one press statements, twenty-eight magazine profiles, forty-nine public addresses, and nine appearances before committees of Congress. Finally, in 1923, Hoover distilled his thinking in a slim volume titled *American Individualism*. Hailed in *The New York Times* as "among the few great formulations of American political theory," the book established Hoover as an intellect to be reckoned with—and as a man on a mission.

All these elements, some clearly defined and others intangible but just as powerful, mingled in Hoover's mind as he considered making a White House bid. Squinting against the afternoon sun, lulled by the rise and fall of the rolling Pacific swells, Hoover turned them over carefully in his mind, searching for pitfalls, weighing the risks. Just what weight he assigned to the different, sometimes competing factors he never spelled out. What is clear is that, after two tedious days on the ocean, Hoover landed no sailfish—that conquest would have to wait—but he'd made up his mind to enter the race.

TWO

A POLITICAL DIPTYCH

Herbert Hoover's conquest of a hostile Republican Party, and the resounding victory he registered in the presidential election, is one of the more remarkable stories in the annals of American politics. It was a function of time and place, a constellation of factors that allowed an avowed outsider to usurp the conventional party organizations at a time when parties were central to the electoral process.

Hoover's triumph was also a function of Hoover himself, his character and his extraordinary trajectory. He was a nettlesome, idiosyncratic loner, peevish, restless, rarely at ease when not wielding a fishing pole. But he was also driven, broadly capable, and supremely confident of his own acumen. He was able to surmount what seemed to be impossible odds largely because he believed he could, and was able to inspire that belief in others.

Thus, upon his return east in the summer of 1927, Hoover was a sort of political diptych—a long-shot outsider, and the front-runner on the inside track. He was an outsider in the sense that he was scorned by the party regulars, who had united behind Coolidge but had failed to coalesce around any of his potential successors. And he was front-runner because, in practical terms, nobody from either party could match Hoover's name recognition or public stature.

This dual profile was especially useful given the particular contours of American politics at the time. The defining political event of the period was Teapot Dome, the oil-field kickback scandal that shattered the Harding administration and may have led to Harding's death in office, of a heart attack, at age fifty-three. When a Senate inquiry and the show trial that followed exposed bribery and a desperate cover-up, the public turned against the stalwarts of both parties. It was only by the most assiduous cultivation of his good-government credentials that Hoover, a prominent member of the Harding cabinet, had managed to avoid the general taint.

Hoover recognized the value of his unique, inside-out political stature and he was determined to maintain it as long as possible. He waged a concerted drive for the nomination and the presidency, but it looked like no campaign anyone had ever seen. He outlined his vision in a conference that August in New York with his friend Ed Rickard. "He will make no move publicly toward securing nomination," Rickard explained in his diary entry that night. "He will not resign from Commerce; he will not have a political manager nor a national committee, nor does he desire any funds raised." It would be a noncampaign, a stealth operation that would upend the conventional political process.

But a campaign nonetheless. Over the next several months Hoover and his aides mobilized a national network of friends and disciples that had been building since Hoover's war relief efforts, former aides and volunteers who were now business and community leaders in their own right. As with Ralph Arnold in California, these Hoover acolytes worked quietly, each developing his own informal organization and helping sustain the claim that Hoover was simply answering the call of a popular movement.

At the same time, Hoover quietly assembled a team of the most sophisticated political operators in the Republican Party, fixers and fundraisers so unsavory that Hoover tried to obscure these connections even in the face of congressional inquiry. Some had been directly involved in Teapot Dome; others were implicated during the campaign for making bribes to secure convention delegates for Hoover. Watching his friend orchestrate these dubious contacts, Edgar Rickard voiced concerns that he dared not even raise with Hoover. "I know that Chief does not want to have them working for him," Rickard mused, "but [he] can hardly help himself."

A third contingent in Hoover's ad hoc organization consisted of aspiring government officials hungry for a more activist administration. Some came from the legislature and others from the bureaucracy; one was a sitting member of the Coolidge cabinet. Prominent among these were two dynamic and enterprising young prosecutors, Mabel Walker Willebrandt and Bill Donovan, deputy attorneys general who were blazing new trails in federal justice administration.

Willebrandt was a character ahead of her time, a prototype of the liberated woman Gloria Steinem would conjure for a later generation. Bold and independent, Willebrandt was just thirty-one years old in 1921 when her appointment to lead Prohibition enforcement at the Department of Justice made her the highest-ranking woman in the federal government. She brought to the job a piercing intellect and a steely zeal—she began each day with an ice-cold bath before she sallied forth to administer justice. During the period of Hoover's presidential run Willebrandt was famous, controversial, and among bootleggers and their corrupt friends in government nationwide widely feared.

Bill Donovan was not so famous as Willebrandt, but he's better known today, legendary as the founding director, under Franklin Roosevelt, of the Office of Strategic Services, forerunner to the CIA. But Donovan was Willebrandt's equal at Justice, a deputy attorney general. And he was a genuine war hero, having collected the Distinguished Service Cross, the Distinguished Service Medal, the Congressional Medal of Honor, a Silver Star, a Purple Heart, and perhaps his most enduring accolade, the nickname "Wild Bill" Donovan, for his exploits as a infantry commander in France.

Hoover and Donovan first collaborated when Donovan took over the antitrust division at Justice. Until then prosecutors stood ready to challenge any instance of collusion between firms which might bear on product prices. Donovan brought a more nuanced approach, encouraging a degree of cooperation between firms—just the sort of policy innovation Hoover was pushing for at Commerce. In effect, Donovan became a cross-agency partner with Hoover. The two had personal ties as well, Donovan having studied law under Harlan Stone, the attorney general under Coolidge and a Hoover ally in the Coolidge cabinet. Hoover sponsored Donovan's membership at the exclusive Cosmos Club in Washington, and attended dinners with Lou at Donovan's Georgetown home, just a mile from the Hoover house on S Street.

Donovan and Willebrandt saw Hoover as a candidate who would transcend the tawdry nature of party and sectional politics; other young strivers in the Hoover camp were simply opportunistic. Principal among these was Walter F. Brown, a Progressive Republican who, like Hoover, backed Theodore Roosevelt when he split the party to launch his Bull Moose campaign for president in 1912. In the years since, Brown learned to play an insider's game, backing Warren Harding for president and becoming the undisputed political boss of Toledo, Ohio.

Early in 1927, even before Coolidge announced his retirement, Hoover brought Brown to Washington as assistant secretary of commerce. It was the most overt political maneuver of the incipient campaign, and the press took notice, labeling Brown "slick, suave, smooth, poker-faced." The maneuver raised hackles in Congress as well. Charles Brand, an Ohio Republican who knew Brown firsthand, lodged a protest in March of 1928. Hoover's department "is now honeycombed with politics," Brand declared from the floor of the House. "We have seen Mr. Hoover come out into Ohio and pick up an ex-political city boss and bring him down here and make him an assistant secretary of commerce, next in position to himself." Brand denounced Hoover for "using money out of the United States Treasury for the purpose of a private political campaign" and called for his resignation; Hoover offered no public response.

Other politicos who enlisted for Hoover included James Good, a former congressman who became one of several campaign managers; Walter Newton, a sitting representative from Minnesota, who drafted and scheduled speakers to appear at Hoover rallies; and Hubert Work, Coolidge's secretary of interior. Work, a former physician and veteran party activist, began working for Hoover in secret and later emerged as the head of the campaign.

While Hoover wrestled to keep a handle on this unwieldy operation, he sought to finesse one of the few genuine obstacles that stood in his path to the

White House. That was his wife, Lou, his helpmate in every endeavor since their marriage in February 1899. Lou had enrolled at Stanford two years after Hoover and pursued the same course of study, but she set aside any thoughts of pursuing her profession as his career took off. When journalist Paul Leach was invited to dinner with the Hoovers in 1928, he asked Lou if she indeed had a degree in geology. "That is correct," Lou replied, "but I have majored in Herbert Hoover since."

That was a more involved task than for most wives, even the most dutiful, for Bert Hoover, as he was known at home and to his friends, was a singularly distracted husband. Like the archetypal absentminded professor, Hoover tended to forget—to pay bills, to answer invitations, even to keep hold of personal belongings. Lou learned to search "coat pockets or books and out-of-the-way places" for receipts and other telltale slips of paper. And when Hoover traveled out, Lou explained to a friend, "he always returns with about a fourth of his impediments missing. Clothing, shoes, toilet articles and above all, books, get simply scattered by the wayside! So the family moral is never to let him be in possession of anything we should mind him losing."

If Lou fussed over Bert Hoover like a mother hen, that should not be taken to indicate a retiring nature, or even a homebody. Tall, lanky, and athletic, with dark brows and striking pale blue eyes, she learned from her father to hunt and fish, and packed a pistol when she and Bert were besieged in China during the Boxer Rebellion. In later years she proved as much an activist as her husband, jumping in when he did to assist American travelers stranded by the outbreak of the world war, and then, after returning with her children to California, raising funds to support Belgian Relief. When Bert was called to Washington, Lou joined him there and took command of their twenty-two-room, three-story mansion on S Street, in the tony Dupont Circle district.

She also made time to pursue a slate of causes, including women's athletics and the Girl Scouts, of which she served as national president from 1922 to 1925. Lou was thoroughly modern but she was no feminist: she wrote checks to support the League of Women Voters in the years after women won the right to vote, but steered clear of the more radical National Women's Party.

For all Lou's varied interests, Bert came to rely on her to provide him a safe and stable oasis in a very busy life. Her task was complicated by her indulgence of their growing boys. The whole family was partial to pets—Bert used to feed his favorite dog, a German shepherd named King Tut, from his breakfast plate—but Allan took it to extremes, collecting cats, birds, turtles, and two white ducks that he trained to sit on the front porch. At one point his menagerie also included two alligators—the gift of a family friend—but before the year was out, the pair was surrendered to the Washington Zoo. Lou had a staff of servants at her command, but she also had the gardens to keep track of, and guests for nearly every meal, and her own charities and causes to pursue.

Lou Hoover considered these various responsibilities part and parcel of her marriage to her increasingly important husband. But she regarded his engagement with electoral politics with some trepidation. Writing to her sons in April 1927, before any concerted campaign got under way, Lou was clearly becoming unsettled at the prospect. "I should like it if the friends who started this talk about the presidency would see it through or drop the subject . . . when we had never wanted it in the first place." Lou was clearly not among those who sensed her husband's larger ambitions. "Daddy had fought it off altogether as long as he had the strength."

By early 1928 the implications of Hoover's gathering momentum were becoming inescapable, even to so reluctant an observer as his wife, Lou. "Affairs are going with uncanny rapidity toward making your Daddy president," Lou Hoover wrote in January. "Even he is perfectly amazed at it, and sometimes says it just does not seem possible that this can all be happening on its own impetus, and practically without any effort on his part."

It's hard to read that last line without wondering at the degree to which Hoover was deceiving Lou—or perhaps even himself. Clearly he was showing one face to his growing team of campaign operatives, and another at home. But that may simply demonstrate the depth of Hoover's allegiance to the idea that he was answering the call of the American people, and not just personal ambition. At any rate, Lou adopted the official doctrine of the campaign. "Daddy himself is just going along running the Department of

Commerce," Lou told her sons. Hoover's own engagement in the campaign, she said, was limited to "listening to accounts of what is being done by his friends, and giving them advice sometimes. Dr. [Hubert] Work is concerning himself most about it, and whole heaps of other friends."

Another letter, undated but apparently written just a week or two later, suggests that Lou was indulging in a little self-deception as well. With her husband now the acknowledged front-runner, Lou was reconciling herself to a change of station. "Politics goes along just as well as can be expected," Lou told her younger son. "Part of the time my inclination is to believe those people who say nothing in this world can stop him now." Here it was Lou's turn to feign indifference. "I am not the least excited about it . . . It really does not worry me at all, the possibility of winning, I mean." This was the sound of Lou whistling in the dark. "I think we can go ahead and live our own lives fairly easily, and that there is no need to be quite as imprisoned in a glass cage as the last few generations have been."

Lou delved further into her efforts to make sense emotionally of developments that would change the life of her family in ways profound and unforeseen. This she made clear in a letter written in the months before the Republican nominating convention. The letter was prompted by a brainstorm, a flash of insight she decided to share with her sons.

"I have just been having a new conception of this game of Daddy's which I think will make it much easier for us to live through," Lou wrote. She said the idea was still taking shape in her mind. "It is simply, that it is a *game* of Daddy's—a game of *Daddy's*."

Lou then described her sense of how the game was being played. "He is not going to be elected because he is the most important man in the country, or the best . . . but because he, and a certain lot of his friends particularly, have learned how to get a certain few delegates. This is all an election amounts to in the end—influencing a few very keynote men, for one or another reason that especially appeals to each—all political reasons, mostly, personally political, that is. 'The people' and the man's qualifications have nothing to do with it."

The election, the advisors, "the people"—those were Bert's business. Lou's concern was how she and her sons should handle life in the shadow of politics. "The most important things will go on just the same," Lou wrote bravely—but she promptly contradicted herself: "a whole lot of very wonderful things we would love to do, we can if this [campaign] fails, but would have to forego doing if it wins." Ultimately, Lou fell back on her abiding faith in her husband and his endeavors. "As I said in starting, I am going to take it all as his game—and help when I can—realizing that whether he wins or loses he will have great vitality left to go on doing many splendid things for years to come, and be happy doing them, and we happy watching and helping."

Hoover's mastery of the political game was put to the test that June at the Republican convention in Kansas City. Hoover did not attend in person, but he sent out a raft of political operatives from what the press was now calling a "well-oiled Hoover machine." They faced off against the party's core leadership—several favorite-son senators hoping to capitalize on a deadlocked convention, and a broader, unfocused group clinging to the hope that Calvin Coolidge might yet "choose" to run after all.

The most critical maneuvers at Kansas City lay in settling the status of several contested delegations from the South. From the time of the Civil War, electoral politics in the old Confederacy had been dominated by the Democrats, who preached white supremacy and barred blacks from the polls. Yet Republicans remained a meaningful presence in the South, largely on the strength of GOP control of the presidency. So long as the head of the party resided in the White House, political functionaries in Washington and in the state party organizations got to dispense thousands of local federal jobs, most in the postal service but also in the Justice Department and a variety of other agencies.

In addition, and crucially, state-level Republican Party organizations selected delegates to the national convention. That meant that every four years Southern delegations accounted for as many as a third of all convention delegates, and their votes could easily decide the presidential nomination. Theodore Roosevelt failed to win the Southern delegations in 1912 and lost the nomination to William Howard Taft; Coolidge cultivated them in 1924 and thwarted better-funded opponents.

But if the local parties were influential, they were themselves divided over race. Some were almost exclusively black, with a few whites mixed in; these came to be known as black-and-tan, "tan" being slang for whites who consorted with blacks. They were opposed by reformers who argued that mixed-race organizations could never mount a meaningful challenge to Democrats in the South. Some of these white activists were genuinely seeking to foster political change while others were plainly racist, but the effect was the same: these "lily-whites" formed their own rival parties, and sent their own slates of delegates to Kansas City.

In the week before the convention opened, then, the officers of the national committee were charged with deciding which delegates would be seated. Here Mabel Walker Willebrandt stepped in to play a critical role for Hoover. Through two days of party caucuses she orchestrated a string of victories—seating twenty-two delegates for Hoover out of twenty-four contested spots. She neatly sidestepped the question of race, choosing whom to support simply on the basis of their allegiance to her candidate. For Mississippi it was the black-and-tans; for Texas it was the lily-whites—both delegations committed to Hoover. It was all part of the "game" Lou Hoover described; Bert's choice of delegates was not guided by race, but by expedience.

These contests over delegates were critical but they were also preliminary. According to the arcane rules of the convention the decisions of the national committee had to be confirmed by the Credentials Committee. Here once again, the Hoover forces proved adroit, and in the afternoon of the convention's official opening day Mabel Willebrandt was elected chairman of that panel. The review of delegate status commenced at three o'clock that afternoon and dragged on until well after midnight, and Willebrandt proved indefatigable and unstoppable. Commanding a two-to-one majority on the fifty-member committee, she won a blanket endorsement of the National Committee votes confirming the Hoover delegates.

Willebrandt delivered these results before the full convention the following morning. Despite just four hours sleep she appeared "as fresh and unruffled and, apparently at least, as unwearied as any of the carefree women in the stage boxes," a *New York Times* correspondent recorded. Dressed in a black two-piece frock with "crisp white collar and cuffs," *Time* magazine judged her to be "shapely, smartly dressed, full of vitality."

Her ten-minute report, and the delegate selections, were approved handily, and with it, Hoover's nomination was all but assured. The only real question was who would stand for vice president; in that day, running mates were selected independently. The laurel went to Charles Curtis, senator from Kansas, one of the favorite sons who announced against Hoover early on. Curtis was a curio in American politics, a Native American, the son of a Kaw Indian who played his heritage for folksy charm but always hewed close to the Republican party line.

When Hoover's nomination was announced on the radio it was after midnight in Washington, but the street in front of the Hoover home was soon jammed with gawkers, and his lawn ringed with a circle of news photographers. The candidate stayed true to form, stepping out on the porch to acknowledge the crowd but declining to make any public statement. When he finally broke his silence weeks later, it was only to declare that he would not speak a word on politics until his official "notification" by the party in August. Further queries were referred to Hubert Work, who informed reporters that this campaign would be "quiet, dignified, instructive, and educational."

Hoover's reticence seemed ill-suited to courting public favor. But at a time when popular culture was awash in fads and bathtub gin, voters appeared attuned to sober leadership, and the press was happy to go along. "Hoover brings character and promise to the Republican ticket," the Cleveland *Plain Dealer* enthused. "He is a new kind of candidate in a day surfeited with old forms and old habits in politics." The editors of the *Idaho Statesman* shared the sense of Hoover as fitted to the times: "Here is a case, if ever there was one, of the presidency seeking the man instead of the man seeking the presidency."

Herbert Hoover finally broke his silence on Saturday, August 11, when he traveled home to Palo Alto to make formal acceptance of his party's nomination. He met his public and embraced his future before a crowd of seventy-five thousand on the sun-splashed turf of the Stanford football stadium. It felt like a pep rally, with daytime fireworks, airplanes swooping between tethered miniature blimps, and half a dozen bands led by John Philip Sousa, then seventy-four years old and at the height of his fame.

Hoover had made hundreds, perhaps thousands of appearances in what was already a long public career, but this would be his first political speech, designed not just to argue a point but to capture votes. He labored over it for weeks, and it gave a fair survey of his thinking and the case he would press over the coming weeks.

It opened with the campaign centerpiece, postwar prosperity. It was a theme Hoover would hammer on, and to which the Democrats could have little response. The Peace of Versailles, Hoover recalled, was followed by a severe depression—"a precipitant nation-wide deflation which in half a year crashed the prices of commodities by nearly one-half. Agriculture was prostrated; land was unsalable; commerce and industry were stagnated; our foreign trade ebbed away; five millions of unemployed walked our streets. . . . Fear of the future haunted every heart."

That was 1921, the year the Republicans were returned to power. What ensued were seven years of growing prosperity, which Hoover reviewed in its minutiae. Lower taxes, with the largest cuts "made in the particular interest of small taxpayers." GNP up 25 percent. Exports up 58 percent. Three million new homes, six million new telephones, seven million radio sets, fourteen million cars. And then the question, a staple for prosperous incumbents ever since: "Every man has a right to ask of us whether the United States is a better place for him, his wife, and his children to live in, because the Republican Party has conducted the government for nearly eight years."

In one passage Hoover didn't mention himself or the race, but turned to a disquisition on "the fundamental correctness of our economic system." In its rapid economic recovery, America had far outdistanced even her allies— and Hoover explained why. It was in "the hardworking character of our people," but it was also in understanding the proper roles of government and business, and in "the stronger growth of associations of workers, farmers, business men, and professional men with a desire to cure their own abuses and a purpose to serve the public interest." Cooperation was key. Cooperation between firms, cooperation among associations, cooperation with government. This was the Progressive ideal, updated, streamlined, and put into action by Hoover at Commerce. The implication was clear: Hoover would bring the gospel of cooperation right into the White House.

The speech was a bit like Hoover himself—deliberate, earnest, thorough. He touched on the key constituencies he sought to connect with: agriculture, "the most urgent economic problem in our nation today," which he addressed at some length; organized labor; and women, whose recent addition to the electorate "means higher political standards." He vowed to defend the tariff—truly a litmus issue for a Republican—as a principal support for American living standards. And he touched on his own record at Commerce. For seven years he had worked to "build up a system of cooperation between government and business," efforts that were "successful beyond any expectation . . . without interference or regulation by the government."

Prohibition warranted a special mention. Hoover offered the conclusive declaration, "I do not favor the repeal of the Eighteenth Amendment," but he added a subtle distinction, setting moral overtones aside and classing the question as one of efficient execution. Prohibition was the law of the land, and as president he would enforce the law with vigor. "Crime and disobedience of law cannot be permitted to break down the Constitution." Anything less would be "nullification"—fighting words for the wets.

There was one topic where Hoover allowed himself to exceed the bounds of expertise, and venture into the hyperbole of a typical stump speech. That was on the question of poverty. Hoover was quite specific: the poverty he had in mind was "the grinding by undernourishment, cold, and ignorance," the kind of destitution he had encountered in the relief work that had made him famous. As a technocrat, as a bureaucrat, as the handyman of the Republican cabinet, Hoover vowed that, "We in America today are nearer to the final triumph over poverty than ever before in the history of any land. The poorhouse is vanishing from among us."

It was, of course, rash to the point of reckless, defying even the Bible's express admonition that the poor will be with us always. And this at a time when, for all the advances Hoover touted in his speech, large sectors of American society had been bypassed by the surge of prosperity, left behind in city tenements, in Appalachian hamlets, in mining camps and sharecropper shacks. Hoover appears to have recognized that his reach was exceeding his grasp, for he promptly added a caveat. "We have not yet reached the goal," he acknowledged, "but given a chance to go forward with the policies of the last eight years, we shall soon with the help of God be in sight of the day when poverty will be banished from this nation." The implications were inescapable, and in the years to come would color Hoover in tones of naïveté and hubris that he never quite deserved.

THREE

FLASHPOINTS, AND A LANDSLIDE

HERBERT HOOVER OPENED HIS 1928 CAMPAIGN FOR PRESIDENT with a late-August visit to his hometown of West Branch, a farming village located west of the Cedar River in southeast Iowa. It was a sentimental destination but it was also strategic, plotted to remind voters that this worldly executive and cosmopolitan bureaucrat had begun life in a humble Quaker village.

That afternoon West Branch was swamped with an estimated fifteen thousand visitors. Most were farmers from Iowa and Illinois; most were attending a presidential rally for the first time. They wandered through town to find the tiny, two-room cottage where Hoover was born, then gathered under a huge white tent to see the candidate deliver his address. It was just the sort of speech one might expect for such an occasion—relatively brief, tailored to a rural audience, and, on personal matters, highly selective.

Hoover recalled for his listeners, and for a national radio audience still learning his story, the first ten years of his life, when he and his siblings cut wood for fuel, fished with bait in Wapsinonoc Creek, and hunted the fields for prairie chickens. Conjuring the spirit of Norman Rockwell, then painting covers for *The Saturday Evening Post*, Hoover said of his childhood, "It is the entry to life which I could wish for every American boy and girl." West Branch was, he remembered, a "Republican village," home to "self-reliant, rugged, God-fearing people of indomitable courage," men and women who had tamed a wild frontier.

It was not the full précis of Hoover's remarkable story arc—orphan boy to wealthy mining engineer, and thence to the highest councils of the government—but it served to soften the edges of a man whose own friends feared that he appeared "too much of a machine." Who could hear the tales of children traipsing through the fields, of icy sledding on a winter morning, of the young Hoover's "wonder at the growing crops," without kindling a sense of amity for a boy who had come so far?

Yet there was so much of the story that Hoover didn't tell—that day or ever after. There was hardly a mention of his parents; there was a single reference to his "Aunt Hannah," and a tip of the hat to Mollie Carran, his teacher in the first grade, but not a word about Hoover's mother, Hulda. Indeed, in a three-volume memoir published toward the end of his life, Hoover refers to his mother only twice. Hulda is recalled as if from some fairy tale—"a sweet-faced woman who for two years kept the little family of four together." Again, just in that phrase, so much unsaid: the "little family of four" being the widow Hulda and her three children; the "two years" (in truth it was three and a half) being the period between the death of Hoover's father and Hulda's own decease.

It's hard to say whether Hoover painted his Iowa childhood in halcyon tones because that's what he actually remembered, or because he considered it a sign of weakness, or somehow wrong, to dwell on the adversity he faced. But there's no question a full accounting of his youth would convey quite a different feel than the stories he liked to share.

Hoover's father, Jesse, was a tradesman, a small-time entrepreneur who ran a blacksmith shop. He was moderately successful, and in 1879 he closed the smithy, opened a farm supply store, and moved his family into a two-story house with a parlor and a new, oil-burning stove. By now there were three children: Thad, then nine years old; "Bertie," aged five; and their sister, Mary, a toddler of three.

Of his early family life Bert Hoover recalled very little. His mother was known for "an unusually fine intelligence and quick wit," and she ran her crowded little household with "stern but kindly discipline." At the same time, Hulda was active in the community, a member of Young People's Christian Association and an officer in the local chapter of the Women's Christian Temperance Union. Privation was always present. Clothes were homespun and hand-dyed; one year, when coffee was just too expensive, Jesse made do with a brew steeped from roasted wheat and sorghum.

Like most people in West Branch, Jesse and Hulda were Quakers. Sundays were spent in the Friends clapboard meetinghouse, where services were observed largely in silence as the members waited for "the spirit" to move them to declamation. This was "strong training in patience," which Bert Hoover recalled years later as "intense repression upon a ten-year-old boy who might not even count his toes."

Life was precarious in those early days on the prairie. Hoover suffered and sweated through all the plagues sent his way: mumps, measles, croup, diphtheria, chicken pox. Nor were the maladies confined to children. In December 1880, just over a year after moving his family to their new abode, Jess Hoover came home with a fever. As his condition grew worse, Hulda sent the children off to stay with an uncle. Late on a cold Monday night she sent a messenger to retrieve them, but it was too late. By the time they arrived home Jesse Hoover was dead. An obituary memorialized his "pleasant, sunshiny disposition," but this was largely lost on young Bert. "My recollection of my father" he wrote later, "is of necessity dim indeed."

Jesse's demise seemed to awaken a venturesome spirit in Hulda. Even before his death she had broken with strict tradition and begun singing hymns in church, persisting even when some Friends walked out of the meeting in protest. Now, following a schism among the local Quakers, Hulda fell in with the "fast" branch of the Friends, who embraced singing and sermons at the services. She proved so gifted a speaker that she was appointed to preach at the Quaker meeting in Springdale, four miles east of West Branch, by consensus of the congregation there. Before long Hulda was traveling as far as Kansas to deliver her sermons.

In the summer of 1881 Hulda farmed out her three children to give her time to travel the preaching circuit. Bert landed with an uncle, Laban Miles, U.S. Indian agent to the Osage tribe, in Oklahoma, for a period of "eight or nine months." Bert boarded with the three Miles children, attended the Indian school, and learned from his new friends to make bows and arrows. The next summer found him living in an earthen dugout as ward of another uncle, a brother of Hulda's who was breaking sod for a new farm in northwest Iowa, three hundred miles from West Branch.

Even when Hulda had the children home with her, life was far more chaotic than before. "I have so much to do all the time," Hulda wrote in the fall of 1883. "I just keep myself ready first for service of my master"—that being God and the church—"then to work at whatever I can do to earn a little to add to our living, and then the care of my little ones." In this accounting, at least, the children came last.

By this time the loss of his father and the disorder surrounding him began to take a toll on Bert's progress in school. After he completed third grade, in June 1883, his teachers decided to have him repeat the year. Hulda's attempts at guidance had little effect. "I have often tried to get Berttie to write," she told her sister later that year, "but he always says he can't write good enough."

That November, with the hard Iowa winter setting in, Hulda wrote her sister again, to express concern for an ailing sibling and to report that, "I never had better health in my life." Three months later, she made a midweek visit to Springdale to prepare for an upcoming meeting. Hardy as ever, Hulda returned to West Branch on foot. She caught cold that night, and for two weeks, despite the ministrations of her neighbors, she steadily declined. On Sunday morning, February 24, diagnosed with typhoid and pneumonia, Hulda Hoover died. Thad, Bert, and Mary were now orphans.

The following year the children were divided, each sent off to live with different relatives, a separation none of them wanted and which they sought for years to remedy. Bert lived for the next eighteen months with yet another uncle, Allan Hoover, on a farm about a mile north of West Branch. He developed a special love for his Aunt Millie, and bragged about her cooking ever after. But in the evenings, in the empty silences of the Iowa prairie, young Bert Hoover missed his mother terribly, and on many nights he cried himself to sleep.

———

Candidate Hoover did not tarry long on this sentimental layover in Iowa. He made a quick side trip to Cedar Rapids to address a conference of agriculture journalists, and then he was back on the train, talking strategy with Bill Donovan on the long run to Washington.

Arriving in the capital, Hoover opened two separate headquarters for his campaign, one in a rented mansion and a second in the Barr Building, a new office tower close by the White House, where Hubert Work set up shop. But after this brief flurry of action Hoover seemed to fade from the scene. For the balance of the race his entire public role consisted of venturing forth every week or two to give a speech—a grand total of five appearances—before heading quickly back to Washington.

Even at headquarters, Hoover continued to play cat-and-mouse with the newspaper correspondents. Instead of formal press conferences, Hoover would make occasional, unscheduled appearances in the "small, uncurtained ground-floor reception room" that was converted into a press office. The room was ringed with desks and typewriters for fifty reporters, all hungry for scraps of news. Once or twice a week, Hoover would drop in unannounced, stride to the center of the room, take a seat, and field questions. As the correspondents chimed in, Hoover's answers were abrupt, curt, and always off the record. Once the queries trailed off Hoover would depart, without signal or salutation, "as suddenly as he came."

Hoover's isolation appeared all the more stark by comparison with his counterpart, Al Smith, the Democratic nominee. A four-term governor of New York, Smith was raised in the immigrant, predominantly Catholic tenements of the East Side and learned his politics from the ward heelers at Tammany Hall. He spoke in the lilting brogue of the streets, his long face split by a toothy smile and crowned with his trademark brown derby.

With Hoover holed up in Washington, Smith spent September and October on the road, making speeches at train stations and auditoriums across the country. To Thomas Stokes, a young reporter covering his first national campaign, the contrast was startling. At the outset he was assigned to cover Smith and had "one of the most enjoyable experiences of my life." The garrulous Smith clearly liked what he was doing—the banter, the daily

press conferences, and the speeches, which were always salted with spur-
of-the-moment amendments that "made it fresh and alive."

Stokes was then transferred to the Hoover campaign. The difference
was immediately apparent. "There was much formality" at the Hoover
headquarters, Stokes observed. The candidate was largely absent, and
staffers eyed the correspondents with suspicion. "The whole prospect was
gloomy and forbidding." This came as a surprise to Stokes, who had attended Hoover's press conferences at Commerce, where the secretary was
"easy, fluent, expressive." Now Stokes saw "the almost physical horror, the
evident recoil, when Herbert Hoover made a public speech. He was a timid
person before a crowd."

Hoover's aversion to the podium was an extraordinary defect in the
makeup of a candidate in an era when oration was the principal weapon
of political combat. But it was there for anyone to see. "There are probably
few such lamentably bad public speakers in the United States as Herbert
Hoover," historian and journalist Henry Pringle pronounced in the cover
story of a national magazine at the height of the campaign. "When hundreds
of people are in front of him, inhibitions seem to rise in his throat and choke
his vocal cords. One hand is kept in his pocket, usually jingling two half-
dollars placed there to ease his nerves. He has not a single gesture."

Ad-lib was simply not in his repertoire; nor eye contact. Hoover's aides
sometimes used a tall lectern to force him to raise his head, but to no avail.
"He reads—his chin down against his shirt front—rapidly and quite without expression," Pringle reported.

These differences in style distinguished Al Smith as a natural politician, and Hoover as an unlikely one, but that was not enough to decide this
contest. America in 1928 was still predominantly rural, and while Smith was
strong in the cities, Hoover assembled an electoral team of field operatives
and proxy speakers that reached into every section of the country. It was a
strategy that won him wide support, but it also generated the only real controversy in the campaign.

The most divisive of Hoover's surrogates was Mabel Walker Willebrandt,
the deputy attorney general who proved so useful in Kansas City. Wille-

brandt always insisted that she did not allow politics to color her endeavors as a prosecutor, but she forced the issue just after the convention in late June when she staged a spectacular booze raid in Al Smith's hometown of New York. Assembling in secret and deploying just after midnight, a strike force of 160 state and federal agents ranged up and down Broadway, padlocking the city's swankiest and most famous nightclubs, driving crowds of patrons into the street and jailing scores of club owners and staff.

The raid took place the day before Smith accepted the Democratic nomination in Dallas. The timing alone was enough for the newspapers. Reporters dubbed Willebrandt "Mad Mabel" and "a modern Portia," and immediately ascribed the raids to campaign politics. To some the obvious goal was to slam Al Smith on his home turf, spotlighting his supposed willingness to ignore the law of the land. To others it was simply an effort to impress Herbert Hoover, whose candidacy Willebrandt had already endorsed. One prominent Democrat complained of Willebrandt "using her office for political effect."

Willebrandt made headlines again in September. This time there was no question of mixing politics with official business; by now Willebrandt was on the stump, rallying the forces of temperance to the Hoover cause. Addressing a convention of Methodist ministers in Springfield, Ohio, the firebrand attorney scored New York as "the center . . . of lawlessness and disregard of the Constitution."

Willebrandt believed that Smith, wet and Catholic, would bring the same sensibility to the White House. "The inevitable result of his leadership would be to increase disregard for law, evasion of responsibility for enforcement, and large avenues of nullification of the Constitution," Willebrandt warned. "No dry Congress could prevent that."

The speech was widely reported and caused an immediate uproar, stoked again two weeks later when Smith made a major speech denouncing a "whispering campaign" to destroy his candidacy. Willebrandt had not actually mentioned Smith's Catholicism, but the religious overtones were easy to assert. "There's separation of church and state for you," Smith protested.

Their public duel now caught fire in the press. The New York *Daily News* led the chorus with an editorial suggesting that Willebrandt be muzzled, but, "no one in authority puts brakes on her ninety-seven horsepower tongue." But she found supporters as well. One New Jersey paper sang her praises in verse:

> *Snarling foes will not unnerve her*
> *As they scorn her from the Dark*
> *May the Grace of God preserve her*
> *Prohibition's Joan of Arc.*

Smith's challenge to Willebrandt sent reporters scurrying back to the Hoover campaign for reaction. They caught up with the candidate at one of his rare press conferences. The exchange went as follows:

Q: Would you dispose of Mrs. Willebrandt in a word or two—her connection with you or the national committee?
A: I don't think I ought to go into that either. I am not managing this campaign.
Q: Mr. Hoover, you said in connection with Mrs. Willebrandt that you are not managing this campaign. Do you mean it is up to Dr. Work?
A: I would rather you would not bring these matters up to me.

Hubert Work met the same questions at a separate news conference. His answers were no more convincing: "She is a sort of free lance, and of course you know she is a Justice Department official. I don't know where she speaks or when she speaks or anything about it."

Hoover and his campaign manager were just as furtive in their pursuit of their most ambitious goal of the 1928 election—to make dramatic gains, and political history, by carrying one or more states in old Dixie.

The principal agent of this stratagem was Horace Mann, a longtime associate of Claudius Huston's from Tennessee. Colonel Mann, as he liked to be called, was a large man with a pleasant voice and an instinctive feel for the racial undertones of Southern politics. He operated largely undercover, working with the lily-white factions in several states and quietly dispensing cash to local chieftains in key districts. He reported occasionally to Huston and occasionally to Work, but always sought to present himself as a power in his own right.

Hubert Work was careful to distance Mann from himself and from the Republican National Committee by having the Tennessee colonel set up his own offices, keep his own books, and spend funds without consulting the party organization. Their cover was blown in late August, however, when party officials opened a Hoover campaign office in Louisiana. Hoover's state manager, aptly named A. O. Cotton, told reporters that he was reporting to Horace Mann, and that he had budgeted $70,000 for the Louisiana campaign. Queried that same day in Washington, Work and other party officials denied any formal connection with Mann; a week later they acknowledged him as the "southern division manager" for the RNC. The connection remained murky, however, and subsequent press accounts called Mann "Hoover's mystery man," or, on one occasion, "Hoover's political viceroy in the South."

Horace Mann's strategy was to exploit Southern fears of Al Smith as a wet, Catholic urbanite and thereby encourage mass defections from the Democratic Party. The trick was to get these crossover voters—"Hoovercrats," they came to be known—to disregard the long alliance between Republicans and black Americans. This Mann attempted by encouraging black Democrats to publicize their support for Smith, and by promoting lily-white Republican leaders, all to convince Southern white voters they might safely vote Republican.

This would appear a patently racist strategy, but ethical judgments were never that simple in the moral fun house of the Deep South. Several black advisors to the Hoover campaign explicitly endorsed the strategy as the best chance to oust the Democrats, even if Southern blacks would have to watch from the sidelines.

The Democrats countered with race-baiting of their own. It was a nasty campaign, underscored by allegations that Mann coordinated his efforts with the Ku Klux Klan. Hoover might have been friendly with blacks, the wizards of the Klan figured, but the wet and Catholic Al Smith presented a bigger threat.

Another Republican operator in the South was Bascom Slemp, a Virginia politico and onetime secretary to Calvin Coolidge. As Hoover was well aware, Slemp had been exposed, just a few years before, for peddling influence and selling public offices, but nobody had more sway than Slemp in Virginia. On July 20 the affiliation was made official when Hubert Work announced he was putting Slemp on the RNC staff as assistant to the chairman.

Most of Slemp's campaign activities took place out of sight, but one particular service he did for Hoover and the party was exposed two years later in hearings before Congress. Slemp, it turned out, acted as a secret conduit between E. C. Jameson, a New York insurance executive, and James Cannon, a bishop with the Methodist Episcopal Church, a veteran of the political wars in Virginia and, in 1928, the nation's most influential defender of Prohibition. Jameson found an immediate affinity with Cannon, and eventually supplied $65,000 to Cannon's operation.

Slight, shrewd, and severe, Cannon was only too happy to repay his sponsors, denouncing Al Smith's Catholic Church as "the mother of ignorance, superstition, intolerance and sin." His base was in Virginia but Cannon's influence reached much further. In early August, for example, he traveled to Florida to address a convention sponsored by the Anti-Saloon League, the Women's Christian Temperance Union, and the Methodist Ministers of Jacksonville. It was the kickoff to a "Dry Democrats" drive that spawned pro-Hoover and anti-Smith clubs across the state. They catered to different constituencies but shared the same goal, and fostered a Republican groundswell.

These were the flashpoints of the 1928 election, but they did not define the contest. For all their differences in demeanor, Hoover and Smith shared the same fundamental outlook. Both considered themselves inheritors of the Progressive movement, both were skeptical of bureaucracy, and both sought to reduce taxes and trim spending. More important, both were friendly toward business and wanted to minimize government intervention in the market. Their only real division was Prohibition, which Hoover endorsed and which Smith heartily opposed.

This policy accord reflected a general sense of satisfaction on the part of the American people. The year 1928 marked the crest of a tide of prosperity that had been rising since 1921, a circumstance for which Hoover and the Republicans claimed much credit. Smith recognized he could not break in upon this policy redoubt, and he didn't try. Instead he emphasized his urban roots and his affinity with working people. Smith was an engaging character, a harbinger of where America was headed, but there was little chance he would win the White House that year.

For his part, Hoover made prosperity his core message. At his few carefully scripted appearances Hoover dwelt at length on the many facets of America's economic success, which he credited to a "progressive economic system" and "vigorous cooperation by the government." To Hoover, cooperation was the key. It was "a new policy in government," which he had introduced at Commerce to foster efficiency and growth, "not by law or regulation, but by purely voluntary action." This modern mode supplanted the strife that characterized the other industrialized economies and helped preserve the unique American values of personal freedom and individual initiative. By standing as an oracle of progress, Hoover kept the focus narrow, and the outcome foreordained.

When the voting commenced the wisdom of this simple approach was quickly confirmed. The first returns arrived from the villages of New Ashford, Massachusetts, and Mount Washington, New Hampshire, where polls had closed early; they reported two to one for Hoover.

That result set the tone for the day. Hoover won in a landslide, collecting 21 million votes to Smith's 15 million, with an electoral college advantage of 444 to 87. Hoover had garnered more votes than any prior president—owing to a larger electorate, but also to a commanding victory. Republicans increased their majorities in both houses of Congress, achieving a margin of over 100 seats in the House and 16 in the Senate. Al Smith had captured many of the great cities previously considered Republican turf— New York, St. Louis, Boston, San Francisco—and made inroads in many more, but there was no question the vote represented a resounding victory for Hoover and his party.

Hoover's most pronounced success came in the South, where he took Virginia, North Carolina, Florida, and Texas, delivering them to the Republican column for the first time since Reconstruction. There were other highlights to his sweeping victory; outside the South, the only states he failed to carry were Massachusetts and Rhode Island. Most remarkably, Hoover carried Al Smith's home state of New York.

The months that followed were marked by quiet confidence in a nation unified behind its brainy, earnest leader. "The whole country was a vast, expectant gallery, its eyes focused on Washington," the journalist Ann O'Hare McCormick observed soon after. "We had summoned a great engineer to solve our problems for us; now we sat back comfortably and confidently to watch the problems being solved." For McCormick the emphasis was not the "problems"—they did not appear especially urgent—so much as the idea that Hoover represented something new, a leader who would elevate science and intellect above crass ideology. "Almost with the air of giving genius its chance, we waited for the performance to begin."

There was no sense of foreboding, no indication of the powerful economic storms that lay just over the horizon. Few from either party would dispute Hoover's assessment, during a campaign statement in September, that "no dangers lie in store." Fewer still recalled the statement of Hoover's campaign manager in September, warning of the dangers that would attend putting the reins of power into Democratic hands.

Hubert Work was discussing the issue of tariff protection, but then shifted to the general state of the economy. The remarkable prosperity of the postwar decade was founded on personal credit, and could be suddenly washed away. "Today a large amount of our people have more at stake than their profits or their jobs," Work told reporters at a Boston news conference. "They owe money on their homes, their radios, their automobiles, their electric washing machine and many other luxuries.

"They have laid wagers on continuing prosperity," Work cautioned. "Let there be a break in the endless chain of prosperity and this whole structure of personal credit will collapse and bury millions beneath it with hardship unprecedented in any former period of depression."

At the time, Work's statement was taken in the spirit it was intended—as a partisan political blast. It was only later, in hindsight, that the Denver physician-turned-politico would look like a soothsayer.

FOUR

"HOOVER THE SILENT"

Herbert Hoover marked his resounding electoral triumph with another disappearing act—he set sail aboard a U.S. Navy dreadnought for a two-month goodwill tour of South America. It was a masterful bit of news management, allowing Hoover to emphasize a new, more pacific foreign policy—as opposed to the Big Stick of Teddy Roosevelt—while evading the queries of the Washington press corps. In that day the interregnum between presidential administrations was six weeks longer than now, and Hoover was loath to endure four months of daily speculation over cabinet appointments. "I should keep entirely out of Washington" until the inauguration, Hoover explained at the time to a friend. "It is partially with this in mind that I have undertaken the South American journey."

The tour was a success, to judge by the great crowds that turned out in Lima and Buenos Aires and Rio de Janeiro. But the time abroad did nothing to ease the burdens that awaited the president-elect. In fact, during Hoover's absence the forces that would soon drive the American economy into crisis were rapidly gathering force.

Heading for Washington directly upon his return, Hoover was dismayed to find that, in the eight weeks since his departure, prices on the New

York Stock Exchange had surged, gaining 25 percent in what analysts were calling the Hoover Boom. Banks and major corporations had committed great sums to support speculators in a rush for fantastic profits. The market was setting records daily for trading volume and volatility. Summing up his reaction in a letter penned ten years later, Hoover recalled, "Immediately [when] I picked up the threads of the American situation, I was appalled at the extent of the boom."

The jump in market values did not arrive overnight. For several years, as the Roaring Twenties crested, Americans of every rank and class had been captivated by the seemingly inexorable rise in stock prices. At first it appeared a simple reflection of robust economic growth, but it soon took on the near magical quality that so reliably signals an overheated speculative market—steadily rising prices that bear little relation to profits, earnings, or any other familiar measure of value. In an era of excess, the rising market emerged as the greatest fad of all. "You could talk about Prohibition, or Hemingway, or air conditioning, or music, or horses," a visiting British journalist observed, "but in the end you had to talk about the stock market, and that was when the conversation became serious."

Alarmed at the huge amounts of cash flowing into the markets, the Federal Reserve early in 1928 raised interest rates in a bid to dampen speculation, at the same time selling government securities to tighten the supply of money. But stock prices kept climbing, as did unemployment, with some business sectors showing persistent weakness. Keeping interest rates high to combat speculation might derail the entire economy. In early August the Fed backed off its tight-money policy and went into a period of virtual inaction. Soon after, with the election of Herbert Hoover, the market took off again.

Hoover was quite out of touch with the state of the economy during his South American sojourn, but he caught up quickly upon his return. His first day back, January 7, he stopped by the White House to brief President Coolidge on his tour. It was just a formality, a gesture of respect from a cabinet secretary who would soon be replacing Coolidge in the executive mansion. But Hoover called again the next day, and this was strictly business; Hoover wanted to talk about the surging market. "I went to Mr. Coolidge and urged that he should ask the Federal Reserve Board to put brakes upon the mis-use of credit for speculative purposes," Hoover explained later.

This request immediately took Coolidge out of his comfort zone. The president did not accept the idea of the executive branch meddling in the affairs of the Federal Reserve. It violated his conception of constitutional limits on the presidency, and his inclination to let the various departments of the government operate without interference. Nor did Coolidge accept the idea that the markets had entered dangerous territory. "He could not believe that anything was really wrong," Hoover recounted.

Hoover agreed in theory with strict limits on the role of the executive. But he had always been a policy activist, and he could not sit by in the face of what he perceived as a dire threat. In this instance he put his reticence aside and, by his later telling of the story, requested "permission" from Coolidge to engage directly on the question. It is not clear what authority Coolidge could confer, or how, but it was enough to satisfy Hoover's scruples, and he promptly contacted key members of the Federal Reserve Board.

According to the account in his memoirs, Hoover made his first approach to Fed chairman Roy Young, a Minnesota banker who had assumed his post just eighteen months before. Hoover said Young shared his concern over excessive speculation in the market. "I conferred several times with him and found him fully alive to the situation," Hoover wrote. "He agreed to use the full powers of the board to strangle the speculative movement."

Another Fed governor Hoover buttonholed during this interval was Adolph Miller. One of the original governors of the system, Miller was the board's only trained economist, a professor at Cornell and then the University of Chicago before his appointment to the Fed in 1914. Argumentative and independent-minded, Miller tended to alienate his fellow governors with lectures on policy. He was also a resident of the Dupont Circle neighborhood in Washington, and a social friend of Hoover's.

For some time Miller had been pressing the board to strike against the market fever by raising interest rates. By January the board majority was swinging around to that view, but now Miller's prescription was beginning to shift. He believed stock prices had reached the point that hiking interest rates would no longer bear much influence on the market plungers. Borrowers pursuing a hot stock were paying 20 percent or more for funds, while "legitimate" borrowers seeking business loans were being driven from the market. Raising rates would only injure business, with no effect on speculation. As Miller put it later, "Control by rate action in a speculative gale of such fury as swept the United States in 1929 is a good deal like spitting against the wind."

Instead of rate hikes, Miller proposed that the board focus more narrowly on the practice of banks extending credit to brokers and stock speculators. He sponsored a policy of "direct pressure," by which the Federal Reserve would admonish member banks not to lend money to finance stock buys. This regimen was simpler in theory than practice—just how regulators were to restrict the use to which borrowed funds would be put was never fully answered—and the policy was immediately controversial on the board.

To some degree, this division over policy reflected the rudimentary state of the Fed. The system was just fourteen years old, and the board was still feeling out its role and its powers. Some of its principal founders felt the board had no role to play in stabilizing the market, that the system's sole charge was to fight inflation. *The Wall Street Journal* championed this strain of orthodoxy when it asserted, "Checking stock speculation is none of the Federal Reserve's business." Moreover, some Fed governors had only vague notions of banking and monetary policy. Selected primarily to satisfy regional interests, the Fed governors included two farmers and two lawyers with limited financial experience. Some critics attribute all the ills of the Depression to the ineptitude and stasis of this group.

But others reject the idea that Fed policy could have altered the great dynamics of price and production that threw the global economy into its epochal stall. Experts still disagree over which policies were appropriate, and what results they might have produced. In any event, in this instance it was the academic economist Miller who pushed for direct pressure, and it was his policy that carried the day.

In theory direct pressure would avoid the blunderbuss quality of across-the-board rate hikes. As such it was a new avenue around a policy conundrum, just the sort of innovation a Progressive like Hoover could embrace.

As Hoover put it in his memoirs, "Governor Young contended that the banks could curb loans for speculation, just by simply refusing to make such loans. I held with the Governor."

This statement is, in fact, incorrect. Young was actually among the board minority opposed to direct pressure, and the record shows he made a point of correcting Hoover's misconception at the time. That Hoover persisted in his error says something of his management style—at Commerce and then as president, he tended to assign a problem to one or another of his subordinates, and then assume that they followed the same policies he would. Hoover may also have been leery, in this rendition, of divulging the full scope of his dealings with Adolph Miller. Writing years later, he exaggerated his contacts with Young, and obscured his contacts with his former neighbor and personal friend.

In any event, on February 4, with the board sharply divided, it voted against raising interest rates and adopted instead the policy of direct pressure. With investors borrowing all the money they could find to finance new stock buys, the Fed put the policy into motion, ordering the reserve banks to restrict lending to "legitimate" purposes. Hoover's inauguration was still a month away, but already he had taken his first steps to grapple with the looming crisis in the economy.

Hoover had been down this path before. In 1925, with the postwar boom well under way, he became concerned with a recent, sharp rise in the amount of loans made by banks to finance stockbroker operations. These so-called brokers' loans had averaged about $1 billion per annum through the first part of the decade; they doubled in 1924 as the speculative impulse began to take hold. In 1925, with brokers' loans approaching $3 billion a year, Hoover decided he ought to do something—anything—to intervene.

Here as later, Hoover raised his concern with Adolph Miller. As Miller recalled it, Hoover burst into Miller's S Street home on a Sunday afternoon in November, bounded up to his second-floor office, and asked in great urgency, "Are you as worried about this speculation as I am?"

The answer was yes. In this instance, Miller had been urging his fellow governors to raise interest rates to dampen the market fever. But as he would

find again in 1928, his was a minority position. The shifts in the financial sector were ambiguous indicators at best, and with recovery proceeding apace,
and no sign of price inflation, the board was content to sit tight. In short,
Miller told Hoover, he'd been stymied, and the board would continue holding rates down.

Undaunted, Hoover turned to another capital ally, Irvine Lenroot, a
senator from Wisconsin and member of the Banking and Currency Committee. Together with Hoover, Lenroot composed a probing letter to D. R.
Crissinger, chairman of the Federal Reserve Board, proposing that speculation in New York could spread to commodity markets across the country,
threatening "the greatest calamities upon our farmers, our workers, and
legitimate business." The letter drew a haughty response from Crissinger,
who dismissed fears of larger impacts from stock speculation. Any damage
from inflated values, Crissinger said, would be limited to the speculators
themselves.

When Hoover and Lenroot responded with a second letter challenging Fed policy, it provoked real heat among the Fed governors. Crissinger
suspected that Lenroot had formed his queries with information from inside
the board; he quickly divined that Adolph Miller had been leaking material
to Hoover, and that Hoover "had egged on" Lenroot. Treasury Secretary
Andrew Mellon, an ex-officio member of the Federal Reserve (a dual status
now barred by statute), shared Crissinger's resentment; he was particularly
annoyed when Hoover approached him personally to criticize board policy.

That was as far as Hoover went, however. He refrained from taking
his critique of the board public, and confined his remarks on speculation to
the Commerce Department's statement on the economic outlook for 1926.
Prospects were bright, Hoover offered, but the financial sector's growing
fascination with Wall Street was ominous. "Over-optimism can only land us
on the shores of over-depression," the commerce secretary warned. "What
we need is an even keel in our financial controls."

Hoover raised his fears again two years later, after the Fed governors
voted in July 1927 to lower interest rates despite robust economic performance. The policy was designed to prop up the principal economies of
Europe, which were struggling to reinstate the prewar gold standard, and

needed help to stem a drain of bullion to America. But monetary ease in a U.S. economy risked channeling funds into an already overheated domestic stock market.

When Hoover learned in August of the decision to lower rates he was incensed. "What Europe needed," he wrote later, "was not credit but disarmament, balancing of budgets, harder work and more production." This time the commerce secretary went to Crissinger directly, but to no better effect. Crissinger dismissed Hoover's fears as "parochial," and promised that the board "would not let the situation get out of hand." Hoover then raised his concern with President Coolidge and Andrew Mellon. Again, nothing; neither felt Hoover's sense of alarm, while Coolidge instructed Hoover in his view that Congress had created the Federal Reserve "entirely independent" of the executive branch, and that he was not inclined to interfere.

Hoover was left to commit his fears to writing. He did so in a memo that he delivered to Crissinger at the Fed. "The safety of continued prosperity will depend on caution and resistance to expansion of credit which will further limit speculation," Hoover wrote. "The real test will be whether we can hold this prosperity together without an era of speculation and extravagance with its inevitable debacle."

In early 1929, destined now for the nation's highest office, Hoover kept secret his meetings and deliberations over the market. He did the same with the more prosaic tasks of his layover in Washington—principally, the vetting and interviews attendant to composing the cabinet of his new administration. He conducted this business from a suite of rooms at the Mayflower, an opulent new hotel off Farragut Square, two blocks north of the White House. There Hoover received a steady stream of visitors, not leaving his rooms even to take lunch at home.

Through it all the president-elect said not a word, to the point where copywriters began taking potshots. "Hoover the Silent," the *New York Evening Post* headlined; the *Times* dubbed him "the best listener Washington has had in a generation," a sobriquet that paid some deference but also implied frustration at Hoover's unbending reserve.

The press was learning only now that as president Hoover would continue in the detached mode he had established during the campaign. But Hoover's drawn-out deliberations over filling his cabinet suggested another feature of his coming term—that his predilection for searching out every potential negative would come to haunt him. Candidates were ruled out for reasons of geography or public profile; for too much fame or for not enough; for reasons that Hoover couldn't or wouldn't name. All the good men were already occupied, Hoover complained, with jobs or family obligations or both. "Hoover is very surprised and not a little grieved," Ed Rickard observed, "to find such difficulty filling his cabinet."

Hoover did not lack executive capacity. At Commerce, and in the relief projects he ran during the war, he was renowned for instinctive leadership and snap decisions. He might agonize over the final outcome, as Lou well recognized, but this lingering hesitation was something new. Close observers felt there was something else at work, some internal voice that stifled the conviction and self-confidence that had marked Hoover for leadership early on. It was as if, having finally attained the high station he sought, he found himself afraid of heights. Formerly sure-footed, he was now tentative.

It may be that Hoover was simply overawed by his new office. Certainly the awe was there. His reverence for the presidency bordered on the "fanatic," one Hoover admirer said later. The writer Eugene Lyons considered Hoover a personal friend, but he could not escape the conclusion that Hoover's performance as president was sometimes compromised. "He found himself muscle-bound by his profound respect for the dignity of that office."

It was natural enough, considering how far Hoover had come. He implied as much back when he landed his party's nomination. Hoover recalled then his beginnings as "a boy from a country village, without inheritance or influential friends," and reflected on "the burdens and responsibilities of the greatest office in the world." Listeners could almost feel him tremble as he summed up the presidency: "No man could think of it except in terms of solemn consecration."

Clarence Dill noted Hoover's transformation, from effective cabinet officer to the guarded and cautious president, up close. Dill was a congressman from Washington state, a Democrat but not especially partisan, who sat first in the House and then in the Senate. He worked with Hoover in crafting a regulatory framework for the new medium of radio, and found the commerce secretary to be flexible and constructive. "He was one of the most affable, agreeable, helpful men in the cabinet," Dill said in 1967 during an oral history interview.

But something changed upon Hoover's election. "It seemed to me that he lost his political charm, if I might call it that," Dill said. "He no longer had that friendly, affable attitude when he became president. He was distant. He had a high respect for the office."

Many Hoover acquaintances remarked on his reticence in the years before he attained the presidency. But in Dill's view, Hoover's reserve became distinctly more pronounced after his election. It was the same transformation that the journalist Thomas Stokes noticed during the campaign, when he remarked on Hoover's formality, and how the "easy" secretary of commerce now appeared "timid."

Dill said he made two early trips to the Hoover White House to discuss legislation, and was surprised on both occasions to find that the president, whom he formerly considered a friend, wouldn't even look at him. "He'd look at the ceiling or he'd look at the floor or he'd look out the window while I was trying to talk to him." Dill found the visits so disturbing that he avoided any further encounters with the president.

Dill never lost his respect for Hoover, and to the end considered him "a great character," one of the standouts he'd met in the course of his career. But the presidency, Dill said, smothered Hoover's better qualities. "I think the office [of president] impressed him so much that he lost much of his effective personality in trying to respect the office," Dill said. "I always felt that Mr. Hoover was so impressed with the office that he couldn't be the free, open man that he was."

After two weeks of nonstop, secret meetings at the Mayflower, Hoover departed the capital again, this time for a fishing vacation in Florida. He traveled in the company of family and staff, and was met in Florida by several close friends, including Edgar Rickard, Judge Harlan Stone, and the journalist Mark Sullivan, a boon friend of ten years' standing who was only too happy to find that his old chum was now president-elect. Hoover's destination was Belle Isle, one of several artificial islands fabricated at the height of Florida's great land boom. The bubble had burst two years before but the islands remained, linked by causeways to the shore, and to Miami Beach.

There Hoover and his entourage took up residence at the estate of J. C. Penney. The retail chain mogul was away in Europe but had left his Italianate limestone villa at Hoover's disposal. A neighbor's home was also vacant, and with outbuildings the entire stretch of waterfront was converted to Hoover's base of operations. He designated a nearby boathouse as the pressroom, chose a stand-alone cottage for his personal office, then retreated inside the Penney mansion.

Hoover said he came to Florida because he needed a break, and the reporters believed it. His face was deeply lined, one writer observed, and he was "obviously in need of a rest." For Hoover that meant fishing, and as soon as his lodgings were settled he departed for Long Key, thirty miles south of Miami. He spent several days trolling the edge of the Gulf Stream with Mark Sullivan.

After a long weekend under a tropical sun Hoover trained back to Miami to resume the business of politics. The first of his visitors was Horace Mann, "chief undercover Hooverizer of the South," as he was termed in *Time* magazine.

Mann was undercover during the election, but no more. While Hoover was out fishing Mann had obtained a suite of rooms at the swank New Fleetwood Hotel in Miami Beach, charged it off to the state Republican organization, and presented himself to reporters as Hoover's "patronage advisor" for the South. The papers went along, tagging Mann "the busiest man in Florida," as he hustled office seekers in and out with promises he would relay their appeals to the president. Hubert Work, never quite so sharp as Mann—or Mann's sponsor, Claudius Huston—had actually played into Mann's scheme. Work was on hand in Miami but not invited on the fishing expedition; uncertain as to his role, he made visits to Mann's suite at the New Fleetwood that were reported in the press, boosting Mann's reputation as a political wheel.

Hoover's advisors took quick notice of Mann's posturing. George Akerson, managing Hoover's affairs in Washington, raised sharp objection in a January 26 telegram addressed "to Chief." Remarking on a spate of news coverage in the "eastern papers," Akerson was alarmed to find Mann portrayed as "in charge of all patronage in the South," and a member of Hoover's circle, even to the exclusion of Hubert Work. Worse, some of the stories had reprised Mann's role in the campaign, his promotion of lily-white Republicans and his unproven but widely suspected affiliation with the Ku Klux Klan, which had branded Al Smith a Romish threat to American values. "This creates a very bad taste," Akerson tersely advised.

Hoover had much the same reaction; he met with Mann the day the Akerson telegram arrived, and immediately afterward Mann publicly repudiated his newspaper title of "patronage dispenser." Soon after, and with little fanfare, Mann announced he had "retired voluntarily from his political activity in behalf of the Republican Party." In fact, as the future would show, Mann was not done with politics, but he was through with Hoover, and Hoover was through with him.

Next in conference was Hubert Work, and this encounter was chilly as well. Hoover had grown increasingly dissatisfied with Work through the course of the campaign, and had several times countermanded the initiatives of his top manager. It probably didn't help that a campaign staffer reported to Hoover sometime in January that Work was itching to sweep the Hoover loyalists out of the offices of the Republican National Committee. He'd had enough, Work was overheard to say, of the "Hoover sun-worshippers."

Just what was discussed was not disclosed. But during the vacation in Miami and in the months that followed, it became clear that while Hubert Work had been instrumental to Hoover's remarkable electoral success, he had lost the allegiance of his star candidate.

While the president-elect busied himself with aides and appointments, the press corps was coming to grips with the idea that Hoover the politician would be quite a different animal from Hoover the avuncular bureaucrat. The candidate's furtive manner during the campaign was just the beginning; now in the interregnum, reporters were actually sequestered, quartered in the boathouse on the J. C. Penney estate. "Hoover we saw only at a distance all during that month we spent in Florida," groused pool reporter

Thomas Stokes. "We caught a glimpse of him occasionally as he rode by in his car. He did not hold a single newspaper conference. We were never inside the house."

The correspondents were effectively corralled, but their growing discontent was finding expression. In mid-January the trade weekly *Editor & Publisher* reported that during his South American tour, Hoover had required reporters to submit their stories for review before sending them back home. His designated examiner was George Barr Baker, a writer who had befriended Hoover in Europe, where he was posted as a naval censor during the war.

Baker acted with restraint during the Hoover tour, amending few stories and spiking none. But the article described an "atmosphere almost of intimidation," and pronounced the reporters on board ship to be "indignant" over their treatment. Even aside from the censorship, the simple fact of the story appearing in print was extraordinary. There was no discounting the fact that the house organ of the Fourth Estate had unleashed a broadside criticizing Hoover even before he took office.

During Hoover's stay in Miami the grumbling increased until it could be heard in Washington. On February 1 Hoover received a telegram from Franklin Fort, a congressman from New Jersey who helped manage the campaign in the East. "There seems to be some growing feeling among the newspapermen of objection to the lack of news they are getting," Fort said. The discontent was exacerbated, he added, by the extraordinary access afforded to Mark Sullivan, which generated "none-too-gracious comment" among his fellow scribes.

Complaints were being noised around Washington, Fort said, and were "beginning to appear" in print. That may have been a reference to the South America censorship story; Fort didn't specify. But *Editor & Publisher* did not back off its critical stance; a week later, Fred Essary, Washington correspondent for the Baltimore *Sun*, found space in *E&P* to muse over the shape of coverage to come. "Observers of Mr. Hoover during and since his campaign are wondering how he will react to criticism, once the criticism begins," he wrote. Already, Essary observed, Hoover had demonstrated his prickly thin skin. "He has proven himself more sensitive to censure, since his nomination, than any man in public life."

Fort, for one, urged Hoover to mend fences. "As many of the men who are at Miami will undoubtedly be in the White House press group, it is important that something be done if possible to smooth them out." Hoover got the same advice from Walter Strong, publisher of the *Chicago Daily News*, and an early Hoover backer. Strong was vacationing in Miami himself when he heard from his Washington correspondent of the professional jealousy that was building over Hoover's close relations with Sullivan and Will Irwin, another of Hoover's small group of intimates in the press corps. Strong decided to take up the matter in person with Hoover.

The meeting took place in Miami. It was a friendly enough encounter, a chat between Hoover, Strong, and Hoover's friend Harlan Stone. Strong made his pitch, warning Hoover that his favoritism could alienate the other reporters covering the White House. Hoover replied "somewhat dourly," Strong recalled later, asserting "that he had always chosen his friends and confidants, and would continue to do so." Judge Stone interjected that Strong had proposed "an idea that was well worth considering," but Hoover gave no ground.

Edgar Rickard was another friend who voiced fears over the restive press corps; in this instance Hoover made clear that the antipathy was mutual. Rickard said a mutual acquaintance, an editor both of them respected, "was very concerned over the attitude of reporters toward Herbert Hoover." Hoover merely shrugged. "In general the majority had been for Smith and were against him," he told Rickard. Smith had "spoiled them," Hoover said.

For all the talks and meetings Hoover conducted in Florida, he returned to Washington in mid-February with his affairs still very much unsettled. He had yet to decide on his cabinet appointments and was struggling to compose his inaugural speech. Hoover had plenty of advice to work with, but the decisions lay with him alone.

Of all the questions crowding in, the status of Bill Donovan remained the most troubling. Charming and charismatic, Donovan had emerged in the campaign as a Hoover confidant; now Hoover was keeping him at arm's length. It was "a mystery," the *Times* pronounced. More than that, it was a reckoning: the time had come for a confrontation, the sort of showdown best conducted in person.

At that moment Donovan was in Santa Fe, dispatched on assignment by President Coolidge. Hoover assigned his aide Larry Richey to call him in, but when the two spoke, Donovan demurred. Donovan had heard that Hoover had already selected another candidate for attorney general, and he "didn't want to come East if it were simply to be a discussion over taking the Governor Generalship of the Philippines." That was not the case, Richey insisted, and so Donovan boarded a Friday night train.

Arriving in Washington on Monday, a week before the inauguration, Donovan went straight to the Hoover home on S Street. "I have two things I want to talk to you about," Hoover began, but it soon became apparent there was only one subject on his mind: he wanted Donovan for the Philippines after all. Hoover made his pitch, which Donovan later recorded in his diary: the islands were of strategic importance, the post was tough to fill, and Donovan was the right man for the job.

Donovan's response was immediate and emphatic: "It is impossible," he said simply. More to the point, Donovan reminded Hoover that he had told him, "here in this room, that you wanted me in your cabinet and you needed me there." Hoover responded with a halfhearted offer of secretary of war. Donovan said he would accept the post "if you want me to do it," but when Hoover equivocated Donovan cut the meeting short. He would head back to Santa Fe that night.

Not just yet, Hoover said. First he wanted Donovan to meet with some of his political allies, presumably to give them a chance to sway him. Donovan reluctantly agreed. He first consulted Mark Sullivan, who advised Donovan to look to the future, and the natural path that led from the Philippines to the vice presidency, and finally to the White House. It was the same course pursued by William Howard Taft just a few years previously, but Donovan dismissed the scenario as "contemptible."

Justice Harlan Stone then stopped by Donovan's home to commiserate. When Stone offered a desultory defense of Hoover's position, Donovan was blunt. "Et tu, Brute?" he asked his former professor. "You can't leave public life," Stone answered. He then offered a partial explanation for Hoover's decision not to place Donovan at Justice, adding there were some considerations that arose from Hoover's "peculiar reticence." And what were those? Stone declined to say.

That was all Donovan cared to know. Of Hoover, Donovan told Stone, "I expected nothing of him but honesty, and that I have not received." Later, in his diary, Donovan said the encounter with Stone left him feeling "sick."

There was one more act in this lugubrious leave-taking. Stone pressed Donovan to accept still another audience with Hoover, and Donovan couldn't resist. Back he went to S Street, where he explained again that he considered the Philippines job to be beneath him. Hoover was intransigent—that was the job he needed filled—and the attorney generalship was out of the question.

In his fulminations over Donovan, Hoover had developed many reasons for rejecting him. He outlined them in an internal memo; perhaps the most telling entry was Hoover's emphatic reference to press support for Donovan, which Hoover attributed to the lawyer's "vast capacity for intrigue, which resulted in starting of opposition press campaigns."

There is little evidence to suppose Donovan had engaged in "vast" intrigues; it's hard to escape the impression that Hoover was rationalizing a decision that rested on grounds he was reluctant to name. The crux was the overarching political question of Prohibition, a point Lou Hoover made clear in her remark regarding Donovan that she jotted down two years later: "Daddy said he simply could not have him there, as he was so extremely wet, and the Attorney General had to be sincerely Dry," Lou wrote to one of her sons.

Donovan saw things differently, of course, and he told Hoover so at their last encounter. Hoover was making a mistake, Donovan said, in pandering to the dry activists like Bishop Cannon and in spurning the services of a devoted acolyte like himself. Hoover's honeymoon with America would end soon enough, Donovan warned, "and you will need someone to stay here who can pull the sword for you." His answer to Donovan was brusque. "I don't think so, Bill," and with that Donovan was gone.

Hoover had his own premonitions of difficulties that might lay ahead, but losing Donovan's counsel was not among them. Rather, Hoover was fending off doubts about himself.

He shared his misgivings with journalist and author Willis Abbot. The two were settled near the shore one evening toward the end of Hoover's Florida vacation, seated by an open fire. Breaking a moment's silence, Hoover offered, "I have no dread of the ordinary workings of the presidency." He paused to gaze out over Biscayne Bay. "What I do fear is the result of the exaggerated idea the people have conceived of me. They have a conviction that I am a sort of superman, that no problem is beyond my capacity." Hoover didn't ponder whence this idea arose, but he readily recognized the risk it posed. "If some unprecedented calamity should come upon the nation . . . I would be sacrificed to the unreasoning disappointment of a people who expected too much."

FIVE

BRIGHT WITH HOPE

THE 4TH OF MARCH BROKE COOL AND GRAY, CASTING A PALL over the festivities planned for the inauguration of the nation's thirty-first president. Hoover had said repeatedly that he wanted a sober and dignified ceremony—"An inauguration as simple as any in the history of the country." The gloomy weather seemed to fit the bill.

Hoover began the day as usual, rising early at his S Street home and sharing breakfast with Lou, Herbert Jr., and two grandchildren. Judge Harlan Stone stopped by for a neighborly chat, and then Hoover prepared for his accession. Kosta Boris, a Serbian butler who entered Hoover's service during the war, helped him into formal morning clothes, including Hoover's trademark high collar and a silk top hat. For her part, Lou chose a plum velvet outfit and one of the close-fitting, helmet-shaped caps that were the current style.

George Moses, the Senate's president pro-tem, arrived just after 10 a.m. to escort the Hoover family to the White House. They gathered in the Blue Room, the ceremonial center of the executive mansion, with Vice President–elect Charles Curtis and a handful of wives and dignitaries. Grace Coolidge did her best to stall while the outgoing president tarried upstairs. She and

Calvin had spent three months packing their belongings—many of them gifts from five years' residence—into 150 boxes for transport to the duplex in Northampton, Massachusetts, that the Coolidges called home. It now appeared the president who did not choose to stay couldn't bring himself to leave.

When Coolidge finally joined the official party he was curt, as usual. "Time to go," the president chirped, and off they set for the Capitol, Hoover and Coolidge riding in an open car, preceded by a cavalry escort and followed, in a second car, by Lou and Grace. As per tradition, the vice president was to be sworn in inside the Senate chamber, with the main event to be held immediately afterward on the reviewing stand outside.

Hoover and Coolidge had never been close, but considering the prosperous, peaceful, and intra-party circumstance of this transition, the principals looked curiously glum. Neither Coolidge nor Hoover exchanged a word through the entire ninety minutes from the White House to the swearing-in. Newsreels show them stoic, eyes fixed in the distance. Hiram Johnson, the irascible senator from California, observed the proceeding at close hand and with a distinct sense of disdain. "I would have given much to be able to sketch their countenances," Johnson wrote in a letter home. "Every lineament was sour and disgruntled, and no human expression once illuminated those stony faces."

Not everyone was caught up in the gravitas of the ceremony. Lou Hoover and Grace Coolidge wandered off, touring the Capitol galleries and discussing White House responsibilities until they lost track of time. The first ladies missed the Curtis swearing-in altogether and their husbands were growing annoyed. When the principals were called to the outdoor stage, Hoover waited five more minutes and then sent George Akerson to search for them. It was only when Grace heard the first notes of "Hail to the Chief," signaling the beginning of the oathtaking, that she grabbed Lou by the arm and "made a break" for the platform. All were relieved when they arrived, eight minutes behind schedule, just as the cloudy skies commenced a steady drizzling rain.

Coolidge and Hoover stepped to a rostrum already occupied by Chief Justice William Howard Taft. Costumed in a jurist's robe, a silken skullcap, and his luxuriant walrus mustache, Taft brought an oriental accent to administration of the oath he himself had sworn to twenty years before. Just as the moment passed, Coolidge surprised everyone by turning to Hoover, grasping his hand, and baring a warm smile, as if it was only now that he could finally let go of the burden that was so quickly settling on Hoover's shoulders. The unscripted gesture sparked a ripple of applause that grew as it spread and broke what had been up to that point a somber mood.

As if beckoned by the ovation the misting drizzle gave way to a downpour. Umbrellas sprouted and the throng fell into silence as Hoover delivered his address in strong, slightly metallic tones, his cadence flat and even. Rain spattered his face and soaked his clothes but Hoover did not falter.

He opened by reprising his winning campaign theme of Progress, commending America as "a new civilization great in its own attainments," and praising Coolidge for "wise guidance in this great period of recovery." That was how Hoover saw it—the whole decade had been a project of recuperation from the Great War.

Hoover then sounded a new theme, a call for strict observance in the face of widespread disregard for Prohibition. He called for sweeping changes in federal law enforcement in order to restore "rigid and speedy justice." More than complain, Hoover laid out a plan for a blue-ribbon commission that would review "the whole structure of our national system of jurisprudence." This emphasis on law and order was the sort of scare speech one might expect in the heat of a campaign, not the statement of a grateful magistrate to the people who had chosen him. But Hoover underscored the point when, after taking his oath, he opened his Bible to Proverbs 29:18: "Where there is no vision, the people perish; but he that keepeth the law, happy is he." There had been just about enough high living, Hoover seemed to be saying, and with his election the party was over.

But this was the only sour note to Hoover's address. Even he, for all his gloomy predilections, could find little to darken the prospect before him. "Ours is a land rich in resources," Hoover said in closing, "blessed with comfort and opportunity." He had a weakness for soaring platitudes, and he deployed one here. "I have no fears for the future of our country," Hoover pronounced in the driving rain. "It is bright with hope."

As Hoover closed he turned and shook hands with Coolidge. This time it was good-bye, Coolidge heading with Grace for Union Station and the train that would take them back to New England and life as ordinary citizens; Hoover heading a few blocks west, to the White House.

The festivities resumed there, with a buffet lunch for two thousand, the White House staff getting a thorough workout from their new masters. A glassed-in reviewing stand had been erected just north of the White House for viewing the inaugural parade, and after lunch Bert and Lou took their stations. They watched for just over two hours—Hoover's prescribed time limit—as military aircraft, including a dirigible and four blimps, wafted in and out of view in the clouds overhead. With the pelting rain the whole affair felt a bit bedraggled, but the participants marched gamely, bands from half the states of the Union and soldiers from every service, men and horses drenched to the skin. There was a full complement of "real cowboys" from Texas, a contingent of Indians in full war paint, and twenty aged Confederate veterans from Mississippi, replete with the Stars and Bars, a sop to Hoover's new friends in the South.

With the parade over the Hoovers walked up to the grand, colonnaded entrance at 1600 Pennsylvania Avenue. Another reception was already under way, a tea for fifteen hundred, to be followed by a dinner for Hoover's extended family—his brother, sister, and children, as well as Lou's sister, were all in town—and a few close friends.

Charles Curtis relieved Hoover of one further duty—that of presiding at the charity ball. Curtis, a widower, would be accompanied by his half sister, Dolly Gann, to whom he accorded all the privileges of a vice president's wife.

Even before the ceremonies were over, Hoover slipped upstairs for a quick survey of what would be his new home. He promptly selected for his study the office suite that Abraham Lincoln had used for his workplace and cabinet meetings. And he immediately began giving orders—a globe, a large clock, and built-in bookcases all had to go. It was the beginning of a period of constant, even compulsive household management, as the Hoovers set about making the executive mansion their own.

Lou took the lead the next morning, sending some furniture to the attic, pulling other pieces down, repurposing rooms, and expressing her sense of style with potted ferns and palms, and in one airy parlor, rattan furniture. It was customary, of course, for new residents to put their own stamp on the White House. But to staff members like Chief Usher Irwin "Ike" Hoover, whose initial task in the mansion was to install its first electric lights in 1861, the Hoovers—Ike's namesake but no relation—took matters entirely too far. "The Hoovers came in and upset the whole private part of the house," Ike Hoover groused in a diary published as a posthumous memoir. "Never was the place so changed up, so torn up, so twisted around."

The Hoovers had a different version of the transition. Upon arrival they found the furnishings to be dreary, and the upstairs living quarters in particular to be "as bleak as a New England barn." Change was imperative, they decided, to introduce "a more livable feeling." It was a reasonable enough proposition. And the Hoovers had a long history of converting strange new domiciles into households—what today would be called "nesting."

But there was something else at work, something in their determination to see every whim realized, that appeared to reflect more than a delicate taste in furnishings. Walls went up, walls came down. Furniture was moved, removed, recalled. Within three months of moving in, "there was not a room on the second floor that had not been completely altered," Ike Hoover observed, "and not one that was finished."

This appeared to be a pattern with the new president, a concern with detail that seemed to signal a yen for control, a compulsion to demonstrate his mastery. It was not enough, for example, that Hoover commissioned the largest building in Washington to house the burgeoning bureaucracy at the Department of Commerce; when he found the roof tiled green, in conformance with the other government buildings nearby, he ordered the tiles painted red. There was no particular reason to do it; Hoover did so, it would seem, just because he could.

More functional, at least, were the changes Hoover ordered to the staff offices, both in the White House and in the adjoining executive office. The basement of the mansion, used for a century for storage, was fitted out for clerical staff and the White House switchboard operators. Upstairs, a new lobby was installed.

But the biggest changes came in the West Wing, where carpenters crammed new offices for Hoover and his several secretaries. The idea of more than one secretary was an innovation in itself; up through Coolidge, no president had more than a solitary personal assistant to handle his affairs.

This was simply inadequate for Hoover. He arrived not as a politician, concerned solely with matters of policy, but as a seasoned administrator accustomed to leading a team of subordinates. The offices and staff he found at the White House were "inadequate to his methods of working," as Hoover put it to Ed Rickard, and so they would change. Instead of the sole secretary, Hoover would have four—Larry Richey, Hoover's personal gumshoe; George Akerson to handle the press; Walter Newton, only recently resigned from the House, as liaison with Congress; and French Strother, former editor at *World's Work*, who would serve as a combined literary and research assistant.

There was no explicit title for the White House chief of staff as there is today, but Richey exercised those powers. He was "the big boss," one staffer recalled. From a personal office next door to Hoover's, he maintained strict control over all personal access to the president. Akerson would do the greetings and the introductions, but only after Richey gave the green light.

Richey effected the same firm grip on the rest of the staff. "We were all scared to death of him," recalled Ruth Durno, a White House secretary. "He was very strict, and he had control of personnel." Durno's anxiety was job-related, not personal. "I liked Mr. Richey very much," she said later in the same interview. Others found him harder to accommodate. The windows of his office had Venetian blinds and he always kept them drawn, adding an air of mystery to his imperious manner. "Mr. Richey could be rather difficult at times to maneuver," said Alonzo Fields, a White House butler. "He could be very unfriendly."

This crew of aides was just a shade of the bustling bureaucracy that would characterize the executive branch just a decade hence, but Hoover was breaking the mold and the press naturally took notice. Correspondents dubbed Hoover's executive team "The Secretariat," or, more biting, "The Vestal Virgins"; they observed, only half in jest, that the plurality of aides only made it harder to get through to the president. Another sign of the times, and of Hoover's new, all-business approach to the job: Hoover was the first president ever to equip his desk with a telephone.

Hoover was asserting himself and exercising command, but he quickly felt overwhelmed by the routine conventions of the chief executive. In his first two days in office he was inundated with callers—glad-handers, petitioners, old friends, and official visitors, all seeking as much time as the protocols and Hoover's secretaries would allow.

By the time Hoover got to his desk, at 9 a.m. on his first full day as president, he found the anterooms near his office crowded with hundreds of visitors waiting patiently to see him. An hour later, the line reached out the door and into the street, where the hopefuls persevered despite steady rain. Around noon, a "cowboy band from Texas" launched into a half-hour set, rewarded when the president stepped out to have his picture taken with the lead vocalist. By the end of the day Hoover had received and greeted more than 2,800 people.

On the second day the throng had diminished, but still they came. Party leaders from Ohio and Tennessee stopped in to tout favorite sons; Texas, where all things were done bigger, sent two delegations, one Republican and the other Democratic. For someone of Hoover's retiring nature, the constant greetings soon became an ordeal.

By the end of the week Hoover had developed his own distinctive hand-shake. "The new Chief Executive extends his hand well forward so that those he greets are held at quite a distance," according to a news report. "And he has substituted a quick, full grasp for the sort of half-catch of the hand that he employed during his campaign."

The experience earned Hoover a new appreciation for one piece of friendly advice he'd received from his predecessor: "You have to stand every day three or four hours of visitors," confided the prickly Coolidge. "Nine-tenths of them want something they ought not to have. If you keep dead still they will run down in three or four minutes. If you even cough or smile they will start up again." This strategem likely served in some circumstances, but upon Hoover's first grappling with his public duties it did not suffice.

Besides the constant distraction from the more practical business of the presidency, the stream of visitors soon took a physical toll. "It was a tax-ing procedure," noted Joel Boone, the White House physician. To Hoover's great relief, his new doctor advised against the practice, and within a few weeks the custom of a public, noonday reception, instituted under Coolidge, was dropped. The White House remained the people's house, however, and in conformance with tradition the first floor was opened daily, from 10 a.m. to 2 p.m., to anyone who might stroll in.

Joel Boone, a Navy physician decorated for heroism in the world war, shared a moment of crisis with Hoover in San Francisco in 1923 when both attended the stricken President Warren Harding in his final hours. They resumed their acquaintance when Boone was assigned to join Hoover aboard ship on his South American tour. This led to one of the distinctive features of the Hoover presidency—the Medicine Ball Cabinet.

It began during the goodwill cruise, when Boone rolled out a leather medicine ball, about the size of a basketball but weighing more than a dozen pounds, and proposed a game akin to volleyball that would allow spirited exercise on the confined spaces of a ship's deck. Later, at the White House, Boone insisted that Hoover needed a "regular form of adequate exercise," but Hoover demurred. He hated the calisthenics routines he'd done intermittently, usually on long trips aboard trains or ships. "I would be bored to death," Hoover declared. What about a team game, Boone asked. What about medicine ball? The president seized on it, and on his third day in office composed a list of the men he'd like to join him. They included six members of his new cabinet, Hoover's journalist friend Mark Sullivan, and Judge Harlan Stone. Larry Richey was not named on the list but was a charter member, along with Boone.

The group commenced meeting daily, at 7 a.m., regardless of the weather, on the lawn southwest of the White House. Lou Hoover helped make the players comfortable, laying out a flagstone-floored bower under a magnolia tree for coffee service and orange juice after the half-hour contest. Exercise was the primary object—former college footballer Harlan Stone actually knocked some of his opponents to the ground with his heaves—but there was more to it than that. For all his prickly and often abrupt demeanor, the new president wanted—needed, some would say—constant companionship. "Mr. Hoover is a man peculiarly dependent on his friends," Stone wrote in a letter describing the new fitness regimen. "I think the gathering of them every morning and the exercise do him good."

William Hard, one of that small group of journalists who was, like Mark Sullivan, a personal friend of the president's, explored the riddle of Hoover's social dependency in a magazine profile. "The President has a very great reputation for loving solitude," Hard averred, grounded in "emotional dispatches . . . written about his delight in going off into the deep woods and being by himself."

"The fact is that when he goes into the deep woods he goes virtually always with companions," Hard wrote. "The fact is that if he completes the work on his desk he will summon almost any friend rather than be alone for any great length of time. The fact is that if he finds himself facing an empty evening he will almost invariably fill it up with visitors summoned abruptly by telephone"—unless Lou Hoover had guests lined up already.

Hard said a friend of Hoover's summed up this particular riddle of the new president's emotional makeup in a phrase: Hoover was "a gregarious hermit." To this formulation, Hard posed his own: "The president is a lonely soul who just hates to be alone." Either way, his friends agreed—Hoover was not the autonomous loner he sometimes appeared, but a secluded spirit; sensitive, vulnerable, unable at times to articulate his needs, even to himself.

The morning games were just the first of the many daily group events that crowded Hoover's schedule from the first days of his White House tenure. After medicine ball came breakfast, then lunch, then a tea service—sometimes as many as three a day—and then dinner, always with invited guests. Lou was a partner in all this sociability—the teas were largely her affairs—and she directed the preparations and comings and goings like a field marshal.

"Mrs. Hoover held regular cabinet meetings before and after each large social affair at the White House," Ike Hoover recalled. This was not the presidential cabinet, of course, but a reference to the staff of more than fifty servants that ran the executive mansion.

It was natural that the head of state would entertain, and the White House has long been the setting for balls, performances, and state dinners. Still, the Hoovers were exceptional. "They never sat down alone," said Lillian Parks, a longtime White House maid. As the weeks wore on and the events accumulated, Lou dispensed with the business of reception lines and individual greetings; now visitors were herded through in groups. Ike Hoover never did warm to the Hoovers, but one can sympathize with his disdain for the constant parade of visitors. Speaking to a journalist at the time, the gossipy head usher said he was agog at the number of visitors entertained in the first six months—by his count, more than fifteen hundred for breakfast, lunch, and dinner.

Some of these occasions were informal; at breakfast Hoover, like Coolidge before him, liked to share his eggs and ham with one or more dogs, whom he sometimes fed with his fork from his own plate. But the dinners especially were always done in full, with Hoover in a tuxedo and Lou an evening gown. The evening meal featured as many as seven courses, with the staff trained to move with precision, Lou giving signals by hand so as not to interrupt conversation.

Not only were these formal affairs so frequent as to be numbingly rote, they were sometimes strange, a consequence of the curious deportment of the host. Simply put, Herbert Hoover had what can only be called atrocious table manners—or, it appears, none at all. He ate voraciously, and rapidly, commencing as soon as a plate was laid in front of him. And since White House protocol called for the president to be served first, that often meant Hoover had cleared his plate before his guests had even been served.

"He ate faster than anyone I ever saw," Bascom Timmons, a journalist and biographer, said in an interview for an oral history. "He would have his food eaten before I hardly started." Timmons's interviewer, Ray Henle, also a former journalist, agreed, terming Hoover "a flash at the plate." The physician Joel Boone put it clinically. "He did not masticate his food as he should—he would eat too hurriedly." Boone said he advised Hoover to change his diet, and told him "to try to relax." "He would complete his meal long before the other guests had completed," Boone recorded; "in fact, at times he was pretty near completed before all, if there were a number of guests, had been served."

Boone noted that Hoover was oblivious to his singular approach at the table. "He was unaware that he was hasty," Boone wrote. "I knew it was not an act, a procedure of discourtesy, but rather a nervous compulsion."

The physician did not speculate as to the source of such a "compulsion," but Hoover's childhood is a likely candidate. He grew up as an orphan, after all, sometimes in impoverished circumstances, and often in company of strangers. That he would develop an impulsive urgency at the table is not especially surprising; that he would carry this deportment, unvarnished, into the White House, has to be regarded as remarkable.

Somehow Hoover had gone through his adult life without anyone checking this behavior; certainly now that he was president nobody did. But it made for some awkward moments, with the sometimes tongue-tied and often brusque president glowering over an empty plate at a table full of munching guests. "He is a fast and voracious eater," according to one critical account, who "consumes his food with his eyes on his plate." If a conversation broke out, Hoover would offer a comment or two and then "lapse into a seemingly sullen and somber state."

It was all a reflection of Hoover's conflicted soul, his professed desire for solitude and his need to be surrounded by friends, his yen for human contact and his painful shyness. "Hoover dreaded eating alone," noted one contemporary biographer. Hoover never acknowledged his neediness, of course; he acted the curmudgeon, who tolerated the intrusion of friends and guests only grudgingly. But those close to him, like Harlan Stone, recognized Hoover's "peculiar dependence." Lou, in particular, understood Hoover's need and catered to it. "He always wants to have people around him," she explained to one of his advisors. "The more he has, the happier he is."

Once his guests were arrayed around him, however, Lou was vigilant. "She protected the president," said butler Alonzo Fields. "She would even protect him at the dinner table from conversations." Sitting close by her husband, she would keep an ear cocked to catch any discussion that threatened to discomfit him. "In a flash, she would change that conversation to get away from what they might be driving at to get the president into something that he wouldn't care to talk about. . . . Mrs. Hoover protected her husband at all times."

These were intrinsically domestic arrangements, as the White House staff got acquainted with the new boss, and Hoover with them, and with his new and in so many ways unique role as president—"the instrument by which national conscience is livened," as Hoover himself termed it. At the same time, and on a more public stage, Hoover set about the business of running the country.

Hoover announced his cabinet on March 5, his first full day in office, by sending his slate to the Senate for confirmation. For all his labors, his final selections comprised a distinctly mediocre group. What united them, if anything, was lack of stature; none were likely to vie with Hoover for leadership or limelight. Some appointments were purely political, as with James Good, one of Hoover's campaign managers, a former congressman with no military background who was named secretary of war. Walter Brown, the Ohio politico and campaign operator who spent a brief tenure at Commerce, was named to the patronage-rich Post Office. Two selections were holdovers from the Coolidge cabinet—Andrew Mellon at Treasury, and Labor Secretary Jim Davis. Perhaps the best of the lot was Ray Lyman Wilbur, a close friend of Hoover's, who left his post as president of Stanford to join the administration as secretary of the interior.

Reaction to the cabinet roster was buffered by good feeling for the new president, but tepid nonetheless. "The Cabinet is obviously not one of All the Talents," *The New York Times* observed delicately, adding, "there has been a good deal of puzzlement" over his choices. Hoover's decision to pass over the popular William Donovan drew the sharpest reaction—anger among Donovan's many friends, and a more generalized sense of surprise that Hoover would bow to Prohibitionist partisans.

The decision seemed especially puzzling when it was learned that Robert Lamont, the new secretary of commerce, was a director of the Association Against the Prohibition Amendment. Lamont promptly quit that post, telling reporters he was "playing the game with this administration." As usual, Hoover offered no public explanation for his decision on Donovan.

Hoover created a stir in Congress as well when he asserted that the holdovers from Coolidge should not have to face confirmation a second time. This was clearly a bid to protect Mellon, who had won numerous critics over eight years in office—populists suspicious of his fortune, principally, and Prohibitionists frustrated with his lackadaisical enforcement efforts. Just why Hoover wanted to keep Mellon on is nearly as mysterious as his rejection of Bill Donovan. At seventy-three years old, Mellon was expected to retire of his own volition, and in their years in the cabinet together, the treasury secretary had never developed much affinity for Hoover. It may be that Hoover simply couldn't settle on a replacement.

But in asserting executive privilege, by declining to present either Mellon or Labor Secretary Davis for confirmation, Hoover managed at once to magnify the resentment against Mellon, and to redirect some of that umbrage toward himself. While some in the Senate talked of impeaching Mellon, the question of holdover appointments was sent to the Judiciary Committee. The episode soon blew over—Mellon's critics were eager but outnumbered—but the fact remained that Hoover's first official contact with the Senate had been contentious.

Hoover did better when, that same, first day in office, he met with the Washington press corps. Addressing more than two hundred correspondents at a noon gathering in the White House, Hoover proposed dramatic changes in protocol that would promote "a more intimate relationship" between the president, the press, and ultimately the public.

This was partly Hoover's response to the resentment among reporters at the silence he'd maintained since his election, but it was also typical of his general approach to the job. His new administration was to be a breath of fresh air in Washington.

Formal White House news conferences were first introduced by William Taft in 1909, an equalitarian response to the personal favoritism by which Teddy Roosevelt had successfully manipulated the press. Subsequently each president developed his own system for managing news. Coolidge, for example, in his early years employed the device of the "White House spokesman," a screen by which his statements would be attributed to the institution, but not to the president himself. By the end of his tenure, however, no statements were being issued, and the press despaired of getting any news at all.

Hoover would change that, he said, by allowing direct quotation. As a demonstration, he invited reporters to quote his statement on the new press policy. It was a startling change of pace. "I am anxious to clear up the twilight zone," Hoover offered, "between authoritative and quotable material on the one hand, and such material as I am able to give from time to time for purely background purposes on the other." This won unvarnished praise from *Editor & Publisher*, which saluted Hoover's "courageous and noble stand."

There were devils, however, in the details. With that preamble Hoover asked the correspondents to form a committee that would consult with him to develop explicit rules. Its first meeting took place that very night, but the results were mixed. Yes, Hoover could be quoted directly, but only from written statements handed out by press aides. Remarks at press conferences might be quoted, but could be attributed only to a "high White House authority," a proviso that smacked of a return of Coolidge's "White House spokesman." A third category, the "purely background" material Hoover had mentioned, was not to be attributed whatsoever.

The lines between these categories soon blurred, and the official handouts routinely failed to address the written questions submitted by reporters. Presidential statements appeared only rarely, and before long reporters resumed their resentment at Hoover's systematic silence.

Hoover's dealings with the press were colored by his nagging preoccupation with dignity and decorum; "They have no respect for the office I hold," Hoover thundered at one point.

But if Hoover held the presidency in august regard, the rest of official Washington looked on the executive mansion and its new occupant with a detached irreverence. Jocund banter has always been part of the lexicon of the capital; whether it stung, and how deeply, depended upon the character of its target.

The first great guffaws directed at the Hoover White House were not for the president, in fact, but derived from a kink in the lines of official protocol that centered on Vice President Charles Curtis. Or, more particularly, on his half sister, Dolly. Curtis was a widower who resided in Washington with his sister and her husband, attorney Edward Everett Gann. Dolly Gann worked in her brother's office when he first arrived in Washington; after Charlie's wife died, in 1924, Dolly became his regular social companion. Taller than her brother—and wider, with her weight estimated at over two hundred pounds—the "statuesque" Dolly accompanied him to his vice presidential inauguration, and Curtis then pronounced Dolly his "official hostess." Dolly was to be the Second Lady, as it were.

This lofty status stirred unrest in the parlors of Washington society. It was not so much a particular objection to Dolly, as to the implications of her elevation for the status of other official wives. Secretary of State Frank Kellogg, for example, in one of his last acts in office, ruled that the wives of foreign diplomats would take seating precedence over Dolly, drawing a letter of protest from Curtis, and throwing the unseemly muddle into the lap of Kellogg's replacement, Henry Stimson.

President Hoover kept his silence, but the press corps had great fun with what they quickly termed "a social war." When Stimson, likewise, announced the State Department had nothing to say on the question, *l'affaire* Dolly Gann only festered.

The next installment of this petty imbroglio came in May, when Eugene Meyer, a financier and power broker in Washington, and his wife, Agnes, threw a large dinner. Those invited included the vice president, several foreign diplomats, and Nicholas Longworth, speaker of the House. By rule—unless the rules were changed—Longworth's wife, Alice Longworth, daughter of President Theodore Roosevelt and the closest thing at the time to American royalty, would be the ranking woman at the party. But Agnes Meyer let slip to Alice that Dolly would be given precedence. Whereupon the Longworths and Vice President Curtis *both* declined to attend. Here was an impasse that "made fashionable Washington gasp."

SIX

THE WALL STREET FRANKENSTEIN

T WO DAYS AFTER HIS INAUGURATION, ON MARCH 6, PRESIDENT Hoover met with officers of the Federal Reserve to discuss the unnerving condition of the New York Stock Exchange. This wasn't to signal any particular bent or emphasis on economic policy for the new administration; it was simply that the warning bells from Wall Street were becoming too loud to ignore.

Stocks had been unsettled for weeks as the markets responded nervously—and erratically—to the Federal Reserve policy of direct pressure. Announcement of that policy happened to coincide with a second market shock, a sharp hike in interest rates by the Bank of England, and in mid-February American markets were swept by waves of selling and "heavy liquidations," with brokers complaining of the Fed's "outrageous interference" in the market. Early March saw what the press termed "violent buying," as brokers reversed course, celebrating the renewal of the "Hoover Bull Market."

It is not just in hindsight that these panicked shifts in the market presaged a full-blown crash. Paul Warburg, one of the architects of the Federal Reserve System, voiced the fears of many insiders when he denounced "orgies of speculation" that had floated stock prices far beyond any measure of intrinsic worth. Speaking March 6, the same day Hoover met with the officers of the Fed, Warburg warned that unless the gambling on stocks was throttled back, "the ultimate collapse is certain not only to affect the speculators themselves, but also to bring about a general depression involving the entire country."

This should not be taken as the clarion call that ought to have reversed the course of history. There were many such warnings, as is often the case when markets get out of balance, but there were also confident pronouncements of optimism, and stock prices soared again after Warburg's jeremiad. The fact is, then as ever, uncertainty was the dominant feature of the market. Even for policymakers who shared Warburg's fears—President Hoover among them—any drastic response threatened to bring on just the sort of destructive breakdown that Warburg feared so much. Moreover, in March as in January, Hoover's financial advisors remained divided and uncertain over how best to calm the speculative frenzy.

Hoover raised his concerns again on March 12, at the second meeting of his cabinet. But he got no direction from this newly assembled panel, nor, in particular, from his treasury secretary, the principal federal officer for economic policy. "He thinks something should be done to curb speculation," Andrew Mellon noted dryly in his diary entry that day. When Hoover posed the question, all heads in the room turned to Mellon, but he demurred in his whispery voice. "Everything possible has been done," Mellon said.

This was true only by a very narrow interpretation of the phrase "everything possible." In fact, as Hoover knew, the governors of the Fed could have raised interest rates, which was the first of the standard anti-inflationary measures available. Another option was to commence open market operations, a device that in many cases proved even more effective in managing the nation's money supply. Under this strategy, the Fed seeks to adjust the amount of money outstanding by directing reserve banks to buy or sell large quantities of government securities—sales of securities draw money into the banks' vaults, while purchases inject funds into circulation and expand the money supply.

Both these options ran into the same problem, however. Expanding the

currency available would only encourage the market plungers, while raising rates or restricting the money supply would punish business and could
bring on recession. Thus, following their initial consultations with Hoover
in January, the Fed had adopted a third course—Adolph Miller's policy of
direct pressure.

Mellon was uncomfortable with any of these alternatives. Retiring, reed-
thin, physically the antithesis of the industrial titan, Mellon was hailed in his
day as "the greatest Treasury Secretary since Alexander Hamilton." But as
Hoover would discover later in quite explicit terms, Mellon was a liquida-
tionist, leader of a conservative faction among policymakers who subscribed
to the theory that the best way to respond to inflationary speculation was to
do nothing. By this thinking, the proper response to a cycle of speculation
was to keep hands off, allowing the bubble to rise until it burst, and then
watch the inflated values burn out through "liquidation"—the closure of
unprofitable operations and conversion of the remaining assets to cash. It
would be painful, but to support overvalued assets with easy money would
only make the inevitable reckoning worse.

Hoover rejected this approach as a hoary artifact of laissez-faire
economic policy. Much had changed since Mellon had come of age—
establishment of the Federal Reserve; full-blown revolutions in production,
management, and social science; a world war. To Hoover, these developments called for new and more sophisticated economic policies; to let the
market simply crash, and then sort through the wreckage, was simply unac-
ceptable. He was convinced, as he put it later, that "we should use the powers
of the government to cushion the situation."

The division over policy was not limited to Hoover and his new cabinet. The
vote to invoke direct pressure was taken over "a formidable opposition," as
Miller recorded later, prompting "acute differences over the leadership of
the Federal Reserve System."

The board implemented its new policy in careful steps. First, a letter
was sent to the reserve banks decrying "the excessive amount of the country's
credit absorbed in speculative security loans," and warning members of their
"grave responsibility" to avoid loans that would support the runaway mar-

ket. A week later, the board released its letter to reporters, making public for the first time that it would wage a concerted campaign against speculation. The stock market broke sharply on the news, but recovered in less than a week.

At the same time, directors at several Federal Reserve Banks notified the board they would refuse to implement the order. This defiance tested the entire apparatus of the Federal Reserve System. At its inception, the architects of the Fed were determined to avoid the single central bank that was the centerpiece of most European financial systems. Instead they fashioned a hybrid featuring autonomous Federal Reserve Banks in twelve districts across the country, and a Board of Governors in Washington. The banks exercised policy through the rates they set on loans they offered private banks within their districts. In turn, the board could recommend policy to the twelve reserve banks, but its only real authority was the right to veto rate hikes. The system was decentralized to avoid reposing too much power in a single agency, but the result was an ongoing contest for control between the board and the regional banks.

Now the regional banks were putting up resistance. The key actor here was George Leslie Harrison, director of the Federal Reserve Bank of New York. Schooled at Harvard, a former staff counsel to the Fed Board in Washington, Harrison learned his banking from Benjamin Strong, his predecessor at the New York Fed and for years the most influential voice in American finance. Harrison had been Strong's personal assistant in New York, and was the obvious choice to replace him when Strong died in 1928. Harrison did not inherit his mentor's gravitas and steely will, but he retained Strong's international outlook, and his readiness to test Washington's authority.

As it happened, just days before the board in Washington voted to adopt direct action, Harrison was meeting in New York with Montagu Norman, governor of the Bank of England. Norman had been a close friend and collaborator with Strong; now he was seeking the same kind of cooperation from Harrison. The booming American stock market was draining off investment funds that Europe sorely needed, Norman explained to Harrison. He had come to New York to seek Harrison's help piercing the stock bubble and restoring order to the financial markets. Failure to do so, Norman warned, would destabilize the international gold standard.

Norman's prescription was for a dramatic hike in interest rates that would break "the spirit of speculation" in the United States. It was the same policy the Fed had just rejected, but to Harrison it was much preferable to direct pressure, which forced upon his bank the uncomfortable chore of dictating to borrowers what they might do with their funds. Thus, in the first week of February, just as the board issued its order for direct action, George Harrison traveled to Washington to press Roy Young in person to revoke direct action and instead raise interest rates. A full-point rate hike could spark a market panic but, as Harrison explained it, better "to have the market fall out of the tenth story, instead of the twentieth later on."

Harrison got nowhere with the Fed; nor did the board persuade Harrison. Returning to New York, Harrison led the governors of the New York Fed to defy the board, reject direct action, and vote, on February 11, to raise interest rates from 5 percent to 6. In answer, the board in Washington exercised its one true lever of authority, a veto prohibiting New York from raising its rates. As Montagu Norman recorded upon his return to London, at this juncture the leaders of the Federal Reserve were "at odds with one another, drifting and not knowing what to do."

There was no question as to the urgency of the predicament: on inauguration day, even so staid a voice as *The New York Times* dubbed the market "a Wall Street Frankenstein." "The truth of the situation," the editors asserted, "is that the existing stock market has broken loose from every influence except those which feed the appetite for speculation."

It wasn't just the president who wanted to see action. Members of Congress eagerly joined the debate. Wall Street was "the most notorious gambling center in the universe," averred Alabama senator Tom Heflin. "The government owes it to itself and to its people to put an end to this monstrous evil." But as all recognized, drastic intervention could bring on the crash that many now believed to be inevitable. The head of the state bankers' association in New York spoke for the entire financial sector when he warned, "Neither the Federal Reserve Board nor any other agency has the moral or legal right to take any public action which will create a panic in the minds of the people and thus jeopardize the investing public's money."

California senator Hiram Johnson spelled out the dilemma in a letter home. "There is a feeling here in Washington," Johnson wrote his sons, "that something should be done, of one sort or another, to curb the wild orgy of gambling so prevalent in the stock market. The difficulty is that there are so many people here, like myself, who recognize that there is something radically wrong, but who are utterly unable to understand the intricacies of the system." Here Johnson focused on the key conundrum. "I cannot see for the life of me how in a stock market a distinction can be made between investment and speculation—that is, between honest exchange and mere gambling; and until I can it is impossible for me to say what is to be done."

Hoover did not suffer those inhibitions, but as a new chief executive he was not yet prepared to overthrow the established policy apparatus. Inclined by nature to work in the shadows, in these early days the new president pressed his agenda discreetly.

Meeting with Roy Young in mid-March, Hoover praised the board for refusing to raise interest rates above 5 percent, and adopting the policy of direct pressure instead. When Young reminded Hoover that he, Young, had opposed direct pressure, Hoover argued the point. Young had to concede that, at the outset, the policy appeared to be succeeding in stifling speculation. The proof was in the interest rates on brokers' loans, now exceeding 20 percent. The high rate indicated a genuine scarcity of funds for stock speculators.

Was this not precisely the result the board was seeking through direct pressure, Hoover asked Young? The Fed chairman grudgingly agreed. Was it not better for business conditions to let rates rise for stock brokers, Hoover asked, but to keep general interest rates down? Again, Young acknowledged the point. Rates for nonstock lending were relatively low, the speculative bubble was under pressure, and business appeared prosperous.

Hoover was satisfied that the Fed was on the right course, but that was not the extent of his engagement. Soon after raising his concerns within his cabinet, the president contacted Eugene Meyer, a private sector financier who, like Hoover, had accepted appointment to key federal posts during the war. The two had collaborated on financial policy under Coolidge, and

Hoover once asked Meyer to join him at Commerce. For his part, Meyer always felt Hoover's reputation for crisis management a bit overblown. "I thought he was all right," Meyer said later, "but I didn't think he was a wizard."

Hoover posed the question to Meyer days after his inauguration. What could be done, asked the president, with the "crazy and dangerous" stock market? It was a dilemma, Meyer conceded. The Fed so far had proved ineffectual. Nor should Hoover make personal pronouncements on the market; no president, Meyer said, should adopt the role of national investment counselor. Meyer captured some of the perplexity of the moment when he recalled the conversation later, during an oral history interview. "I didn't know what he could do about it sitting in the White House that could put the brakes on and keep the thing under control within reason from going completely into collapse."

There was, however, one maneuver that Meyer said might alter the dynamic of the market. Some authority at Treasury, or the Fed, could "start a campaign for people to buy bonds," which were selling "at prices as low as stocks are high." Such a statement would serve through suggestion the same goals direct pressure sought by coercion—to channel investment funds out of the stock market and into the more useful mode of corporate finance.

"That's the only thing I can think of offhand," Meyer told the president.

Hoover took this counsel without expression and without response. This was his custom in private conference as well as public appearances. Some advisors found Hoover's reticence strange and off-putting, as if he failed even to listen to their advice. But there were many instances where Hoover clearly did listen, and later took action; his stoic demeanor was a facet of his intricate internal defense, a psychological shield that preserved his options and allowed him to follow his own compass.

Hoover's conference with Eugene Meyer serves as a case in point. Days later, without a word to Meyer, Hoover summoned Andrew Mellon and pressed him to launch the buy-bonds campaign Meyer had outlined. Mellon resisted. He didn't think much of the policy, and the reclusive treasury secretary was always leery of personal public exposure. But the president insisted, and on March 14, after another "extensive" meeting with Hoover, Mellon did his duty. "The present situation in the financial markets offers an opportunity for the prudent investor to buy bonds," Mellon told reporters. It was as gentle a directive as he could make. "This does not mean many stocks are not sound investments." The wan oracle of high finance added, under questioning, he found it "doubtful" that a move into bonds would have any impact on speculation in the market.

This was as far as Mellon would go. He didn't approve of meddling in the market, and he didn't like being told what to do. Besides, over the eight years they had served in the cabinet together, Mellon had never much warmed to Hoover. This encounter only confirmed to Mellon his sense of Hoover as a rash experimentalist, willing to embrace untried innovations that were, to Mellon's mind, "frequently unsound."

Mellon's halfhearted announcement had little apparent impact on the market. In fact, dealers reported a huge sell-off in bonds as investors sought to fund new speculation. In the week that followed interest rates spiked again, led by the rate on broker loans. This came despite the influence of direct pressure. The policy appeared to be working—banks were withholding credit—but now corporations and other nonbank lenders were crowding into the market, hoping to cash in on the market fever. The torrent of funds flowing into Wall Street continued unabated.

To Hoover this was just another indication that nothing could be done to check the market. "The fever was beyond control," Hoover opined. Better to affect an attitude of quiet confidence and let the drama unfold. With investors jittery, Mellon made a point of telling reporters, on March 21, that he'd spoken "casually" with the president, and that Hoover "had not exhibited unusual interest" in the credit markets.

This bland assurance was forgotten the following day, however, when reporters spied Mellon scurrying from a cabinet meeting at the White House to an extraordinary meeting of the Federal Reserve Board. Mellon declined comment and board officials quickly announced that no action was taken and none anticipated. But these furtive movements were followed by an unprecedented session on Saturday. The board was keeping mum, but word of the "credit parley," as the meeting was dubbed in the press, and the prospect of concerted action to limit speculation prompted a genuine scare on Wall Street. When the Fed resumed its meetings the following week, the market went into free fall. Tuesday, March 26, was another record-setting day, the trading so heavy that stock tickers fell ninety minutes behind the action. At day's end, stunned traders tallied the worst declines ever seen on the stock exchange.

This was the whole point of direct pressure—to deflate the market by starving the speculators of credit. Though the methods were different, the goal was much the same as that described by George Harrison: a break in the market—softer, presumably, than what might follow, but enough to restore some semblance of sanity to stock prices. Now that break was at hand. As Hoover termed it later, direct pressure had produced "a stranglehold on the stock market when the Reserve Banks had so tightened the call-loan situation that a moment arrived when there was no money available to the market."

But at this critical moment, with the market staggering and investors scrambling to cover their losses, the fissures in the edifice of the Federal Reserve broke open, shattering the policy of direct pressure and instigating a new round of speculation. The breach was brought on by Charles Mitchell, president of New York's National City Bank and, beginning in January, a new director at the Federal Reserve Bank of New York. A natural showman and a dogged optimist, "Sunshine Charlie" had built National City into the world's largest bank by underwriting the spectacular rise in stocks, and he wasn't going to let the Fed governors in Washington gore his bull. So that week in March, as panic seized the stock exchange, Mitchell announced that National City stood ready to channel $25 million into broker loans, supporting any stock ventures the public might seek.

Mitchell's gambit brought immediate calm to the market. Evidence of the week-long crash "evaporated" the very next day, and stock prices rose across the board. But all recognized the immediate price response as superficial; the real question was what were the implications of Miller's defiance of the Federal Reserve? Where did the power lie in the American system? Who was in charge?

Senator Carter Glass, former treasury secretary and author of the bill that created the Federal Reserve, immediately weighed in. Charlie Mitchell's announcement "vigorously slaps the Board squarely in the face," Glass told reporters at a news conference. "Mitchell's proclamation is a challenge to the authority and announced policy of the Federal Reserve Board," Glass said; it should be "promptly met and courageously dealt with." But a day later, Robert Owen, former senator from Oklahoma and Glass's coauthor of the original Fed bill, rose to Mitchell's defense, asserting that excess speculation was a question for the stock exchange and not the Federal Reserve. The Fed's monitors, like the governors themselves, were split.

In his memoirs Hoover fully endorsed Glass, but in the event he ignored the senator's appeal that someone step forward to assert authority over the melee at the Fed. As a consequence, the system remained divided through May and June and on into August. Ten times in that span, George Harrison and the New York Fed petitioned the Federal Reserve in Washington to raise interest rates, and each time the board answered with a veto. As the crisis deepened, the reserve banks in Chicago, Philadelphia, and Boston all joined New York in seeking authority to raise rates they considered "absurdly low." Mitchell's defiance of direct pressure had largely gutted the policy, but over the summer Adolph Miller's narrow majority held sway, and the governors of the Fed refused to give ground.

On one trip to Washington, in April, New York's George Harrison tried to enlist Hoover's support for a rate hike, but he was unable to get past Hoover's handlers. "While I have been informed that the president is concerned I understand he prefers to keep hands off at this juncture," Harrison reported to a friend. Just who was the source of Harrison's "understanding" he did not say, but Harrison convinced himself a direct approach would be indiscreet. "We might only embarrass him by seeking an audience right now."

In the meantime, Treasury Secretary Mellon vacillated. In March he voted with the board majority against rate hikes, though he considered them "inevitable"; in May, after an extended debate at the board, he switched sides and voted to raise interest rates, but the measure failed. A week later, Mellon sought to break the impasse with a direct appeal to Hoover. Meeting with

the president on May 23, Mellon criticized his fellow Fed governors for failing to boost interest rates, but Hoover stuck with the board majority.

Mellon made no record of Hoover's remarks, but soon after, the president
expressed his continued approval for the policy of direct pressure. Speaking
confidentially with governors Young and Charles Hamlin, Hoover said the
heated dissents from the Fed banks only showed that the policy was working. Separately, at a meeting with Young and several prominent bankers, he
added with satisfaction that of all the federal agencies, the Fed was entirely
free from politics, and he had no intention of disturbing that independence.

Hoover had already compromised that very independence, of course,
when he weighed in with Young in favor of direct pressure. This became
a pattern of his presidency; Hoover often endorsed the idea of managerial
autonomy, but he rarely restrained his instinctive reactions to issues as they
arose. In this instance, Hoover did both—he supported Adolph Miller in the
policy disputes at the Fed, and he reached outside the formal policy apparatus to exercise what other influence he could.

In April Hoover sent Los Angles banker Henry Robinson to New York,
"to talk in my name to the promoters and bankers in the market." Robinson was an old friend who had served with Hoover after the Armistice
on the World War Foreign Debt Commission, setting terms for managing
international debts. Robinson had since settled in Los Angeles, where he became president of Security First National Bank. Hoover relied on Robinson
throughout his term for candid and impartial advice.

The trip to New York was a futile venture, as Robinson reported back
to the president. "The New York bankers all scoffed at the idea the market
was not 'sound,'" Hoover wrote icily in his memoirs. "They were certain
this was a 'New Era,' to which old economic experience did not apply."

In the same vein—that is, operating outside the channels of formal
authority—Hoover summoned to Washington Richard Whitney, vice president of the New York Stock Exchange, to urge self-regulation of the trading
floor. Hoover had "no desire to stretch the powers of the federal government
by legislation to regulate the stock exchange," he told Whitney; better that
the exchange "control its own members."

These several, modest steps toward arresting the runaway stock market comprised the total of Hoover's engagement with the economy in the early months of his presidency. It was, in hindsight, clearly not enough, and in his memoirs Hoover sought to dress these up as a full-fledged campaign to avert the coming depression. Upon entering office, Hoover wrote, he was "fully alive to the danger inherent in this South Sea Bubble and its inevitable reaction. . . . It was obvious there had to be a vast liquidation of paper values."

Obvious in retrospect, perhaps, but not quite so clear at the moment. As is often the case with a speculative boom, the bull market of the late 1920s had cheerleaders all the way to its final collapse. Nor were these all promoters in the mold of "Sunshine Charlie" Mitchell. Even Irving Fisher, America's foremost economist in that era and still considered an authority on interest rates and deflation, was so enamored of the market that he announced, that summer, "Stock prices have reached what looks like a permanently high plateau." In the same vein, the financier Bernard Baruch, a principal backer of Al Smith's campaign but also an occasional advisor to Hoover, proposed in June that "the economic condition of the world seems to be on the verge of a great forward movement."

Hoover can be excused, then, for failing to mobilize the agencies of the government against an economic threat that had yet to present itself. Still, one often hears of the fortunes made and saved by those who were sagacious enough to anticipate the fall. Ironically, and perhaps tragically, we can count Hoover among that number. In April, around the time he received the report from Henry Robinson, Hoover told his friend and financial advisor Edgar Rickard that it was time to get out of the market. Rickard was making his first trip to visit his friend and mentor in the White House, and on the second day of the visit, the president took him aside to talk politics and business. "Hoover thinks we should liquidate out of Pitney Bowes [one of Hoover's larger personal investments] and settle our bank loans," Rickard noted in his diary. "Possible hard times coming."

SEVEN

THE SPECIAL SESSION

THE CONSTERNATION OVER THE STOCK MARKET WAS MAKING headlines and producing jitters in Washington, but few truly believed that after years of heady growth the country was on the brink of unprecedented economic disaster. Hoover was already pursuing a full agenda, and he was not going to be sidetracked by market gyrations that seemed menacing principally to those wealthy enough to play the game. At this point Hoover's concerns lay elsewhere.

The apex of the opening round of his presidency, the point to which Hoover brought all his electoral momentum to bear, was the special session of Congress he announced on April 15. Such extraordinary sessions are rare today, but in that era the Congress elected in November did not meet until thirteen months later, unless called in by the president. The schedules of the government were reset by constitutional amendment in 1933; before that, special sessions were a means by which the incoming president might give substance to his top priorities.

Hoover exercised that prerogative with a written message he sent to both the House and the Senate. His object was "to lay the foundations for a new day in agriculture, from which we shall preserve to the nation the great values of its individuality and strengthen our whole national fabric." The incoming president was explicit in assigning his motivation: the voters had delivered a "mandate," and Hoover wanted to answer. The special session would "redeem two pledges given in the last election—farm relief and limited tariff revision."

Hoover was invoking the promises he'd made to voters, but he also had a more specific obligation in mind—an explicit pledge he'd given William Borah, the charismatic senator from Idaho, widely regarded as a true champion of the American farmer. Famously, fiercely independent, Borah surprised many by campaigning hard for Hoover, delivering stump speeches in the South, East, and Midwest. In the course of this service, Borah notified Hoover privately that his support was contingent on calling the new Congress into special session to address the ills of agriculture. Hoover readily complied.

Helping the American farmer was a popular notion, but the politics of the special session were daunting from the outset. The intractable problems of agriculture had been a source of strife in Congress ever since the war. And tariffs were a principal skirmish line dividing free market Democrats and protectionist Republicans—the parties holding positions quite the opposite of those they later represented. Just twenty years before, William Howard Taft launched his presidency in similar fashion, calling a special session to reduce tariffs, but it launched a political donnybrook that split his party and resulted in higher trade duties.

In Hoover's case, the party was already divided. Republicans were dominant in Congress, claiming a margin of 106 votes in the House and a sixteen-vote cushion in the Senate. But the party also harbored a restive faction of larger-than-life mavericks known collectively as "the insurgents," onetime Progressives distinguished principally by their deep-seated disinclination to follow any particular platform. Their willingness to align with Democrats against the administration—be it Harding's, Coolidge's, or, now, Hoover's—made the Republican majority a shaky legislative foundation. In laying out such a grand agenda for the special session, Hoover was showing hubris, or ambition: should he accomplish agriculture legislation and tariff reform together, the success of his presidency seemed assured.

Taking on the intractable ills of the American farmer was a gamble, but this was more than a stab in the dark for the new president. Agriculture had been a focus of Hoover's attention for all of his years in government. On this issue in particular, the division was not between parties so much as between the Congress, where farm bloc legislators had floated a series of dubious relief plans, and the executive branch, where those plans were repeatedly vetoed. As a cabinet officer for successive presidents Hoover had been the strongest critic of the congressional ag-aid projects; now was his chance to put into place a fully developed program of his own.

How Hoover developed that program says much about his method, and ultimately about his curious brand of leadership. Hoover's first engagement in the question arose out of his bureaucratic rivalry with Henry C. Wallace, secretary of agriculture under Harding. Reasoning that half of America's domestic product at the time was farm-based, Hoover sought to bring agricultural "marketing" under his purview at Commerce. Wallace, naturally, resisted.

There was no question the American farm was in trouble. Beginning around 1920, the combination of ramped-up wartime production with postwar recession led to a global agricultural slump. In the United States, the weak prices for commodities meant rising debt and possible failure—farm foreclosures ran at under 5 percent in the years 1913 to 1920; for the period between 1926 and 1929, that figure more than tripled, as one in five American farms went bankrupt. When growers expanded their plantings to chase new revenue, prices sank further.

The response from the farm states was to demand that the federal government boost exports, selling them at low cost abroad and compensating farmers with an "equalization fee" that would match high domestic prices for foodstuffs. This two-price system, with exports subsidized by taxes or fees, became the centerpiece of a succession of bills from farm-bloc leaders Charles McNary, Republican senator from Oregon, and Iowa representative Gilbert Haugen, also a Republican. Wallace embraced these bills, Hoover criticized them, and Presidents Harding and Coolidge vetoed them.

There was a second organized response to the postwar depression in agriculture, this one arising in California and outside the formal political process. This was the cooperative movement, led by an attorney from Oakland named Aaron Sapiro, who exhorted farmers to band together collectively and bypass the great grain exchanges and other middlemen. The "Sapiro Plan" won the endorsement of the American Farm Bureau Federation and spread to the Midwest and north into Canada until, by 1925, some 900,000 farmers had signed on.

The cooperative movement had everything Hoover needed to answer Agriculture Secretary Henry Wallace. It arose among the farmers themselves. It sought collective responses to internal issues like waste in distribution. And it rejected the idea of subsidies and price supports. By adopting the cooperative movement as his own, Hoover could edge out Wallace in the cabinet debates while building his reputation with the politically potent farm bloc.

Still, the whole idea of cooperative marketing was that it be done by, for, and among farmers, but that was not enough for Hoover. With agriculture in trouble, he wanted the government to step in with financing, information, and expertise. This raised a contradiction that stood at the center of Hoover's general outlook; he was an apostle of "cooperation" in every economic sphere, with government standing on the sidelines, but he was also a relentless activist, generating projects, systems, bureaucracy. He built Commerce into a bureaucratic juggernaut under the banner of cooperation, and he saw a role for government on the farm as well.

The vehicle for these ambitions was a new Federal Farm Board, to be staffed by economists and marketing experts who would assist cooperatives in moving and selling their produce. In addition, the board would provide financing to help launch new cooperatives, and to conduct price "stabilization" operations—purchasing product in weak markets to support prices until prices recovered. This last function violated Hoover's own precepts on government intervention in the market, a point he always finessed.

Hoover floated his idea for a federal Farm Board as early as 1923 and saw it incorporated into proposed legislation in 1924. Reaction was mixed: the nonpartisan Farm Bureau was "cordial," but other ag organizations were more skeptical. The *California Fruit News* knocked Hoover's plan as "paternalistic and highly hazardous." Sapiro himself became a sharp critic, and farmers generally remained wedded to the McNary-Haugen program. More important to Hoover, however, the scheme won favor from President Coolidge.

This quickly evolved into a full-bore cabinet confrontation, with Hoover pushing his Farm Board and Secretary Wallace backing McNary-Haugen. The feud was cut short by Wallace's death in October 1924 at age fifty-eight. That moved the dispute outside the administration; for the next five years American farmers and their advocates in Congress touted the export subsidies of McNary-Haugen, while Hoover promoted "cooperative marketing" at Commerce, on the campaign trail, and now at the White House.

The contradictions in Hoover's thinking were still there. He proposed, in an address to Congress opening the special session, "creation of a great instrumentality clothed with sufficient authority and resources to assist our farmers." This would put the Farm Board on a par with the Federal Reserve and the Interstate Commerce Commission. But there would be no taxes, no fees, no price supports, no buying or selling of commodities. The goal was to "transfer the agricultural question from the field of politics to the realm of economics." But just how this "instrumentality" should operate, with what budget and what goals, Hoover did not say.

What did become clear was that Hoover had no intention to further describe or explain the farm program he sought. This attitude appeared an extension of Hoover's tight-lipped deportment in the campaign. Once he made a statement, his auditors were left to fill in the blanks. This approach was not unique to Hoover—Calvin Coolidge made a point of saying as little as possible about legislation until it reached his desk—but Hoover was a man of such strong and such particular opinions that his silence appeared incongruous, and came as something of a surprise.

Hoover's demeanor rose to the status of policy in late March, when the House Committee on Agriculture held hearings to prepare for the special session. That week several House Republicans visited Hoover to ask just how he'd like them to proceed, but returned empty-handed. When reporters asked what was amiss, they were told that Hoover "does not intend to write bills and impose them on the Congress." This terse explanation was attributed to "a friend of the president"—not so far a cry from the little lamented "White House spokesman."

Hoover's silence, here at the outset of his presidency, incited a quiet but incredulous buzz in the press gallery. *The New York Times*, in an editorial, reprised the precedents. "McKinley was a great stickler . . . for the absolute independence of Congress," it found, while Theodore Roosevelt "leaned far in the other direction," and Woodrow Wilson went even further. It was largely a matter of personal style, the paper advised, but, "Sooner or later the time comes when he [Hoover] must indicate what kind of legislation he prefers."

Sooner or later, but not quite yet. Hoover was still riding the wave of enthusiasm that had swept him into office, and on this, his opening initiative, he was not to be thwarted. "The president is so immensely popular over the country that the Republicans here are on their knees and the Democrats have their hats off," one senator wrote to a friend. Sure enough, after a brief flirtation with export debentures—the core provision of McNary-Haugen that Hoover had been fighting against for years—the Congress gave Hoover his Farm Board, replete with a half-billion-dollar fund to help underwrite new crop collectives and other ambitious projects. The press trumpeted the vote as Hoover's "First Big Victory."

It was a promising start, but the second tier of Hoover's opening call to Congress—revision of the tariff schedules—presented more difficult terrain. "Protection" by trade duties was a principal mode of governance at the time, a way to encourage domestic industry and, for many years, a major source of funding for the federal government. It was also an easy way for elected representatives to bestow favors on specific industries from timber to wool, from goldfish to bottle caps.

Against this backdrop, Hoover's taciturn style brought out the worst in American politics. His message to Congress expressly specified "limited" changes in trade duties to protect farmers from cheap imports. But in practice there was no limit. Once under way, lawmakers seized the opportunity to raise and extend trade barriers, swapping votes, twisting arms, and bending the rules of logic. By May, the House produced a bill authorizing rate increases on 845 classes of material.

When the Senate took up the bill, in June, William Borah took on the mission of paring the bill back to the "limited" revision that Hoover had described at the outset. Borah filled a strategic role in the Senate—leader of the insurgents, a faction of Progressive Republicans who frequently aligned with Democrats to challenge the Republican establishment. More than that, he was considered a peerless orator in an era when the spoken word was revered for art and influence. "When Borah speaks," one political foe lamented in 1927, "the whole world is led to believe that he is fresh from a conference with the gods."

Borah authored a resolution for a limited tariff, and on June 16 took the floor of the Senate to denounce the excesses of the House bill. Raising industrial tariffs along with agricultural duties defeated the whole purpose of the revision, he said; whatever benefits went to the farmer would be lost in higher prices for farm equipment and other tariff-protected goods. Borah was eloquent as ever, but he was flying in the face of raw self-interest. And he was flying solo—through weeks of debate over the tariff, President Hoover refrained from any statement suggesting his preferences for the bill.

At the close of the day the roll was called and Borah's resolution lost by a single vote. It was Borah's defeat, but it was also Hoover's—he lost both the reasonable, limited tariff he first proposed, and now also the allegiance of Borah and the Progressive Republicans. The liberal journal *Outlook and Independent* marked the frustration of the insurgents. "They comment sarcastically on the president's pledge to place agriculture on an equality with industry," the editors of the magazine lamented. "They hold him responsible for not curbing the House appetite for increased tariff rates."

With the vote on Borah's resolution, the Congress dispersed for its summer vacation, but the special session would resume in the fall, its work unfinished. In the meantime, the Senate Finance Committee remained in session, taking testimony all through the summer from a thousand witnesses and grinding through a wholesale tariff revision. It was a crass display of legislative logrolling, and for many an unsettling reminder that in the first real test of his leadership, Herbert Hoover had fallen short.

While the new president found his political skills tested by the insurgents in his own party, his avowed foes mounted an institutional opposition that would dog Hoover through the length of his term. The instigator was the industrialist John J. Raskob, head of finance for Du Pont *and* General Motors, chairman of the Democratic National Committee, and a principal backer of Al Smith's presidential campaign. Raskob had few genuine differences with Hoover—he was himself a former Republican, and later would be an early critic of Franklin Roosevelt—but he was a confirmed wet and devoted to Smith.

In that day the political parties went into hibernation between the national elections, but in June Raskob broke the pattern by committing a million dollars to fund a full-time Democratic Party operation. He hired Jouett Shouse, a publisher and former congressman from Kentucky, as the party's first salaried executive chairman; a week later, Shouse brought in Charley Michelson, Washington bureau chief for the New York *World*, as the Democrats' director of publicity. No longer would the war between the parties be limited to specific campaigns, but henceforth would be a continuing, incessant contest.

Michelson became the spearpoint to the Democratic thrust. Lanky and lean, with unruly white hair and a sharp, sarcastic wit, Michelson was sixty years old, a veteran journalist who understood how news worked. Knowing his fellow correspondents would discard party handouts as soon as they arrived, Michelson eschewed press releases in favor of statements and speeches that he planted with Democratic congressmen and other presidential critics. Always, his goal was to hook an editor with a catchy dig at Hoover that would find a place high up in a political story—what would today qualify as a sound bite.

It was tough sledding at the outset. "The country was happy in the high tide of prosperity," Michelson recalled in a memoir. "President Hoover was still the magician of the campaign picture, and there were few who doubted that he would make good the extraordinary promises" that had carried the election.

But the special session, with its wrangle over farm policy and tariffs, presented an opportunity. "It was easy to get before the country a picture of slavish legislators closeted with representatives of those industries whose owners contributed most largely to the Hoover campaign," Michelson said.

And so it began, the seasoned old scribe holding forth at the National

Press Club, playing endless rounds of bridge or dominoes, deftly stoking the frustrations of longtime pals and cub reporters stymied by the sphinx in the White House. Gradually, steadily, Michelson's barbs found their mark. A year later, a Republican writer reported that Michelson "more than any other has helped to mold the public mind in regard to Mr. Hoover, magnifying his misfortunes [and] minimizing his achievements."

For his part, the president was appalled. Michelson represented everything that Hoover feared and loathed about the press, a product of "the smear departments of yellow journalism," as he put it later. But Hoover saw no way to strike back at his tormentor. "A president cannot with decency and with proper regard for the dignity of his office reply to such stuff." Hoover's status as a political outsider worked against him as well. "In my case," Hoover wrote, "some of the old-guard Republican leaders in the Senate and the House, who had been defeated in their presidential ambitions in 1928, certainly did not exert themselves energetically in their traditional duty to counterattack and expose misrepresentations." Nor, he might have added, did the insurgents rally to his support. Almost from the outset, Hoover was on his own.

For all these early tribulations, Hoover gave no indication of concern at his political isolation. As the spring gave way to the muggy heat of the Washington summer, Hoover responded as he always had—by toil, putting in longer hours, staying through the weekend. "Daddy gets overworked at times," Lou Hoover wrote her son Allan in April, "but not more than normal." She added, as if to reassure herself, "It is exactly as I expected."

And on some weekends, Bert and Lou were able to get away. This was by design, a project the couple had embarked on before they entered the White House—recognizing, perhaps, that the president would need a ready escape from the demands of a job that could at times feel overwhelming. In April, after months of negotiations, the Hoovers obtained a tract of remote, brushy land in the Blue Ridge Mountains, high above the Virginia Piedmont and watered by the small but lively Rapidan River. There they planned a rustic hideaway and fishing retreat.

Bert and Lou bought outright 164 acres on the border of what would soon become the Shenandoah National Park, leased another two thousand acres, and obtained fishing rights to ten thousand more. After Hoover left office he deeded the entire spread to the government. The terrain was rugged and the plot could be accessed only on horseback, but was soon transformed by a squad of about four hundred Marines, who built a road and raised a cluster of pine-board cabins under the thin pretext of a training exercise. The first surveys were conducted by Hoover aide Larry Richey, who searched under the criteria of good fishing, proximity to the capital, and elevation, to beat the summer heat. Once the site was secured, plans for the camp, from the design of the cabins to the layout of paths and outbuildings, fell to Lou.

The camp rose quickly and combined eclectic taste and rustic luxury in a mix that marked Lou's sense of style. Cabins featured oversized, fieldstone chimneys, and were furnished with raw-wood furniture, and hung with textiles from the American Southwest mixed in with braided rugs, some made locally by the "mountain folk" of the Blue Ridge. Meals were served at a communal "mess hall" by liveried Filipino houseboys, transfers from the presidential yacht *Sequoia*, which Hoover had mothballed.

Lou paid special attention to the grounds, which had been cleared of small brush and were landscaped according to her close direction. Here she showed her father's trained eye; she wanted indigenous plants brought in from the nearby hills, she told the Marine tenders. She asked them to seek in particular "morning glories, wild cucumber, black-eyed susans, yellow-eyed susans, butterfly weed, spireas, hardy asters, trilliums, jacks-in-the-pulpit, columbines, mimulas, goldenrod, violets, ladyslippers, Virginia creeper, common 'red' swamp lilies (almost orange color), tiger lilies, day lilies (wildish), Solomon seals (the *real* kind—much 'false' Solomon seals already present), fox gloves, gentians, iris, lupines, gourds (*all* kinds), larkspur."

Plantings were to be made throughout the camp, wherever sun reached the ground through the canopy of oak and pine and hemlock, but "no formal beds," Lou directed; better they should "ramble off into the surroundings." And she saw that her will was done. "Mrs. Hoover was a person who definitely knew what she wanted," said Frederic Butler, assistant director of public buildings and parks in the District of Columbia during the Hoover presidency. "There were no ands, ifs, or buts. She knew how to get what she wanted and she wasn't happy until she got what she wanted."

There is little question the constant chores and the social demands of her station were taxing for Lou; she rejoiced, for example, at Bert's morning exercise routine, as it left her an hour of peace at the start of every busy day. At the end of April, writing to Allan, she allowed herself to muse wistfully, "If I were not married to Daddy, or connected with him in any other way, I could think of so many exciting things to do." But that was a passing fancy; most days, she took it all in stride, and by May she reported to Allan, "We are beginning to feel perfectly at home."

Lou was accustomed to her husband's dogged approach to whatever task he might confront, but for those on the White House staff it required some adjustment. By July, Joel Boone, the White House physician, was advising the president to take some time off. "He was working harder than I had ever seen anybody work in my long periods in the White House," Boone recorded in his memoir. "I felt he needed at least ten days' respite from the environs of the White House and the pressure of it."

The special session dominated his schedule, but Hoover pursued a broad, Progressive agenda that kept him busy on several fronts. He ordered public disclosure of oversized tax rebates, and froze oil drilling on federal lands—a response to corrupt practices exposed at Teapot Dome, and a first step toward limiting production in a glutted market. At Justice, on the recommendation of Mabel Willebrandt, he drafted the Progressive reformer Sanford Bates to clean up the federal prison system. At Interior, Hoover and Ray Wilbur moved quickly to fire the haughty managers at Indian Affairs and replace them with prototypical Hoover reformers—Charles Rhoads and Henry Scattergood, both Quakers, both successful businessmen, and both active in the Indian Rights Association. And Hoover built on Teddy Roosevelt's legacy in selecting the conservationist Horace Albright to run the National Park Service.

And then there were the commissions. The Wickersham Commission, empaneled in May to carry out Hoover's pledge to study Prohibition, was just one of a raft of panels floated by Hoover to foster reform inside and outside the government. There was a National Advisory Committee on Education, a Committee on the Conservation and Administration of the Public Domain, and the White House Conference on Child Health and Protection, which convened in July with 2,500 delegates.

As spring turned to summer, Lou and Bert talked about a trip west; he was thinking of a visit to Death Valley, and both were eager to attend Allan's graduation from Stanford in June. But when the special session devolved into paralysis, Lou saw her hopes for the summer slipping away. On May 30 she wrote Allan to report that, "Everything is going very well here except the Senate. And that isn't Daddy's fault—he didn't elect 'em." Lou was still anticipating a vacation west, but she could not make firm plans. "If Congress vacations shortly we *might* go west for a month," she wrote.

By the second week in June that prospect was gone. There would be no trip, not even to Stanford. "I am distressed beyond words that I have demanding duties here which prevent my actually seeing you walk the plank," Lou telegrammed Allan. It was her husband's duties that interfered, and not hers, but Lou was accustomed to running interference for Bert, even within the family.

Bert didn't share Lou's propensity for euphemism. It was still early in his term, but already he was feeling trapped in his high station, fettered by many and mounting obligations. Visitors to the White House found him dour and sardonic. Congress was in recess, but with the Senate Finance Committee conducting hearings daily, Hoover could not allow himself the luxury of more than a weekend's respite at the mountain camp on the Rapidan. He was, he told visitors, "condemned to stay here all summer."

EIGHT

THE CRASH

As AUTUMN ARRIVED IN 1929 THE WALL STREET CRASH WAS weeks away but the Great Depression—the historic economic disaster that befell Hoover and the nation—was in some manner already under way. The stock market, heaving and squealing like a maxed-out steam engine, peaked in September. Steel production, a more fundamental barometer of industrial activity, began slipping in June; residential construction had been in a slump for several years.

In the popular mind the Depression begins with the crash—the spectacular collapse of stock prices that wiped out billions of dollars in private and corporate wealth and was followed by business failures, an industrial slump, and deep unemployment that lasted ten long years. It's a valid checkpoint; useful for marking the transition from the Roaring Twenties to the Somber Thirties, a reflection and a cause and an emblem of a historic debacle.

But economists will tell you the crash was just one factor in the onset of the Depression, the stock market a victim as much as a catalyst of the general economic breakdown. (One respected analyst goes so far as to assert, "No causal relationship between the events of late October 1929 and the Great Depression has ever been shown.") Precise reasons remain in dispute. Vari-

"SOLD OUT"

Americans had no idea yet they were facing a historic
Depression, but a sense of foreboding swept the
nation after the stock market crash of October 1929.

ous theories ascribe the Depression to mismanagement of the money supply, income disparity, the stock bubble, the real estate bubble that preceded it, the agricultural depression that preceded *that*, the Treaty of Versailles, international capital flows, or, more esoteric, a confluence of business cycles—of fifty years, nine years, and short-term, all meeting, at the bottom, in 1929.

Each of these models has its adherents, but a serviceable consensus holds that an economic event so profound as the Depression can only derive from a combination of factors coming together in a grim convergence of historic accident. These theorists allude to a weather analogy—the perfect storm, borrowed from the title of the Sebastian Junger adventure tale—to capture the scope and menace of the forces that drove America and all the world from a decade of growth and promise into an era of privation and decline.

It would be beyond the scope of this account to adhere too closely to any one underlying theory of the Depression. But whatever the causes, once the crisis settled in, the White House quickly emerged as the command center in formulating a national response. Herbert Hoover charted his course personally, weighing in on every policy question from agriculture to poverty relief, from interest rates to the international gold standard. The record he compiled tells us much about him; it also speaks to the nature of the Depression, the policies that were deployed and how they fared. It is ground that yields fresh insight with every new appraisal.

What should be kept in mind is that events that took on special significance in hindsight—"Black Thursday," followed by "Black Tuesday"; even the crash itself—were part of a continuum that unfolded only slowly. In truth it took months before the crisis revealed itself as anything more than another sickening swing in the course of a roller-coaster market, and months more before it was perceived in its awful magnitude.

When the reckoning on the stock market finally arrived, after a long summer of dips and runs, it did so with a bang. It began on October 24—Black Thursday, the first in a week of black days, when the market lost 10 percent of its value in a single, hectic morning. The avalanche of stock sales slowed that afternoon as Wall Street's leading financiers, led by "Sunshine Charlie" Mitchell and Morgan senior partner Thomas Lamont, pooled funds to support stocks at their new, lower prices. The market steadied as speculators stood back, dazed by the new reality of plunging shares and lost fortunes.

The next day's session opened with relative calm, and Hoover stepped forward at his regular press conference that afternoon with his initial answer to the crash. His first goal was to observe the Hippocratic stipulation "Do no harm." "Obviously," Hoover wrote later, "as President, I had no business to make things worse in the middle of a crash." So Hoover chose his words carefully, offering a written statement calculated to calm the markets and limit the collateral damage. "The fundamental business of the country, that is, the production and distribution of commodities, is on a very sound and prosperous basis," Hoover pronounced. Prices for commodities remained steady and the cost of labor was rising, he said, indicators that the sell-off was an aberration of the market and not some broader ailment.

Hoover chose not even to mention stock prices; he had long disparaged the "orgy of speculation" in New York and saw no reason to intervene in the inevitable reckoning. The bankers who organized a fund to break the fall on Thursday pressured Hoover to reassure investors that stocks were now available at bargain prices, but the president stuck to his script. Hoover was not trying to salvage Wall Street; he was trying to stave off a national calamity.

Hoover's statement was terse and narrow, not the sort of message that might galvanize the populace, but it hit the right notes, and he had plenty of company. The press, politicians of every stripe, and the financial community in New York all echoed the wishful theme that the sickening price declines of the past week were behind them. "The market situation is firmly in hand," *The New York Times* asserted in a front-page analysis. "The wave of financial hysteria has definitely passed." Except the wave had not passed.

On Monday the slide resumed with the opening bell. This was not a panic so much as a wholesale capitulation. Most small investors had already been driven from the market; now it was professionals—banks, financiers, investment trusts—that saw their fortunes disappear. The selling went on all day, a clinical bloodletting by which great fortunes were reduced and exhausted. It was the worst day ever seen on Wall Street—worse even than Black Thursday—until Tuesday arrived. Black Tuesday. It was the final day of the rout, marked by monstrous, inconceivable losses. On the New York exchange $9 billion in value evaporated; adding tallies from the smaller markets across the country, the total grew to $15 billion, or roughly 10 percent of the gross national product, over the course of a single day.

On Black Tuesday it was Julius Klein, Hoover's friend and the assistant secretary of commerce, who carried the message for the administration. Speaking to the nation on radio after the markets closed, Klein acknowledged that stock prices had "gone down materially since Friday," but that should have no bearing on the larger economy. Many individual investors had lost money to "speculative gyrations," but they represented a tiny fraction of the population. "There has been no change in the situation of the overwhelming majority of American families," Klein said.

That was the point, the line that Hoover and his administration would hammer on for the duration of the crisis: the economy would easily absorb the losses in the market if Americans maintained their confidence. "All of us are justified," Klein emphasized, "in a profound confidence in the general economic future of the country."

The markets calmed in the days that followed, the rout having run its course, and a stunned nation picked over the wreckage to assess damage and assign blame. Democrats in Congress took their first swipes at the Hoover administration, asserting the truism that, "The stock crisis belongs to the party in power." But so many had shared in the market mania that the charge was necessarily muted; it wasn't six months before that John Raskob, the Democrats' principal financier, had authored a piece in the *Ladies' Home Journal* advising Americans of modest means to park their savings in the high-flying stock market. The article was titled "Everybody Ought to Be Rich."

The collapse of stock prices touched off a searching discussion inside the White House as Hoover and his advisors sought to answer a stunning economic shock. There had been ample warning that stock values were inflated—some of those warnings emanating from Hoover himself—but as with so many calamities, the actual event caught policymakers flat-footed.

Hoover's leading economic advisor was, of course, Andrew Mellon, but

Mellon was shaken by the debacle; he had seen the spectacular rise of the market but never accepted the corollary that collapse would surely follow. Now he had few answers. "Mellon seemed depressed by the break in the stock market," one Fed governor observed. It was not any personal financial loss that rattled him, but the sense of shock. Mellon had "always said that no harm could come from the New York speculation," this colleague recorded.

Now called to account by the president, Mellon reverted to the hands-off mantra of laissez-faire economics: "Liquidate labor, liquidate stocks, liquidate the farmers, liquidate real estate," he told Hoover. Mellon sounded, as well, a note of moral censure for a decade of extravagance that he had witnessed with bemusement. "It will purge the rottenness out of the system," Mellon said. "High costs of living and high living will come down. People will work harder, live a more moral life."

The president needed more than that from his august advisor. Long before, Hoover had emphatically rejected laissez-faire as a rudimentary throwback. Unfettered markets failed the test of "social and economic justice" by concentrating economic rewards in the hands of the few, Hoover wrote in his book *American Individualism*. More than that, Hoover was a disciple and an advocate of a new school of public policy that afforded government a critical role in operation and management of the economy.

Hoover first aired this thesis at the height of the postwar recession, in 1921, when he persuaded Warren Harding to convene the President's Conference on Unemployment. It was typical Hoover—tackling social ills with a well-publicized conference—but it also represented a distinct advance in federal administration, a commitment to the simple idea that the government had a role to play in the operations of the economy. Hoover captured the sense of mission in his opening address: "What our people wish is the opportunity to earn their daily bread," he told delegates assembled at the Commerce Department auditorium where the conference was held. "Surely in a country with its warehouses bursting with surpluses of food, of clothing, with its mines capable of indefinite production . . . we possess the intelligence to find solutions."

The sharp unemployment of 1921 eased off that winter as the nation swung into its decade of prosperity, but for Hoover the conference was seminal. Ever after he subscribed to the New Era axiom that the economy was too complex, its parts and people too interdependent, to be left on its own. But at a time when many took that same notion as an impetus to social-ism, Hoover sought a third path between state control and the unfettered market. Government might facilitate private business through regulation, by fostering cooperation, and by assembling information and statistics, but it should never seek to supplant individual enterprise in the market, Hoover believed. In an important sense, his eight years at Commerce were devoted to defining the useful, limited role for government. Now, eight months into his presidency, the crash offered him an opportunity to put those ideas into action.

With Andrew Mellon disengaged at this critical juncture, the impetus for the administration's economic policy fell to Mellon's top deputy, Treasury Undersecretary Ogden Mills. It was Mills who helped Hoover formulate his first, crucial public statement on the Depression—that "the fundamental business of the country . . . is on a very sound and prosperous basis." And it was Mills who stood at Mellon's side during press conferences, taking the tough questions and facing down the more aggressive reporters.

Ogden Mills was something of an anomaly in Hoover's circle—a man with a public reputation independent of the Chief, with excellent political contacts in Washington and the Republican Party. Where Hoover's advisors often catered to the president, telling him what they hoped he wanted to hear, Mills took an opposite tack, drawing Hoover into his orbit with un-wavering confidence, statistical mastery, and steady, consistent advice.

In his personal life Mills was everything Hoover was not—gregarious, loud, and arrogant, an unabashed drinker, a high-stakes gambler. He col-lected lavish estates, savored Mediterranean summers aboard his 160-foot yacht, and bred racehorses at his celebrated Wheatley Stables, home to Seabiscuit and other legendary steeds. Save for his boss at Treasury, Mills was the richest man in Washington.

Mills's fortune was a product of high birth—he was born at Ocean View, a showcase villa in Newport, Rhode Island, and spent his youth shuttling between the family town house in New York, residences in Paris and California, and their winter retreat on the Hudson, a sixty-five room, fourteen-bath Greek Revival mansion, now preserved as a state park. His father was a wealthy banker and his mother, Ruth Livingston, a direct descendant one of New York's founding families.

After graduating from Harvard and then Harvard Law, Mills dove into New York's rough-and-tumble political scene, ringing doorbells and watching polls for the Republican Party. He ran for Congress in 1912 and lost, but was elected to the State Senate two years later, effectively launching his career. "I was possessed of a fortune," Mills once explained, "but I wanted to put myself, as a matter of personal pride, in a position where I was not dependent upon the income I had inherited."

The Great War provided another opportunity for Mills to prove his mettle. He left his State Senate seat to enlist in the Army, shipped out to France, and served at the rank of captain. Upon returning home he won election to Congress from the Upper East Side of Manhattan and distinguished himself as a respected analyst of tax policy. But his manner was off-putting. His speaking voice was strong and clear but also nasal and high-toned; he managed the rare feat of at once sounding reedy and bombastic. He was impatient with his allies, sarcastic with his foes, and generally unpopular with his fellow lawmakers.

In 1926, Mills served his party in a doomed gubernatorial run against the ever popular Al Smith. Calvin Coolidge rewarded him with a posting as Mellon's second in command at Treasury. Two years later, when Hoover threw his hat in the presidential ring, Mills was among the few party regulars to embrace the upstart from Commerce.

With his high birth, his swaggering confidence, and his ease at the podium, Mills seemed just the type to set Hoover on edge. But the president appreciated Mills's direct manner, and bore him no grudge against his family fortune. Hoover considered worldly success to be a mark of character, and he often selected leaders of industry for his commissions and advisory boards. Back when he was considering his presidential run, he professed admiration for Al Smith as a "useful citizen and governor," in part because, as he told Edgar Rickard, Smith's humble background allowed him to appoint "men of wealth and social standing" without fear of being condemned for catering to "the reactionary wealthy class." It appears Hoover felt the same immunity applied to himself.

Though Mills was a sportsman, he never did join in Hoover's Medicine Ball Cabinet. Rather, he took his morning exercise at home, beginning each day with a round of boxing with a personal trainer. But he was readily on call, and in afternoon conferences would indulge with the president in a shared pastime of smoking large, custom cigars—Mills favoring Benson & Hedges, and Hoover, pale-wrapped Coronas, custom made at the Hotel Ritz in New York.

President Hoover rode out the uneasy aftermath of the October crash in silence, but within the administration he and Mills honed and hardened the official line. Confidence remained the principal message, now elaborated by a theory of surplus capital that marked the crash as a positive benefit. By this supposition, the runaway stock market had sucked in all the funds that would otherwise go to genuine business investment. "The ultimate result of the events of the last two weeks will be to release large amounts of capital from the speculative market for employment in business and industry generally," an unnamed administration official told reporters.

With such clear benefits to be anticipated, reaction to the crash became a measure of moral fiber. "The effect of the collapse upon productive business, if there is any at all, will be purely psychological," posited a source "in high official circles."

These quotes surfaced anonymously, but they carried Hoover's tacit endorsement and gave a fair impression of Mills's approach. When he did speak for the record, early the next year, Mills asserted that he found conditions to be "distinctly encouraging." Truculent by nature, Mills cast his prognosis as a test of character.

It all appears in hindsight as an extreme case of wishful thinking, but it should be kept in mind that this was a moment of extraordinary uncertainty. A decade of unprecedented prosperity had closed with a resounding collapse; the bankers and the viziers could not know then the tide had fully turned against them. Commentators from across the political spectrum called for calm and appealed for conviction. "The great task of the next few months is confidence," the editors of *The Nation* pronounced. William Randolph Hearst, assuming the mantle of popular tribune, addressed his appeal directly to Hoover. "Some reassuring utterance by the President of the United States," Hearst advised in an open letter, "would do much to restore the confidence of the public and make them realize that the present situation is not a disaster, but an opportunity for legitimate investment."

Hearst had more, as was his wont. Always pushing, always wheedling, Hearst challenged Hoover to live up to the standard of his office. "The people expect as much from you, Mr. President, as an able, an active and experienced business man, as they would have expected from your strenuous predecessor, Mr. Roosevelt, under similar circumstances." Hearst so relished the point that he repeated it. "Undoubtedly President Roosevelt would have taken some such vigorous action, and the Wall Street leaders would have known that he was in earnest and would not have hesitated to cooperate."

A telling thrust, but a curious case of hagiography for Hearst, who never thought much of Theodore Roosevelt and had actually sought the nomination to run against him in 1904. Roosevelt in fact confronted a very similar crisis in 1907, with a panic and a financial freeze on Wall Street. In the event Roosevelt had done nothing—he was on vacation for the first days of the crunch—and he stood on the sidelines as J. P. Morgan corralled the bankers of New York in his personal library and strong-armed them into concerted action. Wrote one TR biographer, the episode "persuaded some men that Roosevelt was fiscally retarded."

The irony wasn't lost on Hoover. He was cognizant, as he wrote in his memoirs, that no president had ever acknowledged any government responsibility in answer to a market crisis or financial collapse. He cited his antecedents by name—Van Buren, Grant, Grover Cleveland, and, yes, Theodore Roosevelt. "No matter what the urging on previous occasions, presidents steadfastly had maintained that the federal government was apart from such eruptions."

As a consequence, Hoover wrote, "we had to pioneer a new field." But new fields were Hoover's forte. He had experience, he had a strategy, and he had a program. Charles Evans Hughes, jurist, diplomat, and Republican mainstay through the 1920s, once remarked that, "If any difficult situation should arise, the man who more than anyone else could be depended upon to bring the widest knowledge and the greatest resourcefulness to the devising of means to meet the emergency would be Herbert Hoover." Now, in November 1929, with the nation in crisis and Hoover in the White House, that moment had arrived.

Hoover launched his systematic response to the crash the morning of Thursday, November 21, at a three-hour conference in the Cabinet Room at the White House. His guests were selected from the top tier of American business. Some of his visitors are unknown today but were titans of the time—diplomat and industrialist Owen Young, General Motors chairman Alfred Sloan, AT&T president Walter Gifford, and Julius Barnes, president of the Chamber of Commerce. Others at the table remain household names today—the munitions maker Pierre S. duPont, and automaker Henry Ford.

These were Hoover's peers; this was his milieu. And the conference exemplified the Hoover Method—to let government lead by exhortation, by hosting gatherings and fostering cooperation, rather than impose policy by fiat.

Hoover opened with an appraisal far more candid, and more gloomy, than anything he shared with the public. He had called this group together, said the president, only because he "viewed the crisis more seriously than a mere stock market crash." This was an instinctive judgment; there were, as Hoover pointed out, no means available to gauge the depth of the damage. But Hoover felt confident in warning that "we could expect a long and difficult period at best, [and] that there must be much liquidation of inflated values, debts and prices with heavy penalties on the nation."

Hoover's point was not to incite fear—there was plenty of that to go around. His goal was to instill awareness of the gravity of the moment, and a sense of mission going forward. Their "immediate duty" was "to consider the human problem of unemployment and distress." Previous crises had seen the immediate "liquidation" of labor, with wage cuts and layoffs; Hoover opposed such steps "with every instinct." Labor was "not a commodity," he insisted, but an entity comprised of "human homes." Besides, slashing payroll would magnify the shock of the market collapse "by suddenly reducing purchasing power." Wage cuts might prove inevitable, Hoover told this assembly of the nation's greatest employers. But wages should fall as a last resort, delayed at least until the cost of living came down—another likely result of prolonged economic doldrums. Hopefully then the worst hardships might be avoided.

This was not just an ad hoc plea to cushion the shock of the crash. In seeking to sustain payroll and wages, Hoover was invoking a central tenet of New Era economics, the idea that modern technology allowed American manufacturers to pay high wages while producing in such quantity as to keep prices low. Some modern economists, framing the question more narrowly, call it the "doctrine of high wages." It may appear an obvious point, but it was revolutionary at the time, a bold departure from the age-old thesis that producers profited strictly by keeping costs—particularly labor—as low as possible. By cooperating, rather than clashing over scant margins, employers and labor would both come out ahead, as would society as a whole.

Hoover outlined his Progressive views while still at Commerce. "We are a long way on the road to new conceptions," he said in 1926. "The very essence of great production is high wages and low prices, because it depends on a widening range of consumption only to be obtained from the purchasing power of high real wages and increasing standards of living." Here again, cooperation was key: "For both employer and employee to think in terms of the mutual interest of increased production has gained greatly in strength. It is a far cry from the conceptions of the old economics." Hoover was the great governmental exponent of this New Era thinking; Henry Ford—author of the $5 daily wage and the low-price, high-utility Model T—was its emblematic industrialist.

High tariffs were a key component of the high wages doctrine. Critics said the tariff was designed to protect industrial profits, but for Hoover it was always a matter of preserving American wages. "The purpose of the tariff is not to balance the books of business corporations but to safeguard the family budget," Hoover explained during his presidential campaign. "With increasing pressures from countries of lower living standards it has become the fundamental safeguard of the American workman and the American farmer."

Hoover was drawing from this New Era playbook, then, in pressing business leaders to sign on as first responders in the national emergency. And for the moment, they were happy to play along. Henry Ford, a curmudgeon but also a showman, startled everyone by announcing that he not only would hold the line on wages, he would raise them.

Ford made his announcement outside the White House as reporters crowded in seeking headlines from the presidential conference; his remarks were printed on a two-page statement distributed by his secretary. Ford offered a typically eccentric take on the crash; the market was not the problem, he said, so much as "a serious withdrawal of brains from business," as investors focused on profiting from speculation. A second problem, more to the point, was "under-supply of purchasing power." The answer, Ford asserted, was "a movement to increase the general wage level." And he would set the example, raising his industry-leading daily wage from $5 to $7.

"The only thing that should be high-priced in the country is the man who works," Ford declared. The rise and fall of reckless investors should not trouble the workaday world, Ford advised. "A year ago the country was expecting something to happen; now that it is over and past, the road ahead is clear."

Henry Ford stole the headlines that day but Hoover stuck with his program. That same afternoon he met with labor leaders, including John L. Lewis of the United Mine Workers and William Green of the American Federation of Labor. They readily endorsed the doctrine of high wages, of course; what Hoover sought from them was an agreement to maintain labor peace, and not to seek wage hikes during the crisis—Henry Ford's magnanimity notwithstanding. The labor leaders promptly fell into line. "The President of the United States was quick to sense the danger," William Green pronounced the next day.

Hoover unfolded the balance of his policy over the course of the next week. He proposed a dramatic expansion in federal public works to augment employment, and called for the states to do the same. And he called for tax cuts, a measure already in the works but now seen as a spur to business investment. These were standard, Progressive-era ideas, the fiscal-stimulus

measures adopted by consensus after the Harding unemployment conference. But Hoover was pursuing them on a scale never seen before. His appeal to the states was unprecedented, and he sought to expand his capital
improvement program by inviting private business to join in.

The early returns were impressive. Public officials across the country
vowed munificent budgets for 1930—$35 million for public works in the
city of St. Paul; half a billion in the state of Texas. Private industry was even
more open-handed: electric utilities committed to spend $1.4 billion on new
construction and another half-billion on maintenance; U.S. Steel announced
a three-year expansion budgeted at $250 million.

It got to the point that some executives began celebrating the crash as a
boost for business. Buoyed by the White House conferences, the president of
the Philadelphia Stock Exchange predicted a new bull market. And a bankers' sheet in New York proposed that, "The collapse of the inflated price
structure may be correctly regarded as a favorable development from the
point of view of general business." The one real danger, according to the
Guaranty Survey, was "unwarranted pessimism."

With momentum building, Hoover on December 5 convened another
industrial conference, this one hosted by the U.S. Chamber of Commerce in
its massive, colonnaded new building on H Street, facing the White House
across Lafayette Park. The sheer size of the gathering—more than four
hundred business leaders from across the country—attested to the rising
momentum of Hoover's recovery program.

This convention had the air of a pep rally, with cheers and applause as
Hoover mounted the dais in the Chamber's marble-clad Memorial Hall. The
president was less pessimistic than at the prior, White House conference—
presumably because this time reporters were present—but the message remained the same: to combat "undue pessimism, uncertainty, and hesitation
in business."

Speaking in his flat, metallic monotone, Hoover focused on the centerpiece of his recovery program: "to undertake through voluntary organization
of industry continuity and expansion of the construction and maintenance
work of the country." It was a convoluted, typically Hooverian mouthful,
to be sure, but translates simply enough into classic countercyclical stimu-

lus. Investment by private business would augment the promised spending of federal and local governments. Such expenditures, Hoover explained, could provide "a great balance-wheel of stability," structural investments that would provide jobs and support consumer demand without disrupting normal operations of the market.

"All of these efforts have one end," Hoover emphasized: "to assure employment, and to relieve the fear of unemployment." And, crucially to the president, it would be accomplished by voluntary organization, not through the agencies of the government. "The very fact that you gentlemen have come together for these broad purposes represents an advance in the whole conception of the relationship of business to the public welfare," Hoover told his audience of bankers, industrialists, and executives. "You represent the business of the United States, undertaking through your own voluntary action to contribute something very definite to the advancement of stability and progress in our economic life. This is a far cry from the arbitrary and dog-eat-dog attitude of the business world of some thirty or forty years ago."

The conference closed by appointing Julius Barnes, chairman of the chamber, to lead a "continuing economic committee" that would "spread throughout America the stimulating conclusions" reached in Washington. At the same time, the Commerce Department would organize a new division to "coordinate" public works by state and local governments.

In the end, it was all very in-house. Commerce was Hoover's bailiwick, and Barnes was a member of Hoover's personal circle, a former aide in the wartime Food Administration and a partner with Hoover and Ed Rickard in several business enterprises. Hoover let the press carry his message from there. The coverage was reflected in *The New York Times*, which obliged with a front-page story that saluted "The great machine which grew out of President Hoover's business stimulation conferences."

It was a masterful performance, winning accolades for the president in the wake of the crash and raising his profile just as the 72nd Congress was assembling in early December for its first full session. The stock market steadied at a new—albeit lower—price plateau, and labor leaders joined business executives to extol Hoover's leadership.

The leading economists of the day added their enthusiastic endorsement. "A more significant experiment in technique of [economic] balance could not be devised than the one which is being performed before our very eyes," marveled Columbia University professor Wesley Mitchell, an expert on business cycles. William Foster and Waddill Catchings, popular writers who championed the new thesis of countercyclical interventions by government, were even more effusive. "Now, for the first time in our history, we have a president who, by technical training, engineering achievement, Cabinet experience, and grasp of fundamentals, is qualified for business leadership. And for the first time in our history the heads of our largest business enterprises are prepared to follow such leadership."

Yet there was something hollow in this apparent triumph of jawboning over the age-old cycle of economic boom and bust. For all his action and conferences and phone calls, Hoover never made a major public speech on the crisis or its aftermath. He issued a single, three-paragraph statement on October 25, assuring the public that "the fundamental business of the country" was "very sound." That was all.

This was not just a function of Hoover's careful approach to managing fallout from the market crash. Relations with the White House press corps had been deteriorating from the first days of the presidency, when Hoover had set out his rules for quotation and attribution. Since then the twice-weekly press meetings had become sullen, desultory affairs, with the president making a few terse remarks and correspondents accepting brief, typed handouts in lieu of live interviews. The crowd of reporters, which initially numbered more than a hundred, dwindled to as few as a dozen.

Once the crash hit, the pattern continued. On Black Tuesday, Hoover opened his press conference by saying, "I'm sorry, but this is one of those days when I haven't anything I can very well discuss." Three days later, the refrain was the same. Finally, on November 5, Hoover relented, sharing with reporters a ten-minute discourse on "the business situation." He was candid enough, ruminating over possible causes of the crash and comparing the situation—favorably—with the crash of 1907. But the talk produced no news; at the outset of his remarks, Hoover said he was speaking "not from the point of view of publication at all—simply for your own information.

"I see no reason for making any public statements about it, either directly or indirectly," Hoover explained. He had heard the calls, from Hearst and others, entreating him to make a public statement, a display, to take a visible leadership role. But that was never his style, and he wasn't going to change now.

Hoover addressed his auditors and the question of leadership during his speech at the Chamber of Commerce in December. After reprising the "emotions" raised by the crash—"fear, uncertainty and hesitation in business"—Hoover asserted, "These are potential difficulties which cannot be cured with words." Words were cheap, in Hoover's estimation. "The cure for such storms is action," the president said. "The cure for unemployment is to find jobs."

There was no disputing that logic, but Hoover reserved his principal statements on the crash for bankers and businessmen, whom he addressed in person. To the American public, traumatized by the greatest stock crash anyone had ever seen, the president appeared remote, secluded, possibly even disinterested. Their fears were dismissed as "hysteria," as Julius Klein put it, or as Hoover said himself, "any lack of confidence in the economic future or the basic strength of business in the United States is foolish."

While much of the press was busy applauding the president's activist response to the crash, some observers took note that, even at this early stage, Hoover's message of confidence failed to resonate beyond the nation's boardrooms and executive suites. Hoover might have the diagnosis, but he didn't have the bedside manner.

William Allen White, the Kansas editor and a great supporter of Hoover's, tried to capture this particular shortcoming in a letter to a mutual friend. "The president has a great capacity to convince intellectuals," White wrote in December, soon after the White House conferences. But, "He has small capacity to stir people emotionally," and so failed to rally political support. Trying another tack, White used an agricultural metaphor. "He can plow the ground," White wrote, "harrow it, plant the seed, cultivate it, but seems to lack the power to harvest it and flail it into a political[ly] merchantable product."

Hoover's inability to connect with the populace was a terrible handicap for the leader of political system rooted in the public will, and it came to haunt his administration. The president's friends would approach on occasion and ask him to "dramatize" his efforts in the White House, to ease off the "policy of silence," but Hoover had a ready answer. "This is not a showman's job," he said more than once. "I will not step out of character."

Hoover's inability to make an emotional connection with the citizenry appeared all the more glaring in the bully pulpit of the White House, where Hoover could not avoid comparison with some of history's great communicators. "I got the impression of Mr. Hoover," said Washington correspondent James Thomas Williams, "that public sentiment, the public sentiment which Lincoln was talking about when he said, 'Public sentiment is everything . . . ,' was an absolute stranger to Mr. Hoover."

It was true, as administration officials pointed out at the time, and as historians of the crash wrote later, that only a small fraction of the American public—under one percent—were speculating in stock. But that didn't change the fact that the collapse of the market had spread a great fear across the country—fear of the future, fear that the heedless years of the 1920s would come a cropper. Nor could it change the news that was already filtering in, even as Hoover's confidence conferences got under way, that job losses and layoffs—unseasonal, unexpected unemployment—were beginning to mount.

NINE

THE PRESIDENT'S
HAIR SHIRTS

O NE EARLY CASUALTY OF THE WALL STREET CRASH WAS THAT most innocent of bystanders, the new federal Farm Board. The washout of fortunes in paper portfolios had little direct impact on the hardy tillers of the American soil. But the shock from such a fearsome financial collapse sent tremors through the commodity markets, global and domestic, where values were already soft. The sudden pressure pushed the board into a disastrous course of price support, and forced Herbert Hoover to abandon principles he had long held dear.

It's not that the Farm Board shrank from its duties. To the contrary, in the midst of the market breakdown leaders of the new agency stepped into the breach, expanding their operations to head off an accelerating crisis. What nobody yet realized was that this movement in prices was a sea change, a massive shift that would swamp any effort to block its path.

The ill-starred strategy was outlined by Farm Board chairman Alexander Legge. Appointed in July, soon after the agency was created, Legge was a natural fit for the job. Raised on small farms on the Western plains, he was an indefatigable worker who rose through the ranks to become president of International Harvester, America's first agricultural equipment conglomer-

"THE BELATED YULE LOG"

There was little mirth in the holiday season of
1929–30.

ate. Legge entered public service during the Great War when he helped coordinate arms production at the War Industries Board. Like Hoover, Legge
was in Paris during the peace talks and worked with the U.S. legation in
settling terms for the Armistice. When Hoover called on him ten years later,
Legge promptly relinquished his $100,000 corporate post for the title of
Farm Board chairman and a government salary of $10,000 a year.

Legge unveiled the Farm Board's initiative on Saturday, October 26—
two days after Black Thursday, and two days before Black Monday. The
panic in stocks had migrated to wheat, where several days of frantic selling
had driven prices down until farmers lost money on every bushel of grain
they sold. "This unsatisfactory price level is chiefly due to the rapid or dis-
orderly movement which is putting a large part of the year's supply on the
market within a short time," Legge said. Nearly half the annual harvest had
been sold just that past week, and sellers set peacetime records for volume,
and for single-day price breaks.

The impact of Wall Street turbulence on the price of grain was exceptional, Legge said, and unfair. "The unprecedented liquidation of industrial
stocks and shrinkage in values within the last few days has also had an effect
on wheat values which is entirely unwarranted and wheat producers should
not be forced to sell on a market affected by these conditions," Legge announced.

The solution Legge outlined was to advance enough funds to farmer-
led cooperatives to purchase all the wheat that remained, effectively closing
down the market until order—and more reasonable prices—were restored.
The Farm Board had $100 million readily available, and authorization for
more if needed.

Technically speaking, this mode of market intervention qualified under
the strategy of the price stabilization that was part of the original charge to
the Farm Board. But until this time nobody had attempted, or even contem-
plated, such an ambitious effort. To set a floor under the price of a major
commodity traded on exchanges across the world was a novel venture for
any peacetime American government, exceeding the careful proscriptions
laid down by Hoover himself, and the press took immediate notice. "An economic revolution is under way," declared the *Philadelphia Record*. "It means

that the government, despite all protests, is itself going into the business of agriculture," a *New York Times* editorial noted.

This audacious and potentially rash policy was in some degree forced by the crash, but it was also a consequence of the fuzzy thinking that went into creation of the Farm Board in the first place. Hoover's farm policy was always experimental, designed more to fend off the MacNary-Haugen price support scheme than as a comprehensive farm policy in its own right. There was no plan so much as a collection of ideas; the details would be worked out in the doing.

Hoover's best move here was his first—the selection of Alexander Legge as Farm Board chairman. Tall, broad-shouldered, and plain-spoken, Legge was just the sort of person to head up a high-profile and controversial new agency. He understood the farm economy from lifelong experience, but it was character that set him apart. "He has a rare combination of talent for leadership and gentleness," one friend said of Legge. "He knows human nature, he is a very shrewd trader, he is straight as a die and an unbeatable fighter."

Hoover engaged closely with Legge at the outset, meeting with him over three days in July to develop policy and strategy. Legge shared Hoover's key priorities: the principal effort was "to build up farmer-owned and farmer-controlled institutions" that would give growers new leverage in the market. The board would not be a "relief organization," but would work to eliminate the "cause of distress." Direct intervention to support commodity prices would be avoided, though such "stabilization" might be held in reserve as a last resort.

These were untested ideas, a set of principles in search of a system. "No man presumes to know the answer" to the nation's farm problem, Legge confessed after his conferences with the president. "We all start together from scratch and think collectively." Hoover never shared his uncertainty with the public, but Legge was instinctively forthright. "I have read the Act twenty times," Legge told a congressional panel that fall, "and if you understand it, you have me beat."

But Legge started out gamely, leading his new agency in establishing the Farmers National Grain Corporation, capitalized at $20 million, and the United Growers of America, private entities designed to assist local and regional farm cooperatives—to the exclusion of private growers—in marketing their produce. This was the institutionalized "cooperation" that would raise up the fortunes of the growers' cooperatives.

Both firms were launched with great fanfare—United Growers named Hoover's friend Julius Barnes as chairman and ag-cooperative trailblazer Aaron Sapiro as counsel—but soon both ran up against the limits of their prescribed roles. The fact was, farm cooperatives were already in place across the country, and there were already grain elevators and other shipping and purchasing entities ready to receive crops. In large measure, the new "farmer-controlled institutions" envisioned by Legge and Hoover were redundant. The real problem of agriculture—not enough demand for too much supply—lay undisturbed.

Certainly the farmers needed all the help they could find in moving their crops. Over its first month of operation the Farm Board heard from scores of cooperatives and hundreds of individuals seeking loans, facilities, and other assistance. In August, with the clamor mounting, the board suspended all operations, issuing a plaintive press release to explain, "The board is attempting to organize a staff . . . attempting to create a loan division," and, "endeavoring to set up a legal division." Such efforts would "demand the full efforts of the board for some time."

Even as the staff found their desks, mounting pressure threatened to overwhelm the new agency. Early in the summer a bumper crop of wheat from the American and Canadian plains combined with a big harvest in Argentina to glut the global market. By July millions of bushels of wheat were piled up in rail cars and grain elevators from Baltimore to Galveston, and the American export market was all but frozen. Prices fell through the summer, as grain accumulated in the largest surplus on record.

Finally, in October, the stock market crash forced Legge's hand. The collapse in share prices accelerated the historic declines in wheat until prices sank to a dollar a bushel—half the wartime high. The cooperatives were well enough, but without direct price intervention thousands of farms across the American West would be ruined.

The mass purchases to shore up the grain market won wide approval, but they marked a turning point for the Farm Board and for President Hoover. Facing the first of what would be a series of great shocks to the national economy, Hoover was immediately forced to compromise his beliefs and rework his policies. A man of firm convictions and slow deliberation, Hoover would have to improvise.

The president had good reason to fear the effects of price supports. During his tenure as food administrator under Woodrow Wilson, Hoover had himself been charged with boosting production to answer the needs of both the domestic market and the Allied armies in Europe. He had done so through price hikes, quickly obtaining the surge in output he needed, but also sparking dissension among growers, processors, and shippers. Now, years later, in a giant case of unintended consequences, the very production he had stimulated was swamping the global market. His experience left him confirmed in his adamant opposition to price controls. "I have done more of it than any man who lives," Hoover said in 1927, "and I would not propose price-fixing in any form short of again reentering the trenches in a World War."

Rather than attempt to manipulate the market by setting prices, Hoover insisted the best way to assist farmers was to foster cooperation. But it was essentially an ideological position, untested and uncertain; an article of faith. "I confess I do not know how to go about it at the moment," Hoover wrote a friend in 1926, "but if we could get 25 sensible men in a room without the pressure of either publicity or politics I believe the agriculture industry of the United States could be put on a basis more stable than any other industry."

With the board finally in place it was time for that confab of sensible men. On Labor Day, with wheat prices sagging, Hoover invited Legge and several other members of the Farm Board to spend Labor Day at the Rapidan Camp. They hiked and they fished, but they also talked policy—the role of Farmers National, and how to build out the infrastructure of cooperative marketing. But in the end it all came back to the commodity prices. Hoover never quite acknowledged that he was drifting into the same mode of price support the farm advocates in Congress had sought for so long, but in October the president signed off on Legge's plan to support the price of wheat.

"We now determined," Hoover wrote in his memoirs, "that the Farm Board should give indirect support to prices which had seriously declined."

Hoover never publicly acknowledged the conundrum of his farm policies, but he did so privately the following spring. Speaking offhand with his friend Edgar Rickard, Hoover said he was "not at all pleased" with the operations of the Farm Board, but that he was "trying to guide its operations." It was clear he had yet to resolve the dilemmas posed by price supports and other market-related activities; the best the president could hope for was that the board's role "not be too drastic," as he told his friend. But Hoover still professed his principled opposition; "When it is through it will be a lesson for all time against government interference" in the market, he told Rickard.

The dilemma over the proper role for the Farm Board was more than academic, and it soon forced Hoover into a ticklish confrontation with his old friend Julius Barnes. As a leader in the grain trade Barnes had endorsed the Farm Board's new national cooperatives; as president of the Chamber of Commerce Barnes took a lead role at the president's conferences in November to coordinate a national response to the stock market crash. But when the Farm Board announced its plans to support the price of wheat, Barnes stepped into the opposition.

Barnes's dispute with the Farm Board was twofold. He objected to price supports in principle, on the very sure ground that above-market prices would encourage more planting and only make the surplus worse. But he also opposed systematic aid to the farm cooperatives, as it gave them an edge in the grain exchanges over the private grain dealers who carried on the bulk of the trade. Taken to extremes, the operations of the Farm Board would put growers and shippers in direct contact, rendering the merchants superfluous. "The middleman, like Othello, is about to find his occupation gone," trumpeted one farm-state paper.

Here Barnes exposed another unspoken but essential element of the Farm Board concept—that in raising up the farm cooperatives, the board was siding with growers against the private grain dealers, including most of the great firms represented on the Chicago Board of Trade. Barnes would know—he had made his fortune during the war as head of the quasi-public United States Grain Corp., which handled all the shipping for Hoover's Food Administration. U.S. Grain had ceased operations, but Barnes remained active in a major grain export firm. He was also a principal in the Intercontinental Development Company, a holding company with headquarters at 42 Broadway in New York. His partners included President Hoover and their mutual friend Ed Rickard.

Barnes first voiced his criticism of the Farm Board in December, when the Farmers National Grain Corp. began operations in the wheat market. The occasion seemed innocuous enough; Alexander Legge assembled a clutch of major grain dealers at the Chamber of Commerce building in Washington to announce the selection of attorney Edward Flesh to run Farmers National. Flesh was a former executive under Barnes at U.S. Grain, and another close associate of Hoover's.

It all appeared very clubby until Barnes arrived at the conference to declare that "the grain trade throughout the country was threatened with chaos" by Farm Board operations. Barnes made his remarks privately but they were widely reported the next day and set off a flurry of accusations that continued into the following spring. In April Barnes led the Chamber in denouncing the Farm Board for engaging in "discriminatory competition" against the private grain traders, and called for revisions in the law. Legge answered back in kind, suggesting that the Chamber supported the idea of farm aid "only until they find out it works." The board would continue to work for the farmer, Legge vowed, and "not for the benefit of someone else."

Hoover felt obliged to placate both sides. After the initial flare-up he put out a statement suggesting that Barnes had made no effort to challenge the policies of the Farm Board; nor was there any breach between the president and Alexander Legge. The president did not try, however, to conceal his irritation. "As Mr. Hoover had appointed all members of the Farm Board," the statement read, "it was to be expected that he [Barnes] would support the board's policies." This was as far as Hoover went publicly; in private, he confessed to being "upset" with Barnes's obstinate opposition to the Farm Board.

———

Annoying as Barnes was becoming in the public sphere, he was proving to be just as irritating within Hoover's private circle. Like so many others, Barnes took a severe hit in the stock market and was leaning on his business partners for credit. "His actions are rather desperate," Ed Rickard noted after a lunch with Barnes in October.

In November Hoover and Rickard discussed Barnes at length. Hoover was still seeking to unload shares in several corporate properties he'd held since before entering the presidency, many bought at Barnes's behest. Now, when he sought to push them back, Barnes had to beg off. Worse, Barnes was trying to leverage his position on corporate boards to command questionable extensions of credit. "Barnes has some unethical ideas about business," Hoover and Rickard agreed, "which neither of us can conciliate with his public utterances."

Those public utterances were themselves beginning to wear thin. Nobody outshone Barnes when it came to optimism, and nobody better carried Hoover's message in those uncertain days after the crash. "We are now putting to practical test the quality of self-reliance in American business," Barnes told a national radio audience in November. "We are testing as well the capacity of leaders in government to cooperate with the leaders in industry." But inside the president's intimate circle, as with the "business community" in general, Barnes's cheerful pronouncements quickly grew stale. Hoover intimate Lewis Strauss offered an unvarnished appraisal of Barnes in a December memo to Larry Richey. "About the Barnes committee," Strauss began. "It seems to me the whole thing has achieved its purpose in restoring confidence. There is now the danger too much will be expected and if there is some business recession during the first two months of 1930, as seems probable, it will be said that the president's efforts were futile to prevent it."

Strauss now offered a blunt prescription that could apply to Barnes as well as his committee. "The best thing that could happen would be to get the whole thing chloroformed or, at any rate, off the front pages of the newspaper."

———

While his Farm Board ventured onto uncertain ground, Hoover's other signature initiative, the tariff, was stuck in political quicksand. The Senate returned early from its summer recess—the House, having completed its draft of the bill, stayed home—and resumed its tariff duel September 13. The committee hearings of August had produced little change: a bill that raised some rates to protect farmers, but also raised many more duties to favor industries already well protected. It was, one Senate Democrat snickered, a "most signal victory" for D.C. lobbyists, and of no discernible benefit to American farmers.

The ostensible political division was between Republicans, who favored tariffs as an instrument of policy, and Democrats, who favored the principle of free trade. But the crux of decision rested with the dozen Republican insurgents, who championed the farmer and sought to cleanse the party of its Harding-inspired reputation for kowtowing to moneyed interests.

At the center of this political triad stood Hoover, tight-lipped, taciturn. He set the tone in June: when William Borah sought White House backing for his resolution limiting tariff revision to agriculture, Hoover had disappointed his campaign ally by withholding endorsement and declining any statement.

The Senate went into recess soon after, but several committees remained in session, grinding on through a hot and bone-dry summer, "one of the worst I can remember," as one Georgetown resident complained. Every product on the tariff schedule had its day, the process painstaking but politically lucrative, the committee hearings crowded with manufacturers seeking trade duties that would protect or enhance their profits. As the weeks wore by the duties ratcheted higher, and pressure again mounted for Hoover to declare whether he would countenance the feeding frenzy that was clearly under way, or would stick to the "limited revision" he had first proposed.

Hoover's refusal to address the question incited partisans on both sides. DNC chair Jouett Shouse goaded the president in September. "What sort of chief executive is it who would sit back and permit his own Congress to make a larcenous hash of its whole session—the session he called for a specific purpose, farm relief—when by a word he could direct the flow of legislation into any channel he desired?" Senate majority leader James Watson then leapt into print, declaring the president "would sign cheerfully" any bill produced from the Republican committee. Still, no word emanated from the White House.

At this point Senator Borah confirmed his status as leader of the insurgent Republicans in the Senate by conducting a series of closed-door meetings to coordinate opposition to the tariff revision. He met with Democrats as well, announcing after one session that, "We have a complete understanding." Then, in brazen defiance of political convention, Borah authorized Shouse to reprint more than a million copies of his June speech denouncing Hoover's farm plan and the tariff revisions. More than that, Borah allowed the Democrats to use his franking privileges in distributing the speech, saving them thousands of dollars in postage.

DNC chief Shouse made sure to maximize Hoover's embarrassment from the episode. "It goes without saying that the Democratic National Committee does not necessarily endorse all the views of the Republican Senator from Idaho," Shouse told reporters, "but it is certainly of educational value to let the people know what Mr. Hoover's pre-election advocate thinks of the only piece of legislation passed by the Hoover administration."

Hoover watched all this unfold with a sense of mounting frustration. He wouldn't engage on debating tariff schedules for individual products—the list ran into the thousands and the issues were contentious and technical (Just what *were* the cost factors for wool in New Zealand?). Besides, the president continued to profess reluctance at meddling with the legislative branch.

But Hoover wanted to promote an overriding feature that he believed could resolve the whole interminable wrangle over the proper levels to set for import duties: recasting the federal Tariff Commission, a technical agency charged mainly with gathering data, into an advisory body that could adjust tariff rates up or down, subject to a presidential veto. A "flexible tariff" administered by a bipartisan commission would rationalize a process that was thoroughly politicized when tariff rates were set solely by legislation. Hoover wanted to get politics out of the tariff by moving the tariff out of Congress.

Hoover first raised this point in his speech to open the special session in

April; now, "the flexible tariff was taking a beating in the Senate," as Hoover termed it later, and he decided to hammer on the question with a public statement. At this point he still believed William Borah to be his legislative partner—or at least wished him so—and invited him to a series of meetings culminating in a White House dinner. Hoover thought he had satisfied Borah's concerns, but that may just have been his tentative approach—when requesting help Hoover could be so gingerly as to leave his auditors wondering just what it was that he sought. Borah, too, was being cagey, and "gave no indication of opposition," at least in Hoover's estimate.

So the president met with reporters September 24 and delivered a statement demanding that tariffs be set and adjusted by a revamped Tariff Commission. He opened cautiously, as was his wont, dancing around his constitutional reservations before handing out his printed remarks. "I haven't thought that the president was ever in a position to discuss schedules [for individual tariffs]," he said, adding that, "the business of the Executive was to limit himself to the consideration of principles." With that caveat, Hoover issued his statement. "The flexible tariff is one of the most progressive steps taken in tariff making in all our history," Hoover wrote. "I regard it as of the utmost importance in justice to the public."

This set the stage for what turned out to be a full-scale political double-cross. Taking the floor of the Senate two days later, with battle lines drawn and eager crowds gazing down from the gallery, William Borah turned on the president he had done so much to elect. He broadsided Hoover, blasting him for abandoning agriculture to appease the industrial East.

Borah began with an attack on Hoover's intervention into the Senate's business. "It is not my idea of the division of the departments of government under the Constitution," Borah said. But he was not going to quibble over prerogatives—not this time. He wanted to return to the ostensible purpose for this special session: the question of agriculture. By refusing to join Borah in limiting tariff review to agricultural products, Hoover had allowed a general revision, with rates climbing for industry and agriculture once again left behind. Now the going was getting rough, and Hoover would have to speak out. "Having put his hand to the plow," Borah intoned, "the president cannot turn aside because of rough furrows. Having undertaken to shape this bill, the president must go through to the end."

"The real fight here is between the agricultural and industrial interests. The most important question to the country, the one thing which will be fought out here until the snow falls, is whether these [increased] industrial schedules are justified. . . .

"I ask from the floor of the Senate that the president advise this body and advise the country, as he did with reference to the flexible tariff position, whether he approves of these industrial schedules in this bill. . . . And finally, will he advise us whether this bill meets the pledges and the promises which he made in the last campaign?"

It was a landmark performance, vintage Borah, principled and partisan at the same time, the senator flaying the lines of party allegiance as he returned to his accustomed place in opposition to the administration. For the next week Republican insurgents took turns denouncing the tariff revisions in general and Hoover's flexible tariff in particular, and on October 2 the Senate voted to limit the president's role in tariff rates to forwarding recommendations of the Tariff Commission, without comment, to the Congress.

The import of the vote echoed off the pages of the major daily papers in headline salvos. "Senate Rejects Hoover's Plea," blared the Baltimore *Sun*. "Senate Snubs Hoover," said the administration-friendly *Washington Post*. Thirteen Republicans joined thirty-four Democrats to carry the decision 47 to 42; by that margin, seven months into his term, Hoover lost control of his party and of the Congress. The debate over tariffs would drag on another six months, but Hoover's honeymoon with Congress, never especially amorous, was now officially over.

Hoover made no public acknowledgment of his stinging defeat in the Senate. He issued no statement, and instead busied himself with preparations to spend a long weekend at the Rapidan Camp in company with Ramsay MacDonald, the British prime minister, who was making his first visit to America.

But if the president remained outwardly aloof to the noisy political game unfolding at the Capitol, he was taking muted but firm measures to rein in the insurgents and put his personal stamp on the party. The designated slugger in this mission was Claudius Huston, the campaign advisor

from Tennessee who combined long-standing ties to the GOP and intense
fealty to Hoover.

Immediately following Hoover's election Huston had laid low, leaving
the limelight to Hubert Work, the ostensible manager of the 1928 campaign.
But Hoover had never much liked Work, and in June the president enlisted
Work's old mentor Will Hays, and a persistent Larry Richey, to push Work
into retirement. Work had considered Hoover's success to be a personal triumph, the capstone to a career in politics, but he now found, as William
Donovan and Mabel Willebrandt did before him, that Hoover's fidelity
could be fleeting.

Huston meanwhile continued his close association with the president,
stopping by the White House quietly but frequently. Early in August, *The
New York Times* took official notice of Huston's rising stature, profiling the
Tennessee politico as "a real Mysterious Stranger"—a curious reference to
the central character of Mark Twain's last, unfinished novel. The story went
on to assay the character of the president's latest proconsul. "This new figure in national politics moves with catlike tread. . . . He enjoys a whispered
reputation for political acumen."

The second shoe dropped in September, when Huston was elevated
to Work's former post as chairman of the Republican National Committee. The import of the decision was sounded immediately in the opposition
press. "This choice of Mr. Huston, dictated by Mr. Hoover, should dispose of
the last pretense that the president is above playing the political game in the
traditional way." Versed in the byways of political payoffs and party discipline, Huston was expected to restore order in a party divided by section and
by rival ambitions. The party's old guard, another correspondent reported,
was "openly jubilant."

Huston had two charges in his new position. The first was to make
good on Hoover's electoral success in the South. There was no subtlety here;
Huston's role was emblazoned in bold-type headlines. "Republican South
Expected of Huston," the *Times* pronounced on September 8. "For the first
time the party will be dominated by a man of the South determined to take
advantage of defections in that section and build up an organization that
will commend itself to liberal Democrats." Speaking to reporters the next

day, Huston promised to conciliate "warring elements" in the Republican South.

This was not so innocuous a task as might appear. In practical terms it meant cracking down on corruption and squeezing out the black-and-tan Republicans, a delicate operation that ran the risk of alienating black Republicans North and South. But party officials—and Hoover—believed Huston's wide connections and his unctuous manner nicely suited to the job.

Hoover's second priority for Huston was to restore harmony within the party establishment—principally by bringing the Republican insurgents to heel. This was another tall order, as the insurgents were, to a man, headstrong, irreverent, and popular with their home-state constituents. Hoover might have done better to meet these in-house rebels head-on, but being intrinsically averse to personal conflict, he cultivated surrogates more accustomed to political knife fights. By October at least, and probably sooner, the president was meeting with Huston daily, conferring on politics and policy, and people.

Initial party reaction to Huston was positive, but it lasted only so long as he kept his initiatives to himself. The politicians wanted their patronage, and if Hoover would not listen to them, Huston would have to. He got an earful in late October, when Senator Frederic Walcott of Connecticut hosted a "private luncheon," ostensibly to better acquaint Huston with the Senate Republicans. Huston could hardly refuse the honor; Walcott was a former Hoover assistant from the Food Administration, elected to Congress in the Hoover landslide.

But if Walcott was a Hoover man, that didn't make him a Huston man. The fete turned to ambush as the lawmakers loosed their resentment at the cool treatment they were receiving from the White House. Already Hoover had scrapped, in the name of good government, the time-honored practice of allowing senators to confer federal jobs on their friends and supporters; now they weren't even being notified. Senators from Illinois and Missouri, Oklahoma and California told Huston they had learned of federal appointments by reading the newspaper; some were so angry they had deserted Hoover to join the insurgents on the tariff and other key votes.

Huston was conciliatory, suggesting that "accidental" oversights were to be expected from a new administration. He promised that in future their advice in appointments would be "sought more freely." But Huston saw himself as more than an apologist for the administration. He could appease, but it was more in his nature to rebuke, and to punish.

Huston's harder edge was on display the night after the Walcott luncheon. He was back in New York, guest of honor at a Republican dinner at the posh University Club. There it was announced that Otto Kahn, of the banking firm Kuhn, Loeb, had agreed to become treasurer of the Republican National Committee. That meant lavish funding for the party's incumbents, but it was also seen as a direct threat to insurgents like William Borah and George Norris. "Selection of Mr. Kahn was seen as something of a war measure," the *Times* advised, "aimed as much against the members of the so-called Republican Progressive group in the Senate as against the Democrats."

Huston was the moving force behind the appointment, but there was no mistaking that the event, and the strategy, bore Hoover's imprimatur. Otto Kahn was, after all, a partner from the same firm as Hoover intimate Lewis Strauss, and the host for the dinner was top Hoover donor Jeremiah Milbank. While the president did not make the trip himself, his contingent was there in force, led by Vice President Charles Curtis, cabinet secretaries Walter Brown and Robert Lamont, and presidential aides Walter Newton and Larry Richey. Already serving as Hoover's vizier in the South, Huston was now emerging as Hoover's political strong arm at the RNC.

Hoover was catching flak from ostensible allies as well as the political opposition, but this was all within the bounds of the game as he understood it. What nettled Hoover more, what drove him to literal distraction, was insinuation and calumny from enemies he couldn't see, the threat of secret schemes to besmirch him. As he climbed higher in the public sphere, these threats took shape as exposé books floated by his political opposition. Hoover never minced words when it came to such "smear books"—on different occasions he termed them "slander," "vague insinuations," "absolute malice," and "filthy political defamation"—and he enlisted his closest friends in an effort to root them out.

An early instance of such plots arose in the closing days of the 1928 campaign, when a former New York policeman named James O'Brien made headlines with the allegation that Hoover had employed serfs and convicts "in the condition of semi-slavery" at his foreign mining operations. O'Brien had close contacts with John Raskob and the Democratic National Committee, but Raskob disavowed the accusation, and reporters dropped the story. Not Hoover, however. At the height of the campaign, with O'Brien's innuendos still circulating, Hoover dispatched his aide Larry Richey to London to track down any court documents or other public records that might bear on Hoover's career abroad.

The episode lay quiet until a year later when a British immigrant named John Hamill approached Hoover's financial advisor Edgar Rickard with a most surprising proposition. Hamill said he had been hired by James O'Brien to help develop the aspersions against Hoover into a book-length exposé. Hamill had agreed to go along, but felt guilty for abetting such a nefarious project. He was "sick at heart of the whole business," and wanted to make amends. Hamill contacted Rickard in December, and was invited to stop by Rickard's office in Manhattan.

After arranging his meeting with the mysterious stranger, Rickard contacted Hoover aide Larry Richey. Richey, in turn, called on J. Edgar Hoover, a personal friend then in his sixth year as director of the Federal Bureau of Investigation. Hoover arranged for his agents in New York to track Hamill in the days before the meeting with Rickard.

When at last they sat down, Hamill told Rickard he was engaged in a full-blown plot to defame the president, and that he would do whatever he could to assist Hoover and his team in their defense against O'Brien. But Rickard was forewarned; the FBI reported that just the day before, Hamill had met with O'Brien at the public library, where together they had perused reports on Hoover from old mining magazines.

With that shadowy backdrop, the meeting did little to clear the air. In the days afterward Rickard and Richey then each pursued the Hamill affair in their own fashion. Rickard consulted attorneys, including George Wickersham, the head of Hoover's law enforcement reform commission. In turn, Wickersham brought in Isidor Kresel, one of the top lawyers in Manhattan, and placed him under Rickard's command.

Kresel made a close review of the facts and got back to Rickard just before the turn of the year. He was unequivocal. "I think this man is a dangerous character. He impresses me as an adventurer who would not stop at anything." To Kresel, Hamill's motive was obvious. "I think the man is looking for money. I think he has obtained all that he could get from the other side and is now looking to sell what dribble he has to us." There was no question how to proceed. "My advice would be to have nothing further to do with the man."

Larry Richey agreed with Kresel's assessment, but he was less inclined to break off his researches on Hamill; he had an investigator's curiosity to learn more about O'Brien, about the Democratic National Committee, and about what damaging material Hamill had turned up. And he had a boss who always wanted to know all he could.

J. Edgar Hoover was another principal in the John Hamill surveillance who wanted to pursue the matter further. When he sent Richey the field reports his agents filed on Hamill in December, the FBI director asked, in a cover memo, for "any suggestions that you can offer concerning future action that we should take in this matter."

But Richey was too savvy, or knew J. Edgar too well, to admit the insinuating young lawman into the president's confidential circle. He was willing to use the FBI on a short-term basis, but preferred to conduct sensitive investigations on his own.

Rather than J. Edgar Hoover, Richey chose to enlist the services of Lewis Strauss, the banking attorney and friend of the president's. Richey and Strauss had long been friendly, but after Hoover entered the White House the connection appears to have deepened. Beginning that summer they maintained a steady correspondence, with memos on Southern politics and Wall Street financial conditions mixed in with reports on fishing prospects and invitations to dinner. In December, Strauss commissioned a pair of custom-made fishing boots for Richey; a month later he sent along several pairs of red-top socks from Abercrombie & Fitch to complement the boots.

Not only was Strauss friendly with Richey, but he brought his own intelligence contacts to the project. One of Strauss's partners at Kuhn, Loeb was

William Wiseman, head of British intelligence in America during the war. Another close friend was Paul Foster, recently retired as head of the U.S. Naval Intelligence office in New York.

Strauss brought these connections to bear in January, when Wiseman reached out to friends in England for background on Hamill. The findings were all negative; contrary to reports, Hamill had no record of employment with either the War Office, the Foreign Office, or Scotland Yard. The trail was cold, but that didn't stop Hoover's closest friends—and Hoover himself—from their determined efforts to expose and destroy the plots against the president.

Herbert Hoover had yet to spend a full year in office but it was fast becoming apparent that his would be a turbulent passage through the presidency, even by comparison to his immediate predecessor, the puckish but primly distinguished Calvin Coolidge. The market crash had been predicted for years, but now it was Hoover's headache; in the meantime his principal political initiatives were drawing fire from friend and foe.

This was not the sort of debut the thin-skinned super-administrator had anticipated. But at this stage Hoover strove to contain his disappointment and compose his difficulties as standard accouterments of his high office. Usually tight-lipped about anything approaching a personal revelation, Hoover offered at this juncture a rare—and revealing—discourse on this inner equanimity. The occasion was a holiday dinner held by the Gridiron Club, then as now a unique institution, consisting of fifty top Washington journalists and devoted exclusively to staging semiannual dinners featuring satirical skits put on by club members, and off-record speeches by guests from the political establishment, up to and including the president.

When Hoover stood to deliver at the December dinner, he opened with what was apparently meant as a humorous disquisition on hair shirts, the itchy, purposely uncomfortable garments worn by monks of the Middle Ages to remind them of their mortal sins. "Many years ago," Hoover proposed, "I concluded that a few hair shirts were part of the mental wardrobe of any man. The president differs from other men only in that he has a more extensive wardrobe"—of hair shirts.

"I am not complaining," Hoover continued. "I am only explaining one of the things that train his soul and his public conduct in urbanity." Now Hoover explained himself. "You could discover from these proceedings why presidents seldom worry about anything. They have so many troubles in the closet or stowed away in the icebox that when one of them gets tiresome they can always send for another, and by great variety maintain interest and a high cheerfulness of spirit."

Hoover was professing to be undisturbed, which was in keeping with the self-effacing but also paternalistic tone of his wit. But his insouciance seemed a bit forced, and the hair shirt was an odd place to find inspiration. This wasn't the belligerent, even bellicose confidence of Teddy Roosevelt or Woodrow Wilson. Nor was it the calm, self-composed reserve of Calvin Coolidge. Hoover's brand of leadership, virtually unknown to the public until revealed by his conduct in office, was also rooted in self-confidence, but of a plaintive, narcissistic mode that evoked more pity than belief.

In years to come the reference would appear repeatedly, but rarely in sympathy or in approval: Hoover, our hair-shirt president.

TEN

"THE PECULIAR WEAKNESS OF MR. HOOVER"

THE NEW YEAR OF 1930 OFFERED HERBERT HOOVER THE CHANCE to make a midcourse correction. The nation was poised somewhere in the shadowland between crash and depression, with business leaders and most Americans averting their eyes in the wishful belief that the October sell-off was just about stocks, and not the entire economy. Congress was in session, but lawmakers continued preoccupied with the tariff to the exclusion of almost all other business. The moment was ripe for the sort of gesture that would reclaim for Hoover the stature he'd squandered over the course of the special session.

But there would be no reset. Rocky as the early stages of his presidential term had proven to be, Hoover was destined over the next several months to confirm his reputation for political ineptitude. It was a trait that initially worked in his favor, setting him apart from the usual run of favorite sons and party hacks. But now Hoover executed a series of clumsy gaffes that brought his judgment and his character into question. Instead of standing above the fray, Hoover appeared artless and ineffectual.

The first and best opportunity for Hoover to reclaim the mantle of leadership came early on, when declining health forced the resignation of

"HEY, LET GO!"
Hoover's refusal to cut loose Tennessee politico
Claudius Huston, shown here clinging to the GOP
tail, cost him dearly.

William Howard Taft, the former president and now chief justice of the Supreme Court. Here Hoover might set the national agenda by exercising the prerogative that was his alone: selection of a new leader for the high court.

Within the White House as well as without, it was assumed that Hoover would seize the opportunity to name Associate Justice Harlan Stone to Taft's seat. Stone was widely admired and considered by many the natural choice to lead a notoriously hidebound bench in a new, more Progressive direction. And his elevation would leave an open seat, allowing Hoover to name a new associate justice—essentially a twofer that could mark a fundamental shift on the court. In addition, Stone was Hoover's close friend, an ally in the Coolidge administration, a fishing companion, and an original member of the Medicine Ball Cabinet.

Taft made his resignation official on Monday, February 3, and White House correspondents spent the afternoon awaiting the announcement that was sure to follow. Around 3 p.m. Hoover aide George Akerson strolled into the press room and said, in a stage whisper audible to all, "It's Stone."

This notification was informal; the official announcement was scheduled for Hoover's regular Tuesday press conference. But Akerson's utterance set off a commotion as correspondents scrambled to file their stories for the next day's papers. It apparently set off a commotion inside the White House as well, as word of Akerson's statement circulated through the offices. An hour after his offhand announcement, Akerson was back in the press room. This time he made no statement, but passed around slips of paper with a terse, momentous correction: the nomination would not go to Stone after all, but to Charles Evans Hughes.

Hughes was not an especially controversial selection. He was a Republican Party stalwart, a former associate justice on the high court who had resigned to mount a stiff challenge to Woodrow Wilson in the 1916 presidential election. He was also secretary of state under Presidents Harding and Coolidge, and a former governor of New York. Hughes campaigned hard for Hoover in 1928 and had the backing of the core, "regular" Republicans.

His nomination won immediate praise. "Never was there a clearer case of the office seeking the man," *The New York Times* pronounced. Benjamin Cardozo, sitting on the New York Court of Appeals and already a leading voice in jurisprudence, declared Hughes "a great choice of a great man for a great office."

But the applause for Hughes could not drown out consternation over the president's bungled and altered announcement. The Baltimore *Sun* termed Hughes's selection "the biggest surprise of [Hoover's] administration." So big a surprise, in fact, that for years many believed that Hoover made the appointment by mistake—that he intended Stone for the post but offered it first to Hughes as a courtesy, only to be surprised when Hughes accepted.

More than that, the switch away from Stone dashed the hopes of many voters who expected Hoover to instigate a season of change in the American courts. "The president's friends counted on him to liberalize the institution," one liberal columnist surmised. "The Stone appointment was taken for granted because it gave the president a chance to demonstrate what we thought was his real attitude in an effective and non-political manner."

For some Hoover backers, the court choice proved that their support was in error. "Progressives now concede that what they mistook for liberalism was no more than humanitarianism," the disgruntled scribe continued. "The Hughes appointment, to our mind, has discouraged this wing of the Republican Party more than any policy or appointment of such a stand-patter as Calvin Coolidge." Many had seen Hoover as a return to the party's reformist roots, but now, "we find the Progressives to be grievously disappointed."

When he first learned of Hoover's selection, George Norris, chair of the Senate Judiciary Committee and a leading Republican insurgent, said flatly, "There is no objection to Mr. Hughes' appointment." But a week later, when Majority Leader James Watson called for nomination by unanimous acclamation, Norris took the floor to launch a blistering attack upon Hughes. "We have reached a time in our history when the power and influence of monopoly and organized wealth are reaching into every government activity," Norris proclaimed. "No man in public life so exemplifies the influence of powerful combinations in the political and financial worlds as does Mr. Hughes."

The speech—and the change of heart—were typical of Norris, a prairie populist who viewed most political action through the lens of class interest. His calls to the ramparts were usually ignored by his Senate colleagues, but now Norris struck a nerve. Suddenly, the swirling political frustrations left over from the special session, and the fear and suspicion engendered by the October crash, were unleashed on the floor of the Senate. It was an early sign that economic strife stifled under years of growth would find soon a forum in the Congress.

William Borah, always game for a political donnybrook, took up the cudgel the following day. He focused on a pair of obscure Hughes cases—one concerning radio licenses and another municipal rate-setting authorities—and construed them to portray the veteran jurist as a servant of property. Hughes's viewpoint, Borah declared, "if carried to its logical conclusion, must result in great economic oppression to the people of the United States."

The denunciations were unexpected, and stunning. "Not in a century have such attacks been made upon confirmation of a chief justice," noted the lead story in the *Times*.

They were also a bit overwrought. True, in the years since he had left the Supreme Court, Hughes had represented well-heeled clients before the tribunal. But that was largely the nature of the institution—a forum where powerful interests tested their reach. In fact Hughes hailed from the same liberal tradition as Hoover and many other Republicans of the day. Like Henry Stimson, another New York Republican, Hughes broke into public life investigating corrupt utilities and insurance companies, and he was elected governor of New York as a Progressive closely aligned with Theodore Roosevelt. During his first term on the Supreme Court, from 1910 to 1916, he challenged the reigning doctrine of laissez-faire, expanding the scope of the Constitution's commerce clause. And as secretary of state, Hughes championed disarmament, and collaborated with Hoover to suppress a federal injunction against striking railway workers.

Charles Evans Hughes was not the monopolists' shill that the Senate insurgents were gunning for, and they knew it. As much as Norris and Borah blasted away at Hughes, the obvious target was the White House. The president had deserted them in the tariff fight, and now they were frustrated with the court appointment. It may be, too, that they sensed weakness in the gyrations around the appointment. These political warhorses responded to power as much as policy, and when Hoover faltered, they were quick to break ranks.

The rage against Hughes—or, more properly, against Hoover's selection— blew for three days through the Senate, culminating with a contentious seven-hour debate. In the end Hughes was confirmed handily, by a 52-to-26 margin, but the lopsided tally could not paper over the changed mood in Washington. President Hoover could not have been surprised, then, when his next court nominee quickly foundered.

The president returned to the arena of Senate confirmations again in March—sooner than he would have liked, perhaps, his hand forced by the unexpected death of an associate justice at the relatively early age of just sixty-four. Two weeks later, Hoover nominated John J. Parker, a North Carolina native and federal appellate judge sitting on the Fourth Circuit in Virginia.

It was a distinct shift from Hoover's choice the month before. Where Hughes had been a safe and cautious selection, Parker was a bold one. Having ignored the South while he assembled his cabinet, Hoover was finally paying his debt to the Hoovercrats who had helped him break in upon the Democrats' Solid South. In the words of Paul Anderson, a veteran Washington correspondent writing for *The Nation*, the appointment was "purely political . . . intended to strengthen the Republican Party in the South, and particularly in North Carolina."

Parker certainly fit the profile of the new Southern elite that Hoover hoped to raise up. Just forty-four years old—half the age of the senior justice on the court—Parker was already a star in North Carolina politics and law, a leader of the state's lily-white Republicans and a genuine threat to the dominant Democrats. While still in private practice Parker ran in a series of longshot campaigns—for Congress, for attorney general, for governor— and while he lost them all, in 1920 he polled 230,000 votes, the best Republican showing for any office in that state, ever.

But Parker's extrajudicial appeal invited a spirited opposition that also arose outside the customary domain of the courts. First to speak out against the Southern jurist was William Green, president of the American Federation of Labor. As successor to AFL founder Samuel Gompers, Green was generally amenable to Hoover's doctrine of economic cooperation. But Green was not above grandstanding for his constituent unions, and in Parker he found an irresistible straw man.

Parker's defect was a 1927 order barring labor activists from attempting to organize mineworkers already covered by a nonunion contract. Such "yellow-dog contracts" are illegal today, but in the 1920s they were a hated corporate tool, widely used to stave off labor organizers. Yellow-dog contracts, and the court injunctions employers often obtained to enforce them, enjoyed the explicit endorsement of the Supreme Court, which in 1917 upheld "freedom of contract" over the rights of labor protest.

To Parker the contest over the Red Jacket Mining Company was a fairly innocuous case presenting questions already settled by precedent, but for Green and the labor federation it was a litmus test. Yellow-dog contracts and labor injunctions left workers "in a condition approximating industrial servitude," as Green termed it, and over the next two years he would campaign hard for new legislation banning the practice. In the event, a week after Hoover named Parker, Green called a press conference to declare that he would fight Parker's confirmation. By ruling in favor of Red Jacket, Green said, "Judge Parker placed property rights above and superior to human rights."

A week after the labor federation denounced Parker's nomination, adversaries just as adamant arose from the staff and leadership of the National Association for the Advancement of Colored People. Clinching the case was a yellowed newspaper clipping sent to Walter White, the organization's acting secretary and a part-time journalist, soon to become NAACP president. The article, from a 1920 edition of the Greensboro, North Carolina, *Daily News*, excerpted a Parker speech accepting his party's gubernatorial nomination. He was addressing a charge by state Democrats that the Republicans would enfranchise blacks and ride their votes to victory.

"The negro as a class does not desire to enter politics," Parker declared in his speech. "The Republican Party of North Carolina does not desire him to do so. We recognize the fact that he has not yet entered the stage in his development when he can share the burdens and responsibilities of government. This being true, and every intelligent man in North Carolina knows that it is true, the attempt of certain petty Democratic politicians to inject the race issue into every campaign is reprehensible."

Presented with this trenchant oration by Parker, White felt his course was clear. "Plainly this attitude would constitute a grave threat to the future of the Negro" should Parker be seated on the Supreme Court, White wrote later. Over the next several weeks White contacted every NAACP chapter in the country, calling on individual members to write their senators opposing the nomination, and to alert "church, fraternal, labor, civic, educational, and other bodies" to do the same. Prominent leaders in the NAACP, including Arthur Spingarn and W. E. B. Du Bois, spoke to large audiences and distributed telegraph blanks preaddressed to specific senators.

The results were impressive. By early April, letters and telegrams opposing Parker were pouring into the NAACP offices in New York, and into Senate offices in Washington. As the piles of mail mounted, senators from Northern states with large numbers of black voters began to waver. Labor was a shifting faction, often aligned with the Democrats, and their demands might be balanced, but black votes were a Republican mainstay. Now those votes were in jeopardy; as one telegram reminded both the senators from Ohio, "Parker is seriously objectionable to 90,000 Cleveland Negro citizens."

The night of April 10, with protests mounting, the unthinkable happened: James Watson, the majority leader, made an evening visit to the White House to advise Hoover that Parker's nomination was in serious trouble. The following day Vice President Charles Curtis stopped in to offer the same counsel.

Only now did the depth of the problem start to become clear: Parker was reaping all the fallout of Hoover's troubled Southern strategy. From the earliest days of his presidential campaign, Hoover and his strategists had chosen not to pick sides in the race-riven South, but to take the Southern parties as they found them. Black-and-tan or lily-white, Hoover cared not, so long as they vouched him their support. Hoover's silence on questions of race left black Americans to their own interpretations, and his attacks on patronage corruption convinced them Hoover was conducting a racial purge of the party. Nominating a lily-white like Parker seemed to prove the point. To Walter White, to the NAACP, and to blacks across the country, Hoover was "the man in the lily-White House."

Even as the Senate Judiciary Committee was thrashing Hoover's court selections, a second Senate committee was eyeing the activities of the president's top political counselor. The ostensible project was to investigate influence peddling in connection with the tariff, but it soon appeared the goal was to the bring down Claudius Huston.

George Norris empaneled the lobbying subcommittee at the height of the wrangles over the tariff in the fall of 1929. But under the direction of Chairman Thaddeus Caraway, a moon-faced, sharp-tongued former prosecutor from Arkansas, the committee inquiry soon began to wander, settling in February on the huge federal power facility at Muscle Shoals, a small town on the Tennessee River in northern Alabama. Erected during the closing stages of the war, the plant had become the focal point of national debate over public versus private power generation. At the same time, it was the forum for the first collaboration between Claudius Huston and Herbert Hoover.

This alliance dated to the early 1920s, when, as secretary of commerce, Hoover was seeking a private firm to take over operation of the plant, which came to be called by the name of the town where it was located. At that time Huston was a rising jack-of-all-business-trades in Tennessee, and as such, an officer in the Tennessee River Improvement Association. Both Hoover and Huston voiced keen support in 1921 for a bid by Henry Ford to step in at Muscle Shoals; the plan foundered, but the association between Huston and Hoover grew stronger over the years.

Huston formally resigned his post at the TRIA nine years later, when Hoover made him chairman at the Republican National Committee. But Caraway was intrigued by Huston's link to Hoover, and called Huston before the committee on March 12. The chairman probed for any hint that Huston had exercised undue or illicit influence through his connection with Hoover, but Huston and the president came through unscathed.

The senators then turned to the finances of the Tennessee River Improvement Association. Huston said he had personally contributed more than $50,000 of his own money to float the TRIA in lean times, he said, but he had kept no records, as "it is not a deductible item." Thomas Walsh, one of the committee's two Democrats, aired the panel's bemusement. "The trouble about it is, you have nothing to conceal but you have nothing to reveal."

Huston held his own through three days of testimony, but during his fourth appearance, on March 18, the committee struck a nerve. Leaving policy aside, they pressed Huston on two large contributions to the TRIA that he had solicited just the year before.

The source of the funds was Union Carbide. That was natural enough, as Union Carbide was one of the industrial firms seeking development rights at Muscle Shoals. But by Huston's own testimony, the TRIA had been all but moribund since 1925, holding no meetings and ceasing to pay a salary to the executive director. Why then did Huston approach a Union Carbide executive in February 1929 and press him for a contribution of $20,000? Why did that executive respond by writing Huston a personal check? And why, rather than sending that check on to the TRIA in Tennessee, did Huston deposit the funds in a personal bank account in New York? Just what happened to the money?

The senators spent the day hammering on Huston, filling in details and pressing for more. They learned Huston didn't handle the money himself, but ran it through an agent, who passed it on to a Wall Street brokerage firm, which placed the funds in a stock-trading account maintained for Huston. From there things only got worse. Huston's agents, called and placed under oath, explained that Huston's brokerage account was maintained solely for stock trades, and that his calls for "contributions" to the then moribund TRIA coincided with margin calls on underperforming stocks. It developed later that the first check, for $22,000, served to cover Huston's brokerage debt of $19,391.07, and the second, in June, for $14,100, was put up on margin to purchase a new round of stocks.

There was nothing criminal in the transactions, but it was so very unseemly. The president's close advisor, the "mystery man" he'd placed atop the RNC, had been hustling his donors and using them to cover large bets

on the bull market—sharp practice that looked all the more tawdry after
the crash. Republican lawmakers immediately sensed potential damage in
the midterm elections, now just eight months away. The day after Huston's
stock transactions were confirmed in sworn testimony, a caucus of more
than twenty Republican senators demanded his resignation from the RNC.

At this point it was clear President Hoover was in full retreat. Not only
was Huston mortally wounded, but the spectacle of the Senate inquiry had
rendered the Parker nomination untenable. It wasn't just the prospect of
corruption: Hoover had raised up Huston as the arbiter of patronage, the
man who would clean up the corrupt party organizations in the South. Now
Huston was the object of scorn, and his sponsors—Hoover, principally, but
also the Republican Party—appeared his dupes.

"We cannot refrain from having a quiet laugh at the expense of the
President of the United States with regard to those Southern Republicans,"
W. E. B. Du Bois, the NAACP firebrand, wrote in May. Here was Huston,
"appointed for the express purpose of cleansing these Augean stables for the
benefit of Hoover majorities at the next presidential election," now exposed
in sordid self-dealing. Du Bois felt moved to sarcasm: "All of which con-
vinces us of the spotless purity of the white Republicans of the South and the
unforgivable perverseness of Negroes in not following their able teachings
and shining example."

Once a harbinger of renewal and reform, Hoover's Southern strategy
now looked crude and cynical. And Judge Parker stood as the inadvertent
standard-bearer for that strategy—polished, professional, lily-white, and
chosen by the president.

America in 1930 had not yet reached the point that racial offenses would
doom a candidate for national office. But the concerted opposition of labor
and black Americans put Parker's Supreme Court nomination in jeopardy.
Added to that, Hoover's overriding disdain for "politics" rendered him inert
and ineffectual in his battles with Congress. Hoover aide French Strother
spelled it out at the time: the president "was handicapped because he didn't
understand playing the political game well enough—trading and swapping
one thing for another."

When it came, the decision was excruciatingly close. Forty-nine senators voted against Parker, and forty-seven in his favor. A single additional vote for Parker would have deadlocked the Senate, allowing the vice president to decide the question in favor of the administration. But that vote was never cast, and Parker was rejected, the first time in thirty-six years a Supreme Court nominee had failed confirmation, and only the ninth time in the nation's history.

Hoover responded to the rejection of Judge Parker in characteristic fashion. He said nothing, enduring without comment his repudiation by a Congress where his own party controlled both houses by commanding margins. Two days later he nominated Owen Roberts, a Philadelphia attorney who did a brief turn as a Teapot Dome prosecutor, to the open court seat. He did so without even a mention to the press, simply sending to the Senate a message bearing Roberts's name.

After all the derision heaped on his first two candidates, Roberts was confirmed with barely a murmur.* But Hoover could not delude himself that the drubbing he took in the debates over Charles Evans Hughes, Claudius Huston, and Judge John Parker might escape notice.

Of all the imbroglios to mar Hoover's first, extended encounter with the Congress, the tariff was perhaps the most costly. It dragged on incessantly, it brought out the worst in the legislators, and it highlighted Hoover's weakness as a leader—all in service of a bill that nobody much liked in the end.

The final version of the tariff bill, authored by Utah senator Reed Smoot and Representative Willis Hawley, of Oregon, engaged in wholesale rate hikes covering 887 specific products—a far cry from the limited revision first proposed by Hoover. After winning House approval in May, the bill engendered a groundswell of protest, including a public letter from 1,028 economists demanding a Hoover veto. But that was impossible; hav-

---

* Roberts would win court fame in 1937 for the "switch in time that saved nine," his swing vote upholding the minimum wage. In prior cases Roberts had struck down key elements of the New Deal, prompting FDR's plan to remake the court. Many believe that Roberts "switched" on the wage vote to help thwart the attack on the court, though Roberts denied playing strategy with his vote.

ing stood by as the bill made its tortuous way through Congress, the president could hardly turn his back on a measure endorsed by a clear majority of his own party. Privately, Hoover disparaged the bill as "vicious, extortionate, and obnoxious," but on June 17 he signed the Smoot-Hawley tariff into law.

Passage of the bill was a victory for no one—least of all the president who endorsed it. As with the controversies over his judicial nominations, the details in dispute tended to blur, and the focus of criticism inevitably shifted to the president, his character and his leadership. In all these controversies, Hoover was the common denominator.

New York Democrat Robert Wagner posed the question in March in a speech from the Senate floor. The issue was the tariff, still mired in committee, but Wagner spoke on the question of leadership. "Who is responsible for the tariff delay? Where, precisely, does the fault lie?" That the Senate Republicans were divided, Wagner readily admitted. But who should answer for that? "When this breakdown occurred in the Republican Party the president did not come forward and exercise the leadership which was the prerogative of his office."

"Instead he was undecided; he was undetermined; he vacillated." This was the price of Hoover's silence; his critics stepped into the stillness and supplied the motives for him. "He drifted," Wagner said derisively, "he permitted every tide and every wind of popular fancy to shift his course."

Democratic National Committee chairman Jouett Shouse drew the indictment even more sharply in a speech in Florida. Like Wagner, Shouse took the divisions over the tariff as his case in point. "The Republican majority in the Senate is split in three divergent sections because the president could not, or would not, lead his party."

Shouse then expanded on the role of the chief executive. "The American people do not expect that the President of the United States shall dictate to Congress, but the American people expect of the man chosen as their chief executive, when his party is in control of both branches of the legislative arm of the government, a degree of constructive leadership that will get results." This was more than a matter of style, Shouse said, and would come to define Hoover's tenure in the White House. "Every president in our history who has made a marked success of his administration has been able to lead Congress and to lead the people of the country. Those who have failed have failed because of lack of these attributes."

These were partisan attacks, of course, and Hoover and his team could dismiss them as such. But as the Democratic sharpshooter Charley Michelson wrote later, he never had to trump up the charges he leveled against the president. "There was no necessity for misrepresentation, no excuse for slander," Michelson said. "A man sat in the president's chair who didn't fit."

Indeed, the heaviest blow Hoover sustained was delivered by a former friend, the pundit and literary analyst Walter Lippmann, in a cover story for *Harper's Magazine*. Back in 1920, Hoover and Lippman traveled in the same social circles in Washington; Lippmann thought so much of Hoover then that he floated the idea of pairing him with Franklin Roosevelt on a Progressive presidential dream ticket. But that was a decade ago; now Hoover was a sitting president, and Lippmann composed a searching and intensely personal portrait.

This landmark essay, published in June, found the president deficient not just in conduct but in character. Under the title "The Peculiar Weakness of Mr. Hoover," Lippmann reprised the careful plans Hoover had laid for his administration, and "the refusal of circumstances to fit the specification." Thus a "limited revision of the tariff" became a wholesale rewrite of the duty schedule, and a damaging political embarrassment; a bipartisan study of Prohibition only stoked a running controversy. There were more fiascos Lippmann might have touched on—"reform" in the South certainly qualified—but the point was clear enough: Lippmann wondered "why it is that events have so spectacularly eluded the control of a man who with fine purposes and high abilities had set himself the ideal of controlling them?"

In deference to the president, Lippmann laid part of the blame on Hoover's campaign-burnished reputation for competence and expertise. By raising public expectations so high, Hoover and his boosters had set him up for an inevitable fall. Much of the disappointment in the president's performance was simply an adjustment to reality. "Hoover is blamed for not

achieving things which nobody would ever have expected" of his presidential predecessors, Lippmann allowed.

But preconceptions were only part of the problem. A year in the White
House had revealed new dimensions to Hoover's character, features that surprised and dismayed even some in his inner circle. After an opening stanza,
Lippman cut to his critique. "My own notion is that a close examination of
Mr. Hoover's conduct in the critical matters will disclose a strange weakness
which renders him indecisive at the point where the battle can be won or
lost." This was a mortal flaw in a political figure, but one that rang familiar
to the Hoover allies, in and out of Congress, who had sought to interpret his
agenda.

Lou Hoover credited her husband's tendency to agonize over decisions
to his scientific mind and engineer's training, but Lippmann was less generous: "This weakness appears at the point where in order to win he would
have to intervene in the hurly-burly of conflicting wills which are the living tissue of popular government." As Michelson suggested, the pattern was
there for all to see: when lines were drawn and the contenders looked for
conviction, Hoover tended to fade away, his voice mute and his purpose obscure.

Knowing Hoover was new to elected office, Lippmann laid the president's failings to the vagaries of the democratic process. "He is baffled and
worried . . . his action paralyzed by his own inexperience in the very special
business of democracy." Some might see Hoover's remote bearing as arrogance, but Lippmann felt otherwise. Again, the source was in the system.
Hoover prized certainty, Lippmann wrote, and was "excessively diffident in
the presence of the normal irrationality of democracy." Hoover was quickly
emerging as a caution to those who saw the dry logic of the engineer as an
antidote to the practice of politics. "In the realm of reason he is an unusually
bold man; in the realm of unreason he is, for a statesman, an exceptionally
thin-skinned and easily bewildered man."

It got to the point that the president's supporters in newsrooms far from
Washington felt moved to sound an alarm. From Iowa, the editor of the
Cedar Rapids Gazette wrote to implore the president for a change in tone.

"All the press needs to know is what is going on," came the plea. "I almost weep when I think of the possibilities for constructive publicity that are being passed up."

Another seasoned journalist, writing this time to Hoover's friend Mark Sullivan, sounded a parallel but more universal theme. The American public was "dazed" by the market crash and the political smash-up in Washington; it was time for the president to seize the initiative. "I don't believe an administration should be content with calm, factual statements when the obvious need of the hour is for somebody to say something with a heroic ring to it—a battle cry rousing the spirits of the people. . . . Silence is no guide, and calm statement, however sound, has no inspiration."

More insistent, and more detailed in his critique, was Alfred Kirchhofer, managing editor of the *Buffalo Evening News*. A boon friend and political supporter of William Donovan, Kirchhofer had served the 1928 campaign as one of Hoover's media advisors, and later was a repeat guest at the presidential retreat on the Rapidan. Now in 1930, following a July visit to the White House and a lengthy conversation with the president, Kirchhofer composed a nine-page letter analyzing Hoover's public image and his "ever-present problem of press relations." Here at the height of this season of political setbacks, Kirchhofer was deferential to Hoover but severe in his assessment. "If I would be helpful, I must be frank," the editor warned the president.

Kirchhover was good to his word. "The public, generally speaking and without regard to party, thinks the administration to date has been a failure." Here his thinking echoed that of William Allen White, editor from Iowa. "The main reason for this," Kirchhofer wrote, "is the fact that your story has not got across to the public."

Kirchhofer cited as a case in point "the terrific campaign" waged against the tariff, to which Hoover and his team made "no effective answer." Kirchhofer had discussed the matter in his visit with the president, but now raised it again for emphasis. "It is a fact, according to my observation, that a large selection of public opinion feels that you either haven't stood your ground or have backed down in your encounters with Congress. They have a feeling that you bow down too easily to opposition."

Claudius Huston was another example. Huston was at the time continuing his defiant holdout at the RNC; "It would have been better to make a clean sweep," Kirchhofer advised, "than to let Huston rather than the president be the boss."

Kirchhofer readily acknowledged that the press corps was part of the problem, but he insisted the solution lay with Hoover. "I think you could make friends if you'd just give the rank and file something to write about." That didn't mean quotes and personal interviews, but program, policy; news. And it had to come from the president. "I know you feel that what you say should have the most careful thought," Kirchhofer wrote. But Hoover needed to relax and open up with the press, as he had before the election. "I know that you can, upon occasion, let go of the word or thought that will hit the front page." This was not, Kirchhofer realized, the sort of advice Hoover wanted to hear. But he pressed the point anyway. "You can't put over your job without selling it to the public," he wrote. "I think it is as important as anything you can do."

Kirchoffer said he was concerned with the success of Hoover and his administration, but he had an ulterior motive as well. He had looked to Hoover as an antidote to the compromises and corruptions of politics-as-usual. "Your triumph is essential to putting in a minor place selfish politicians and unscrupulous partisans," Kirchoffer wrote. "I mean that unless you do succeed in a measurable way, the politicians, perhaps for generations to come, will have the excuse that we need a politician rather than an accomplished man of affairs in the presidential office."

Hoover was insulated, he was isolated, but he was not oblivious. He recognized that he was having problems with Congress, that some initiatives had been sidetracked and others stalled. What distinguished the president was his interpretation. Where others saw a lack of presidential leadership, Hoover saw blind opposition from his enemies, and disloyalty and cowardice on the part of his allies. He conceded "errors" on his part, but only tactical. It did not occur to him that his basic approach to governance might be wrong.

Faced with mounting resistance in and out of Congress, then, Hoover responded with a redoubled campaign to smoke out his enemies. This came in various forms, none publicly acknowledged, but, in one case, controversial at the time, and in another, documented in records that turned up much later.

The latter episode consisted of a renewed inquiry into James O'Brien's purported exposé of Hoover's alleged perfidies abroad. Toward the end of May, word surfaced that O'Brien was getting ready to publish. This prompted a secret meeting at the Manhattan office of Hoover's friend Lewis Strauss. On hand were Strauss, his associate Paul Foster, and Glen Howell, Foster's former Navy subordinate, then serving as head of Naval Intelligence in New York.

Strauss led the meeting. He described O'Brien's early work for Raskob, and their apparent falling-out. It appeared, however, that O'Brien was still connected to the Democrats through a party functionary who owned the Salmon Building, a Manhattan office tower. O'Brien maintained an office there where he'd stored all the documents he'd assembled on Hoover's pre-presidential career. Strauss was bold in describing for the group his own close connection with Hoover. "The president is anxious to know what the contents of these mysterious documents are," Strauss said. He had been directed to get hold of the O'Brien papers and "arrange for a secret look at them by one of the president's secretaries," Strauss said; that he'd been "authorized by the president" to use "any one of our government's secret services" to obtain them. Glen Howell was familiar with the principals in the administration, and quickly surmised that the secretary involved was Larry Richey.

According to entries Howell made in his personal journal, he took a second meeting with Strauss and Foster at the end of May, and decided then to go ahead with his espionage. He confessed in his journal to a "private dislike of Mr. Hoover," but considered the job for Strauss to be a matter of "duty." On June 5, accompanied by a private detective in his employ, Howell went to the Salmon Building, found the office next door to O'Brien's—a printing shop—and represented himself as a government agent tracking a foreign spy. Suitably impressed, the proprietor agreed to let Howell's private eye pose as a new employee.

During the visit, Howell chanced to get a peek into O'Brien's open door and saw "a handsomely furnished office . . . padded office chairs, rugs on the floor, and pictures on the wall." But there was too much traffic in the building to make a move. That night, Howell's gumshoe obtained a soap impression of the key to O'Brien's office, and made himself a copy.

Howell and his partner decided to move early on Monday, before tenants showed up for work. They arrived at the Salmon Building before dawn, waited until just after daylight, and then entered. What they found presented Howell with "one of the greatest surprises of my life," as he put it in his journal. "The room was absolutely empty. There was not a stick of furniture in it." Over the weekend O'Brien had moved out. The plot had come to nothing.

Howell promptly made his report to Strauss. That same day, Strauss sent a note to Richey. "My Navy friends report that our bird in the Salmon Building has flown from the nest and moved out, lock, stock, and barrel," Strauss wrote. He assured Richey their plots had not been discovered, and said the surveillance would continue. "We are now endeavoring to find the new perch."

Forty-two years later, another Quaker president would commission a burglary of Democratic offices to learn what damaging information his opposition might have on him. As with Hoover, the burglary failed to produce the information he sought. The principal difference was that, in the latter case, the burglars themselves were caught.

The second instance of espionage by the Hoover White House involved his critics in Congress. This arose, like the O'Brien break-in, in early May, at the height of the controversy over Judge Parker. On May 5, a Monday, three senators told reporters that their offices had been broken into and their papers rifled. One, Democrat Kenneth McKellar, of Tennessee, made clear he believed it a product of government spying. "Probably some Secret Service agents or somebody who wanted to get something for their benefit and to my detriment."

Such a break-in would cause a major uproar today, but McKellar made light of the incident. "It seems to me quite unnecessary to pull off raids in the Senate Office Building," McKellar told reporters. "If the raiders would notify Mr. Alden, superintendent of the building, which offices they wanted to get into I have no doubt he would arrange with Senators so that their offices could be examined by such Secret Service agents."

Another Senate burglary, perpetrated just a few weeks later, provoked a much sharper reaction, but this time in private. The object of this caper was Hiram Johnson, the California Progressive and an avowed political nemesis of Hoover's. Johnson arrived at his offices inside the Capitol on a Friday morning in May to find they had been burglarized, his files ransacked. A shocked Johnson called in the Capitol Police; their searches were fruitless, but Johnson felt confident that the White House was behind it. He shared his thinking in a letter to his sons. "I am beastly angry, of course," Johnson wrote. He said "every receptacle in the office" had been opened and rifled. He was convinced it was a political job.

"I recognize that we are in an era of espionage, and that there are more detectives connected with this administration than all the other administrations since [the American] Government was founded," Johnson wrote his sons. They were grown adults—one practicing law in San Francisco, and the other in college—and Johnson felt free confiding in them as peers. "I recognize that Hoover is so enamored of detectives that he utilizes them for every conceivable thing, and one of the principal Secret Service men is one of his principal secretaries. I am unable to reach any other conclusion than that some of these detectives did the job."

Johnson conceded that his evidence was solely circumstantial. "I may be utterly mistaken in my suspicions," he conceded, "but I cannot fathom why anybody else would attempt such a thing, and it certainly is in line with the present mode of running things here."

A week later, dropping by his office on a Sunday morning, Johnson found several locked cabinets in his office with the doors hanging open. Johnson described his reaction in another letter to his sons in California. "There was nothing like the disorder of the previous day, but there was no doubt at all that some intruder had been up to his tricks again," Johnson wrote.

It says something about the press of the day that Johnson shared his story with reporters, and they responded in jocular fashion, but that no stories were produced. The jokes come in reference to an incident in the fall, when Hoover hosted the Republicans of the Senate at a White House dinner, but Johnson's invitation had gone astray. "It is all extremely mysterious," Johnson wrote of the second burglary. "The solutions have varied from the humorous references of the press men that the White House sleuths were searching the office to find the lost [dinner] invitation to the White House, to those who seriously think material was sought by the Hoover people to be utilized in the [congressional] campaign in California this year."

Hostile as he was to Hoover, Johnson realized that without evidence he could say nothing publicly about the break-ins. He decided he would share his hunches with his sons, but nobody else. "It is perfectly useless to indulge in suspicion because they are only suspicions," Johnson wrote. "I feel I am justified in saying that someone in authority in this city, exercising authority over a miserable little employee of the Capitol, entered the office with the use of one of the master keys in possession of the custodian of the building. Beyond this I cannot go."

Johnson kept his silence, and the incident will have to go down as a mystery, a Washington whodunit for the ages. But it was no secret that Hoover considered every challenge to his standing or his program a personal affront, that he had placed a private investigator at the pinnacle of his administration, that Larry Richey would deploy any agency of the government in the service to his Chief. Profoundly sensitive, haunted by a childhood spent alone and friendless, Hoover had brought his fears to the White House. Now those fears, distilled through the gimlet eye of his private, personal detective, were becoming a hallmark of his administration.

Private and guarded in all his communications, Hoover generally kept his darker premonitions to himself. But he opened up to his intimates—to Larry Richey, presumably, to Rickard, sometimes, and to others when the occasion required. Beginning in 1930, and continuing on and off though the end of his term, one of those others, a new presence in Hoover's inner circle, was a former congressman named James MacLafferty.

A native of San Diego, MacLafferty served two terms in Congress as a representative from Oakland. After he failed reelection in 1924, Mac-

Lafferty spent eighteen months at Commerce as an assistant to Secretary Hoover, then moved back to California to take a job in the shipping industry. MacLafferty happened to be back in Washington the week of Hoover's inauguration and made sure to stop in and congratulate his former boss. Taut and precise, drawn to power, MacLafferty shouldered his way into the foyer to make sure his was the first face Hoover saw when he entered the White House.

A year later MacLafferty again presented himself to the president, and this time he offered his services. He would sign on as an unpaid political consultant, an undercover operator with hands-on experience in Congress. He realized that Hoover already had a former congressman on staff, in the person of Walter Newton. But MacLafferty could see, as could most, that Hoover needed help.

Hoover readily agreed. According to MacLafferty's notes of their meeting, the president counted off "the many perplexities confronting him. Enmities in the Senate. Determinations to wreck his effort. Lack of loyalty at times even among those who were supposed to be his supporters." The impasse over Claudius Huston was downright embarrassing; Hoover even conceded to MacLafferty that Huston's appointment had been a mistake.

At Hoover's request MacLafferty returned the following week, and thus began a continuing, sub-rosa collaboration. The two met regularly, MacLafferty slipping in and out of the White House early in the morning or late in the day, without the knowledge of the press or even most White House staff. Between visits MacLafferty haunted the cafeterias and lobbies of Congress, touting the policies of the administration and sounding the sentiments and loyalties of his former colleagues in the legislature. Then he would report back to Hoover, serving the president as conduit, fixer, and sometimes simply as sounding board.

Of all the issues on Hoover's agenda heading into the summer of 1930, the first he raised with MacLafferty was the question of veterans' benefits. The American Legion and its allies had just pushed through Congress a bill extending disability pensions to veterans of the Spanish-American War, whether or not the disability was related to military service. The bill carried a price tag of $11 million, but invited a much costlier expansion.

Hoover vetoed the bill on May 28. It was the first veto of his presidency, but it hardly slowed the movement in Congress. Four days later, during a break in the tariff debates, both houses voted to override. Now, in June, the Senate was moving to expand coverage and benefits for the millions more veterans from the Great War.

It was a new chapter in an old fight. Since the Civil War the federal government had managed veterans' affairs piecemeal, dispensing pensions and health benefits in broad but haphazard fashion through the Veterans Bureau, the National Home for Disabled Volunteer Soldiers, and the Bureau of Pensions. The patchwork left wide gaps in coverage, and after the Armistice, the discharged soldiers, organized under the new American Legion, began pressing for added benefits, including backdated "bonus" compensation for wartime service. The scheme was politically popular, but not with presidents, and both Warren Harding and Calvin Coolidge vetoed bonus bills as extravagant. Now it was Hoover's turn to hold the line.

This new initiative in the Senate was not the bonus, but it was a big bill, with costs estimated at $102 million, nearly ten times that of the Spanish-American War bill. It presented, Hoover told MacLafferty, "the most serious thing confronting me." Pacing the floor of his office, his smoldering cigar clenched in a fist, Hoover complained that the bill wrought "injustices" in the disparate treatment of soldiers, and expenditures that would precipitate a "financial panic." He raged against the "cowardice" of congressmen who pandered to the "soldier vote." MacLafferty was impressed. "I never saw Mr. Hoover in as deadly earnest in my life as he was in this instance."

It was a signal moment. On issues ranging from the tariff to political patronage, Hoover's priorities seemed to get lost in the tangled interface of policy and politics. But the hard logic of the balance sheet seemed to clarify things for the president. When it came to government spending, Hoover shed his timidity and his prevarication. To his mind, limiting spending was a matter of "protecting the American people," a duty he embraced with verve. For the most part Hoover had muddled through his first year in office, preaching cooperation but failing to define himself with Congress or with the public. Now he had found his mission.

MacLafferty was delighted to see the president in such a combative mood. Like so many others, he saw Hoover's central problem to be one of leadership. He wanted Hoover to hit harder, to drive his enemies, to rule even his friends through fear. Watching Hoover vent his outrage over the pension bill, MacLafferty egged him on. The lawmakers who lined up against him had done so for fear of constituent backlash; the answer was to make those politicians fear Hoover even more. "Let them all know . . . if they are not for you, you are not for them," MacLafferty told Hoover. "Make them fear you."

For the next week, Hoover worked systematically, with MacLafferty and Walter Newton, meeting with individual lawmakers and arranging his allies. On June 25 Hoover exercised his second veto, rejecting the expanded benefits, and denouncing the projected price tag as "a serious embarrassment to the government and to the country." The next day, in a carefully scripted progression, House Republicans narrowly sustained the veto, then joined the Senate in sending to Hoover a substitute bill of his own design. The bill comprised an artful compromise, restricting total payments but also eliminating distinctions between service-related and nonservice disabilities, making all disabled veterans eligible for government pensions. Estimated to cost $70 million a year, it answered the president's budget fears but won praise from the American Legion. Hoover signed it into law, capturing his biggest legislative conquest to date.

To MacLafferty, Hoover's handling of the veterans' benefit bill showed the president coming into his own, exposing a dominant streak that he had seen in the past but which seemed to have deserted him in the White House. "This trait in his character will continue to develop," MacLafferty projected. "Before long he will have his cohorts marshaled behind him and he will be irresistible."

This was not the Bert Hoover that Lou Henry knew; nor was it the apostle of cooperation who had presided over the Department of Commerce. But a year of ridicule and reversal had wrought a change in the president. No longer popular, no longer even respected, Hoover had to relinquish the tools of consensus and public opinion that he had once relied on to carry his agenda. Henceforth he would govern by intimidation and legislative threat, a mode that would win results but would also broaden the gulf between the president and the American people.

The dynamic would transpire with increasing frequency as the crises mounted around him—Hoover, besieged, seeking some sort of leverage over his enemies, while his advisors pressed him to slug it out. "Again, I urged that men went in opposition to his wishes because of fear," MacLafferty recorded in his diary. "He, in turn, must make them fear to oppose him."

PART II

WAR ON A THOUSAND FRONTS

ELEVEN

CHALLENGING FACTS

IF EVER YOU HAVE LIVED THROUGH AN EARTHQUAKE YOU KNOW the unusual, incremental manner by which it reveals itself. There is the first great shaking, a fearsome phenomenon experienced by everyone in the quake zone. At home, at first, the impact appears minimal. Maybe some windows crack, maybe some china spills from a shelf, crashing to the floor.

Then comes silence. You might hear car alarms, or sirens in the distance, but otherwise it's stillness. You turn on the television—unless the electricity is out. Then you get your news by old-fashioned transistor radio—and you learn, as word filters in, what it was that happened. It could be nothing more than your broken plateware and rattled nerves. But if it was a big one, the reports would arrive sporadically; a downed freeway overpass, a collapsed apartment building, power outages, fatalities. It might be months before the full extent of the damage becomes clear.

That is how the Depression revealed itself to Herbert Hoover, and to America, in the aftermath of the October crash. True, the spectacular collapse of the high-flying securities market provided ample notice that a decade of unprecedented growth and prosperity was over. But Hoover had answered the crisis in unique fashion, securing commitments from various sectors of the private economy, and mobilizing government entities in Washington and in a hundred municipal road crews, all in the interest of limiting the damage from the crash.

For a time it appeared it may have worked. Some of that could have been wishful thinking, as local boosters, the business press, and the president and his team sought silver linings they could relay to a jittery public. But there was also genuine optimism, rooted in confidence that the engineer-president knew just the mix of exhortation, countercyclical spending, and macromanagement needed to pull the economy back onto solid ground.

In January 1930 the National Business Survey Conference, an offshoot of one of Hoover's November industrial conferences, reported that "business had returned so far toward normal that no emergency methods were required." In March, another of Hoover's business committees reported a double-digit increase in capital spending by utilities across the country, part of a broad, "moderately upward swing" in productive investment since the crash. At that stage it was possible to believe that the combination of the Federal Reserve—still a recent innovation in American finance—and an activist president like Hoover had actually prevailed over the old, inexorable cycles of boom and bust.

But contrary reports were coming in as well, stories of economic dislocation too various, too grave, and just too plentiful to ignore. On the same day Hoover learned of the optimistic utility projections, for instance, the American Federation of Labor announced its own survey that found unemployment had reached the point of "serious danger." More than 20 percent of its members were out of work, the labor federation reported, and in the building trades the rate of unemployed was more than 40 percent.

Anecdotes drove the point home. The Charity Organization Society of New York reported in January it was ministering to double the number of families as the year before, and "swamped with appeals." In Boston, where the destitute were invited to earn groceries by chopping wood, the city woodlot was crowded with six hundred men—ten times the usual number. In Illinois, the director of the state employment agency said Chicago was suffering its worst unemployment in ten years.

Later, in March, New Yorkers witnessed the first of what would soon become an emblem of the new era: a breadline stretching two blocks long.

Still, there had been sharp market breaks in the past—1907, for example, or even 1921, the sudden postwar depression that immediately preceded the boom years. These recessions were deep but they were also brief, convincing many observers—Hoover among them—that the post-crash economy would soon recover. It was only later, and in hindsight, that the whole mosaic came together, the many discrete reports and observations fleshing out the picture of a seminal event, the worst economic breakdown the country, and the world, had ever seen.

The delay was in some degree inescapable, as the government at that time simply did not have the macroreporting capabilities that have been developed since. Those seeking to evaluate the state of the economy—from the president on down—were flying blind.

That conundrum was illustrated in January, when President Hoover asked the U.S. Employment Service to provide him an accelerated, short-term profile of unemployment. The USES was established during the Great War to find prospective workers for jobs that needed filling; now the problem was reversed. There was another federal office charged with compiling such figures—the Bureau of Labor Statistics. Both were administered under the Department of Labor, but the BLS figures tended to come late, incomplete, and with a downward bias. The president wanted something more immediate.

Hoover got his first, expedited survey from the USES toward the end of the month, and was pleased to find a projected boost in hiring based on statements from steel, iron, auto, and other heavy industries. This was what he wanted to hear; it was also good for stoking confidence, which he firmly believed was key to recovery. Hoover promptly called a press conference to share the report. "The tide of employment has changed in the right direction," the president announced. The good news was transmitted across the country.

Among those reading the story the next day was Frances Perkins, labor commissioner for the state of New York. A trained scientist and an early feminist, Perkins had her own independent sources of employment data for her state, and they directly contradicted Hoover's report. Perkins immediately called her own press conference to assert "the truth": unemployment was growing steadily.

In the years to come, Perkins would become a committed Hoover adversary, and in 1933 she followed her boss, Franklin Roosevelt, to Washington. But at this point her objection was more principled than political. In March, speaking at a conference on unemployment, Perkins made a point of acknowledging "a great debt to President Hoover" for his initial, aggressive response to the crisis.

Hoover and those around him, however, took Perkins's challenge in partisan terms. A day after the Perkins January press conference in New York, Labor Secretary Jim Davis announced in Washington that employment was indeed trending upward. "Unfortunately there is developing an inclination in some quarters to make politics out of our employment situation," Davis said. Quickly, perhaps inevitably, one's assessment of the economy became a test of political allegiance.

The president's official optimism was a matter of economic doctrine: confidence at the top would broadcast confidence among the populace, which itself would aid the recovery. As Hoover explained his outlook later in the year, "unnecessary fears and pessimism" were a principal drag on the economy, "the result of which is to slacken the consumption of goods and discourage enterprise."

But there was an ulterior reason for Hoover's official, stubborn optimism: he was hoping to head off the rising clamor in Congress and around the country to do something—to do *many* things—to restore the national economy. For despite mixed reports and the official squabble over the level of unemployment, the simple fact of the Depression was settling over the land, fueling political unrest and bringing the entire social order into question.

New York was a hotbed of ferment. A Conference for Progressive Labor Action held there in January called for massive spending on public works, and dismissed Hoover's early business conferences as "a huge publicity stunt in an attempt to influence the mood of business and the public"—which, to some degree, is just what they were. Two weeks later the National Unemployment League, also of New York, chimed in, terming the economic situation "acute and menacing," and calling for a transcontinental highway project that would provide thousands of jobs. Their inspiration, they said, was Hoover himself, and his prescription, after the famous unemployment conference he led in 1921, for public spending to balance out the business cycle.

It wasn't long before these same notes were being sounded in Congress—the demand for public works in particular. This followed on the Hoover policy, not just of 1921, but of November 1929, when the president had called on states and municipalities to help soften the blow of the market crash. But when it came time to outline an explicit, countercyclical spending program, Hoover hedged. Thus, in a November telegram calling on state governors to launch new projects, Hoover touted public works as "one of the largest factors that can be brought to bear" on unemployment, but then cautioned that such efforts must be "energetic yet prudent." In his first State of the Union address, delivered early in December, Hoover's message was similarly mixed. "We cannot fail to recognize the obligations of the government in support of the public welfare but we must coincidentally bear in mind the burden of taxes and strive to find relief through some tax reduction." His only explicit reference to new public works was distinctly muted: "We have canvassed the federal government and instituted measures of prudent expansion in such work that should be helpful."

Later, in his memoirs, Hoover cited expanded public works as one of his principal policy responses to the Depression. But considering the guarded nature of his initial approach, it's hard to escape the notion that Hoover's enthusiasm was tempered by his weighty responsibilities as chief executive. This may have been an aspect of Lippmann's "peculiar weakness," Hoover's general aversion to political discord. Or it may have reflected the waxing influence of Ogden Mills, a man of simple and firm convictions. All through Hoover's tenure, Mills was adamant in pursuit of fiscal restraint. "Balanced budgets," Mills told an assembly of publishers and editors in February, were the "first fundamental requisite of any sound system of public finance."

So it was that Hoover called Republican leaders of Congress to a White House breakfast conference on a chilly Monday in February to warn them that indiscriminate spending could drive the government into deficit and bring on a sizable tax increase. Flanked by Mills and Andrew Mellon, Hoover tallied spending proposals he'd received from all over the country, which together would add nearly $2 billion to a federal budget then running at about $4 billion.

Presiding over plates of eggs served on White House china, Hoover acted the benevolent but conscientious patriarch, inclined to indulge his rambunctious charges but obliged to invoke the bounds of prudence. It was a role that suited Hoover's professorial self-image, but it didn't play so well with the grown-ups in the opposition. "The whole thing is bunk," sniffed Carter Glass, the Virginia Democrat, of Hoover's appeal for restraint.

More than that, the president's message was contradictory. "In his new role as autocrat of the breakfast table, President Hoover has confused the situation worse than ever," scolded Pat Harrison, a Mississippi Democrat. "A while ago he was urging increased public works in order to avoid unemployment. Now, apparently, he has shifted his position again."

Glass was back at it the next day, excoriating Hoover for setting up federal extravagance as a straw man by which to chastise Congress. The whole episode, Glass said, comprised "a cheap exhibition of partisan politics." Hoover, stung, came as close to a retreat as his pride would allow. At a press conference that same day, the president took pains to point out that the clamor for new spending that he objected to did not arise in Congress, but from "the different sections of the country and from various groups and organizations which are vigorously supporting their own projects."

Still, Hoover's message remained the same. "I hope that the people at home will realize that the government cannot undertake every worthy social and economic, and military and naval expansion. . . . We have enough resources to take care of the budget, and such necessities as the marginal cases of disability in various groups of veterans, and to take care of the speeding up of public works which we have undertaken all over the country with a view to assisting employment. . . . But this is not the time for general expansion of public expenditure."

The way Hoover saw it, he had met the unprecedented crash of October with an unprecedented response, mobilizing private industry, contributing a measured public works program from the government, and averting the sort of financial panic that could turn a temporary setback into a calamity. What he couldn't understand, what he couldn't accept, was the idea of anyone else meddling with his formula. If his program was correct, no amendment was necessary.

It was a prickly, insular approach to policy, poorly suited to the public arena. Sure enough, Senator Robert Wagner rose in Congress to stake out his own strategy for addressing unemployment. A lifelong friend and political ally of Al Smith's, Wagner shared Smith's sharp elbows, his urban brogue, and his modern commitment to government action on behalf of working people.

Taking the floor of the Senate March 3, Wagner called for "sober consideration" of the "challenging facts" of unemployment. Mincing no words, Wagner scored President Hoover for "political manipulation of unemployment figures," and called for a new federal commitment to assist the jobless. Wagner insisted he was not motivated by "partisanship," but he did not shy from taking another swing at the president: "It has been amply demonstrated," Wagner said, "that we cannot continue to have prosperity by proclamation or employment by exhortation."

This was not Wagner's first venture into the field of unemployment. Two years before, making his first speech in the Senate, Wagner had challenged the complacency of the boom years. There were no comprehensive job figures, Wagner observed, but his analysis of reports from the Bureau of Labor Statistics showed that, even then, in 1928, employment was falling off sharply from its peak the prior year; by his count unemployment had already climbed above four million. Now, with the crisis at hand, Wagner proposed three separate bills: one mandating a modest program of countercyclical public works, another that would replace the United States Employment Service with a new consortium of federal and state job banks, and last, a bill ordering the secretary of labor to produce a monthly survey of unemployment.

None of these proposals was especially radical; during his years at Commerce, Secretary Hoover had floated some version of each of them. But with hard times already pressing, tempers and partiality were beginning to flare. During his oration on March 3, Wagner was interrupted by David Walsh of Massachusetts—another urban Democrat—who rose to declaim not just unemployment, but official indifference. People out of work "appreciated the difficulty" of providing relief, but they wanted the government to tackle the problem directly, Walsh said. Instead, the administration was attempting to "deny the facts," an effort grounded in an "apparent lack of sympathy with the unemployment problem."

Walsh was turning the policy debate into a moral argument. "The complete failure to recognize the existence of the problem, to express a kind, sympathetic word to those who are suffering, seems to me to be indefensible."

A politician accustomed to gratuitous slights of legislative debate might shrug off such grandstanding, but with Hoover it tended only to incite. At his regular press conference three days later Hoover adopted a new, more combative stance. "The low point of business and employment" had already passed, the president said; "the situation is very much better now than it was then." The Department of Labor had not yet completed a full survey, but early reports showed that "unemployment amounting to distress"—a new category for the jobless—was limited to just twelve states, primarily in the urban East. For the rest of the country, "abnormal unemployment is rapidly vanishing" and had wrought "no particular strain" on local communities.

Hoover was so confident that he ventured a prediction. "All the facts indicate that the worst effects of the crash on employment will have passed within the next thirty to sixty days."

Hoover should have known better than to hitch his public reputation to so uncertain a steed as the faltering national economy. But there were other, powerful factors driving the president: the administration's commitment to the policy of confidence was a line he could hardly abandon now, and the goading from Congress may have clouded his judgment and stoked his ire.

Even as the odds got longer, Hoover doubled down. On May 1 he painted what must have seemed a startling new version of the Depression so far, delivered in a major address to the Chamber of Commerce in Washington. With his friend Julian Barnes sitting at the head table, Hoover acknowledged the Depression as "one of those great economic storms which periodically bring hardship . . . upon our people," but then he proceeded to minimize it.

Hoover came very near to putting the crisis in the past tense; as he put it, it was an event "we have been passing through." Already, he said, "We have succeeded in maintaining confidence and courage. We have avoided monetary panic and credit stringency. Those dangers are behind us." Looking forward, he said, "I am convinced we have now passed the worst and with continued unity of effort we shall rapidly recover."

Hoover was especially pleased to compare current conditions to the storms of the past—principally the recessions of 1907 and 1921. In this latest crisis, he said, wages were maintained, and strikes and lockouts avoided "for the first time in the history of great slumps."

Hoover's principal thrust was to extol the "great economic experiment" by which the danger had been averted. It was cooperation, he said—between government, industry, agriculture, labor, the press, and the finance sector—that had softened and shortened the effects of the crash. "I believe I can say with assurance that our joint undertaking has succeeded to a remarkable degree."

Later, in June, the president went even further. Faced with a delegation from the National Catholic Welfare Council, pressing him for a new round of public works to aid the unemployed, Hoover turned confrontational. "Gentlemen, you have come sixty days too late. The Depression is over."

These pronouncements were not quite so absurd as they appear in hindsight. The first part of the year had seen a strong revival in the stock market, and later economic studies find "an actual increase" in industrial production for early 1930—albeit from the low levels set in November and December.

Hoover believed, as well, that his call for increased investment in public and private construction was bearing fruit. In the main, major employers had kept their commitment not to slash wages or payroll. Several key industries—railroads and electric utilities, in particular—had made good on their plans to invest in new plant and equipment. And, for all his prevarication, public entities had responded to Hoover's call for new spending. The federal government boosted spending on public works by 35 percent, and the states pitched in with a 13 percent increase.

These were the key planks in Hoover's countercyclical strategy of "stabilization," but they were not enough to pull the economy out of its slide. For one thing, ramping up government spending was simply not the macroeconomic tool that it can be today, because government was a much smaller entity then than now. Federal spending amounted to just 2.5 percent of the gross national product, about a tenth of today's figure. State spending was also smaller then—just half the federal total—meaning that even a big boost in public spending still provided a very modest stimulus.

Moreover, these small gains were more than offset by declines in the private sector. Real estate, which had been the subject of intense speculation even before the stock market, led the slowdown. Residential construction, already off a third from the peak year of 1926, sank a further $1.6 billion in 1930, that one figure easily canceling all the gains registered by the Hoover program.

A snapshot survey of other indicators confirmed the general impression: commodity prices had dropped 10 percent in a year, freight car loadings were down 15 percent from 1929, and steel production was off a third, with plants operating at just 57 percent capacity. The rout was on; a national economy defined by growth and prosperity was now in free fall.

Isolated inside the White House, Hoover was the last to know. He was committed to his program and believed more time would yield better results. He dismissed his critics as politically motivated; the Democrats were cynically seeking to buy votes with profligate spending, and their Republican allies were personally disloyal, or "cowards," or both.

Hoover was buttressed by unanimous support from inside the administration. When the first alarms were sounded on widespread unemployment, Labor Secretary Jim Davis predicted a "speedy recovery," and proposed that Hoover's initial response to the crash "beyond all doubt saved us from disaster." A month later, after Robert Wagner's speech in the Senate, Davis acknowledged "distressing unemployment," but insisted that "the situation is greatly improved." And Ogden Mills was always ready to push the correct mode of thinking. In February, speaking to top editors and publishers in

New York, Mills delivered the administration line: "A man would have to be one of pretty poor spirit and courage," Mills said, "not to look forward to the future with complete confidence."

But as the months went by it got harder to keep the story straight. Toward the end of June, Commerce Secretary Robert Lamont announced that a new survey, based on house-to-house sampling conducted for the next census, showed unemployment running at 1.9 percent. As with Hoover's statement in January, this drew sharp rebuttals from Frances Perkins in New York, and from the American Federation of Labor.

This time, however, protests arose from inside the government, as well as without. Charles Persons, the census official who led the survey, objected to the form of the report, which listed seven different categories of employment, of which only the first—"Those out of a job, able to work and looking for a job"—counted as unemployed. Persons proposed that many workers in the several other categories, including part-time workers and those laid off on a "temporary" basis, should be included in the count. When his objections were ignored, Persons resigned.

It was still too early, even then, to know for sure that this "business depression" would be worse than any ever seen, that prices and production would plummet for months to come, that unemployment would continue to rise and would persist for another decade. But Hoover's belligerent optimism was beginning to work against him. Assaying the public mood in July, one Republican stalwart worried that "a spirit of criticism and depression" had settled over Washington, and that the president was only making it worse.

Ted Clark, former secretary to Calvin Coolidge, stopped by the White House on a Tuesday morning in July and wrote his former boss to describe the mood inside the administration. Hoover's advisors were frustrated, Clark said, with the president's missteps, and concerned with his sinking reputation—though Clark did not speak for Hoover himself. The principal gaffe, Clark said, the one that could cause lasting damage, was Hoover's audacious prediction of a swift recovery.

"Everyone here, including the White House, realizes that the 'sixty days' announcement was a mistake," Clark wrote to Coolidge. It was a simple political calculation, Clark explained: There was little to be gained by such a prediction, and much to lose. "If it was based on actual facts it would have come anyway and the credit given would not have been enhanced." If it were wrong—and sixty days had already passed since Hoover's Chamber of Commerce speech—the upshot was something close to political disaster. "The net result has been to discount and destroy confidence"—the very object of Hoover's strategy—"and to create the impression that the federal government has failed in an attempt to bring back better conditions."

Clark implied that Hoover was alone in pressing his prediction of renewed prosperity. "I know that Mr. Mellon was virtually forced to give out a bright picture where he really did not believe it himself," Clark confided. Hoover's insistence on the strategy clearly nettled Clark; revisiting the question later, he again termed the president's prophecy "unwarranted." "The only justification was the idea that a prediction of prosperity would create it," Clark wrote. He was skeptical enough that he presumed an ulterior motive must be at work. Hoover "could not resist the impulse to show by this prediction a flash of that super-ability which had been so widely advertised in '28." If that were the case, it had been "a terrible failure."

Clark's expertise was in politics, not economics. He was not venturing to suggest which way the economy might be headed. But he sensed a lasting shift in public perceptions of Herbert Hoover, and his personal estimate was evolving as well. It was not the political reversals that caused Clark to doubt Hoover—not even the historic rejection of Judge Parker—but rather Hoover's tremulous handling of the early Depression, Clark began to lose faith. "Somewhere, somehow, there must be something fundamentally wrong—a lack of certain attributes of character which are perceived even if they are not definitely analyzed and put into words," Clark mused.

"I know that the memory of the American people is notoriously short and I have no doubt that with a return of normal conditions, the president could be made a hero who pulled us through a desperate crisis." Even so, Hoover's uneven performance had left his reputation indelibly tarnished. "It seems to me," Clark told Coolidge, "something has been lost which can never be regained."

TWELVE

FRICTION AT THE FED

HERBERT HOOVER'S PRONOUNCEMENTS ON PROSPERITY WERE his principal public acts in response to the oncoming Depression, but they were not the extent of his engagement. Hoover was cerebral and conscientious, and in the moments he was able to carve from his crowded schedule he thought deeply on the nature of the economic problem and how to answer it.

There was a fair degree of consensus over the cause of the crisis. All agreed it was essentially a consequence of the excesses of the postwar boom. Hoover felt he had seen it coming and had tried to mobilize the monetary authorities at the Federal Reserve, but that was water under the bridge. There had been such crises and such adjustments in the past; they were painful but they soon passed. Now the collapse had come and it was time for the nation to dig itself out.

But Hoover was concerned there was a larger phenomenon at work. The rise of industrial mass production had brought unprecedented prosperity but also widespread dislocation, and required its own difficult process of adjustment. There was, Hoover believed, "a constant stream of unemployment which comes from perfecting the process of production and distribution." These displaced workers needed new jobs, along with the job seekers added by simple population growth. This meant economic expansion even beyond that required just to climb out of the hole opened by the market crash.

Hoover sought at least the germ of a solution by surveying the field of employment and job creation for bottlenecks, obstacles that might be cleared away, and he found just that in the credit structure of the housing industry. Home mortgages at that time were limited to just half the value of the new structure; aspiring homeowners were expected to cover the other half out of pocket. Mortgage loans ran just three to five years, at which point they had to be paid off or refinanced. And second mortgages, sometimes used to augment the initial construction, carried interest rates as high as 20 percent.

Hoover's new focus on home finance and its ramifications for the Depression represented an important insight. Studies conducted much later, with data unavailable to Hoover at the time, showed residential construction to be a leading factor in the general collapse. Of twelve sectors broken out for a 1971 study, construction showed the sharpest, deepest dive of all. Well before any other voice was raised, Hoover noted "a distinct proportional decrease in the amount of credit available" for home building, and observed, "This comes to the front in times of depression when credit available for this purpose almost disappears."

Recognizing the ailment, Hoover also saw opportunity. Building homes would generate substantial new employment, not just from construction, but in producing building materials and furnishings. At the same time, Hoover believed, "Increasing improvement in housing conditions is of the utmost social importance."

Hoover outlined his views in March, in a letter to Roy Young at the Federal Reserve. This was not the obvious venue for creative housing policy, but Hoover was thinking in large scale. That is, he was hoping the staff of the Federal Reserve might be put to the task of formulating new credit facilities for the housing sector, along the lines of the existing Federal Land Bank System, founded in 1916 to underwrite agricultural mortgages. In addition, Hoover proposed that residential mortgages be qualified as collateral for interbank loans. This would enhance the value of home loans for banks, and expand the credit base for the Federal Reserve.

It was a promising, innovative proposal—too inventive, as it turned out, for the Fed. Young dutifully turned Hoover's letter over to E. A. Goldenweiser, director of research for the Fed. The answer came back two weeks later. Home building was indeed a "promising field," Goldenweiser found, and mortgage financing was "in an extremely backward stage of development." However, the report found that many American cities were already overbuilt. And Goldenweiser was firm in holding that mortgages were unsuitable for the balance sheets of the Federal Reserve, which had little use anyway for new classes of assets.

The staff did acknowledge that a new entity devoted to home finance might be in order, and offered to study the question further. But the message to Hoover was clear: if he wanted to tamper with the larger framework of the American financial system, he'd have to do it himself.

Emanuel Goldenweiser was a Russian immigrant, a fact finder with a PhD from Cornell. He joined the Federal Reserve in 1919 and developed the Board's research capabilities until it rivaled the Commerce Department as a leading source of data on the American economy. He was also the first official economic advisor to the Fed, and his policy views generally mirrored those of the board.

Goldenweiser's memo to Hoover illuminated the stasis that characterized the agency's approach to the growing crisis in the economy. The Fed had been instrumental in mitigating the immediate impact of the October crash, slashing interest rates, moving assets, and buying securities to channel cash to the member banks, thereby heading off the bank runs that had magnified the shock of previous breaks in the market.

But once the dust settled, the Fed Board slipped into uncertainty. It was still not known, after all, the depth and extent of the trough the economy had fallen into. Credit was strained, but it remained available, and at lower rates than in the months preceding the crash.

And there remained a fundamental division in the system, between the Federal Reserve Bank in New York and the Federal Reserve Board, in Washington.

George Norris, board member from Philadelphia, spoke for the majority when he wrote in January, "We feel that we should not interfere . . . unless the situation clearly calls for some action and we cannot see that it does." In June Norris went further, explaining that to his mind the recession was due to "overproduction and excess capacity . . . rather than to financial causes." Easy money, therefore, "would not help the situation but on the contrary might lead to further increases in productive capacity and further overproduction."

In his memo to Hoover, Goldenweiser echoed the board's sense of complacency in regard to credit. "Our banking system at the present time has $7,500,000,000 of eligible paper, including government securities, and it is not likely to have use for an amount approaching that total for a great many years to come." Here in the spring of 1930, six months after the Wall Street crash, Goldenweiser was almost condescending in his blithe confidence. "This means that, in so far as obtaining Federal Reserve Bank credit is concerned, the channels into the reserve banks are adequate for all present and prospective needs of the country."

This prediction would prove terribly, even disastrously wrong before the year was out, but so would many others. That is not to say that the board of the Federal Reserve was stupid, as some historians appear to believe. The point is that, then as now, economics was an uncertain science, subject to conflicting theories, agendas, and data.

There were other currents of opinion at the Fed. Some financial managers felt that far more aggressive policies were in order. But these voices were lost in the cracks between the various, quasi-independent entities that comprised the Federal Reserve System. Designed to avoid the concentrated power of a single central bank, in practice the system served to frustrate the development of coherent, proactive monetary policy.

The principal structural rift in the system lay between the Federal Reserve Board in Washington, technically an advisory body but empowered with a veto over changes in interest rates, and the twelve purportedly autonomous Federal Reserve Banks. The largest, in New York, often clashed with the board in Washington. It had done so in the summer of 1929, making repeated requests to dampen speculation by raising interest rates, which the board repeatedly vetoed. Now George Harrison and his fellow directors in New York sought to push rates down, in an attempt to rally private business. As before, the board in Washington was skeptical, but this time gave ground.

It did so incrementally. Thus, the first New York rate cut, in November 1929, from 5 percent to 4.5 percent, went through without comment. But a second, voted in New York January 30, was vetoed by the board on a tie vote. When the New York directors returned a week later, again calling for a half point cut, from 4.5 percent to 4, the board again rendered a split decision, but this time one governor changed his vote because he thought it wrong to set policy on a tie vote, and the rate cut went through.

The votes continued in this halting fashion through the summer, with the New York rate finally bottoming out at 2.5 percent. But the rate would have gone lower, and faster, were it not for the opposition in Washington. More troubling, at least in hindsight, was the Fed opposition to proposals from New York for a campaign of open market purchases, another measure designed to ease monetary conditions and spur business activity.

In this case the resistance came from the Open Market Policy Conference, not the Fed Board. This entity, one of the several policy arms of the unwieldy Fed system, consisting of the presidents of each of the twelve reserve banks, was even more cumbersome than the Board of Governors, and more difficult to manage. New York had, on its own, initiated a quick, high-volume purchasing program in November, after the crash, and in March and June the New York directors sought clearance for continued large-scale purchases. But here the executive committee of the Open Market Policy Conference intervened, finding that "at present there is no occasion for further purchases of government securities."

The policy divide reflected the wide range of opinion within the system. For instance, the governor of the Federal Reserve Bank of Chicago, a charter member of the Conference, wrote to Harrison in July to assert there was "an abundance of funds in the market," and that expanding the supply of money by purchasing securities would only encourage a new round of speculation.

These debates and divisions all took place outside public sight, and President Hoover made sure publicly to commend the Fed for its response to the October crash. In private, however, Hoover kept a close eye on credit conditions, and in March voiced support for lower interest rates, thereby siding with New York over the board in Washington. In late April Hoover posed a direct query on Fed policy to Andrew Mellon. He'd received a letter from "a very able business man and economist" who suggested that an active bond-buying program "would make money cheaper everywhere." The economist proposed that by its inaction, the Fed was incurring "risk of the business depression being deeper and longer than is necessary." What, Hoover wondered, did Mellon make of this critique?

The president received no formal response to that memo, and his contacts with the Fed and its officers trailed off. As the months dragged by and the division in the system grew more pronounced, it appears Hoover came to focus on Roy Young as the source of the trouble. According to Adolph Miller, the president's friend on the board, "Hoover considered Young a rather weak man," and a "failure" as chairman.

Toward the end of August, despite his repeated insistence that the Fed was autonomous and beyond the purview of the executive branch, Hoover decided to make a move. Working quietly, his steps still hidden today, Hoover engineered what amounted to a coup at the Federal Reserve.

Just how far Hoover stretched his powers in this maneuver is hard to say, but it appears the door was opened by Roy Young, who recognized it was time for him to leave the board. Young had served just three years of a ten-year appointment, but as he told the story later, he began looking for a way out as early as March. He said he had confided his yearnings to Andrew Mellon, but to no one else. In any event, toward the middle of August, Young learned of an opening at the helm of the Federal Reserve Bank in Boston.

Young had a plausible enough reason for leaving—he stood to double his salary in the move to Boston. It was one of the imbalances in the system that the officers at the twelve reserve banks earned generous, private sector salaries while the system governors in Washington were paid at more modest, government scale. Not yet fifty years old, Young said he wanted to boost his earnings while he still could. In addition, he believed the moment of financial crisis had passed. Like Andrew Mellon at Treasury, Young believed the economy to be on the mend; "It is clearly evident," he wrote Hoover in tendering his resignation, "the credit position of the country is in an easy and exceptionally strong position."

But if Young left of his own accord, the White House clearly helped orchestrate his departure. Young's letter of resignation was vetted by Ogden Mills and submitted to Hoover for his advance review; Mills also set the time for its release to the public.

While selection of Fed governors was a presidential privilege, in practice Hoover's predecessors had for years deferred to the expertise of Treasury Secretary Mellon in selecting new governors. In this case, however, Hoover had his own candidate in mind—Eugene Meyer, the financier who would later gain fame as publisher of *The Washington Post*.

By 1930 Meyer had long experience on Wall Street and in government service, and Hoover considered him "most able." When first assembling his administration Hoover had offered Meyer several different positions, but so far Meyer had rebuffed him. Still, Meyer had been a frequent visitor at the White House, consulting with Hoover on the state of the economy and the performance of the Fed. Now Hoover came on strong. With Young's resignation confirmed, Hoover called Meyer and declared, "There's a vacancy on the Federal Reserve. I'm going to appoint you a member and appoint you governor."* Recounting the phone call later, Meyer said the president ended the call abruptly. "I won't take no for an answer," Meyer quoted Hoover. "And then he hung up. That was the beginning and end of it."

But that was not the end of it. The Federal Reserve charter expressly barred seating more than one board member from each of the twelve reserve districts, and there was already a member from New York—Edmund Platt, a newspaper publisher from Poughkeepsie and former representative in Congress. Platt was just embarking on a second, ten-year term on the board. If Meyer was to come, Platt had to go.

---

*The nomenclature for the Fed is tricky. Members of the board are called "governors," as are the directors of the twelve semiautonomous Federal Reserve Banks. And the chairman of the Fed Board is also called "the" governor; governor of all the governors, as it were. Thus Hoover is not being redundant when he says "I'm going to appoint you member," and, "I'm going to appoint you governor."

Now, just days after Young agreed to terms with the Boston bank, Platt received his own timely and unexpected job offer from a prospective employer. This was a bank holding company in Buffalo, which happened to be seeking a new executive. The salary would mean a hefty raise in pay. Platt readily accepted, and Meyer's path to the board was open.

These sudden turns made for dizzying headlines—on September 4 *The New York Times* called the clause blocking Meyer's appointment "insuperable"; a day later the obstacle was "surmounted"—but the real confusion came inside the Fed. The mystery turned on the status of Edmund Platt.

According to later testimony, Platt met in late August with his prospective employer and agreed to consider the job in Buffalo. He never speculated on the timing of the offer, or what might have prompted it, but there were clearly other interests at work.

The same week of that meeting, on Friday, Platt was visiting fellow reserve board member Charles Hamlin at Hamlin's home in Massachusetts when he received a call from Roy Young. It was two days after Young's resignation, but the outgoing chairman felt obliged to relay a message to Platt—that Treasury Secretary Andrew Mellon wanted to see him, if possible the next morning, in New York. Platt and Hamlin's other guests believed Mellon might offer Platt the Fed chairmanship but Hamlin knew better; he believed Mellon would "induce Platt to resign."

Platt's meeting with Mellon took place two days later, on Labor Day. Mellon opened by saying he had heard of Platt's job offer, and that he hoped Platt would accept. Speaking in his customary, understated manner, Mellon "gave him to understand," as Platt put it, "by necessary implication, that President Hoover hoped he would accept, as he had someone he desired to appoint in his place." At last Mellon revealed that Hoover wanted Eugene Meyer on the Fed Board. When Platt mentioned that he was thinking of staying on with the Fed until October 1, Mellon corrected him; "Hoover wanted him to resign at once."

Platt now realized he was being pushed aside. He made no protest at the time, but voiced his resentment to Hamlin a week later. "If they make any more fuss about it, I may not resign at all," Platt announced.

Hamlin, for one, was shocked at the maneuver. "It is extraordinary for Hoover and Mellon practically to force Platt off the board in this manner," he fumed in his diary. But it was not "Hoover and Mellon" moving against Platt; as Mellon pointedly informed Platt, he had nothing to do with choosing Meyer. Adolph Miller, also taken by surprise, was likewise left out of the loop. In this instance, the president was acting on his own.

With Congress out of session, Meyer's was a recess appointment, subject to subsequent Senate confirmation. During those hearings, the following January, Hoover's critics accused him of plotting to remove Platt and even Roy Young, but the charges were roundly denied and quickly put to rest. After all, appointments to the Fed were and are the express province of the president. In later years the episode was cloaked in singular silence: Hoover did not mention Meyer's appointment in his memoirs; nor did Meyer discuss the incident, except to assert his belief that Young left the Fed solely to seek better pay. Neither said a word about Platt, and Platt raised misgivings only at the time, in conversation with Hamlin.

But the maneuvers around Platt created real friction on the board, leading to a rift between some members—Hamlin especially—and the new chairman. Even if all Hoover did was nudge, he was violating the statutory autonomy of the Fed and his own avowed strict fealty to the separation of powers. Platt's ouster suggests that, when the occasion called for it, Hoover's principles were more flexible than he would care to admit. It also reveals a more active, more decisive Hoover than his customary demeanor would suggest. In this instance, having decided whom he wanted at the Fed, Hoover brushed aside institutional obstacles and his own inhibitions.

The quiet coup at the Fed also rebuts the thesis that Hoover was disengaged or disinterested in the financial phases of the Depression. Even during a lull in the tempest that followed the October crash, Hoover was keeping a firm grip on the wheel.

Eugene Meyer was a financier who, like Hoover, made his fortune early and moved into public life out of a sense of duty. Aged fifty-five at the time of his appointment, he was born in Los Angeles, the son of a French immigrant who partnered with the Lazard brothers to help build an international financial house. Rather than follow his father into banking, Meyer launched his own investment firm and quickly rose to prominence as a Wall Street maverick. During the war he signed on under Woodrow Wilson as a dollar-a-year man, guiding the War Finance Corporation and then the Federal Farm Loan Board. Astute, skeptical of fads, Meyer sat out the speculative abandon of the 1920s and emerged from the crash unscathed. At the time Hoover drafted him for the Fed Meyer had a mansion in Washington, an estate outside New York in Westchester County, a cattle ranch in Jackson Hole, and a reputation for confidence, vision, and independence.

Hoover and Meyer were friendly enough, but both were headstrong, and Meyer never joined up with what he called Hoover's "ardent crowd of followers." Meyer set the tone of their relationship soon after his appointment to the Fed, meeting with the president to press for a dramatic reduction in debts and reparations stemming from the Great War. It was a potentially transformative proposition, but politically radical—a startling overture for a new appointee.

The layered edifice of financial obligations erected after the war was the great Gordian knot of the era, with payments totaling more than $10 billion and stretching sixty years into the future. Technically debts and reparations were separate—the debts were the huge sums loaned by the United States to finance the Allied armies, while reparations were penalties the victors levied against the Axis powers at Versailles. But in practice they were intrinsically linked, with Britain and France relying on reparations from Germany to pay installments on their debt to the Americans.

These obligations were an ongoing source of international friction, with America's former friends coming to disparage their erstwhile ally as "Uncle Shylock." The debts were also subject to constant revision, as successive diplomats adjusted the payments to what they believed the Europeans could carry. For his efforts in one such mission, in 1924, Charles Dawes received the Nobel Peace Prize.

In his approach to Hoover in October, Meyer proposed a new and dramatic revision, slashing American claims on Continental debtors by at least half and perhaps more. It was not a question of right or equity, he insisted. With unemployment surging, German anger over reparations had led to the

breakup of its parliamentary coalition and the rise of the National Social-
ists, who vowed to repudiate the Versailles treaty. Meyer had spent time in
Europe and he believed he could see where things were headed. The international financial order, already battered by deflation, could crumble. "Germany will default and repudiate," Meyer told the president. "Then France
and England will follow, and we will go in on top of the heap."

Hoover had been over this ground before. In 1922 he was named, along
with Andrew Mellon and Charles Evans Hughes—and Henry Robinson—
to the World War Foreign Debt Commission, one of the first efforts by the
United States to rationalize the decisions taken at Versailles. Hoover proposed then that America simply cancel all loans made during the war, and
seek to recover only the advances made since the Armistice—about a third
of the $11 billion in debts outstanding. "This would have strengthened our
moral position," Hoover explained later. But the more practiced politicians
on the commission assured him the scheme would never fly with Congress.*
Hoover persisted, suggesting that the United States at least repudiate the
interest on the loans, but again he was outvoted.

Hoover apparently took this tutorial in realpolitik to heart, because just
six months later he performed a complete about-face. In 1922, answering
growing popular sentiment for cancellation, Hoover declared in a major
speech that the war debts were a "moral and contractual obligation," and
that "repudiation [of the war debts] would undermine the whole fabric of
international good faith." At the time, Germany was just entering the painful spell of hyperinflation that prostrated its economy, but Hoover never altered his public stance on the debts.

Now, sitting in the Oval Office with the new chairman of the Federal
Reserve, Hoover reprised the same political factors, explaining to Meyer that
debt reduction for Europe simply wouldn't fly. Meyer answered sharply. "I
don't agree with you," he told the president. "I think there would be a lot of
support politically for that in this and every other country."

---

*Calvin Coolidge, an intrinsically political animal, waved off European complaints as buyer's
remorse. Legend credits him with the quip, "They hired the money, didn't they?," though later
research disputes the attribution.

Hoover was skeptical. "Where do you get that idea?"

It was just instinct, Meyer said. "I think they would be glad to hear somebody who has the courage to speak frankly and truthfully," he told the president. Hoover wouldn't bite. "Why shouldn't Britain or France make the proposal?" he asked. That was hardly a serious suggestion; as Meyer pointed out, no British or French politician could propose cuts in German payments and survive the next election. But Hoover was unmoved, and dismissed the subject with the remark that there was "a whole lot of propaganda" in the controversy.

The issue of debts and reparations would return soon enough; in the meantime, this initial encounter set the tone for what would remain a prickly association. Hoover came to regard Meyer as "stubborn," while Meyer refused to defer to the president. "A lot of people thought he was gospel . . . so I examined his statements and sometimes found that he was rather hasty in his judgments and extreme in his views," Meyer said in an oral history interview. "When I said so, I was viewed with great suspicion because I dared to challenge the scriptures."

As a self-made financial success, as a Jew who navigated America's Protestant establishment, Eugene Meyer took great pride in his independence. But as a newcomer to the Federal Reserve, Meyer was careful not to violate the bounds of orthodoxy. "Governor Meyer takes hold of his work with perfect assurance," board member Charles Hamlin noted after Meyer's first session in mid-September. Three weeks later, however, Hamlin rendered a different finding: "Governor Meyer, so far, has shown no sign of having any fixed policy."

With powerful forces of price deflation already in motion, pressure was building in and outside the Fed to expand the nation's money supply. But Meyer opted for caution. As Hamlin noted in his diary, "Some newspapers say [Meyer] believes in more credit for business, but he has accepted without any dissent the Governors' recommendation for holding the status quo."

Hoover's friend Adolph Miller is often portrayed as one of the Fed's more conservative voices, but at this point he was the strongest advocate inside the system for an easy-money policy. Toward the end of September Miller explicitly pressed the board to "consider the purchase of a large amount of government securities to ease credit conditions." But when the idea was put to Meyer he rejected it out of hand. More than that, Meyer said the Federal Reserve "had nothing to do with the stock market or the general money market." While the former was true enough, the latter was curiously inapt; it only confirmed that, while he was renowned as an investor and market analyst, Meyer actually had little experience in banking. At the Fed, he would be learning on the job.

Up to that point, Hoover had stayed out of debates over interest rates. Early in 1928 he sided with Adolph Miller in the debate over rate hikes versus direct action, but since then he left questions of monetary policy to the experts. But now in October, seeking perhaps to sound the views of his new Fed chairman, Hoover referred Meyer to a letter from Will Wood, a Republican congressman from Indiana, who proposed to address the nation's economic torpor by "raising the price level." This would be accomplished through "an aggressive easing policy" that included new reductions in interest rates "and purchase of several hundred of millions of securities."

By today's lights the proposal was surprisingly sophisticated, identifying deflation as the critical issue of the moment and encompassing the primary policy tools available to the Fed. This prescription takes on more weight in light of the Fed's response to the recession of 2008, which included a massive open market purchasing operation known as "quantitative easing." Recent research posits that in 1930 a policy of monetary easing roughly on the scale proposed by Wood could have blocked or even reversed the course of the Depression.

In the event, Meyer rejected the scheme out of hand. That wasn't surprising, as the Fed Board had voted repeatedly against easing, as had its member banks. But Meyer composed a detailed policy memo that provides a clear statement of his thinking, and of federal policy, at a critical stage in the advance of the Depression.

To Meyer's mind, the sinking prices for commodities were a function of overproduction, and he doubted whether "any conceivable course of action" by the Fed could have "any material effect." Moreover, echoing Roy Young, Meyer said "credit conditions in this country have been very easy for a number of months," and noted that the Fed currently held more government securities than ever before. That was true, but as Meyer acknowledged, the purchases were more than offset by reductions in loans outstanding to member banks, negating any impact on price levels. By September, even the purportedly conservative Adolph Miller told the board that in his view, "Money is not really cheap nor easy."

Meyer sidestepped the question of easy money to get to his main point, which was that any "radical easing" to check deflation would threaten the Fed's gold reserves. Here was the familiar riddle presented by the international gold standard: lower interest rates in domestic money markets would induce foreign creditors to call their deposits, squeezing bank reserves and defeating the original policy. "In the gold standard world," Meyer lectured, "the movements of gold impose definite limitations upon the influence of central bank policy."

As we have seen, Hoover had wrestled with this conundrum himself in 1925, when he and Adolph Miller had protested the Fed's easy-money policy. Their fears were dismissed by Benjamin Strong, director of the Federal Reserve Bank in New York, who kept American interest rates low, despite speculative bubbles in stocks and real estate, to help the central bank in England defend its gold position. Hoover later scorned Strong as "a mental annex of Europe."

Five years later, the situation was reversed; disregarding the slumping economy, Meyer wanted to keep interest rates relatively high, to protect the American gold position. But Hoover didn't see a parallel with Strong and his policy, or if he did, he didn't mention it. Hoover at the time was wrestling with his own monetary conundrum: he firmly believed "ample" credit at low rates of interest was essential to recovery, but he was equally sure that "inflation" was the principal cause of the Depression—and that applied to "inflations of currency and credit," as well as the more notorious inflationary bubbles in land and securities. With his own mind divided, Hoover deferred. He signed off on the Meyer memo and threw his weight behind his selection as the new leader of the Fed.

THIRTEEN

THE GROUND GIVES WAY

The disputes at the fed, and president hoover's maneu-
vers there, were critical to the progress of the Depression, but the controversy was muted. Monetary policy was esoteric and its impacts unknown;
even the state of the American economy, soon to be recognized as danger-
ously unwell, was still subject to debate. What was clearly in crisis, and what
threatened to drag the rest of the country into economic disaster, was American agriculture.

The proximate cause of trouble in agriculture was overproduction, the
annual surplus that Hoover and the Congress sought to address when they
established the Federal Farm Board. But now American farmers were getting whipsawed from the opposite direction. What started in December as a
dry spell had shaped up by April as a full-blown drought, reaching from the
eastern slopes of the Rockies across the Mississippi Valley and all the way to
Maryland.

With prices fallen to the point that every harvest produced a loss, even
bad news came as good tidings. In June, commodity traders were crediting
the prospect of drought-driven crop failures—along with the Farm Board
buying program—with preventing wheat from falling even further. So sen-

"WHEN THE LEVEE BROKE"

Hoover's reputation for Mississippi flood relief
informed this image of the Depression as a
torrent sweeping all before it.

sitive was the market that good news—reports of scattered showers in the Midwest—drove prices down, on fears that the dry spell might be breaking.

Those fears proved premature. The drought persisted into July, aggravated now by a heat wave that brought record, hundred-degree temperatures to a dozen states. Twenty-four deaths over three days were attributed to scorching heat; the fatalities included a farmer in Nebraska and another in Missouri, who perished while working their fields. In Kansas, growers harvested wheat by moonlight to avoid the searing sun. In Kentucky, the storied bluegrass turned white.

In this dark and difficult year, silver linings wore thin. Despite the widespread crop damage the international markets remained glutted. There would be no price relief, and no reprieve from the heat. By August the toll of the calamity was coming clear—massive failure of the corn crop, heavy damage to wheat, and spot shortages in dairy, fruit, and cotton. A telegram to the Farm Board from the Ohio grange told the story in shorthand: "Most disastrous drought ever known. No feed for live stock. Farmers must have financial assistance. Cows not producing."

Suddenly, the crisis on the farm came to rival the larger breakdown in the economy. The emergency facilities of the Department of Agriculture, even augmented by the new agency of the Farm Board, were quickly overwhelmed. Inevitably, the demands and appeals of the farm states found their way to the White House.

It came as some relief to President Hoover, after his travails with Congress, to grapple with a problem not of his own making. This was, moreover, emergency relief, Hoover's specialty. He knew just what to do.

Hoover swung into action in early August with a series of meetings with Alexander Legge and with Agriculture Secretary Arthur Hyde. As with the early returns on urban unemployment, the president's first instinct was to minimize the severity of the problem. Obtaining detailed reports from the stricken states, Hoover found "a great deal of variation in the effects of the drought," but acknowledged, "it is of the most serious character in some localities, and unless it is remedied there will be a great deal of suffering." Several days later, the president was more sanguine. The "acutely affected area" contained just 12 percent of the nation's livestock, he noted, and while some herds had no feed at all, others had plenty—"So that the total amount of the problem is much less than the total figures might indicate."

Still, almost grudgingly, he acknowledged a role for benevolent intervention. "Nevertheless, there will be a good deal of privation amongst families in the drought area due to the loss of their income and their inability to carry their stock without assistance over the winter."

In consequence, Hoover announced a White House conference on drought relief and invited governors from the thirteen hardest-hit states to join him. At the same time he laid out a four-point program for aid: reduced rail rates, road projects to provide work for idled farmers, loan guarantees for stock feed and for spring planting, and, where local charity would not suffice, material assistance by the national Red Cross.

This was necessarily an ad hoc, incident-specific project. Federal disaster aid was far from automatic; the Federal Emergency Management Agency would not be founded for another forty years.

It was typical of Hoover to formulate his plan, and even set parts of it in motion, before the arrival of the governors whom he ostensibly hoped to consult. He knew he must answer the fast-moving crisis on the farm, but he wanted to do so on his own terms. The governors had been invited not to help craft the program, but to carry it out.

Sure enough, the state officials came to the capital in a fervent and vocal mood; "It is money we need and money we must have," one governor told reporters as he entered the conference. But Hoover was not offering money, or at least, not such funds as might be lavished on prostrated farmers with families to feed and debts to pay. In the course of a formal, three-hour session, and in after-dinner talks late into the night, Hoover convinced the governors to sign on to his "cooperative" scheme.

Hoover's strongest ally here, his accomplice in optimism and understatement, was John Barton Payne, chairman of the Red Cross. Payne was a Southern aristocrat of the old school, a lawyer, jurist, and Democrat from Virginia who had served two years as secretary of interior under Woodrow Wilson. He was seventy-five years old in 1930, and shared Hoover's emphatic views on private charity and self-help.

On Hoover's invitation, Payne met with the president three days before the governors conference opened. The two had worked together in managing emergency response to the Mississippi flood; together they had weathered the censure of the NAACP for spotty relief efforts in some of the same districts now parched by drought. In this instance, Hoover told Payne he expected that Northern states like Ohio and Illinois, with their "great wealth," could manage the emergency on their own, but that the poorer regions to the south, some of them not yet recovered from the deluge of 1927, would likely require aid.

Payne agreed with Hoover's assessment, and also with the president's suggestion that together they play down the degree of assistance the relief agency would deliver. Better to keep the emphasis on local responsibility, not outside aid. Visiting the White House two days after the governors had departed, Payne told reporters that the Red Cross had received just fifty-six "inquiries" about drought aid at its national headquarters and its regional office in St. Louis combined; just a third of those were actual requests for aid. Payne said the agency's $5 million standing reserve fund would be sufficient to cover any exigencies.

At this point both Payne and Hoover were being disingenuous. While both publicly discounted the projected cost of drought aid, in private both anticipated a much heavier toll. In his initial meeting with Payne, Hoover had suggested that the cost of assistance would easily surpass the $17 million the Red Cross had spent after the 1927 flood, the total possibly mounting to several times that figure. Similarly, after suggesting in public the effort would be routine, Payne warned the chairmen of the agency's local chapters that drought relief activities would be "extensive."

The line was the same, but in their deceptions each was following his own agenda. To Payne and other Red Cross officials, the sheer scope of the drought presented a natural calamity so vast as to overwhelm the entire organization. According to its charter, the Red Cross was conceived to respond to natural disasters like fire and flood, but explicitly excluded "hazards of farming" like a bad harvest. In its initial response to the drought, agency officials stuck to the script, specifically ordering local chapters not to address problems associated with crop failure.

Hoover had broader responsibilities than Payne, and different reasons to discount the severity of the crisis. Foremost in his mind was the gnawing problem of urban unemployment. As much as he and his deputies disputed the numbers, there was no denying the unsettling new commonplace of jobless men, hungry and adrift, crowding the sidewalks of a hundred cities. If Hoover endorsed federal aid for the farmer, how could he deny assistance to this much larger group?

At the same time, Hoover was painfully aware of the approach in November of the midterm congressional elections. Claudius Huston had finally resigned, clearing up the logjam at the Republican National Committee, but the House Republicans were in full retreat, and the party's comfortable majority appeared in jeopardy. In his meetings with James MacLafferty, Hoover confessed fears that, should the House fall, his second presidential term might already be in jeopardy.

Having built his public reputation on his exploits in disaster relief, Hoover knew he could not shirk responsibility for widespread suffering. But he was determined that relief remain a local, and not a federal obligation. He made the distinction in his first statement on the drought, declaring "there will be no stone unturned by the Federal Government in its assistance to local authorities to deal with the situation." It was a subtle point, but anyone presuming that the president's promise would open a font of federal dollars was soon disillusioned.

The question of federal aid for destitute citizens struck at one of the core contradictions in Hoover's character and his public record. He rose to fame as the Great Humanitarian by running relief projects in both private and government stations, yet he rejected the idea of the government accepting responsibility for responding to public emergency.

Hoover's opposition to public aid rested on two pillars, enunciated at different times and on different occasions. The first was the old and familiar argument against government assistance—that dispensing aid would reward shirkers and discourage enterprise. Second, but no less fervently, Hoover believed that replacing local relief with federal dollars threatened to "stifle" that neighborly impulse to charity that Hoover saw as essential to the American character.

It was a matter of principle that Hoover had long enunciated, but had sometimes allowed to blur. In his great relief projects he always emphasized private donations, but the primary source of funds for his aid to Belgium, and for his postwar famine relief to Russia, was the American government. Now, ensconced in the Oval Office and facing a national emergency, Hoover drew a hard line. No longer the advocate for faceless victims of invading armies, Hoover now embraced a new role, defending his conception of civic virtue.

When the drought-state governors arrived at the White House, then, Hoover presented them with a three-tiered "cooperative" scheme that afforded only a limited federal role while rooting primary responsibility at the local level. Aid would be directed by county committees chaired by, in Hoover's term, "a leading citizen," and including representatives from the local department of agriculture, the Red Cross, and at least one banker. These committees would report to state relief committees appointed by the governors, which in turn would report to a National Drought Relief Committee in Washington.

To fund the relief effort, including "support of families over the winter," Hoover proposed that the county committees seek loans from local banks or, better, that they establish agricultural credit corporations that might obtain loans from federal entities including the Federal Land Banks, the Farm Board, and "other federal agencies." These operations would be coordinated by still another committee, a panel of bankers supervised by Hoover's Los Angeles friend Henry Robinson. As a last resort, the Red Cross would step in to address needs unmet by the loan program.

It was a convoluted and cumbersome system, certainly, with built-in gaps and bureaucratic overlap. But it won the support of the assembled governors, and at first blush from the press. In Hot Springs, Arkansas, the heart of the drought zone, the *Sentinel Record* proudly proclaimed, "The farmer isn't yet in a position to be fed in a soup line." In his syndicated column, the humorist Will Rogers spoke in the plain manner that made him famous: "It's like old times to have Mr. Hoover taking personal charge of our heat and drought calamity."

It felt auspicious, too, when on the same day the president hosted the governors at the White House, heavy rains broke over the Allegheny Mountains, the first in a series of storms that brought respite from a drought pattern that would continue for several more years in the American West. For the moment, in Washington and across the nation, the break in the weather felt like a welcome change in fortune.

Even as Hoover was reaping plaudits for his energetic response to the drought, the continuing breakdown of the larger economy was becoming too grave to ignore. The rapid progression from recession to outright depression had introduced a sense of insecurity deeply unsettling to a nation only a year removed from what appeared to be invincible prosperity. And it was only getting worse.

Unemployment is just one measure of economic performance; all through 1930 other indicators were heading in the same direction. The Wall Street crash was bad enough, wreaking precipitous declines in industrial production and personal income, but, remarkably, the slide accelerated after that. In the twelve months after the October crash, U.S. gross national product fell by a third, corporate profits were off two-thirds, and commodity prices, led by wheat and cotton, hit lows not seen since before the war. Writing at the end of the decade, the pioneering economist Joseph Schumpeter recapped the behavior of commodity prices for 1930; his language serves just as well to describe the state of the nation. The first half of the year was "satisfactory," Schumpeter wrote, but in the second half, "People felt the ground give way beneath their feet."

Hoover was skeptical of the figures and he was leery of the idea that people should need help from the government. In his own experience, privation was part of life; nothing he'd want to replicate, but nothing to fear, either. But popular outcry at the deepening distress finally forced his hand. Even apart from the looming midterm election, he recognized that if he didn't take the initiative, Congress would.

Hoover announced his new program at a press conference on October 21. He would create a national committee to tackle unemployment, a sort of sister to the drought committee, aimed at fostering local self-help. As Hoover termed it, "We propose to develop an organization for cooperation with industry, and especially cooperation with the local welfare bodies, state authorities, but nothing as to method has been worked out.

"We have running parallel with the unemployment problem, the drought problem, which we have to develop coincidentally in cooperation with the other. In the main, the job is to secure the cooperation of the whole community—local, municipal, state, federal—in working out systematic handling of the whole question."

The committee would be Hoover's own, a demonstration of his personal commitment, working under the title President's Emergency Committee for Employment, or PECE.

But here the president digressed, hoping to enlist the White House correspondents in his doubtful view of the crisis. "There is one thing I would like to suggest to you just privately, and that is that all these things can be very much exaggerated," Hoover advised. "The actual amount of unemployment, just for your own information, taking the base of the census of April 1 . . . probably at the present moment is somewhere about three and a half million."

As we have seen, hard numbers for social statistics were unavailable at that time, but subsequent studies place the actual number of unemployed in October 1930 at 4.3 million. Even that figure is an estimate, however; the best way to reckon may be from the firmer, annual estimates. By that count, Americans in 1930 were passing from full employment, with a 1929 jobless rate of 3 percent, to the 1931 figure of 16 percent. In October 1930, then, joblessness had just entered double digits, and was climbing steadily.

In his statement, working from his low estimate, Hoover began to stipulate:

There are always a million unemployed or thereabouts of general estimates of people shifting from one job to another. The people who had employment in July, about a million of them, or some portion of them, not a million, go out in August and come back in September. So that when you talk about 3½ million unemployment you are not talking about people without some income, interrupted income. And furthermore, the census will show you that there are an average of about 1¾ breadwinners per family in the United States. So that when you talk about 3½ million, or reduce it to 2½ million of people who are continuously out of employment, you are not talking about 2½ million families; you are talking about a lesser number of families without breadwinners.

Here the president was demonstrating, for any members of the press who didn't quite get the concept, what it meant to be a nonpolitician. Addressing a situation that clearly called for effusions of sentiment and sympathy, Hoover was parsing the numbers, weighing the sufferings of his citizens by degree. And he wasn't done.

"You also have another statistical factor in the problem and that is that our statistics of employment embrace all the local communities, where the intimate personal associations are much more potent than in the larger municipalities, and where the local communities have their own difficulties, so that the actual burden of the problem is nothing like even what the statistical numbers would indicate."

Hoover didn't say, but may as well have, that this sharp-eyed appraisal of the gross statistics harked back to his hardscrabble beginnings, when his widowed mother scavenged the root cellar and took in sewing to make it through the cold Iowa winter. All through his political ascent Hoover and his team had played upon his upbringing, the orphan boy who saved his pennies, who, in college, did other students' laundry to earn his spending money. The story was heartwarming, and won Hoover plaudits and votes. With hard times closing in, Hoover was showing the toughness that had carried him through.

"I am not minimizing the problem at all," Hoover told the reporters, when of course he was doing just that. Then he proceeded to diminish it further, suggesting that, "We have a substantial problem to overcome," but adding, "It amounts to a good deal less than half of that being borne by countries abroad, so that we shall get through it and we shall get through without any suffering."

The transcript of the press conference records a single follow-up question. "You mean without actual individual suffering?"

"That is the object of the organization," was Hoover's terse reply. "To prevent individual suffering."

Inside the White House, the discussion was a bit more candid. The same

day he announced the PECE, Hoover proposed formation of an "Unemployment Cabinet," a sort of internal council that would include the secretaries of War, Labor, Treasury, and Agriculture, along with Eugene Meyer
of the Federal Reserve, all under direction of Commerce Secretary Lamont.
Hoover invited the other members of his regular cabinet to sit in on this first
session, and as Henry Stimson noted later, "We all did."

Andrew Mellon was the official representative from Treasury, but he
was not in attendance that day. It was his undersecretary, Ogden Mills, who
was on hand, and it was he who set the tone. "Mills was particularly clear
and practical," Henry Stimson observed in his notes of the session. Though
the midterm vote was just two weeks away, Mills was thinking ahead, to
the session of Congress set to commence in December. "Unless we took the
lead in some sort of constructive policy before Congress meets there will be
bills at once introduced for payment of large relief funds," Mills pointed out.
"These bills would undoubtedly pass unless we have a counter proposition
all ready."

There was no question Hoover shared Mills's concern. He didn't think
much of legislators to begin with, and was especially leery of laws forged in
the heat of passion. "The most dangerous animal in the United States is the
man with an emotion and a desire to pass a new law," Hoover pronounced one
evening at the Gridiron Club. The semiannual gridiron dinners there were
dedicated to satire and humor, but in this case, the president wasn't joking.

Hoover named Arthur Woods, a former police commissioner in New York
renowned as a Progressive social reformer, to head the new PECE. Woods
was a rare character, a patrician whose polished manners and open nature
won access to the highest circles of society and a long-term role as advisor to the Rockefeller Foundation. He first came to Hoover's attention after
the Armistice, when Woods was placed in charge of the Emergency Employment Commission for Soldiers and Sailors, established inside the War
Department out of frustration with the slack performance of the U.S. Employment Service.

Woods succeeded there due to the simple fact that employer demand
far outstripped the supply of returning doughboys. Two years later, at the

height of the brief, sharp, postwar recession, when Warren Harding named Hoover chairman of his President's Conference on Unemployment, Hoover drafted the colonel to coordinate the efforts of municipal, state, and federal governments. Now in 1930, he called on Colonel Woods again.

Woods tackled his new post with enthusiasm, coming to Washington the day after he was named, meeting Hoover at the White House that evening, and speaking with reporters that night. He would move with his family to the capital, Woods said, and he was bringing "all the energy and vigor we can summon. . . . This is a race against human misery."

But from the outset, Woods was careful not to exceed the president's parameters. He and his committee worked out of offices in the Commerce Department, with borrowed staff and statistical resources at hand. There would be no spending and no jobs program. "The principal part of our work is cooperating with local organizations," Woods told reporters. "It's a coordinating sort of thing."

A day later, President Hoover weighed in for emphasis. "The spirit of voluntary service has been strong enough to cope with the problem for the past year, and it will, I am confident, continue in full measure of the need," Hoover said in a written statement endorsing his new committee. "Colonel Woods is receiving the most gratifying evidence of this from the governors, mayors, industrial leaders, and welfare organizations from throughout the country."

That's not all Woods was hearing. As unemployment turned chronic it began to take on new dimensions. Vagabonds became a familiar sight, as tens of thousands of men took to the roads looking for work. Apple growers in the Northwest, saddled with a bumper crop and shrinking demand, hit upon the scheme of advancing fruit to jobless men and letting them do the retailing. Soon they were shipping millions of apples east; beginning in the autumn of 1930, ragged apple vendors became a lasting hallmark of the Depression.

All of this was apparent to Woods, but for Hoover the story of the PECE was one of "gratifying" progress. Should anyone miss the point, Hoover made it explicit; Congress need not concern itself. "No special session is necessary to deal with employment," Hoover declared in October.

Over the next few weeks Woods walked a fine line: breathing fire in his exhortations to the press and public, but always with the caveat that it was a self-help model he was pursuing. Woods and his advisors pressed a growing slate of mutual-aid schemes: shorter shifts in factories, unpaid furloughs for those who could afford them, accelerated maintenance schedules for industry, home remodeling and "spruce-up" projects, and a back-to-school campaign "to keep the young off the labor market." But neither PECE nor the federal government would provide the answer. "We can win this battle if we all work together," Woods told a national radio audience. "No one can do it for us. We must do it ourselves."

With his stopgap committees up and running, Hoover finally turned his attention to the business of politics. Midterm elections are notoriously difficult for first-term presidents, as the newcomer's novelty has worn off and the problems facing the administration come into sharper focus. In Hoover's case those problems were exacerbated by Charley Michelson, who was having fun and great success pinning blame for the Depression on the president and his party. Hoover wanted to fight back. "We are not attacking enough," he declared to James MacLafferty, now echoing MacLafferty's urgings of June and July.

Hoover's initial impulse was to rely on surrogates, pushing ranking Republicans like House Speaker Nicholas Longworth to flog the party agenda. But he recognized, too, that he had his own role to play. For a politician who loathed politics, the idea of campaigning in an election not his own was particularly odious. But duty was Hoover's impetus, and if public appearances were part of the job, then the president would do his part. He decided, in a case of overkill, to make four speeches in the first week of October—two of them on the same day. Once the schedule was set, he bent to his work. Noted Edgar Rickard, during a visit in late September, "Hoover under great strain."

Hoover wanted the others in his party to challenge the Democrats, but he had no flair himself for political fisticuffs. Instead he fell back on his paternalistic, pedagogic instincts. He took to the dais hoping to inspire the electorate by invoking the resilience of the American character, but his message felt strangely off-key. Standing at a podium in one great hall after another, eyes down, intoning in his nasal, almost robotic voice, Hoover succeeded principally in exposing the gulf between himself and his audience.

Hoover had learned, apparently, to avoid the blunder of prognostication, but he could not seem to shake his inclination to minimize the crisis. Several times in this flurry of October appearances he trod perilously close to referring to the Depression in the past tense. Twice, speaking at a bankers convention in Cleveland, he congratulated the assembled actuaries for having "carried the credit system of the nation safely through a most difficult crisis."

Repeatedly, remarkably, he reminded audiences that other people, in other times and other places, had suffered more than they. "Our problems . . . are less difficult than those which confronted generations before us," he said in North Carolina. "We are suffering far less than other countries," he said in Cleveland. The postwar recession of 1921, he said, was "far more severe."

Rather than commiserate, Hoover touted his ideal of mutual aid. In Boston, addressing the American Federation of Labor, he commended "the fine cooperation" of federal and local governments, railroads, and utilities in "taking up the slack of unemployment." He pressed his theme like a door-to-door salesman. "Nationwide cooperation and team play . . . have greatly ameliorated the hardship of this depression," he asserted.

In some instances, he seemed inclined to forget the Depression altogether. At Kings Mountain, a Revolutionary War battleground in South Carolina, he waxed on what he called "the spirit of America." Looking back over a century of progress, Hoover found himself "filled with justifiable pride in the valor, the inventions, the contributions to art and literature, the moral influence of our people." Surely, this was exceptionalism misplaced. "We glow with satisfaction at the . . . benefits and blessings amongst us." Hoover even reached back to the language of his electoral campaign, conjuring again "that ultimate goal of every right-thinking citizen—the abolition of poverty of mind and home."

It was enough to make one wonder what Hoover was talking about, and whom he was addressing. This was, after all, no marginal setback the nation had encountered, but a deepening wound that gave no sign of healing. The

American people were not acting like the plucky patriots of Hoover's caricature; they were reeling in the face of loss, dislocation, and in the drought region, impending famine. Hoover could not have been ignorant of the deepening gloom. Bob Lucas, who replaced Claudius Huston at the Republican National Committee, had canvassed "every part of the United States," and found "the people" in a "state of utter despondency and an apathetic waiting for something worse." These were folks who needed solace, not a scolding.

Nor did Hoover actually believe the rosy picture he was painting, a nation animated by "cooperation and team play which have greatly ameliorated the hardship of this depression." In fact, within the councils of his administration, the president acknowledged a far darker prospect. "It seems to me that any hope of industrial recovery between now and winter is rapidly vanishing," Hoover wrote to Secretary of Commerce Lamont October 1, a day before heading out on the hustings. "We will need to face a very serious problem of unemployment."

Hoover was not lying in his professions of optimism; he was doing what he believed a president should do: resisting pessimism, fighting fear. But Hoover took it to the verge of bald-faced denial, and at that point he left his audience behind. They could feel the impact of the Depression in the workplace and in their bank accounts, regardless of what Hoover might contend. It was a predilection of his, exhorting people to do as he felt they ought, rather than frankly sharing his true beliefs, but it was better suited to a schoolhouse than to adult civic discourse. In this instance it only made him appear cold and remote.

Hoover grasped the idea that the crisis had wrought a steep toll in the sufferings of the people. "It is not a problem in academic economics; it is a great human problem," Hoover told the bankers in Cleveland. But in his next sentence, even as he detailed the distress, he reduced the human toll to a matter of ideology. "The margin of shrinkage [in the economy] brings loss of savings, unemployment, privation, hardship, and fear." These natural feelings should be rejected, he said; they were "no part of our ideals for the American economic system." Even when he voiced the words, Hoover couldn't seem to summon notes of actual empathy.

From the moment he announced as a candidate for president Herbert Hoover presented Americans with the riddle: what did it mean to place a nonpolitician—an anti-politician—in high political office? By now an answer was beginning to emerge. Hoover was striving to perform the intrinsically political task of rallying the electorate to his party standard, but there was no resonance, no sensation. The bond that connects a leader to the people might be ineffable, but now, with the country wounded and seeking direction, its absence felt uncomfortably real.

For Secretary of State Henry Stimson, returned from negotiations in Europe and now frequently in intimate contact with the president, Hoover's peculiar isolation evoked feelings very close to pity. One evening in October, before Hoover set out for his appearance in Boston, Stimson telephoned the president to praise the speech he'd made in Cleveland. Hoover's obvious gratitude for the friendly call prompted Stimson to reflect: "Underneath his shyness he is so sensitive and really human that it is a tragedy that he cannot, apparently, make that side of his nature felt in his public contacts."

A month later another observer, directly engaged like Stimson but not so close to the president, remarked on the same phenomenon from a slightly different perspective. Ted Clark, staff secretary in Calvin Coolidge's White House, maintained a steady correspondence to keep his former boss informed of doings in Washington. Writing soon after polls closed for the congressional elections, Clark shared an observation that struck him "very forcibly": "That is, the seeming failure of Mr. Hoover to impress upon the average citizen even a vague picture of his character and personality."

A veteran Washington observer, Clark said this failure to make an impression was unique to Hoover. "Certainly it is not true of Wilson, Harding, and yourself," he confided to Coolidge. "If you ask a man if Hoover is cool or friendly, sincere or insincere, confident or vacillating, fearless or temporizing, it will be generally found that he has not made up his mind." Just one quality shone through: "about the only definite impression is that he is most ignorant of what they call 'politics.'"

Clark felt this pervasive ambiguity might actually redound to Hoover's benefit; that it could insulate him from the public's natural impulse to blame someone for the Depression. But there was another aspect that went unmentioned, more intangible but possibly more fundamental: What of leadership? What did it mean for a suffering nation to cast its eyes toward the White House to find only reproach and indifference?

FOURTEEN

PLAYING POLITICS
WITH HUMAN MISERY

Herbert Hoover had reason to feel optimistic entering the midterm election of 1930. For all his problems with Congress, he had seen his veto of the veterans' pension upheld and his own compromise bill put through. He had won applause for his handling of the drought. And he had preached his gospel of recovery until he almost believed it himself.

But outside Washington the skirmishes and triumphs of the Hoover administration rang hollow. In the great cities the soup kitchens and the breadlines were proliferating. Factories were running half-time shifts to spread the work around. And in the rural byways farmers stared out at crops that would only sell at a loss. Ten years of Republican leadership had brought them to this point; voters were ready to try something new.

They registered their shifting allegiance in the congressional elections November 4, delivering a resounding rebuke to the ruling party. The Republican majorities in Congress—16 votes in the Senate, and 103 in House—were erased. It was not unprecedented; Taft and Harding had both seen their party sustain heavier losses at the midterm. But it did not augur well for a president already at odds with Congress.

James MacLafferty visited the White House two days later to go over the results with the president. Hoover looked pale, grave and weary. "There was discouragement in his voice," noted MacLafferty. Personally MacLafferty considered the vote a "disaster," but with the president he tried to stay on the bright side. In some districts, he said, Prohibition was the deciding factor; in others, "there has been a sort of dissatisfaction because of unemployment." But MacLafferty said he had spent a month on the campaign trail himself, meeting with candidates and delivering speeches, and all that time he found no antagonism to the administration. The mention of Hoover's name always elicited "a fine response," MacLafferty said. "This is not a rebuke to you," he told the president.

That last bit of counsel was hard to buy. Later that day Henry Stimson stopped in to discuss several small matters from the foreign desk. When talk inevitably turned to the election, Hoover appeared "rather sad and depressed and said he saw no way of looking at it except as a vote of lack of confidence in him." Stimson did not contradict him, but shared his recollections of William Howard Taft facing the same sort of result. Stimson assured Hoover he would remain "absolutely loyal," and Hoover thanked him earnestly, "almost pathetically."

But if Hoover was wounded, he and his staff did not let it show. Three weeks after the election Ted Clark was able to report, "the feeling in the White House was one of disgust rather than surprise," and that the president was "firm in the belief that there is no real rebuke to his administration." In this version, the ousted congressional incumbents had brought it on themselves, paying the price for failing to cohere as a bloc and stand by their president.

Even as the pundits and the politicians were scrutinizing the returns from the polls, the disaster in the rural South and East took on new and frightening dimensions. Distress wrought by the drought raised new and even more pressing appeals from the nation's heartland. With winter coming on, schools in the Arkansas countryside reported thousands of children could not attend classes for lack of shoes and clothing. A Red Cross field survey in Lee County, bordering the Mississippi River, found "not only suffering but actual starvation."

For lawmakers in Washington, Joseph Robinson, the Senate's Democratic leader, put the crisis in personal terms. The week of the election he'd traveled home to Arkansas and found conditions worse than he'd ever seen—farmers barefoot, their children hungry, livestock sold or slaughtered for lack of feed. "If I took this entire day," Robinson told his fellow senators, "I should still leave an inadequate picture of the misery, the desolation, and the suffering that exist in many sections of the drought area."

Conditions in the South were complicated, as usual, by the dynamics of race. Landowners who employed black sharecroppers to raise cotton asked that aid be delayed until after the crop was in, the better to control their indentured workforce. "A food program would be extremely harmful to the participants, and would disturb economic conditions," was the racially coded message from one Mississippi relief advisor.

It wasn't just cruelty on the part of the growers; the drought had devastated crop yields, leaving them unable to pay their mortgages or seed loans, let alone labor. Moreover, the global collapse in commodity prices meant that even though production was down, prices continued to fall.

In late November, the combination of maladies found a new outlet—a cascade of bank failures, beginning in Arkansas but quickly spreading east, through Tennessee, Kentucky, and North Carolina, and north, into Missouri, Indiana, and Illinois. During one five-day stretch, eighty-one Southern banks failed. Nationwide, in the last two months of 1930, 608 banks closed their doors, most of them in the drought region.

It's a shocking tally in any context, but it should be understood that banking in that era was a completely different animal than what we know today. From the time of Andrew Jackson, endemic suspicion of the "money power" had inhibited every effort to centralize the financial sector, resulting in a plethora of institutions and a division of regulation between the national authorities and the states. In consequence, banking had long been a dicey business; even during the boom decade of the 1920s, an average of more than six hundred banks failed each year.

Most of those that failed, however, were vanishingly small. Two thirds had capital stock of $25,000 or less. Eighty percent were located in towns of just 2,500 people, and 40 percent in towns of just five hundred residents or fewer.

These numbers tell us much about the character of the institutions. Located in rural areas, such banks were closely tied to the cycle of agricultural credit, extending loans and mortgages based on crop yields and land values. During agriculture's "Golden Era," from the turn of the century to the Great War, the number of banks more than doubled, from 13,925 to 30,395. After the war, big harvests brought low prices and some dislocation; in 1930, the drought hit the rickety rural banks like a sledgehammer.

The catalyst came in early November with the sudden collapse of Caldwell and Company, a conglomerate based in Little Rock and known as the "Morgan of the South." Founded in 1917 as a municipal bond house, Caldwell grew to include eight insurance companies, interests in business and industry, and the largest chain of banks in the South. Battered by the stock crash and sinking real estate values, Caldwell in June 1930 arranged a merger with BancoKentucky, a holding company organized by the National Bank of Kentucky. The merger brought an infusion of cash but could not reverse the decline in its portfolio, and BancoKentucky shut down November 14. The National Bank of Kentucky followed two days later, and the rout was on.

The bank failures served as another reminder that this next, lame-duck session of Congress, set to commence December 2, would be concerned principally with addressing the broken economy. And with the election results setting Republicans and Democrats at virtual parity, jockeying for pole position started early.

The first move came from Joe Robinson, senator from Arkansas and Al Smith's running mate in 1928. Sobered by the conditions he encountered in his visit home, Robinson assembled the core of the Democrats' national leadership and persuaded them to join him in a public repudiation of partisan hostilities. In a press statement issued the first Friday after the voting, Robinson; Al Smith; John Nance Garner, the new Democratic Speaker of the House; John Raskob; and three other prominent signators vowed to set politics aside in facing the national emergency. They would join with Republicans to "steer legislation in a straight line toward prosperity," these Democrats vowed, with "no thought of political advantage."

It was, of course, a patently political maneuver. And it was baldly self-serving, the joint statement veering off to reprise the tariff fight and cast the Democrats as exemplars of "patience and caution." But this pledge to country bore the endorsement of the party's top leadership—"seven sages," as they were dubbed in the press, including the last three presidential nominees— and it expressly vowed not "to embarrass the President of the United States." After all the acrimony of the past year, this final session of the 71st Congress was to be marked by harmony.

The statement blindsided Hoover and his administration. "Pure political bunk," Jim MacLafferty termed it, expressing the "belliciose" feeling inside the White House. Especially galling to the president was the fact that he himself had been mulling a similar initiative. On election day, with the polls still open, Hoover told Henry Stimson he was inclined to "appeal to the people for the coming two months to give up politics and try to devote ourselves to curing the financial and economic depression we are under." Now Robinson was the conciliator, and the best Hoover could do was to follow his lead.

All through the weekend following the Democrats' announcement, Hoover's political aides labored with ranking party officials to compose an answer. They drafted an angry retort, but when they showed it to the president on Sunday he rejected it out of hand. "The country would think the Democrats want to be helpful and we refused their cooperation," Hoover said. "It won't do."

Hoover ordered his team to take the opposite tack. The result was a magnanimous statement that Senate Republican leader Jim Watson delivered on Monday, pronouncing his party "very happy" with the Democrats' bipartisan proffer. Watson even took the opportunity to chide the insurgents in his own party, suggesting it was now their "duty . . . to cooperate."

Hoover put his personal stamp on this charm offensive two days later, making known that he'd sent a telegram to Robinson "urging close cooperation" in the upcoming session of Congress. Officially the story was a leak; it was sourced to "a close friend of the president." Warming to this pantomime, Hoover put out word the next day that he'd spoken with leaders of both parties, he said, "with a view to securing cooperation." Reporters attributed the story to a statement "authorized by President Hoover."

Cooperation was the official line, but inside the White House it was quite a different story. The president and his aides remained incensed at the Democrats' proposal. The wily Joe Robinson had stolen Hoover's thunder.

Hoover voiced his resentment to Henry Stimson the day his telegram went out, telling him the missive was "intended to put [Robinson] in a hole." Stimson, more practiced in the ways of politics, tried to back the president down. "I begged him not to be so suspicious, and to go on his own feelings and not on the advice of political smart-alecs."

But Hoover was already in combat mode, with plans in motion. Meeting with MacLafferty later that day, Hoover told him to prepare for battle once Congress got under way. "We need fighters now," Hoover told his deputy. "We've got to be mean to them; we've got to start them fighting among themselves." According to MacLafferty's notes of the meeting, Hoover then gave the directive: "Organize the right kind of group [in the Senate] and plague them to death!"

His one caveat was to remind MacLafferty to keep secret his link to the White House. "Leave it to me, Chief," MacLafferty gamely replied. "Our discouraged Republicans throughout the country will jump up out of the grass when they hear one good war whoop."

Some Democrats had the same reaction to the idea of a legislative truce, and they didn't mind making it public. Carter Glass, the long-tenured, hot-tempered, Democratic senator from Virginia, made quick to distance himself from Robinson and his fellow sages. In a lengthy press statement, Glass extolled the last two prior Democratic presidents—Grover Cleveland and Woodrow Wilson—and confessed "some astonishment that anybody should feel impelled to apologize for an apparent Democratic victory" in the midterms.

One person who appears to have been sincere in this round of blind-man's-bluff was Senator Joseph Robinson. Famous for his scrappy disposition but known also for legislative compromise, Robinson was leery of some of the schemes being floated by his party in the name of Depression relief. Writing to Bernard Baruch, possibly the most influential Democrat *not* to sign the peace pledge, Robinson said he thought it best to "sit steady in the boat," echoing a current Republican slogan. Regarding economic affairs, Robinson wrote, "I grow more and more impressed with conservative action."

On the last Sunday in November, with Congress to open the following day, President Hoover invited Joseph Robinson to the White House. The senator had just returned from his home state flush with a sense of urgency to rush aid to the suffering farmers; for his part, the president was laying the final plank in the legislative strategy he first broached with MacLafferty.

Neither president nor senator spoke for the record following the afternoon parley, but aides made sure the press got the message. "Hoover and Robinson Agree to Expedite Relief Bills," ran the headline in *The New York Times.* The *Herald Tribune* marveled at "the unusual incident of a Republican president planning legislation with the opposition leader."

Bipartisan truce, initiated by Robinson and then adopted by Hoover as his own, appeared to be the order of the day when Congress convened on Monday. Several bills were introduced calling for public works and other forms of aid, but just two qualified under the "program" discussed by Hoover and Robinson—a bill to accelerate public works, sponsored by the administration and carrying a price of $150 million; and a bill to subsist farmers in the drought zone with $60 million in loans for seed, feed, and equipment. For the president, the key was that both measures could be effected without raising taxes.

The ag relief bill was Robinson's personal project. He authored the measure and lined up cosponsors, including sometime Hoover ally Charles McNary of Oregon. A matching bill was introduced in the House by James Aswell of Louisiana, the ranking Democrat on the Agriculture Committee. Robinson's sole innovation was to include food and clothing for the distressed farmers, along with seed and animal feed, among the uses to which the loans might be put.

The $60 million figure had been proposed in the weeks before the session began, and confirmed November 20 in deliberations of Hoover's National Drought Relief Committee, at a convention held in Washington and chaired by Agriculture Secretary Arthur Hyde. According to Aswell, when he introduced his bill the $60 million budget enjoyed broad support. "The Republican members of my committee helped me, as well as the Democratic members," Aswell said later, "and we thought there was no opposition."

All that changed Wednesday morning, when Hoover moved to cut authorizations in the seed-loan bill by more than half, to $25 million. He dispatched messengers first to the House and then to the Senate, delivering to the chairmen of the agriculture committees for each body copies of a new draft for the bill, with the budget slashed and the food-for-farmers provision deleted. The couriers arrived with no warning and no explanation.

Aswell was floored. "I thought for three months I had the enthusiastic support of the Secretary of Agriculture," Aswell told his fellow legislators; Hyde had been "most outspoken in his approval." Delivery of the revised bill came as a revelation. "It was the first time I had any hint of what was going on under cover."

Aswell was not the only one surprised at Hoover's move; by all indications Secretary Hyde had been sincere in his support for the bill, and for the $60 million. This abrupt attack on the drought loan program was undertaken at the sole direction of the president.

Hyde learned only later what had happened. It turned out that, in the hours between meeting with Joe Robinson on Sunday and the start of business on Wednesday, Hoover had contacted the head of the extension office at the Department of Agriculture and asked him to prepare a substitute bill capping the loan program at $25 million. The veteran bureaucrat had long opposed running credit programs through his department, and was glad to find an ally in the president. He promptly wrote the revised bills that Hoover dispatched to Congress.

Word of this intrigue—though not Hoover's role—soon reached Nils Olsen, head of the Bureau of Agricultural Economics at the Department of Agriculture. Olsen promptly ordered not one but two in-house studies to estimate the optimal size of the loan program; both found in favor of the higher figure. Olsen submitted these findings to Secretary Hyde with a cover summary: "It seems that a substantially larger amount than the $25 million would be required to cover the production credit needs of the drought-stricken farmers."

Hyde dismissed the staff protests, and in testimony before Congress supported the president's figure. When Olsen pressed him later for an explanation, Hyde was emphatic. It was Hoover who had requested the revised bill, it was he who set the figure at $25 million, and it was he who dispatched the report to the committee chairmen. "So when the President of the United States wants a thing done," Hyde told Olsen, "it must be done."

Hoover's move to slash the ag loan program rattled both houses of Congress. In the House, James Aswell called it "the cheapest, political, pinhead action I ever had thrust in my face." But he could not keep his Republican colleagues in line, and the Agriculture Committee agreed in a party-line vote to cut the proposed $60 million loan budget to Hoover's figure.

In the Senate the Agriculture Committee held its ground, voting unanimously to retain the $60 million allocation; the full Senate then passed the bill by voice vote. But the challenge from the administration shook confidence in the whole idea of a legislative truce. The first serious note of dissent was sounded by Senator David Walsh, a brash populist Democrat from Massachusetts. Taking the floor to propose a major government job project, Walsh derided Robinson's "harmony program" and denounced the president's relief bills as wholly inadequate. "I am sick and tired of the absence of sympathy and appreciation of this problem," Walsh declared, "and an attempt to talk in the same breath that we talk of relief about saving money from the public treasury."

Walsh's discord was met that night with an equally resounding discharge from Arthur Hyde. Quite aware now that he was to provide cover for Hoover's impetuous maneuver, Hyde denounced the Robinson bill, focusing particularly on its allowance for food and clothing. "There are a great many objections to the government making loans for human food," Hyde told reporters. Such a provision "approaches perilously near the dole system and would be a move in the wrong direction."

Hyde said the Red Cross was ready "to take care of all cases of distress," and that extending loans to purchase food would encourage "the shiftless and ne'er-do-well to accept the loans and then repudiate them . . . a form of charity much more damaging than relief by the Red Cross."

Now President Hoover joined the fray in person, delivering a blast at his weekly press conference that brought Robinson's short-lived peace pact to a shuddering close. In a terse written statement, Hoover said he felt compelled to speak out against extravagant programs that would require increased taxes or new government borrowing. "Prosperity cannot be restored by raids on the public treasury," the president scolded.

Bills had been introduced in the new session, Hoover said, "mostly under the guise of giving relief of some kind or another," that would more than double the government's annual expenditure, pushing the federal budget $4.5 billion into deficit. This was quite an exaggeration; while several lawmakers, including David Walsh, had floated their own pet schemes for public assistance, the only bills to advance were the administration's public works bill, and Robinson's drought loans. What had piqued the president, it appeared, was the Senate's temerity in spurning his bid to slash Robinson's program.

It was a startling broadside, echoing the swipe Hoover took at lawmakers during debates over the Wagner unemployment bills early in the year. Hoover had backed off then, and now he appeared to do so again, offering toward the end of his statement that, "many of these measures are being promoted by organizations and agencies outside of Congress." He also suggested that "the leaders of both parties" were "cooperating" with him to bar such profligacy. But in the same breath he returned to his theme, chiding spendthrift lawmakers for "playing politics with human misery."

It was a strange, muddled message, long on innuendo and overtly inflammatory—if the leaders of both parties were "cooperating," why not work with those leaders to keep legislation in line? And whatever happened to the "legislative program" that Hoover and Robinson had agreed to support?

To Senator Pat Harrison, Democrat of Mississippi, the attack was so egregious that it suggested some sort of psychological basis. "There has not been the slightest quiver of politics in this chamber" in the week since Congress opened, Harrison said in rebutting Hoover's statement. "What is it that has so aroused the president? Why is it that he has lost his usual equilibrium?"

Especially irksome was Hoover's suggestion that some lawmakers were "playing politics with human misery." Hoover's own reputation was built on his good works; now he was rebuking others for answering the same impulse. "There is no man in the history of this country who has won more political favor upon the miseries of people," Harrison observed. "Is this an obsession with the president?"

There was an element of insight here; from the time of his exploits during the Great War, when the question turned to emergency relief, Hoover
considered himself uniquely qualified. But there was another, more prosaic
explanation: this was a political ploy, the war whoop that MacLafferty had
called for.

Harrison picked up on that as well. "President Hoover is trying to put
the Democratic leadership in a hole and he is doing it deliberately." Right
again—Harrison had actually hit upon the very words Hoover used when
he mentioned his plan to Stimson. Hoover's strategy was now evident. "The
distinguished Senator from Arkansas has tried to cooperate," Harrison surmised, "but this soon in the session the president breaks the bond of cooperation."

Hoover had stirred up something of a hornet's nest in Congress, but he and
his advisors considered the attack on the Senate Democrats a success. Hoover
was particularly heartened to find his tough talk had won hearty endorsement from *The New York Times*. Headlined "Irresponsible in Congress," the
editorial reminded readers that Hoover was "head of the government," and
"bound by oath" to protect the Republic from harm. "What could be more
harmful than laws which would bankrupt the Treasury and impose heavy
and cruel burdens of taxation upon all citizens?"

The *Times* was not a strictly Republican paper, but it viewed with alarm
the prospect of Congress adopting heavy spending programs to answer the
Depression. And it accepted Hoover's premise that allocating $60 million for
the drought zone loan program, rather than his figure of $25 million, sig-
naled "a stampede into reckless spending of the public money." The paper
said nothing of the demise of Senator Robinson's much celebrated, but little
mourned political truce.

For his part, Joe Robinson was clearly shaken by the president's ambush. Taking the floor of the Senate a day after Hoover's scathing challenge,
Robinson appeared pensive, dwelling for some time on the desolation in the
drought zone. When at last he took up Hoover's attack, Robinson all but
apologized for him. "The president apparently lost his temper when he issued his statement yesterday," he told his colleagues.

Robinson had a reputation as a pugilist—he was banned from the

Chevy Chase Country Club for once slugging a fellow golfer. But none of that fighting spirit was evident here. "My purpose is to try to do my duty," Robinson told his Senate colleagues. "I recognize that my standards of duty may be perverted or inferior and that they are subject to criticism, but I should like to see this Congress now act in a spirit of greater cooperation."

It was not to be. Through all his years in Washington, Herbert Hoover had proselytized cooperation as a mode of governance and a communitarian ideal. Now in the critical moment, with the country blighted and the Congress uncertain, Hoover abandoned collaboration in favor of a hard line. When Robinson risked the ire of his fellow Democrats to seek common ground with the president, Hoover promised his support and then betrayed him. In later years Hoover would voice "despair at my personal failure to secure any assurance of cooperation from the Democratic side." But here at the outset of a key legislative session, it was Hoover who poisoned the well.

Hoover was using subterfuge to keep the Democrats in Congress at bay; as the winter closed in and the crisis in the cities mounted, he was forced to use similar tactics with his own unemployment committee.

In the weeks leading up to the midterm elections, Arthur Woods had been content to work within the narrow confines marked out by the president; canvassing state and local governments to get better data on the extent of unemployment, and exhorting local charities to redouble their efforts. But these measures were intrinsically marginal, and Woods was soon chafing for a more active role. In late November, operating under his mandate to help coordinate government relief efforts, Woods convened a joint session with his PECE and a national association of state highway officials. The two groups quickly reached a consensus: favoring road-building projects as a means of putting the unemployed to work.

It was the same conclusion reached by Hoover himself at President Harding's unemployment conference in 1921. "It is felt by the committee and by economists generally," Woods announced in a press release, "that the carrying out of a broad and comprehensive public roads program at a time like this is one of the soundest procedures to meet a situation of depression."

Woods and his team actually convinced themselves that Hoover could be persuaded to come around. For the next several days Woods busied himself composing a "comprehensive plan for public works," centered on road-building projects and budgeted at $840 million. But to Hoover, Woods's plan smacked of the job programs being promoted in Congress. He dismissed the committee proposal as "imprudent," citing "certain common-sense limitations upon any expansions of construction work." Any stopgap job programs would have to arise from the states and the cities, not the federal government.

Woods was chagrined, but he wasn't going to contradict the president, and he accepted this rebuff in silence. Word had gotten out, however, about his ambitious public works scheme, and in December, just as Hoover was reprimanding the Congress for playing games with human misery, the Senate made a formal request to see the PECE report.

Rather than comply, Hoover dissembled. "The president's emergency committee has made no report on unemployment," Hoover said in a written message to the Senate. "I have received notes and verbal suggestions from Colonel Woods from time to time, and from the departments of the government on this subject. These were confined to guidance in formulation of the recommendations which I have already laid before Congress. Such notes and discussions are necessarily passing and tentative, and they represent that confidential relation of the president with government officers which should be preserved."

The Senate did not contest this early exercise of executive privilege, and Hoover successfully buried Woods's report. But in doing so he effectively scuttled the work of his principal relief organization. "The president's failure to come through with a suggested program for employment leaves the committee . . . up in the air," one frustrated member wrote in an internal report. "The committee can do little more than act as a clearinghouse."

Hoover's intransigence was alienating even some of his core supporters. But at this point, besieged on all sides, the president dug in. At a time when events seemed to defy his every endeavor, keeping charity out of the federal portfolio was one position he felt he could hold.

"GRAY DAYS IN THE WHITE HOUSE"
With the Depression deepening and the
president's popularity sinking with it,
Hoover's gloom was palpable.

FIFTEEN

THE GHOST OF GROVER CLEVELAND

Herbert Hoover opened 1931 in a flush of confidence and enthusiasm. New Year's Day was the occasion for an annual public reception at the White House, but even this ceremonial chore could not dampen his spirits. So buoyant was Hoover that when he learned two visitors had taken up stations before dawn, hoping to secure first place at the 1 p.m. reception, he invited them to join him for breakfast.

"If there are two men who are as anxious to see me as all that, I won't keep them waiting out in the cold any longer," Hoover generously exclaimed. Escorted in by White House police, the pair was introduced to the holdovers from that morning's round of medicine ball. After polite introductions, the group sat with the president to share plates of bacon and eggs.

Once his surprised breakfast guests had eaten and moved on, Hoover stopped to chat with Joel Boone, on hand in deep blue naval uniform for the day's festivities. The president made a rare display of congeniality, chatting with Boone about the three Hoover grandchildren who had taken up residence at the White House while their father, Herbert Jr., was in treatment for tuberculosis. Better they should spend the holidays on the East Coast, Hoover said, where they might experience "a real winter," rather than home in ever-sunny California.

Hoover was cheered as well by his efforts over the past few days to line up major public figures to help promote a fund drive for the Red Cross. He was in a "fight," Hoover said, "for a fundamental principle of government," which was to divorce charity from the purview of the government. Such benevolence must be a private concern, or it would soon evolve into a "dole," whether disguised or in plain view. Boone promptly endorsed Hoover's stand.

"I told the president that the American people, as I observed, were with him," Boone recorded later, "that they were convinced he was fighting for them." It was the kind of advice he tended to get from his staff and his aides—the kind of advice Hoover wanted to hear.

With that, the president was off to the Blue Room, the great oval reception hall on the second floor, dominated that day by the official Christmas tree. It was a scene of pomp and pageant—diplomats in full regalia, generals festooned in gold braid, all moving to the cadence set by the Marine Corps Band. After enduring the more taxing afternoon reception, Bert and Lou Hoover sat down with two close friends for a private dinner. The tribulations of the Depression must have felt like just a bad dream.

Three days later, outside a rural hamlet called England, Arkansas, a tenant farmer named H. C. Coney received a visit from a neighbor. Approaching him in tears, the woman told him her children hadn't had a bite to eat for the past two days. Coney was forty-six years old, the father of five, and had his own brood to feed. But he was moved by the plight of his neighbor, and so set out in his farm truck, his wife seated beside him, headed for the Red Cross depot.

They encountered there an unhappy crowd gathered in the street. The local Red Cross agent had run out of application blanks and was sending the hungry farmers away empty-handed. Coney gazed briefly at the group milling about the depot, and at that moment made a decision. "Climb on," he shouted; they would roll into town and get what they needed, Red Cross vouchers or no.

Arriving in England, Coney and his new friends sought out the mayor and then the chief of police. The crowd grew and the complaint became more pointed: "We are not going to let our children starve!" After a brief standoff several merchants opened their doors, and before the day was out more than three hundred people helped themselves to provisions.

The "food riot" just twenty miles outside Little Rock seemed to encapsulate all the distress brought on by the drought just as Congress returned from its holiday recess. "A situation has developed that no one can ignore," said Senator Thad Caraway. A former sharecropper himself, Caraway decried Red Cross food grants that ranged as small as a dollar a month. "That is no relief," the former prosecutor spat; "that is an insult."

Caraway paid respects to the Red Cross but said that, facing disaster on this scale, the organization was simply overmatched. His answer was to sponsor a $15 million authorization for food aid that would be tacked onto the latest drought loan bill, a compromise measure set at $45 million. It was no coincidence that the price tag now totaled $60 million—the figure set initially by Hoover's own drought advisory council, and then rejected by the president.

Red Cross chairman John Barton Payne answered Caraway the next day. Called to testify before the Senate Appropriations Committee, Payne stuck with the strategy his agency had followed since the fall—to minimize the problem and discourage outside intervention. The funds and staff at the local chapters were more than sufficient to the emergency, Payne said; of the $5 million drought reserve set aside by the national organization, less than half a million had been spent.

Pressed to explain the reports of desperation in Arkansas, Payne offered his blithe assurance. "I, with great modesty, say that no such situation exists." He had conferred with President Hoover, Payne said, and affirmed to him that matters were well in hand.

This sanguine statement was a strategic blunder. The startling news from England, Arkansas, spurred the nation's press corps, and over the next few weeks reporters from the industrial East made their way out to the hinterlands and confirmed the worst—sharecroppers without food or funds, mothers huddled in drafty shacks, their children in rags, their husbands gone. Suffering was everywhere present, and famine appeared imminent.

But the advocates for aid blundered, too. The same day Payne spoke before the Senate, New York representative Fiorello La Guardia stood in the House to demand that any food aid for farmers be matched by aid to the unemployed. This would expand a project conceived to assist an estimated million drought sufferers to cover at least five million more people, a program so expansive that all but the most ardent liberals in Congress shied away.

The disarray in Congress suited Hoover nicely. He had recognized, as Judge Payne apparently failed to do, that the Red Cross had sorely underestimated the extent of privation in the drought zone. The onset of deep winter cold would push many thousands to the brink of outright starvation, and only a major feeding program, administered from posts stretching from Virginia to Texas, could answer the emergency.

Hoover's answer was the fundraising drive he'd mentioned to Joel Boone. Such a campaign would reprise some of the great moments from the president's wartime exploits. At the same time, keeping the focus on the Red Cross would deflect attention from the idea of a government feeding program.

This was a contest Hoover believed he could win. "The president seemed quite cheerful," Henry Stimson wrote January 16, the day Hoover broached his plan to his cabinet. "I was delighted to find that he was full of fight," Stimson noted, especially that it was "constructive fight, entering the contest in a way which showed his old genius for organization."

The only trick was to get Judge Payne on board. An appeal for funds would certainly prove embarrassing, as Payne would have to contradict his own testimony of just days before. But with suffering from the drought now getting front-page coverage across the country, to feign ignorance was no longer an option. On Saturday, January 10, less than a week after his insouciant appearance before the Senate, Payne visited Hoover at the White House. Following a conference with the president, Payne addressed reporters in a distinctly new tone. The charity's national reserve fund, so sound four days before, was now "melting down very rapidly."

President Hoover followed up at his next press conference on Tuesday. Acting now in his capacity as honorary president of the Red Cross, Hoover called for "a very material increase in the resources of the Red Cross," a national campaign to raise $10 million for drought relief. It was the only viable option, Hoover said; "The American Red Cross is the nation's sole agency for relief in such a crisis." He then weighed in with a public letter calling on the "active sympathies toward our fellow countrymen."

Over the next week the campaign unfolded like clockwork. On Monday, John Barton Payne sent telegrams to three thousand local Red Cross chapters announcing an "immediate campaign . . . to prevent untold suffering and actual starvation of thousands of families." *The New York Times*, now an actor in this drama, chimed in with a series of editorials praising the Red Cross and the very idea of charity. "The nation's response through this channel will have a moral value which no outright Congressional appropriation could have," one column advised. Voluntary gifts would make coercive taxes unnecessary. More than that, "The generosity of such a response would make of a disaster a triumph of man's spirit over the material thing."

By now the lines were becoming clear; while Congress was laboring to devise a meaningful aid program, Hoover had enlisted the Red Cross—and the establishment press—in his bid to keep the government out of the business of direct relief.

For the next several weeks Congress wrestled with the fundamental question: Would emergency relief remain a private affair, or should the government shoulder the burden? While the battle raged in Washington, newspapers across the country carried the latest reports from the drought zone. The Red Cross was now assisting hundreds of thousands of people, but untold thousands more were eking out the most bare existence. Turnips grown from the first Red Cross seed packets were now the principal staple of the rural South. People were calling them "Hoover apples."

President Hoover took his Red Cross appeal to the airwaves, along with major public figures like Calvin Coolidge and Al Smith, and entertainers Will Rogers and Amos and Andy. All joined in a marathon national broadcast beseeching public support for the $10 million drought aid campaign.

Throughout the fund drive, Hoover stressed that he considered the Red Cross to be something more than a vehicle for charity. "It is essential that we should maintain the sound American tradition and spirit of voluntary aid in such emergency and should not undermine that spirit," the president proclaimed. Typically, his message felt more cold than warm, a call to duty rather than a heartfelt expression. The folksy Will Rogers, after visiting the White House to discuss the fundraising drive, ribbed Hoover for his habitual reserve. Writing in his syndicated column on the prospect of a government grant to the Red Cross, Rogers quipped, "He sincerely believes (with almost emotion) that it would set a bad precedent."

Hoover was a poor pitchman, but there was substance to his notion of charity as a core feature of national life. For Americans today the Community Chest is familiar only as a quaint category from the Depression-era board game Monopoly. But in 1930 there were Community Chests in every major city—more than three hundred in all—along with community trusts, service clubs, and neighborhood welfare councils.

Some charities were closely targeted, like the Association for Improving the Condition of the Poor; others were more generic. Nationally, there were groups to coordinate groups—the Charity Organization Society, the National Trade Union Amity League. This layered fabric of private philanthropies was one facet of the "associationalism" Hoover saw as the alternative to laissez-faire capitalism.

Hoover won plaudits as secretary of commerce by relentlessly promoting cooperation, but the combination of drought and economic dislocation convinced a broad section of Congress that something more must be done. They were a fractious and disparate group, encompassing Republican insurgents and urban Democrats, but they were united by the growing conviction that government must provide an answer.

Thwarted on one tack, they promptly tried another. If the Red Cross were to be the agency, then the Congress would make a $25 million donation to the drought fund. Judge Payne declined the offer outright, but that was beside the point. And what about the Farm Board surplus? Why not donate last season's wheat, stuffed into silos and awaiting a market rebound? Proposals for distribution of Farm Board wheat were raised inside and outside Congress, but all were steered aside. The Agricultural Marketing Act, Alexander Legge pointed out, had no provision for giving away surplus grain.

Hoover sought to avoid the fray, limiting his public remarks to repeated endorsement of the Red Cross fund drive. But at his insistence his allies in Congress rejected every effort at compromise, and before long the coalition seeking government action trained their argument, and their criticism, on the president himself.

Joe Robinson, spurned sponsor of the bipartisan peace initiative, pronounced himself bewildered by Hoover's hard line. "It is difficult for the human mind to grasp that the government, as it is now being administered, manifests such complete indifference toward the sufferings of its citizens," Robinson declared from the Senate floor.

Thad Caraway, Robinson's colleague from Arkansas, was more pointed. The campaign to raise funds for the Red Cross was a ruse, Caraway said, "a political screen behind which the president is undertaking to shirk his responsibility to see that the suffering and the starving are relieved."

"I protest," the senator declared. "If the president himself wants to become an oppressor of humanity, let him do it in his own name and not degrade this institution which is known as the Red Cross and is loved by millions of American citizens."

As the brickbats flew Hoover hunkered down, sticking to his preferred strategy of letting his critics blow themselves out. But in this case the umbrage continued to mount, with only an occasional protest raised in the president's defense. The longer the conflict dragged out, the more isolated Hoover became, and the more unpopular.

The struggle over relief was just one in a series of disputes between Hoover and the Congress. There was George Norris's bid for public operation of Muscle Shoals, another veterans' bonus bill, and renewed controversy over appointment confirmations, particularly Fed chairman Eugene Meyer. Each dispute was bound to be contentious, but all seemed to boil down to another attack on the president. Hoover expected rancor from the Democrats, especially after his treatment of Joe Robinson's truce. But he was disappointed in how slow his ostensible allies were in defending him and his agenda, especially in the House.

The president vented his frustration with political advisor James Mac-Lafferty, who met with him daily now that Congress was in session. In mid-December Hoover directed MacLafferty to assemble a "select group" of lawmakers in both branches of Congress to serve as surrogates for the administration. They should speak out every time he was "unfairly attacked," Hoover said. "Let them nail each lie one by one as the lie is uttered and proclaim it as dirty politics and nothing else."

MacLafferty set out gamely but encountered resistance even among Hoover's strongest supporters. John Q. Tilson, Republican floor leader in the House, flat declined to participate. "It would be foolish and not good strategy," Tilson said, "to answer every cheap attack made on the president."

When MacLafferty reported this exchange to Hoover, the president suggested he try his luck with Arthur Free, a Stanford graduate and the congressman representing Palo Alto. Free proved more amenable than Tilson, but said the president must first repair his personal relations with Congress. Hoover needed to speak with key representatives in person, to share his legislative strategy, to enlist their support. But above all, Free maintained, Hoover had to do away with his aide George Akerson.

It was a lot to ask. Akerson had been with Hoover for five years, at Commerce, through the campaign, and halfway through his first term. He was loyal and affable, but had been whipsawed in his role as presidential buffer. Tasked as gatekeeper to the press and the legislature, Akerson took the blame for a president who made no secret of his disdain for both groups. The White House correspondents had recently issued a call for Akerson's ouster; now the lawmakers were demanding satisfaction as well.

Hoover was saddened at the prospect of firing such a dutiful aide. Akerson had stayed for years in a job at which nobody else had lasted more than eighteen months. And he understood the nuances of the position—how to fend off the inquiries and intrusions that drove Hoover mad, and also how to tolerate the stale air of the president's inner circle, where toil was a given and rewards only implicit.

Fortunately, Hoover had ties to Hollywood—through personal relationships with several studio chiefs, and with former RNC chairman Will Hays, now the film industry's top censor. A day into the New Year, Hoover announced that Akerson had accepted a job at Paramount Studios.

The House Republicans had gotten their pound of flesh, but that did little to alter the tension between Congress and the White House. Hoover continued to press his narrow agenda, to oppose every bill not of his own making, and to hear treachery in every opposition voice.

Hoover's dubious political compass didn't make his path any easier. He created a sensation in January, for example, when he presented to Congress the report of the Wickersham Commission—the panel he created to study the problems of Prohibition. Eighteen months in the making, the final report was an uncertain muddle, with seven of the eleven commissioners advising some sort of change, either in enforcement or of the underlying amendment. Hoover then contradicted the obvious drift of the committee by declaring that his own duty remained unchanged: "to enforce the law with all the means at our disposal without equivocation or reservation." In one simple statement Hoover had disappointed the wets, cut off any avenue to compromise, and discredited his own handpicked commission. Charley Michelson could not have asked for more.

As the congressional session wore on Hoover grew steadily more combative. When the Democrats floated a new, more expensive version of the veterans' bonus, Hoover ruled that his people would make no effort to improve the bill. He wanted it "as bad as it is possible," the better to assert his planned veto. It was a cynical strategy that Hoover described through clenched teeth. "He was very tense," MacLafferty observed. "He was cutting his words short and his voice, never loud, was low."

"I don't want a compromise," the grim-faced president told his political aide. "I want the bill . . . to go to the limit so that it will arouse the country so that it cannot pass over a veto."

MacLafferty, who always saw political matters in black and white, encouraged Hoover's intransigence. "My advice is that you figuratively kick them in the face," MacLafferty told the president. "Don't show any mercy right now. If you do it will be heralded as weakening on your part. Your enemies won't have it any other way. The public will say you are weakening. Don't give them a chance to say it."

MacLafferty liked to incite Hoover—he felt he was doing the president a service—but in the battle to keep the government out of direct relief Hoover needed no stiffening. As early as August, when the damage from the drought was first coming into view, Hoover and Ogden Mills pressed the Red Cross to step in expressly to head off calls for public intervention.

At that point, support for the Red Cross appeared much in line with Hoover's established reputation as a humanitarian. But once the drought matured into a full-blown crisis, Hoover's determined opposition to relief appeared to contradict his character and his record. "The attitude of the President of the United States is incomprehensible to his most intimate friends," Joe Robinson mused during one Senate speech. "Before he became president he was the recognized leader of the relief movements in this country and throughout the world." Now that he was head of the government, why would he change his stripes?

From outward appearance it was hard not to conclude that Hoover was intrinsically indifferent, heartless at his core. But there was more at work than temperament. Robinson's initial instinct was correct; the key to Hoover's outlook lay in his personal story.

Hoover's role in sending emergency aid to postwar Russia provides some perspective. It was the last of the outsized relief projects that established Hoover the world over as the "Great Humanitarian." But to compare the problems facing America in 1930 with those confronting postwar Europe was to misconstrue the facts, and to sorely underestimate Hoover's earlier accomplishment.

Consider: while Bolsheviks battled czarists and Soviet armies laid siege to the Baltic states to the west, conflict and drought drove the Volga River region into outright famine. By the winter of 1921, starvation was killing an estimated 100,000 people a week. Emaciated bodies were piled in the streets and set upon by dogs.

At that time Hoover was serving his first term as secretary of commerce, but continued to hold his volunteer post as director of the American Relief Administration. At the personal entreaty of Maxim Gorky, Hoover put the ARA into action. Funded with $100 million in U.S. government funds, Hoover's team delivered shiploads of food to shattered Baltic ports and employed tens of thousands of Russians to distribute rations along the Volga. At its peak, the ARA was feeding ten million people a day and, by Gorky's estimate, saved nine million lives.

Against that backdrop, the problems of the American drought in 1930 were of a distinctly lower order. Hoover might be the Master of Emergencies, but that distinction cut both ways. Like a weathered sea captain, he could not bring himself to treat a squall, gusty as it might be, like a full-blown hurricane.

Hoover's wartime experience also shaped his outlook on the role of government. Hoover was speaking from firsthand knowledge that December when he told an audience of journalists that the war had brought on "a period of centralization of power never hitherto known." This was essential in wartime, but introduced a warped new conception of the state in peacetime. "There has grown up among our people the idea that the government is a separate entity, endowed with all power, all money, all resources; that it can be called upon at any hour to settle any difficulty."

That was a dangerous delusion, Hoover believed. Reliance on government bred bureaucracy and corruption, and stifled innovation. It was an ideological point that Hoover had settled in his mind well before the Depression hit, and which he emphasized during his presidential campaign. Under Woodrow Wilson the federal government had become "a centralized despotism," Hoover said in one of his last major addresses, a speech at Madison Square Garden. "However justified in time of war, if continued in peacetime it would destroy not only our American system but with it our progress and freedom as well."

In Europe, reliance upon the central government had produced the most important social innovation of the postwar era—cash payments to the unemployed. Americans watched this development with interest that soon evolved into disdain. Even before the onset of the Depression, the term "dole" had become a knee-jerk epithet in American discourse, a dose of political kryptonite shunned by politicians of every stripe.

This was not about hard hearts or failed vision; it was a matter of simple observation. First Britain and then Germany had implemented systems of unemployment assistance, and each then had entered a period of economic descent. It was hard to say which came first, the dole or the decline, but they appeared to go hand in hand. In Germany, payments to idled workers in the industrial Ruhr Valley helped bring on the hyperinflation that resulted in a historic economic collapse; in England, disillusion with the dole prompted repeated attacks on social spending and the ultimate collapse of the Labour government.

So pervasive was American suspicion of anything approaching a dole that even advocates of direct aid to the unemployed were careful to disparage the detested dole. Despite the many relief bills floated in Congress, Republican functionary Ted Clark held, "I cannot believe that this is a serious menace with the example of England before us." Hoover shared that view, but where Clark was sanguine, Hoover was vigilant.

Another reason Hoover adopted such a firm stance against public relief was that he didn't believe the suffering was quite so severe as the tribunes of the downtrodden would have it. Here again, Hoover's personal history helps to explain his outlook.

Even considering the rural beginnings of many of his contemporaries, Hoover had an especially disadvantaged childhood. From his few memories of his widowed mother Hoover recalled that she took in sewing to make ends meet; Hulda confirmed her son's impression of privation in her correspondence. Soon after she was widowed, she opened a letter to her mother with the line, "You will laugh at my poverty if I tell you I could not scratch up enough to pay my postage, but it has been so."

Life got no easier for young Bert when he was sent out from Iowa to spend his teenage years in Oregon, living with his uncle John Minthorn. He spent one summer boarding in a neighbor's barn and picking onions for pocket change; another summer was spent pulling stumps.

Tales of rural poverty wakened no fear in Hoover; nor did stories of dislocation, or even of systemic financial breakdown. The president didn't say so publicly, but in a lengthy, off-record interview with a trusted correspondent, Hoover discounted the general climate of despair as, "A condition of hysteria in the country."

Raymond Clapper was not one of those favored reporters counted among Hoover's inner circle, like Mark Sullivan, or the *Times*'s Richard Oulahan. But Clapper was an enterprising, mid-career journalist, head of the United Press Capital bureau, and in February 1931 he sat down with the president for a background review of his first two years in office. Clapper kept a typed transcript that is startling for Hoover's candor.

Hoover opened by stating the obvious. "Of course our big job and our first job is to get out of this depression we are in. Everything else naturally has to be subordinated to that."

But while the president acknowledged the urgency of fashioning some sort of policy response to the Depression, he could not muster much sympathy for its impact on individual lives. When it came to breadlines and soup kitchens, he was downright dismissive. "Nobody is starving," Hoover dryly pronounced. "The hoboes are better fed than they ever were before." The president mentioned an anecdote from the current news. "Did you see where one hobo in New York got 18 meals in one day? These are boon times for hoboes."

Hoover's skepticism extended even to conditions in the drought zone. Despite detailed reports from Red Cross staff describing widespread hunger, the president twice insisted on sending his own representatives to report back to him in person. This drew another joke from Will Rogers, more barbed this time than usual. "He could have sent a blind man and found out," Rogers wrote.

The president's skeptical view of the nation's emotional response to social distress was more than a difference of opinion. To Hoover it fed a sense of panic that threatened to force government into new and improper channels. "I think a large part of this depression can be traced to psychological conditions," Hoover told Clapper. "There seems to be a condition of hysteria."

Just breaking the spell could break the back of the Depression, Hoover suggested. "What the country needs is a good big laugh," he said wistfully. "If someone could get off a good joke every ten days I think our troubles would be over in two months."

There is irony in this, to hear the dour Hoover calling for a good laugh, but his exasperation at the public's fixation on the plight of the jobless was shared by elected leaders throughout the industrial West. A year before Hoover's conversation with Clapper, Winston Churchill was sounding the same notes in an essay for *The Saturday Evening Post*. The obsession with unemployment had developed into "a mood of insane hysteria," Churchill wrote, and had reduced the British government to "groveling in the poverty complex."

Churchill had reason to complain; his Conservative Party had been voted out of office the prior year. But there was no disputing his contention that, in the years since the Great War, British national elections were "nearly all fought upon the numbers of the unemployed." By the midterm elections of 1930, that was true of America as well.

All through December and January, while Hoover's stiff opposition to public aid for drought victims held Congress in deadlock, William Borah stood on the sidelines. Borah was never a reliable partner to Hoover, but he was a lifelong Republican and he accepted the party's credo of limited government.

When the short session was just getting under way, Borah warned against free-spending schemes to stimulate a recovery. "There seems to be a widespread belief that you can restore prosperity from the public treasury," Borah declared when Robinson first proposed direct food aid. "That is not only a false theory, but a vicious theory."

But as the debate wore on Borah began to waver. A true politician, he seemed to feel in his bones the mood of the people, and he had a thespian's instinct for timing. For Borah the critical moment arrived February 2, after the House voted to back Hoover and reject Robinson's bill for food aid. Just when the cause appeared doomed, Borah stepped forward for the first time to demand government aid both to the drought zone and to the unemployed.

It was one of Borah's great performances, a rousing Senate speech that sparked an ovation from a packed visitors' gallery and hosannas from both sides of the aisle. He set his argument in stark moral terms, and cast Hoover as the villain.

Borah opened by challenging the idea that feeding individual citizens would set a precedent for the government. "There is no new principle involved; there is no precedent to be established." In particular, Borah said, it was "no less than intellectual dishonesty" to equate food aid with a dole. "When before, when there has been a fire or a flood or an earthquake, has there been talk of establishing a dole?" Borah asked. "In no sense does the dole system apply."

Borah dramatized his point with an anecdote from a Red Cross field report, of a widow reduced to feeding her four children johnny cakes made from rancid grease and sour corn meal. "Imagine this mother," Borah demanded. "We are told that if we feed that woman and feed those children that we will undermine her initiative and destroy her self-reliance so that she will no longer be a fit citizen of the United States. It is a cowardly imputation, conceived for a wholly different purpose by those who are accusing us of proposing to establish a dole."

Borah made sure to acknowledge the efforts of the Red Cross, but said the agency was overmatched by the combined effects of drought and depression. Borah roared, "To take care of people in twenty-one states, a million and a half people, and five to six million unemployed, with from eight to ten million dollars, is an absurdity." Now he began banging on the podium, his indignation filling the venerable chamber. "I am willing to accept the challenge. I am willing to take it to the American people. I want to know whether this government will take care of its people when they have been grievously afflicted by an act of God."

By the animated response in the Senate, from the banner headlines Borah got in the press, it was clear that he had struck a nerve. His righteous tone was infectious and the sufferings of a widow and her little ones hard to ignore. Certainly it got the attention of the president.

Herbert Hoover recognized that his opposition to food aid had left him open to a passionate emotional appeal. "It is not an easy thing to say that food shall be withheld from hungry people," he said wistfully during a strategy session in January. But now that Borah had laid down his challenge, Hoover dug in to mount a full-dress defense of his policy on public assistance.

There was no thought of compromise. Hoover discussed two approaches with Henry Stimson—one "bitter" and the other "calm and reasonable." At Stimson's urging, the president opted for the latter, hammered out the next that night, then rehearsed the final draft before the full cabinet the next morning.

Hoover delivered the final product at his noon press conference Tuesday, February 3, just twenty-four hours after Borah's thunderous Senate speech. It was a remarkably short turnaround for the painstaking president, but that may have been fortunate. Goaded out of his accustomed reserve, Hoover produced a clear and cogent statement of his thinking on the critical question of public relief.

"I do not wish to add acrimony," Hoover said at the outset, "but would rather state this case as I see its fundamentals." And so he did, framing his address principally around the question of private charity versus public relief.

"This is not an issue as to whether people shall go hungry or cold in the United States," the president insisted. "It is solely a question of the best method by which hunger and cold shall be prevented." There were two choices: "mutual self-help through voluntary giving and the responsibility of local government"; and, "appropriations out of the federal treasury." Hoover said he was deeply committed to the former, partly because he considered the government to be inherently inefficient, but also because he wanted to nurture the individual impulse to help one's neighbor. To Hoover that propensity was crucial, "something infinitely valuable in the life of the American people."

While private charity was beneficial both to the benefactor and to the recipient, the alternative was fraught with danger. Reliance on federal intervention "struck at the roots of self-government," Hoover warned. More concretely, it would settle a new charge upon the central government that would forever alter its role in national life. Once the example was set, Hoover said, "We are faced with the abyss of reliance in the future upon government charity in some form or other."

Here Hoover invoked a presidential precedent: the veto by Grover Cleveland in 1887 of a bill to spend $10,000 providing seed to drought-stricken farmers. That instance matched nicely the circumstances facing the nation in 1930, and Cleveland had taken the occasion to issue a seminal statement on limited government. "The lesson should be constantly enforced," Cleveland said, "that though the people support the government, the government should not support the people."

During his two terms in office Grover Cleveland cast 584 vetoes—more than any other president before or since. Most were used to block a stampede of bills expanding pension benefits for Civil War veterans, but in this case

Cleveland was addressing the question of public benevolence. Hoover quoted him directly: "The friendliness and charity of our countrymen can always be relied upon to retrieve their fellow-citizens in misfortune," Cleveland said in a statement that might have sprung from Hoover's own pen. "Federal aid in such cases encourages the expectation of paternal care on the part of the government and weakens the sturdiness of our national character."

Hoover then added his own explicit endorsement of voluntary aid. There were "an infinite number of agencies of self help" in communities across the country, Hoover said. To operate through those entities, to let them shoulder the burden of relief was "the American way."

The Red Cross embodied this mode of relief, and Hoover insisted the agency was managing distress in the drought states "with sympathetic understanding." "No one is going hungry," Hoover said; "no one need go hungry or cold." Unemployment was a separate question, the president acknowledged, but the combination of expanded public works and volunteer agencies "in every town and country" was sufficient.

Hoover then signaled that, behind his cool and stern facade, he could feel the barbs slung his way. "I have indeed spent much of my life fighting hardship and starvation," he said. "I do not feel that I should be charged with lack of human sympathy for those who suffer."

Then he went further, drawing on his personal experience to suggest that "the foundation" of all his prior relief work "has been to summon the maximum of self-help." His projects relied heavily on government grants, but he added, "these appropriations were but a tithe of that which was coincidentally mobilized from the public charity of the United States and foreign countries."

Comparing his past endeavors to the present circumstance, Hoover said postwar Europe had been "so disorganized by war and anarchy that self-help was impossible." Today, at home, he held, "there is no such paralysis." In this crisis, the American Way should prevail.

Rather than impugn the motives of those calling for public relief, Hoover acknowledged their "natural anxiety" for the fate of their neighbors. He then made a dramatic gesture: "I am willing to pledge," Hoover declared, that if voluntary agencies and local governments could not handle the job, he would deploy the resources of the federal government, "because I would no more see starvation amongst our countrymen than would any senator or congressman."

Hoover's statement effectively closed this seminal debate over government assistance. It did not carry the emotional charge of Borah's Senate speech, but bore the weight of the presidency at a time when the nation was adrift and uncertain. More to the point, it convinced Joe Robinson that holding out for an explicit grant of food aid to victims of the drought would be futile.

In the days that followed, with Senator Jim Watson serving as go-between, Robinson agreed to face-saving terms with the president. There would be an additional $20 million appropriation on top of the seed-and-feed loans; this would also be limited to agricultural loans, but under the loose category of "farm rehabilitation," which might cover any purchase necessary to a farming operation. The press termed it a compromise, but the administration gave no ground on the crucial point, and the final bill gave no specific authorization for the purchase of food. In the end, Robinson and his allies had not been persuaded; they had been co-opted.

It was a mark of Hoover's ideological commitment to his position that his statement on relief rested on central tenets that were demonstrably false. As contemporary Red Cross field reports made clear, it was not true that everyone in the drought zone was free from hunger and cold. Assistance varied substantially from one county to the next, depending principally on the staff of the local Red Cross chapter; in many areas relief was minimal or wholly absent. More broadly, it was simply not true, as Hoover averred, that his European relief operations were funded in equal measure by private and public funds. By far the greater part of the budgets for Belgian Relief and for the American Relief Administration had come from the governments of Britain, France, and the United States. Hoover's statement to the contrary was a case of wishful thinking—or worse.

But if Hoover occasionally played loose with the facts, he was adept at wielding conventional wisdom. Americans of that era were a hardy, self-reliant people, most of them raised on farms, and genuinely skeptical of expansive government. The major press, from *The New York Times* to the

New York *World*, closed ranks behind the president, castigating the Senate for making "fine flourishes" that were "rapidly disgusting the country." The populists in the Senate might speak for the people, but Hoover spoke for the center, and thus far, the center held.

While Hoover was willing to tell an occasional fib to support his idea of the greater good, he was no hypocrite. All through his adult life Hoover made a practice of personal philanthropy, making anonymous gifts to friends of friends, or to complete strangers whose misfortune came to his attention. As president, of course, his chance encounters with the public were limited, but the office of the presidency was a magnet for supplicants of all stripes. With the onset of the Depression requests for financial and other help streamed into the White House, and under Hoover's administration each got careful consideration.

Bert and Lou Hoover considered these appeals to be personal and familial obligations, not charges against the state. Within the household, they became Lou's responsibility. Early in 1931, while the aid debate raged in Congress, the flow of letters grew to the point that Lou designated one of her secretaries—on household and not government payroll—to open a file on each plaintive letter, to investigate its claim and seek some sort of resolution. For Lou, who felt obliged to work just as hard as her toilsome husband, the handling of these appeals became a full-time job.

The individual cases provide live illustration of the Hoover mode of charity. A small number were found to be fraudulent, and some, while heartfelt, were simply untenable—requests for a year's mortgage, for example, to save the family farm. But most were susceptible to some simple, practical intervention, and these were handled through a remarkable personal network that included family friends like Ed Rickard, but also Red Cross chapters and local aid societies in towns across the country.

One typical appeal began with a letter from Anna Heidler, a resident of central Pennsylvania and mother of thirteen children. Her husband was ill and her family impoverished. "We need some clothes and eats," was Heidler's plea. "If you can help me I will thank you many times."

Lou and her secretaries had no personal contacts in the area, so they referred Heidler's letter to Highland Hall, a small, private school for girls located nearby. The Highland Hall headmistress responded three weeks later. She had contacted "the community nurse," who had commended the Heidlers as "self-respecting people" come upon hard times; the father was behind his rent on a cobbler shop and the mother, Anna, was "completely worn out by the care of such a large family." Thereupon, reported the head-mistress, "We made up a pocket book of $50 or $60 from the school and the girls are going to give their old clothes when they pack up next week." They also gave food to the Heidler family; "a bushel of potatoes, a sack of flour, a sack of corn meal, sugar, oleomargarine, a ham, eggs. . . . We will try to help them some each week."

Not all the appeals got such concrete results, but all received personal attention and some sort of referral to a local agency. And in keeping with the Hoover family ethic, these inquiries and Lou Hoover's interventions were all kept confidential. The work was done for charity, not publicity.

President Hoover left most such casework to his wife and his staff, but in one particular instance he, too, brought his expertise and resources to bear. This episode arose in the coalfields of Appalachia, where poverty seemed as endemic to the region as the rugged landscape. With slack industrial activity driving down the demand for coal, some mines had cut their working days by half; others simply closed down. The resulting distress forced a reckoning among Hoover's small cadre of aid workers.

PECE chairman Arthur Woods first raised the question in February, approaching Judge Payne to assert the "vital need" for the Red Cross to as-sist in the mining districts. Woods explained that the miners suffered from a Depression trifecta—drought, unemployment, and the special problems of the coal industry—but Payne demurred. His charge was solely to relieve vic-tims of the drought; he would not accept responsibility for the unemployed, urban or otherwise.

Woods took this impasse to the president. Hoover moved carefully; with Senate negotiations still under way, he could not afford a public falling-out among the relief agencies. So he asked Payne to have the Red Cross move "very quietly and unobtrusively" to supplement whatever aid work was al-ready taking place in the coalfields. Payne grudgingly agreed.

The friction persisted, however, exacerbated now by labor conflict, as the United Mine Workers and other, smaller unions answered wage cuts with strikes. In these districts particularly, the Red Cross refused to get engaged. After one unionist denounced the policy at a Senate hearing, Judge Payne called a press conference to insist that jobless miners did not qualify as drought sufferers, and would not warrant consideration for relief.

Deeply concerned, Woods sent an aide to West Virginia to assess the situation on the ground. The results were grim; according to one report, local Red Cross chapters had completely exhausted their funds. "The result has been that in many sections the counties have been forced to feed the starving and some of these have either run out of money or are about broke." In other cases, Red Cross staff refused to feed hungry miners out of allegiance to the mine owners. Things were approaching a state that Hoover the humanitarian, even in his elevated station as president, could not ignore.

In early April the president made another run at Payne, but this time the aged attorney refused outright to undertake aid in the coalfields. Hoover would have to improvise, but he would continue to do so through private entities, not the government. He directed staff from the PECE to ask the American Friends Service Committee if they might step in. Hoover had clashed with the Quaker leadership when they partnered with him to provide postwar relief in Europe, but that was years ago. Now he needed their expertise. If they would supply the staff, Hoover advised, the Red Cross would supply the funds.

The Quaker leadership mulled the question for weeks. They were accustomed to choosing their own projects, and like the Red Cross were leery of getting enmeshed in labor strife. But the need was pressing, and it was clear nobody else was ready to step in. Finally in July, Hoover invited a committee of four senior Friends to the White House to press his case. "He spoke with a depth of understanding and appreciation which strengthened our confidence," recalled Clarence Pickett, executive secretary to the Friends Service Committee.

The president also informed them that the Red Cross would not fund the project after all—Judge Payne had refused to assist in any fashion. But Hoover had secured the money himself; he would make available $225,000 left over from the American Relief Administration's children's fund, provided the Friends raised a matching sum from their usual donors. The Quakers agreed, and within five months had established a program that fed forty thousand impoverished children in 563 communities, ranging from Pennsylvania to Tennessee.

Unfortunately for his presidency and for his legacy, Hoover kept this intervention secret. It was a recurring, damaging dynamic: in his concern for his privacy, in his refusal to explain himself, Hoover allowed himself to appear cold, remote, and unfeeling. But his stern calls to duty and his principled refusal to feed hungry farmers left the public disappointed and confused.

It didn't have to be that way. In Joe Robinson, Hoover had a legislative partner who shared his aversion to major spending programs and who risked the censure of his own party to find common ground with the president. But Hoover insisted on winning every point, a divisive approach that inspired florid rhetoric and lasting outrage.

To a degree, this was just another manifestation of Hoover's famous aversion to democratic process. Charles McNary, one of the few Republicans to stand by Hoover in the Senate, lamented the president's inflexibility in a letter to his brother. "If the engineer . . . had more political acumen," McNary wrote in December, "mole hills would not be viewed as mountains and tempests would take place at sea rather than in the teapot."

Hoover liked to consider his intransigence a matter of principle, but he was too extreme, too sharp-edged, to claim such high purpose. His obstinacy was something more fundamental, an intrinsic mark of character. Despite his high station, Hoover remained conflicted and insecure, convinced of his special abilities but also fearful of exposure, of being found inadequate. It was hard for him to share credit, hard to acknowledge other points of view.

To the public Hoover projected a cool, placid demeanor, but behind the facade he would seethe with frustration and misplaced anger. It was true that he had aides like Jim MacLafferty prodding him, but MacLafferty was only there at Hoover's invitation. Within the redoubt of his awkward personal reserve, Hoover trained a jealous eye on friend and foe alike.

In consequence, Hoover made a poor advocate for the things he cared about most. There was real merit, for example, in his resistance to government intervention in the face of natural disaster, as the survivors of such latter-day storms as Katrina and Sandy would attest. Had Hoover given ground at the outset, and acquiesced to Joe Robinson's $60 million drought loan program, he might have successfully defended the notion of volunteer aid and private relief as America's core mode of emergency response. Instead, he attacked Robinson, embittered his allies, and turned the battle over drought aid into his Waterloo. The message that resonated over that lean, hard winter was not Grover Cleveland's admonition to mutual aid, but William Borah's rousing call that the government "take care of its people."

Come the next session of Congress, Hoover would find himself too isolated to head off appeals for government action. It was no longer a question of principle; by then, the issue had become personal, with Hoover in the role of the stern, moralizing patriarch. He had earned his sobriquet as the Great Humanitarian over years of ceaseless toil, but his single term as president erased that stature from the public mind. From that time forward, Americans would remember Hoover as the man who refused them in the time of their greatest need.

SIXTEEN

CREDIT CRUNCH

W HEN THE 71ST CONGRESS WRAPPED UP ITS WORK IN EARLY March 1931, Herbert Hoover believed he had weathered the greatest threat to economic recovery. With the politicians out of town, the president could pursue his agenda without fear of panic legislation or personal vilification.

Hoover's program for combating the Depression remained in its basic elements the same that he had pursued over the eighteen months since the Wall Street crash—maintain wages, keep interest rates low, and expand public works to provide a degree of support for the jobless.

His principal addition to the formula in 1930 was to sharply curtail immigration as a threat to the domestic labor market. Just before the midterm elections Hoover announced an executive order restricting immigration to those with jobs already in hand. It was a popular measure that Hoover included in every subsequent policy statement on the Depression, though its impact was limited by the fact that, with jobs scarce, immigration was already sharply down.

The other change to Hoover's program was more gradual, a retreat from his commitment to countercyclical public works. He continued to tout expanded government payrolls "as an aid to unemployment," but began increasingly to lay on caveats, citing "common-sense limitations" on the pace of expansion. More broadly, Hoover gave priority to the simple refrain, "Economic depression cannot be cured by legislative action or executive pronouncement."

This shift in emphasis was partly political, to throw a damper on the demands in and out of Congress for a massive jobs program. But it was also acknowledgment that, for more than a year, the government had tried and failed to achieve meaningful job growth. In the first two years of the Depression the federal government tripled hiring for construction and roadwork, but that brought a total of 655,000 new jobs—just a fraction of the several millions idled since the Wall Street crash. And in the meantime the federal deficit was starting to balloon. This was as much a consequence of sinking revenue as new expenditures, but to Hoover and others in the cabinet it was a sign to put the brakes on spending.

State and local governments were facing the same problem. Though the federal government had doubled its grants to encourage state and county road projects, many local entities had seen revenues tail off drastically. Spending on public works in several key states, including Pennsylvania, Florida, and California, actually declined.

The president was satisfied, then, to play both sides of the question. He was quick to claim, as he did in June, that "For the first time in history the federal government has taken an extensive and positive part in mitigating the effects of depression." Yet he could also announce that, by setting limits on federal engagement, he had managed to "avoid the opiates of government charity and the stifling of our national spirit."

Hoover was not simply playing politics here. His views fell very much within the bounds of mainstream economic thinking at the time—more proactive than the "liquidationists," but more tempered than the fiscal activists. The leader of the big spenders, champion of a nebulous $5 billion work program, was William Randolph Hearst—a good indication of the idea's popular appeal, but perhaps not its worth.

Even John Maynard Keynes, intellectual author of strategic stimulus, was lukewarm on the policy in 1931. Keynes never viewed public spending as more than a bridge strategy to prod private investment, but even so, he felt that in America the time for such measures was not ripe. Visiting the United States that spring, Keynes told a radio audience that, "I think the argument for public works is much weaker in this country than it is for Great Britain. . . . Deliberate public works should be regarded much more as a tonic to change of business conditions, but the means of getting back to a state of equilibrium should be concentrated on the rate of interest." Easy money, not state spending, was Keynes's preferred formula.

Hoover was not so theoretical as Keynes, nor so populist as Hearst. The president took his own counsel, in regard to the Depression as in most everything. And in the first months of 1931 a chance conversation helped crystallize Hoover's thinking about the state of America's wounded economy.

The president related the story in his interview with Ray Clapper. Hoover did not name his interlocutor, but it was clearly a formative encounter. He brought it up to illustrate his conviction that, as he put it, "Our main trouble is psychological." Hoover explained: "A man told me not long ago that it was a question of how long a mob can stay in one mood." His point of reference was the depression of 1873–96, a severe slump that swept Europe as well as America and which remains to this day the longest-lasting economic contraction on record.

"Things were worse then than they are now," Hoover told Clapper. "The country was in a hell of a condition." Hoover's friend told him the "feeling of fear" lasted for nineteen months, "and then everything began to change." Hoover did his own figuring, and decided the country's mood was due to swing March 1.

The lesson for Hoover was that the best response to the continuing Depression was to ignore it. "I believe if the newspapers would quit talking about unemployment our troubles would be over in a couple of months." Already, the president said, "Sentiment is more optimistic."

It's hard to read these lines in hindsight without wincing at the apparent absurdity of such prognostication. The country had changed dramatically since the crash. In small towns and large, tired and desperate men stood for hours outside factory gates or languished in tumbledown shacks. New buildings raised during the boom years stood half empty, the owners facing bankruptcy. Unemployment was high, homelessness was spreading, and the Red Cross was continuing to operate feeding stations in a dozen states.

But in that particular moment, there were indeed early signs of economic recovery. Commodity prices leveled off after months of steady decline. Industrial production ticked upward. Breadlines began to peter out. Across the country, 120 cities closed their emergency relief programs.

In the drought zone, the ag-loan program was making a real impact. By mid-March more than a hundred thousand farmers had received small loans to get them started on a new planting, with a hundred thousand more loans in process. That spring and summer, a total of $47 million was loaned to 385,192 farmers in thirty-one states, with allotments ranging as low as a hundred dollars. Some contemporary observers dismissed such figures as "pitiful," but it was an early instance of microlending, and in turn, restoration of farm operations stemmed the rural banking crisis. Small banks continued to fail, but at lower, manageable, pre-drought rates.

Things had calmed to the point that the president felt free to take some time to himself. In early March he traveled to Asheville, North Carolina, where Herbert Jr. was confined for his tuberculosis treatment. The president traveled on a standard train in company of his wife, aide Larry Richey, physician Joel Boone, and five reporters.

Traveling through a spring snowfall, Hoover and his party arrived in Asheville late on Saturday, and departed the next evening. It was far too quick a trip to be termed a vacation, but Hoover was glad to find his elder son making a full recovery, and cheerful enough on his return that he consented to step out of his Pullman to greet the crowds gathered at whistle-stops along the way. It was his first trip away from the White House in five months.

A week later Hoover decided he could go even further. Late on a Sunday evening the president surprised a jaded press corps by announcing he would shortly depart on a ten-day vacation tour of the Caribbean. He would sail on the battleship *Arizona*, with stops at Puerto Rico and the Virgin Islands. There was some business to do—Hoover would visit Teddy Roosevelt Jr., whom he had appointed governor of Puerto Rico in 1929—but the principal goal of the cruise was rest. Lou stayed in Washington for this excursion, but the president enjoyed his naps on deck, movies in the evening with the crew, and all the pomp of a foreign tour.

Upon his return Hoover set about some basic houskeeping. There were two major changes in his personal staff; French Strother, the ex-journalist charged with research and assisting on speeches, joined George Akerson in his exit from the White House. The two positions were combined, and filled by Ted Joslin, White House correspondent for the *Boston Evening Transcript*.

To Ted Clark, always alert to news from inside the White House, Joslin was "a typical Hoover appointment," a lackluster political writer who had alienated most of the Republicans in Washington, as well as much of the press corps, with his "bumptiousness." Writing to inform Coolidge of the new hire, Clark shared the pointed remark of a Hearst correspondent; Joslin's move to the White House was "the first known instance of a rat joining a sinking ship."

Certainly, Joslin was eager. At forty years of age it was his first job outside a newroom, and he was taken with the pace and the pressure of the post. "This is the hottest spot I was ever on," Joslin marveled after a month inside the White House. He quickly settled in to the ethic of loyal and devoted service that Hoover expected of his inner circle. At the same time, Joslin kept a detailed diary, and later published a book, which together provide an important, additional source close to the taciturn president.

Other changes carried larger policy implications. Alexander Legge departed the Farm Board, to be replaced by James Stone, a member of the board and organizer of a short-lived experiment in cooperative marketing of tobacco. Hoover said he accepted Legge's resignation with "intense regret," but all acknowledged his had been a thankless—and hopeless—task.

At the time of Legge's departure the Farm Board had amassed holdings of 100 million bushels of wheat, and 1.3 million bales of cotton, and still the price of both key commodities was sinking. Stone vowed, upon taking his post, to hold to the same course charted by Legge, but within weeks announced that the board would make no more purchases to maintain commodity prices. On the news, the price of wheat dropped another 10 cents, to 67 cents per bushel, the lowest since 1895.

Stone would soldier on in the job for the next two years, but it was really just a mop-up operation. The Farm Board had become the symbol of all Hoover's perplexing contradictions, and of the frustrations he'd met in his presidency. Despite his professed skepticism of government, Hoover had personally floated this great, richly endowed program. It was designed to restructure agricultural markets on cooperative principles, expressly as an alternative to price support schemes. Instead it had been sucked into just such an endeavor, a desperate effort to maintain farm prices. Now it was abdicating, its assets washed away, its message of mutual self-help lost in the general collapse.

Arthur Woods of the President's Emergency Committee for Employment was another casualty of the president's spring cleaning. Even more than the Farm Board, the PECE had been conceived as a substitute for direct congressional action, and with no real program to pursue, it was fading from the scene.

Hoover was so encouraged by the signs of recovery that he felt free to pursue some long-range projects that had been sidelined since the stock crash. Among the more intriguing of these was his hope to establish some sort of private system that would provide financial security against illness, job loss, and old age. A patchwork of such policies—some run by state governments, and others associated with large companies or labor unions—covered several million workers, but most Americans remained on their own.

Hoover had long harbored a theoretical interest in economic security as the next frontier in social justice. The reform movements of the Progressive era had brought many abuses to light, but material improvements for most citizens remained an elusive goal. Midway through his presidential term Hoover had a practical motive as well; he expected unemployment insurance to be an "overshadowing issue" at the next meeting of Congress in December, and he wanted to be prepared.

Hoover's partner in this pursuit was Frederick Ecker, president of Metropolitan Life, the nation's largest insurer. Hoover first enlisted Metropolitan ten years before, in his first stint as secretary of commerce. He had asked the company to develop a variety of plans based on employer and worker contributions, thus to stay "the blighting hand of government." The result was an unemployment insurance bill fashioned for the state of New York. Metropolitan presented it to the state legislature in 1924 but got no further, due largely to the opposition of union leader Samuel Gompers, who put first priority on keeping the state out of the affairs of labor.

As president, Hoover revived the project in correspondence with Ecker. Once again he sought actuarial input—figures showing what level of contributions would deliver what sort of benefits. On pensions in particular, French Strother wrote in 1930, "The president feels strongly that it is a duty of society by some means to solve this problem so as to remove the fear of old age from the minds of every member of society."

The Metropolitan study came back with mixed results. The numbers were promising—$1,000, paid in by age thirty, would yield $50 a month at age sixty-five. But the premiums were too small to yield a profit to a private insurer, and the major firms too absorbed with the Depression to engage in novel projects.

Now, in March 1931, Hoover tried again, inviting Ecker to visit the White House overnight. Ecker told the president that large employers were growing more interested in unemployment coverage, and that he was just then sending three company executives to Europe to study the private and public plans operating there. Hoover was enthusiastic, and provided each of the travelers with letters of introduction.

But that was the end of the project. As Hoover explained in his memoirs, "The height of the world's greatest depression was no time to introduce such ideas." And as spring turned to summer in 1931, the smoldering embers of the Depression came roaring back to life. This time, the flames broke out in Europe.

Word of mounting trouble across the Atlantic was delivered in person, in early April, by Montagu Norman, the eccentric, enigmatic governor of England's central bank. A mentor to other international bankers—he'd been very close to New York Fed leader Benjamin Strong—but coy and furtive with the press, Norman had been making periodic visits to America since 1921, seeking to concert the policies of the world's two greatest economies.

This trip began in New York, where the elfin Norman, who favored tweed hats and a Vandyke beard, was hosted by George Harrison and the directors of the Federal Reserve Bank. It was represented as a "purely social affair," but that was just for show; in private Norman was warning of the "very gloomy situation" in Europe.

Proceeding to Washington in company with Harrison, Norman made the official rounds, meeting publicly with the governors of the Federal Reserve, with Fed chairman Eugene Meyer, and with Treasury Secretary Andrew Mellon. In addition, in private, he met with President Hoover. While eddies of haggard, unemployed men crowded street corners in cities and towns across the nation, Hoover and Norman talked about gold.

Norman's primary concern was France, which was accumulating gold so rapidly as to destabilize the other economies of Europe. This was something of a monetary accident; as late as 1927 France had endured a round of inflation nearly as debilitating as Germany's. The result was a devaluation that restored French trade and brought in a steady flow of bullion. Now that hoard had grown to outsized proportions, draining capital from Germany and England and leaving banks in those countries scrambling for coin.

Norman saw two important steps the United States could take to ease the pressure in Europe. The first, which he raised with the bankers in New York, was to create a new lending consortium that could support the weaker European banks with loans from France and America. But with American banks already in retreat the plan found little support.

Norman presented his second option direct to Hoover: drop the high-wage policy and "deflate" pay scales dramatically, in concert with England. "Unless [the United States] began that movement, took the lead in it," Norman told Hoover, "America would probably come to the dole next winter."

Hoover recounted this conversation for his cabinet the next day, and then offered his response. He would hold the line, Hoover said; the high wages Americans earned were a consequence of technological advance, not artifice, and should not be sacrificed to satisfy our trading partners. There followed "a good long discussion," as Henry Stimson saw it, which "cleared the air and put our policy upon the basis upon which alone I think we can stand, one of pure expediency to preserve our humanitarian standard."

Norman returned to England empty-handed. His last recourse was to appeal directly to the French, in a letter to his counterpart at the Banque de France. The French central bank must ease off its gold position to relieve the pressure on England and Germany. "Unless drastic measures are taken to save it, the capitalist system throughout the civilized world will be wrecked within a year."

Montagu Norman sounded the alarm, but it did nothing to disturb the underlying web of fear and animosity that kept Europe's bankers at odds. In particular, France enjoyed the leverage her gold stocks afforded over her old rival England, and had little sympathy for the vanquished Germans. As events turned out, the only error in Norman's prediction was timing: the wreckage was just weeks away, not months.

President Hoover followed the fortunes of Europe in daily conferences, beginning in May, with Henry Stimson at State, Andrew Mellon and Ogden Mills at Treasury, and Eugene Meyer at the Fed. The meetings were tense and incessant, lending to the air of mounting crisis.

The first great fissure came on Monday, May 11, when authorities in Austria announced a loss of $20 million over the prior year at Credit Anstalt, one of the largest banks in Europe. The shortfall should not have posed a mortal threat to an institution claiming assets of $250 million, but as would soon appear, the loss was substantially more than first advertised and the asset valuation dubious.

It wasn't just losses from bad loans that put such pressure on the Austrian bank. Like most banks in Europe, Credit Anstalt had relied on short-term foreign loans to paper over its flimsy balance sheets. As those foreign lenders came under pressure at home, they stopped renewing their positions. The Austrian government stepped in to guarantee deposits but withdrawals only accelerated. Foreign investors began to fear for the stability of Germany and Hungary, Austria's two primary trading partners, and within days investors were pulling funds from banks in both. As Hoover recalled later, "Apprehension began to run like mercury through the financial world."

Hoover shared that anxiety. In early May, just before the troubles in Austria, the U.S. ambassador to Germany made an urgent, unscheduled trip to

Washington to deliver a full and disturbing briefing. The problem there was the same afflicting Austrian banks; Germany's rapid recovery from hyper-inflation had been accomplished largely through short-term foreign credit. Those loans were not being renewed, leading to domestic capital flight and massive unemployment. The Weimar Republic might survive the month, but "unless the tide should turn by autumn, Germany would collapse."

Hoover recognized that, for all the damages and penalties arising from the war, Germany remained Europe's great industrial power, and her break-down would carry grave implications. For the next several weeks the president closeted himself in his study, poring over statistical reports from the departments of State and Commerce, and consulting experts from government and private industry. His focus was the status of Europe, but his concern was the American financial system.

In the eighteen months after the October crash the Federal Reserve and the major banks had successfully papered over the precarious condition of banking in the United States. There had been the rash of rural bank failures in the autumn of 1930, and in December the Bank of United States, head-quartered in Manhattan with fifty-seven branches and $200 million in assets, became the first major urban bank to give way. It failed in spectacular fashion, angry depositors clashing with mounted police outside a Bronx branch office as a crowd of twenty thousand spectators looked on aghast.

Such scenes fueled a general sense of fear, but these early bank failures were essentially isolated events. Like Caldwell and Company in Tennessee, the Bank of United States was a renegade operation, plagued with insider loans and crooked subsidiaries created expressly to hide weak investments. These bad practices were exposed by the end of the boom years, but did not reflect the larger problems facing the financial sector.

Far more menacing was the threat posed by the general deflation. After any dramatic run-up in values, prices of stocks and real estate eventually can be expected to fall back to some intrinsic core value. But after the prolonged boom of the 1920s, the collapse was so sharp and so widespread that values plunged right through what used to be the floor, eroding the foundations of the system as they went.

The upshot was a vicious cycle that came to be known as debt deflation.

In an economy built on a foundation of debt and credit, declining prices magnified the debt load, as debtors had to make payments with dollars more scarce than when the loans were issued. When distressed debtors sold assets to pay their debts, prices fell further. And, at the same time, the sinking asset values "froze" those assets held by the banks—that is, loan collateral credited on the balance sheets was no longer worth the sums that had been loaned against them. To cover these potential losses banks had to call in more loans and restrict new issues, shrinking the supply of money and thus the level of prices. More price declines forced more businesses into bankruptcy, further hollowing bank balance sheets.

The washout of the rural banks in the American South showed what such depreciation could do, but that was in a very narrow framework, with the assets in question limited to land and crops. Now the malady of frozen assets was spreading to banks of all stripes, and in every modern nation, as commodities led the decline in prices worldwide. International lenders were suddenly pulling back, cutting off the short-term loans that had floated the reconstruction of Europe.

Here was another vicious cycle: without new loans to cover payments on the old ones, all the loans extended to European banks faced imminent default. As much as $2 billion in those short-term German loans originated with American banks; default there could mean widespread bank failures across the water.

What was especially galling to the president was that this European financial seizure arrived just as the United States appeared poised to break out of its doldrums. By his personal economic survey Hoover had seen promising indicators of incipient recovery: banks flush with capital, low interest rates, even payroll gains. Now all that was in jeopardy. "Things were about to turn," a disappointed president told Stimson in May. Instead, Stimson reported that at meetings of the cabinet in early June, "the atmosphere was pure indigo because of the continued slump."

Quietly, consulting several advisors but working the details on his own, Hoover developed a strategic response to the threat from Europe. He would make a bold stroke outside the channels of bank finance and credit that would at least carve out a breathing spell and could break the momentum of the panic.

His target was the network of international payments established by the Allied powers at Versailles. These consisted of reparations imposed on Germany, and payments to the United States on loans made to finance the war effort. As we have seen, these onerous obligations for years had been the subject of politically charged international negotiation; now, with a simple, single-handed gesture, Hoover would sweep them all aside.

The idea was not unique; leading bankers in New York had been advocating some sort of suspension of reparations payments for some time, partly as it appeared that Germany simply couldn't keep up with the payments. But suspension was unpopular, especially with insurgent Republicans like William Borah and Hiram Johnson, who were always skeptical of making accommodations with Europe. Hoover made the point in the fall, in his contentious meeting with newly appointed Fed governor Eugene Meyer; now, in June, he argued the same line. "Politically it is quite impossible," Hoover told a banker from J. P. Morgan. "You have no idea what the sentiment of the country at large is on these intergovernmental debts."

Yet for all his trepidation, Hoover was coming to recognize that suspending debt payments was one of the few measures available with potential to defuse the onrushing financial crisis. He began toying with the idea early in May, discussing elements of his plan with Stimson and with Ogden Mills, but keeping the full scope of the proposal to himself. Finally, late one evening, Ted Joslin entered Hoover's study to find him writing longhand on an oversized yellow pad. Joslin turned to leave but the president asked him to wait while he jotted another few lines. Finally he put down his pencil, pushed back from the desk, and pronounced, "This is perhaps the most daring statement I ever thought of issuing."

Hoover then read the draft aloud. He would call for a blanket moratorium on reparations and debt payments alike. If the nations of Europe would join him, it would lift a billion dollars in liability from the world's industrial economies. The United States stood to lose the most—$250 million in loan receipts—but that gave Hoover the moral high ground.

The strength of the plan was its simplicity—Suspend all payments!—

but it was delicate in application. The proposal far exceeded the reach of Hoover's ostensible authority, as funding and debt were the purview of Congress. In Europe as well, the United States had no legal standing to intervene in reparations; these payments were imposed at Versailles, in direct treaties between Germany and her continental neighbors. Hoover would have to lead by exhortation.

Having struck upon his strategy, Hoover began the arduous process of weighing the pros and cons. By now he was in full crisis mode, working incessantly, scouring every report and every cable for word on European finance. This was the phase that Lou and Hoover's other intimates knew so well—the agonizing, the incessant doubts. Nobody would arraign the plan more severely than Hoover himself.

Fighting through his misgivings, the president presented his plan on June 5 to Andrew Mellon, Ogden Mills, and Henry Stimson. Left out of the loop, tellingly, was Eugene Meyer. The president could not have relished the smug condensation Meyer would surely display when he learned Hoover had changed his tune.

Of the advisors he consulted, Mellon questioned whether such a move was necessary, and Mills wondered if Hoover had the authority to carry it out. Only Stimson offered his full endorsement. "It involved a bold emphatic proposition to assume leadership," Stimson noted in his journal that night. "I myself felt more glad than I could say that he was at last turning that way."

But reaching a decision was one thing; living with it another. For the next several days Hoover vacillated, worrying through all the complex history of the war debts since Versailles. America had always made a point of treating debts and reparations as separate and distinct issues. To conflate them now would spark outrage at home and "drag us into the European mess," Hoover said; at one point, he announced, he would "never consent to it."

The drama dragged on for weeks. Hoover's advisors huddled inside the White House and out, sweating through a triple-digit heat wave, drafting new plans and tossing them aside while they waited for Hoover to move. "I recognized that the president was following his usual psychological reaction to a proposition like this," Stimson wrote June 13. "In every important crisis which I have had with him . . . he has always gone through a period in which he sees every possible difficulty and gets terribly discouraged over it."

In that interval Hoover would argue against his own plan as vigorously as he first argued for it. In the end, he would stand his ground "with great courage," Stimson wrote, but only at the cost of much tension. "The trouble with his method is that it is terribly wearing on those who have to work with him and help him carry it out, because the agony of going through so much fear and hesitation beforehand is a very great burden."

It probably helped that Andrew Mellon chose just that moment to depart on a vacation to Europe, leaving Mills in charge at Treasury. Conferring with Mills, Stimson found the undersecretary had "completely come over" from his initial hesitation. More than that, they now agreed, along with Eugene Meyer, who at last had been briefed on the plan, that the moratorium should extend for two full years. Together they agreed their job now was to shore up the president's resolve.

All through June the pressure mounted. Day by day Germany drifted closer to default, but still Hoover kept his debt moratorium proposal under wraps. He spoke with bankers, he consulted his advisors, he canvassed key Democrats to see if they would back his hand.

Events seemed to portend a true global smash-up. Elected governments teetered in England and France, Austria and Germany. A chain of banks failed in Chicago. Bolivia and Peru went into default; Argentina, Uruguay, and Brazil were considering a joint renunciation of all foreign debts. Revolution toppled governments in Spain, Chile, and Costa Rica. Hoover pressed on, drafting Bernard Baruch to quietly tout the moratorium among Democrats, while Henry Stimson placed calls to Ramsay MacDonald in England. Inside the White House, the pace recalled a military siege. "The situation is quite like war," Stimson recorded in his journal. Echoed Ted Joslin, in his own private account, "It reminds me of wartime."

France loomed as the biggest obstacle to international cooperation. Knowing their bellicose neighbor too well, the French regarded the Germans with suspicion; they were especially alarmed in March when Germany announced a new customs union with Austria. France reacted sharply, using the finance crisis for leverage. Rather than rescue Credit Anstalt, French officials demanded immediate payment of their short-term loans unless the Austrians renounced the alliance with Germany.

Hoover and his advisors considered the move sheer blackmail. Still, France was critical to any European solution. Stimson met quietly with the French ambassador, and decided some collaboration was possible, though he did not dare divulge the proposed moratorium; later he asked Ramsay Mac-Donald to sound out possible French reaction, but the prime minister had no better sources in Paris than did the Americans. The best approach, Hoover and Stimson decided, was to surprise the French with the plan. They would either have to fall in line or be isolated as a pariah in Europe.

Further complicating matters were several speaking engagements—dedications, a homage to Warren Harding—that required Hoover to be out of Washington just as events reached a crescendo. There was talk of canceling the trip, but the president insisted he do nothing to arouse suspicion. Meanwhile, Stimson pressed for an immediate declaration, fearing that Germany wouldn't survive the week. So adamant was Stimson that Joslin thought he would resign his post, but Hoover stuck with his schedule. Off he went, to Indiana, Illinois, and Ohio, delivering speeches, meeting local dignitaries at whistle-stops, all the while secretly communicating with his team in Washington.

The day he returned to Washington, June 18, Hoover received a cable direct from Paul von Hindenburg, Germany's beleaguered president. Circumstances had reached "a climax," the urgent missive warned. "The economic crisis from which the whole world is suffering hits particularly hard on the German nation," leading to a wholesale withdrawal of loans critical to the survival of the banking system. With Europe hamstrung, help must come from America. Hindenburg didn't specify what form such aid might take, but "relief must come at once."

Still Hoover waited, spending the next two days working the phones, tracking down thirty members of Congress, most in their home districts far from Washington, to secure consent to his plans. The president hoped to delay even longer, to cajole perhaps even the cooperation of the French, but the secret was out, and several papers were planning to break the story in their Sunday editions.

Finally Hoover pulled the trigger, calling a press conference for Saturday afternoon. The unusual day and hour signalled that something big was afoot, and the correspondents crowded in—hundreds of them jammed into the press briefing room where Hoover read them his dramatic announcement. The brunt of the statement was delivered in a single, opening sentence. "The American government proposes the postponement during one year of all payments on intergovernmental debts, reparations and relief debts."

After all the fear of leaks and exposure, the announcement came off as planned, a surprise measure that stunned executives in government and finance the world over. That it came out of the blue, that it came from America—"Uncle Shylock"—all added to the sense of wonder and relief.

Most surprising of all, it came from Herbert Hoover. Such bold action seemed to contradict the character of the bemused, frustrated, and so often silent president. But for those who recalled the Hoover of wartime relief and two successive cabinets—a man of decision and constant initiative, sponsor of expansive programs in and out of government—it came as a flash of recognition. In Ted Joslin's view this was "Hoover at his best—the type of man the people pictured when they elected him."

For a brief moment, in the capitals of Europe to the plains of the Argentine, the gloom of economic depression was replaced by optimism and outright delight. "The effect on the market has been magical," Henry Stimson enthused two days later. The drain of deposits from German banks halted overnight, stocks rose in Berlin and New York, even the price of commodities ticked upward. Stimson was not so naive as to believe that global fortunes had been reversed, but he fully appreciated the immediate impact. "Of course it cannot last at this rate," Stimson wrote, "but the need of a changed psychology was made evident by this tremendous effect."

Even Hoover was able to drop his dour manner long enough to savor a rare public relations coup. As soon as the press room had cleared, the reporters dashing off to meet their evening deadlines, Hoover called Joslin to his office. The president leaned back in his chair, puffing on a cigar. To Joslin it appeared the tension from weeks of constant, anxious negotiation had fallen away completely. "Well, Ted, we've had a hard siege. Get your wife and the boys and we'll go down to the camp for Sunday." For once, Hoover allowed himself a break from his trials.

The president enjoyed a twenty-four-hour turnaround at his mountain camp and returned looking "transformed," as one advisor put it—smiling, vigorous, energetic. He arrived to find a stack of telegrams from governments as divergent as parliamentary England, fascist Italy, and imperial Japan, all commending his dramatic announcement. Acclaim sounded from unusual quarters; *The Nation* deemed it "the most praiseworthy step taken by an American president since the treaty of peace." It may have been the first time Hoover found himself favorably compared to Woodrow Wilson, one of his heroes.

It was a triumphant moment, but no more than that. It's possible that, in his agonies of decision, Hoover had waited too long, allowing the bank panic in Europe to gain too much momentum; it may be that the situation was simply irredeemable.

The immediate problem was France. By Tuesday word arrived from Paris. The French were "very responsive to the call of the president," according to the foreign minister. But, "Many problems of the first order are implicated in which France wants a delay." Now the game was afoot: however Hoover might upbraid them with professed good intentions, France had no interest in letting Germany off the hook.

That was the risk Hoover had run. His plan outstripped the actual powers of his office, resting principally on hopes that the nations of Europe would follow his good example in renouncing all intergovernmental debts.

For most of the countries involved it was easy to agree, as most gained by the formula, or broke even. France was a different matter. Having suffered the greatest carnage in the war, she received the largest sum in annual reparation payments, and so would lose the most by the moratorium. At the same time, French popular opinion would brook no compromise with their hated enemy. Prime Minister Pierre Laval might privately embrace Hoover's effort to stabilize a volatile situation, but he had to present a hard face to Germany or his own government would almost certainly fall.

These circumstances, and the particulars of the French position, took days to unfold. In the meantime, the jolt of optimism delivered by Hoover's surprise announcement began to fade, and with it confidence in Germany's finances. Within days, the runs on German banks resumed; only a new, $100 million loan raised by bankers in New York and London staved off immediate collapse.

For the next several weeks Hoover was fully consumed in the frantic effort to stabilize global finances. It so happened that Henry Stimson, like Andrew Mellon, had scheduled a European vacation for late June; by July both Mellon and Stimson were plying the diplomatic byways of Europe, and communicating with the White House via the technological marvel of transatlantic telephone. At his end Hoover relied on Ogden Mills at Treasury, George Harrison in New York, Fed chairman Eugene Meyer, Undersecretary of State William Castle, and Charles Dawes, the vice president under Coolidge and now ambassador to Great Britain but at that moment on hand in the capital.

For the president it was much like the wrangles with Congress, except that instead of two political parties he was coping with the heads of several sovereign states. Observing him at close hand, Dawes remarked on Hoover's "clearness and quickness of comprehension—his equipoise and calmness," and judged him to be "always the alert, competent, compelling executive." And yet, results eluded him. First the French held back, and then the bankers, until the fast pace of the growing financial debacle overwhelmed his plans.

The runs against the German banks continued, domestic depositors making withdrawals and foreigners calling their short-term loans, demanding payment in gold. On Monday, July 13, President Hindenburg declared a bank holiday, closing all the nation's banks by decree in a bid to break the fever. In the meantime the panic jumped borders all through Central Europe. Banks in Austria, Hungary, Poland, and Czechoslovakia closed their doors, barring entry to angry depositors.

Herbert Hoover watched these events unfold with a growing sense of dread. Henry Robinson, his banking friend in Los Angeles, warned him of another type of liability that had hitherto gone unnoticed—"bank acceptances," or short-term loans made against future trade, which had been widely marketed in America by the German banks. Hoover asked the Treasury for a new accounting of these acceptances, and found that U.S. banks held close to $2 billion such notes, and European banks as much as $5 billion.

"I don't know that I have ever received a worse shock," Hoover said of the Treasury report. "The explosive mine which underlay the economic system of the world was now coming clearly into view."

Just at that moment, diplomats meeting in Paris seeking to manage the crisis proposed a new loan to Germany, a total $500 million from England, France, and the United States. Henry Stimson was in attendance and relayed the plan by phone to Hoover, but the president demurred; the half billion was "wholly inadequate" to resolve the liabilities in question, and was "merely partial relief of banks at government expense."

Hoover countered now with another innovation: he proposed a "standstill agreement" whereby all short-term foreign claims against German banks would be frozen. This would buy time for Germany to straighten its accounts, and would prevent the global bank failures that would result from an immediate, strict accounting.

The scheme put Stimson in the delicate position of selling the new proposition while fending off support for the more conventional but far more risky loan. As it happened, within hours of his conversation with Hoover, Stimson learned that Ramsay MacDonald was proposing just such a standstill. That augured well for the idea, but added the new wrinkle of who could claim credit, the American president or the British prime minister.

On July 20, as the diplomats moved their talks from Paris to London, Stimson, joined now by Andrew Mellon, decided the surest strategy was to keep mum on the Hoover plan and follow MacDonald's lead. He begged Hoover to go along and the president complied, but only overnight. When he learned the next day that France was again pushing for a loan—which would carry political terms that Germany was sure to reject—Hoover decided to make his plan public.

It was exasperating for Stimson; to his mind the president was jeopardizing delicate and momentous negotiations simply to ensure he got credit for the plan. But Stimson was adroit, and managed to cast the plan as "an

Anglo-American notion." On July 24 the London conference closed with an agreement that the Bank of International Settlements, established just the year before to manage reparation payments, would supervise a three-month freeze on claims against Germany. In his autobiography, Stimson and his coauthor termed the negotiation "one of the neatest and most successful of his [Stimson's] career."

It was another triumph for the American president, another demonstration of poise and purpose in the international arena. But it was also just another a stopgap. All he could hope for, Hoover mused later, was "that Central Europe had struck bottom," and the worldwide depression along with it. Instead, as with the moratorium, the standstill provided only temporary respite in a season of unremitting disappointment.

As the frustrations mounted and the long days piled in one after another, Hoover started to show the strain. "The president is dog tired," Joslin noted in July. "How he stands up under the pressure is a mystery to me."

Seeking somehow to ease Hoover's burden, Joslin played a wild card— he contacted Byron Price, the well-liked Washington bureau chief for the Associated Press. The president needed someone to alter his outlook. "He is in a state and maybe a talk with you will do him good." Joslin made clear this was not a matter for publication. "It's not an interview," he told Price. "Just a talk."

Price was intrigued and, upon being ushered into Hoover's office, astonished. "He didn't look to me like the Hoover I'd been seeing," Price recalled later. "His hair was rumpled. He was almost crouching behind his desk, and he burst out at me with a volley of angry words—not against me or against the press, but against the politicians and the foreign governments—with absolutely unbridled language."

In the midst of the tense and interminable negotiations, Hoover was boiling over. Price made careful notes of the encounter, and provides a verbatim quote from the embattled president: "And now I am asked to take the blame," Hoover fumed. "Is it my fault that those selfish men over the whole world have refused to see the folly of their policies until it was too late? . . . Is it my fault that France, our ally, has stood blindly in the way of settlement and cooperation?"

Hoover was mad at France, but his anger encompassed the whole economic disaster that had so compromised his term in office. "Over a period of years, as president and in the Cabinet, I have done all I could to avert the terrible situation we are in today, but it was not enough," Hoover complained to Price. The original sin was committed at Versailles, Hoover said, and those follies aggravated by "stupidity and stubbornness."

Whatever Ted Joslin was thinking when he arranged this encounter, it appears to have worked. Price kept his confidence, and Hoover invited him back repeatedly, always off the record, always to vent his anger. But of all Hoover's dark days, the summer of 1931 may have been the most frustrating, the most emotional. It was only then that Hoover realized, however far he might reach, however hard he might push, the global economic collapse that began twenty months before was not going to turn or come around like the depressions of the past. He recognized now, as John Maynard Keynes had written a few months before, "We are living this year in the shadow of one of the greatest economic catastrophes of modern history."

"EXORCISING THE DEVILS"

By October 1931 Hoover was trying any means
he could to restore confidence
and revive the flagging economy.

SEVENTEEN

THE GIBRALTAR OF
WORLD STABILITY

Dᴜʀɪɴɢ ʜɪs ᴊᴜɴᴇ 1931 sᴘᴇᴀᴋɪɴɢ ᴛᴏᴜʀ, ᴜɴᴅᴇʀᴛᴀᴋᴇɴ ɪɴ ᴛʜᴇ midst of the secret negotiations over his European moratorium, President Hoover made the most essential statement of his presidency. The global debt crisis helped him recognize for the first time the scope and the depth of the challenge he was facing, and now he offered a commensurate response.

Political writers immediately billed this seminal speech the opening salvo of the presidential campaign of 1932—and it may well have been. It was delivered in the course of a speaking tour through the key electoral states of Illinois and Ohio, and offered to a partisan audience, five thousand members of the Indiana Republican Editorial Association at the fairgrounds in Indianapolis.

Mounting the stage in sweltering heat, Hoover invited his listeners to doff their coats, then launched into a lengthy discourse on the state of the economy. He did not make reference to the opposition party, and did not discuss ballots or votes. Instead he made a comprehensive, affirmative defense of free enterprise, and of the individualism that he had always placed at the center of his political thought. At the very moment when the global capitalist order appeared on the verge of collapse, Hoover vowed allegiance to the principles of what he called "the American system."

"Our people can take justifiable pride that their united efforts have greatly reduced unemployment which would otherwise have been our fate," Hoover said. It might feel like faint praise, but to the president it was a sign of progress. "Great as have been our difficulties no man can contrast them with our experiences in previous depressions or with the condition of other important industrial countries without a glow of pride in our American system and a confidence in its future."

In this Hoover was not confronting his political foes, but something larger and more fundamental—the bewilderment of a nation stunned by an epic reversal of fortune. The blind optimism of the 1920s had been replaced by a dull sense of loss, and a yearning for answers. James Mead, a Democratic representative from Buffalo, gave early and eloquent voice to that sensibility during a speech on the floor of Congress. "What a strange situation confronts us today," Mead said in late 1930. "Will not our grandchildren regard it as quite incomprehensible that millions of Americans went hungry because they produced too much food, that millions of men, women and children were cold because they had produced too much clothing?" Mead's query wound down to a simple paradox that defined his era. "Today we are suffering want in the midst of unprecedented plenty."

Not content to pose the question, many Americans were ready to condemn the system outright. "The present economic structure in this country is an absolute failure," William Green told the Massachusetts Federation of Labor in August. In this view, the Depression was not a problem of capitalism, but a symptom. Capitalism didn't need fixing, it needed replacing.

The most popular variant of this thesis was to call for economic planning in the mode of the emergent Soviet Union. By the summer of 1931 calls for five- and ten-year plans had become "a national chorus," *The Literary Digest* noted. This appeal, addressed by the National Civic Federation to six hundred industrial executives, was typical: "Economic adjustment is as necessary as the air we breathe. . . . We need to meet the cold-blooded Communist Five-Year Plan with a warm-blooded ten-year plan of democratic idealism."

To all this, Hoover answered directly, defiantly, "We have many citizens insisting that we produce an advance 'plan' for the future development of the United States," Hoover told the journalists in Indiana. "I am able to propose an American plan to you. We plan to take care of the twenty million increase in population in the next twenty years. We plan to build for them four million new and better homes, thousands of new and still more beautiful city buildings, thousands of factories; to increase the capacity of our railways; to add thousands of miles of highways and waterways; to install twenty-five million electrical horsepower; to grow twenty percent more farm products. We plan to provide new parks, schools, colleges and churches for this twenty million people. We plan more leisure for men and women and better opportunities for its enjoyment. We not only plan to provide for all the new generation, but we shall, by research and invention, lift the standard of living and security of life to the whole people. We plan to secure a greater diffusion of wealth, a decrease in poverty, and a great reduction in crime."

Reporters covering the address were struck by the president's manner as much as his message. The droning incantation of particulars was classic Hoover, but the audacity and energy in his delivery were something wholly new. As the *Times* correspondent observed, "There was more vigor and emphasis than noted in any of his speeches within the last two years."

Hoover was being dynamic; he was also being a bit facetious. Hoover had no plan, and that was the point. Planning was fine for bureaucracies, it was an important tool for an individual business, but it was noxious to the operations of a capitalist economy. "This plan will be carried out if we just keep on giving the American people a chance," the president said. "Its impulsive force is in the character and spirit of the people. They have already done a better job for one hundred twenty million people than any other nation in all history."

Just what prompted the president to tackle these expansive issues at the Indianapolis fairgrounds is hard to say. It was the first of four speeches he made on the trip, but each of the others served a specific function—to salute a refurbished Lincoln memorial in Illinois or to dedicate a new memorial in

Ohio to Hoover's old friend Warren Harding. But this initial oration Hoover made on his own initiative, unbidden and in some degree unexpected. It was a personal manifesto.

Hoover composed the statement with extra care. He wrote and rewrote, laboring through fourteen drafts while his advisors wrestled with the Austrian bank failure. "Never have I seen a man work harder trying to get his words down on paper," Ted Joslin marveled in his diary.

Whatever the precise impetus, Hoover's statement came at a critical juncture, when the girders of global capitalism were under maximum stress and on the verge of giving way. Hoover had a pedagogical bent to his politics; he may have felt that now was the time that the system needed its best defense.

Hoover was always an explicit proponent of capitalism. In his 1922 treatise, *American Individualism*, he identified socialism—exemplified by the Stalin's Soviet Union—as "an economic and spiritual fallacy." He acknowledged the "great inequalities and injustices of centuries" that led to the October Revolution, but the practice of communism he could already write off as having "wrecked itself finally upon the rocks of destroyed production and moral degeneracy." The only question for capitalism, Hoover believed then, was how best to manage it, by mitigating the excesses of monopoly and better distributing the fruits of enterprise.

Now, ten years later, the Soviet Union had survived its birth pains. Leftist revolution was spreading across Latin America, matched on the right flank by authoritarian fascism in Italy, and statist movements in Hungary, Chile, and elsewhere. Capitalism had not triumphed, it had faltered, and now Hoover felt obliged to speak in its defense.

It was not capitalism per se that Hoover praised at Indianapolis, but capitalism as it had evolved in the United States—his American system. The key distinction lay in the role of the government. In America, Hoover said, the state served the individual. "The other idea is that we shall directly or indirectly regiment the population into a bureaucracy to serve the state."

In that formulation, the central planning so many Americans were calling for wasn't a solution; it represented a mortal threat. Better to leave the initiative for economic recovery in private, not public hands. On this Hoover was unequivocal. "Nothing can be gained in recovery of employment by detouring capital away from industry and commerce into the Treasury of the United States, either by taxes or loans, on the assumption that the government can create more employment by use of these funds than can industry and commerce itself."

The state could, and should, stay on the sidelines. "While I am a strong advocate of expansion of useful public works in hard times, and we have trebled our federal expenditure in aid to unemployment, yet there are limitations on the application of this principle." Unless closely monitored, government projects easily devolve into fiscal boondoggles. "The remedy to economic depression is not waste," Hoover said, "but the creation and distribution of wealth."

Continuing his defense of his program, Hoover identified unemployment insurance as another key test for the American system. He endorsed the insurance concept, but only on a private basis—a pact between labor and industry. "The moment government enters into this field it invariably degenerates into the dole," Hoover said. And once introduced, the dynamic of electoral politics ensured that calls for federal largesse would only grow. "Nothing can withstand the political pressures which carry governments over this dangerous border."

This was familiar ground to Hoover and to his audience, not a far step from the rhetoric of his campaign. What was different was the circumstance: Hoover's presidential campaign had been waged at the height of postwar prosperity. His Indiana speech was delivered at a time verging on outright panic.

Harder to explain is where Hoover derived his supreme confidence in the nation's economic system. Near the top of the speech Hoover cited "no less than fifteen depressions in the last century . . . though none has hitherto been so widespread." Some took these successive disruptions as a sign of encroaching doom, but to Hoover it was a comforting notion. "We have come out of each previous depression into a period of greater prosperity than ever before. We shall do so this time."

In his closing Hoover returned to his hopeful premise. "We should have full faith and confidence in those mighty resources, those intellectual and spiritual forces, which have impelled this nation to a success never before known in the history of the world. Far from being impaired, these forces were never stronger than at this moment."

Confidence had been Hoover's mantra ever since the October crash, but this was not another of his rosy prognostications. This was more transcendental, a statement of faith. For the balance of his term Hoover made it his mission to preserve the United States as the third option, the choice between collectivism and autocracy. At a time when others were losing their bearings, Hoover held more tightly to his.

Even as the president was extolling the virtues of capitalism, he and his advisors were striving to manage its historic breakdown. The moratorium had been designed to calm markets and investors overseas, but the chaos in Europe had numerous, direct effects on the American financial system. It may seem odd that a crisis launched by a failed bank in Austria would lead to pressure on America, but it was all one integrated process.

The most direct impacts derived from the international holdings of the European banks. When Credit Anstalt suspended operations, for example, the payments due on American loans, and the receivables due to American firms, were immobilized. These frozen credits formed an immediate drag on the balance sheets of U.S. banks. And the process worked in reverse, as foreign depositors, suddenly under pressure, called for the funds they had parked in America.

Fear worked against the banks in other ways, harder to quantify but just as debilitating. The most immediate impact was a rash of domestic bank runs. With the newspapers full of European bank failures, nervous depositors decided to convert their savings to cash. "Hoarding," as it became known, grew steadily through the summer of 1931, draining American banks of close to a billion dollars. This outflow generated its own effect, as the banks sold assets to pay off the depositors. Forced sale of bonds and other holdings on an already depressed market drove the price of assets down, further eroding portfolios. Thus the banks were hit from both sides; with assets undervalued, even healthy banks had trouble answering short-run claims from depositors.

The result was a new surge in bank failures. After the relatively mild month of April, when sixty-four U.S. banks suspended operations—roughly the average tally for a month in the 1920s—failures jumped in June, the month following Credit Anstalt, with 167 closures; and again in August, with 158. There was no single spectacular collapse, but the surge in hoarding evinced a powerful undercurrent of fear—a "suppressed panic," Hoover called it in talks with his advisors.

This was just the sort of crisis the Fed had been founded to answer; by serving as "lender of last resort," the central bank could provide the credit banks needed to calm panicked depositors and answer their demands. But the Fed covered only part of the banking system—most state banks, smaller and far more numerous than federally chartered national banks, did not have access to Fed reserves.

The shocks to American banks from the credit squeeze in Europe prompted a further contraction of domestic credit, as U.S. banks cut back on loans and conserved their assets, the better to answer any prospective run. This in turn further throttled down economic activity. Between April and September U.S. industrial production, already depressed, fell by another 18 percent. Construction dropped 30 percent, and stocks sank by nearly half. It was a sickening descent, just when many expected the economy to turn around.

As the summer wore on and the slump deepened, President Hoover focused on the bottleneck at the banks. He recognized that the problem was intrinsic to the system: the bankers were so caught up in the struggle to stay afloat that nobody was addressing the larger question of keeping open the channels of credit. This was a paradox, but to Hoover it also presented an opportunity to invoke his cherished ideal of mutual self-help. In September, with the financial world facing unprecedented challenges, Hoover called on the bankers to reform the system themselves.

The president broached this concept during a September 8 meeting with Eugene Meyer at the White House. Hoover's initial concern was the huge trove of deposits and investment-grade assets that had been immobilized by bank closures since the October crash—over a billion dollars, representing the savings and property of more than a million people. Most of this capital was still viable—the depositor dollars were still on hand, as were the assets taken as loan collateral—but they were frozen pending liquidation, a huge and daunting task that awaited the attention of state banking authorities.

The solution, Hoover proposed, was that "our banking system must now organize itself." At the very least, the president said, a system should be devised allowing loans to be made on "some portion" of the assets of the suspended banks, and these proceeds returned to depositors, providing crucial relief to them and returning that much cash to general circulation. In a memo to Meyer after their meeting, Hoover noted that such innovation fell outside the formal authority of his own office and of the Federal Reserve, but that should not stifle reform. "The method of effecting this relief," Hoover proposed, "seems to me a problem which the country has a right to expect that the banking community can solve."

It was up to the bankers to act, but Hoover had a plan for them to follow. He wanted to see them contribute funds to underwrite a National Credit Corporation, which would make loans against the assets of suspended banks, restoring liquidity to the financial system. This prospective entity would also be able to supplement the Federal Reserve by lending to banks outside the system, or to those in the system with assets ineligible for loans under the rules of the system.

Hoover proposed an initial pool of half a billion dollars, with the banks to put up more if needed. As a voluntary association of the nation's largest lending institutions, the mere existence of the National Credit Corporation would help reassure the public that the bankers were moving to address the crisis.

For two weeks after meeting with Meyer the president was in constant consultation with bankers and financiers, sounding out enthusiasm for his plan and the temper of the financial markets. It was still just an idea, but events soon confirmed Hoover's sense that some extraordinary action was required. In September bank closures accelerated again, reaching 305 closures, doubling even the high rate of the prior month.

————

Hoover wanted to see the leaders of the American financial system take charge, but it was clear the initiative would have to come from inside his administration. That meant reliance on Hoover's principal economic advisors, a small group that had yet to form a cohesive unit. In fact, the ostensible leader of that core group was on his way out, his advanced age and his habitual caution putting him out of step with the Hoover program.

Andrew Mellon had sailed for Europe in June with plans for a quiet retreat on the French Riviera, but had been drafted into weeks of tense negotiations in hammering out terms for the moratorium. He returned to Washington in August acting every bit of his seventy-six years of age; tired, peevish, distracted. In conference at the White House he slipped easily into reminiscence, returning to the current crisis with evident strain. The treasury secretary was "living more and more in the past," Ted Joslin remarked. "He is little more than a dead weight."

Eugene Meyer was a good deal more vital than Mellon, but not much more useful to Hoover. In the year since his elevation to head of the Fed Meyer had yet to settle on a distinct monetary policy, his views oscillating between monetary expansion to spur business activity, and raising interest rates to defend U.S. gold stocks. In consequence the Fed was largely inactive in this critical period.

Meyer's principal concern at this stage was to assert his personal standing. Still new to the Fed, he was secretive about his movements and domineering with staff, leading to friction with his fellow Fed governors. And while he was more deferential toward the president, Meyer was always concerned that Hoover was not giving him enough credit for policy. It was a shortcoming Meyer shared with Hoover himself, with the result that neither confided much in the other.

Hoover's call for a bankers pool drew a typical response from Meyer. Yes, he agreed with Hoover that fresh credit was crucial to breaking the economy's free fall. But Meyer had another plan: call Congress into special session and win authorization for a new financial entity modeled on the War Finance Corporation, an agency established by Woodrow Wilson in 1918 to underwrite the war effort. Eugene Meyer had served as director.

Meyer's plan paralleled Hoover's except in two key particulars: it would be a government, and not a private agency; and it would require calling a special session of Congress. Both were anathema to the president, and he insisted on first trying the voluntary association. Meyer took offense, recording in an oral history, "He didn't back me up in the way he should have." Doubtless Hoover felt the same.

With Mellon moribund and Meyer obdurate, Hoover was left with George Harrison, governor of the Federal Reserve Bank of New York, and Ogden Mills. Harrison was dutiful with the president, readily providing candid assessments of the banking situation, but he was closely engaged in New York and afforded little opportunity for direct consultation. Mills was more available than Harrison, and more deferential than Meyer—"a perfect servant," was Meyer's wife, Agnes's, arch assessment of the undersecretary. But while Mills was industrious and forceful, he lacked imagination. If Hoover was going to improvise to address the financial crisis, he would have to do so on his own.

Andrew Mellon made that point painfully clear in September, when the banking panic reached his hometown of Pittsburgh. The pressure focused on the Bank of Pittsburgh, the only bank in the city not controlled by the Mellon family. It was a relatively healthy institution with seventeen thousand depositors, but a run by panicked depositors had left it gasping for cash.

The treasury secretary hurried back to Pittsburgh on a Saturday for an emergency conference with the city's financial leadership. Mellon had resigned his presidency at Mellon Bank when he took over at the Treasury in 1920, but banking remained the basis of his fortune and his field of expertise.

With Mellon in transit, President Hoover took a direct hand in managing the emergency from Washington. This became a practice of his; with banking panics hopping from city to city like flares in a wildfire, he worked the phone, seeking firsthand reports and trying to encourage the principal players. In this case, Hoover helped to shape a rescue package of loans from a syndicate of local investors, including Mellon's brother Richard and his nephew William.

The plans were in place; if Andrew Mellon would contribute a million

dollars to the $3 million already raised by the syndicate, the Bank of Pitts-
burgh and its $57 million in assets could be saved. But when the moment
came, Mellon could not suppress the instincts that had made him America's
most powerful and feared financier. No, Mellon said. He would step in and
put up his cash only if the directors of the Bank of Pittsburgh would grant
his family a majority share of the bank's stock. The directors refused, and on
September 21 the Bank of Pittsburgh closed its doors.

When Hoover learned of the denouement in Pittsburgh, he was furious
with his treasury secretary. At a time when the president was seeking to rally
the American financial community to the banner of cooperation, its leading
statesman had declined his assigned role, placing private interest above the
public weal.

The damage rolled on for weeks, as a total of fifteen area banks and trust
companies failed in a fiscal chain reaction. Andrew Mellon's reputation was
another casualty. Once revered for wisdom and generosity, he now found
himself vilified in the same capacity as his boss. It was around this time that
Mellon's son Paul ran across a memorable bit of doggerel scrawled above a
urinal at a gas station rest room:

> *Mellon pulled the whistle,*
> *Hoover rang the bell,*
> *Wall Street gave the signal,*
> *And the country went to hell.*

The same day the Bank of Pittsburgh went under, the American financial
system received much more shocking news from across the water: Great
Britain was going off the gold standard.

It was an epochal moment, a turning point in economic history. For
close to a century the advanced nations of the world relied on the British
pound, backed by gold, as the single scale of value that would enable trade
and facilitate credit. Now that core mechanism was teetering, and with it the
ethic of multilateral cooperation that made the global system hum.

The trigger, once again, was the failure of Credit Anstalt. For weeks
after the financial collapse of Central Europe the flames of panic followed

the money trail to the source. Creditors from near and far presented their pounds to the Bank of England, draining its gold reserves and forcing a final reckoning. And in the week after England capitulated, nine more countries, including Canada, India, and all of Scandinavia, had followed suit. By the end of the year a total of twenty-five countries abandoned gold.

This was more than a simple mathematical exercise, countries switching denominators from shillings to francs. Remember: under the gold standard, all the countries involved promised to redeem their currencies at a value set in some immutable relation to gold. Conversely, when a country left gold, that meant it would no longer redeem its currency at the agreed-to rate. Anyone holding that currency immediately lost whatever was the difference between what was promised, and whatever value was lost at the new, adjusted rate of exchange.

When England left gold, for instance, the pound promptly lost a third of its value, erasing equity in that proportion the world over for the traders, investors, and governments that held their wealth in pounds sterling. Burned by Britain, those same traders and central banks promptly sought to exchange whatever dollars they had for gold, for fear the United States would soon follow England.

In the event, the immediate impact in America was sudden and dramatic. On September 22, the day England left gold, foreign governments and investors cashed out $116 million from U.S. gold stocks—the largest one-day drain on record. Over the next five weeks, that figure climbed to $750 million, threatening to push Fed bank holdings of gold below the legal minimum. In the financial district of New York in particular, the outflow presented a full-scale emergency.

For Herbert Hoover, this portentous new challenge only confirmed his sense of the United States facing an existential challenge. "We were plunged into a battle against invading forces of destruction from abroad," Hoover said in a speech a year later. The challenges were several, and severe: "To counteract the terrific forces of deflation aligned against us; to protect the debtor class who were being strangled by the contraction of credit and the demands for payment of debt; to prevent our being pushed off the gold standard, which in our country would have meant disaster to every person who owed money; and finally to preserve the savings of the American people.

"We were fighting to hold the Gibraltar of world stability," Hoover said of this critical juncture. "Only by holding this last fortress could we be saved from a crashing world, with a decade of misery and the destruction of our form of government and our ideals of national life."

Few Americans had a more ardent, more personal attachment to the gold standard than did Herbert Hoover. During the twenty years he spent abroad Hoover directed vast international capital enterprises, and he understood how useful it was to be able to coordinate values of disparate currencies through a single, stable medium. Hoover may have had a psychological attachment as well; after a childhood of constant insecurity, gold's promise of unwavering stability could have an irresistible allure.

Recounting the story a year later, Hoover said that in the midst of "this hurricane"—the European financial meltdown—he and his advisors "kept a cool head and rejected every counsel of weakness and cowardice." He saw his role in terms of duty and he embraced it. "We determined that we would stand up like men and render the credit of the United States impregnable."

In the moment, as was his pattern, Hoover kept his dire presentiments to himself. It was part of his strategic calculus, his conviction that a candid assessment would only spread fear and panic. But his silence kept Hoover isolated, from the lawmakers who might sign on to his program, and from the citizenry, who were left to weather these climactic events on their own. Those who looked to the president for direction got only Hoover's starched white collar, terse homilies, and petty procedural announcements. To a suffering, wounded people, the White House appeared distant and implacable.

Even on the event of England leaving the gold standard, news the president and his advisors considered nothing less than disastrous, Hoover made a show of unconcern at his regular press conference. After emphasizing that, "I cannot make a public statement," Hoover offered a few offhand remarks. "The course resolved upon by the British Government creates some temporary dislocations in the international world," which would bring "a certain amount of confusion," but no great shocks.

Remarkably, Hoover offered a perceptive and specific appraisal of the internal effect of England's momentous decision. "It should act as a stimulant and thus should increase employment and increase the demand again for raw materials," he said.

That is precisely what happened in the months that followed. And in later years, students of the Depression reached a consensus that leaving gold—which had the practical effect of devaluing a currency—was key to jump-starting economic recovery. But that came later, after hard-won experience. At the time just a small group of economists, John Maynard Keynes principal among them, endorsed the radical step of leaving gold.

Even so, England moved only because there was no other option—her gold was already gone. America, on the other hand, could boast a mountainous gold reserve—one pillar of strength in a world gone soft. Along with most American policymakers, Hoover was determined to preserve it.

His conviction was stirring, but one can hardly fail to wince at reviewing the text of his September statement on Britain and gold. At the time, at his press conference, in his pivotal line, Hoover stated, "Altogether the action, no doubt necessary on the British side, is not, we feel, going to have any great effect in the United States. The probabilities are that it will considerably improve the situation in England, and we will benefit in the long run."

Hoover could see "considerable" benefit to England, but it did not occur to him the United States might follow the same course to achieve the same result. Instead his attention was fixed on the disruption to the international order.

Had Hoover used at home the same logic he applied to England, had he relinquished the gold standard when Britain did, history might have taken a different course. As it was, in late 1931 the long slump that opened with the Wall Street crash moved to a new, even more fearsome stage. To quote one economic historian, "that is when the severe depression in Europe and North America that had started in the summer of 1929 in the United States, and in the fall of 1928 in Germany, turned into *the* Great Depression."

Hoover was adamant in his defense of the gold standard, but he was not alone. The rest of the financial establishment, from the New York Fed to the Treasury Department, was party to the consensus, and in the first days after the announcement from England, officials in America moved to shore up the gold position and uphold the dollar.

The standard way for a country to avert runs on gold was to prove to investors that it would "defend its position"—that is, in the case of the United States, to demonstrate that it would continue to convert dollars to gold at the official rate. This was accomplished by raising the interest rate on loans offered by the Federal Reserve. That would attract new foreign capital, shore up the system's balance sheet, and—more to the point—convince foreigners that their dollars would remain "good as gold."

This was a useful mechanism for maintaining price equilibrium, but it imposed powerful constraints on economic activity. That is, a country facing a recession might want to lower rates to spur business, but to do so would weaken its gold standing. Repeatedly after 1929, as recession settled across the globe, central banks raised rates to build or preserve gold reserves despite mounting unemployment and failing banks. In September 1931, when Britain abdicated its gold position, it was America's turn.

Reaction from U.S. financiers was deliberate but unequivocal. At its first opportunity, in early October, the board of the New York Federal Reserve Bank voted to increase interest rates by a full point, to 2.5 percent. Answering concern that higher rates would erode bond values, George Harrison cited "foreign fears concerning the dollar." A week later, this time with Eugene Meyer in attendance, the board raised the rate another point—which, tacked onto the previous hike, meant the Fed had more than doubled interest rates in just two weeks. When this drastic action raised fears about the impact on business activity, Meyer answered forcefully: "An advance in the rate was called for by every known rule"; that is, the rules of the gold standard. "Foreigners would regard it as a lack of courage if the rate were not advanced," Meyer said.

This was the manly response expected by President Hoover; in the circles of high finance it was considered imperative. "A decidedly wise move," opined the *Commercial and Financial Chronicle*.

Orthodox, definitely. Courageous, perhaps. But also, certainly, counterproductive. Just as the cycle of deflation was squeezing profits and throttling businesses, the grim logic of the gold standard required higher interest rates and tighter credit.

More than most of his contemporaries, Herbert Hoover recognized the unfolding disaster of 1931 not as the death throes of capitalism per se, but as a crisis of credit, a transient breakdown in the system. He had the audacity and the initiative to attack the problem by demanding that timorous bankers take a fresh approach through a wholly new institution. But when he came face-to-face with the core financial convention of his time, his vision failed him. His commitment to saving the international economy by upholding the gold standard meant stifling any chance of domestic recovery.

Raising interest rates was the standard response to international market turmoil, but Hoover was convinced the rash of bank failures that began in June required a more resolute response. As was his wont, the president moved in secret, calling forty of the nation's top banking and insurance executives to a furtive meeting the night of Sunday October 4 at Andrew Mellon's six-bedroom flat, just off Dupont Circle. There in the spacious living room, under the gaze of priceless oil paintings that "breathe an atmosphere of loveliness," as one visitor recalled, the titans of American finance listened as the president lectured them on their duty.

Britain's departure from gold was "approaching disaster," Hoover said, spreading panic among depositors at a time when many smaller banks were already weakened by defaults on farm and mortgage loans. The weaker banks were forced to sell assets to answer the calls for cash, driving asset prices down. And the major banks in the great cities were making matters worse, calling loans from secondary centers to shore up their balance sheets even as they ignored the credits available from the Federal Reserve. The pressure was coming from Europe, Hoover acknowledged, but the responsibility rested here at home. To his mind, this was "a bankers' panic."

Having given his critique, Hoover turned to his prescription. The billions in frozen assets, the hundreds of millions in deposits withdrawn—these were beyond the capacity of the Federal Reserve. The bankers must save themselves, the president said.

The vehicle, Hoover advised, was the voluntary credit pool he had first proposed to Eugene Meyer—the National Credit Corporation. This new entity would lend freely to assist wounded banks and salvage the assets of closed ones. In addition, Hoover called for suspension of foreclosures on underwater mortgages, and proposed new rules for the Federal Reserve to encourage banks to extend more loans.

Now Hoover leaned in, "went after them rough shod," as he characterized it later. For years, Hoover told the bankers, he'd been fighting their battles for them, fending off legislation with promises that business would govern its own affairs. Now was the time to show that they could. If not he would call Congress into session and invite them to tackle the problem. It would open the door to socialism, Hoover warned; he would recommend creation of a government finance corporation but, once begun, there was no telling where it would end. "God help you when they get through with you," Hoover warned.

The assembled bankers shifted uneasily on the antique furniture. They had come only reluctantly, traveling together from New York in two private rail cars, and had agreed en route that they would resist any call for them to put up their own capital. Now, gathered in Mellon's ornate hall like schoolboys called in for detention, a few spoke up in favor of the plan—but just a few, and "they constantly reverted to a proposal that the government do it," Hoover crossly recorded later. They were missing the point. What Hoover wanted to see was "American private enterprise demonstrate its ability to protect both the country and itself."

Ogden Mills spoke next, followed by Andrew Mellon, but their arguments were "without visible effect" on the recalcitrant financiers—not surprisingly, in Mellon's case, his exploits in Pittsburgh having surfaced in the press. Hoover and his Treasury chiefs then retired from the room, leaving Eugene Meyer to try his hand.

Meyer opted for candor. He never did buy into the idea of a voluntary pool, he confided to the bankers. He thought it too small and too limited in its powers to interrupt the ongoing meltdown of the banking system. But Hoover was the president, and committed to his ethic of cooperation. The only option was to play along, Meyer advised; then, should the National Credit Corporation fail, he would throw all his weight behind reviving the War Finance Corporation, the government entity he had directed under Woodrow Wilson. "I practically promised them," Meyer recalled later.

This gambit was not the betrayal it might appear. Meyer believed the assembled bankers would reject the credit pool outright if he did not promise a ready substitute. But it undermined Hoover's moral authority and stripped the urgency from his injunction. The bankers didn't say yes that night, but they didn't say no, and they quietly returned to New York to take their counsel. At the end of the evening, Hoover recorded later, "I returned to the White House after midnight more depressed than ever before."

The president headed out the next day on a rare excursion—a trip to Philadelphia, to take in the third game of the World Series, between Connie Mack's A's and the St. Louis Cardinals. It was meant as a distraction—for the press, who had yet to learn of his surreptitious banking conference; and for Hoover, who needed a break from weeks of crisis management. The president enjoyed the baseball, but got little respite from his troubles. When fans learned of his presence, they voiced their feelings with scattered boos that evolved into a chant: "We want beer!" Be it Prohibition or Depression, Hoover's instincts seemed ordained to contradict the popular will.

Hoover dove back into crisis mode the next day. He learned from George Harrison that the bankers would acquiesce in forming a new self-financed lending agency. That evening Hoover moved to confirm his victory, assembling thirty-five members of Congress in the Lincoln Study to present the voluntary credit pool. Reeling the lawmakers in from their home districts during recess was a logistical feat—Jack Garner of Texas only made it by taking his first ride in an airplane—but it helped underscore the sense of urgency, and in the end Hoover had the endorsement of both parties.

For the second time in three nights, Hoover's conference ran past midnight, this time with scores of reporters corralled under the main portico outside as the president, Mills, and key congressmen worked to draft a news release. The National Credit Corporation was announced the next day, "dropt egglike from a shell of silence and secrecy," as one jaded scribe put it. In his announcement, Hoover emphasized the ideas of confidence and cooperation. "It is a movement of national assurance and of unity in action in an American way."

Reaction to the new credit agency was quick, broad, and universally positive. Key Democrats gave their endorsement, and bankers across the country promised to participate. The headlines were resounding. "No one could ask for better publicity," Ted Joslin enthused.

It was much like the war-debts moratorium—an innovation, hashed out for weeks, and finally sprung to widespread applause. And like the moratorium, it had a positive, short-term impact, but it addressed a problem that was bigger and deeper that any stopgap measure could resolve. Hoover recognized this at the time—"He knows it is only one step," Joslin recorded at the time; "many others must be taken"—but that was the nature of the emergency. Events were moving at a frantic pace, and Hoover was scrambling to keep up.

In the weeks that followed it became clear that the financiers were not so flexible as the president, less willing to innovate and more cautious about how to deploy their assets. George Harrison outlined those reservations after meeting with a committee of New York bankers. Hoover's plan was "a most constructive and important step in the present emergency," Harrison said in a memo to the president, but there were key elements that were simply not feasible.

Making loans against the assets of closed banks, in particular, involved "technical difficulties" that made this element of the credit pool "unwise if not impossible," and should be dropped. More subtly, Harrison pointed out that the plan was designed to inject liquidity in banks that were healthy but for their assets being frozen. That was fine in some cases, Harrison said, but far more frequently the problem facing American banks was not liquidity but solvency. Even if they counted their frozen assets at face value, such banks would still be unable to cover their obligations. In layman's terms, they were already broke.

Harrison's argument was technically correct, but it missed the larger point of Hoover's initiative. The impetus of the National Credit Corporation targeted a more ephemeral but more immediately consequential liability than frozen assets, and that was generalized fear. Something had to be done to knock down the panic that was driving depositors across the country to empty their bank accounts.

On that score, the National Credit Corporation worked a small wonder. It was makeshift, it was inadequate, but it was timely, and it instantly broke the fever that had seized the nation's depositors. In the week following Hoover's announcement the torrent of currency flowing out of the banks eased by two thirds, to $42 million. Bank closures peaked in October at 522, then fell in November to 175. The free fall that commenced with England's departure from gold was cut short.

Early the next year, George Harrison testified before a Senate committee on the effect of Hoover's credit pool. "The whole psychology of the bankers' mind—especially the smaller country banker—was immediately changed," Harrison said. He was fully cognizant of the shortcomings in the design, but those were secondary. "The mere existence of the fund, the mere evidence of the fact that the banking community of the United States stood ready to act with solidarity . . . restored confidence, the evidence of which was immediately obvious."

The collapse of the international gold standard was just one of a series of fundamental challenges Hoover faced in this period of economic transformation. The breakdowns multiplied—defaults by foreign debtors, a collapse in the price of railroad bonds, the bankruptcy of major cities like Detroit and Chicago, where schoolteachers worked without pay for months—while old problems, persisted, only partly resolved. In the drought zone, the weather had broken but the misery had not. "Tens of thousands of families have had their savings swept away and even their subsistence endangered," Agriculture Secretary Hyde wrote Hoover in the fall.

In August, preparing for a meeting with advisors on a recent plunge in the market for cotton, Hoover voiced his growing exasperation. "In this emergency, it is just one fixing job after another," he railed to his press secretary. "There is an international crack to fill up, then an industrial leak and next an agricultural flood. I am just a repairman. I don't have time to do anything new."

It was true, the relentless pace of the crisis, but Hoover's self-assessment was a bit unfair. The kaleidoscopic array of problems forced him to test basic assumptions, to reject some and to overhaul others. He tackled each in turn, churning out policy initiatives in a season of continuous bureaucratic creativity.

The first of these fundamental challenges was a yawning budget deficit. The Depression meant declining revenue across the board, and in January the deficit for 1931 was projected at $700 million. On top of that, Congress in February passed a veterans bill that would provide cash loans against a pension "endowment" that had been set aside in 1924 with a maturity of twenty years. This "bonus" came with a price tag of more than $1 billion—a third of the entire federal budget. Hoover vetoed the bill but was quickly overridden.

The prospect of a major deficit from the bonus put Hoover in a quandary. Ever since the Armistice, the government had operated in the black, covering spending from receipts and even retiring a substantial portion of its war debts. Now the president would have to choose, between raising taxes or incurring debt.

Hoover always kept a strict eye on government spending, especially in a depressed economy. This was partly an expression of his moralistic worldview, but also part of his fear that government borrowing weighed heavily on private enterprise. All through his presidency, Hoover drove government officials to cut spending and reduce staff, even while he ramped up public works. "Rigid economy," Hoover chided his department heads, "is the real road to relief."

By the same token, Hoover opposed raising taxes. In the spring of 1931, after weighing the growing deficit and the need to maintain the operations of the government, Hoover opted for deficit spending. The president shared his thinking with his cabinet and reached a consensus among his advisors. "After a long and very interesting discussion," Henry Stimson recorded in May, "practically everybody agreed that it was our business first to restore good times and then . . . balance the budget." Hoover had the last word. "The president likened it to war times," Stimson wrote. "He said in war times nobody dreamed of balancing the budget."

This was a remarkably flexible view for a man of Hoover's precise, almost mechanical mind, and it did not hold. When Britain left the gold standard, Hoover's determination that America must become the Gibraltar of the world economy carried with it a new and exclusive emphasis on credit. That had implications for the banking system; it also meant a new approach to the budget.

Again, the driving force was fear. That is, foreign investors seeking safe harbor considered government deficits a sign of weakness, which could lead to new drains of gold. At the same time, experience from the war showed that, with credit scarce, government borrowing would drive up the cost of loans, suppressing private investment. In both cases, the markets argued for new taxes over higher debt. With the choice now between deficits and stability, the president opted for safety. Henceforth, budget balance was assigned top priority.

Hoover had to let go another of his basic beliefs in September, when five major corporations announced they would implement a 10 percent wage cut. For two years the country's major corporations had accepted Hoover's directive to maintain pay scales, but now they broke ranks, following the lead of U.S. Steel, whose giant mills were operating at just a third of capacity. "It was the very action the president has been battling against for months," Ted Joslin lamented.

The immediate question was how to respond to the wage cuts. Hoover wanted to say nothing, for fear of inciting strikes and labor conflict, but Joslin and Walter Newton insisted. Finally a terse statement was issued: "The President's anxiety for maintaining the standard of living in this country has been constant and is unaltered." Despite the assertive tone, it was the swan song for Hoover's consumer-oriented, demand-side recovery strategy.

One policy Hoover upheld without qualms or revision was his determination to keep aid and charity a strictly local affair. All summer, unemployment persisted in double digits and it was clear the coming winter would be even worse than the last. But Hoover's response was rote and programmatic. The president had fought that battle already; his response this time would be the same.

He would have to start from scratch, however, as Arthur Woods and his colleagues had disbanded. Finding a second slate of volunteers for a new unemployment committee was more difficult than the first time around. Hoover set his sights on Walter Gifford, head of AT&T, for the top post. Gifford did not have the same cachet as Woods, but he was president of the Charity Organization Society in New York, and a social acquaintance of Hoover's. Still, it took some doing to get him on board.

Hoover hosted Gifford at the White House twice in August, discussing economic problems at length and pressing him to accept the assignment. But

Gifford had seen the travails of the Woods committee, and he knew the burden New York aid societies had carried through the winter of 1930. On his
train ride back to New York, Gifford spent the whole time trying to think
of a reason to refuse the job.

Gifford finally accepted the call to duty, and Hoover in August announced formation of the President's Organization for Unemployment
Relief. It was a new name for a new organization identical to the one he established the year before: voluntary, strictly advisory, with no official duties.

Hoover went through the same exercises, too, in discounting the extent
of the problem. Queried by reporters in August as to the current state of
unemployment, the president declined even to offer an estimate. Any such
number would be "theoretical," Hoover said, and to attempt a measurement
"is not merely bewildering but misleading." For now, he said, government
actuaries were conducting an "exhaustive" study.

It was the kind of distant, antiseptic approach that earned the president his reputation for cold-hearted indifference. And it was deserved, at
least in the case of unemployment; from the beginning of the Depression,
Hoover treated the question of job loss as an annoyance to be papered over
more than a grave social problem.

But it was also true that, in the big picture, unemployment was a
by-product of a systemic economic breakdown, and Hoover was fully engaged in the effort to repair that system. Hoover may well have cared about
the personal misfortunes of the jobless—he certainly said he did—but he
made little attempt to appease public sentiment. He believed that restoring capitalism would resolve the problem of unemployment, while providing public relief, especially in the fashion adopted in Europe, would only
drag the economy down further.

It was in pursuit of this larger goal, the effort to pull American capitalism out of its death spiral, that Hoover devoted his creativity, his acumen,
and his enormous capacity for work. In this regard, the crisis brought on by
the collapse of the gold standard marked a period of insight, of innovation
and executive action.

The moratorium on international obligations was the most sensational
of these innovations, and the National Credit Corporation was perhaps the

most innovative. But there were many other proposals; new rules to ease terms of credit with the Federal Farm Loan Board, new rules at the Federal Reserve to expand the kinds of assets that member banks might use as collateral, plans for a new system of Federal Home Loan Banks. It was not a single plan, not a program per se; it was Hoover's American plan, a redoubled commitment to credit and capital as the lifeblood of the American economy.

Toward the end of the year, with winter coming on and the new Congress due to convene, Hoover faced still another challenge to his core beliefs, another fundamental choice. This conundrum went to his core mission of salvaging capitalism, and the ethic of cooperation that Hoover believed was its highest expression. In the end it gave rise to a wrenching ideological retreat, one of the real tests of his presidency.

The challenge originated with Eugene Meyer and his continuing argument that the National Credit Corporation should be reformulated as a major government entity. Meyer never dropped the matter. When the bankers dragged their feet in raising the capital stake for the NCC, he goaded the president. Only the government could coordinate and compel monetary operations of such scale, Meyer insisted. But Hoover held on, to his program and to his associationalist ideal.

Initial response to the credit pool suggested that Hoover had been right after all. In a florid tribute, *The Literary Digest* saluted the president for "Smashing at the incubus of hard times with all the power of his great office"; the American Bankers Association gave the new agency a unanimous endorsement.

And the National Credit Corporation quickly achieved its initial purpose, dampening the bank runs and easing the sense of panic. But the idea that bankers might recognize their larger obligations in the name of self-interest; that they would pool resources to save the weaker banks, and thereby the system, proved to be a fallacy. Sure enough, they put up the initial stake of $500 million and assembled a board of directors for the corporation, but lending progressed only haltingly.

By December, despite much talk in the press of confidence and cooperation, the National Credit Corporation had loaned out just $10 million. Hoover offered this dour postmortem in his memoirs: "After a few weeks of enterprising courage the bankers' National Credit Corporation became ultraconservative, then fearful, and finally died. It had not exerted anything like its full possible strength."

In the meantime, bank failures were rising again, and hoarding had returned in full fury. Between August 1931 and January 1932 the amount of currency kept in U.S. banks fell 17 percent—the fastest drain on record—as millions of Americans sought safety in cash. The price of bonds, a key asset in most bank portfolios, fell drastically as more banks sold them off in a scramble for liquidity. And the high interest rates set by the Fed succeeded in stanching the outflow of gold, but also in further stifling the economy.

Hoover had seen enough. "Vast liquidation," the president concluded, had left the country in a state of "credit paralysis." In the face of renewed, wholesale financial breakdown, Hoover accepted the counsel of Eugene Meyer and proposed to Congress creation of the Reconstruction Finance Corporation, with initial funding at $500 million, and authority to borrow up to $2 billion more.

For the president it was a complete capitulation. Hoover had to forsake his cherished ideal of keeping government and business separate, and he had to abandon cooperation as the organizing principle for a successful capitalist society. But he had little choice, and he made no fuss over his surrender. "Certainly the public will not blame the administration," Hoover confided to his commerce secretary, "if, upon inability of private enterprise to save the situation, the government should do it."

Hoover offered perhaps a more candid expression of his sensibility when he recounted in his memoirs the White House session he conducted in October, when he presented his plan for a voluntary credit pool to key members of Congress. The assembled lawmakers "seemed shocked," Hoover recalled, "shocked at the revelation that our government for the first time in history might have to intervene to support private enterprise."

It was true that some congressmen would question the Reconstruction Finance Corporation on such grounds, but that came later. The issue in October was the National Credit Corporation, and it won nearly unanimous praise. If anyone was shocked that night, shocked at the prospect of peacetime government intervention in the economy, it was more likely Hoover himself.

EIGHTEEN

RECONSTRUCTION

IN THE FIRST WEEK OF DECEMBER 1931 MORE THAN A THOUSAND leftist hunger marchers converged on Washington, most hailing from the Eastern seaboard but some trekking from as far as Los Angeles and Seattle. They sang "The Internationale" and heard speakers denounce President Hoover as the "chief engineer of the New York Stock market."

Police lined the roadways to hem the demonstrators; a week before, a self-proclaimed "vanguard" of fourteen were arrested when they unfurled banners in front of the White House. But the December march came off without incident. After consultation with the White House, Pelham Glassford, chief of police for the District of Columbia, even arranged for sleeping quarters in a vacated Marine barracks. Glassford then led the protest parade down Pennsylvania Avenue, riding ahead on his blue police motorcycle.

Organizers of the march hoped to galvanize "the hungry millions" idled and left penniless by the national calamity that was just then coming to be referred to as the Great Depression. Yet far from stirring anger in the populace and fear in the government, the protest did little more than enliven the opening day of Congress. The protesters disbanded three days after they arrived, another case of impotence in a time of dysfunction.

The demonstration had come off without a hitch, but the organizers misread the mood of the people. Instead of seething with anger at their plight, Americans were feeling despondent. "Beyond the Potomac there is silence," mused one correspondent for *The New York Times*. "The politician in power is left in a vacuum; no life-giving breath of popular enthusiasm or popular indignation . . . refreshes the devitalized atmosphere of government."

It was a matter of simple exhaustion, as the nation entered its third winter of depression with no end in sight. But it was also a general recognition in this season of malaise that there were no easy answers, no obvious culprits. The ranks of millionaires—that exotic economic stratum that flourished through the 1920s—had been decimated, membership falling from 513 to 149. With bankruptcies everywhere, it rang hollow simply to pin the blame on "the rich."

Without enemies but also without prospects, Americans turned inward. "The indifference towards politics and government," worried the Baltimore *Sun*, "has grown until it almost seems impenetrable." It wasn't just Hoover whom the public turned against, but the full panoply of presumed social leadership. "President, politicians, bankers and industrialists are alike discredited," one analyst reckoned.

It was a mark of the times, this public indifference, but it also reflected the mode of leadership emanating from the White House. Within the councils of the administration, Herbert Hoover was a dynamo, working incessantly, driving his team. "He exhausts his associates," Edgar Rickard noted approvingly that fall; Hoover's advisors were "not accustomed to continuous, non-relenting work."

Yet none of Hoover's industry and none of his spirit of policy initiative came across to the public. The president's penchant for secrecy, his spite for the press, and his overriding fear that disclosure of the difficulties facing the nation would only make things worse, meant that the Hoover White House operated as the political equivalent of a black hole, a collapsed star that allowed no sound or light to escape its gated premises.

From his distant perspective in London, watching the drama of clashing interest rates and collapsed currencies, John Maynard Keynes studied

Hoover with bemusement. "The President of the United States turned in his sleep last June," Keynes wrote in late September, making reference to the debt moratorium. "Yet the magic spell of immobility which has been cast over the White House still seems unbroken." Closer to home Hoover's stoic isolation was put in less lyrical terms: "He is an unpopular and unloved man," wrote one caustic critic, "harder to get at than King Tut."

The nation was weary of politics, but politics remained the blood sport of the capital. And with Congress in town and the presidential election less than a year away, the jockeying for place was already under way. Hoover stood at the pinnacle of the process, leader of his party and occupant of the nation's highest elected office, but for him the prospect of a long campaign brought up all his old ambivalence, all his inner conflicts.

As early as January 1930, having held his office less than a year, Hoover was already talking about being a one-term president. He said this as if it were his preference, as if it mattered not to him or to the country. It would be better, Hoover posited at one point, to limit the office to a single term. "Three-and-a-half years would satisfy me," he said with airy indifference. The trials were too great, the rewards too meager. Hoover felt no president could earnestly hope for a second term, that the incumbent running again "is apt to be a coward, in the sense that he wants to get out of office, but is afraid of being called a quitter if he deserts."

Hoover recognized that he had fared poorly in office. Congress was hostile, the press had turned against him, and the Depression overshadowed all his achievements. To this he responded with feigned indifference. "I don't give a damn, Ted, whether I am re-nominated or not," Hoover told Joslin in November. "I shall not turn a hand to get another term."

This was the diffident Hoover, the thin-skinned outsider so poorly suited to the huckstering that politics required. But Joslin knew better. He was a newcomer to Hoover's inner circle but he recognized the ambition that his boss tried, but failed to conceal. "It riles the president to talk politics with him," Joslin observed in his diary. Yet, "He wants another term more than he wants anything else."

The next election was on Hoover's mind constantly, often manifesting as an obsession with Calvin Coolidge. The former president showed no sign of returning to public life, rarely surfacing from his retirement in Northampton except to pen political homilies for newspaper syndication. But in April Hoover worried aloud about a "plot" among party regulars to draft Coolidge at the convention in June; by September, Hoover had reversed field, encouraging a "draft Coolidge" movement in order to force the former president to renounce any such ambition.

Hoover was obsessed, as well, with a "smear book" produced by John Hamill, the British factotum retained by sometime Democratic Party operative John O'Brien to gather material on Hoover in 1928. It was O'Brien whose office was the subject of the failed burglary commissioned by Hoover aide Larry Richey in 1930; now Hamill had split with O'Brien and was proceeding on his own.

Hamill's book, a compilation of allegations from Hoover's years abroad, was published in the fall as *The Strange Career of Mr. Hoover Under Two Flags.* Based loosely on news reports and court documents but rife with innuendo, the book got little notice in the press, but received constant attention from Hoover and his inner circle. Edgar Rickard, in particular, engaged attorneys and private investigators to keep tabs on Hamill and his associates; in turn, Rickard stayed in close contact with Larry Richey at the White House, and with Hoover himself, delivering updates and requesting advice.

The idea was twofold; to discredit the book by exposing errors in fact, and to reveal it as a political hit piece by showing that it was published with funds provided by Democratic activists.

Several times the president was advised to drop the inquiry, that he would do better simply to ignore Hamill. But Hoover and his team were "determined to go forward," and did so on several fronts. They shadowed Hamill and his publisher, using Justice Department attorneys, Post Office inspectors, and the Office of Naval Intelligence to build their files. And they retained Arthur Train, a former attorney for Hoover, to compose a detailed refutation of the book. Train met with Hoover in the White House to discuss the project, and the president took a hand in directing the research.

It was not rivals or slanders, of course, but the continuing Depression that posed the greatest threat to Hoover's reelection. In moments of clarity, the president and his advisors recognized that if the economy did not turn, Hoover and his party were headed for defeat, and possibly a devastating one. But that prognosis was provisional. "They are entirely confident," one insider wrote in late September, "that an upturn by next summer will bring a victory to Mr. Hoover."

In his heart, Hoover was even more hopeful. "I can win," Hoover told political aide Jim MacLafferty in December. "I can win with economic conditions no better than they are right now." This came at a time when polling was rudimentary and politics was more instinct than science. But already Hoover's camp was finding money harder to raise, because many of the usual donors were facing lean times, and because Hoover was simply unpopular. And the party's national committee had never recovered its footing since the Claudius Huston debacle. All things considered, the flame of optimism that Hoover cultivated appears a bit naive, almost wistful. Externally so stern, Hoover's interior was draped in sentiment.

Before any campaign could get under way, Hoover would have to face the new Congress. That presented problems of its own—political and psychological. Hoover's experience with the 71st Congress had been bruising enough, and this new class included many Democrats—and several Republicans—elected expressly in opposition to the president. The Democrats held the majority in the House, and in the Senate the Republicans were so divided that Hoover proposed letting the opposition party organize the committee leadership.

This was a fairly ham-handed version of Machiavelli. That is, Hoover wanted the Democrats running the committees because then they would have to share blame for the Depression. Should prosperity return, Hoover figured, he would be glad to share the credit.

It was a sharp angle for the president, perhaps, but sure to further alienate the leadership of his own party. "It never occurs to him that these chairmanships are the very pinnacle of the political careers of the men in the House and Senate," complained an exasperated Ted Clark in another missive to Coolidge. These Republicans were "vitally important in influencing the type and character of legislation," Clark noted, and should be cultivated, not pushed away. More than that, Hoover's approach was impossibly self-centered. "The thought has never entered his mind," Clark groused, "that he is asking these sacrifices to make his path to re-election easier and for no other purpose."

Hoover failed to look out for his friends, and he was overtly hostile to his foes. The painful confrontation over Red Cross relief at the last Congress had only left him embittered; in particular, in drafting his recovery program, Hoover disdained any effort to conciliate the opposition. His greatest fear, he said, was that "the Democrats would agree with everything he proposed."

Hoover's belligerence was gratifying to a political pugilist like Jim Mac-Lafferty, but to the more seasoned statesmen of the administration, Hoover was acting out of character and out of his depth. "The president told me that for the remaining eighteen months (of his term) he intended to fight everything," Henry Stimson noted late that year. "He was very bellicose."

Stimson had seen the president's evolution and was leery of this new iteration. "During the past two years I have many times wished he would fight more," Stimson confided in his diary. "Now I am afraid that he is in the situation of a man who does not like to fight, and once he gets started to fighting, he fights foolishly."

Hoover was not the only one playing politics during the lean winter of 1931. Congressional Democrats well remembered the way Joe Robinson's plea for cooperation had been abused just the year before. When Congress opened in December, the opposition party proved just as bellicose as the Republican president.

The immediate object was Hoover's debt moratorium. It was a silly point to contest—the initial sensation of that dramatic announcement had long since passed, and the debtor nations could hardly now be called to account for the suspended payments. But the country was in a sour mood, and revulsion at the idea of renouncing legitimate claims to foreign funds made the moratorium a tempting target.

Hoover's most bitter critic here was Louis McFadden, the Republican representative from Pennsylvania who led the opposition to Eugene Meyer's appointment to the Fed. McFadden was a banker and chairman of the House Committee on Banking and Currency, but he was also paranoid and

The future president: Herbert Hoover acknowledges well-wishers the day after he wins the Republican nomination.

Hoover in Perth, Australia, age 23.

Humble beginnings: The cabin where Hoover was born.

Prairie girl: Lou Hoover
as a teenager.

Newlyweds, 1899:
Seated behind Lou and Bert are
Lou's father, Charles; her sister,
Jean; and her mother, Florence.

Herbert Hoover in 1932.

First Lady Lou Henry Hoover.

Fast friends: Bert and Lou Hoover visit postwar Venice with Edgar and Abbie Rickard.

Oath of office: Former President and current Chief Justice William Howard Taft swears in Hoover as Calvin Coolidge looks on.

Presidential transition:
"Every lineament
was sour."

BELOW: Grace Coolidge
(left) and Lou Hoover
nearly missed the
inauguration ceremony.

A fractious team: Hoover flanked
by advisors Hubert Work (left)
and Claudius Huston.

13

Trial by microphone:
When Hoover took the
podium, "inhibitions seemed
to rise in his throat."

14

Splendid isolation:
Hoover found solace
in working a stream.

15

The Palo Alto house,
designed by Lou, on
campus at Stanford
University.

16

Hoover's presidential camp on
the Rapidan River in Virginia.

17

Bert and Lou relax
by the Rapidan.

18

Big news: Hoover
never got used to the
attentions of the press.

The Lincoln Study:
Hoover made it his own.

Hoover's White House
days started with a
round of medicine ball.

He meets his public:
Hoover chafed at his
ceremonial duties.

What a difference five years make: The top photo shows Andrew Mellon in his prime, in 1927, with his assistant Ogden Mills. The same two men pose again in 1932 (right), but now Mills is Secretary of Treasury, and Mellon is in his dotage.

Bank run: Police tell depositors their bank will not open today.

25

The Depression saw thousands of small banks close their doors, like this one in Kansas.

26

Changing horses: Outgoing Fed Chairman Roy Young (left) looks on as Eugene Meyer receives his commission from Andrew Mellon, September 1930.

27

Brooklyn breadline: Hunger stalked the cities.

Red Cross aid: Hoover supported seed for farmers, but not food.

Hooverville: Shantytowns became commonplace, like this one outside Seattle.

Friends in high places:
Hoover found reluctant partners in
John Barton Payne (above left)
of the Red Cross, and
Walter S. Gifford (above right).
Henry Ford (right) supported
Hoover's high-wage policy, but
deserted him in the banking crisis.

33

Sparring partners: Hoover's foes in Congress included Democrats Joe Robinson of Arkansas (above left), Jack Garner of Texas (above right), and Carter Glass of Virginia (lower left); Republican William Borah (lower right) was an ostensible but uncertain ally.

Some Hoover intimates left diaries that
help illuminate their reclusive Chief.
They included political advisor James
MacLafferty (above left),
and Secretary of State Henry Stimson
(above right). Press aide Ted Joslin (right)
shared many a tense moment with his boss.

Hunger march: 1931 closed with thousands of protesters marching on the Capitol.

Washington's own Hooverville: The Bonus Army set up camp along the Anacostia River.

Citizen soldiers: Veterans march to appeal for government aid.

Flash point: Veterans battle police as the protest boils over.

43

District of Columbia Police
Chief Pelham Glassford.

A break in the action:
General Douglas MacArthur
takes a breather as Major Dwight
Eisenhower (far left) looks on.

46

A doomed campaign: Lou feared her husband would not survive his bid for reelection.

SPECIAL
BALTIMORE & OHIO R R
TRAIN

No love lost: Herbert Hoover and Franklin Roosevelt ride in silence to FDR's inauguration.

anti-Semitic. These traits would grow more pronounced as his career progressed; at this point, he was simply a loudmouth.

McFadden aired his charges soon after Congress opened, his speech filling most of a December afternoon. Hoover's moratorium was "an infamous proposal," McFadden said, a bid to "take the money away from the men and women and children of this country and give it to Germany." The president had consulted Congress only because "he was afraid to do this thing alone at the bidding of the German international bankers . . . and all their followers."

Hoover was unpopular, certainly, and opinion was divided over the moratorium, but in this show of spite McFadden went too far. He was answered immediately, Republicans and even some Democrats rising to the president's defense, and in the days that followed Hoover enjoyed the most sympathetic press coverage he'd received in some time.

Treasury Secretary Mellon was another target of militant Democrats, and this, too, worked in Hoover's favor. Early in January, Wright Patman, a freshman congressman elected after campaigning against "Mellonism," moved to impeach the aging financier. Patman made a scattershot attack, with charges ranging from insider trading and Prohibition violations to tax evasion.

Hoover harbored little love for his treasury secretary, retaining him largely out of deference for the only man from the Harding cabinet still holding office. Now, Patman's attack opened the door to one of Hoover's bureaucratic sleights of hand. In February, Hoover appointed Mellon ambassador to Britain. The current ambassador, former vice president Charles Dawes, would return to join the administration's fight against the Depression, while at Treasury, Ogden Mills would step into Mellon's place.

This moved Mellon off the hot seat—a frustrated Wright Patman promptly shut down his impeachment drive—and it confirmed Mills as one of Hoover's closest advisors.

These were the politics of party and power, the continuing contest over who should rule. The drama was critical to the players and grist for headlines, but in a time of national emergency it was all window dressing. What really counted was the Depression, and finding some path to recovery. Hoover understood this, and he crafted a program to ensure that the debate took place on his terms.

He laid out his plans in his annual address to Congress, a printed document delivered to the Capitol for its opening session December 7. It was the State of the Union, at a time when the union had never been in such a state. Hulking factories shuttered, shantytowns skirting the great cities, threadbare drifters on the highways—an America transformed from the one that elected Hoover president.

Hoover labored over his text for six full weeks, sending a total of twenty-two drafts to the printer. So pleased was he with the result, he previewed the speech with Republican floor leaders at a White House dinner, and arranged for it to be read verbatim—all seven thousand words—by two House clerks over a national radio network.

A State of the Union speech will often tend toward omnibus, and Hoover touched on a long list of concerns, from military readiness to public power. But this was no ordinary occasion. The emergency of wholesale economic collapse was at hand. Something had to happen, and now was the time for the president to say what that might be.

Hoover opened with his customary search, now become maddening, for glimmering hints of optimism. "If we lift our vision beyond these immediate emergencies we find fundamental national gains even amid depression," Hoover offered. He even ventured to cite a decrease in infant mortality as evidence that "our people have been protected from hunger and cold."

The argument verged on the preposterous, but Hoover's thrust was clear: he was not going to engage in a dialogue over new modes of direct aid. Instead, under the heading "Further Measures," he turned to the looming phenomenon of "credit paralysis," which he placed as the greatest obstacle to economic revival.

"If we can put our financial resources to work," Hoover intoned, "I am confident we can make a large measure of recovery independent of the rest of the world." Here was the core of the president's program, the product of a year spent in crisis management.

The plan rested on two pillars; on the one hand, new support for banks through the Reconstruction Finance Corporation, fashioned along the lines advanced by Eugene Meyer. On the other hand, balancing the federal budget through sharp reductions in federal spending and a substantial hike in taxes.

The credit side of the program was still in formation. The Reconstruction Finance Corporation would be a federal program modeled after the War Finance Corporation, but would operate simultaneously with the voluntary credit pool. Hoover was still ambivalent over establishing such an imposing state entity, suggesting that, "It may not be necessary to use such an instrumentality very extensively." He then proposed a series of similar innovations in the nation's credit facilities: a new system of Home Loan Banks; expanded funding for the Federal Land Banks; systematic disposition of the assets of closed banks; some means of returning to circulation the funds in savings accounts offered by the Post Office—a service long since discontinued but at that time the chosen refuge for half a billion dollars pulled from banks by wary depositors—and some means for shoring up railroad bonds, one of the most common assets in institutional portfolios, and among the hardest hit in the general deflation. It was a broad, flexible program targeting the weakest links in the nation's wobbly capital structure.

Hoover detailed his tax plan in a separate address, but here he gave a general outline that was alarming to a nation accustomed to balanced budgets. Federal receipts had fallen by more than a billion dollars in two years, Hoover said, while spending climbed steadily. After a decade of surplus, the deficit for 1931 ran to more than $900 million; the deficit for the coming year was projected at $2 billion. "Several conclusions are inevitable," Hoover admonished. "We must have an insistent and determined reduction in government expenses," and, "We must face a temporary increase in taxes."

In political terms it was a daring speech, even foolhardy. The tax increase would naturally be unpopular; not because it was the wrong response to a slack economy—that thesis had yet to be demonstrated—but simply because heavier taxes in such a lean year would be a genuine burden. And committing public funds to new credit agencies devoted to shoring up bank finances, while at the same time denying funds to relieve widespread destitution, seemed designed to invite ridicule.

But these were not normal times. By and large, the public and even the politicians managed to put aside the temptation to score points with easy attacks on the president. Walter Lippmann's *Herald Tribune* voiced the general mood, suggesting that, "The businesslike quality prevailing in Mr. Hoover's message will be exceedingly welcome to a country beset by radicals and perfectionists." The editorial saluted the president's technical response throughout the crisis. "As each financial emergency has arisen, Mr. Hoover has approached it with clear eye and steady hand."

But if the speech scored points on policy grounds, it failed to gener-ate the sort of heat that might shake the nation from its torpor. *The New York Times*, rival to the *Herald Tribune* and often friendly to the president, deemed Hoover's message "correct but cold."

What was correct was the economic program, the focus on credit and the balance of restraint and targeted action. It reflected the president's "un-usual powers of analysis," and "points out accurately what must be done." The *Times* endorsed in particular the call for budget cuts. "There is nothing for our government but the most severe and continuous economy. . . . The main principle upon which Mr. Hoover insists is perfectly sound."

But that was not enough. "The effect is, it must honestly be said, to leave Americans still longing for a public man who could rise to the great crisis in a great way and utter words which would not only be watchwords of debate in Congress, but which would carry cheer and hope to thousands of despon-dent homes throughout the country."

In terms of policy and procedure, the president was performing as ad-vertised. But called to account on the more intangible, human elements of the job, the ineffable qualities of warmth, vitality, and leadership, Hoover had no answer.

Over the last weeks of December and into the New Year Hoover worked with Eugene Meyer and Ogden Mills, at his end, and the committees of Congress on the other, to win authorization for the Reconstruction Finance Corporation. Funded at $500 million, with authority to issue bonds up to a total $2 billion—more than half the entire federal budget—it would com-prise the largest peacetime government intervention into the private credit markets in history.

The proposal quickly became a vehicle for a variety of strategic priorities. First precedence was to foster credit through direct loans to banks. Then came several critical sectors that were, like the banks, sinking for lack of credit. The Treasury sought an amendment allowing loans to railroads, which were losing volume and freight charges. Railroad bonds were the single largest category of investments in bank and insurance company portfolios; poor performance by rail carriers was a drag on the entire financial system.

Hoover himself proposed two specific, additional provisions: one would allow the RFC to issue notes secured by the assets of closed banks, and another that would qualify RFC bonds as collateral at the Federal Reserve. Both would further extend the volume of credit the new agency could inject into the economy.

Members of Congress had their own ideas for the new federal entity. Senator Joe Robinson wanted to include agricultural credit corporations; another senator sought a set-aside for loans to small farmers, to be administered through the secretary of agriculture. And, in a measure that would shift the focus of the whole project, senators from New York and Chicago proposed that the RFC serve as a backstop to the strapped cities, making loans against future tax receipts.

Hoover opposed this last proposal in particular, part of his determined effort to have individual states deal with the crisis independent of the central government. But the president didn't address each innovation specifically. Rather, he pressed for action—any action—as soon as possible.

Hoover did much of the lobbying himself. By his own count he met in person with more than 150 congressmen to urge his program. Twice he called members of key committees to the White House for breakfast. And he publicly pleaded that Congress skip or abridge its Christmas recess in order to move legislation. The idea got nowhere, but Hoover continued to press lawmakers over the holiday. Quick action after the break, Hoover aides told reporters, was "uppermost in the president's mind."

Negotiations over the RFC got serious in mid-January. By then some critics had found their voice; Fiorello La Guardia denounced the entire scheme as a "millionaire's dole." La Guardia understood the goal of thawing the frozen credit markets, but could not abide the irony of aid to moneyed institutions—even sickly ones—in a time of destitution. "It is a subsidy for broken bankers—a subsidy for bankrupt railroads—a reward for speculation and unscrupulous bond pluggers."

But if the bill was an easy target for ridicule, it was also the centerpiece of the government's response to the Depression. With circumstances so dire, outright opposition would be symbolic, and futile.

More telling were the objections set forth by Carter Glass, Democrat of Virginia and the principal author, in 1913, of the Federal Reserve Act. Glass was deeply conservative, especially in regard to money and credit, and he considered much of the thrust of the RFC an ill-disguised effort to spark inflation. It was a fine distinction, between expanding credit and inflating the currency, but Glass was determined he would have one without the other.

To that end, Senator Glass mounted a dogged resistance to one of the key elements of Hoover's RFC—the proposal that the secured debts issued by the new agency be acceptable as collateral for loans from the Federal Reserve. That status would render those securities more marketable and amplify the benefit to the overall credit picture—just the aims the RFC was designed to achieve. But Glass feared the banks would dump their overvalued RFC securities on the Federal Reserve and quickly swamp the system. "I am suggesting," Glass said at a Senate hearing, "that we would not have a Federal Reserve System if these debentures, made eligible, should in very large measure get into Federal Reserve Banks. They would absorb the present excess lending power of the Federal Reserve Banks."

Glass inveighed, too, against clauses that would allow the RFC to make direct loans to industrial firms or to public entities seeking to finance public works. Glass and his allies opposed this for the simple reason it invested the directors of the new agency with too much power. In the same vein, Glass also imposed far tighter restrictions on bank eligibility for RFC loans than proposed by the administration. Here was a stark irony; Hoover, so wary of public action in the private sphere, headed off by Democrats fearful of government overreach.

Hoover acceded to the Glass amendments, showing a spirit of compromise often missing from his legislative strategy, but he could not resist one final display of partisan pique. It so happened that, when the measure was delivered to the White House for his signature, the president was meeting in the Lincoln Study with three opposition senators. Rather than share credit for the bill, Hoover had Ted Joslin set up newsreel cameras in a small side office. At a signal from his press secretary Hoover left his guests, crossed a hall, and conducted the signing ceremony in secret. Joslin chortled afterward, "The three Democrats did not have the slightest idea what had taken place."

Once established in law, the Reconstruction Finance Corporation swung into action with remarkable speed. Even before the bill was signed, President Hoover named its two top executives—Eugene Meyer, chairman, and Charles Dawes as president. For Meyer it meant a second post, simultaneous with his duties, already demanding, as chairman of the Federal Reserve. For Dawes it was yet another way station in a remarkable career that included high-profile postings as diplomat, brigadier general, and vice president, but also the very relevant jobs of private banker, comptroller of the currency, and director of the federal budget.

The dual appointments were typical of the president; leery of settling too much power in any single pair of hands, he opted for divided rule. Dawes was better known but had other commitments, particularly to his banking interests in Chicago; Meyer was more deeply engaged in the new entity, and resented the idea of shared authority. But at the outset there was plenty of work for both. Meyer had better contacts and built the new bureaucracy out of his former staff—the secretary, general counsel, and chief bank examiners all hailed from the War Finance Corporation. And he designed the agency along the same lines, with thirty-three regional offices from Birmingham to Spokane to receive and vet loan applications.

Staffing these offices was complicated by the fact of the Depression itself. The new agency created six hundred immediate job openings but drew ten thousand applicants, many claiming congressional sponsors; it was up to the RFC board to sort out the logjam. At the same time, Meyer, Dawes, and Ogden Mills were each working to process individual loan applications. They had to: in a ringing confirmation that credit was indeed a fundamental problem in the economy, the RFC received thousands of applications for loans. On its first formal day of operation, on February 3, the RFC loaned $15 million to bail out the Bank of America, the largest chain banking operation in the country. By the end of the month the new agency had put out $45 million in emergency loans to banks and another $25 million to major railroads.

The agriculture side of the agency proved equally active. Weighing in just in time for spring planting, Agriculture Secretary Arthur Hyde supervised distribution of $40 million in RFC funds. The loans were capped at $400, but helped 200,000 farmers get a crop in the ground.

While Hoover's advisors toiled to get the RFC up and running, the president pressed on with the balance of his program. Restoring credit was Hoover's core concern, but that covered a broad field of endeavor. Fighting the Depression was like wartime, he said on several occasions: "it is not a battle on a single front but on many fronts," or, giving the phrase a different turn, "This battle is upon a thousand fronts."

One initiative was a public campaign against hoarding. By January 1932 fearful citizens were sitting on more than $5 billion, squeezing bank assets and thus the amount of credit available. Hoover made the connection clear when he announced formation of the Citizens Reconstruction Organization. This was a distinctly Hooverian project, with a conference of fifty business and labor leaders at the White House, appearances by Charles Dawes, Ogden Mills, and Eugene Meyer, and a statement—not a speech—from the president. "Credit is the blood stream of our economic life," Hoover said, and holding money out of circulation cut back on credit. "Every dollar returned from hoarding to circulation means putting men to work." The appeal struck home, or at least it appeared to; by the end of March the Treasury reported that the drain had been reversed, and bank deposits grew by $200 million.

Other credit initiatives required continuing collaboration with Congress. Some measures sailed through; after the House voted $100 million in fresh capital for the Federal Land Bank System, the Senate promptly voted an additional $25 million, calling for a moratorium on farm foreclosures. Hoover was pleased to sign the bill just days after creation of the RFC. It should, he said, "bring relief and hope to many borrowers"; in particular, it would allow a billion-dollar expansion of rural credit.

Creating a parallel system for federal aid to home owners proved much more difficult. That was partly due to the fact that, unlike the Land Banks, there was no precedent for such an agency, no apparatus in place. Launching a new system, even when all agreed that urgent action was needed, required a degree of comity that simply was not present.

Leading the opposition to Hoover's proposed Federal Home Loan Banks was Republican insurgent James Couzens, a onetime partner of Henry Ford who split with the automaker and entered politics when he was appointed to the Senate in 1922. Couzens considered himself an expert in finance, and deemed mortgage assistance to be useful "for the emergency period," but an encumbrance afterward. Short-term aid to homeowners, he said, would better be administered through the new RFC.

With a key Republican declaring against the plan in the Senate, House leaders sidetracked the bill. The plan didn't come up for a hearing until July, and even then, Couzens succeeded in restricting the loans to half the value of the property, with a cap of $20,000. Hoover believed the restrictions effectively gutted the program, and came to resent Couzens as "a curiously perverse person." In his memoirs Hoover singled him out for direct censure: "Although he called himself a 'progressive,' he was, without knowing it, a profound reactionary."

Aside from creating new lending entities, Hoover had still another strategic initiative aimed at releasing the credit bottled up in the nation's financial system. He wanted to revise the rules of the Federal Reserve System to free more funds for lending by the member banks. It required intrusion on the complex balance of gold, currency, and bank reserves; it also required another Hoover parley with the senior senator from Virginia.

Carter Glass is known today as a champion of government regulation, author of the famous Glass-Steagall Act, which separated commercial, or depository, banks from the risky activities of investment banks. But that bill was something of an anomaly for Glass, who was a small-government, states' rights conservative best known for a Southern drawl and a sharp tongue. One of Glass's predecessors as senator from Virginia once described Glass as "a snapping turtle—mighty dangerous if you poke him."

Glass held strong views on the Depression. He blamed the "riot of credit and inflation" that preceded the crash, and faulted the managers of the Federal Reserve for underwriting the speculation rather than safeguarding the stability of the currency. One response was his bid to separate commercial banks from investment banks; he also wanted strict limits on the kinds of assets banks could use as reserves to back their loan operations, which would restrict the amount of money they could lend out.

This latter proscription drew Glass into direct opposition to the president. Since the early summer Hoover had been seeking some means to make basic changes in the reserve requirements of the banking system, admitting new categories of stock and corporate debt as collateral for loans to banks from the Federal Reserve. Simply put, Hoover was seeking to expand credit and liquidity, which Glass considered the root of monetary evil.

Glass developed his views at a leisurely pace, collecting testimony as chairman of a banking subcommittee and testing his ideas in a reform bill, authored in 1930, as "merely a tentative measure." When he was installed in December 1931 as head of the Senate Banking and Currency Committee, he was ready with a more developed, more restrictive bank reform bill.

Through the first two years of the Depression Hoover and his advisors were content to let Glass make his own way, but the banking crisis forced the president onto Glass's turf. Their first encounter came in October when, as part of his proposal for the National Credit Corporation, Hoover recommended basic changes in the reserve requirements of the banking system. As with Hoover's bid to qualify RFC bonds as Federal Reserve collateral, Glass would have nothing to do with the plan.

Indicating, perhaps, that he was learning how the game was played, Hoover catered to Glass in his State of the Union speech, inviting Congress to "investigate the need for separation between different kinds of banking"— Glass's top priority. But when Hoover asked Glass to incorporate elements of the administration's credit-easing agenda in his bank reform bill, Glass brushed him off.

Events quickly put this standoff into eclipse. By mid-January it became apparent the economy had entered a new, sharp, downward spiral. Bank closures were surging, with more than seven hundred in December and January. Frightened bankers throughout the system were selling assets, calling in loans, and shutting down lending operations in a desperate scramble for liquidity.

Gold was another key factor. According to the rules governing the Federal Reserve, the twelve reserve banks were required to maintain a 40 percent gold "cover" for currency in circulation, with the rest backed by high-grade bonds and securities. But the decline of so many classes of stocks and bonds created a sudden shortage of such paper, meaning that Fed managers had to keep far more than the 40 percent minimum gold on hand. And foreign governments, sensing weakness, were calling in gold at an accelerating pace.

With alarm bells sounding all around, Hoover called Glass to an evening conference at the White House and leaned on him hard. Credit was being squeezed at the federal spigot, Hoover told him, and the threat to gold was "seriously impugning our national stability." Glass turned Hoover down flat; he would accept no amendments to his banking bill. Any effort to ease collateral requirements, he wrote later, he considered "an assault upon the very integrity of our banking system."

Hoover hated this business of courting the opposition. "You have no idea how I had to demean myself before these Democratic swine!" he raged to a friend early in February. But he kept at it, making concessions when needed and seizing advantage when it appeared. At a White House dinner for Jack Garner, the new speaker of the house, Hoover pressed on him the urgency of the situation and found Garner ready to join forces. Now Hoover had split the Democrats; Glass would be forced to deal.

Hoover made his move the frosty morning of Wednesday, February 10. He called Glass back to the White House, along with the five other key senators, and sat them down with Eugene Meyer, Ogden Mills, and Charles Dawes. They met over breakfast, but there was little comity in the room. Glass disdained the president, considering him to be "densely ignorant, pitifully ignorant, on banking questions." The Hoover team felt the same about Glass; Ogden Mills, remarking on the senator's reputation as "a great authority on banking," told a friend in April that "my personal observation leads me to believe that there is no ground for any such belief."

It was not harmony that carried the day, but urgency—the sense that something needed to happen. Dawes made the point with a characteristic display of temper, his voice booming through the hallways, his fist hammering the table and "sounding like the barking of a machine gun." Dawes was a diplomat, but was rarely accused of being diplomatic.

Finally Glass gave ground. He agreed to set aside his banking bill in favor of Hoover's proposal to ease the collateral requirements of the Federal Reserve. But he did so in classic legislative fashion, trading his concession for Hoover's agreement to relinquish his plan to rehabilitate the assets of closed banks. Glass supported the idea, so much that he wanted to incorporate it in his own banking bill as "bait" to win votes.

With Glass on board at last, Hoover that same day hosted a second meeting, this of the House leadership, including Speaker Garner and Henry Steagall, chair of the Committee on Banking and Currency. Steagall was Glass's counterpart in banking reform; he also agreed to sponsor Hoover's bill, and agreed to table the banking bill until later in the session.

The resulting Glass-Steagall bill—referred to as the "Bank-Relief Bill"—was introduced in both houses of Congress that week, but in the Senate Carter Glass promptly laid on amendments to limit the range of banks entitled to the new Federal Reserve credits. This was not simply because Glass was obstreperous, though he certainly was that. The fact was that, under the pressure of the renewed banking crisis, Glass and Hoover were joined in an uncertain alliance to subvert economic principles that both held dear. Glass was just a bit more reluctant.

Glass and the president agreed that a stable currency grounded in gold was critical to recovery, both globally and within the United States. Yet both recognized that immobilized credit was the single biggest obstacle to recovery. Hoover's strategy, to which Glass grudgingly acquiesced, was to aim for that most intangible of targets, "reflation" of the currency. They wanted to stop the deflation, but outright inflation was heresy; Hoover and Glass each hoped to split the difference.

Even that modest goal had to be concealed. France and other gold standard nations were watching closely for the slightest sign of devaluation, while at home, orthodox bankers demanded the Federal Reserve wield "a club of iron to beat down inflationist tendencies." And, sure enough, foreign governments met the quick progress of the Glass-Steagall bill by redeeming more of their U.S. dollars for gold.

Hoover tackled the European reaction at a press conference in January, insisting that, "The emergency measures we have taken are the use of government credit to loosen up frozen credits in institutions, and that is not inflation." Likewise, when he introduced his bill in the Senate, Carter Glass vowed that it would not be used for "excessive inflation of the currency." Within the White House, and confiding only to his diary, Ted Joslin was more candid. "It is really an inflation measure making for greater credit," Joslin wrote, "but it's the last thing we will say publicly."

There was one final aspect of Glass-Steagall that was the most inflationary element of the bill, but also the most subtle. That is, the new reserve requirements Hoover requested for the Fed sharply reduced the amount of gold that had to be set aside to back currency issues. In turn, that allowed Fed governors leeway to push more currency into circulation. They did so the same week the president signed Glass-Steagall, voting to reduce interest rates by half a point, and to commence purchasing government securities.

The Glass-Steagall bank-relief bill sailed through Congress almost without opposition. The financial press gave the program unanimous applause; *Business Week* christened it "the most powerful offensive force imagination has, so far, been able to command."

The only real protest came from the political opposition. Democratic leaders complained that the president was stealing all the plaudits by labeling the package of laws aimed at economic stimulus and reform "the Hoover program."

It was hard for the president's foes to swallow, but it was also hard to deny—Hoover had outlined the program in his State of the Union address, and pushed it through an opposition Congress in what can only be considered a legislative tour de force. The Democrats could take credit for cooperation, but the initiative, and the agenda, belonged exclusively to the administration.

Nor did Hoover and his team relax when the votes came through. By February, Eugene Meyer, who had done so much to put his stamp on the

program, was splitting his days, working mornings at the Fed and after-
noons at the RFC, both exacting, high-pressure jobs. He was an alpha type,
always seeking more authority, but this was more than he could handle.

Early in February, Meyer's wife, Agnes, contacted Ted Joslin and asked
for a private conference with Hoover. She called it "secret"—presumably
from the press, but also from her husband. Agnes Meyer was a blue-eyed,
fair-haired socialite, one of the arbiters of the Washington dinner circuit,
but she was also worldly and politically active, a delegate to the Republican
convention in 1924. She had no trouble leveling with the president.

Meeting with Hoover in the White House, she told him her husband
simply could not continue working at the present pace. In particular he
needed help dealing with the constant clamor from applicants seeking jobs
at the new RFC. "I frightened him thoroughly by telling him Eugene would
break physically unless Hoover would help protect him," she recorded. The
president surprised her by avowing his firm allegiance to her financier husband. "Eugene Meyer is the most valuable man I've got," Hoover declared,
adding that his "chief occupation" was "to keep Eugene well."

Agnes Meyer was touched by this encounter. She had heard from Eugene only of his conflicts with Hoover; now she found the president persuasive, "even when I cannot believe the pictures he paints." To Agnes, Hoover
appeared "old and worn," but entirely sympathetic. "I shall never get over
my liking for him."

For the first few weeks after passage of the bank bill it all seemed worth
it. Bank failures dipped again to pre-Depression levels, depositors began returning funds, and the RFC performed as planned, cranking out 974 separate loans to banks, insurance companies, and mortgage lenders by the end
of March. Eugene Meyer was so encouraged that he told his fellow Fed governors he believed the tide of the Depression had turned. He added one
crucial caveat, however: "If the damned hoarders would cease hoarding, and
if the damned banks would begin loaning, all would be well."

But that was the rub. Even as their reserves piled up, fearful bankers
refused to put new funds in the hands of even their most reliable customers.
RFC loans might thaw frozen assets, but that did not push the money out
the door.

Hoover tracked the situation via correspondence and phone calls with business executives all over the country. A utility president in Kansas reported that the Central National Bank of Topeka was holding $6 million in deposits and just $1 million in loans—the reverse of normal lending ratios. Banks in Kansas City had stopped lending altogether. A banker in New York shocked a visitor from Chicago by proposing that, "1931 would be remembered as the year of the Depression, and 1932 as the year of the Great Panic." Another correspondent told the president that, after months of crisis, bankers he'd known for decades "have turned vicious and mean."

Hoover considered the bankers' continued anxiety to be "perfectly disastrous." By April, Meyer, too, was losing heart, a colleague at the Fed noting that, "His former optimism has entirely gone." Nor were the problems strictly financial. Industrial production continued its long, dismal decline, and unemployment its commensurate climb, these critical indicators impervious to all efforts to brake their grim progress.

Still, Hoover and his financial team stuck with their program. At a meeting of the Fed's Open Market Policy Conference in April, Meyer, Ogden Mills, and Hoover's old ally Adolph Miller squared off with the more conservative members to demand a renewed effort at credit expansion. "Congress and the administration had done all they could in developing remedial action," Mills said, "and yet deterioration was taking place steadily." The one tool remaining was to accelerate the open market purchasing program.

Faced with the dire economic data and a united administration team, the Fed governors signed on. Commencing April 12, the Fed Reserve entered into the largest bill-buying program in the short history of America's central bank, purchasing a billion dollars' worth of government securities in just four months.

Nothing happened. Despite the weekly injection of large amounts of cash into circulation, no more lending took place, and business activity did not increase. Banks used the easier credit terms to further boost liquidity, reducing their borrowings from the Fed, and stockpiling excess reserves. At the same time, alarmed to see the Fed shift into what appeared a baldly inflationary posture, France and other gold standard countries began a new round of gold withdrawals. This brought a new round of pressure on banks across America, and spread more fear among depositors.

Bank closures began to climb again, news that Hoover kept close tabs on in Washington. In mid-May, Secretary of State Stimson, arrived from another diplomatic sojourn abroad, took lunch with Hoover but found him sorely distracted. "The poor man was very much distressed by the economic situation," Stimson recorded. "That was the only thing on his mind. He started our luncheon conversation by saying that he could only hope that the country could avoid a crash for three weeks and he would feel happier than he was today."

Herbert Hoover was prone to pessimism but in this instance his misgivings were well placed. The bank failures spiked again in June, with Chicago at the center of the storm.

Chicago was especially vulnerable to financial contagion due to widespread misfeasance by both public and private interests. The city best known for the flagrant depredations of gangsters like Al Capone was also poorly managed and nearly bankrupt; in March the municipal government suspended all payments to city employees. The private sector ran along the same lines. Bank balance sheets were rife with overvalued real estate loans, and the April bankruptcy of Sam Insull, the city's biggest utility tycoon, wiped out many thousands of stockholders.

One immediate casualty of the problems in Chicago was Charles Dawes, president of the Reconstruction Finance Corp. As with Mellon in Pittsburgh, Dawes was technically insulated from the operations of his family's bank in Chicago but remained the genius behind it, and with trouble mounting he decided his only course was to return to Illinois. He announced his intention to Hoover in late May, but the president pleaded for time. By June 6, with withdrawals from his Central Republic National Bank running at $2 million a day, Dawes resigned the RFC.

The crisis accelerated from there. By June 24 runs had forced forty Chicago-area banks to close. That afternoon, a Saturday, large crowds appeared in the downtown Loop, converging on the five major banks located there. At First National Bank, the city's largest, president Melvin Traylor averted closure only by calming a panicked depositors with a speech delivered from a plinth in the bank's marbled lobby.

That night Dawes decided that come Monday morning he would call in creditors and depositors and close his family's bank for good. Here Traylor intervened. Dawes had to hold on, he insisted; if Central Republic were to close the rest of the banks on the Loop would have to follow suit, leaving the Second City without a single functioning fiduciary institution and threatening a national crisis. When Dawes resisted, Traylor insisted on a call to the president in Washington.

President Hoover was up at his Rapidan retreat for the weekend, but was quite aware of the debacle unfolding in Chicago and he readily accepted Traylor's call. He promptly consulted Ogden Mills and Eugene Meyer and determined the RFC should step in to keep the bank open. That night and all of the next day the president was on the phone, talking with the officers of the RFC and principals in Chicago to cobble together a prospective bailout. When the New York banks declined to participate, it was decided the federal government would put up $90 million from the RFC against a paltry $5 million commitment from other institutions in Illinois. The main point, as Hoover emphasized in calls to Chicago, was to "Save that bank!"

The deal wasn't settled until the early hours of Monday morning, Hoover working the phones constantly to keep the bankers on track. But come the beginning of business hours Dawes's Central Republic opened its doors, as did the other major Chicago banks. All parties agreed to keep the RFC loan a secret, as exposure would only highlight the bank's vulnerability. But closure had been averted, at least for the moment.

By the middle of June the policymakers at the Federal Reserve were coming to question their commitment to quantitative easing. Member banks had piled up the highest level of excess reserves on record, with no appreciable increase in lending. And while the new reserve requirements gave more flexibility under the gold standard, the renewed gold drain once again pushed several Federal Reserve Banks up against their reserve limits. By July, despite objections from Eugene Meyer and George Harrison, the Fed voted against continued purchases of government securities.

Meyer and Harrison were Hoover's advocates at the Fed, but in this case the president aligned with the board majority. When it came to monetary easing, Hoover had seen enough. He acknowledged in his memoirs that credit expansion through open market operations was "one part of the theory upon which the Reserve System was founded," but decided, after four months of aggressive purchases, that "the public was not disposed to take advantage of the increased credit." With the public fearful and investors pessimistic, Hoover said, monetary easing "had no effect whatsoever."

Hoover rendered this verdict in 1952, twenty years after the moment of decision. His thinking at the time was less sharply defined—it was he, after all, who sponsored the policy just a few months before. But he considered the initiative experimental, and the results appeared inconclusive at best.

Nor was there any theoretical guidance on the effects of monetary expansion. Congress held hearings on banking policy that spring—part of a continuing search for answers to the maddening paradox of the Depression—and the testimony showed expert opinion to be fundamentally divided.

Irving Fisher, the debt deflation theorist and America's best-known economist, endorsed the policy of easing, as well as proposals for heavy spending on public works. But, as he acknowledged during an appearance before the Senate Committee on Banking and Currency in May, these policies could well require "varying the gold content of the dollar"—a euphemism for moving off the gold standard.

Come July, Fisher went further, endorsing a novel but wildly impractical proposal for a "stamped dollar," which would encourage spending by requiring holders to affix a one-cent stamp each week it remained in their possession. Ideas of this sort proliferated in the dark days of the crisis—and confirmed Hoover in his skepticism of such innovations.

Hoover was more taken with the thinking of Edwin Kemmerer, a Princeton economist and, like Fisher, a former president of the American Economic Association. Hoover consulted Kemmerer at the White House in late 1931, and maintained a correspondence thereafter. Like Fisher—and like Hoover—Kemmerer considered the supply of money critical to recovery, but he was chiefly concerned with how that money was used. That is, he focused on the "velocity" of money—how often each dollar changed hands—as opposed to the number of dollars outstanding.

This led Kemmerer to put greater emphasis on the intangibles of confidence and stability than Fisher and some other expansionists. In one missive to Hoover, Kemmerer deplored "the radical and half-baked monetary plans that such a period always bring forward," and suggested that continued expansion would drive the country off the gold standard. In turn, that would lead to more fear and more liquidation. "All this would spell deflation," Kemmerer insisted.

Economists have been debating these questions since the time of the October crash, and today there is a clear consensus in favor of monetary ease. One of the leading architects of that consensus was Ben Bernanke, who spent years studying the Depression as a professor of economics at Princeton. In 2002 George W. Bush named Bernanke to the board of the Federal Reserve, and after the crash of 2009 Bernanke responded with an unprecedented program of quantitative easing to achieve monetary expansion. His patron had so imbibed Bernanke's credo that President Bush himself pronounced in 2004 that, "Aggressive monetary policy can make a recession shorter and milder."

As a corollary, Bernanke and his fellow Depression scholars believe that, once the deflation had set in, adherence to the gold standard was the principal factor in prolonging the slump. For evidence they point to the fact that, once Great Britain renounced gold, recovery began almost immediately; the same was true for most of the countries that followed her lead. In the countries that stuck with gold, mainly the United States and France, recovery came much later.

There was no such policy consensus in 1932. Faced with shattered paradigms but also a terrible urgency to chart a coherent course of action, Herbert Hoover had to innovate. He had done so from the time he took office, beginning with the Farm Board, then with his industrial conferences, his public works program, and then the moratorium on international debts. No matter how fast he moved or in what direction, the financial tsunami of the Depression seemed to wash out all his endeavors.

So it was with the effort to boost credit. Hoover recognized the ravages of deflation and the importance of resuscitating the financial system. Recognizing, too, that a policy of "reflation" ran counter to the imperatives of the gold standard, he managed to craft, with Carter Glass, new reserve requirements for the Federal Reserve that would make room for monetary easing. But that only staved off a final reckoning. When, after four months of rapid expansion, the central bank was again pushing the limits of the gold standard, Hoover was forced to choose.

In sampling and setting policy Hoover proved flexible and smart, even if he appeared indifferent to individual suffering. But when the crisis closed in around him and his administration, Hoover prized security above all—the security and stability of gold.

PART III

THE BITTER END

NINETEEN

ROOSEVELT RISING

LATE IN 1931 JAMES MACLAFFERTY RESUMED HIS POSITION AS Herbert Hoover's covert, unofficial political aide. Most of the men arrayed around the president were expert in particular aspects of policy or executive management, but with Hoover's reelection campaign looming in November, MacLafferty focused solely on the business of political warfare. "Every morning when I awake," he recorded in December, "the first thing I think is, 'What harm can I do Democratic prospects today?'"

Taut, circumspect, and disciplined, MacLafferty sometimes sought to stiffen the president's nerve, but usually he was satisfied simply to ascertain just what he could do for his Chief. MacLafferty was worldly and well informed, but he was also a true subordinate, narrow in his thinking and loyal to a fault.

Ruminating in his diary in late January, MacLafferty worried that Hoover was neglecting matters critical to his candidacy. The tide was running against him but nobody had the nerve to say so. "It is surely a test," MacLafferty acknowledged, "when one dares go to the President of the United States, at the beginning of another, for him, terrible day and tell him of things that have solely to do with his politics and things that can only be worrisome to him."

That day, and indeed through much of that winter, MacLafferty was juggling two distinct problems. The first was, simply put, Hoover's dismal standing with the public. "People all over the country who belong to his party are saying he should not run again but that he should step aside for someone else who will have a chance to win," MacLafferty worried. "The very people he is trying to save are many of them literally cursing him."

Hoover himself was not so sure. At one point, perusing press coverage of one of his speeches, the president gazed out the window over the White House grounds and wondered aloud. "I wish I had some way of knowing how that speech was taken by the man in the street," he told MacLafferty. It was impossible to say at a time when polling was in its infancy, but that uncertainty provided Hoover with a margin of comfort. "Business is fickle," Hoover said on another occasion, "but the common people have never been very far away from me."

"I hope they are," was MacLafferty's immediate response, but that was the best he could muster. As he well knew, for several weeks both he and the president had received only bad tidings from even fellow Republicans. Hoover told him soon after the New Year that he heard that Senator Arthur Vandenberg was seeking to draft Charles Dawes to run in Hoover's stead. Around the same time, Harold Knutson, longtime Republican representative of Minnesota, told MacLafferty flat-out, "Hoover is sunk."

In MacLafferty's tendentious mind, the blame for Hoover's crumbling support could not rest with the president himself; it had to lie without. That led naturally enough to the second problem, which was the combination of forces arrayed against his hero. Political animal that he was, MacLafferty saw these forces rooted in power, not policy; the elemental contest over who would rule. "Hoover's enemies in the party and out are feeding all the poison they can," he mused darkly. The most dangerous of these hostiles, MacLafferty posited, hailed from the Republican old guard. "I shall not cease to suspect and watch those who, before his nomination, did all in their power to destroy him."

It was treachery, then, that was doing the damage, and driving popular opinion before it. MacLafferty wrestled with these competing themes as he composed his journal, managing to fuse them into a single vindication of his beleaguered leader. "How true it is," wrote the onetime congressman, "that a president becomes more and more isolated as he continues in office, and largely because his friends, because of the intrigues of his enemies, are driven from his confidence."

Unfortunately for Hoover, it never occurred either to him or to MacLafferty that their shared sense of suspicion and persecution only made matters worse. Nor did they consider that, by repeatedly rejecting every initiative from the Democrats, the president ensured that all the anger and frustration arising from a historic economic collapse would accrue to him alone.

The president and his counselors did not need to seek further than the Capitol dome to turn up the single glaring cause of Hoover's sinking reputation. There, beginning in December, Senate Committee on Manufactures chairman Bob La Follette was conducting an open-ended hearing on the state of unemployment.

Hoover found the whole subject tiresome—hadn't this all been hashed out just a year before?—but there was no escaping a phenomenon that, over the course of the year 1931, had grown from a sectional social problem to a fearsome, unprecedented scourge. At some point between 1930 and 1931 the jobless rate entered double digits; by New Year's Day of 1932 the rate exceeded 20 percent.

Those are national figures, stark but sterile, broad enough to smooth over regional and local conditions that seem hard to credit. Consider: a survey in Chicago found 40 percent unemployment among men and women "customarily" employed, with 100,000 families on public relief. Smaller industrial towns like Dayton and Akron saw unemployment spike over 80 percent; in other locales, further afield, modern economic life all but ceased. The town of Tenino, Washington, was reduced to barter when its last bank failed; the local Chamber of Commerce put out wooden nickels to keep business moving.

These dire circumstances were described during the Senate hearings by a succession of public officials and social workers. They won sympathetic consideration from some of the Hoover administration's most ardent critics—La Follette, New York Democrat Robert Wagner, Republican in-

surgent James Couzens—but there was no need to embellish on the witness
testimony. Speakers like Gifford Pinchot, Progressive governor of Pennsylvania, made the connections for them, denouncing administration policy as
"vicious."

President Hoover endured this stretch of opprobrium in silence. The
committee did, however, call Walter Gifford, of the President's Organization for Unemployment Relief, to speak for the administration. Two days
before his appearance, Gifford huddled in the White House for forty minutes with Hoover, but preparation did not appear to help their cause. Under
skeptical inquiry Gifford could offer no firm estimate of the current number
of Americans out of work, but blandly insisted that local committees had
resources sufficient to get through the winter. As to a role for government,
Gifford stuck to Hoover's script. "My sober and considered judgment is that
at this stage. . . . Federal aid would be a disservice to the unemployed."

It was an awkward and difficult performance that persuaded nobody—
not even, apparently, Walter Gifford. His appearance before the Senate
was his last public act as head of the POUR; within a month he was telling friends privately that the federal government must step in after all, that
mass unemployment was too much for private charity and local government
to handle. To Hoover it was another case of a man failing to live up to expectations. "He's been a sorry disappointment," Hoover said of Gifford in
February. "He lacks the qualities I thought he possessed."

In the first few weeks of the 72nd Congress Hoover coolly ignored the renewed clamor for some sort of relief to the unemployed. Instead he hammered on the theme of cutting costs, placing the balanced budget at the
center of his reform program. "Our first duty as a nation is to put our governmental house in order," the president said in January. "With the return
of prosperity the government can undertake projects both of a social character and in public improvement, but we just cannot squander our way into
prosperity."

As in the debates over food aid a year before, Hoover's hard line drew
a shower of epithets from his critics. The president suffered the calumny in
solitary silence, stalking the hallways of the White House tight-lipped and

distracted. His intimates felt his anguish keenly. "I here give my testimony that Herbert Hoover wants people to like him and that it is a cause for grief when he thinks they do not," James MacLafferty effused that gloomy winter. "More than that, he is one of the greatest humanitarians the world has ever known."

To be reviled for doing right, MacLafferty decided, was the price of Hoover's high station. "He is now suffering under the bitter disillusionment that comes to all those who are placed in life as he is. He is having his Gethsemane."

But if it's true that Hoover suffered, it was not in lonely sacrifice to lofty convictions. Hoover's zealous defense of the public purse won the endorsement of much of the political establishment at the time. It was a policy Hoover believed in, but it was also one he thought would win him a second term.

The point was emphasized repeatedly in discussion inside the administration. There had been a raft of relief bills introduced early in the session—they were put on hold long enough to establish the RFC—and Hoover's advisors were spoiling for a showdown. Such a confrontation "would cause the sane people of the country to line up behind him," MacLafferty told Hoover in February.

Hoover would not get that satisfaction. At this early stage, the advocates for relief were divided over leadership and strategy. Bob La Follette authored what might be termed the baseline relief bill for that session—$375 million in grants to the states for direct, cash relief. Rather than join forces, Senator Robert Wagner advanced his own bill, this for $750 million, but charging the funds as loans to the states against future federal road projects. A third bill, from a separate clutch of Senate Democrats and again funded at $750 million, would loan only to states that could no longer borrow, and provide only work relief—no dole. Against this array administration allies mounted a solid front in opposition, rehearsing the old arguments against pork-barrel spending, the evils of the dole, and the erosion of state and local responsibility.

With the activists in Congress divided, the La Follette bill was rejected in the Senate by a twelve-vote margin on February 16. Robert Wagner, inveterate champion of the unemployed, introduced his replacement bill the next day, but at this point Hoover and the administration clearly had the upper hand. By March, Hoover was getting impatient for Congress to advance a jobs bill just so he could strike it down. "I mean it," he complained to his press secretary. "The country is ripe to spike any move against [government] economy." Two weeks later, Ted Joslin confirmed to the president that, in conversations with constituents from all over the country, he was hearing a "universal demand for the utmost government economy."

And so Hoover pressed what he called a program of "drastic economy," which consisted of "resolute opposition" to any rise in spending, and increased taxes. Even so, Hoover noted ruefully, the government would incur a deficit for 1932 of more than $2 billion. "Nothing is more important than balancing the budget with the least increase in taxes," Hoover reiterated in March.

One principal reason Hoover was able to stave off federal assistance to the unemployed, even as the country entered into a third winter of depression, was that his political opponents never mounted much of an alternative. Cries for vigorous action were raised in the Senate by lawmakers from both parties, but the Democrats who controlled the national party in 1932 agreed in principle with most of the Hoover program.

It was more than just a political question. To some degree the general accord favoring government austerity was rooted in a collective sense of guilt left over from the heady and heedless time before the Wall Street crash. "Our troubles today are in very large part due to the theory that anything our hearts desired . . . could be had painlessly and promptly by borrowing money," Walter Lippmann chided. "The nations borrowed to pay for the war," Lippmann recounted. "Then they borrowed in order to finance prosperity. Then they borrowed to finance the depression." It was high time to end this spiral of spending, Lippmann held. "It is a sign of returning sanity that the Administration has at last decided to begin paying its way by economy and taxes rather than by contracting more and more debts."

That conviction was nearly as strong among Democrats as Republicans. The dominant figure in the Democratic Party at the time was, in fact, a former Republican—John Raskob, the party chairman who bankrolled the op-

erations of Jouet Shouse and the poison-penned Charley Michelson. It was
Raskob who made Al Smith a national candidate in 1928, and after Hoover's
victory, Raskob invited Smith to take up offices in his new skyscraper, the
Empire State Building. With the approach of a new electoral cycle Raskob
was again backing Al Smith, or, as a second choice, Woodrow Wilson protégé
Newton Baker—both fiscal conservatives—for the Democratic nomination.

In the same vein, the leading Democrat in Congress, speaker Jack Garner, was just as adamant as Hoover that taxes should be raised to cover the
deficit. Garner was a politician defined more by character and friendships
than by party affiliation. He shared a car with his predecessor, Republican
speaker Nicholas Longworth, and joined Longworth in hosting regular,
after-hours, illegal drinks in a capitol garret that they dubbed the Board of
Education. Coarse like the Texas district he hailed from, Garner earned the
sobriquet "Cactus Jack" for his earnest but failed campaign to see the bloom
of the prickly pear named the state flower. Not one to trouble with ideological consistency, Garner was a big advocate for federal jobs programs, but he
was the president's strongest ally on the question of a balanced budget.

Garner's commitment to fiscal restraint produced a moment of high the-
ater in March, after House Democrats rejected a sales tax initially proposed
by leaders of their own party as the best means to balance the budget. Garner
was so shaken by the reversal that he felt obliged to take the floor and, evan-
gelical style, lead a profession of faith. "I am now opposed to a sales tax," he
told his raucous congregation of representatives. "But gentlemen, if I find it
impossible to balance the budget and restore the confidence of the world and
our own people in our government without some such tax I would levy any
tax, sales or any other kind in order to do that."

Garner then called upon the members to show their allegiance, asking
those who believed in a balanced budget to rise from his seat. On cue, the
entire body stood, a demonstration of solidarity but also of utter confusion.

President Hoover responded to the imbroglio in the House cautiously,
even generously. His advisors pressed him to "take a fling at Congress,"
judging that "the country is ripe for a crack at the nation's legislators." But
Hoover recognized it could only accrue to his benefit to have leading Democrats promoting his principles. On this occasion the president counseled co-

operation. "My role must be that of pacificator," Hoover told Ted Joslin. "I must strive to bring the contending factions together."

Standing outside the circle of congressional Democrats, emerging as a power in his own right, was the ebullient governor of New York. Franklin Delano Roosevelt shared the same home state as Al Smith, and had succeeded him as governor from the same party, but Smith never found in Roosevelt the deference he felt was his due. For his part, Roosevelt never abandoned the national ambitions put on view when he accepted the party's nomination for vice president in 1920.

Roosevelt's rise was knocked off course in 1921 when he contracted polio, which left him paralyzed from the waist down. But the illness proved a political blessing, holding him out of the dismal Democratic defeat of 1924 while making him a sympathetic, even tragic figure. Recovering his strength to win election as New York governor in 1928, Roosevelt so concili-ated Gotham's Tammany machine with the state's rural Progressives that he was returned to office in 1930 by a record 750,000 votes—double the high-est margin ever posted by Smith. With personal ties to the South, where he converted a resort in Warm Springs, Georgia, into a polio treatment center, and his prior turn in the national spotlight, Roosevelt emerged by 1932 as the front-runner for his party's nomination to take on Hoover.

Roosevelt was popular and free of political entanglements, but he suf-fered for his airy demeanor and a reputation as something of a dilettante. *The New Republic*, in 1931, deemed him "a liberal-minded man, of excellent intentions," but "not a man of great intellectual force." A year later Walter Lippmann scored the governor for cynically—and obviously—embracing both sides of the "great questions" of the day. Roosevelt was "too eager to please," Lippmann sniffed; "He is a pleasant man who, without any impor-tant qualifications for the office, would very much like to be president."

But the skepticism of the kingmakers freed Roosevelt from the pol-icy consensus of the establishment in both parties. As governor Roosevelt showed a lively interest in the plight of the unemployed and the elderly poor; the Depression seemed to warrant exploring such themes on a na-tional scale.

Entering the election season in earnest, Roosevelt moved to placate the isolationists of his party by repudiating U.S. participation in the League of Nations. But any notion he would close ranks with the old guard and battle Hoover for the political center Roosevelt erased with a national radio address in April. There he denounced Hoover's recovery program as a top-down strategy that did nothing to answer the privations afflicting "the little fellow." This was his "Forgotten Man" speech, where Roosevelt cast his lot with "the infantry of our economic army."

It was a startling change in the tenor of the national discourse, and it was Roosevelt's alone. Distancing himself from the Democrats of the Senate, he dismissed the idea of "a huge expenditure of public funds" as "only a stop-gap," one of "the illusions of economic magic." Nor did Roosevelt propose any specific alternative plan. Instead he derided the Reconstruction Finance Corporation as "the two billion dollar fund which President Hoover and the Congress have put at the disposal of the big banks, the railroads and the corporations." In Hoover's single-minded focus on the salvaging America's credit apparatus, Roosevelt found "a national administration which can think in terms only of the top of the social and economic structure. It has sought temporary relief from the top down rather than permanent relief from the bottom up."

In the months to come Roosevelt would alter course repeatedly, first in his drive for the nomination and then in the national campaign. But he never strayed far from the theme he laid down in that seminal April address. Henceforth, the Squire of Hyde Park, as he was known to friend and foe, would stand as tribune for "the forgotten man at the bottom of the economic pyramid."

The politician most startled by Franklin Roosevelt's unexpected appeal to the economic underdog was Al Smith. Taking the podium two weeks later, at the Democratic Party's annual Jefferson Day Dinner in Washington, Smith lashed out against his rival.

"I protest against the endeavor to delude the poor people of this country to their ruin by trying to make them believe that they can get employment before the people who would ordinarily employ them are again restored to conditions of normal prosperity," Smith said, offering a tacit endorsement of Hoover's recovery program.

The Happy Warrior was known for his pluck and his verve, but he was far from happy that day. "I will take off my coat and vest," Smith vowed, "and fight to the end any candidate who persists in any demagogic appeal to the masses of the working people of this country to destroy themselves by setting class against class and rich against poor!"

We can presume that President Hoover shared Smith's disdain for the way Roosevelt depicted the administration's recovery strategy, but he did not share Smith's anger. To the contrary, Hoover firmly believed that the American electorate held the same views as the established political parties. Like Lippmann, the president considered Roosevelt too changeable, too baldly political, to be taken seriously. After all, Roosevelt had for years hewed to Hoover's line that relief for the unemployed was a strictly local affair; only now was he endorsing federal intervention. "He's a trimmer," Hoover judged at one point, "not a constructive leader." Several times that winter, Hoover and his advisors asserted that Al Smith and Newton Baker were the candidates they feared, and not Roosevelt.

This was more than just lip service. Days after Smith's Jefferson Day tirade against Roosevelt, MacLafferty informed Hoover that a staffer at the Democratic National Committee was trying to peddle damaging political dirt on Roosevelt. Hoover warned him to stay away. "I hope they do nothing to destroy Roosevelt politically before his nomination," the president said. "We want him for the candidate."

Hoover's aides, always ready to defer to their Chief, followed his lead. "I would prefer Roosevelt to almost any other leading Democrat for the president's opponent," Ted Joslin recorded in February; the candidate Joslin feared most was the streetwise Al Smith.

In March, MacLafferty was pleased to report that Roosevelt was gaining strength among what he termed Progressives and radicals. "They are more and more proclaiming him as their leader," MacLafferty told the president, "and that will scare even the small home-owner to death."

A month later Hoover's team took a more direct role in promoting the future nominee. They learned from Walter Gifford in New York that Smith and Raskob, the leading stop-Roosevelt Democrats, had quietly teamed with Bernard Baruch to throw their support to the prominent industrialist Owen Young. Hoover wanted to scuttle this plot in the offing. "Their game is to keep this arrangement secret," Ted Joslin recorded in his diary. "As it is to our advantage to keep Roosevelt as far out in front as possible, I leaked the information." When word surfaced that the Democrats were cutting deals to sabotage Roosevelt, Young promptly pulled his hat from the ring.

It wasn't just a question of policies and ballots. Hoover believed he held a physical advantage over Roosevelt, whose rehabilitation had progressed to the point where he could make appearances and deliver speeches, but who still needed heavy, painful leg braces just to stand erect. "He shouldn't think of running," Hoover exclaimed in April, after Roosevelt lost a major primary. "He's a sick man," the president said sharply. "He wouldn't last a year in the White House."

There's no reason to doubt the authenticity of these remarks, recorded by Hoover's closest advisors, but one cannot escape the sense that, to some degree, the president was whistling in the dark. It was Hoover, after all, who was showing the strain from years of unbroken crisis and work. And it was Roosevelt who was steadily gaining endorsements and momentum.

These intangibles were brought into close focus at the end of April, when governors from more than half the states gathered for an annual conference in Richmond, Virginia. As per custom, Hoover invited the governors to join him at a White House dinner for the following day. In addition, Hoover decided to address the governors at Richmond. He did so impulsively, but also imperiously, requesting, at the last minute, a formal invitation. The governors could hardly refuse the president, and the request was extended, with a special session scheduled for his appearance.

In the event, there was an uncomfortable juxtaposition at Richmond— uncomfortable for the president, anyway. Hoover was all business. He arrived by train at 1:56 p.m., reached the conference at 2:05, addressed the governors five minutes later, and departed five minutes after his speech was done. Hoover kept his trip secret until the day prior, believing a sudden, surprise appearance would "galvanize the attention of the country." In contrast, Roosevelt was on hand for two full days, hobnobbing with reporters and fellow governors, reaping headlines and chatting easily about election prospects.

The speeches, too, were different and distinct. Hoover's was a stern warning that the states had to cut back spending, just as the federal government was doing, or all would face "national impoverishment." He then expounded on "the difficulties that all executives face," lecturing on budget cuts and tax schemes in a mode that the governors could only find condescending. Maryland's governor responded that afternoon, telling reporters that his state "did not need the president's advice."

Roosevelt's address, given at a separate conclave that evening, was more fanciful, but carried a sharp edge. He took as his theme George Washington, to whom the conference was dedicated. Some historians considered Washington "ultra-conservative," Roosevelt suggested, but his policies were "far reaching and liberal for the time." The founder should serve as a model, Roosevelt said, "at this hour . . . when new problems and new valuations call for a new leadership." That was the first of several digs at Hoover; another proposed that Washington "reasoned directly from what he saw to what he thought ought to be done by the government, not disturbing his mind by mere efforts to reconcile conflicting schools of economic theory." It was a novel rendering of the Sage of Mount Vernon, but the reference to the current administration was clear.

The minuet of upstart and incumbent resumed the next evening at Hoover's reception for the governors. Roosevelt arrived at the White House separately from the others, entered by a rear door, and had a butler assigned to assist him, all to help conceal his disability. Once the group was assembled, however, they stood for half an hour to await Hoover's arrival, a delay that Eleanor Roosevelt suspected was intentional, "as though he were being deliberately put through an endurance test." But if malice was intended, it gained Hoover no advantage. Roosevelt breezed through the dinner, and during a whistle-stop on his way in from Richmond was hailed by a platform crowd as "the next president."

Nor did Hoover's appearance at the governors conference accrue to his advantage. That weekend the president made his first visit that year to his Rapidan retreat. He did some fishing, caught an afternoon nap, and spent the evening in company of more than twenty friends, including several members of his cabinet, settled under the trees in their rough-hewn, stand-alone cabins. They gathered that night before the great fireplace in the main cabin to look at newsreel footage from his appearance at Richmond. But the evening was spoiled as the black-and-white images flickered across the screen. The president was appalled to find himself looking worn and haggard, while Roosevelt, posing for still photographs, appeared young and vigorous. "They made me look as though I was 82 years old!" Hoover complained to his press secretary. The contrast was so disturbing that Lou Hoover broke down in tears.

There was no denying the truth of what the newsreel cameras revealed. Voters of every era are familiar with the rapid aging that presidents undergo—the premature gray, the new lines to the face—but Hoover was an extreme case, his eyes hollowed, his visage haunted with disillusion.

It couldn't be helped. The continuing, historic breakdown in the economy was bad enough, but that was just the most pressing of the incessant claims on his energy, his attention, and his time.

Foreign pressures alone could have kept the president and his administration fully occupied. In September 1931, a week before England abandoned the gold standard, Japan invaded Manchuria. This incursion into mainland China posed the first great test for the several international treaties then in place—the Nine-Power Pact, Kellogg-Briand, and the still new League of Nations—and drew Hoover and Secretary Henry Stimson into a protracted and vexing consultation.

Both Hoover and Stimson condemned such unprovoked aggression, but where Stimson wanted to challenge Japan with some sort of threat, either military or economic, Hoover would go no further than diplomatic pressure. In particular, Hoover rejected economic sanctions as "war measures"—a first step toward armed intervention. Here the president and his secretary of state divided over basic principles: where Hoover was a committed pacifist, he considered Stimson "at times more of a warrior than a diplomat."

After several months and much debate the two hit upon a compromise:

formal notice to Japan that the United States would refuse to recognize any territorial gains obtained by force. This came to be known as the Stimson Doctrine, but in truth it was a compromise position that Stimson chafed under and at times resisted. It suited Hoover, however, and he made it the standard for American foreign relations. It was especially useful in application to Latin America, affording principled grounds on which to challenge internal revolts and invasions by neighbor states without resort to direct intervention.

Through this same period Stimson was negotiating a new round of disarmament talks in Geneva. This again exposed the division between the executive and the State Department; when Hoover suggested in April that Stimson propose a series of drastic measures—abolition of all tanks, large guns, and most military aircraft—Stimson bridled. To his world-weary eye, the president's plan was "just a proposition from Alice and Wonderland." In the end they were both proved right. When Hoover floated his proposal through an ambassador in Geneva, it won endorsement from thirty-eight nations, but was adopted by none.

Inside the White House, the threat of war in Asia was matched by the intensity of the incessant conflict with Congress. Several times Stimson had to defer consultations with the president because Hoover was so hard-pressed. "I could see his work was lying very heavily on him," Stimson wrote of Hoover in February. "Things are going very badly in the country and he is under great pressure." Three months later the refrain was the same. "The president is, of course, in his terrible battle with Congress and can think of nothing else."

It was not just at Hoover's end. The unremitting economic crisis, combined with the intensity of resentment against Hoover's intransigence, kept the entire legislature on edge. "This has been the most strenuous session we've ever had," said Mississippi Democrat Pat Harrison. Nevada's Key Pittman, first elected to the Senate in 1913, was sorry to pronounce, "conditions of the War were nothing like these."

Hoover's intimates used a similar analogy to describe the president's situation. "The effort now is twice what it was nine months ago," Ted Joslin wrote in January, "and then it was greater than at any time since the World

War." Joslin was familiar with Hoover's work ethic, but with the pressure building, the pace seemed only to accelerate. "This cannot continue indefinitely," Joslin ruled. "There has to be a breaking point somewhere."

Hoover did not break, but he did begin to bend. He had learned something from his earlier setbacks at the hands of Congress, and where formerly he drew a hard line, he began to compromise. He did so partly in service to his urgent priority on fiscal and monetary policy, which required a degree of collaboration with lawmakers of both parties. But it's hard not to suspect that sheer fatigue played a role as well.

Hoover showcased his new approach to Congress upon the retirement in January of Oliver Wendell Holmes from the Supreme Court. Hoover's first instinct was to turn the seat over to William D. Mitchell, his attorney general, but he recognized it could stir a rebellion in the Senate as had the appointment of John Parker two years before. After some reflection, Hoover settled on New York appellate judge Benjamin Cardozo, a Democrat and a confirmed liberal.

Hoover chose Cardozo out of respect for judicial balance, recognizing Holmes as a leader of the liberal wing on the court. But there were also "political considerations," as Ted Joslin recorded in February. "The president must look to the East this year for re-election," Joslin wrote, "with that and avoiding a bad Senate fight in mind, he gave Cardozo the post."

It was not an undisputed selection. Two of the more conservative associate justices asked that the president not "afflict the court with another Jew," but Hoover ignored them. In the event, Cardozo was confirmed swiftly, and shared lunch with Hoover at the White House the following day. Senator Clarence Dill, Democrat of Washington, took to the radio soon after to pronounce Hoover's selection of Cardozo "the finest act of his career as president."

Hoover compromised, too, when Congress voted in January to donate forty million bushels of Farm Board wheat to the Red Cross for distribution to the hungry and the unemployed. He still believed that grants of free food would undermine individual initiative, but he couldn't stand the prospect of another emotional battle with Congress. "I can't afford, at a time like this, to say this must not be done simply because it violates a correct principle," Hoover said after the vote. "The only thing I can do when the bill reaches me is to sign it."

When the bill arrived in March, Hoover stalled, consulting with John Barton Payne of the Red Cross and Attorney General Mitchell to sort out technical issues in the law. But the outcome was never in question; the Farm Board was sitting on 160 million bushels, half the 1931 crop was still on the farm, and wheat was still selling below cost. With nowhere else to put the stuff, Hoover authorized the transfer.

Hoover dodged another Senate fight when Congress passed an anti-injunction act, which barred the yellow-dog contracts that figured so large in the defeat of Judge Parker. Senator George Norris, the Nebraska insurgent and sponsor of the bill, had pulled it from consideration in 1930 partly because he believed Hoover to be adamant in opposition, though Hoover never did make public comment on the bill. Two years later, with Democrats stronger in Congress and with yellow-dog contracts now considered an emblem of employer exploitation, Norris drafted Fiorello La Guardia as his partner in the House and the bill won quick passage.

Hoover harbored no love for Norris, and while he had always maintained friendly relations with organized labor, he weighed the new bill carefully. So did Attorney General Mitchell, who raised several small criticisms, but advised that Hoover would do better to sign the law than dig in for a battle with the Senate. Political aide Walter Newton and Labor Secretary William Doak both reached outside the White House to propose minor amendments, but when the bill reached Hoover's desk in early March the president signed off without objection.

These were small concessions, examples of the sort of flexibility that would have served Hoover well early in his term, but which he always resisted. It's hard to attribute this shift in attitude solely to the upcoming presidential election; it could well have been a simple matter of progress on the learning curve. At long last, Hoover was figuring out how to play the game.

But in May Hoover made another, more fundamental compromise, one that contradicted his strict doctrine against federal action in local relief. This was clearly a case of the president changing course to meet the electoral challenge of the Democrats. Such an accommodation is not particularly shocking, even when it involves so obstinate a candidate as Bert Hoover. What is surprising here is that it was not Roosevelt that Hoover feared, but one of his dark-horse Democratic rivals, Owen Young.

The catalyst for the president's about-face was Joseph Robinson, the Arkansas Democrat and Hoover's sparring partner from the 71st Congress. On May 11, Robinson offered a major new relief bill—$300 million in loans to the states to help with aid to the unemployed, and another $2 billion for infrastructure projects that would put people to work. "I believe the time has arrived," Robinson told the Senate, "when action should be taken by the federal government."

The announcement came as something of a wake-up call at the White House. Having driven the relief bills from the field in February, Hoover and his advisors felt they were in full control of the national agenda. Just a week before, Hoover had blistered the Congress with another of his stern declarations, asserting that, "Nothing is more necessary at this time than balancing the budget." That meant cuts in operations, raising new taxes, and a "determined stand in defeating unwise and unnecessary legislation."

Hoover's message won praise from the press, which by and large subscribed to the idea of a balanced budget, and blamed the Democrats for Congress's failure to achieve it. His tone was "bitter and savage," the Baltimore *Sun* pronounced, but it was only what the Democrats deserved. The president "stands forth as a figure of consistency and stability in contrast with a Congress destitute of purpose and will." *New York Times* correspondent Arthur Krock was even more taken with Hoover's initiative. "It was a bullseye," Krock announced in a news analysis. "Like Washington's surprise victory at Trenton."

But while the pundits and the party leaders were focused on the budget, it was the deepening despair of the poor and unemployed that captured the attention of mainstream Democrats like Robinson. As early as January, Bernard Baruch decided he could no longer adhere to the idea that poverty was strictly a state concern; in March, he proposed to Robinson a new jobs program based on federal funding for "self-liquidating" public works—

projects like toll bridges and hydroelectric dams that would pay for themselves. This was a challenge to Hoover; it was also an answer to Roosevelt, and his appeal to the Forgotten Man.

Up to the moment Robinson rolled out his proposal Hoover was occupied solely with his "economy program"—his drive to cut government spending. But he quickly came around, his progress marked by stages in Ted Joslin's diary entries. On May 10, a Tuesday, word reached the White House that Robinson would float a jobs plan, but that Owen Young was its true sponsor. Joslin told Hoover this would play right into the president's hands, that "the people would not stand for such use of government funds." Hoover was not so sure.

A day later, once Robinson's speech in the Senate confirmed the rumor of a big jobs program, Hoover was furious. He'd been planning a jobs program himself, he told Joslin, based on self-liquidating projects to be funded through the RFC. He hadn't mentioned it publicly yet, but there it was, now in Robinson's name. "It's a complete steal!" Hoover fumed. And immediately, he ascribed blame. "Gifford leaked," the president snapped; he'd shared his plans with Walter Gifford, who had talked to Owen Young, and "Young had given the ideas to Robinson."

Whether Hoover actually had such a plan—and whether Gifford leaked it—is hard to say. None of the jobs proposals were especially new, of course; variants had been floating around Washington for months. But the prospect of Owen Young stepping into the picture gave Hoover the shivers. Unlike Franklin Roosevelt, Young had the sort of solid, real-world credentials Hoover respected and feared. Young was a self-made man, raised on a farm, who parlayed a law degree into a career as a corporate executive and a part-time diplomat. Like Charles Dawes, he figured prominently in the protracted talks over international war debts. There was a Dawes Plan, the fruits of one round of talks, and then, in 1929, a Young Plan, for which *Time* magazine named him Man of the Year.

Hoover had tried to keep Young close, appointing him to several of his commissions, at Commerce and then at the White House. Now, faced with the specter of Young as a presidential candidate, Hoover made a decision. "We have got to prevent Robinson and the Democrats from snatching all the credit for aid to the states and for relief work," the president told Joslin. Thereupon, the president "went into action immediately," meeting with James Watson, Charles Dawes, Ogden Mills, and Eugene Meyer, and then calling in a startled Joe Robinson.

The next day, May 12, Hoover made an announcement of his own. He was sponsoring a billion-dollar plan to stimulate business, relieve the states, and assist the unemployed.

The president opened with an explanation. "The policy steadfastly adhered to up to the present time has been that responsibility for relief to distress belongs to private organizations, local communities, and the states. That fundamental policy is not to be changed." Until now.

"But," Hoover continued, "since the fear has arisen that existing relief measures and resources may prove inadequate in certain localities and to ensure against any possible breakdown in those localities," the Reconstruction Finance Corporation would loan to the states up to $300 million. Second, the RFC would be authorized to make loans to both state and private enterprises, provided in both cases that they be "self-liquidating"—meaning they would generate revenues to cover their cost.

Hoover's announcement was larded with caveats—projects must be "of a constructive replacement character," loans would be made "without entering the field of industry or public expansion," the RFC would avoid "works of largely artificial character"—but there was no disguising it: this was a federal relief bill, and complete reversal for the president.

Among those whipsawed by Hoover's conversion to federal aid was Eugene Meyer. Already close to collapse from his dual duties at both the Fed and the RFC, Meyer resisted the idea of expanding the responsibilities of the RFC to financing public relief and private business. Disappointed by the failure of the Fed's open market operation, isolated at the RFC and at the Fed, Meyer was now losing the confidence of the president.

The New York Times, generally sympathetic with the president's themes, if not his personage, framed Hoover's maneuver in gauzy terms. "The latest proposals mark a great improvement over earlier measures," the editors observed, and Hoover's plan "protects the taxpayer . . . in theory, at least." But if Hoover could claim a corrective influence, he could not claim authorship. "It represents in substance, if not in form, a victory for Senator La Follette and Senator Wagner and the rest who have hitherto poured their pleas for federal aid into deaf ears."

Hiram Johnson, always leery of his fellow Californian but jaded with politics in general, found the whole episode amusing. "The most interesting event of the past week," Johnson wrote home to his sons, "is the remarkable somersault turned by the president and the leaders of the Democratic Party." Johnson was agnostic on the policy question, but attuned to the evident hypocrisy. "Both the Democrats and Hoover camouflage their new scheme, but, nevertheless, it is federal aid extended for unemployment and for the destitute, the principle of which they have most emphatically denied in the past."

TWENTY

THE CONFLICTED CANDIDATE

THE COMMUNIST HUNGER MARCHERS WHO CONVERGED ON Washington to greet the new Congress in December failed to spark a revolution, but it appears they started a trend. In January a second march arrived in the capital, this one less militant but a good deal larger.

This was led by James Cox, a charismatic, activist priest who ran a soup kitchen outside a shantytown in Pittsburgh. Cox was struck that the thousands of newly poor in residence there had rejected the rhetoric of the left, and he reached out to them with an activist "social gospel." He found success where communist organizers had failed, mustering more than six thousand men for a trek to Washington.

Cox gave speeches along the way, marking his band and his movement as peaceable, but not docile. "Our president is still trying to give money to the bankers, but none to the people," Cox told an audience in Johnstown, seventy miles outside Pittsburgh. "We are going to rededicate this country to the principle that every man has a right to life, liberty and the pursuit of happiness. We have that old Liberty Bell yet in Philadelphia and it's still ringing for us!"

Making their way east, crossing Pennsylvania in the depths of winter,

"THE SKIPPER SIGHTS LAND AGAIN"
Hoover's eagerness to pronounce a turning point in
the Depression led to blunders, and to ridicule.

their numbers swelled as they went, jobless men clambering aboard hundreds of jalopies and old farm trucks. By the time they reached Washington they comprised the single largest public demonstration ever seen in the capital—between fifteen and twenty thousand spirited, hungry protesters.

Cox and his horde arrived on a dark night in the middle of the week, soaked with freezing rain, and famished. As with the hunger marchers a month before, official Washington offered these bedraggled protesters a warm welcome. Police officers met them at the district border and escorted them to Maryland Avenue, where the Army had set up field kitchens to serve hot meals. Officers put some marchers up at the National Guard armory, hunted down vacant buildings to shelter others, and found restaurants willing to donate coffee and bread.

Hoover's advisors looked askance on Cox and his flock. "We will not see this man," gatekeeper Larry Richey said in a directive to White House staff. "If he has a petition we will be glad to receive [it], but he will not see the president."

But Hoover himself was more accommodating. The day after Cox arrived in the capital the president greeted him personally, along with twelve of his fellow protesters, as thousands more massed outside the White House gates. Jim Davis, Hoover's former labor secretary and now a senator from Pennsylvania, was a longtime friend of the cleric, and he served Father Cox as an escort. That morning Cox had presented his petition in Congress; now Hoover offered his salutation. "I have intense sympathy for your difficulties," Hoover told the Pittsburgh priest.

Not to be diverted, Father Cox had his say. He called for a billion-dollar jobs program, free medical care and public-owned utilities, with costs to be covered by new taxes on the wealthy. Hoover answered earnestly, but in a fashion unlikely to placate the hunger marchers—he recited once again his own legislative agenda. "I have considered that the vital function of the president and of the federal government was to exert every effort and every power of the government to the restoration of stability and employment in the country," he said.

But Hoover rejected the sort of intervention Cox was seeking. The battle against the Depression "cannot be won by any single skirmish or any panacea," the president admonished. "The real victory is to restore men to employment through their regular jobs. That is our object."

Father Cox and his thousands did not tarry in Washington. Leaving the White House, they trekked out to Arlington National Cemetery, where Cox gave a moving benediction. This was the climax; the protesters were on the road back to Pittsburgh the next day. Inevitably, there were stragglers who missed the caravan; when police reported 276 penniless, stranded men, Andrew Mellon, then still at Treasury, ponied up the train fare to send them home.

Another round of road-weary protesters began to filter into Washington toward the end of May. This was the first vanguard of the Bonus Expeditionary Force, a makeshift army named for the cause for which they marched—full payment now of the veteran's "bonus," the sum that the government had voted, in 1924, to pay its war veterans twenty years hence.

The movement started in Portland, Oregon, at a small gathering of the National Veterans Association, when scrawny former sergeant named Walter Waters proposed that letters and petitions were not enough; if veterans wanted to cash out their bonus now they must present their appeal in person. Unemployed and a father of two young children, Waters decided to lead the march himself. In May he gathered three hundred fellow indigent veterans and they set out for the capital, nearly three thousand miles distant.

Waters and his cohort were on the road for a month. Newspapers covered their progress, and as word spread of a Bonus Army marching on the nation's capital, thousands of other veterans, also unemployed and cut adrift, responded to the call. Some fell in with Waters; many more marched on their own.

Once again, the men around the president recoiled at the idea of receiving or accommodating any of these malcontents. To RFC president Charles Dawes, a brigadier general during the war, the BEF represented nothing less than open rebellion; he pressed Hoover to "meet the bonus marchers at the district line with troops with their bayonets fixed." Once again, within the councils of the administration, Hoover declined to treat the marchers as a threat. But he made no official statement, and in his silence left the press and the public to draw their own conclusions.

The official who took charge of the bonus marchers upon their arrival was District of Columbia Police Chief Pelham Glassford. He greeted the BEF with an official escort, warm food, and temporary quarters. He also issued an edict requiring them to limit their stay in the capital to forty-eight hours.

Glassford was a veteran himself—the son of a cavalry officer, a graduate of West Point. He had shipped out to France in the world war and was named the Army's youngest brigadier general, before decommissioning at the rank of major. But Glassford was also a peace officer, and there were numerous reports of unruly and even criminal action by the BEF on its way across the country, including forcibly blocking rail lines. Moreover, avowedly communist organizers were cheerfully piggybacking on the veterans' cause. In several states, impatient governors ordered up trucks to move the marchers through, rather than to allow them to set up camp.

Glassford sought to keep order by keeping the veterans off the streets. With most of the marchers still making their way into Washington, he approached Patrick Hurley, secretary of war and a favorite of Hoover's, to request equipment, food, and bedding for the incoming troops. When Hurley declined, Glassford went to the White House in person. He was met by Walter Newton, who also turned him away.

Glassford was a soldier, but he wasn't intimidated by authority. He promptly fired off a telegram to Hurley complaining of the stonewall at the War Department, then distributed it to reporters. This got President Hoover's attention, and he quietly directed Hurley to cooperate with the district police. Beginning May 31, Hurley ordered the transfer of several field kitchens and hundreds of tents, cots, and bedclothes to Glassford. Other federal officials designated several parks and available public buildings to quarter the veterans.

Here as in so many cases, Hoover kept his assistance to Glassford secret. So did Glassford, who resented his initial clash with Hoover's subordinates, and likely was never informed just why it was they changed their minds. From the outset of the BEF occupation of the capital, Chief Glassford, the veterans, and the press all considered the president to be inflexibly opposed to the demonstration; Hoover's silence appeared to be confirmation.

Hoover's direct communications contradict this view. He opposed the bonus and he was leery of the demonstrators, but he would accommodate them just as he had Father Cox.

On June 2, with veterans now streaming into town, Ted Joslin proposed—as had Charles Dawes—that they be stopped with force at the border of the federal district. Hoover rejected the idea out of hand. "That would almost certainly end in bloodshed," he warned. What if they wanted to meet the president? Hoover would not sit down with communists, he said, but if the veterans sent a committee, he would see them.

Unlike Father Cox, however, no meeting with the bonus marchers took place. Ever after, this was taken as a sign of Hoover's hostility—"There seemed no excuse for his refusal to see their leaders," New Deal historian, Arthur Schlesinger wrote in 1957—but it appears more likely a sign of Hoover's customary reticence. Tellingly, a search of records and communications for the period turns up no sign of a request from Waters or the BEF for a meeting with the president.

Hoover expressed what appear to be his candid views of the BEF in an exchange with Bruce Barton, a Madison Avenue advertising executive and friend of the president's. Barton wrote in early June to propose that Hoover "would stir the country and greatly strengthen your hands" if he were to issue a sharp, firm message sending the veterans home. "My dear Barton," came Hoover's blithe reply. "There has been no disturbance of the peace in Washington yet. It is improbable that there will be." There was no animosity toward the protesters in the president's tone, no edge of resentment. "As a matter of fact," Hoover wrote, "except for a few New York agitators these are perfectly peaceable people that are coming in here."

Soon after, with the veterans overflowing their camps, Hoover made another important concession, agreeing to put on hold the demolition of several buildings on Pennsylvania Avenue slated for imminent replacement. This was a major project from the government's much maligned jobs program, but the work was only half done, and Glassford needed more space.

The site included auto showrooms, wholesale warehouses, and a cheap hotel, all gutted but sufficient to shelter vagabond veterans. Upon Hoover's intervention, the old brick hulks were turned over to police administration.

When the soldiers moved in, three blocks from the Capitol and a half mile east of the White House, they dubbed their new quarters "Camp Glassford."

By now crowds of veterans were gathering in every public square in Washington, jostling like the restless crows of the Hitchcock film. Some saw them as a menace but to Hoover they were just a sideshow in a period of crucial action and decision. He was under enormous stress, wrangling with Congress, restructuring his economic program, and anticipating national nominating conventions for both parties.

Besides, so far as the president was concerned, the question of the veterans' bonus was moot. Hoover believed he had put the matter to rest eight months before. In September, at the height of the panic over Great Britain leaving the gold standard, he had made one of his sudden sorties out from Washington, this time to Detroit, where he addressed the American Legion at their thirteenth annual convention.

Hoover traveled all night, but completed his address in just ten minutes. He built the speech around the government's growing deficit—since the onset of the Depression, receipts from federal income taxes had dropped by half, while the pressure to spend rose steadily. "The imperative moment has come when the increase in government expenditures must be avoided," Hoover intoned behind banked microphones in Detroit's cavernous Olympic Auditorium.

Hoover did not once mention the bonus, but all knew it was the reason for his talk, the object of his trip. "Nothing would give a greater glow of confidence to our country today than your enlistment . . . to prevent additional burden on the government."

After a faltering start, Hoover warmed to his speech, and by the end the great hall was ringing with applause. The president's performance was, in Ted Joslin's estimation, "a ten-strike." At the close of the convention, with the president back in Washington, the Legion voted to oppose immediate funding of the veterans' bonus certificates. And without the backing of the Legion, there was little chance the bonus would go through.

The question of veterans' compensation arose again in December, as it had in every new Congress since the war; in this case more than twenty bonus bills were introduced. Some legislators saw the bonus as means to combat the Depression through monetary inflation; others were simply courting the votes of the nation's million veterans.

Leading this parade was Wright Patman, the Texas populist who was at the same time so heartily denouncing Treasury Secretary Andrew Mellon. Patman, himself a Legionaire, won standing early in 1932 for a bill requiring full, immediate payment of the bonus, a measure that would cost the government a lump sum of $2.4 billion.

Hearings on the bill occupied much of April, but by now there was a growing movement against making a large cash grant from an overdrawn Treasury. Benefits had been expanding for years, growing to cover disability for soldiers who never saw combat, and pensions for veterans with as little as seventy days' service. Nicholas Murray Butler, president of Columbia University and a celebrated public intellectual, marked out a broad consensus in April when he denounced "organized raids upon the treasury by war veterans and their families" as "a shocking example of the misuse that may be made of the word patriotism."

"No one would deny to any man injured on the field of battle . . . the fullest measure of protection and care," Butler said. But, "This sentiment of justice and gratitude has been taken advantage of" by hale and healthy veterans "to compel Congress to give them doles."

Congress, however, was resisting. In the debates over the Patman bill fiscal conservatives were joined by advocates of public relief, like New Yorkers Fiorello La Guardia and Robert Wagner, and even the Nebraska insurgent George Norris, who wanted any government largesse directed toward the ten million unemployed, rather than former soldiers. Even Franklin Roosevelt, always tricky to pin down, came out with a flat statement against the bonus.

In 1930, Hoover had seen his veto of new pensions for veterans of the Spanish-American War quickly and easily overridden. Now, two years later, Congress didn't even send him a bill; Patman prevailed in the House, but in June, with thousands of anguished veterans milling about the Capitol Plaza, the Senate rejected the bonus bill by a three-to-one margin.

The president kept an eye on the vote that night, but less out of trepidation than spite for his political foes. "I don't give a damn what the Senate does," Hoover told Ted Joslin. "I'll have that bill back before Congress with my veto in ten minutes."

There were hungry veterans in the streets and hostilities with Congress, but what preoccupied Hoover that season was the upcoming presidential election. Both parties would hold conventions in June, in Chicago, and while the Republican choice was never in doubt, the national spotlight would require a clear statement on the issues. For Hoover that meant confronting the one dispute that disturbed his sleep and unsettled his mind—the moral quandary of Prohibition.

It is one of the ironies of history that while the Depression was the event that would define Herbert Hoover's presidency, the great political question all through his term was the constitutional ban on alcohol. And while in hindsight the wrangle over strong drink appears almost quaint, Prohibition was something profound and, for many, sacrosanct, the product of a century of heartfelt social action. At the same time, twelve years of enforcement had changed the face of America, fostering criminal gangs and flagrant violation at tens of thousands of speakeasies. The question was always hotly contested.

Over his first three years in the White House Hoover never wavered in his support for Prohibition. In 1929 he signed the "Five and Ten Law" making every liquor violation a felony, and his Justice Department ramped up federal enforcement. "We enormously increased the jail population," by jailing Prohibition violators Hoover recalled in his memoirs. "We multiplied the fines, padlocking, and confiscations." Yet all this aggressive action he ascribed to his duty as a constitutional officer, not to his actual endorsement. On this basic political question, Hoover declined to share his feelings and refused to act on them.

Hoover's stern and corporal approach to Prohibition served him nicely in 1928, allowing him to stand pat on a matter of apparent national consensus while Al Smith, an avowed wet, paid the price of his convictions. But as with the debate over veterans' claims, much had changed by June 1932. The Wickersham Commission, conceived to clear the air, had ended in confusion, its final report sharply criticizing enforcement efforts but recommending no changes in the law. Meanwhile the advent of the Depression added new arguments for repeal: legalizing beer, at least, would create new jobs, boost tax revenue, and open a new market for grain. After ten years of increasing strife, popular support for Prohibition began to wane.

During the 1928 campaign Hoover famously saluted Prohibition as "a great social and economic experiment, noble in motive and far-reaching in purpose." But three years later, surely the test had been run. The question now was, which way from here? It was a matter of leadership, requiring a statement of faith as well as policy. In his few and careful public remarks on the issue, Hoover had managed to avoid the simple, human question of what he actually thought. With the nominating convention looming, the pressure grew on President Hoover to explain himself.

This was the ground where Hoover was least comfortable. For a born politician like Al Smith, personal declaration was the natural instinct that led him into politics in the first place. But Hoover treated his inner life as a sanctuary and a secret, a forbidden zone that he protected so fiercely that he appeared to fear even his own inquiries. Here in the shadows of individual experience and true feelings, Hoover was conflicted.

Born and raised in a Quaker family and a Quaker community, Hoover was weaned on the social movement that gave rise to Prohibition. His mother, Hulda, had been secretary to the local chapter of the Women's Christian Temperance Union, and Hoover recalled spending one day parked at the polls, where Hulda gathered a troop of women outside the voting booth "in an effort to make the men vote themselves dry."

Even then, in Hoover's wry telling the question of drink took on a partisan political edge. "There was only one Democrat in the village," Hoover recalled of West Branch. "He occasionally fell under the influence of liquor; therefore in the opinion of our village he represented all the forces of evil."

That was his childhood training, but Hoover soon moved on. In his early adulthood he drifted away from the Quaker church and developed a taste for wine and sometimes harder stuff—though as one lifelong friend recalled, "Mr. Hoover never took more than one cocktail." That did not in-

dicate strict sobriety, however; this same friend told the story of one carous-
ing evening in Paris, when she and Hoover happened to pass by a bandstand
outside a hotel dining room. "I guess we had a little more than one bottle of
champagne, because Mr. Hoover stopped and took the baton from the orchestra leader and led the orchestra himself." These were the carefree days
that Lou Hoover liked to think back on as well, the time before all the toil
and ambition of the Washington years.

When Prohibition was repealed by the states, just nine months after
Hoover left office, the ex-president resumed his acquaintance with the cocktail; in later years, he made a ritual of drinking two martinis every evening.
And yet he never gave up his professed moral opposition to booze. "Strong
alcoholic drinks," Hoover intoned in his memoirs, "are moral, physical, and
economic curses to the race."

The point here is not to expose Hoover as a hypocrite, but to suggest the
division in Hoover's heart. On the question of Prohibition, as in so many
other issues, Hoover was torn between personal inclination and his sense of
duty.

When Prohibition first came into force this internal conflict was easy
to resolve. As a government official Hoover would pay strict observance
to the laws. He made that clear the day the ban went into effect in January 1920. Bert and Lou were hosting a small dinner party, and the evening
began, as was their custom, with the Hoovers' butler serving a tray of mixed
drinks. As the story goes, Lou Hoover "sprang up from her chair and hurried across the living room" to remind Bert of the new law. "Take them all
out!" her husband promptly declared, and the household was dry from that
day forward.

But personal abstinence was a far simpler course to chart than the
correct public policy, or the politics involved. And Hoover's task was
complicated by his own internal uncertainty.

One clue to the unsettled state of Hoover's mind was his continuing reversion
to the subject, year after year. Late in 1930, not long before the Wickersham
Commission completed its long-delayed report, Hoover shared with Henry
Stimson his "doubts as to the wisdom of constitutional Prohibition"; he told

Stimson that "he was very doubtful now as to whether it could be made workable." But two weeks later, with delivery of the Wickersham report imminent, the president pronounced himself "a conscientious believer in Prohibition . . . a dry, as he expressed it; and he couldn't give up his conscience." On another occasion he told Stimson "that he believed thoroughly in total abstinence," and that "in fifty years he believed the whole country would be dry."

It was typical of Hoover to find that the dictates of his conscience ran athwart his personal inclinations. His fondness for alcohol was something he shared with those millions of fellow Americans—perhaps a majority of them—who crowded into speakeasies across the country, the miscreants including several members of his cabinet and his staff. But Hoover couldn't respond to that common chord; he answered instead to mores instilled through a hard and lonely childhood.

He was under constant pressure to change his mind. In New York, Hoover intimates Edgar Rickard, Lewis Strauss, Jeremiah Milbank, and George Barr Baker struggled to craft some sort of position that would answer to the growing movement for repeal. In early 1931 Milbank worried that a dry stand would undermine fundraising for the 1932 campaign. But the president appeared intransigent. "No one can read a glimmer of hope" that Hoover might show "any liberality" on the question, Baker reported.

Hoover did waver on occasion, but he was checked by his doubting nature. Soon after the midterm elections he told James MacLafferty that he wanted to punt the whole question of Prohibition to the states. This was "resubmission," a middle road that would acknowledge the problems with federal enforcement and allow the drys to fight it out at local level. But with the Democrats already wet, such a compromise appeared impossible. If the Republicans appeared to waver, Hoover said, "we would be the followers of the Democratic Party and we would be beaten." Still, Hoover encouraged MacLafferty to seek support in Congress for "some sort of concession to the tremendous and increasing wet sentiment in the country today."

It wasn't just the Democrats that had Hoover spooked. He feared that open support for resubmission would split the Republicans the way Teddy Roosevelt's insurgency had in 1912. Talk of a third party was rife, quietly encouraged by ardent drys like William Borah.

Always allergic to the vagaries of democratic process, Hoover at one point proposed to Henry Stimson a "special constitutional convention," limited solely to Prohibition. It should be sponsored by a bipartisan coalition of dry and wet congressmen so as to render the debate "as free as possible from any other politics."

Stimson was sympathetic, but he would not join in the president's delusion. "I told him . . . that whether we liked it or not, this question was in politics, and it was going to be in politics all through the next two years, and that I hoped he would take a strong lead in it rather than put it aside as if it wasn't in politics."

Hoover readily agreed, but with his internal conflicts and outward reticence, that strong stance never materialized.

By early 1932 little doubt remained as to the mood of the electorate. Respondents to a national mail-in survey conducted by *The Literary Digest* in February and March endorsed repeal of the Eighteenth Amendment by a four-to-one margin. Residents of Ohio, the birthplace of Prohibition, sent in 112,026 ballots for repeal and just 43,284 for keeping the ban on booze. Kansas was the only state to poll in favor of Prohibition.

While the poll results were still coming in the president conducted a study of his own. He drew up a list of states along with their electoral college votes and arranged them under two columns—"Repeal," and "Doubtful," neither column signifying strong support for Prohibition. Southern states were not included—they were predominantly dry, but Hoover fully expected they would return to the Democratic fold in this election. The result was daunting: if voters allowed Prohibition to be their guide, the opposition would account for 323 of a total 531 electoral college ballots.

Hoover recognized the situation. The country was swinging hard and fast, from dry to wet. Prohibition, a controversial law that banned a practice Hoover personally enjoyed, was doomed, as were the prospects of any politician who clung to it. Yet the more the pressure mounted to change his ground, the more Hoover dug in.

Hoover invited MacLafferty to stop by on a Friday morning in March to review his tabulations. They seemed to confirm MacLafferty's worst fears; mulling the question the next day, he confided to his diary, "If the Democratic platform is wet and the Republican platform is dry the Democrats will win next November." Hoover shared those fears, but he regarded the hard numbers fatalistically. In the end, he said, he had no choice: "I must stay dry."

As the June convention drew near, Hoover continued to vacillate. He determined at one point that he should set the tone for his party and for the nation with a bracing personal statement. He changed his mind in April; he must *not* declare personally, but would devote his energies to ensuring that the party stayed dry. These peregrinations were secret, but they were also obvious. "He was afraid to take the lead and he was afraid not to dictate," discerned Walter Lippmann. It was, Lippmann deemed, another iteration of Hoover's "peculiar weakness."

Prohibition was, in truth, the only real question for the Republicans at their nominating convention in Chicago. Nicholas Murray Butler, attending as a New York delegate and a leader in the Association Against the Prohibition Amendment, was planning a floor fight, and Hoover was determined to head him off. "That convention is dripping wet," Hoover groused in June. "We can't do anything with them."

Hoover remained in Washington for the proceedings, but he was thoroughly represented in Chicago. Seven members of his cabinet attended as delegates, as well as Walter Newton and Larry Richey. Moreover, the state delegations were packed with government employees and officials, the federal phalanx recalling the "Hoover steamroller" of 1928. Despite repeated avowals from the White House that Hoover was "entirely neutral" on policy questions, the president was on the phone constantly, dictating terms of the party's Prohibition plank and monitoring the state of the opposition.

The statement that emerged from the platform committee was one of those orphans that committees so often produce—difficult, convoluted, beloved of none. It saluted obedience to the law, but recognized the "nation-wide controversy" over the Eighteenth Amendment; it supported amendment but not repeal; it endorsed state conventions but no referendum. It was, in the parlance of the time, a "straddle."

Press reaction was quick and sharp. "It is wet and dry; it opposes repeal and proposes it," the *Times* reported. A follow-up editorial was more blunt: The Republican plank on Prohibition was "perhaps the worst jungle of verbiage that even platform-makers ever devised in order to conceal their thought." H. L. Mencken summed up the statement as "quite unintelligible to simple folk."

As ever, Hoover feared the worst. On the day the proceedings formally opened, with Butler still driving hard for repeal, Hoover threw a bit of a tantrum. "If the convention goes for repeal," he announced to Ted Joslin, "I shall refuse to accept the nomination."

Joslin knew his boss too well to rise to the bait. "You can't do that, Mr. President."

"Yes I can," came Hoover's petulant reply. "I shall have to."

But he did not. Later that day Butler's bid for repeal was voted down 690 to 460. Hoover and his team had wrought the result through force and threat, but the opposition did not go down quietly. On June 15, the night before the vote on the party platform, wet delegates joined twenty thousand local citizens in the galleries of the new Chicago Stadium in a raucous demonstration, showering the platform committee with lusty boos and chanting, "We want repeal." Noted one reporter, "It seemed as if the whole hall was in rebellion against the administration plank for resubmission."

It was an embarrassment, but the party chiefs controlled the key committees, and the uprising soon played itself out. On June 17, the president, his wife, Lou, and two of her secretaries repaired to the Lincoln Study to listen to the convention finale on a radio broadcast. With them were Ted Joslin and George Akerson, returned from Hollywood to help on the campaign. When the ballots were cast and Hoover's renomination announced there were no congratulations, no audible response from his official family. Hoover stood and said, "Well, it wasn't exactly unexpected," then turned and headed out into the hallway.

The only sign of emotion came from Lou. When the president stepped out she dropped her knitting and hurried after him, catching the president on his way to the elevator. She left him there, and he returned to his work.

Hoover had his victory, but he may have sealed his fate. When the Democrats arrived in Chicago—they would hold their convention in the same new stadium the Republicans used—there was more drama and a more sus-penseful choice. But it was Roosevelt after all, and upon his nomination, he faced all the moral complexities of Prohibition and sliced them clean through. "This convention wants repeal!" Roosevelt declared in his accep-tance speech. "Your candidate wants repeal." Now the cheers were rising around him. "The people of the United States want the Eighteenth Amend-ment repealed."

Roosevelt had to wait a moment to let the applause die down; then he added his coda: "From this date on the Eighteenth Amendment is doomed."

Here was the strong, clear position that Henry Stimson had asked for, but which President Hoover was unable to deliver. Roosevelt did, however, and the impact was immediate. A *New York Times* editorial the next day commended the "forthright and bold act of the candidate to take his stand squarely" in favor of repeal. It was brave, but more than that, "It is wise of him to emphasize what may easily prove to be the winning issue of the campaign."

As much as Hoover was flummoxed by the politics of the impending cam-paign, he was beset by the continuing breakdown of the American economy. He had launched a policy revolution in January and February, committing the government to intervention on an unprecedented scale, but it was clear by May that initiative had to be revamped. And while those changes were technical and abstract, they turned on personalities, parties, and, ultimately, politics.

That was especially true, of course, when the revisions had to come through Congress. Integral to Hoover's "somersault" on relief was his agree-ment with Joseph Robinson that federal aid to the states and the new round of public works projects be channeled through the Reconstruction Finance Corporation. Hoover took the opportunity as well to expand the lending authority and the capital funding for the new agency.

This was a delicate legislative maneuver. When it was created in Janu-ary the RFC was widely accepted, the central plank of the president's recov-ery program. But five months later, with the Depression grinding on, the idea of pushing millions of dollars into the hands of banks and railroads had become distinctly unpopular. Rewriting the charter to boost the powers of the RFC required legislative cover, and coupling these changes to relief was the answer.

Well enough, so far as Hoover and Robinson went, but the senator from Arkansas could not answer for the entire Congress. In the House, "Cactus Jack" Garner took the legislative reins and promptly killed all pretense at comity. Announcing in May that a new coalition would sponsor a "nonpartisan" relief bill, Garner outlined a specific role for Hoover.

"If the president will refrain for thirty days from making double-barreled statements, this frozen confidence will naturally melt," Garner told a clutch of reporters gathered in his Capitol office. "His statements have done more in the last six months to freeze confidence than all other sources put together."

Most observers took Garner's remarks as predictable political fare—Garner was just then vying with Roosevelt for the presidential nomination—but Hoover took it hard. He slugged back in the closing days of the session, denouncing as "disastrous" the relief bill Garner's coalition had produced. He singled out for censure a clause granting the RFC authority to lend to private companies or individuals. Hoover had proposed just such a provision in December, only to see it blocked by Senator Glass; now he scored it as making the RFC "the most gigantic banking and pawnbroking business in all history."

A chagrined Congress quickly excised the offending clause from the relief bill. But, in a backdoor move, the irrepressible Carter Glass tacked onto the bill a rider that would grant these same lending powers to the Federal Reserve. Hoover instinctively reacted with outrage, until he sat down with Meyer and Ogden Mills, who recalled him to the single and overriding goal of their entire policy, which was to open the channels of credit. Hoover recovered himself, and decided to embrace Glass's new language.

All this got back to Glass, who got a good laugh in telling the story to friends at the Federal Reserve. "Well, the administration went into a spasm over my amendment, pulling every wire in order to defeat it," Glass chortled in a gossipy phone call. "Now the administration is in a spasm for fear they will *not* get it!" Glass said both Mills and Meyer had each dropped by to tell him the tale in person.

Congress finally passed the Emergency Relief and Construction Act just before the end of its session in July. In his signing statement Hoover took a swipe at Garner, primly advising that provisions for "a gigantic centralized banking business had been removed." The president made no reference to the Glass amendment, which provided for unprecedented, direct lending to private business from the Federal Reserve. Saluting the act as "a strong step toward recovery," he left the public to decide who now was playing politics with human misery.

A similar contest for praise and recognition plagued the principal federal agencies charged with arresting the Depression—the Fed and the RFC. The key actor here was Eugene Meyer, who held the top jobs at both.

Hoover installed Meyer as a financial mastermind who would shake the Fed out of its doldrums, and it only seemed natural that, having pressed hard for the RFC, Meyer should lead it as well. But by May the president was beginning to have his doubts. Meyer had been given everything he asked for—unprecedented powers, new staff, control over close to half the federal budget—but where were the results? Economic recovery seemed just as distant as ever. Meyer was proving human after all.

Waiting closely on the president that spring, Ted Joslin got an earful of Hoover's shifting attitude toward his financial chief. "The president is losing confidence in the officials of the Reconstruction Finance Corporation," Joslin noted March 16. "Governor Meyer, however, more than the others. There are times he would like to boot Meyer the length of Pennsylvania Avenue."

Hoover was more explicit a week later, after another round of bad news on the state of the economy. "It is exasperating to lay the foundation for constructive action only to reach an impasse because the agencies set up do not function properly," Hoover stormed in one of his occasional fits of pique. "I have brought about the Credit Pool, broadened the base of the Federal Reserve and established the Reconstruction Corporation. All of these agencies should be functioning, but they are only operating at 60 [or] 80 percent efficiency. That is the difference between success or failure."

It was the classic insider's, bureaucratic critique: it was not the system or the strategy that was at fault, but the manager, and the quality of his execution. "Gene will do well to watch his step," Joslin surmised, "for the President is dissatisfied with him."

This was not really fair, of course. Despite the appeal from Agnes Meyer in February, Hoover never scaled back the demands he made on his principals, especially those responsible for financial policy. Thus Meyer was engaged in both the Board of Governors and the Open Market committee of the Fed, as well as launching the RFC; he frequently attended the president during legislative and policy conferences; and, with Ogden Mills, he was called upon to defend the administration before Congress.

Clearly, the strain was taking a toll. By July, fellow board member Adolph Miller assigned his wife to accompany Meyer on his regular rail commute between New York and Washington; the financier was so "perplexed" that Miller did not want him traveling alone.

Even then, Hoover's concern was not with Meyer's health so much as his acumen. The same week Miller asked his wife to look after Meyer, the president asked Miller if George Harrison, the president of the Federal Reserve Bank in New York, "was not abler than Governor Meyer." Miller was no fan of Meyer's, and was thoroughly versed in the apparent futility of the government's economic program, but gave Meyer his unqualified endorsement. "There is no comparison," Miller told the president. "Governor Meyer is far abler."

By now Meyer was catching it from all sides. At the Federal Reserve, ironically, the governors complained that Meyer was too close to the White House, too engaged with the RFC, and too secretive in his various roles to be of service at the Fed. When Meyer was called to advise Hoover on the Glass-Steagall credit bill, for instance, the Fed governors were informed only after the fact. "Not a member knew of this!" Charles Hamlin cried in his diary. "Under Governor Meyer the Board has practically ceased to exist!"

The status of the board was important, but these concerns start to feel petty. In May, with financial pressures building, Hamlin and Adolph Miller agreed that Meyer "had no time and only a languid interest in Federal Reserve Board matters." Hamlin worried that board deliberations were curtailed to allow Meyer to pursue the affairs of the RFC, "where his heart really is."

One senses that much of this dissatisfaction arises from Hamlin's principal, recurrent complaint—Meyer's failure to cooperate. "Governor Meyer has a total incapacity to work with anyone else," Hamlin wrote. "He plays a lone hand!"

Fellow officers at the Reconstruction Finance Corporation agreed, but they chalked it up to partisanship. Texan banker Jesse Jones, one of three Democrats on the seven-member board, found Meyer to be effective but abrasive. Meyer and Ogden Mills dominated the early operations of the RFC, Jones said, and while he credited Meyer "for having set up a good organization," he said that "several months passed before Secretary Mills found it necessary to regard the Democratic members as their equals." This attitude, Jones said, "brought on clashes."

It came as a relief to all concerned, then, when Hoover decided in July to replace Meyer at the RFC. Charles Dawes had bowed out a month before, to rush home to Chicago and attend personally to the three-alarm banking crisis there. Moving Meyer out would allow a fresh start for an entity that had opened with promise, but had yet to reverse the steady march of insolvency.

This was another of the many amendments tacked onto the Relief and Reconstruction Act in May, a clause removing the governor of the Fed from the board of the RFC. In Meyer's place Hoover named Atlee Pomerene, a former Democratic senator from Ohio—no partisanship here!—distinguished as the lead prosecutor in the Teapot Dome scandal.

Meyer continued on at the Federal Reserve, and despite continuing personal friction he remained, with Ogden Mills, a principal financial advisor to the president.

That Eugene Meyer had an autocratic streak there is little doubt. But some degree of tension was inevitable in the hothouse circumstances of monetary management in 1932. Even when the president got into the act—*especially* when the president got into the act—tempers flared and fingers pointed.

One such instance arose when in May it became apparent that for all the RFC loans and Federal Reserve purchases and other measures to boost liquidity, the banks were still refusing to extend loans, preferring instead to keep all their assets close at hand. At a meeting of the Fed's Open Market Policy Conference, on May 17, board member and Hoover intimate Adolph Miller said the Fed's massive bill-purchasing operations were not enough; that the Fed should establish a system of ad hoc committees, one in each Federal Reserve district, where bankers, industrialists, and business executives could sort out credit conditions and agree on regional plans of action.

It was a likely scheme—so much so that, three days later, *The New York Times* reported the creation of just such a committee, "called together" by George Harrison of the New York Fed, and chaired by Owen Young.

Now the fur began to fly. The diarist Charles Hamlin noted that Harrison had opposed the idea in the committee meeting just days before, and that, "Something has evidently speeded him up!" Then, later that day, President Hoover announced to the press that "I am much gratified at the action taken in New York," and that he hoped to see the other Federal Reserve districts "proceed in a similar way."

Hamlin was aghast. "Hoover has stolen the board's thunder, and pushed it aside, in an effort to claim sole credit for a plan with which he had nothing to do, and which was originated by Miller and C.S.H."—that is, Hamlin himself.

The plot thickened from there. Hamlin soon learned just where Hoover had gotten the idea of forming a chain of industrial credit committees. It turned out that Adolph Miller had presented the idea to him at a private meeting at the White House. Hoover liked the plan but bluntly told Miller that he had no confidence in the Federal Reserve Board running the committees.

As the two Fed governors surmised, Hoover had then tabbed George Harrison to float idea of the New York committee—a directive Harrison kept to himself when Miller proposed establishing district committees at the policy meeting May 17. Miller and Hamlin now decided they could not trust Harrison, their fellow governor and the director of the most important bank in the system. As for the president, Hamlin recorded in his diary, "Hoover is a glutton for the limelight!"

Miller was particularly exasperated with the constant meddling from his erstwhile friend. "Hoover tries to run everything from the White House," he complained to Hamlin. Miller then alluded to Jack Garner's snide attack on the president, just then in the headlines. Garner had been "very undiplomatic" in suggesting that the Depression would be resolved if Hoover would only keep quiet. But, Miller said, Garner was "in part, at least, justified."

Nor was Hoover done with this particular round of meddling. At the direction of the Fed Board, Meyer had continued traveling the country to organize banking and industrial committees under the jurisdiction of the Federal Reserve. Come June, however, Hoover notified him he wanted the committees transferred to the jurisdiction of the RFC. Meyer recoiled, convinced now that Hamlin was right: this was clearly a bid by the president to claim credit for a Fed program.

This prompted another visit to the White House by the intrepid Agnes Meyer. She told Hoover he was running a great risk, as his attempt to "grab the committees" could backfire in a wave of Democratic resignations. The president answered in "loud, angry tones," Agnes Meyer noted in her diary, protesting that he had conceived of the committees, and that Owen Young was using the New York committee as a platform for a presidential bid.

"Eugene thinks I am nothing but a politician, but there has got to be leadership in this situation," Hoover declared. "I am the president for better or worse and I have got to do the leading!" As with Adolph Miller, the episode prompted Agnes Meyer to revise her estimation of the president. "Eugene is trying to save the country," she recorded in her diary, "and the president is trying to save Hoover."

In the end all this grasping and recrimination came to naught. Hoover backed off, leaving the committees to operate under Federal Reserve auspices. But like so many of the initiatives launched by Hoover and from every other quarter, these committees had little impact on the underlying dynamic of the Depression. Week after week, prices, production, and employment continued to fall, and no matter how much money was sluiced into their coffers, the bankers of America refused to push any back out the door. Credit remained impossibly scarce, and assets, and confidence, frozen.

Mark Sullivan Jr., son of the journalist and welcome in Hoover's intimate circle, used to visit Washington during his college days, sometimes riding up to the Rapidan Camp with his father and the president. On one of those trips Hoover said something to his father that stuck in young Sullivan's mind forty years later. He couldn't quite place the moment he heard it, but it may well have been uttered during this difficult time. "The only trouble with capitalism is capitalists," the president told his journalist friend. "They're too damned greedy."

"SHOW IT IN"

Veterans' spending was the single largest
discretionary item in the federal budget, and
Hoover was keen to keep it in check.

TWENTY-ONE

EVIL MAGIC

THE DEFEAT OF THE VETERANS' BONUS BILL IN THE SENATE, ON June 17, promised to end at least one of the serial crises bearing down on President Hoover that summer. There was no more reason for the continued encampment of twelve thousand destitute and disgruntled veterans on public grounds around the Capitol. Their cause was finished. It was time to return home.

But there was no exodus. For many of the veterans there really wasn't much "home" to go to. Like thousands of their civilian counterparts across the country, jobless and in many cases homeless, these onetime soldiers were drifting aimlessly, unmoored from any lasting attachment. The makeshift encampments close by the Capitol would serve well enough.

President Hoover sought to move them along—gently. He was tempted to issue an edict clearing the city—"I don't want to appear weak before the American people," he cried at one point—but instead he chose the carrot over the stick. On July 6 he asked Congress to set aside $100,000 to provide for rail fare and subsistence in transit—at the rate of 75 cents per day—for any veterans willing to leave the federal district. Thousands of dispirited marchers accepted the offer, but many more did not.

This friendly gesture seemed only to galvanize those protesters who remained. Walter Waters, voted "supreme commander" of the Bonus Expeditionary Force early in the protest, resented the departures and sent squads of toughs to harass them as "deserters." It got to the point where Police Chief Pelham Glassford had to assign officers to protect the outgoing soldiers at the Veterans Administration, where they applied for travel vouchers, and at the train station.

From that point forward, the situation of the protesters in the capital grew steadily more tense. Without a bonus bill to focus on, the veterans began to splinter, some adhering to Waters but others finding new leaders to follow. These included a small but vocal band of communists, who quickly made peace with Chief Glassford but who disparaged Waters as an incipient fascist. As if to confirm the charge, Waters selected a posse of men to maintain order and drive out suspected subversives. He dubbed this squad the "Khaki Shirts of America."

These developments were the subject of growing concern inside the White House and among the district commissioners, a three-member panel which in that era governed the semiautonomous District of Columbia, including the police force. The commissioners pushed for more forceful handling of the protesters, but Glassford resisted that approach, much as Hoover did with his advisors.

But while Hoover and Glassford shared the same sense of restraint, they were suspicious of each other. Glassford assumed, by Hoover's silence and by the foot-dragging of his aides, that the president deeply resented the presence of the veterans, while Hoover believed Glassford—so affable that he was nicknamed "Happy"—was abetting and inciting the protests. Not once during the escalating crisis did the two principals actually speak.

These accidental allies were drawn into collaboration July 14 when a breakaway faction of veterans defied a standing agreement between Waters and the police and set up camp just outside the Capitol steps. This so disturbed Vice President Charles Curtis, one of several officials with technical authority over the building and its grounds, that he called out the Marines. A squad of sixty men was promptly dispatched—via streetcar.

Now Chief Glassford got involved. Fearing that military force might quickly ignite this constitutional standoff, he rushed to the Capitol to confront Curtis. When the vice president refused to back down, Glassford collared a senator who was friendly with Hoover and asked him to phone an appeal to the president. Hoover responded immediately, recalling the troops and insisting that the incident be resolved peacefully. Press coverage of the episode painted Glassford as a friend to the veterans, while assuming the timorous Curtis spoke for the administration. Hoover's role went untold.

Toward the end of July what had begun as a high-spirited mass protest by the Bonus Army had settled into something less. The crowded camps sweated in the summer heat, peopled by bored and testy men, some with wives and children to feed. The private donations that flowed in the early days of the protest dwindled, and many now subsisted on black coffee, stale donuts, and bread from a camp bakery.

There were roughly twenty-five billets scattered around town, several of them clustered in the so-called Federal Triangle, framed by Pennsylvania and Constitution Avenues. But the largest camp was located on the mud flats east of the Anacostia River, about a mile from the White House. There some seven thousand men—and a thousand-odd women—erected Washington's own Hooverville, with shacks fashioned from reclaimed lumber, scrap metal, and cardboard, interspersed with broke-down jalopies and canvas tents on loan from the Army. The place had a certain fantastical, crazy-quilt appeal, but the filth, the flies, and the reek of open latrines robbed it of any charm. The veterans called it Bonus City.

In their poverty and their raw idealism, the plucky veterans of the BEF became a sort of mascot for a suffering nation. Reporters profiled their sufferings, while the former doughboys valiantly proclaimed their patriotism. They emphatically rejected any larger political mission; Waters and his Khaki Shirts made sport of confronting and sometimes assaulting any suspected "reds." Their mantra, repeated by Waters at every opportunity, was at once defiant and utterly futile: "We stay here until 1945!"—the year the bonus came due.

After two months of occupation the officials in charge of the federal district reached their limit. Assistant Treasury Secretary Ferry Heath, director of the government's $700 million building program, moved to break the stalemate on July 20, informing Chief Glassford and the district commissioners that he must at last take possession of the abandoned buildings on Pennsylvania Avenue. The demolition contractor had waited as long as he could; the delays were driving him into bankruptcy.

No action took place that day, but on the next, Ferry Heath was joined by U.S. Grant III—grandson of the president and a colonel in the Army, then posted as the custodian of public buildings in the District of Columbia—who went a good deal further, asking the district commissioners to clear all federal property. The commissioners, who had chafed under the continuing occupation, were glad to oblige, and ordered Glassford to proceed forthwith.

Glassford balked. Governance of the federal district was badly convoluted—it remained so until passage of the Home Rule Act in 1973— and the chief held that the commissioners had no authority to enforce the evictions. His doubts were confirmed by the district's legal counsel, and at a conference the next day with representatives from Treasury, the United States marshal, and the attorney general, it was decided that Treasury would have to obtain a court order. As for the protesters, when Walter Waters learned of the eviction order—albeit in abeyance—he vowed to "declare war" rather than surrender.

Confusion reigned for the next week. President Hoover had much else on his plate, and came only reluctantly to take a direct hand. He finally stepped in on July 27, designating Attorney General William Mitchell to coordinate federal action. The first eviction would be limited to Camp Glassford—of all places—and federal troops would be called only if police could not maintain order.

While the administration was laying plans at the White House, Chief Glassford was meeting with the district commissioners to lay plans of his own. He had Commander Waters of the BEF on hand, but the commissioners declined speaking with the protest leader in person, so Glassford served as intermediary. By the end of these talks Glassford, Waters, and the commissioners appeared to have an understanding; Waters told reporters that night he had agreed to the partial evacuation.

Come Thursday morning, the actors were in place before the National Guard Armory, the first of the buildings to be evacuated. Waters said now that Chief Glassford had promised him a four-day stay, but Glassford, backed by a hundred officers, said the critical moment had arrived. After an initial standoff the veterans filed out of the building, and Waters repaired across the Anacostia to Bonus City. Come noon the building was secured, calm prevailed, and Glassford and his men broke for lunch.

In the meantime, three blocks away, Attorney General Mitchell called reporters to his office and issued his own, more expansive order. He was moving to enforce "summary evictions" from all occupied government properties in the district, and to enforce "all criminal laws and ordinances of the district," including panhandling and blocking traffic, of which many bonuseers were clearly culpable. Mitchell had yet made no move to bring such enforcement, but his tone was clear. The Bonus Army had overstayed its welcome. "It is high time this conduct should end," he said.

Word of this escalation soon reached Bonus City, and Commander Waters promptly swung into action, alerting the camp and sending several truckloads of men over the river to the armory. Thousands more followed on foot, and the police were quickly surrounded by protesters, described by one officer as a "mad, seething, howling mob." When three of the veterans attempted to reenter the armory, a melee broke out. Suddenly the air was full of bricks, the ex-soldiers pelting the officers. Chief Glassford was struck twice and went down; when another officer stepped up to cover him, he was dropped by a brick that fractured his skull.

The action stopped five minutes after it started, when a squad of Waters's enforcers intervened on behalf of the police. There was an uneasy truce, but violence flared again an hour later, fifty yards down the block. This time four police officers found themselves cornered inside a building, pressed by a small but aggressive crew of about twenty squatters. The cops and the veterans slugged it out until one officer drew his weapon. He fired once and then again, striking a veteran in the chest and killing him on the spot. A second officer opened fire but Chief Glassford arrived moments later, recovered from the first altercation and backed with reinforcements. The casualties from this incident included one protester dead, another fatally wounded, and three of the four police officers seriously injured. After weeks of building tension, the Bonus Army had finally come to blows.

President Hoover was paying little attention to the Bonus Army when the violence erupted on the Federal Triangle. His longtime friend, Los Angeles banker Henry Robinson was Hoover's guest at the White House that week, and the two were in close consultation on the revised operations of the RFC. On Thursday, Hoover was at lunch when an aide informed him that the district commissioners had called; the protest had turned violent, and they were requesting federal troops to back up the police.

Hoover moved with caution, relaying word to the commissioners that he would not act on the strength of a phone call. He needed their message in writing, a statement that should incorporate the views of Chief Glassford.

The letter arrived within minutes. From their Pennsylvania Street offices the commissioners had seen the veterans streaming by and had held several urgent meetings with Glassford. There had been that morning "a serious riot," the commissioners informed the president, with police outnumbered and several officers injured. The only option short of "free use of firearms" was to call in federal troops, which they hoped could restore order "with far less violence and bloodshed." This was the opinion of Chief Glassford, the letter said, as well as the commissioners.

Hoover now faced a critical moment. For the first time in his presidency, he was called upon to exercise his powers as commander in chief. He had managed so far to escape that part of his duties by pursuing an explicitly nonviolent foreign policy, sometimes to the frustration of his secretary of state. Now the responsibility was thrust upon him by violence at home, an uprising by former servicemen in the streets of the capital. And, in what must be considered a twist of fate, his counterpart in command was among the most decorated and headstrong soldiers ever to wear an American uniform—General Douglas MacArthur.

According to Ted Joslin, who was in constant contact with Hoover that day, the president weighed his decision with all the gravity one might expect of a committed pacifist. "He took this action under the deepest emotion and with the greatest reluctance," Joslin wrote later. He actually proposed to his secretary of war that the troops be sent in with police batons instead of fire-arms. Hurley scoffed at the suggestion—he "didn't want to see the United States Army defeated by a mob"—and Hoover backed down, a first instance of his deference to military command.

The president then directed Hurley to assemble troops at the Ellipse—the spacious, oval, manicured lawn behind the White House—and to hold them there. Hurley relayed the order to MacArthur, then in his second year as the Army's chief of staff.

MacArthur responded like a peacetime soldier yearning for action, which of course he was, donning full-dress uniform and preparing to take personal command of the force. This approach startled his staff aide, a sol-dier who would later make his own mark in military history, then-Major Dwight D. Eisenhower. So upset was Eisenhower that he objected on the spot, telling MacArthur that personal intervention in a domestic police ac-tion by the highest-ranking officer in the land was "highly inappropriate." "He paid no attention to my dissent," Eisenhower recalled later. There was "incipient revolution in the air," MacArthur told his aide, and he would meet it in person.

Still Hoover stalled. Once the president had issued the order to assemble troops, Hurley pressed him hard to sign a proclamation declaring a domes-tic insurrection and invoking martial law, which would give the military carte blanche in dealing with the protesters. MacArthur specifically sought such authority, which would allow him to place the bonuseers in detention and transport them under guard out of Washington and back to their home states. But the president refused to issue such a sweeping order.

With Hoover holding his ground and the troops restricted to the Ellipse, Hurley called MacArthur. Perhaps the swaggering war chief could persuade the president in person. MacArthur arrived at the White House in full regalia—high boots, spurs and a riding crop, medals on his chest, and a peaked hat. Hurley waited for him outside the Oval Office, and when they were admitted Hurley immediately pressed the case. "Now here's a general, Mr. President. He's been down there and he said the police can't handle this deal."

Hurley could have dispensed with the introduction. Hoover was quite aware of who MacArthur was. It was Hoover who, in 1930, passed over several more senior candidates to name MacArthur chief of staff at a time when he was, at age fifty, the youngest major general in the Army. Hoover's choice elicited much grumbling—one more senior general deemed him "a rotten choice"—but the president never doubted his appointment of the intense, willful commander.

Now conferring with the president in the Oval Office, his troops gathered on the lawn before them, MacArthur brought all his charm and influence to bear. He was convinced, based on a sketchy report from Army Intelligence, that the Bonus Army had been infiltrated by radicals and organized communists armed with machine guns and other weapons. According to this report—overblown as such reports tend to be—any bloodshed in Washington "is to be the signal for a communist uprising in all large cities." The presence of a vocal communist cadre among the BEF—albeit a group ostracized by the other veterans—seemed to lend credence to the story.

The combined pleadings of MacArthur and Hurley held some sway. Besides, circumstances clearly required some kind of action. One man was already dead, the police were cowed, and there were thousands of angry protesters in the streets. Finally, at three o'clock, three hours after the first flare of violence, Hoover yielded. He placed MacArthur in command and ordered the troops into action.

At the same time Hoover granted his order, he released a statement to the press that bore further mark of MacArthur's influence. Hoover reiterated his principal concern, that the bonuseers were holding up construction work in the Federal Triangle. But, for the first time since the veterans arrived in Washington, the president expressed concern that "a considerable part" of the Bonus Army were not ex-soldiers at all, but were "communists and persons with criminal records."

Even so, the order Hoover issued was very much his own. He did not proclaim martial law, as Hurley and MacArthur requested. Instead he gave explicit instructions that troops solely clear the neighborhoods around the Federal Triangle, and that the protesters be returned to their camps—not driven from the district. The Army was to "Cooperate fully with the District of Columbia Police Force which is now in charge." Last, MacArthur was to "use all humanity consistent with the due execution of this order."

What ensued that afternoon is the famous rout of the Bonus Army. For two hours the tattered and woebegone veterans retreated before full-dress soldiers marching in close formation down Pennsylvania Avenue, backed by six tanks under command of Major George Patton. Tear gas was freely deployed, and where knots of veterans put up resistance, mounted cavalry rode them down.

The infantry was well armed but there was no gunfire. Bayonet and saber were the weapons of choice, steel glinting in the hot sun, the cavalry striking blows with the flats of their swords. They inflicted stinging punishment but injured relatively few. Some retreating veterans set fire to their billets in pitiable acts of defiance; where the hovels were left standing, troops stepped in to finish the job. Spectators lined the boulevard, jeering the soldiers and cheering the underdog veterans until clouds of tear gas broke up the crowd.

At 6:30 p.m. MacArthur had cleared most of the downtown area, and called his men to a halt. They mustered at the foot of Pennsylvania Avenue, close by the Anacostia Bridge, and stopped there to eat and regroup.

Chief Glassford was presumed by Hoover to be in charge of the operation but he was quickly reduced to crowd control. This was fine with Glassford—he had attended West Point when MacArthur was first captain, the outstanding member of his class, and Glassford conceived then his life-long wish to see MacArthur elected president. Now he was serving in the field with his hero, and though he was the ranking civil official on the scene, there was little question who was in command.

Glassford did at one point ask MacArthur to "clean up" a particular group of squatters, but MacArthur declined the request. Likewise, the District Commissioners asked MacArthur to move against two camps near the Capitol, but MacArthur refused. He was pressing forward with his offensive and refused to be side-tracked by civilian authorities. As he put it to Glassford that afternoon, he "had orders from the Chief Executive to drive the veterans out of the city. . . . We are going to break the backs of the BEF." Having swept down Pennsylvania Avenue, his next target was the main body of the protesters in Bonus City, across the Anacostia River.

This last target exceeded the explicit bounds of Hoover's initial directive. Sometime late in the day the president learned of the general's plan and immediately moved to stop it. Hoover gave his order to Pat Hurley, who dispatched a staff general to deliver the message in person. The messenger easily located MacArthur, took him aside, and explained that Hoover did not want troops crossing the bridge that night. MacArthur was "very much annoyed"; Dwight Eisenhower, who was on hand, quoted MacArthur saying "he did not want either himself or his staff bothered by people pretending to bring orders."

MacArthur's reputation for flouting authority was already so well established that Hoover and Hurley decided to send a second messenger that night; this envoy, too, quickly found MacArthur and "explained the situation to him fully." There is no question that MacArthur had received, loud and clear, a direct order from the commander in chief and the secretary of war.

MacArthur methodically circumvented the order. Soon after nightfall, a deputized envoy from the BEF stepped out on the Anacostia Bridge waving a white shirt over his head, asking for time to evacuate the women and children of the camp. He was granted a one-hour truce, while MacArthur massed his force. At ten o'clock, he ordered the advance into Bonus City.

Almost immediately, before the first rank of infantry entered the camp itself, small fires sprang up among the shacks and tents and lean-tos, the flames climbing until the entire field was ablaze. Several of the commanding officers on the spot recorded their impressions. "The rioters lost heart in the face of a power they could recognize as overwhelming," MacArthur wrote in an after-action summary he composed for the president. In his memoirs, Dwight Eisenhower adopted a different tone. "It was a pitiful scene," he recalled. "These ragged, discouraged people burning their own little things."

With resistance at an end, General MacArthur left his subordinates in charge and repaired to the White House. He joined Patrick Hurley and for the next half hour described the day's action for the president. There is no record of the meeting, but afterward Hoover promptly retired to bed. He left it to the military men to treat with the press.

Addressing the White House correspondents at eleven o'clock, MacArthur made a point of praising Hoover's "gentleness" and "consideration" for the veterans, then sketched in the administration's emerging line. "There were, in my opinion, few veteran soldiers in that group we cleared out today—few indeed." He quickly acknowledged that he had no actual facts to support that assertion, but that did not give him pause. He spoke with equal confidence on their motives. "That mob down there was a bad looking mob," the general opined. "It was animated by the essence of revolution." There was no mention of communists, but MacArthur's inference was clear.

After a round of questions the reporters disbanded, but MacArthur was not done for the night. He returned with Hurley to the smoldering Anacostia camp and commenced what may have been the cruelest phase of the operation. All that night and into the dawn, squads of soldiers and police harassed the broken ranks of the protesters. At the city limits, state police blocked the roads leading to Virginia and Maryland, leaving the confused and humiliated veterans nowhere to turn.

Finally, toward noon, Secretary Hurley persuaded the authorities in Maryland to grant the veterans through-passage to Pennsylvania. The tattered protesters formed ranks and trudged along Massachusetts Avenue and on out of the district, to scattered applause from sympathizers along the way.

The rout of the Bonus Army was a clear case of overkill, the Army using far more force than necessary against a hapless band of men. But just as clearly the protesting veterans had invited their punishment, overstaying their welcome in the capital and, in the critical moments, assaulting police officers without provocation. Early public response to the dramatic events in Washington was uncertain and divided.

In fact—remarkably, in hindsight—initial press coverage was strongly supportive of the president. *The New York Times* weighed in while troops were still clearing the streets, denouncing the BEF's occupation of the capital "a scandal" and "a national reproach." As to Hoover's response, the *Times* held, "the president could do no other than call upon the army." A day later, editorial reaction was virtually unanimous. "President Hoover was fully justified" in calling out the Army, the *Newark Evening News* insisted; "No other course was possible," agreed the *St. Louis Globe-Democrat*.

It took a series of blunders by Hoover to clarify the question, and rally the public against him. Here he would confirm, if there was still any doubt, that he was most assuredly not a politician.

His biggest mistake was his first one—failing to repudiate MacArthur for disobeying his direct order. He had the opportunity, either during the evening conference with Hurley the night of the riot or, by another account, in a face-to-face meeting the morning after, while the hovels of the BEF still smoldered on the mud flats by the Anacostia River. According to one version, MacArthur actually tendered his resignation, but Hoover refused him in an act of misplaced loyalty that bound him unalterably to MacArthur's bellicose and ultimately erroneous version of events. There is no official record of this encounter, but it was described later by two Hoover intimates in oral history interviews.

As the story goes, MacArthur acknowledged to the president that he had violated a direct order; that rather than corral the BEF veterans, he had attacked and routed them. In one account—credited to a statement from Hoover himself—the president told a friend that he "upbraided" MacArthur for his insubordination. "He bawled MacArthur out," Hoover's friend told his interviewer. Bawled him out, but then let the matter rest.

The other version, passed on secondhand from a Hoover business associate, purports to recall what Hoover told his errant general.

"I know you disobeyed orders," Hoover is alleged to have said. "But I believe you did what you thought you should do under the circumstances. You have an outstanding career in the Army and you have a brilliant future ahead of you. I have a broad back and can take the criticism which will result from what has happened. I refuse to accept your resignation."

It is too much to expect that Hoover's remarks were captured verbatim in this decades-later, secondhand account. Yet there is a distinctly Hooverian feel to the statement: the condescending attitude, the vainglorious sense of personal sacrifice—"I have a broad back." And it jibes with the ingenuous reverence Hoover reserved for people whose aptitudes ran foreign to his nature. Hoover appears to have been awed by MacArthur, a born soldier, already famous for exploits in combat, in the same way Hoover was reverential toward the consummate politician William Borah, or even his personal sleuth, the dapper sportsman Larry Richey.

More than that, Hoover's indulgence of the insubordinate MacArthur jibes with his warped sense of personal loyalty—the same instinct that led him to jettison Mabel Willebrandt and William Donovan, and to pass over Justice Harlan Stone, but to stand by the political grifter Claudius Huston to the bitter end. It was as if the surest way to win Hoover's allegiance was to commit some crucial act of malfeasance.

Whatever may have transpired between the president and the general, it resulted in MacArthur retaining his post, and Hoover accepting personal responsibility for all that had occurred. The morning after the rout of the veterans, Hoover spent another hour in conference with Secretary of War Patrick Hurley. Promptly thereafter, the president adopted a new and much more severe tone regarding the BEF and the actions of the Army.

Hoover signaled his approach by ordering a grand jury to investigate the central allegation in the administration's new, hard line: that the riots were triggered by radical instigators, not the long-suffering veterans. Attorney General Mitchell named one of his assistants as a special prosecutor to lead the inquiry.

The same morning, Hoover fired off a caustic letter to the district commissioners, underscored by a statement to the press. Addressing reporters toward the end of the day, Hoover announced that, "A challenge to the authority of the United States Government has been met, swiftly and firmly." A day before he said the protesting veterans were "no doubt unaware" of the "communists and persons with criminal records" who had led them astray; now the BEF was a "mob" perpetrating "organized lawlessness."

Hoover's letter to the commissioners went further, suggesting that "subversive influences . . . inaugurated and organized this attack" on the police. More than that, the president implied that the police themselves—and, by implication, Chief Glassford—were to blame; that "the mobs . . . were undoubtedly led to believe that the civil authorities could be intimidated with impunity because of attempts to conciliate by lax enforcement of city ordinances and laws."

This new attitude contradicted the spirit of patience and toleration with which Hoover had treated even the avowedly communist demonstrators who marched on Washington that winter. When throngs of discouraged veterans began arriving in May, the remote silence Hoover maintained was never very endearing, but at least his scruples afforded him some claim to moral high ground. Now his new, vengeful tone cost him even that vestige of humanity. It did not suit him, and it did not serve him.

Hoover's patronizing letter to the district commissioners drew a sharp response from a most unexpected quarter—the chief of the District of Columbia Police. Pelham Glassford never did like being paired with the dour and unpopular president, and he clearly felt conflicted about sending armed soldiers to roust his fellow war veterans. Now Glassford openly turned against Hoover, announcing to reporters that he had not, in fact, requested reinforcements from the Army, and that he and his officers never did need their assistance. Tellingly, he did not quarrel with the commissioners over the request they made to Hoover; his dispute was with the president.

Paired with Hoover's new, tougher tone, Glassford's announcement changed the politics of the Bonus eviction dramatically. The district police chief now stood alone as the friend of the downtrodden soldiers, while the president emerged as the author of their humiliation, stern and remorseless.

Several key members of Congress, on vacation but still in town, promptly chimed in. Tennessee Democrat Kenneth McKellar vowed to launch an investigation of his own, with blame to be placed on "those who were responsible for this miserable fiasco." Making his own position clear, McKellar said the president had "not the slightest excuse" for calling in the Army.

Evidently surprised at this backlash, the president began to feel exposed. With the heat rising, he suggested to Patrick Hurley that Hurley and General MacArthur step up in a public defense of the administration's show of force. Hurley discussed it with MacArthur, and then declined the invitation.

Hurley phoned his decision in to Larry Richey at the White House, leaving a frank message for the president. MacArthur feared "it would be bragging," Hurley explained to Richey, "putting a man forth in the role of a hero." And Hurley agreed; if it were he taking the lead, it would appear unseemly. "Here I am, a ex-serviceman and so forth. I actually gave the order that moved the troops in. It is a defense of myself to say we didn't kill anybody, and we are nice boys and did a good job."

Besides, Hurley told Richey, the eviction of the BEF needed no explanation. "Why should we defend a just action on which the response to the
president is 99 percent right now? That would be trying ourselves, and you
know how fickle the public is."

Hurley rationalized further. "I would not have [Hoover] think for a moment that I don't want to do it because I could do it and be some kind of
hero. I could get the thing across in fine shape, but I would have to be showing, 'Here is the man who did the job.'" Better for Hoover to accept the
laurels himself, Hurley said. "As it is now, the Chief is standing at the head
where he should be, and there is nobody against him except Scripps Howard
and a bag of scatterbrains.

"My opinion is for all of us to stay off the silver sheet now"—a reference
to the newsreels, which were the most powerful news medium of the moment. "After going over it with his friends and among our people," Hurley
reiterated, "we decided that neither myself nor MacArthur should hit the
foot lights."

One can only wonder how Hoover responded to this memo. Did he
decide that yes, after all, he for once should accept all the credit that he usually shared with his subordinates? Or did it set off another bout of second
thoughts and self-doubt, Hoover considering all the risks of standing alone,
of letting credit—or blame—settle on his "broad back"?

What is clear is that Hoover did stand on his own, continuing ever after
to blame communists and "criminals" for inciting the riot, even after the
grand jury investigation he asked for failed to return a single indictment.
What is clear as well is that the strategy Hurley offered and which Hoover
followed was a political disaster.

Newsreel footage projected on the silver sheet was especially damaging.
Images of helmeted troops rousting and gassing impoverished veterans of-
fended any sense of fair play. Combined with Hoover's prior opposition to
food aid and his belated conversion to public relief, the harsh treatment of
the bonuseers completed the picture of a cold and heartless president.

One observer who immediately grasped the political implications of the
Bonus riot was Franklin Roosevelt. Reclining in the governor's mansion in
Albany the morning after the melee in Washington, the newly confirmed

Democratic nominee reviewed newspaper photos of the smoke and the mayhem and pronounced them "scenes from a nightmare."

The governor shared with Rex Tugwell, a key member of the inner circle that would come to be known as the "Brains Trust," his frank amazement at the depth of Hoover's blunder. He had planned to spend part of that day reviewing campaign strategy, but it appeared now that wouldn't be necessary, Roosevelt said. So far as he was concerned, the election was all but over.

Roosevelt didn't just gloat at Hoover's error; he wondered how it came to pass. Back in 1920, Roosevelt recalled, he'd been among those touting Hoover for president; the great humanitarian appeared then as "a kind of superman." Eight years later, during his run for the White House, Hoover remained the most admired public figure in the country. But come the crash, he'd isolated himself, relying on "his business friends" and talking about principles. But for all the meetings and all the pronouncements, Hoover "hadn't done anything that was nearly big enough," Roosevelt said.

Now, confronted by "a few poor, unorganized fellows," the president had surrounded himself with guards and "set Doug MacArthur on those harmless vets." It was no longer a question of policy, but character. Hoover had been a very different person during the war years, or perhaps Roosevelt didn't know him as well as he thought. "There was nothing left inside the man but jelly," he mused. "Maybe there never *had* been anything."

Tugwell made no comment as to Hoover's character, but on the political implications of the Bonus rout, he was unconvinced. Republicans were a "pretty traditional" group, accustomed to control of the White House; wouldn't they stick with the incumbent, continue to vote the party line? Roosevelt pointed again to the photos from Anacostia camp and shook his head. Hoover should have sent out coffee and donuts, not troops and gas.

The governor leaned back and lit a cigarette. He wouldn't waste any more time analyzing his foe. Hoover now stood exposed before the public. "Everyone could see what was there, and they wouldn't like it." Neither did Roosevelt. He'd been friends with Hoover in the past, but no more. "I won't feel sorry for him even in November."

Roosevelt felt confident he could handle Hoover, but he was less sure just what he should offer in the way of an alternative. On Saturday evening, July 30, just a day after his conversation with Tugwell, Roosevelt delivered the first address of his campaign, a radio talk, delivered from the comfort of his drawing room in Albany.

It was his first statement as the Democratic candidate, but it appears the nominee was still seeking to appease the different factions of his own party. His speech consisted chiefly of a reprise of the platform devised by the party in Chicago, a centrist document that scored the Republicans for bringing on the Depression, and vowed to restore balanced budgets and a "sound currency." Gone was the veiled class analysis, the appeal to the Forgotten Man that Roosevelt sounded in the spring. Rather, Roosevelt scored Hoover as a spendthrift, and vowed to slash federal spending "by not less than twenty-five percent." In the same vein, Roosevelt settled on the fiscal conservative Jack Garner—and not one of senate militants—as his running mate.

This shift to the center was a curious tactic for the Democratic nominee. As much as he attacked Republicans for "the disastrous policies pursued by our government since the World War," Roosevelt outlined an agenda that appeared quite similar. As one of his key advisors observed later, "Herbert Hoover could have readily endorsed the statement."

It was true that Roosevelt had ventured onto Hoover's turf, and Republicans around the country recognized it immediately. On Sunday morning the White House switchboard was working nonstop as Ted Joslin fielded calls offering advice and assistance. The president himself was energized and optimistic. He saw that Roosevelt was venturing into uncertain territory and he was determined to take advantage. "The thing to do, Ted, is to carry the fight to Roosevelt," Hoover declared, and he spent the afternoon parceling out talking points to Republican senators. "We've got to crack him every time he opens his mouth. Now's our chance."

It was one thing for Hoover to identify a weakness in his opponent, but quite another to salvage his own shattered reputation. The fact remained that, for all his efforts—unseen by Roosevelt or the public at large, but the product of prodigious toil—none of the successive crises of the Depression were solved.

They had simply accumulated, like a bastard litter, each unwanted pup still crying for attention.

On the agricultural front, the Farm Board's massive buying program had hardly slowed the pace of deflation. Prices remained so low that growers lost money on every harvest. In Iowa and on out to Nebraska, frustrated farmers decided on drastic measures—pulling their produce from the market and forcing others to do likewise. The result was a farmers strike, centered in Sioux City, where militant growers set up barricades on rural roads to block any trucks hauling farm produce. In a few instances crews of Khaki Shirts, remnants of the Bonus Army, joined straw-hatted farmers at the roadblocks.

Federal officials watched these developments carefully. J. Edgar Hoover had FBI agents monitor the unrest and relayed their reports to Larry Richey. State and local authorities sent lawmen out under orders to arrest any picketers on charges of inciting to riot. But Hoover's political friends in the Midwest warned him to make "every possible effort" to avoid taking a direct federal role. The movement soon petered out—another act of frustration from men who'd lost everything—but growers remained convinced that the Republicans and their president had deserted them in their hour of need.

Hoover had no more luck with the financial community and the drive to open the channels of credit. Late in July, while most of Washington was preoccupied with the travails of the BEF, Hoover received a report from Eugene Meyer on credit problems in the Ohio district of the Federal Reserve. Despite the best efforts of the Fed and the RFC, businesses still could not obtain loans from Cleveland's "timorous banks."

To Hoover, this signaled just the occasion to invoke the amendment inserted by Carter Glass in the relief bill, the emergency provision that would authorize the Fed to make direct loans to businesses because bank credits had been immobilized. "This statement is a complete indictment of the banking situation," the president wrote in an urgent letter to the governors of the Fed. "The result of these restrictions [on loans] has been to increase unemployment and to stifle business activity."

Hoover was not criticizing the Fed, but pressing it to take action. "We cannot stand by and see the American people, suffering as they are today and to the extent that may imperil the very stability of the government, because of the unwillingness of the banks to take advantage of the facilities provided by the government."

But while most of the Fed governors had supported the Glass amendment, they resented Hoover's approach as an infringement upon their statutory autonomy. When Eugene Meyer presented the president's letter at a meeting of the board July 26, the reaction was quick and sharp. "The board was very angry," Charles Hamlin recorded; even Hoover's old friend Adolph Miller denounced Hoover's advance as "the most offensive assumption of executive authority in the history of the Federal Reserve Board."

There was no question as to the urgency of the situation—the governors of the Fed understood as well as any the prostrate state of the economy—but their concerns were bureaucratic and political. Charles Hamlin sorted his feelings in his diary; "at first," he thought to himself, "this insulting and illegal letter meant that Hoover thought the board was not showing good faith in carrying out the [Glass] amendment." He then decided on a more pejorative interpretation. "On second consideration," Hamlin wrote, "it was but another manifestation of Hoover's desire to dominate and obtain personal credit for everything."

Hamlin felt confirmed in his skepticism in August when Hoover convened a meeting of the ad hoc business and industrial committees that had caused such friction at the Fed in May. Hoover made a point of extending a personal invitation to Hamlin, but when he neglected to include the Fed governors at a reception for the committee delegates, Hamlin took offense.

It was, in the end, a lugubrious affair, lacking the energy and promise of Hoover's initial business conferences after the Wall Street crash, and shadowed by the presidential campaign. The president sought to inject a sense of urgent purpose in the proceedings with a speech that leaned heavily on military metaphors, reprising the story of "invading forces" met by "constant defense and counter-attack." Hoover closed climactically: "The attack on our line has been stopped. But I warn you that the war is not over, we must now reform our forces for the battle of Soissons."

For all his labors the president could not overcome the sense of the administration going through the motions—again. To read the news coming out of Washington, Arthur Krock remarked in *The New York Times*, "one might have believed himself back in 1930 or 1931." There was little more enthusiasm generated inside the conference. Attendees were "disgusted" to find more time devoted to speeches than problem-solving workshops. It was, Hamlin ruled, "a purely political conference."

Some degree of cynicism may have been inevitable, given the weight of a historic economic depression combined with Hoover's tin-eared approach to politics. But by this point even the president's adversaries were beginning to think he was jinxed. "In 1932," Roosevelt advisor Rex Tugwell wrote later, "there seemed to be some evil magic working against Hoover."

TWENTY-TWO

PRESIDENT REJECT

O N A SATURDAY AFTERNOON IN MAY PRESIDENT HOOVER SPENT
a rare, free hour chatting with the journalist H. V. Kaltenborn, a reporter
who made the switch early on from print to the more immediate medium of
radio. It was more a conversation than an interview, and Hoover was feeling free and glib. But he was president, after all, and before it was over the
discussion turned to the upcoming election.

Kaltenborn asked Hoover if he were worried about his campaign prospects. "No, not at all," the president quickly replied. It was obviously too
flip a response, considering the state of the economy and the popularity
of Franklin Roosevelt. After a pause, Hoover decided to explain himself.
"The reason I'm not worried is because I don't give a damn whether I am
re-elected or not." Here was Hoover's old ambivalence about politics, braced
now by three trying years in the White House. It was a candid remark, but
not exactly true, and carried the potential for real political damage.

Kaltenborn ended his visit soon after Hoover's statement; a few minutes
later Hoover called in Ted Joslin, and queried vaguely what he might know
about Kaltenborn. Joslin said he knew him from a few years back as a correspondent for *The Brooklyn Daily Eagle*. Hoover then asked if Kaltenborn

"HE THINKS IT WILL DO"

This image depicts not Hoover but the
Republican Party, portrayed as a befuddled
old burgher, running on the "Theories of
the Harding Administration." Clearly, the
country was ready for something new.

understood the current White House ground rules for reporters—that "all talks with the president are confidential." Joslin couldn't say for sure.

"Then run him down," Hoover barked. "I said something that would cause a world sensation if repeated publicly." Joslin jumped. He caught up with Kaltenborn just as he was leaving the White House, and the story was successfully squelched. It was a typical case of Hoover second-guessing himself, and a nice demonstration of Hoover's divided mind. But for Joslin it was something more—confirmation of Hoover's unacknowledged but ill-concealed yen to be returned to office. "The president may say he doesn't give a damn about reelection," Joslin commented in his diary, "but he wants it more than anything else."

It was a bit absurd, for the highest elected official in the nation to continue, after three years in office, to resent the most basic requirements of his station, but the conflict was intrinsic to Hoover's makeup, and it persisted through the campaign.

In July, for instance, he recalled that in the 1928 campaign he'd made just five major speeches; this time, he decided, he would make only three. That same week, when pressed to make a campaign swing through the far West, where voters felt alienated from distant Washington, Hoover emphatically declined; "He said the trouble was that he couldn't go away without stopping at every little station the train stopped at, and then everybody would have a crowd of people there, and he would have to make little foolish speeches."

It almost became a game with Hoover, as if to remind even his close friends of his intrinsic propriety. As late as September, with his first major campaign trip, to Des Moines, scheduled three weeks hence, Hoover told Joslin that he had decided not to go. Joslin, by now accustomed to these occasional bouts of petulance, asked, simply, "What do you mean?"

"No president seeking re-election has campaigned," Hoover pronounced. "You are all wrong," came Joslin's retort; he himself had traveled with Presidents Taft and Wilson when they were running for reelection. To confirm the point Joslin sent a messenger home to obtain a scrapbook with clippings of stories from those campaign appearances. They were delivered and Hoover was perusing them when political secretary Walter Newton happened by. "I guess, Walter," the president said, "I can make that trip after all."

The one campaign strategy that Hoover embraced was the combative retort, the "hit-back" responses to every utterance by Franklin Roosevelt. It was a tactic that would gratify a political pugilist like James MacLafferty, but, tellingly, rather than do the slugging himself, Hoover designated surrogates like Ogden Mills or, frequently, Patrick Hurley.

The cabinet members sallied forth, but they were intrinsically figures of the second rank, and with Roosevelt taking the field in person, these rhetorical counterpunches began to wear thin. By August, Henry Stimson worried that the public was starting to lose interest in the administration's ripostes; more than that, he worried, "It is getting to be a little bit undignified."

Dignified or not, it was the course Hoover had chosen, and in September he decided the time had come to escalate. He would continue to issue directives answering his rival's speeches, but he also wanted a direct frontal challenge to Roosevelt. This would best be made by "someone from New York," Hoover decided, but Ogden Mills was already too closely tied to the president to be effective. After a routine meeting of the cabinet, Hoover took Henry Stimson aside and told him he wanted the speech to come from him.

For Stimson, this request from the president came as "a dreadful shock." As one of the few members of the cabinet with an independent public reputation, Stimson had been a great help to Hoover in building popular support for the moratorium. But here Stimson drew the line. He considered domestic affairs an improper subject for comment by the secretary of state; he also considered it bad politics. "I told all this to the president and frankly told him I wouldn't do it," Stimson recorded in his diary.

Stimson maintained a high regard for Hoover, for his great toil and for the great obstacles he faced. "I was turning down the first request he had made of me in regard to the campaign and it made me feel very badly," Stimson reflected. "He is very much alone. Nobody is supporting him and nobody is making speeches for him except members of his Cabinet."

Still, Stimson considered Hoover's request a shocking case of overreach. The president was feeling cornered, and he was lashing out against even his strongest allies. "Altogether it was a damned unpleasant interview," Stimson wrote.

To Joslin, charged with managing the press, Hoover's inherently re-active strategy was simply insufficient. Hoover needed to take the lead—present his own agenda, and let Roosevelt do the answering, not the other way 'round. "The president has the 'answer-hit back' complex as have few I have ever known," Joslin grumbled at one point. He tried to persuade his boss to adopt a different tone, but on this question as on so many, Hoover was intransigent. "I have talked until I am black in the face," Joslin told his diary, but without effect. "Oh well."

It wasn't just the demands of the campaign trail that Hoover so resented, or the speechmaking, or even the public scrutiny, though each of those ele-ments he found trying. More than that Hoover disliked the idea that he had to sell himself as a person, to put himself on display. His was the visceral reaction of the recluse exposed to light, involuntary and unreasoning. And it found expression in a burning resentment for the mediators in that process: the press.

In his years at Commerce Hoover made a point of cultivating reporters; upon returning to the United States from Europe, he had even purchased an interest in two newspapers, one of them in Washington. But when he was elected president whatever collegial affinity he felt toward the White House correspondents had evaporated; now, when he needed most to curry their favor, his hostility was absolute.

And it was mutual. By the nature of their office presidents generally believe the press corps is working against them, but there is little question that in Washington in 1932 reporters and editors had a lively antipathy for Hoover, a disdain unmatched by any successor until the next Quaker to oc-cupy the White House—Richard Nixon, some forty years later.

Part of this hostility was due to the essentially populist nature of the press, and the feeling among reporters—as with so many Americans at the time—that Hoover cared little for the travails of the common man. But part of it was more personal, rooted in the correspondents' resentment at the manner of their treatment at the hands of the White House. The early promise of more open and candid communication with the president had quickly faded until the sporadic press conferences were lifeless and dull.

More troubling, reporters whose stories managed to offend the prickly president were subject to investigation by Larry Richey or the Secret Service, and in some cases official complaints to their editors and publishers. Republican operative Ted Clark, corresponding with Calvin Coolidge at the height of the campaign, lamented "the bitter personal hatred which [Hoover] has inspired in so many newspaper men." It was "one of the unfortunate features of the whole Hoover administration," and left the president at a distinct disadvantage. "News has been distorted in an effort to injure Mr. Hoover to a degree that I never imagined possible," Clark wrote.

Clark based this critique on both his intimate knowledge of the Hoover administration, which was the subject of his continuing scrutiny, and of the Washington press corps. Thus he spoke to Coolidge of actions and policies that are difficult to corroborate, but also difficult to ignore. According to Clark, beginning around the time of the moratorium, Hoover and Richey intensified their "ruthless attitude toward the press."

It started with an obsession with leaks—a fixation, it should be mentioned, that seems endemic to the office of the chief executive. "The White House undertook to use the Secret Service to find out the sources of stories which might be perfectly harmless in themselves but which showed that someone near the president had given the press a hint."

Hoover and his team further alienated the press, Clark wrote, by attempting "to directly control individual correspondents by open threats and demands upon publishers that various persons be fired." Among several others, Clark cited the case of Ted Wallen, Washington bureau chief for the *New York Herald Tribune*, who "had to fight for his life against the personal attempt of the president to have him displaced." The episode, Clark said, was "generally known."

Nor was this the limit of the administration's resentment. Larry Richey's loyalty to Hoover had "led him to incredible extremes" in pursuing vendettas. "I know personally that agencies of the government were used for intimidation whenever possible," Clark declared.

Again, there is no documentation of such official excesses, but on one occasion the president himself gave the idea implicit corroboration. In Au-

gust, when Ted Joslin pleaded with the president to invite the press to a
scheduled luncheon, Hoover boiled over. "They have no respect for the office I hold," Hoover said of the correspondents. "Once I am reelected I am
going to clean that bunch out whatever the consequences may be." Hoover
then intimated that he'd compiled dossiers on specific individuals. "I have
enough on fifty of them to hang them," the president thundered. "Let any of
them make one move after November and I'll go for them."

Recording the outburst that night, Joslin could only marvel. "How the
president hates the press!"

The president's retreat on the Rapidan River was a particular source of friction with the press corps. The place was the focus of special interest because
it was the sort of relaxed, convivial setting where the remote and stiff-necked
president might actually unbend. More than that, he spent weekends there in
company with members of his administration and other key people, engaged
in discussions that often resulted in important policy. Yet reporters were
never allowed even to approach the camp. Required by their editors to tail
the president but barred from the premises, they spent those summer weekends in purgatory at a town several miles distant, awaiting whatever scraps
of information Richey or Ted Joslin might toss their way via telephone.

This sore point flared again in July, when construction of a new road
emboldened the correspondents to propose to Joslin that they might trail the
president as far as the Marine post that stood at the entrance to the Rapidan
Camp. When the camp's Marine Corps commander confirmed that he had
no right to bar the reporters from the public road, Joslin granted permission
and then informed the president. "There is nothing for them to see there,"
Hoover shrugged. "But if they stop within five miles of my camp I'll have
them arrested!"

Joslin had divided loyalties. He'd been a member of the press himself
until just a year before; now he worked daily with, and was deeply loyal to
Hoover. He didn't choose sides here, but was struck by the intensity of the
strife. "There is almost as much love lost between the President and the press
as between God Almighty and the devil himself," Joslin wrote in his diary.

In August, Richey and Joel Boone hit upon a plan to restore some amity
between Hoover and the correspondents—a press day up at the Rapidan,

with photographers as well as reporters, and all their spouses invited, with the president and Mrs. Hoover as their hosts. Richey sold the idea to Joslin, and together they convinced Hoover to go along.

On Saturday, August 20, a caravan of press vehicles wound its way up over the Blue Ridge and down to the camp, the journalists getting their first look inside the president's retreat. Richey, Boone, and Joslin readied the president, but Hoover could not seem to get past his resentment at the idea of reporters swarming through his private hideaway. Richey set up a number of activities to perform in front of the cameras, but Hoover refused to engage in even the most banal civilities. "He was none too hospitable," Ted Joslin recorded. "He went though his stunts—fishing, walking with Mrs. Hoover, playing with the dogs and riding his horse—but he did the task mechanically. He wanted to get it over."

Hoover was so disgruntled, so distracted, that when he donned riding gaiters, he put them on backward. Come the lunch break, when all the reporters and their spouses gathered at the camp's central Town Hall, Hoover declined to join them. Making the long drive back to the capital that evening, Richey and Joel Boone rode in silence, "feeling pretty depressed." The press day had been "a fiasco."

Of course, Hoover's bid for a second term had many problems that had nothing to do with the press. Hoover himself was quite aware of them: at one point he enumerated them for Joslin. "We are opposed by ten million unemployed, ten thousand Bonus marchers, and ten-cent corn. Is it any wonder that the prospects are dark?"

Inevitably, Hoover's efforts to fight the Depression and his electoral campaign coursed in the same channel, meeting at the principal agency in the government's economic arsenal—the Reconstruction Finance Corp. After Congress agreed in July to boost RFC funding and expand its role, business and government leaders across the country began looking for movement and for funding. Instead they found stasis. And when the new agency did finally swing into action, it was immediately assailed for what it did do, and what it didn't.

The RFC program that drew the most interest, and the most political heat, was the Emergency Relief Division, charged with dispensing federal loans to states that were unable to sustain relief efforts from their own coffers. This was Hoover's great concession to advocates of federal intervention, like Robert Wagner, but it would also be a point of intense discord, as the principals sorted through clashing values to put ideas into action.

From the beginning, officials at the RFC accepted Hoover's thesis that the first responsibility for aid rested with the states. "This means," said Atlee Pomerene, the Democrat who replaced Eugene Meyer, "that federal funds may be used only when all monies then available or those which can be made available, are not sufficient."

State governors promptly tested these rules, filing applications totaling $200 million, with several seeking the statutory maximum of $45 million. First to be turned down, early in August, was Pennsylvania. There was no question as to need—unemployment was running over 30 percent, and private charities were thoroughly exhausted, their clients reduced to what one social worker termed a state of "primitive communism." But the state constitution barred direct outlays for relief, and when the governor sought authority for emergency spending, lawmakers rejected his bid for an override. In consequence, the RFC board voted unanimously to stand aside "until we know what the [Pennsylvania] Legislature will do for the relief of its own people."

Caught in the middle was Governor Gifford Pinchot, a mercurial Progressive in the mode of George Norris. Rebuffed at his own State House and now by the RFC, Pinchot refused to assign state staff to spend weeks composing a request that might satisfy the federal bureaucrats. "Our people are not in favor of splitting hairs while children starve," Pinchot wrote in a letter to the RFC board. If the funds were not forthcoming, Pinchot would address a personal appeal to the president.

This was a purely political gesture; Hoover and Pinchot had clashed years before, when Pinchot served briefly under Hoover at the Food Administration and quit his post in a policy dispute. But Hoover took the bait, dispatching to Pinchot a terse note asserting the autonomy of the RFC and his support for the "eminent, patriotic, and sympathetic men" on the board.

Governor Pinchot finally revised his state's application, and in September the RFC awarded a loan of $2.5 million. But Pinchot found this figure wholly inadequate, and answered with a letter to Pomerene that was clearly aimed at Hoover and the upcoming election. The RFC and the president cared only for the rich, he charged; "in giving help to the great banks, great railroads and great corporations you have shown no such niggardly spirit . . . our people have little patience with giving everything possible to the big fellow and as little as possible to the little fellow."

Pennsylvania received its loan, however, and having conformed to the system, was now in rotation for monthly allotments that amounted to $27 million over the course of the winter. But the dustup seemed to confirm the image of Hoover as a skinflint and a plutocrat. His pained, grudging concession to appeals for federal relief had gained him nothing.

Hoover fared little better with a second new initiative at the RFC, specifically designed to expand employment. This was the Self-Liquidating Division, charged with financing public works. The title had an unappetizing ring to it but had the virtue of being self-explanatory: this was to be the great jobs generator that the fiscal activists had been clamoring for, but because the projects would pay for themselves, they could be financed and built without raising taxes or adding to the public debt. Here was a policy all sides could get behind.

But that was just on paper. In execution, the Self-Liquidating Division soon bogged down in the same sort of conflicts that had plagued Hoover's earlier efforts to expand public works: major projects required extensive planning, as well as protracted wrangling over which projects to fund, and where.

Added to this was the special requirement that, in order to prevent the government from displacing private enterprise, RFC loans should carry an interest rate higher than that offered on the private market. This could be the difference between profit and loss with a complex project like slum clearance, a category specifically authorized under the Construction and Relief Act. Senator Robert Wagner teamed with former governor Al Smith to propose just such a venture for the East Side of New York, but when the RFC declined lowering its loan rate, the venture had to be abandoned.

Such technical issues, combined with the basic provision that projects generate a positive cash flow, sharply curtailed the number of works authorized by the RFC. By early October, of 243 applications filed with the Self-Liquidating Division, just three had been approved. This was maddening, of course, to public jobs advocates like Senator Wagner, who denounced the RFC for generating "mile upon mile of red tape." In refusing to bend its regulations, the agency "is depriving unemployed workers of jobs and is cruel and dangerous."

Hoover found the delays just as exasperating. Early in August, after a cabinet meeting, Hoover fell into conversation with Henry Stimson and Ogden Mills. Stimson was sharing the thoughts of a financier he'd spoken with early in the week, who advised that he saw signs of incipient recovery under way, but that the timing was delicate, and that it would be a grave mistake to allow politics to influence the timing or the pace of projects undertaken by the RFC. The trick, Stimson said, was to ensure that Democrats enjoyed "strong representation" on key agencies like the RFC, "so that every decision would be nonpartisan."

Here Hoover interjected. "To my surprise," Stimson wrote in his diary that night, "the president broke into a rather impassioned speech in which he said that he had made up his mind that even if the Democrats wouldn't go along with him, he was going to use all the machinery [of the government] to win the election, for he felt that was necessary for the country." With Mills looking on, Stimson told Hoover he was "astounded" to hear him speak in such fashion, but Hoover "kept repeating it." Stimson took it as a sign of the "terrible strain" Hoover was working under, a symptom of his distress "in regard to the effect of this Depression upon his fortunes." Certainly that was true; it was also confirmation that Hoover was, as Joslin put it, "frantic" for a second term.

Unfortunately for Hoover, the harder he pushed, the more it worked against him. In October, with pressure mounting to show some sort of accomplishment, the Self-Liquidating Division approved three major projects, all in California: the Bay Bridge, linking Oakland to San Francisco; a new waterworks for Pasadena; and the Metropolitan Aqueduct, which would carry water from the Colorado River to Los Angeles. These were just the sort of projects Hoover's critics had been clamoring for, but now he was denounced for prostituting his pet program. The RFC was simply, as *The Nation* headlined, "Buying California for Hoover."

Hoover was also haunted by a compromise he'd made in order to push the RFC amendments through Congress—a clause, insisted upon by Jack Garner, making public the recipients of RFC loans. Hoover fought the provision, then relented on Senator Joe Robinson's assurance that loan information would not be made public. Once the bill went through, however, Garner insisted he'd made no such bargain, and in mid-August the first RFC loan report was issued.

The report was not particularly damaging, covering only the first ten days after the vote approving the amendment on July 21. It confirmed the impression of a very active agency, showing $45 million in loans to 437 borrowers for the reporting period, and a total $866 million since the February launch of the RFC. But it also showed that the preponderance of loans went to banks and railroads, helping fuel the thesis that the president was concerned principally with the fortunes of the wealthy.

Hoover tackled the point directly in his August speech accepting his party's nomination. Loans to banks were made "not to save a few stockholders," he said, "but to save twenty-five million American families, every one of whose savings and employment might have been wiped out and whose whole futures would have been blighted had those institutions gone down." It was an earnest argument, but not nearly so catchy as the critics' mantra that the RFC was the "millionaire's dole."

The problems at the RFC were predictable and perhaps inevitable, bumps along the learning curve associated with launching a major and untried financial initiative in the midst of an economic maelstrom. But in the context of a political campaign the performance of the agency reflected on its sponsor in ways he did not anticipate.

And Hoover was not operating in a vacuum. He was facing a challenge from a resourceful, creative, even brilliant politician, and as the campaign got truly under way, Roosevelt began to set the terms of the debate. He did so by hitting Hoover early and often, shifting ground and angles of attack, never holding still long enough for the literal-minded, overworked president to respond.

Hoover tried to. He denounced Roosevelt for his "self-interested inexactitude," and derided him, in one unusually droll formulation, as a "chameleon on Scotch plaid." But the president's retorts always felt late, slow, and defensive. It was like Cassius Clay facing Sonny Liston—Roosevelt floated like a butterfly, and stung like a bee.

The challenger's shape-shifting manner on the stump was not necessarily by design. It was the product of his process—one diametrically opposed to the president's. Where Hoover took pride in writing his own speeches, Roosevelt did not bother even to attempt authorship. The one time he did pen his own lines during the campaign, his wife and advisors found the product tedious and Roosevelt blithely discarded his draft. Instead he relied on a variety of speechwriters who disagreed among themselves over basic policy. Untroubled by the hobgoblin of consistency, Roosevelt read the lines as they came. Thus he might call for balanced budgets on one night, and major new spending programs a week later.

But as Roosevelt cherry-picked ideas from his advisors, the choices he made plotted out as themes in his campaign. One certain drift in his thinking was to insist on change, if only because the status quo had so evidently failed. "Bold, persistent experimentation," he termed it in May; "above all, try something!" Whatever it was that America might need, it had to be something different, a fresh approach, a New Deal.

To Hoover's mind, this was just what he'd been doing for the past three years. The Farm Board, the moratorium, the Reconstruction Finance Corporation, and the Home Loan Banks, each marked a dramatic break with past practice. But the president always stepped carefully, balancing his innovations and couching them in the rhetoric of probity and convention. Thus the Farm Board was conceived to head off the radical price-fixing of McNary-Haugen, and the RFC was formed to preserve, rather than replace, the existing financial system. Now Roosevelt was turning Hoover's painstaking deliberation against him.

More troubling to Hoover, and possibly more damaging, was Roosevelt's effort to align himself with the common man, and Hoover with the economic elite. Hoover felt these slights and insinuations deeply, especially as the accusation came from a man literally born in a country manor. From the time he entered politics Hoover had conceived of himself as a facts-driven Progressive, an administrator whose vision transcended the categories of labor or management, wealthy or poor. For Roosevelt to assail his motives seemed to alter the very nature of electoral politics; rather than argue the merits of his platform, Hoover said later, the governor's campaign "revolved around personal attacks."

This complaint was certainly overwrought. Politics had been an intensely personal game since the dawn of the republic, and no less so in the decade after the Great War. But Hoover's pain was real enough—the result of his famously thin skin, but also of Roosevelt's success in defining his opponent.

It got so bad that in July, Lou Hoover felt obliged to write an extraordinary letter to her sons, to ensure that at least they and their children should know their patriarch as she knew him, and not as portrayed by his foes. "I started this letter when I was much incensed at reading one morning of Democratic and 'Progressive' effusions about the President's having no thought for the little man, but bending all his energies toward saving the bloated plutocrat," Lou explained. "The absolute injustice and downright lying infuriated me—and there rushed through my mind a whirlwind mind-movie of how all that he has been doing so endlessly and so courageously has been for the small individual, the millions of them."

In fact, Lou asserted, Bert only agreed to run for president because the office would afford him the best chance to serve "the least privileged classes of our community."

"This, and this alone, I really believe I can say, persuaded him," Lou told her children.

She proceeded at some length, unspooling her mind-movie, recalling their father's years running huge mining operations in the Australian out-back, in China, in Russia and Burma. "In all of these I have watched from month to month, week to week, day by day, his foremost thought shaping affairs to the best interests of the so-called smaller people."

"Never were his men not the best paid in a community," she wrote in growing indignation. "Never would he permit their well-being to be sacrificed to the shareholders." Then came the war, and Hoover's emergence as the Great Humanitarian; he "worked as few men have ever worked before" in the service of the Belgians, and then of refugees across Europe.

Hoover maintained his benevolent attitudes in the White House, she wrote. "Look back through these past three years, and recognize," Lou admonished, "it is the 'small man' that the president has been working ceaselessly for."

Even so, Lou felt obliged to explain a bit further. It was business that provided the jobs that working people depended upon, and so the president had made business the focus of his recovery program. "His political opponents try to make party or individual capital out of the fact that the dollars are actually loaned to the bank, the railway, the farming cooperative, the big industry," Lou wrote. "But these must in turn distribute it," in wages and salaries, and also in stocks and bonds. "More little men than big go down in these days when a big enterprise fails," she insisted. "And with the banks, the depositors lose as well."

In many cases a diarist or correspondent close to the scene of momentous events will pen such a letter with an eye to posterity, hoping to influence the shape and inflection of the historical record. But Lou Hoover was, like her husband, an intensely private person, and she impressed upon all concerned that her letters should never be made public. It was only upon reconsideration by her son Allan, late in his life and after Lou was gone, that he donated his papers, including her letters to him, to the Hoover Presidential Library, and thus to public view. This letter was not a matter of Lou lobbying for her husband's place in history. It was the heartfelt act of a loving partner seeking to bind up wounds to her family that she feared to be lasting.

Hoover's reaction to Roosevelt's challenge was not so deliberate as Lou's, nor so internally directed. It came in stages, and took the form of campaign strategy. Its first expression came with Hoover's declaration to Ted Joslin at the end of July that his team should "crack" Roosevelt at every opportunity, giving each of his statements a specific response.

Hoover's umbrage escalated in September, when Roosevelt set out to barnstorm the country in a fourteen-city whistle-stop speaking tour. With his rival in full swing, Hoover was still debating, with his staff and in his own mind, whether to abandon his holding pattern and take to the stump.

He raised the question during a lunch break on a Sunday already busy with campaign work. Sitting with Walter Newton and Henry Stimson in the otherwise deserted main dining room, Hoover lamented his poor stand-ing among voters in California, and remarked that of one thing he was certain—that he would not waste time campaigning in his home state.

Stimson answered with a contrary lecture on the state of the electorate. In California as across the West, Stimson said, it had come down to a ques-tion of personality and not program. People were not actually hostile to him, but they were frustrated with the Depression. "Nobody disputed his fidelity or his good intentions," Stimson told the president, but they wondered if Hoover were not too strongly "connected" with the industrial East; "they questioned whether he was not standing too much with property interests." The solution, Stimson advised, was to venture forth. "The best thing to rem-edy the issue would be his own personal presence."

This brought a harsh remonstrance from the president, a statement that appears rooted in the dark side of his personality, source to his constant misgivings and his dark premonitions. There was, Hoover pronounced, "a thorough, strong feeling of hatred against him through all the West." Not dislike, or even mistrust, but, Stimson noted carefully in his diary, "as he called it, a hatred." The only way that hatred could be overcome, Hoover said, was by fear.

This, then, was the president's culminating electoral strategy, laid out before his secretary of state and his political advisor in the echoing silence of the empty, wood-paneled banquet hall. As things stood at present, the election was already lost, Hoover said. "The only possibility of winning," he said, "would be by exciting a fear of what Roosevelt would do in men who had a dislike for the president."

This was the 1930s equivalent of "going negative." Early in the contest Hoover explicitly warned his staff against reference to any perceived personal, physical weakness of Roosevelt's—particularly concerning his crippled legs.

But on points of policy, as the campaign approached its climax Hoover made fear of his rival the core message in a grim and increasingly futile effort.

In October the president took his gloomy themes out on the road. Beginning in Des Moines, on October 4, and continuing through an appearance in New York on the 31st, Hoover made ten major campaign speeches, and scores of whistle-stop appearances in between.

His tone was combative, his focus fixed on the "mistaken statements," the "misinformation," the "deliberate, intolerable falsehoods" raised by his challenger. Hoover answered with numbing discourses on the intricacies of tariff schedules and the federal budget, all with frequent references to the perfidies of the Democrats in Congress, the Democratic candidate, or, simply, the Governor. The administration had pursued a program, Hoover insisted, "which has saved the country from complete disaster," while election of Roosevelt "will end the hope of recovery."

As he warmed to his themes Hoover moved beyond simple fearmongering to frame the election as a clash of values. "This is more than a contest between two men," Hoover said at Madison Square Garden. "It is a contest between two philosophies of government." The one, Hoover's program, emphasized limited government and individual freedom and responsibility, "a society absolutely fluid in freedom to the individual." In the alternative, Roosevelt was "proposing changes and so-called new deals which would destroy the very foundations of the American system."

And Hoover broke it down; in catering to special interests, Roosevelt would expand spending, debt, and taxes. He would inflate the currency—this was not Roosevelt's vow but was Hoover's presumption—and would put the government into the power business. And, of course, the Democrats would reduce tariffs.

Hoover cut to the essence of their differences when he quoted from Roosevelt's statement at the Commonwealth Club in San Francisco, when he proposed that Hoover's beloved ethic of individualism had run its course. "Our last frontier has been reached," Roosevelt said. "Our task now is not the discovery of natural resources or necessarily the production of more goods, it is the sober, less-dramatic administering of the resources and plants already in hand."

Hoover disputed this thesis in toto. "What Governor Roosevelt has overlooked is the fact that we are yet on the frontiers of development of science, and of invention. I have only to remind you that discoveries in electricity, the internal-combustion engine, the radio . . . have in themselves represented the greatest advances in America. This philosophy upon which the Governor of New York proposed to conduct the Presidency of the United States is the philosophy of stagnation, of despair. It is the end of hope. . . . It would be the end of the American system."

Hoover's was a valid analysis, even useful. But his stern, angry tone effectively eclipsed the thrust of his argument. He forecast "tragic disasters" from an inflated currency. Roosevelt's promise to ramp up public work to employ "all surplus labor" would mean "the total abandonment of every principle upon which this government and the American system is founded." Most memorably, Hoover warned that, should tariffs be lowered, "The grass will grow in the streets of a hundred cities, a thousand towns; the weeds will overrun the fields of millions of farms if that protection be taken away." For all his reason and cool exposition, this absurdist, even paranoid prophecy became the passage for which the speech at Madison Square Garden is remembered.

As election day loomed Hoover pressed on in what was now considered, within and without, a doomed campaign. "At this time we are very badly whipped," Joslin recorded in October. "We are as blue as wet stones." Hoover was becoming groggy from the work, the pressure, the looming sense of disappointment, but he kept up the grinding pace. "He fully realizes the predicament he is in, but he just doesn't know the meaning of defeat. He is plugging right along as though victory was assured."

The president sought support from former allies like William Borah, but now they shunned him; even members of his cabinet were reluctant to pitch in. And those endorsements he won were less than helpful. Henry Ford put up a notice in his plant advising that, "To prevent times from getting worse and to help them get better, President Hoover must be elected." But Ford himself had lost much of his popular appeal that March, when unemployed workers staged a hunger protest outside his River Rouge plant. The protest was broken up when police and Ford guards opened fire on the crowd, killing four and wounding twenty. The auto mogul, like Hoover, was not the titan he once appeared.

With the election close at hand, the Republican National Committee was dispirited and ineffectual. On top of that, it was entirely out of money—another sign of Hoover's declining stature. It seemed absurd—a Republican incumbent, his campaign in debt, unable even to pay for poll workers. Hoover asked Ogden Mills to solicit a large contribution from Andrew Mellon, but to no avail. Finally, Hoover prevailed on J. P. Morgan Jr. to put up a half million dollars to float the final push.

It was not until late October that Hoover decided how he would conclude his drive for reelection. He was inclined at one point to accept an offer from Charles Lindbergh to hopscotch the Midwest by airplane. But Walter Newton and Larry Richey "went into action," as Ted Joslin recorded, and "put an end to that foolishness." It is true that, as Joslin feared, the stunt might be seen as an effort to copy Roosevelt, who had made his own dramatic, last-minute flight to Chicago to accept the nomination, but it also would have added a dose of dash and celebrity to a moribund campaign.

Hoover finally settled on a more conventional conclusion—a rail trip from the capital to his home in California. That meant another round of speeches, and through the final days of October, as one aide recorded, "The president worked more furiously and more intensely than ever." If Hoover was to go down, he would do so fighting.

On the afternoon of Thursday, November 3, the presidential train was ready for departure—twenty sleeping cars, two lounges, and a dining car, enough to accommodate Secret Service men, reporters, newsreel crews, telegraph operators, and party functionaries. All were on board, but all were on hold, waiting for the president.

Lou Hoover was waiting, too, sitting in the White House limousine under the shade of the North Portico. When at last the president emerged he looked pale and very fatigued. As he climbed into the car Lou turned to him and said, "Bert, I have been waiting a long time. What happened?" Her husband put her off. "I've been completing one of my speeches." But Lou pressed him. "You look so fagged out. I have never seen you look like this."

The president then slumped deep into his seat. He lowered his voice to a whisper, so that the chauffeur and Secret Service man in the front seat might not hear. "I am so exhausted," he confided to Lou. "I do not believe I will survive this trip."

With that, the president and First Lady proceeded to Washington station. Hoover put up a brave front, but Lou made a point of pulling aside White House physician Joel Boone and ordering him to keep a close eye on the president through the length of the journey. "I'm terribly worried about Bert," she said.

What Hoover intended as a last hurrah proved to be a forlorn and worrisome passage for all concerned. In town after town, speech after speech, audiences could not help but notice Hoover's ashen skin; his nasal monotone was often practically inaudible. Even friendly reporters saw in him "the face of a human creature deeply hurt and pained."

Large crowds turned out along the way. Some were welcoming, but many were not. There was "a great deal of heckling," Joel Boone reported, and an occasional egg splashed against the side of the train. Outside St. Louis, the presidential car was pelted with tomatoes. Always stiff before a crowd, at his whistle-stops Hoover was now further insulated, surrounded by a phalanx of nervous Secret Service agents.

Franklin Roosevelt was winding up his own campaign as well, and the contrast could not have been more distinct. Roosevelt liked crowds as much as Hoover dreaded them, and where the president labored over his carefully composed text, Roosevelt smiled and laughed and traded jokes with his audience. One standby: Roosevelt told of a hitchhiker who breezed across the country by holding up a placard that said, "If you don't give me a ride, I'll vote for Hoover."

The president's expedition reached something of a nadir in St. Paul, Minnesota. Crowds in the street booed Hoover as his motorcade made its way to the Municipal Auditorium, where fifteen thousand listened skeptically to another tedious oration. The president several times lost his place, and when Joel Boone stepped up to the speaker's stand to offer him a cue card, Hoover froze. Boone and the Secret Service men feared he would faint right there.

Later in the speech, Hoover cited a Democratic prediction that a Republican victory would be answered by mob rule. "Thank God," the president responded, "we still have a government in Washington that knows how to deal with a mob." This reference to the Bonus Army sent a nervous ripple through the hall, and a party official asked the head of the Secret Service detail, "Why don't they make him quit? He's not doing the party or himself any good. It's turning into a farce."

Hoover made it home to Palo Alto just in time to vote. Somehow, the students at Stanford failed to grasp that this would be a doleful occasion for their favorite son. They prepared a bonfire for the anticipated victory celebration, which obliged Hoover to climb to his rooftop deck and wave to this last remnant of what had once been his adoring public. The president was so obviously staggering on his feet that one of the Secret Service men had to assist him up the stairs. "I thought I was going to have to pick him up and carry him, he was so far gone," the agent recalled.

If there was any grace to the evening it was in brevity. Around 6 p.m., with the West Coast polls still open, Hoover sat down to an early dinner, in company of a few family members and just a handful of aides. While they were still eating, Hoover's valet, Kosta Boris, brought him a note. Hoover opened it and, without a word, excused himself and left the table.

A few minutes passed, and then a few more, and invited guests arrived, but Hoover still did not return. Finally an aide entered his study and found him alone. More staffers joined them there—Larry Richey, Walter Newton, Interior Secretary Ray Wilbur, French Strother, and Joel Boone. Hoover closed the door and then explained: Boris's note had informed him that Roosevelt had carried New York. That should not have come as a great surprise, but by Hoover's calculations, it clinched the decision: the election was already over.

There was a brief, gloomy conference, as Hoover passed around a draft of the telegram he'd composed, congratulating Roosevelt on his victory. Each of his aides considered the message; Hoover weighed their comments and dispatched his note. He then left his study to make a brief round of the guests in the living room, then returned to the study and his small circle of aides. Lou Hoover followed him in, then stepped up next to him and said, "Bert, the election is over. You must get rest and I want you to come to bed."

Hoover then did something that his aides, loyal to their boss but knowing him well, could not recall him ever doing before. He walked around their circle and shook hands with each of them, a formal gesture of thanks and acknowledgment. Lou then took his arm to lead him out. Joel Boone recorded the president's final salutation to his intimate staff: "Before opening the door he turned and faced us again. He said with a smile on his face, 'Good night, my friends. That's it.'"

Herbert Hoover lost to Franklin Roosevelt in a landslide even larger than the one that ushered him into office. He carried just six states—Pennsylvania, Delaware, and parts of New England—and received less than 40 percent of the popular vote, to Roosevelt's 57 percent. The South, which Hoover had successfully cracked in 1928, gave him not a whisper of support. *Time* magazine dubbed Hoover "President Reject."

It was a historic fall, from one of America's most celebrated incoming presidents to its most reviled incumbent. And while in time Roosevelt would emerge as one of the country's most beloved and most effective leaders, his charisma was not the defining element in his initial national triumph. The editors of *The New Republic* put it plainly: "All informed observers agree that the country did not vote for Roosevelt; it voted against Hoover."

It was the times that changed as much as Hoover, and the nation's perception of its president. He was never a crowd-pleaser, and that worked to his advantage in 1928, when America was ready to sober up from the eight-year binge of the Roaring Twenties. But it wore thin as he continued, stiff and silent, through historic hard times. When Roosevelt appeared, offering compassion and warm sympathy, the electorate was eager to change gears.

And there was the Depression. Later generations of Americans would accept as self-evident Bill Clinton's electoral mantra of 1992—It's the economy, stupid—and it was just as true in 1932. With shantytowns on the fringes of every great city, and breadlines on Main Street; with banks failing in record numbers and collapsed prices driving farmers off their land, it's a wonder more than fifteen million people actually cast their votes for Herbert Hoover.

TWENTY-THREE

INTERREGNUM

THE MORNING AFTER THE ELECTION JOEL BOONE WAS THE FIRST in the Hoover household to rise. The president had winnowed his staff in the waning days of the campaign, until only Larry Richey and Boone remained on hand. Now Boone was dressed and ready when Hoover made his appearance in the hallway.

"Are you up to take a walk with me?" Hoover asked his friend and physician. Boone answered in the affirmative, and off they went, strolling across the Stanford campus and into the hills behind. It wasn't medicine ball, but it gave the day a vigorous start.

When the pair turned to head back to the house, Hoover wondered if Richey was already awake. Boone guessed Richey was still in bed, and Hoover said, "Don't disturb him." He then asked Boone to pass along a directive once he was up. "Tell him I want him to order the train prepared to start us back to Washington tomorrow."

This was not the destination Boone had in mind. Before the balloting, he, Richey, and Hoover had made plans to head out to Hawaii on a fishing expedition, a post-electoral cool-down. Richey and Hoover would pursue their favorite sport while Boone would keep a close eye on the overworked president.

"A STRAIN IN THE OLD TOP-PIECE"

While awaiting the inauguration of a new president,
Americans witnessed a mind-numbing debate over
monetary policy and foreign exchange.

Boone put up a modicum of resistance. "Mr. President, we're not going to Washington from here. We're going to get you some rest on a sea trip to Honolulu."

Hoover parried, gently but firmly. "Joel, we *were* going to Honolulu. We are not going now." Hoover paused, then drew himself up to announce a decision he'd made, one he'd concocted sometime between midnight, when he saw that the election had gone hard against him, and the bright hours of the morning.

"I am going to do something no president to my knowledge has ever done before," Hoover said. "I am going to disclose to my successor all the dangers with which we are faced; alert him to what he must be prepared to do; give him every information that I possibly can, known to me, about our government as it is in this very, very serious hour."

It was true this notion was unprecedented, but in large part that was because incoming administrations—especially from the opposite party—had little interest in what their predecessors had to say. Though circumstances were more dire in the winter of 1932, the politics of the matter were much the same, but Hoover wasn't ready to move on. For so long such a reluctant chief executive, now he found himself energized.

Events conspired to give Hoover a convenient opening by which to launch this uninvited—and soon to be unrequited—effort to "assist" the president-elect. On November 10, just as Hoover told Boone of his plans to hurry back to Washington, Henry Stimson received "a bombshell" at the State Department—a diplomatic letter from England proposing to renegotiate its next payment on its war debts, due December 15. This was followed by a similar note from France. The whole question of debts and reparations, put on hold by Hoover's moratorium the previous summer, was now in play.

Stimson's first move was to contact Odgen Mills, still in Washington and, as treasury secretary, directly concerned with the debt question. Mills and Stimson agreed that Roosevelt should be notified of the note from Britain and, further, that, "We had no interest in the matter except to facilitate the transition period." But first, Mills contacted Hoover.

The call did not go well. As Mills reported to Stimson, Hoover was "full of fight," and more interested in asserting his priorities than accepting the neutered role of quietly handing the matter off to the new administration. Stimson spoke to Hoover that afternoon and found him "much more amenable"; the president asked his two closest advisors to write a telegram by which he would notify Roosevelt of the news from Europe.

When Stimson and Mills sent their draft out to Hoover the next day, however, the president said he would be making changes in the text. The tone of his dissent left Stimson much disturbed. "The president still has the aroma of battle on him," Stimson worried. "It is very hard for him to lift himself up above the plane on which he has been for so many months."

Hoover sent his revised telegram to FDR the next day, a Saturday, from a watering stop for his eastbound train. It was a lengthy and argumentative note, reprising the story of the commission that had first set the terms of the international debts, invoking Hoover's moratorium, and detailing concessions the United States could require in return for reduced payments. "It took away the simple and magnanimous tone which we had tried to get into the telegram," Stimson lamented that evening. "I fear it will have a bad effect."

That same day, Hoover delivered two speeches from his eastbound train—the president who hated public appearances now felt compelled to make himself heard. At Glendale, California, Hoover offered what might be considered his official concession speech, assuring the public—and his rival—that, "The political campaign is over," but then explaining that he was making an "early return to Washington" in order to work for "unity in constructive action."

Hoover's telegram, and word of his public announcements, was received with bemusement in Albany. It didn't help matters that the president had released to the press the text of his telegram hours before it was sent. But even aside from this breach of etiquette, Roosevelt disagreed fundamentally with Hoover over the debt question.

In Hoover's precise and complicated mind, the debts were enmeshed in linkage. Payments from Europe would help sustain the dollar, and perhaps the gold standard; these factors in turn would bear upon a World Economic Conference then being planned for London in the coming year. Further,

Hoover wanted to condition any reduction in payments to cutbacks in armaments, which were now abuilding across Europe. War, peace, and recovery were intrinsically connected, and every move should be closely coordinated.

It all made sense, but it was also all quite presumptuous. The fact was, America no longer had the leverage to bring Europe to heel. Moreover, and more to the point, Franklin Roosevelt bore little of Hoover's certainty and cared little for his agenda. He did not much expect the Europeans to continue their debt payments, nor was he greatly concerned with maintaining the gold standard.

Hoover understood this, and it infuriated him. As during the campaign, Hoover was trying to smoke Roosevelt out, to pin him down, but Roosevelt would not be cornered. He answered Hoover's telegram with a polite but cautious reply; he would be "delighted" to meet with the president, alone and on a "wholly informal and personal" basis. Matters of policy must rest, however, with "those now vested with executive and legislative authority." It would be foolish for the president-elect to commit himself before taking office, and he did not intend to do so.

After talks between the two camps, the "wholly informal" visit between Hoover and the president-elect felt more like a duel under the Irish Code. Each was permitted a second at his side; Hoover chose Ogden Mills, while Roosevelt named Raymond Moley, an obscure professor from Columbia University who had emerged as the linchpin in FDR's Brains Trust.

In the days before the meeting Hoover gave every evidence of frantic anticipation. Twice he scheduled press conferences, and twice he canceled them. By the time the big day arrived, White House staff were struck by "considerable nervousness on the part of all hands." As Henry Stimson observed, the tension began with the president. "He has allowed himself to get so full of mistrust of his rival that I think it will go far to prevent a profitable meeting."

Roosevelt pulled into Washington the afternoon of Tuesday, November 22. It was his first visit to the capital since his election; he would continue on the next day to his retreat at Warm Springs, Georgia. Roosevelt and Moley were met at the train station around 3:30 p.m. by an official limousine.

Entering the White House via the more private South Entrance, they were escorted to the Red Room, where Hoover awaited them under portraits of Grant, Madison, Jefferson, and Adams. The president was grave but polite, while Mills chatted lightly with Roosevelt, his Harvard classmate and near neighbor to his Husdon Valley estate. Everyone lit up a smoke: cigars, for Hoover and Mills; cigarettes for Roosevelt and Moley.

Hoover then commenced an hour's unbroken discourse on the state of international finance. Commenting afterward on the basis of notes he made that night, Professor Moley counted himself impressed: "It was clear that we were in the presence of the best-informed person in the country on the question of the debts." It was also clear to Moley that Hoover had trouble addressing the man who had bested him. Hoover began with his eyes fixed on the floor, and only gradually let them drift up to meet Moley's. "He glanced at Roosevelt only occasionally," Moley observed. "He obviously found it hard to overcome the profound personal disappointment of the election."

The lecture finished, the talks began. Hoover wanted an accord with Roosevelt that cancellation or default on the war debts would bring disaster. In particular, Hoover wanted Roosevelt to join him in appointing a new debt commission to settle the various international claims.

Roosevelt responded in a fashion that would soon became familiar to friend and foe—vaguely encouraging but without commitment. As Moley described it, "FDR nodded his head in partial agreement," leaving Hoover to believe what he liked. The precise terms were left unsaid; what was firm was that each side would issue its own statement the next day. The meeting ended with fifteen minutes of private conversation between Hoover and the president-elect. Said Moley, "It was all very polite."

The simmering resentments boiled over the next day. Mills opened by visiting Roosevelt at the Mayflower Hotel to present him with a lengthy, typed draft of the policy statement Hoover would deliver. But if Mills was seeking an endorsement he was promptly disappointed. All he got from the president-elect was the jocular observation, "You must have sat up all night working on that." As to his own, complementary announcement, Roosevelt said he had been caught up in meetings and would compose his thoughts on the train that afternoon.

After this uncertain encounter, Mills reported back to Hoover and the president released his statement. It was addressed to the governments of Europe, but it was also aimed at Congress, which had previously ignored his call for a new debt commission. Hoover enumerated once more his central premise; the debt payments must resume, but they might be negotiated, through the new commission. On such a settlement rested "the great causes of world peace, world disarmament and world recovery."

Hoover then called to the White House the leaders of both parties in Congress. He detailed for them the notes from England and France, and his fear that unless a new payment schedule was drafted—by a reconstituted debt commission—the Europeans would simply default. Hoover leaned as hard as he could, but the idea of renegotiating the war debts was always unpopular, even more so when the president making the case had already been voted out of office. Hoover's plea was rejected out of hand.

The other shoe dropped that evening, when Roosevelt issued his statement following up the meeting with Hoover. He found himself "in complete accord" with the principles enunciated by the president, Roosevelt said. There was no need, however, for any new debt commission; "existing agencies and constituted channels of diplomatic intercourse" would suffice.

It was a wordy, windy announcement that Hoover correctly discerned as "not wholly cooperative." But the meeting, the pleasantries, the follow-up note, they were all politesse. Roosevelt gave reporters his shorthand version of the entire episode when they caught up with him on his way out of the capital. Tossing the remark over his shoulder, he said of the European debt problem, "It's not my baby." Not until the inauguration, anyway.

This uncomfortable exchange, between the old president and the new, was prologue to a drama that teetered between tragedy and farce all through the winter. In 1932 the interregnum between election and inauguration ran four full months, an interval set in the early days of the republic to allow time for elected officials to travel long distances from the frontier to the capital.

To shorten the lame-duck interval required a constitutional amendment, one that Progressives led by George Norris first proposed as a good-government measure in 1922. Ten years later—a blink of an eye, when it comes to such matters—Congress moved an amendment that would advance the start of the president's term to January 20, where it stands today. The states quickly fell into line, but the deciding, thirty-eighth state did not ratify the amendment until late January 1933. That came too late to spare Herbert Hoover the distinction of being the last president to endure four full months as a repudiated chief of state. There were several other single-term presidents before Hoover, but none experienced so much crisis, and so much palpable unpopularity, as did Hoover.

It wasn't just the continuing economic breakdown that made this interregnum so excruciating for Hoover. It was also his divided mind, a psyche torn between disdain for others' opinions and a deep yearning for their approval. The tension between these two poles had made him an enigmatic candidate—hungry for victory yet resentful of the process—and now rendered him unable to accept his defeat.

Just as, before the election, Hoover made a great show of his indifference toward a second term, now he took every opportunity to assert his contentment with the negative result. In Palo Alto the morning after the vote, Hoover told reporters he'd just had his "best night's sleep in years."

Hoover elaborated on this theme a week later, in a tart response to a preacher in Minnesota who had written to express condolences over the result. "I wonder if you have not a misconception of the election," the president wrote. He then asserted, in peculiar syntax, "It was not a game or a sport for personal gain but an event that as far as the personal side is concerned the victory was to him who lost and the defeat to him who won."

Hoover, then, was claiming a personal triumph in his defeat. "I can say that never in the last fifteen years have I slept more soundly than I have since the election. I have almost a feeling of elation." He added a single caveat. "My only concern is what will happen to the country as a result of the change in policies."

If Hoover believed these lines when he wrote them, he was deceiving himself. Perusal of his writings and a review of his career show the loss to FDR as a distinct turning point in his life. Hoover's memoirs provide a nice example. The third and most important volume was titled, *The Great Depression, 1929–1941*, but fully half the book is devoted to a recap of the 1932 election and its aftermath. In Hoover's mind, that was the central event of the period—not the Wall Street crash, not the drought, not the breadlines, but the election.

The turning point is underscored in years of thought and action. Where previously he'd been a persistent problem solver, a synthesizer of ideas who disdained but tolerated those who disagreed with him, he transformed, post-Roosevelt, to a shellback partisan, constantly on the lookout for "pink" tendencies, indicative of an underlying allegiance to "collectivism." And where, prior to his presidency, Hoover had only occasionally engaged in political spadework, in the decades that followed he haunted the quadrennial Republican conventions, seeking another nomination or, failing that, working to shore up his party's right wing.

All that lay ahead. Hoover signaled his more immediate response in the last line of his letter to the Minnesota minister; he became obsessed with the idea of saving the country from the policies and attitudes of the president-elect.

Despite the resounding verdict of the voters, Hoover never failed in his conviction that he knew the proper strategy for dealing with the Depression. His final State of the Union message, delivered to Congress December 6, had a strangely triumphal ring to it, with Hoover clearly expecting the lawmakers to follow his lead.

He started by reciting accomplishments. Against the prospect of another lean winter, "great private agencies have been mobilized again." Loans to the states from the Reconstruction Finance Corporation "guarantee that there should be no suffering from hunger or cold." And RFC loans to banks, coupled with the first Glass-Steagall Act, amending the rules of the Federal Reserve, "served to defend the nation in a great crisis."

Turning to current legislation, Hoover pointed out "three definite directions" as "necessary foundations to any other action." They were banking reform, a balanced budget, and—here was a new wrinkle, driven by the talks with Roosevelt—international cooperation. The welfare of America, as well as the entire world, rested on "the great causes of world peace, world disarmament, and organized world recovery." A separate budget message contained another Hooverian imperative: deficit spending, he said, "cannot be continued without disaster to the federal finances."

That Hoover was roundly ignored, his political capital thoroughly exhausted, did not seem to faze him. He followed his address in rapid succession with a series of proposed bills, for budget cuts, for government reorganization, for an arms treaty, for bankruptcy reform, for a sales tax—an idea repudiated by Congress earlier that same year—and for the second Glass-Steagall Act, the one that would finally divide commercial from investment banking. Just one of these recommendations—bankruptcy reform—was voted into law under Hoover's tenure.

These were specific proposals, planks in a platform, essentially utilitarian. Hoover went deeper, exploring his sense of history and verging on dark prophecy, in the more informal setting of the semiannual Gridiron Club dinner. He relied on a metaphor that he strained to its limit—an indication, perhaps, of how strongly he felt.

Taking the podium a month after his defeat, he opened with a bit of wry humor. "You will expect me to discuss the late election," Hoover said. "Well, as nearly as I can learn, we did not have enough votes on our side." Having acknowledged his loss, he served up his portent.

> The life stream of this nation is the generations of millions of human particles acting under impulses of advancing ideas and national ideals gathered from a thousand springs. These springs and rills have gathered into great streams which have nurtured and fertilized this great land over these centuries. Its dikes against dangerous floods are cemented with the blood of our fathers. Our children will strengthen these dikes, will create new channels, and the land will grow greater and richer with their lives.
>
> We are but transitory officials in government whose duty is to keep these channels clear and to strengthen and extend their dikes. What counts toward the honor of public officials is that they sustain the national ideals upon which are patterned the design of these channels of progress and the construction of these dikes of safety. What is said in this or that political campaign counts no more than the cheerful ripples or

the angry whirls of the stream. What matters is—that God help the man or the group that breaks down these dikes, who diverts these channels to selfish ends. These waters will drown him or them in a tragedy that will spread over a thousand years.

Hoover had lost his mandate, but somehow that only convinced him of the urgency of his mission to save the country from itself, and from Roosevelt.

On December 12, the MacDonald government in Britain made its debt payment to the United States, on schedule, in gold. But officials there warned that this was the last installment that could be expected until the terms were renegotiated.

The next day, French premier Edouard Herriot proposed to the Chamber of Deputies that they go through with their payment as well. This sparked hours of heated debate that closed with the ejection of Herriot and his Radical government. Belgium, Poland, and Hungary followed France into default. In Germany, where Adolf Hitler had assumed sole command of the state, there was no chance that reparations would resume. The postwar international order was coming apart.

In Washington, Hoover responded to the British note with another telegram to FDR, wheedling him again to join in naming a new debt commission. Strangely, and surprisingly quickly, Hoover was stepping out of the role of chief executive and back into that of bureaucratic infighter, seeking advantage by feint and thrust. It was a mode of combat that served him well enough during his years at Commerce, but now exercised in full public view and from the office of the president, it was simply embarrassing.

Henry Stimson sought to palliate Hoover's temper, then advised him to just desist. "I did not want him to go to the indignity of dragging out the correspondence when it seemed evident . . . that Roosevelt didn't want to do this at all," the secretary of state remarked in his journal. "It makes the president look as if he were trying to hang onto Roosevelt's coattail when Roosevelt didn't want to be hung onto."

Roosevelt responded promptly and politely, but in the negative. Hoover fired off still another note, and then backed off, but not before one more salvo—a press conference where he released copies of all the telegrams, and the terse statement, "Governor Roosevelt considers that it is undesirable for him to assent to my suggestions for cooperative action . . . I will respect his wishes."

This drew a sharp retort from Albany. Roosevelt would "consult freely" with the president, but for now, Hoover would simply have to make his appointments on his own. To Walter Lippmann, this transitional contretemps was all "fantastic." Hoover and Roosevelt were "addressing complicated notes to each other, and proclamations, and messages, and newspaper statements, for all the world as if they were two governments and not two men."

At this point, acting indeed like a government faced with a hostile power, Roosevelt opened a back channel to his rival. On the evening of December 22, the day of his press statement answering Hoover, Roosevelt proposed to a friend, "Why doesn't Harry Stimson come up here and talk with me and settle this damn thing?"

The friend to whom Roosevelt addressed this remark was Felix Frankfurter, a professor of law at Harvard who had begun his career on the team of trustbusters that Stimson ran as a U.S. attorney in New York. Frankfurter promptly called his old mentor and suggested that he come meet Roosevelt alone, in his home, soon after Christmas. Now Stimson, so reluctant to disparage Roosevelt during the campaign, was to serve as advance guard for the new administration. "Altogether," Stimson noted in his journal, "it was a funny occurrence."

Funny to Stimson, perhaps, but not to Hoover. When Stimson, a stickler for protocol, asked Hoover's permission for a meeting with Roosevelt, Hoover took umbrage. "He was against it, I could see, from the first," Stimson recorded. Hoover's mind "was crystallized very strongly against going near Roosevelt." It wasn't just resentment; Hoover believed that this latest exchange of telegrams had given him the edge. "He felt that the situation was in good political shape now so far as he was concerned and he didn't care to reopen it."

Hoover was so pleased with the situation that he decided, at long last, he could step away from it long enough to take a quick vacation—his first

respite since the rigors of the campaign. A getaway now would also spare
him the indignity of presiding over holiday festivities as a repudiated master
of ceremonies. There would be no more reception lines for Hoover.

On December 23, the president boarded a special train with his wife
and a small troupe of good friends—the Rickards, the Sullivans, the Harlan
Stones, Vermont senator Warren Austin. Larry Richey and Joel Boone went
along, as did two secretaries to Lou Hoover. They headed for Savannah,
where the sea trout were said to be running strong.

Hoover returned to Washington on January 3, his mood distinctly lighter
than when he'd left. He had so recovered his equanimity that, when Stimson
told him FDR had renewed his request to meet with the secretary of state,
Hoover relented. He still considered Roosevelt "a very dangerous and contrary man," but if Roosevelt would run the request through the president,
Hoover would allow the meeting to go forward.

This was followed, the next day, by a direct call from Albany. Roosevelt not only asked to meet with Stimson; he wanted another round with
the president. Hoover treated with his rival warily; he insisted on having a
member of his staff listen in, and a stenographer transcribing every word.
Still, he agreed to both requests. The grudging transition was on again.

Hoover was fairly bustling, his face tanned, his vigor renewed, his
schedule crammed with legislative conferences, when a news flash brought
everything to a halt. Hoover's predecessor, and for six years his immediate
superior at the helm of the government, Calvin Coolidge, was dead at age
sixty.

Coolidge had never much liked Hoover, and never gave him much support, but Hoover took his death hard. "It may have been my imagination,
but it seemed to me that in an hour he had lost all the benefit of his southern
trip," Ted Joslin recorded. Just four years out of office, Coolidge had been
the last living former president; there were six surviving first ladies, all wid-
ows now. Hoover "soon became downcast," Joslin observed. "He knows the
presidency is a man-killer."

This was Joslin's surmise, not something that Hoover shared with him.
But it was hard not to notice the melancholy that settled over the presi-

dent, the evident loneliness. At the funeral, in Northampton, on January 8, Hoover was joined by Stimson, Vice President Curtis, Justices Hughes and Stone, and a pack of politicians, but as he made his way into the red-brick church, he might as well have been alone.

"People stood as he entered, but he paid no attention to them," wrote a correspondent who made a brief study of the president. Hoover took up a position in the first pew, closest to the coffin, and waited for Lou to join him. Then he turned to the front, closed his eyes, and lowered his head. "His whole figure seemed to droop . . . people looked at him curiously." When the minister began his oration, "Hoover sat unmoved, his head still bent, as if he had been carved from stone."

Upon his return to Washington, Hoover had lost some of that sense of mission that had driven him so hard, for so long. Ted Joslin was after him immediately, pressing the president to "assume leadership and rally the country to make Congress do what is necessary . . . to combat the Depression." But rather than stiffen, Hoover sagged into self-pitying resentment. "Perhaps my tactics have been wrong," the president said. "What I have tried to do has been to save the people. They don't know what they have missed. They are not appreciative. What I should have done was to have waited until they were half drowned and then waded in and tried to save them. Then they would have known what it was all about."

Hoover was losing his will to fight; he had also lost his clout. Even as his popularity waned Hoover had dominated Congress by bluster and threat, but he could get no traction now. Early in the session he persuaded his old sparring partners, Senator Joseph Robinson and Speaker Jack Garner, now vice-president-elect, to support a sales tax to reduce—though not erase—the deficit for the coming year. Garner and Robinson then met with Roosevelt in New York and came away with what they believed to be his consent.

It appears these fellow Democrats, like Hoover after the parley in the Red Room, had confused Roosevelt's "partial agreement" with consent. Or as a *Times* editorial put it, "The conferees could not agree to what they had agreed upon." In any event, when the sales tax plan was made public, Roosevelt pronounced himself "horrified," and support for the levy evaporated. Hoover felt little satisfaction when Garner approached him soon after to announce, "For the first time in my life I am unable to carry out an agree-ment." In Hoover's telling, this was the last time in twenty years that anyone would attempt to balance the federal budget.

Jack Garner was chagrined to be caught out in this game of shifting al-legiances, but he remained a determined partisan, and in January launched a direct assault on the centerpiece of the Hoover recovery program—the Reconstruction Finance Corporation.

Like most Democrats and many Republicans, Garner was always sus-picious of the "millionaire's dole" and had authored the provision that all RFC loans should be made public. These notices commenced in the sum-mer of 1932, beginning from the date of passage of the Emergency Relief and Construction Act in July. Now, in January 1933, Garner sponsored a bill requiring publication of all recipients of RFC loans, dating back to the time the corporation was formed. This would mean naming 3,600 banks and in-surance companies that had fortified frail balance sheets with federal loans; now their weaknesses would be exposed.

President Hoover and several RFC directors implored Garner to drop this measure, but the prickly Texan gave no ground. "I have consistently said there has been too much secrecy about what has been going on in the past twelve months," Garner said in a press statement. "If the truth scares people, let it come."

To Hoover this was the height of reckless partisanship. He lined up sup-port from the Democrats of the RFC board, as well as Republican insurgents like James Couzens, but Garner was adamant and his bill went through. A month later Hoover pleaded for a repeal, warning that publicizing the loans "is destroying the usefulness and effectiveness of the Reconstruction Corporation. . . . It is drying up the very sources of credit." But where a year before such an appeal had won the votes to launch the RFC, now it was ignored.

The president had no better luck when he aligned himself with the Demo-crats to support their own legislation. With the White House in transition, the Congress had trouble deciding which way to go.

This confusion was exemplified in the fate of the banking bill authored

by Virginia Democrat Carter Glass. Glass had been Hoover's grudging partner in the prior session of Congress, carrying the president's bill to expand
the credit facilities of the Federal Reserve; now Glass was ready to bring
forward the banking bill that he'd been developing over the past two years.

During the campaign Glass had attacked Hoover in his typical, mor-
dant fashion, but with the election over Hoover put that aside and proposed
to Glass a new collaboration. Glass considered Hoover's advance "ironical";
as his biographer put it, "A Republican president whom he had assailed only
a few months before was asking him for help." But both had genuine interest in bank reform—Hoover, to restore credit, and Glass, to prevent the
excesses that preceded the crash.

In particular, both Hoover and Glass wanted to see an expansion of
branch banking, barred in most states out of the general fear of the "money
power." Banks with multiple franchises were far more stable; Canada,
which faced the same drastic price deflation but where most banking was
conducted by national chains, did not experience a single bank failure in the
entire period of the Depression.

Despite suffering after-effects from an extended illness, Glass rose in
the Senate January 6 to introduce his bill. He pronounced branch banking
to be the most important provision in the bill, and warned that hundreds of
banks stood on the brink of failure if the measure did not go through. But
expectations of quick passage were dashed by the "violent speech in opposition" from a newly arrived populist upstart—Huey Long, the Louisiana
Kingfish.

Headstrong, fearless, and happy to step on toes, Senator Long denounced
the Glass banking bill as an instrument of "imperial finance," and focused
his attack on the very provision that Hoover and Glass felt the most critical.
He knew "a good deal more about branch banking" than Glass, Long said,
and styled himself as the defender of small-town, small-scale finance.

Most of his fellow senators quickly identified Long as a loose cannon—
"the most irresponsible, impossible and impervious individual I have ever
seen," Hiram Johnson pronounced—but Long knew the rules of procedure,
and he made the bank bill the vehicle for his first great performance on a
national stage.

On January 10 Long launched his first filibuster, a ploy for which he became famous by the time of his assassination just three years later. In this rendition, Long defied his party leadership to ridicule Glass, to denounce the House of Morgan, and to claim the unspoken support of Franklin Roosevelt. When he tired, he presented the Senate clerk with lengthy documents to be read into the record; when he tired of talking about banking, he outlined pet plans for wholesale redistribution of wealth, and for creating jobs by spending $10 billion on public works.

Long's filibuster lasted eight days. His antics drove most of his fellow lawmakers to distraction, but Long found secret support from James Watson, the Republican leader, who hoped to disrupt Roosevelt's plans by gumming up the Congress and forcing him to call an early, extra session. Glass finally got his bill through, but only after acceding to Long and dropping the branch banking clause.

What role Hoover had in Watson's juvenile scheme to sabotage Roosevelt's debut is unknown; Watson said later he enlisted the help of Charles Curtis, but made no mention of the president. In any event, by mid-January, Hoover was thinking along the same lines as Watson. "The Senate can keep wasting time as far as I'm concerned," Hoover told Ted Joslin. "I don't want them to do anything now."

The loss of the branch banking clause only confirmed Hoover's resentment. When he learned on January 17 of a move to invoke cloture, the president summoned two Senate allies to block the move. "Our game," he instructed, "is to prevent cloture of Long and encourage all filibustering." After his years preaching cooperation, in his last weeks in office Hoover was reduced to obstruction; it was the only option he had left.

Hoover found business with Congress frustrating, but his dealings with FDR were downright excruciating. Having reluctantly granted permission for Stimson to meet with Roosevelt, Hoover had no choice but to endure the rosy afterglow. And while Stimson was sensitive enough to try to spare Hoover's feelings, there was no concealing the fact that, after their first, five-hour encounter, on January 9, the secretary of state and the president-elect had immediately struck up a friendship. As both Stimson and Roosevelt told reporters that day, they had each found their meeting to be "delightful."

It seems petty but also inevitable that these cheery reports left Hoover feeling lonely and superfluous. Those feelings seemed confirmed in mid-January when Stimson notified the League of Nations and American allies in Europe, in stern language, that the United States would stand by its policy of refusing to recognize any territories claimed through aggression. The statement was designed to stiffen the League's response to the Japanese occupation of Manchuria.

This was, technically, Hoover's own view, but Stimson's note was distinctly more forceful than Hoover's customary mode. More disturbing to the president, news coverage of the Stimson note emphasized that he had first cleared the message with Roosevelt. A day later, Roosevelt issued his own statement supporting the policy. When Stimson telephoned to thank Roosevelt for the gesture, Roosevelt said brightly, "We are getting so that we do pretty good teamwork, don't we?"

Hoover was less than pleased, then, when Stimson informed him that FDR would be making another trip to Warm Springs, and again passing through Washington. The governor had requested another conference with Hoover on the European war debts.

This session, convening, once again, in the Red Room, proved larger, less formal, and more contentious. Along with Ray Moley, Roosevelt brought Norman Davis, a Democrat just returned from the arms talks in Geneva; not to be outnumbered, Hoover was attended by Stimson and Ogden Mills. The immediate question was how to answer the British, who, having made their December payment, were seeking an adjustment in terms.

Hoover wanted negotiations to start immediately, but Roosevelt insisted that nothing commence until he was in office. This Hoover promptly accepted, but much dispute ensued over the esoteric question of whether debts would be discussed in conjunction with larger economic matters. Once again, after the meeting, both sides accused the other of ignoring the firm agreements made there.

The import of this encounter was not what was said—or what was not—but how the talks weighed on the outgoing president. Hoover's resentment at the whole process was consuming, his discomfort clearly evident. When Ted Joslin told Hoover, the day before the conference, that the press had requested a group photo, Hoover responded with venom. "I will never be photographed with that man," the president declared. "I have too much respect for myself."

The next day, at the conference, Moley felt that Hoover appeared "close to death." Moley told a friend later, "He had the look of being done, but still of going on and on, driven by some damned duty." This observation was perceptive—duty was always a factor in Hoover's motivation—but not the whole story. As Mills explained later to one of Stimson's aides, Hoover felt "acutely the sense of being in the background." It brought home to him the reality of his defeat, that his moment at the nexus of command and control was over. After the meeting, Hoover told Mills, "He had never been so humiliated in his life."

TWENTY-FOUR

THE SOUND OF CRASHING BANKS

ON SUNDAY, FEBRUARY 5, PRESIDENT HOOVER SPENT MUCH OF his day on the telephone, helping to arrange for an RFC bailout of Hibernia Bank, the largest commercial bank in New Orleans. The banking crisis had receded under the influence of millions in RFC loans; now it returned with a vengeance.

His partner in this fiduciary rescue was Huey Long, who routinely railed against faceless bankers but who was quick to respond when Louisiana was threatened. Hoover had little liking for Long; he bragged to his advisors that he possessed IRS data that would land the Kingfish in jail. But in this instance both senator and president believed that failure of Hibernia could spark a new round of bank failures in the South.

The runs on Hibernia began on Friday, February 3, after the failure of a major insurance company operated by the president of the bank, who was also a regional director for the RFC. When a congressman called for an investigation into the "rotten mess" in Louisiana, out-of-town depositors began pulling their funds. Faced with a sudden crisis, Long worked with the state governor to arrange an abrupt, unscheduled legal "holiday"—Pierre Lafitte, the legendary pirate, was the ostensible honoree—to keep creditors at bay through the weekend. In the meantime, from the White House, Hoover helped arrange a $20 million RFC loan to cover Hibernia's frozen assets. The RFC board agreed, contingent on the bank raising $4 million in loans from local partners.

When the bank opened on Monday—an hour early, no less—Long was on hand to announce there was "no safer place to put the money than right here." That assurance was enough to dispel the panic in New Orleans, but within hours President Hoover was responding to another banking emergency, this time in Detroit. In this case there were two banks involved; the stakes were higher, and the crisis more complicated. Should these institutions fail, the impact would be felt nationwide.

When Ted Joslin reported for work Monday morning the president briefed him on the hectic weekend, and then looked ahead. "With the Detroit situation even more critical I don't know whether a panic can be avoided," Hoover said. He then paused to do a little figuring. "Let's see, we have a little more than three weeks to run"—three weeks, that is, before Roosevelt's inauguration. Hoover then mused ruefully, "I certainly hope the crash won't come before we go out."

Sometime around June 1932, just as the presidential campaign was getting under way, America paused on its dizzying slide into the economic trough. Commodity prices stopped falling. Bank failures tapered off to fewer than one hundred per month—too many for comfort, but a pace more fitted to the Roaring Twenties than the Dismal Thirties. Beginning in July, industrial production actually began to rise.

Several factors contributed to this performance plateau. One, certainly, was the RFC. In its first year of operation it loaned out more than $850 million to more than five thousand banks and trust companies. Many bankers complained that the terms were too stiff, that the authorities required too much in collateral and charged too much in interest; but many more were able to weather credit calls by covering frozen assets with government cash. There was a sense of calm, too, when the British pound stabilized after dropping a third of its value since England left the gold standard.

All through the campaign President Hoover hoped, as he did with every glimmer of good news, that these positive indicators marked a turning point; that prices had at last hit bottom, that the business confidence he had so long invoked had at last arrived. But the respite proved temporary. Soon after the election, beginning in December and accelerating in January, the numbers all went bad. Trade was off, prices resumed their slide, and bank failures began to accelerate.

To Hoover the source of this resumed decline was obvious: Franklin Roosevelt was the new ingredient, the cocked die that changed the game. His allusions to vast job programs, his faint promises to balance the budget, and his plan to reduce tariffs had scared business leaders off planned investments in new equipment and new hires. "The sum of all these matters was to turn the clock of recovery abruptly backward with the election," Hoover recalled in his memoirs.

This sounds like so much sour grapes—Hoover had made these arguments all through the campaign. It's hard to accept that Roosevelt's landslide victory, embraced by Americans of every stripe and in every region, sent a shudder of fear through a business community already prostrated by three years of steady decline.

But the election was prelude to a much bigger shock, delivered by indirection as Roosevelt rebuffed Hoover's entreaties to cooperation. That shock was the dawning realization that Roosevelt would take a far more flexible approach than Hoover to the question of currency and gold. As Hoover termed it later, "The next blow to recovery came from a great fear that currency tinkering would be undertaken by the new administration."

On this score Hoover's analysis of the impact of Roosevelt's election was closer to the target, but he was conflating two distinct things. Without question, the collapse of the gold standard abroad hampered any efforts at recovery inside the United States. And uncertainty made it worse; the American government needed either to abandon gold, or to renew its commitment to the idea of a currency fixed in value. That was the declaration Hoover insisted on from FDR.

But it was not Roosevelt who destabilized the terms of international exchange. A firm commitment to gold might have staved off the crisis, but that would only delay a final reckoning. In the long run gold could only be reinstated as an international standard if the rest of the world agreed to go along. And as Roosevelt and his advisors well recognized, such a prospect was "obviously illusory."

There is no doubt that the United States paid a high price for maintaining allegiance to gold after most of the world opted for deflation. The cost was anticipated by John Maynard Keynes back in 1931, as soon as Britain made her move, leaving France and the United States as the only major powers still pegging their currencies to a fixed weight of gold.

"They have willed the destruction of their own export industries," Keynes predicted, and "must also gravely embarrass their banking systems." Keynes was still an outlier in his field; while most economists considered Britain's decision a tragedy, Keynes was among just a handful who rejoiced at "the breaking of our gold fetters." But in this moment he showed the foresight that would establish him as one of the great intellects of his time. By holding firm to gold, he said, Britain's rivals would be left behind. "The United States had, in effect, set the rest of us the problem of finding some way to do without her wheat, her copper, her cotton, and her motor-cars." And in so doing, the rest of the world would embark, at last, upon recovery.

By early 1933 the effects on the United States were becoming too pronounced to ignore. The results were summarized, ironically, by Hoover himself, in an off-the-record commentary during a press conference in January. "There is no doubt that the countries of depreciated currency have begun to inundate some markets with goods," Hoover advised. There had been some delay in the effect of devaluation, he said, but now it was coming into force. "It"—the flow of imports—"has only begun to be enlarged in its volume during the last four or five months, and it is gradually accelerating in intensity until it has now produced definitely a very considerable unemployment [in America] and is doing further damage to agriculture."

Hoover was not the only one to notice the shift. With commodity prices again hitting bottom, farm state lawmakers began a new push for devaluation. Senator Tom Connally of Texas, hoping to restore cotton to prewar prices, proposed reducing the gold content of the dollar by a third. Elmer Thomas of Oklahoma wanted simply to issue unbacked currency, and cited the performance of Great Britain as the example to follow. Observed *The Commercial and Financial Chronicle*, "The whole question of currency inflation . . . has been stalking the Capitol for weeks."

Sinking commodity prices were the most conspicuous effect; the impact on banks was more subtle, and more dangerous. Growing concern over the stability of the dollar drove businesses and individuals in a new wave of withdrawals from the banks—hoarding, in the pejorative parlance of the administration. From a near standstill in December, these withdrawals drained $2 billion in bank deposits by February.

This erosion of confidence felt like a disheartening reversion to the near panic of 1931, but it was also different, distinguished by a marked preference for gold. During a February conference among directors of the New York Federal Reserve Bank, George Harrison described the trend in certain terms: "This movement represents something more than the hoarding of currency, which reflects a distrust of banks; it represents in addition a distrust of the currency itself and it is inspired by the talk of devaluation of the dollar and inflation of the currency."

The erosion of confidence and flight into gold was a national phenomenon that struck with gathering force at places already weakened by mismanagement or difficult local conditions. When the pressure reached the breaking point, the alarm would sound in Washington, at the Fed, at the RFC, and at the White House. That was the case with New Orleans, and that was the case with Detroit.

The banks of Detroit were a by-product of the auto industry, itself already subject to the boom-and-bust cycles that haunt carmakers to this day. When Ford and General Motors and Studebaker were on the rise, Detroit banks underwrote tens of thousands of mortgages for factory workers enriched by Henry Ford's high-wage model. But now Ford and the others were cutting wages and closing plants. Many of those workers returned whence they came, abandoning houses and payments; many who stayed slipped into default, degrading the balance sheets of banks large and small.

There were many banks in Michigan but most were held by two Detroit corporations—the Detroit Bankers Company, and Union Guardian

Trust—huge holding companies with subsidiaries scattered across the state. Union Guardian was largely a creature of the Ford empire, and Ford's son Edsel was a founding director. But Henry Ford held stakes in both institutions, with $32 million on deposit at Union Guardian, and $25 million at Detroit Bankers.

After the 1929 crash both banking groups found themselves saddled with large quantities of frozen mortgages. Initially, they drained their subsidiaries for cash, until the red ink finally reached their own balance sheets. In July 1932, strapped for liquid assets, the directors at Union Guardian turned to the government for help. Just days after the bailout of Charles Dawes' Central Republic National Bank, in Chicago, the RFC issued to Guardian the first in a series of loans that would total $15 million by the turn of the year.

These stopgap measures kept Guardian afloat until the gold scare hit in January 1933. The first three weeks of the month saw 195 bank failures in Michigan, many of them subsidiaries to either Union Guardian or Detroit Bankers, and massive runs against any banks that survived. By the end of the month both of the holding companies were nearly prostrate. Detroit Bankers was able to liquidate just enough assets to keep its doors open, but Union Guardian was forced to come back to the RFC. They needed $50 million to stay afloat, but RFC rules barred unsecured loans and Guardian's salable assets fell $14 million short of the required sum.

This is where President Hoover stepped in. Collapse of the Michigan holding companies could threaten the financial structure of the entire country—this was the crash he spoke of so ominously with Joslin. To borrow from today's parlance, the banks of Detroit were "too big to fail."

But Hoover wasn't inclined to breach the lending limits of the RFC. His first instinct was always to organize intervention by key principals instead of the federal government; here he wanted the moguls who had built their fortunes in Detroit to help finance a solution.

As a first step, Hoover and Ogden Mills obtained an agreement from Edsel Ford to subordinate the Ford deposits at Union Guardian, granting the government first claim to the company assets as collateral for an RFC loan. That covered about half the unsecured portion of the loan Union Guardian needed; the rest must come from cash contributions.

Over the next two days the president was engaged "unceasingly" in devising an emergency bailout for Detroit. Ogden Mills and the directors of the RFC met late into the night, while titans of industry were called to the White House. Hoover personally secured agreements from Walter Chrysler, and from General Motors CEO Alfred Sloan, to fortify the RFC loan with individual contributions of $2 million each. Key to these talks was Roy Chapin, the new secretary of commerce, who was a former executive at Hudson Motors and happened to be one of the Union Guardian founders.

Hoover needed just $2 million more to close the deal. He turned to James Couzens, onetime partner of Henry Ford's and now the senior senator from Michigan. This required a delicate approach, however, as Couzens had never been close to the president and was one of the RFC's sharpest critics in Congress. He had led a Senate inquiry into the agency's loans to railroads, and after the bailout of the Dawes bank in Chicago, suggested that it might have been better just to "let things slide." How would he feel about such an effort in his hometown?

Rather than make a personal approach to Couzens, Hoover decided he would present his idea at a White House conference attended by Charles Miller, who had replaced Dawes as RFC president, and by Arthur Vandenberg, the junior senator from Michigan. In his caution, when he made his invitations, Hoover did not state the nature of the meeting, leaving Couzens to divine from rumors that he would be asked to approve the full, unsecured loan. It was a most unfortunate misunderstanding.

This crucial financial conference took place just after dark on the wintry evening of Thursday, February 9, with the fate of the Detroit banks hanging in the balance. Hoover hosted in his favorite haunt, the Lincoln Study.

Instead of an opening introduction, Hoover simply turned the floor over to Miller, who began by reading through the Union Guardian loan application. Miller concluded by offering his opinion that, considering Union Guardian's weak management and flimsy portfolio, the requested loan would be "illegal and also immoral."

This was all that Couzens needed to hear. He would oppose any such bailout, he declared with a flourish: "I will shout it from the rooftops and on the floor of the Senate!"

But that was not what the meeting was about. Hoover wouldn't support an unsecured cash transfusion, either. Following Couzens's outburst, Hoover tried to steer the discussion back to his proposal—Ford had agreed to subordinate his capital, and the other carmakers had come forward with "voluntary contributions"; what Hoover sought was a matching, $2 million commitment from Couzens. This would cover the bank's immediate liabilities; it would also satisfy the legal requirements for the RFC loan.

Perhaps it was the reference to his old rival Ford, or perhaps it was the residual heat from his umbrage at the RFC, but Couzens rejected the proposal out of hand. The senator "ranted all over the room," Hoover recalled later; he "threatened the RFC with dire vengeance if the directors gave any assistance" to the Union Guardian group.

Now Hoover got his dander up. He leaned on Couzens, describing Henry Ford's sacrifice of interest and the president's own "great efforts" to secure cooperation from the other automakers. But Couzens would not be pressured. "Why should the RFC bail out Ford?" he shouted in anger.

Hoover tried again, insisting that Union Guardian's assets were necessarily undervalued, but that earnings would soon recover and all loans would be repaid. He then scolded Couzens: "If 800,000 small bank depositors in my home town could be saved by lending 3 percent of my fortune, even if I lost, I certainly would do it." This last reproach drew no better result. After two hours in conference, as Hoover recalled later, Couzens "left in great heat."

After the Michigan senators departed, Hoover convened one more meeting that night, with Commerce Secretary Chapin, Treasury Secretary Mills, and Mills's undersecretary, Arthur Ballantine. Couzens was out, but perhaps he was right after all. Henry Ford was the dominant figure at Union Guardian; why shouldn't he take a bigger role? It was decided to send Chapin and Ballantine out to snowbound Detroit and meet with Ford in person. All was in strict confidence; when reporters called that night in to ask about rumors of important talks at the White House, Hoover ordered a brush-off. "Turn them off any way you can," he told Ted Joslin. "The situation is altogether too critical to let them know anything."

On Sunday, the night before the RFC meeting with Henry Ford, Hoover called the automaker from the White House and spoke with him for ten minutes. The two had a fair amount of history together—Hoover had supported Ford's bid to operate Muscle Shoals, and Ford had visited Hoover at the White House. By the end of their talk Ford had made no commitments, but the president believed he had at least confirmed Edsel's agreement to subordinate the Ford deposits at Union Guardian.

Something happened overnight to change Ford's outlook. It may have been the front page of the *Detroit Free Press*, which carried a startling interview with James Couzens. Still irate, apparently, after his meeting at the White House, Couzens said he now favored a general "moratorium" that would suspend banking operations nationwide, with only sound institutions allowed to reopen. When told of the senator's remarks, Ford said, "For once in his life Jim Couzens is right."

In any event, when Chapin and Ballantine arrived at Dearborn early Monday for their meeting with Ford, they were kept waiting a full hour outside his office; they were told he was busy "inspecting his fields" in the below-freezing weather. When Ford finally showed up, the lean, terse tycoon made short work of the bailout plan. Not only did he refuse contributing to the bailout, he rescinded the agreement Edsel had made to subordinate the Ford accounts at Union Guardian. More than that, Ford vowed that if Union Guardian failed to open, his first move would be to withdraw the $25 million he had on deposit with Detroit Bankers. If Michigan's leading banks were going down, Henry Ford would be the first one out.

Taken aback at this escalation, Ballantine asked if he had heard Ford correctly. When Ford said that he had, Ballantine explored the possible consequences: Should Guardian and Detroit Bankers fail, it was hard to see how any banks in the state would survive, throwing more than three million people into distress. Moreover, the pressure on banks would most likely spread, with bank closures across the entire country.

If circumstances were that dire, Ford countered, why would the government wait for him? "You say all of these terrible consequences might come and yet the government proposes to let this situation come about by refusal to put up $6 million." Ford had a point; Ballantine could only plead that the government was ready to "put up every cent," but that legal strictures on RFC funding required pledges of good collateral, which meant that the government loans must be granted priority over his deposits.

"All right," Ford answered, "have it that way." The bailout would not supplant his personal interest. "I think Senator Couzens was probably right in saying, 'Let the crash come.'"

Not only had Ford refused to help, his vow to pull his millions from whatever banks dared to open Tuesday morning meant that any new cash would simply be siphoned off to Ford. Emergency infusions would be futile. With that threat, Ford effectively killed the bailout, much as Andrew Mellon had in Pittsburgh a year before. Hoover had to wonder then, whether cooperation and capitalism could ever coexist.

With all options closed, RFC officials asked Michigan's governor to declare a bank holiday, as Huey Long had done in Louisiana. The news would come as a shock, but at least that would stop the bleeding. On Tuesday morning, February 14, the deed was done: Governor William A. Comstock suspended all banking operations in the state, freezing $1.5 billion in deposits at more than five hundred banks. The holiday was supposed to run for eight days; it ran nearly a month.

Just how closely Hoover was able to track the decisions being taken in Washington and Detroit is hard to say. That Monday, while the RFC officials were meeting with Henry Ford, Hoover was scheduled to deliver a Lincoln Day speech to the National Republican Club in New York. It would be his last major public address as president.

Hoover took a call from Commerce Secretary Chapin in Detroit at 1:48 that afternoon, but they could not have spoken long; the president's train left Union Station at 2:15. He spent the four-hour trip in the company of his wife and a full retinue, including Ogden Mills, Henry Stimson, and Patrick Hurley. They were met at Pennsylvania Station in New York by two hundred uniformed officers; six hundred more were deployed on the route from the station to the posh Waldorf-Astoria Hotel.

The president and Lou Hoover planned to return to Washington late that night, but they did not travel lightly. The entire fourteenth floor at the Waldorf was set aside for the Hoover entourage, and it took six porters to manage all the president's baggage. The hotel lobby was crammed with guests in evening dress, who applauded as the Hoovers and their Secret Service escort made their way to the elevators. Among those on hand was the

hotel owner; the president greeted him with a cordial, "Hello, Mr. Tschirky";
Lou, close behind, smiled and said, "Hello, Oscar."

Once in their quarters, Hoover had to gather himself for his speech, but
the financial smash-up in Michigan remained very much on his mind. He
made a quick phone call to Ogden Mills, who was staying in touch with the
RFC and other officials Washington. And he squeezed in a brief conversation with his friend and financial advisor, Edgar Rickard.

Busy as he was, Hoover asked Rickard to attend to him while shaving.
There, in shirtsleeves and with a lather on his face, the president shared
his thoughts. He was "greatly disturbed" over the banking situation in Detroit, Hoover said. There would likely be a bank holiday, possibly followed
by "great national unrest." Best to make provisions, Hoover said; He then
asked Rickard to withdraw $10,000 cash "for possible emergency use." For
months Hoover had inveighed against the evils of hoarding, but here he was
simply being practical. It appeared the final crisis was at hand.

The speech the president gave that night in New York was previewed in
the press as his valedictory, but Hoover didn't see it that way. He wanted
to avoid politics, and to look forward, not back. But it was certainly topical,
and could well have carried the subtitle, A Message for Franklin.

The subject was the global economy. For Hoover that meant the gold
standard, and the urgent requirement that it be preserved in America and
resurrected in Europe. Part of his appeal was by now painfully familiar.
Reprising one of the central tenets of his campaign, Hoover reminded the
partisan audience of 1,500 that by keeping the dollar redeemable in gold, his
administration had "maintained one Gibraltar of stability in the world" and
helped to "check the movement to chaos."

Hoover harked back to the heyday of international trade, before the
war, when gold served as the cornerstone for orderly, stable exchange. To
this he added the reverence of a man who spent years in the field, tracking
the yellow metal across the continents. "We have to remember that it is a
commodity the value of which is enshrined in human instincts for over ten
thousand years," Hoover intoned. "The time may come when the world can
safely abandon its use . . . but it has not yet reached that point."

Hoover recognized that Britain's departure from gold had changed the global landscape. "Depreciated currencies gave some nations the hope to manufacture goods more cheaply than their neighbors and thus to rehabilitate their financial position by invasion of the markets of other nations. Those nations in turn have sought to protect themselves by erecting trade barriers." This was a curious argument, coming from a president whose first great initiative in office was the Smoot-Hawley tariff, but Hoover always held that to be a defensive measure to preserve American wages, not to inhibit trade.

Now was different. "These depreciations of currency and regulations and restrictions on imports originated as defense measures by nations to meet their domestic financial difficulties. But a new phase is now developing among these nations that is the rapid degeneration into economic war which threatens to engulf the world."

This war was already taking a toll on Americans. "We are ourselves now confronted with an unnatural movement of goods from the lowered costs and standards of countries with depreciated currencies, which daily increase our unemployment and our difficulties. . . . We will ourselves be forced to defensive action to protect ourselves unless this mad race is stopped. We must not be the major victim of it all."

Modern readers cannot help but see parallels in the picture Hoover painted to the phenomenon of globalism today, not in trade barriers so much as in the international movement of capital and jobs in the ceaseless search for lower costs. Hoover believed the proper response lay in a constant medium of exchange that would allow nations to maximize their natural endowments through trade. In order "to break these vicious fiscal and financial circles," Hoover advised, "The first point of attack is to secure greater stability in the currencies of the important commercial nations." And the single means to that stability was gold.

"It may be that by theoretically managed currencies some form of stability might be found a score or two years hence," Hoover recognized, "but we have no time to wait." There was irony here—Hoover could see the future, but he couldn't see how to get there.

"The American people will soon be at the fork of three roads," Hoover proposed. "The first is the highway of cooperation among nations"—there was Hoover's familiar, elusive ideal of mutual aid, with gold as the integrating mechanism. The second fork was "national self-containment," based on increased tariffs and other trade restrictions. This had been a principal strategy for Hoover's first two years in office; Hoover allowed that such measures might yet be "necessary," but that was beside the point. His principal concern was option three.

"The third road is that we inflate our currency, consequently abandon the gold standard, and with our depreciated currency attempt to enter a world economic war, with the certainty that it leads to complete destruction, both at home and abroad." As bad as things had gotten, Hoover saw a darker side—the path toward which Roosevelt was leaning. Hoover had lost the election but he was convinced he knew the way forward. It was his duty—and of course it was duty that drove him—to make one last bid to save the country from the fate that lay ahead.

Hoover was wrong about sticking with gold. He had witnessed Britain's struggle to maintain the gold standard, but he misread the message. True, with debts mounting and gold stocks nearly exhausted, they had capitulated. But it was not a failure of will on the part of the great banking houses of London. They simply recognized that their time was up. As Keynes observed, "the step was not taken until it was unavoidable."

Hoover saw the same signs—and he had the further example of Britain's first several months of operations with a floating currency. He saw the American recovery stall and the first stirrings of England's incremental but unmistakable renewal. But Hoover dismissed these indicators as economic anomalies and the manipulations of his enemies. He could not bring himself to let go of gold.

This was due in part to Hoover's stoic nature, his grim sense of duty. He was the taskmaster, the orphaned boy grown to stern patriarch, who learned over an eventful life that toil and self-denial were the only reliable roads to success. That was the way of the world, for nations as for individuals. Hoover would never be the sort of speaker who could rouse an audience, warm their hearts or make them laugh; but he always stood ready to pronounce a call to service and sacrifice. Misfortune and adversity were his métier.

That same course of life instilled in him, too, a longing for stability and order that only gold could answer. Setting currencies free to float, cutting the tether to gold would result in global "confusion," Hoover warned, "waves of fear and apprehension." In the mute medium of gold lay the basis for "cooperation"—the Hooverian ideal, the antithesis of chaos. Adherence to gold was a fundamental, even an existential decision. "Any other course in the world today endangers civilization itself."

Hoover was calling for confidence but invoking fear, like a preacher fulminating on the torments of the damned. His professed optimism could not conceal the fact that Hoover was terrified. The Wall Street crash had marked the high-water mark of a great inflation; once the tide turned, the rip currents of deflation carried all before them. In America as in England, it became increasingly apparent that it was futile to resist; that the only recourse was to let go and drift with the current.

That was too much for Hoover. On this most critical test of the Depression era, on the one policy that trumped all the others, Hoover was immobilized by fear. Too scared to let go, he devoted his presidency and his administration to establishing in America a Gibraltar of stability. But as with the concrete fortifications being raised over those same years by the French defense minister André Maginot, the edifice was obsolete before it was even finished.

But if Hoover was wrong about gold, his fears were not entirely misplaced. It was true, for example, as Hoover alleged, that Franklin Roosevelt was waffling on the question of the gold standard. And the corollary is true as well: Roosevelt's refusal to join the outgoing president in a vow to maintain the value of the dollar contributed to the growing pressure on the American banking system.

Roosevelt understood the delicacy of the issue. For much of the interregnum he remained undecided on the direction of his monetary policy; he wanted to bide his time until he took office and make his choices then. But he opened the question inadvertently when he invited Carter Glass to join his cabinet as secretary of the treasury.

The appointment was designed to reassure party centrists like Bernard

Baruch that Roosevelt would not make the sort of rash, inflationary moves that Hoover and so many others suspected and feared. At seventy-five years of age Glass was the embodiment of fiscal stability, the founder of the Federal Reserve, and a foremost foe of deficit spending.

But Glass took himself too seriously to be used as Roosevelt's foil. When offered the post at Treasury, he asked Roosevelt's emissary for the president-elect's policy on the gold standard. The answer that came back was cagey. "We're not going to throw ideas out of the window just because they're labeled inflation," Roosevelt said. That was the end of the talks. Glass told Roosevelt he would defend the gold standard from where he stood, "a roaring lion in the Senate."

The talks with Glass were private, but the deliberations were very much in the public eye. As early as January 30 the *Washington Herald* reported that Roosevelt was considering "controlled reflation," and that in consequence Glass was "hesitating" in accepting the Treasury post. When Glass's final refusal went public, the implications for the gold standard were unmistakable.

Hoover was correct, too, that the move off gold would bring on a convertibility crisis. That was the crash he had mentioned to Joslin; now his worst fears were taking shape.

The suspension of banking operations in Michigan lit the fuse on a new, more advanced stage of the national financial crisis that had been gathering since the failure of Credit Anstalt in May 1931. It was the beginning of a final reckoning that had started in Europe and spread across the globe, as all the advanced commercial nations reset their currencies and their debts, adjustments that had been postponed since the Armistice, fifteen years before.

It marked, too, a new stage in President Hoover's protracted exit from the White House. With his personal and political capital exhausted, Hoover launched an increasingly desperate round of appeals to stave off a financial crash, to protect what was left of his reputation and—here was the tallest order of all—to finally bring Roosevelt into line. The closer he got to the final day of his tenure—March 4, inauguration day—the more frantic Hoover's pleadings, until by the end his antics seemed clearly psychological in nature, the thrashings of a man unable to accept his fate.

This final phase of Hoover's exit from the presidency commenced February 13, during the White House meetings over the crisis in Michigan. With Roosevelt's departure in January for a rest at Warm Springs and a fishing trip in Florida, Hoover had perforce broken off his effort to secure policy commitments from the president-elect. Now, during a conference with RFC chairman Atlee Pomerene, Hoover resumed his pleadings.

The argument was by now well rehearsed. The financial panic was rooted in fears of inflation; the only solution was a commitment from the incoming president to defend the value of the currency. Pomerene was versed in finance and, like most principals in both parties, supported the gold standard; perhaps he could call Roosevelt to his duty. But while Pomerene was a lifelong Democrat, he and Roosevelt "were not mutually congenial," as one contemporary phrased it. Hoover's suggestion went nowhere.

The next day, following his round-trip to New York for the Lincoln Day speech, Hoover collared several congressional Democrats and made the same appeal with them. There was little chance of a message getting through; at that moment Roosevelt was at sea, relaxing on a ten-day fishing expedition, much as Hoover had before his inauguration.

For Roosevelt the vacation nearly ended in tragedy. After landing at Biscayne Bay, he stopped for a brief public appearance before heading home. There an unemployed New Jersey bricklayer named Giuseppe Zangara opened fire on Roosevelt's motorcade. Roosevelt was unhurt, but Chicago mayor Anton Cermak, on hand to curry favor with the new administration, was fatally wounded.

When news of this harrowing incident reached Washington Hoover promptly ordered the Secret Service to increase its escort for the president-elect and telegraphed his concern for Roosevelt to Miami. Hoover then sat down to compose a singular, confidential letter to the president-elect. Now that he was back on land, perhaps he would be ready to accept what Hoover considered to be his responsibilities!

"A most critical situation has arisen in the country," Hoover began, as if the airy Roosevelt might have simply failed to notice a story emblazoned in headlines across the country. There was "a state of alarm which is rapidly reaching the dimensions of a crisis"—a crisis reflected in gold drains, increased hoarding, the breakdown in Detroit, and a surge in bank failures.

This was not the same impetus for "cooperation" that had prompted his first entreaties to Roosevelt—the status of the European war debts—but to Hoover the solution was the same: "A very early statement by you upon two or three policies of your administration would serve greatly to restore confidence and cause a resumption of the march of recovery." Once again, in Hoover's view, Roosevelt's first obligation was to join him in the traces of leadership. And, shallow though he believed him to be, Hoover couldn't conceive that Roosevelt's prescription would differ from his.

So pressing was Hoover's sense of urgency that he dispatched a Secret Service operative from Washington to New York with orders to find Roosevelt and deliver the document in person. The result was something out of a Maxwell Smart spoof—on Saturday, February 18, Roosevelt was sitting with a crowd of close to a thousand people in the ballroom at the Hotel Astor, an honored guest at the annual jamboree put on by a New York press club called the Inner Circle. Sometime after midnight he was approached by a government gumshoe and handed an unmarked envelope. Inside he found the letter, written in Hoover's distinctive, looping scrawl.

Roosevelt took the document home that night and passed it around among two or three friends. It was a strange and labored production, reprising the crises of 1931 and 1932, the steps taken by the administration, and the many failings of Congress. There was much work yet to be done, Hoover said, but Roosevelt could make an immediate contribution by "clarifying the public mind." Hoover then proffered the key talking points. "It would steady the country greatly if there could be prompt assurance that there will be no tampering or inflation of the currency; that the budget will be unquestionably balanced, even if further taxation is necessary; that the government credit will be maintained by refusal to exhaust it in the issue of securities."

Hoover's game was so brash it was hard to credit: election results notwithstanding, he believed he could persuade Roosevelt to discard his own program and pursue Hoover's instead. So it appeared from the letter, and so Hoover confirmed three days later in a confidential note to a friendly senator. He was hoping the Democrats in Congress might be convinced, as he was attempting with Roosevelt, to declare against "inflation" and deficit spending. "I realize that if these declarations be made by the president-elect

he will have ratified the whole major program of the Republican administration," Hoover acknowledged. "That is, it means the abandonment of
90 percent of the so-called new deal."

Roosevelt was quite aware of the ill-concealed effrontery of Hoover's
position—he later termed it "cheeky"—but he said nothing at the time, im-
pressing his advisors with his "extraordinary calm."

Sometime soon thereafter, Roosevelt composed a gentle, unruffled
response—and then he sat on it. Ten days later he sent Hoover a polite note
of apology—the delay was a case of secretarial oversight, he said—but the
result was the same: Hoover was on his own.

Hoover would not accept no for an answer. After two days of silence, he
asked the Secret Service to confirm delivery of his letter to Roosevelt. He
received a "full report" of the handoff; the letter had been received, but it
may as well have been dropped down a well.

The next day, Ogden Mills was scheduled to meet William Woodin, the
man chosen by Roosevelt for Treasury after Carter Glass declined. Seizing a
slim opportunity, Hoover asked Mills to see if Woodin might be able obtain
a statement from the president-elect. Mills took his meeting in New York
and reported back that evening: "positively no statement would be made."

Satisfied, finally, that he would get no help from Roosevelt, Hoover
turned to the Federal Reserve. The governors had been silent through the
crisis so far; now Hoover addressed them in a formal letter. "I wish to leave
no stone unturned for constructive action," he wrote; just what might they
advise? But the Fed Board had no more appetite than Roosevelt to shoulder
responsibility and blame at this late date. The board took two days to answer, and while it agreed the situation was "disturbing," it did "not desire to
make any specific proposals."

The day Hoover received this note, on February 25, a Saturday, the
governor of Maryland declared a bank holiday. With Michigan still in suspension, the crisis was moving rapidly. By now the president was swinging
wildly between the poles of action and accusation. His first reaction was to
announce, to Ted Joslin, that, "There is nothing we can do." Fear of Roosevelt was driving the panic. "The American people are writing off the New
Deal," Hoover declaimed.

But that afternoon and all day Sunday, Hoover plunged back into meetings with Ogden Mills and Eugene Meyer, and Chairman Pomerene and President Miller of the Reconstruction Finance Corporation. There were a number of possible options, but Hoover could not settle on a strategy. On Tuesday, he sent another appeal to the Fed. He acknowledged that, "the board is not the technical advisor to the president," but perhaps they would recommend a plan. Or was it better, Hoover asked, "to allow the situation to drift along"?

By now the board at the Fed was as leery of Hoover as was Roosevelt. Hoover's letter was "evidently designed to make a record for political reasons," the governors surmised, and so they answered in kind. The question was not whether matters should "drift," but what measures were available that would not "create greater difficulty or alarm." So far, the answer was none.

Now, with Roosevelt's inauguration just days away, it seemed to all parties that a terrible crash was at hand. Long lines were forming at banks across the country as depositors large and small sought access to their funds. Foreign governments scrambled to convert dollars to gold. Several states authorized banks to limit withdrawals to a fraction of total deposits. On March 2 six more states closed their banks by decree.

The tension in Washington mounted steadily. At the White House the president toiled incessantly, meeting finance officials and members of Congress, plying the phone and catching just a few hours of sleep. Officials at the Treasury and the Fed and the RFC labored apace, office lights burning well past midnight as they tracked bank closures and considered remedies.

Toward the end of the week Franklin Roosevelt and his advisors took rooms at the Mayflower Hotel pending their move into the White House. From their various stations around the capital the principals eyed each other warily, each wondering how they might escape blame for the break that was sure to come.

The night of March 2 the governors of the Fed decided they could wait no longer. Answering the president's plea of a week before, the board advised him to declare a national bank holiday; put all activity on hold, let the fever burn off and start fresh with a new administration. There was an emergency powers provision left over from the war the president could cite for authority.

Hoover bridled. "I won't go it alone," he vowed, but he wanted some pretext for his reticence. He turned to Attorney General William Mitchell, who rendered a carefully tailored argument, but not a written opinion. And the argument changed—that afternoon, Mitchell told attorneys for the Fed and the Treasury that Hoover had the authority to close all the banks "if he felt the emergency justified it." But that evening Ogden Mills gave the Fed governors a different version; Mitchell had told him "the matter was not free from doubt," and that Hoover should not suspend bank operations "without the consent of the incoming administration."

All this occurred behind the scenes. In the meantime, Hoover remained on center stage, obliged to honor the protocols of an orderly presidential transition. He spent the noon hour in company with Lou, saying good-bye to a stream of friends in and out of government. One guest was Alice Roosevelt Longworth, who had remained loyal to the party of her father. She could not help but feel empathy for Hoover, finding him "all stiff, bruised and wounded."

At four o'clock the president performed perhaps the most difficult chore of his day, joining Lou once again to host Franklin and Eleanor Roosevelt in the Red Room for tea. A sit-down dinner was more customary, but some wise head had switched to the less formal, less demanding idea of a tea service. In any event, as one staff member recalled, "No one seemed comfortable."

With that pantomime over, Lou and Eleanor moved to the Green Room, while Hoover asked Roosevelt to stay put. Hoover then brought in his financial team, Ogden Mills and Eugene Meyer. This was unscheduled, a small surprise sprung to once more try to dragoon the president-elect into service. Fortunately for Roosevelt, White House usher Ike Hoover—aware, certainly, which president would be responsible for his continued employment—tipped him off to the scheme, and Roosevelt had sent word for Ray Moley to hurry over.

When the aides were gathered the talks ran for roughly an hour. It had all been said before—Hoover sought commitments and Roosevelt gave none—their first, historic encounter now reprised as farce. At least Roosevelt was polite, considering the ambush nature of the meeting. In his memoir, Moley remarked on Roosevelt's reserve. "Perhaps it was the look of utter weariness and defeat on Hoover's face that made Roosevelt refrain from answering as sharply as he might have."

Roosevelt departed the White House late that afternoon but the crisis did not let up. The pressure built all through the day, thousands of banks closing and the financial centers of New York and Chicago running out of gold. At 8 p.m., Mills called in from the meetings at the Fed. Roosevelt would take power tomorrow but that was too long to wait; Hoover must move now to close the banks. But for Hoover it no longer was a question of policy; this would be disgrace, a final admission of failure.

Sitting at his desk in the study he had made his own, the president raged at Mills, his voice rising until finally it broke into a wail. "How horrible it is for me to have such a proposal made on the eve of my leaving office!" Now Hoover unburdened himself. "To do so would be passing on to my two sons an inheritance which I would not countenance doing. You should know what my answer would be. No, no, no!" He slammed down the phone, sat for a moment, seething, then stood and paced the floor, hands in his pocket, head down.

Now it was not just his foes that Hoover feared. At this last, desperate hour he was turning against his closest aides.

Later that evening, the Fed governors prevailed on Eugene Meyer to try once again. He called the president and "begged him both as an advisor and a personal friend to issue the proclamation" closing the banks. Hoover rejected the appeal bitterly, using the same tone he had adopted with Mills. Hoover had long suspected Meyer of disloyalty; here was final proof.

That same eventful evening Ogden Mills presented the second version of William Mitchell's legal opinion to the Roosevelt team at the Mayflower—Hoover would sign on but he needed Roosevelt's support. William Woodin, soon to replace Mills at Treasury, understood the need to freeze bank operations and endorsed the holiday; if FDR would go along it would be a consensus. But Roosevelt would not join; he sent back word that state-level action would suffice. Shortly before midnight Hoover called Roosevelt to make the appeal in person, but the result was the same.

Senator Carter Glass was among the many courtiers on hand at the Mayflower that night. When Roosevelt told him of his phone call with Hoover, Glass asked what he planned to do about the banks. "Planning to close, them, of course." Roosevelt would declare a bank holiday after all, but on his own initiative.

Back at the White House, Hoover told Ted Joslin of his talk with Roosevelt. Hoover said they had discussed the bank holiday, but that he felt he was being manipulated. "They want to jockey me into proceeding. But I won't go it alone." Hoover struck a defiant tone. "We told them to go to hell."

Outmaneuvered and outfoxed, Hoover was cross as a skewered bull, but his last night as president was not yet over. With the entire banking sector sliding into panic, the governors of the Federal Reserve remained in session. Shortly after midnight they determined the bank holiday was "absolutely necessary," and drafted a proclamation for Hoover to sign closing all banks until the Sunday inauguration. It would cover just twenty-four hours but could avert an unprecedented fiscal calamity.

At 12:30 a.m. the board dispatched a courier to take their message to the White House. There he was informed the president had gone to bed at midnight and left word not to be disturbed. Someone suggested calling Larry Richey. They raised him on the phone, and a courier was sent back to the White House, but there was no answer from the president.

With no recourse to a national shutdown, the Fed governors stayed on, coordinating with state authorities in New York and Illinois to secure temporary banking holidays in those key states. Arrangements were finalized sometime after 3 a.m.

The next day Hoover fired off an angry note to Eugene Meyer. Since the Fed Board had arranged the shutdowns at the state level, Hoover was "at a loss to understand" why they needed to trouble the president with a request for emergency action "in the last few hours of this administration." But members of the board were just as indignant. When they sent their courier the board did not know, and nor could the president, that the state governors would agree to intervene. So far as Governor Charles Hamlin was concerned, the president had deserted them in the critical hour. "Hoover doubtless drew the bed clothing over his head and cowardly tried to shirk his duty!"

Inauguration day broke cold and gray over Washington, a fitting backdrop for the close of a presidency shadowed by crisis, frustration, and disappointment. For the moment the busy hallways were deserted and the staterooms half stripped of furniture, awaiting the arrival of a new administration.

On the South Lawn of the White House the Medicine Ball Cabinet assembled one last time, but this was not a day for sport. Hoover took the occasion to present to his daily companions sixteen signed, five-pound leather balls as mementos. Taking leave of this cohort, Hoover shared a quiet breakfast with a friend from the RFC, then closeted himself one last time in the Lincoln Study, looking south, out over the Ellipse.

As the hour for the inaugural ceremony approached, Hoover waited with Lou, their sons, Allan and Herbert Jr., and Joel Boone. The president's dejection was apparent to all. The staff was gathered under the Front Portico to see him off, and they agreed afterward, "He looked like a whipped man." Following after her husband, Lou could not resist the impulse to recall better times, when Bert had been the solution, and not the problem. "Maggie," she said furtively to a favored aide, "My husband will come back some day to do great things." As the aide recalled, Lou left the White House with tears in her eyes.

Hoover subjected himself to one last torment—he rode from the White House to the Capitol in the rear of an open car, side by side with Franklin Roosevelt. Photographs from the event capture the essence of the moment, both in top hats, both sharing a car blanket against the cold, but Roosevelt was beaming, and Hoover looked stunned.

On the drive and all through the ceremony, the two hardly spoke. Finally they parted, Roosevelt for the White House, which he would occupy for the rest of his days; Hoover directly to Union Station. A small group of friends gathered there to say good-bye, including Ogden Mills and Patrick Hurley and Henry Stimson. There was a Secret Service detail on the station platform as well, but that was as far as they would go.

Larry Richey objected. He'd arranged for a police escort in New York, where the Hoovers would stay until they sorted out their plans, but what about the journey itself? The railroad had assigned four guards to the Hoover party, the agent in charge explained, but that was it.

The trip came off without trouble, and that evening the Hoovers took up residence at the Waldorf, which Bert would call home for many years to come. Hoover considered the Secret Service snafu a personal affront, a crowning dishonor at the hands of an ungrateful nation. "I had all the security in the world going to the inauguration," he told a friend later. "The moment Roosevelt was sworn in, I was nothing."

It was typical of Hoover, a small and personal view of the office and his role that had made it so hard for him to make any connection with the people he governed. Hoover spent much of the rest of his life seeking to restore his reputation, posing Roosevelt as his nemesis. Yet in all his revisions and literary visitations, he never really came to grips with the full arc of his story.

The people around him may have had a richer appreciation of his saga. Especially for those to whom Hoover had arrived as the embodiment of progress and competence, the master of great endeavors and the bane of foolish politics, his fall appeared epic, even operatic. Agnes Meyer, sharp-eyed wife to Eugene, captured the scale and the tone of his final crescendo. "Hard on Hoover to go out of office to the sound of crashing banks," Meyer wrote in her diary. "Like the tragic end to a tragic story."

EPILOGUE

Upon his departure from Washington Herbert Hoover vowed to sleep for forty-eight hours—an exceptional extravagance for the toilsome ex-president, but less than what he'd lost in the weeks of mounting crisis.

In the event, he was off by a factor of four. But Hoover did manage to sleep twelve long hours, and awakened, like Rip Van Winkle, to a changed world. Where, for four years in office, Hoover stood at the center of events, with every crisis in a troubled nation laid at his door, now he was instantly, widely forgotten, master of his own schedule but little else.

He spent his first day as a private citizen in a leisurely drive out to Connecticut, where he visited Edgar Rickard and his wife at their country estate. Hoover made the trip with Larry Richey and Hoover's son Allan, in a limousine borrowed from Ogden Mills, who was still in Washington. Lou Hoover had not made it as far as New York, deciding instead to part ways with her husband soon after they left the capital. She changed trains at Philadelphia, in company with Herbert Jr., and headed directly for California. Bert was not quite ready for retirement, but Lou definitely was.

The next morning, a Tuesday, Hoover arose restless and early. He was out just after dawn, Larry Richey at his side, strolling over to Fifth Avenue and then up to Central Park, gazing about like a tourist. Much had changed. He had visited the city several times as president, but had always kept such a close schedule that he never really had the chance to look around. The skyline had changed, Hoover remarked later; among other lost landmarks he was surprised to find that the vast Fifth Avenue townhouse of William Vanderbilt, considered the largest private home ever built in Manhattan, had been demolished.

Hoover was back at the Waldorf by eight. He dawdled at the Peacock Alley lounge, a posh new dining court, and then headed up to his suite. Many visitors stopped by that day, but all the calls were social, and none concerned affairs of state.

Hoover remained in his opulent, thirty-third-floor suite for another ten days. It only fed his sense of isolation to know that, down in Washington, his closest White House advisors continued in crisis mode. Mills and Eugene Meyer were working frantically with the new administration to manage the banking crisis that had crested in the final days of Hoover's tenure.

Hoover did have one unfortunate, official obligation to answer. On March 12 Hoover's occasional literary aide, French Strother, just forty-nine years old, died of pneumonia that he contracted during the blustery morning of the Roosevelt inauguration. Three days later Hoover attended Strother's funeral on Long Island, slipping into the Garden City Episcopal Cathedral through a side door and insulated from the other mourners by a cordon of police.

Finally, on the afternoon of Thursday, March 16, the former president, his son Allan, and Larry Richey quit the Waldorf-Astoria for Pennsylvania Station, the first leg of Hoover's long journey to rejoin Lou in Palo Alto. Hoover rode across town with a motorcycle escort, but it was just an echo of the pomp to which he had become accustomed. He was an ex-president without portfolio, a man whose unbroken string of success and mounting accomplishment had come to an abrupt end. For the first time in a busy life he was unsure what to do next. He was fifty-eight years old.

At Penn Station the ex-president was pressed by reporters and by news-reel crews for any sort of statement, but Hoover refused to say a word. Larry Richey filled in, suggesting that Hoover's plans were to "just take it easy for a month or so, maybe doing a little fishing in the California mountains." To most Americans, who counted themselves fortunate if they could even eke out a livelihood, it sounded ideal. But to a lifelong workaholic like Hoover, it looked like purgatory.

While Hoover felt his way into his new and sharply circumscribed status, his successor was making sensational strides in handling the financial debacle Hoover had left behind. It was a demonstration of alchemy over secular science, of the fundamentally social nature of economics, and of democracy in action. Where Hoover had personified the ideal of the nonpolitician as executive manager, Roosevelt was the opposite—the consummate politician who could accomplish real-world feats by invoking the intangible forces of persuasion and inspiration.

It began with his first act, his inaugural address. Taking the podium that slate-gray day in March, Roosevelt treated the nation to a spectacle it had not experienced in a generation—a speech by a president who actually enjoyed making speeches. The effect was electric, and the result far greater than the simple message the oration might imply.

The phrase that has rung down through the years came in the first stanza of the speech: "Let me assert my firm belief that the only thing we have to fear is, fear itself." Roosevelt delivered the line in ringing tones, with a theatrical pause before "fear itself," his voice clearly audible to the 150,000 souls draped like a blanket over the great lawn facing the Capitol.

It was a rousing appeal, nicely suited to the moment, but there was nothing original about it. From the week of the Wall Street crash three years before, "confidence" had been Hoover's drumbeat refrain, repeated so incessantly that by the time of the 1932 campaign his critics were throwing it back in his face. But with Hoover it always came in his stilted vernacular, and it always felt more like admonition than encouragement. "Ceaseless effort must be directed toward the restoration of confidence," he pronounced in one typical incantation, "the vanquishing of fear and apprehension, and thus the release of the recuperative spirit of the world." The message had to fight through the verbiage.

Even as he uttered it, Roosevelt's small meditation on fear already had a history. In 1851, Henry David Thoreau wrote in his journal, "Nothing is to be so much feared as fear," and the remark was included in later collections of his work. Eighty years later, Hoover's friend and investment partner Julian Barnes voiced its modern formulation. As head of the national Chamber of Commerce Barnes often sought to echo and amplify the president's policies; in February 1931 that meant stabilizing business by instilling confidence. Barnes explained to a *New York Times* reporter that, when it came to job creation, "the thing to be feared most is fear itself."

The idea was out there, but it was not until Roosevelt's elocution that the catchphrase found traction with the American people. And when it did, the impact was profound. "Practically everybody feels better already," the tabloid New York *Daily News* effused the day after Roosevelt's inaugural. "Confidence seems to be coming back with a rush, along with courage."

The sudden shift in mood and temper penetrated even the White House, a gloomy place after four years under Hoover's glower. Entering the executive mansion late on inauguration day, Secret Service agent Edmund Starling found it "transformed . . . into a gay place full of people who oozed confidence and seemed unaware that anything was wrong with the United States." To Starling as to millions of Americans, "So far as the spirit of the thing was concerned, the depression ended right there."

Of course, the Depression did not end right there. In fact it persisted through the end of the decade, resisting the ardent efforts of Roosevelt and his advisors. Encouraged to experiment, they tried every available means to restore employment and production—public works, farm cooperatives, currency inflation, central planning. Production recovered modestly, but penury and widespread unemployment persisted until the advent of the next world war. Industrialized warfare provided a solution of sorts, but that could never be embraced as a viable policy tool.

Still, there was more than hokum at work in Roosevelt's determined and vigorous assault on the Depression. His single most successful foray was his first, against the banking crisis that greeted him upon taking office. It was here that the change in leadership could have the strongest real-world impact. In the realm of economics, where a shift in the mood and temper of the people at large could yield meaningful change in bank ledgers and bottom lines, mass psychology mattered.

Roosevelt benefited as well by the best efforts of Hoover's own team of advisors, and by a full year of Hoover's frantic efforts to salvage the banks. In later years Hoover was condemned for the collapse of the banking system, and Roosevelt credited with its restoration, but the story is more subtle than that.

Roosevelt made the financial crisis the focus of his inaugural speech on Saturday, first exhorting against fear, then laying blame for the Depression at the feet of the bankers. "The rulers of the exchange of mankind's goods have failed through their own stubbornness and their own incompetence." Roosevelt couched his wrath in biblical terms: "The money changers have fled from their high seats in the temple of our civilization."

Having established a moral tone for his new administration, Roosevelt swung into action on Sunday with two bracing proclamations. The first called Congress into emergency session and the second ordered the bank holiday that Hoover had begged Roosevelt to endorse. The strategy was useful, Roosevelt decided; it was the alliance with Hoover that he could not abide.

And so the national economy was arrested in its careening death spiral, put on hold long enough for the new president and his advisors to work out a plan for its resurrection. Here, however, they were largely at sea, in part because the crisis they faced was unprecedented, but also because most of the financial acumen and experience in the government lay in the councils of the former administration.

That might present an awkward test for a more doctrinaire captain, but not for the nimble Roosevelt. Even before he took the reins of power, Roosevelt had his new treasury secretary, William Woodin, confer with Ogden Mills and Eugene Meyer in drawing up policy. Both men remained loyal to Hoover and skeptical of Roosevelt, but both committed long hours, along with their senior staff, to formulating emergency policy.

Their first substantial contribution was the actual proclamation closing the banks, which Roosevelt issued at 1 a.m. Monday; the hour was chosen to avoid talking business on Sunday, but also to be sure the banks did not open for business that week. The order itself was the one Meyer had drafted for Hoover and sent to the White House after midnight just two days before. Hoover, beset by his incapacities, had refused the proclamation, but Roosevelt put it into force.

Closing the banks was simple enough; the tricky part was what to do next. William Woodin, an industrialist who had spent five years as a director of the Federal Reserve Bank of New York, had a vague plan to issue scrip from individual, large banks in place of the national currency. But that idea was vigorously opposed by Eugene Meyer and quickly dropped as too unwieldy. Like his boss, Woodin had no particular scheme he wanted to push; once all the banks were closed, Woodin invited a clutch of friendly financiers to visit his suite at the Carlton Hotel and strummed a guitar while the executives mulled policy options.

The hard work, it turns out, was being done by the remnants of the Hoover team at the Treasury. The principals were Mills, Meyer, Mills's deputy Arthur Ballantine, Fed staffers Emanuel Goldenweiser and Walter Wyatt, J. P. Morgan banker Parker Gilbert, and Francis Awalt, the interim comptroller of the currency. These stalwarts began on March 3 to confer in marathon sessions over how to stem the tide and salvage the banking system, while fearful depositors carried off millions of dollars in gold by the hour.

On March 4—inauguration day—Mills called this crew together to spend the day fashioning a plan for reopening the banks. By afternoon he had a "tentative outline," a scheme to divide the nation's banks into three classes—A, B, and C, according to their financial health—to screen them closely, and then restore them in stages to regular operation. This would allow the government to assure a fearful public that, when the "holiday" was lifted, only sound banks would be permitted to open their doors.

The outline of this scheme was presented to William Woodin and relayed to Roosevelt, who promptly embraced it. He then called a Sunday meeting of bankers from the major financial centers—New York, Chicago, Boston, and Philadelphia—and key leaders of Congress, to garner support for the bank holiday. In the meantime, at Treasury, Mills labored on, working with his team to develop legal language and to inventory the nation's banks. Class A banks, judged to be sound, would open first; those in Class B would receive loans from the Fed to ensure their liquidity, based on an expanded range of assets, and open second. Class C banks would obtain special assistance, including possible capital infusions from the RFC in return for stock issues, or else would stay closed and be liquidated. Mills completed his working draft of the plan at 2:30 in the morning of March 7; the next day he and his team plunged into implementation.

It was tough, painstaking work, and singularly thankless. Meyer and Mills both naturally resented the obligation to work for a president who had triumphed over their Chief; Mills in addition was the object of Roosevelt's personal enmity. By the end of his run he was obliged to hide his contributions because, as Francis Awalt termed it later, "the wall of hostility toward him had closed in so tightly." Mills himself termed the work "very disagreeable," and said he received little in the way of recognition from the new administration. "But I am not working for them," Mills told a friend. "I am working for the country."

Franklin Roosevelt proclaimed the bank holiday on March 6, and on March 9, after Congress convened in emergency session, he extended it. That day, too, Congress granted to the Federal Reserve new powers for lending to banks that it had jealousy withheld from Hoover; Carter Glass, in particular, set aside his fears of inflation to allow the bank rescue operations to commence.

Through it all, the public waited patiently. They had little choice—most of the banks had already been closed by state decree—but they were also hungry for leadership, and Roosevelt promised to be a sympathetic ally. The "holiday" ran for six business days, and all that week the country operated on a cash-and-barter basis. But there was no panic; people treated the hiatus less as a crisis than as the holiday it was purported to be.

On March 12, the Sunday before the banks would reopen, Roosevelt prepared the ground by delivering the first of his famous "fireside chats," this one devoted exclusively to explaining the operations of the financial system, the problems faced by the banks, and the reasons behind the holiday. The phenomenon of hoarding, which had so vexed Hoover and which was a principal cause of the crisis that spring, Roosevelt dispensed with in a single line: "It is my belief that hoarding during the past week has become an exceedingly unfashionable pastime in every part of our nation."

In style and tone—it was a chat, after all, and not a speech—Roosevelt could not have differed more than his predecessor. But those seeking a dramatic break in mode of governance between Hoover and Roosevelt will not find it here. In fact this first, seminal statement from the new administration was drafted by Mills's assistant Ballantine, explaining a program designed by Mills himself.

Still, it was FDR's initiative, and that made all the difference. When the Class A banks opened on Monday, official Washington held its collective breath, waiting to see if the runs would resume. Sure enough, the depositors lined up, but they were seeking to put their money in, not pull it out. On that first day the Federal Reserve Bank of New York took in $27 million, with more than $11 million of that in gold certificates. The bank also paid out $18 million, but most of that was loans to member banks, and almost none to fearful depositors. At the close of business that day William Woodin proclaimed himself "delighted."

For the balance of the week the flow of deposits to banks continued unabated. It was more than a change in mood, it was as if a fever had broken. Cash was erupting, like geysers, from hidden springs and deep wells. It wasn't just bank deposits; federal tax offices were suddenly inundated with cash payments. So many first-time filers were lined up at the collector's office on 57th Street in New York that police had to be called in to keep order.

Nor was the flow of funds limited to currency. Depositors brought in gold as well, reversing the drains of February and early March. It was "a gold stampede in reverse," the *Times* reported, "unlike anything within the memory of the downtown financial community." Even more gratifying, the surge of funds sloshed over into business activity. Newspaper advertising rose "decidedly," and in Chicago, commodity prices "shot skyward" in "a whirlwind of almost feverish trading."

With so many evidences of resurgent optimism, there was no disputing that Franklin Roosevelt had pulled off a genuine political miracle. Hamilton Lewis, Democratic senator from Illinois, recognized the feat at the time. "I have never seen within my life such a real transformation in sentiment," Lewis told reporters, "from discouragement to encouragement, from despair to complete hope."

It was real and it was remarkable, but it was not Roosevelt's triumph alone.

After all, once the panic receded, the banks still had to conduct business based on the strength of their balance sheets, and as was amply demonstrated in the weeks after the holiday, most major American banks were solvent and secure.

In total, more than 90 percent of the banks resumed normal operations without additional support. This was in substantial measure the legacy of Hoover's Reconstruction Finance Corporation. For all its limitations, in its first year of operation the RFC managed to inject $2 billion into the economy, advancing loans to one of every four banks in the nation. Despite the fears of the public and the ravages of deflation, the banking system inherited by Roosevelt was essentially solvent, a credit to Hoover's vision and the consequence of his determined effort.

Also forgotten in the flush of Roosevelt's wizardry was the crucial role Hoover's lieutenants played in implementing the procedures for managing the banking crisis. Roosevelt advisor Ray Moley sought to correct the record in 1966, asserting that, "except for the expertness, the information, and the plans at the lower levels of the Hoover Administration, the crisis could never have been surmounted."

Herbert Hoover followed these developments closely, first by telephone, in conversations with Ogden Mills, and then through the press. Removed to the quiet environs of Palo Alto, he was appalled at the dearth of national news in the local papers, so he arranged for airmail delivery of thirty out-of-state newspapers to his home office each day. He read them in solitude— no briefings, no medicine ball with friends and supplicants, no urgent calls for his attention and decision. When Edgar Rickard visited, in April, he found his old friend to be "lonely beyond measure."

Hoover tried to fill the hollow space he felt inside with expeditions. In April, he and Lou joined Ogden Mills and his wife, Dorothy, for a driving tour of northern Nevada, where Mills owned property inherited from his father. After the Millses departed, Hoover kept driving, alone or with his son Allan, visiting fishing camps and natural monuments, and traveling as far as Yellowstone. In July, the former president resumed his seasonal residence among the stately redwoods of the Bohemian Grove. But the warm welcome from old friends could not hold him, and when the revelers broke camp Hoover was back on the road, now headed for his rustic fishing camp on Wooley Creek, close by what is now the Klamath National Forest. Another fishing trip in October took him to the wild rivers in Oregon that he explored as a teenager. Over the course of that restless summer, Hoover logged ten thousand miles on the road.

Through all this incessant motion, Hoover stayed mum about Roosevelt and the New Deal. He saw the country depart the gold standard, embrace central economic planning, and embark on several massive public works programs—all measures Hoover had fought hard to stave off—without speaking a word to the press. He encouraged the Republican opposition in private contacts with individuals, but otherwise he maintained what one historian called "a policy of public silence," much as he did on so many occasions in the White House.

Hoover maintained his stoic reserve for more than a year. His sole public endeavor he undertook in private, collaborating with Edward Eyre Hunt, one of his longtime acolytes, on a revision of his *American Individualism*, a collection of essays that he titled *The Challenge to Liberty*. The challenge referred to in the title was the Depression, not the New Deal, but the book marked a stirring for Hoover, a tentative step back toward the public forum.

The Challenge to Liberty won a respectful audience and became a national bestseller, but Hoover refrained from public statements through the midterm elections of 1934. The balloting bucked the usual trend of reaction against the incumbent administration, instead reinforcing the Democratic majority in Congress. This renewed and enthusiastic endorsement of the New Deal was more than Hoover could stand. Despite the frustrations he endured as the head of his party and the many humiliations of his not-so-distant turn in the White House, despite his resounding repudiation by the American electorate, early in 1935 Hoover returned to the public lists.

He did so by issuing a public letter, a "call to arms" to the annual California Republican Assembly, in Sacramento. Here, for the first time since his doomed reelection campaign, Hoover aimed squarely at Roosevelt and the New Deal. Republicans now confronted "the greatest responsibility . . . since the days of Abraham Lincoln"—that of providing an alternative, a "rallying point," against "the newly created system of regimentation and bureaucratic domination in which men and women are not masters of government, but are the pawns or dependents of a centralized and potentially self-perpetuating government."

Hoover was heartened to find many Republicans responding to his call; he found unexpected support, as well, at home. To this point, over the length of Hoover's career in office Lou Hoover had limited her public engagement to causes in which she had a direct, personal investment—principally, the Girl Scouts of America. But the drubbing her husband took at the hands of FDR, and the universal public embrace of the New Deal, wrought a change in the former First Lady. For the first time, Lou engaged in partisan politics on her own account.

Her chosen vehicle was Pro America, a women's group organized in the Pacific Northwest to draw homemakers and other sometimes reticent constituencies into the electoral arena. Formed in 1932, Pro America claimed as its president Edith Roosevelt, Theodore's widow and a social and political friend of the Hoovers'. Beginning in 1934 Lou took an active role in the organization, corresponding with its leadership and helping to mediate a schism between those who sought to limit membership to Republicans, and others who felt, as Lou did, that it would have more influence as an independent entity committed to "the old, everlasting principles that have guided America so far."

With these encouragements, and as the pain of his tenure in the White House began to lose its sting, Hoover came to see himself as "the only voice in the [Republican] party that carries nationally." And with the approach of the next presidential election in 1936, Hoover began to see himself as a candidate. He would run again, he would expose Roosevelt and the flimsy foundations of the New Deal, and he would redeem himself.

There were two key factors that rendered Hoover's renewed presidential ambitions a moot point. The first was that, for all the positive feedback Hoover received from the party faithful, he remained a most unpopular ex-president, rejected for his policies but also reviled with that extra dose of venom that Americans keep in reserve for their fallen idols.

William Allen White, the journalistic icon from Kansas who cooled toward Hoover during his presidency, but who never warmed to Roosevelt, summed up the popular feeling on Hoover in a letter to former presidential aide Walter Newton in the summer of 1935. "The great mass of the American people hold even after three years the rancor of 1932 which overcame Hoover. Nothing more terrible, more disheartening to our democratic ideals has ever happened in the history of this republic than this mob rage at an honest, earnest, courageous man. Yet it is here. It still hangs on."

The other obstacle confronting Hoover was his timeworn but still fully operational internal conflict between his desire for high political office and his pained diffidence toward public life. Thus through 1935 and 1936, while he burned for the chance to enter the lists again against Roosevelt, while he plotted and schemed for the nomination, he refused to declare himself a candidate. It was a replay of his successful stealth candidacy of 1927, but with the added burden that Hoover was no longer an unknown, but now an all too well known entity.

The upshot was the curious spectacle of Hoover taking to the hustings, attacking the New Deal and defending his White House record, but keeping mum about his own ambitions. Hoover even backed a slate of unpledged delegates in the 1936 California primary, opposing a slate committed to Republican front-runner Alf Landon. The unpledged delegates prevailed, but Hoover still declined to make himself their leader, and at the convention Landon was nominated handily.

Hoover was invited to make a speech, but after he did so he played no further role in the proceedings. When it came to the campaign, Landon was the candidate, but it was Hoover that Roosevelt ran against, and Roosevelt prevailed in another landslide.

The 1936 election cycle set the template for the next several national elections. Each time, Hoover put himself through the emotional trial of silently seeking the nomination, only to be frozen out by his party. And in the general election Republicans would shy from Hoover as a proven loser, while Franklin Roosevelt always invoked the troubled years of the Depression. "You remember the closed banks and the breadlines and the starvation wages," Roosevelt told a labor audience during his last campaign, in 1944, "the Hoovervilles and the young men and women of the nation facing a hopeless, jobless future . . . and the utter impotence of the federal government."

It was, of course, a setup line. "Now there are some politicians who do not remember that far back, and there are some who remember but find it convenient to forget." Roosevelt was happy to remind them. "No," he insisted, "the record is not to be washed away that easily."

The record remained, burnished every four years, and always with Hoover's name affixed, the symbol of economic hardship, and of a time when the government refused to aid its people.

He was shut out from the government and reviled by an electorate that had once idolized him, but Herbert Hoover would not permit himself to be eased off the public stage. Setting his own pace, he traveled widely and spoke often, developing an intransigent critique of the New Deal that defined him more clearly than even his years in the White House. This was the period that completed Hoover's transition from Bull Moose Progressive, to pragmatist president, to strident ideologue.

Not surprisingly, Franklin Roosevelt became Hoover's obsession, and Roosevelt obliged by fulfilling Hoover's most extreme, most fantastic imaginings—creating one state agency after another; running up billions in public debt; seeking, when opposed by the Supreme Court, to remake that court to suit his ends. Confirmed in his suspicions, Hoover cried out against the alleged sins of bureaucracy and "regimentation," signs of incipient socialism that would undermine his beloved American system.

At a time when the America he sought to preserve was finding much to like in Roosevelt's activist state, Hoover was becoming ever more shrill in denouncing the president and all those who collaborated with him. He had forecast this critique during the presidential campaign of 1932, when he spoke of the fateful choice between two philosophies. For Hoover, the passing years only made the division more stark.

"In all the history of the world mankind has found only two ways of doing the work of feeding, clothing, housing, and providing comforts for the people. One is the way of liberty," Hoover proposed late in 1935. "The other way is the compulsion by which men work for slave-drivers or governments, or as dictated by governments." And there was no question on which path the New Deal was leading the American people.

It was an angry and uncompromising vision that failed to connect with a people still traumatized by the privations of the Depression. What did it matter that the government spawned red tape and lumbering bureaucracies, if it provided a job and some sort of stipend for millions of hopeless and hungry citizens? It was the wrong time for Hoover the fight that fight, and his urgency only belied the personal roots of his pique.

Then came the war, and Hoover again found himself out of step and out of favor. He had no illusions about Hitler, whom he considered dangerous and clearly insane, but he had little patience, either, with his nemesis in the White House. To Hoover's mind, Roosevelt was naive and out of his depth when it came to world affairs. A slave to as well as a conductor of popular opinion, Roosevelt was succumbing to the temptation of knee-jerk moral responses that would drag America into war.

Hoover refined his views of the mounting international crisis, and of Roosevelt's policy reactions with an extended tour of Europe in early 1938. It was his first return to the scene of his humanitarian endeavors during the Great War, and it rekindled in him the ambitions to stage great interventions to administer relief, and to steer the United States clear of the fighting. In particular, Hoover believed Hitler's principal rivalry lay to the east, with Joseph Stalin, and that Europe and the United States should stand aside while the two totalitarians beat each other senseless.

The great blunder that brought civilization to the brink of extinction, Hoover believed, was the decision by France and Britain, taken with Roosevelt's encouragement, to guarantee the safety of Poland. Hitler's invasion there was a first step toward Moscow; had he been allowed to proceed unhindered, England, France, and the rest would have gone unmolested.

After his return from Europe in 1938 Hoover spoke often and forcefully against intervention. Roosevelt ignored him, of course, and rejected repeated appeals to place Hoover in charge of a variety of Red Cross and other relief projects. Up to Pearl Harbor, and on through the Allied victory Roosevelt's popularity never waned, and Hoover remained a pariah in American public life.

Roosevelt's death in office, in April 1945, at last released Hoover from his intractable purgatory. Roosevelt's successor was another Democrat, but Harry

Truman did not have the same personal history with Hoover, and within a month of becoming president Truman had invited Hoover to pay him a visit.

This olive branch initiated a modest revival for Hoover, a new round of activity that, while falling short of rehabilitating the former president, allowed him at least to augment his lifelong record of achievement. In 1946, Truman commissioned Hoover to conduct a study of the war damage in Germany and Austria. This return to his humanitarian exploits resulted in school meals for millions of hungry children in Allied-occupied Germany.

Hoover was glad for the useful work; he also appreciated the personal respect Truman afforded him. Truman saw to it that Hoover's name was restored to the Hoover Dam, and he formed a genuine personal bond with his aging predecessor. "The president always speaks to me as the president," Hoover quipped with satisfaction.

In 1947, acknowledging Hoover's reputation for efficiency, Truman asked him to lead a project aimed at streamlining the federal bureaucracy. The Hoover Commission produced a score of reports outlining hundreds of measures to eliminate waste, some of which Hoover had been advocating since the Harding administration. In 1953 Dwight Eisenhower tasked Hoover with a second, similar study. No longer the butt of satire, Hoover was becoming a brand.

He was, by now, very much alone. Lou Hoover was stricken by a heart attack and died in 1944, at the age of sixty-eight. Even before her passing, Bert had prevailed on her to sell the Palo Alto house and move with him into permanent quarters in the apartments set aside by the Waldorf-Astoria for "permanent guests"—among them Cole Porter, the Shah of Iran, and Queen Juliana of the Netherlands.

Continuing in residence as a widower, Hoover maintained the five rooms at suite 31-A as both home and office, with one room reserved for his secretaries, as many as four at a time. During the holiday season, another room was set aside for the gifts of food and liquor that arrived from friends the world over. Hoover called it "the Commissary." His principal social activity was a weekly lunch at the Dutch Treat Club, a men-only retreat for writers and entertainers notorious for strong drinks, ribald skits, and strict observance of members' privacy—a sort of Bohemian Grove East, with skyscrapers standing in for redwoods.

The staff at the Waldorf doted over the ex-president, and he returned their attentions in kind. When the hotel assigned him a waiter, Hoover inquired after his wage, then promptly raised it, supplying the difference himself. And every August, when his birthday came around, Hoover reversed customary practice and ordered birthday cakes delivered to the Waldorf elevator attendants and its 155 telephone operators.

In 1949, Hoover declined one last turn in public office. That year Robert Wagner, Hoover's old Senate foe from New York, resigned his seat due to ill health. Thomas Dewey, smarting from his surprise loss to Truman the prior year but still the popular governor of New York, offered to appoint Hoover to fill out Wagner's term. But the ex-president advised Dewey to confer the post on a younger man. At age seventy-five, Hoover decided he would stick to his base and fight his battles from there.

Quite conscious of his legacy, he kept a small staff and continued to work long hours. One preoccupation was the preservation of a massive documentary collection that he had amassed over his eventful lifetime. From his long engagement in diplomacy and relief work, he had gathered in person and through friends all the papers he could find from the belligerent nations and the various political factions that sprang up; these he bequeathed to the Hoover Institution of War, Revolution and Peace, which he first established, at Stanford, in 1919. It includes, among many remarkable texts, the papers of Rosa Luxemburg and the diaries of Joseph Goebbels.

Hoover founded a separate repository for the papers from his presidency. This came before the government adopted the current practice of assembling presidential papers for posterity, and many such collections were scattered, archived privately, or donated to the Library of Congress. Hoover chose to archive his at West Branch, Iowa, in a facility contiguous to the small prairie cabin where he was born. Now jointly operated by the National Archives and Records Administration and the private Herbert Hoover Presidential Foundation, the Hoover Library and Museum are part of a National Historic Site dedicated to his memory.

Besides conserving his papers, Hoover continued to create them, producing, in his later years, a broad array of writings. They include his three-volume memoirs; four volumes of notes and reminiscences from his far-flung aid projects, gathered under the serial title *An American Epic*; and several collections of his *Addresses Upon the American Road*. It was a mark of Hoover's obstinacy, and of his unique inner drive, that he made his ultimate vocation in the one discipline—English exposition—that nearly got him flunked out of Stanford.

Nor did Hoover confine his writings to reflections on his public career. In 1958 he published *The Ordeal of Woodrow Wilson*, a profile of the president Hoover considered a political mentor. It was a groundbreaking effort, the first book any ex-president ever wrote about another ex-president. Hoover also indulged in a fanciful treatment of his favorite pastime, publishing in 1963 *Fishing for Fun—And to Wash Your Soul*.

His greatest work, however, Hoover left unfinished. He labored over it for twenty years, writing tirelessly, revising endlessly. Among his friends and various secretaries Hoover referred to it as his Magnum Opus; toward the end, before his death, he settled on the title *Freedom Betrayed*. This was not, like his memoirs, a defense of his record, but a massive, systematic indictment of Franklin Roosevelt's foreign policy and his management of the Second World War.

Hoover had the manuscript in a close to final draft by the time of his death in 1964, his ninetieth year. Hoover's heirs—tired, perhaps, of the patriarch's obsession with his nemesis—deigned not to release the book, and it was consigned to storage. There it lay, for close to fifty years, until it was taken up by George Nash, most assiduous of the Hoover scholars, who gave the manuscript a final polish, and appended an annotated introduction that ran to a hundred printed pages.

The result was a fitting monument to the memory of its author—prodigious, erudite and closely reasoned, hard to read but thoroughly original. Herbert Hoover never did escape the shadow of the politician who vanquished him in the depths of America's Great Depression. But Hoover never left off his lifelong effort to bequeath to his countrymen his vision of liberty and freedom as the birthright of every American. To his mind it was a source of strength but also a most fragile inheritance, a resource to be refreshed by each new generation.

ACKNOWLEDGMENTS

My principal debt in this as with my previous books for Simon & Schuster is owed to Alice Mayhew, editor and sage, for her canny direction, for her belief in me and in this project, and, this time around especially, for her patience. I feel fortunate to have Alice as my editor, and can only hope this work does justice to her confidence.

Research on the Hoover presidency took me to the Library of Congress, in Washington, D.C.; the Hoover Institution at Stanford University; the Schlesinger Library, at Radcliffe, in Cambridge; the Butler Library, at Columbia University; and, near where I live in Los Angeles, to the Huntington Library, in San Marino; the Doheny and Von KleinSmid Center libraries, at the University of Southern California; the University of California Los Angeles Law Library; and the Los Angeles Public Library. At each institution the staff shared their expertise and treated me with professional courtesy.

At the Herbert Hoover Presidential Library, in West Branch, Iowa, however, my searches were more extensive, and the staff was required to go beyond the scope of customary duty. During my visits there first Matthew Schaefer and then Spencer Howard, archivists and apparently drawers of the short straw, answered incessant inquiries, explained the arcane filing systems bequeathed by the Hoover White House, and joined me in hunting down—or attempting to—obscure references, forgotten tomes, and mislaid files. Spencer Howard even pitched in with help in transcription, his lightning-fast typing skills allowing me to capture copy-restricted documents that were essential to the project.

These services continued long-distance after I returned to Los Angeles, Matthew and Spencer fielding queries as the process of writing brought into sharp focus the areas where my facts got fuzzy. As well, archivist Craig Wright, responsible for online and digital access to the Hoover collection, was always prompt and cheerful in providing me with electronic copies of oral histories, memoirs, and other key documents. And when it came time to assemble photographs, archivist Lynn Smith answered every request with a range of samples so I might navigate the library's extensive but loosely catalogued collection. My second trip to West Branch was underwritten by a research grant from the Hoover Presidential Foundation, and for that support I am indebted to them.

Thanks as well to Thomas Schwartz, director of the Hoover library, for taking a personal interest in my work and in making me feel at home in West Branch. It was Schwartz who offered the very helpful suggestion that I delve into the trove of personal pique and press disputes that Hoover filed under "Misinformation."

In Washington, I was fortunate enough to draft as hosts for my two research visits Jim Trainor and Rosalie Ryan. They were generous with their home and with their kitchen, and I enjoyed the open hospitality extended by them, Jim's daughter Cathleen, and her husband, Conn Lehane. Thanks also to Ron Stringer, here in L.A., for the introduction.

My professional thanks go to my agent and longtime collaborator Paul Bresnick; and to Stuart Roberts, assistant editor at Simon & Schuster, for wrangling drafts, images, amendments, and urgent messages with aplomb. John Seeley and Will Soper, both of Los Angeles, helped to proofread the manuscript. And I want to acknowledge the generosity of Lauren Post, of San Francisco, executor of the estate of Rollin Kirby, three-time winner of the Pulitzer Prize for editorial cartooning, whose images illustrate this book. When I contacted Post with my interest in using Kirby's images to evoke the feel of the time, she promptly responded with carte-blanche permission to use her great-grandfather's work—with the results you see here.

My personal thanks go to my family—my mother, Ann Crompton, stepfather, Fuzz Crompton (yes, so he is known), and my brothers, Bill and Tim Rappleye, whose support for me never flags. My horseshoe buddies, Sam, Chip, and Kasper, helped keep my roof up and my lines level; my tennis partners, Will and Antonio, allowed me to win every now and then. I want to mention also my longtime friends Dave Cogan, Sara Catania, and Claude Steiner; each has provided me essential, repeat service as ballast and sounding board. My wife, Tulsa Kinney, has shown me care, attention, and support that could only stem from love, and for which I will be forever grateful.

Lastly, I feel fortunate that the conventions of publishing allow me to make special acknowledgment of my progeny—they are children no longer—Dexter and Kelly Rappleye. I have been gratified, largely in the course of writing this book, to see both of them evolve from promising adolescents to young adults of conscience, character, and purpose. They have made their father proud, and I am happy to dedicate this work to them.

NOTES

Abbreviations Used in the Notes

COHC Columbia Oral History Collection
HHPL Herbert Hoover Presidential Library and Museum, West Branch, Iowa
LHH   Lou Hoover Letters, drawn from Allan Hoover Papers, HHPL, and given
      by date.
LOC   Library of Congress
NYT   *New York Times*
OH   Oral History from HHPL
PRO   Public Record Office, London

EPIGRAPH

xi This tribute was penned by Franklin Roosevelt in honor of Nebraska senator
    George W. Norris. Both were great adversaries of Herbert Hoover's, but the
    encomium might best apply to Hoover himself.

INTRODUCTION

xiv *"I'm not Jesus Christ":* Smith, *Uncommon Man*, p. 309. For the campaign slogan,
     see p. 20.
xvi *"was portrayed as":* Schlesinger, "Hoover Makes a Comeback."

ONE: HE DID NOT CHOOSE

3 *Hoover had graduated:* Wert, *The Fishing President*, pp. 105–9; for the name of
   Hoover's camp, see Rickard, Diary, 6/23/25.
4 *"President Coolidge issued":* The telegram is quoted in Nash, "The 'Great Enigma'
   and the 'Great Engineer.'"
4 *these missives called for Hoover:* Hoover, *Memoirs*, II:190.

4   *"I regret the suggestion":* New York *World*, 8/4/27.

4   *Hoover sent out a telegram:* Rickard, Diary, 8/4/27.

5   *a secret, midnight meeting:* Arnold, "Laying Foundation Stones."

5   *Hoover ordered his personal secretary:* Larry Richey to George Akerson, 8/3/27, George Akerson Papers—Campaign and Transition—Correspondence, HHPL.

5   *"I can understand":* Senator T. Coleman du Pont, quoted in the New York *World*, 8/4/27.

5   *"ardently desired":* Dawes quoted in McCoy, *Coolidge*, p. 385.

6   *Hoover and Akerson composed:* Walter Newton to George Akerson, 8/5/27, 8/15/27; George Akerson Papers—Campaign and Transition—Walter Newton, Correspondence, HHPL.

6   *an inspection of facilities:* Wert, *The Fishing President*, p. 149.

7   *"just as he takes everything":* LHH to Allan Hoover, n.d. (1928).

8   *"constitutional gloomy":* Nash, *The Humanitarian*, pp. 371, 372.

8   *"an unpleasant dourness":* Harold Laski, quoted in Schwarz, *Interregnum of Despair*, p. 50.

11 *"Our conception of the problem":* Hoover, quoted in Cornell University Mann Library web exhibit, "Home Economists in World War I: U.S. Food Administration." www.mannlib.cornell.edu/meatlesswheatless.

11 *"Mr. Hoover was the only":* Keynes, *Economic Consequences of the Peace*, p. 274, n. 1.

11 *"the supreme illustration":* The *Collier's* quote, and the statement from Brandeis, are in Ritchie, *Electing FDR*, p. 21.

11 *"Secretary of Everything":* Ritchie, *Electing FDR*, p. 23.

11 *"Secretary of Commerce":* Villard, "Presidential Possibilities."

12 *"Nothing could be more abhorrent":* Hoover to Brand Whitlock, 1/28/16, quoted in Smith, *Uncommon Man*, p. 30.

13 *"The whole idea":* Hoover to William Glascow, 4/12/19, quoted in Lloyd, *Aggressive Introvert*, p. 81.

13 *"abnormally sensitive":* Pringle, "Hoover: An Enigma Easily Misunderstood."

13 *"Above all":* Hoover to William Glascow, 4/12/19, quoted in Lloyd, *Aggressive Introvert*, p. 81.

13 *"The Presidency is more":* Hoover statement to the Republican convention, 6/14/28, in Wilbur, ed., *New Day*, p. 5.

14 *"I don't believe that I want":* Wehle, *Hidden Threads of History*, p. 83.

14 *"imply entry upon":* Hoover to Ralph Arnold, 3/8/20, quoted in Lloyd, *Aggressive Introvert*, p. 81.

14 *"Hoover was always ambitious":* Eugene Meyer, COHC, p. 381, 271.

14 *"has his eyes firmly fixed":* PRO: Geddes to Curzon, 10/17/22.

15 *"He seems to be":* Castle letter quoted in Nash, "The 'Great Enigma and the 'Great Engineer,'" p. 271.

15   *"the Chief's ideas"*: Rickard, Diary, 12/31/25.

15   *"He also senses"*: Ibid., 12/10/26.

15   *"some job of public service"*: Wilson, *Forgotten Progressive*, p. 20.

15   *"I came to believe"*: Hoover, *Memoirs*, II:v–vi.

16   *"great theories"*: Hoover, *American Individualism*, pp. 1, 6.

16   *"created for the sole purpose"*: Burner, *A Public Life*, p. 141.

16   *"among the few"*: NYT, 12/17/22.

TWO: A POLITICAL DIPTYCH

18   *"He will make no move"*: Rickard, Diary, 8/28/27.

18   *"I know that Chief"*: Ibid., 4/11/28.

19   *Donovan became a cross-agency partner:* For Donovan's role in antitrust policy, and for Hoover's, see Himmelberg, *Origins of the National Recovery Administration*, Chapters 3 and 4; for Donovan and Hoover's collaboration, see pp. 70–71.

19   *The two had personal ties:* For Donovan as a social friend, see Dunlop, *Donovan*, pp. 160–61.

20   *"slick, suave, smooth"*: *Time*, 3/11/29.

20   *"is now honeycombed with politics"*: *Congressional Record*, 70th Cong., 1st Sess., p. 1,822.

21   *"That is correct"*: Lou Hoover quoted in Paul R. Leach OH.

21   *"coat pockets or books"*: Clements, *Imperfect Visionary*, p. 193.

22   *Her task was complicated:* For life at the S Street house, see Hoover, *Memoirs*, II:186–87; see also Wert, *Hoover the Fishing President*, pp. 110–11.

22   *"I should like it"*: LHH to "Dear Herbert and Allan," 4/10/27.

22   *"Affairs are going"*: LHH to "Dear Boys," 1/28/28.

23   *"Politics goes along"*: LHH to "Dear Allan," January/February 1928.

23   *"I have just been having"*: LHH to "Dear Boy of Mine," n.d. (1928).

24   *"well-oiled Hoover machine"*: NYT, 6/7/28.

24   *Southern delegations:* For Theodore Roosevelt, see Lisio, *Lily-Whites*, p. 36; for Coolidge, see Medved, *Shadow Presidents*, p. 177.

25   *"as fresh and unruffled"*: NYT, 6/6/28; for an excellent analysis of Hoover's handling of delegates in the South, see Lisio, *Lily-Whites*, pp. 60–61.

26   *"crisp white collar"*: *Time*, quoted in Brown, *Mabel Walker Willebrandt*, p. 155.

26   *he would not speak a word:* NYT, 7/17/28.

26   *"quiet, dignified, instructive"*: Goldman, *National Party Chairmen*, p. 181.

26   *"Hoover brings character"*: The newspaper excerpts are collected in *NYT*, 6/16/28.

27   *"A precipitant nation-wide deflation"*: Hoover acceptance speech, 8/11/28, presented in Wilbur, ed., *New Day*, pp. 9–44. See also Smith, *Shattered Dream*, pp. 3–5.

THREE: FLASHPOINTS, AND A LANDSLIDE

31 *"It is the entry to life"*: Hoover address, West Branch, Iowa, 8/21/28, in Wilbur, ed., *New Day*, pp. 47–60.

32 *"too much of a machine"*: Mark Requa to Larry Richey, 5/27/29, quoted in Fausold, *Presidency of Herbert C. Hoover*, p. 46.

32 *"a sweet-faced woman"*: Hoover, *Memoirs*, I:4, 5.

33 *"an unusually fine intelligence"*: McClean, *Hulda's World*, p. 67.

33 *"stern but kindly"*: Hoover, *Memoirs*, I:1.

33 *Clothes were homespun*: McLean, *Hulda's World*, p. 73.

33 *"strong training in patience"*: Hoover, *Memoirs*, I:7.

33 *begun singing hymns*: McLean, *Hulda's World*, p. 67.

33 *the "fast" branch of the Friends*: The term "fast" Friends is from Burner, *Herbert Hoover*, p. 10; for more on the schism, see p. 79.

33 *Bert landed with an uncle*: Ibid., p. 354, n. 20; see also Hoover, *Memoirs*, I:4, 5; and Wert, *The Fishing President*, p. 13.

34 *"I have so much to do"*: Hulda Hoover to Agnes Hoover, 10/24/83. The letter is reproduced in McClean, *Hulda's World*, p. 128.

34 *his teachers decided*: Cahill, "Herbert Hoover's Early Schooling."

34 *"I have often tried"*: Hulda Hoover to Agnes Hoover, 10/24/83, in McClean, *Hulda's World*, p. 129.

34 *"I never had better"*: Hulda Hoover to Laban and Aggie Miles, 11/16/83, in ibid, p. 130.

34 *cried himself to sleep*: Lane, *Making of Herbert Hoover*, p. 61.

35 *"as suddenly as he came"*: NYT, 9/22/28.

35 *"one of the most enjoyable"*: Stokes recapped the 1928 campaign in his memoir, *Chip Off My Shoulder*. For the quotes see pp. 243–45.

36 *"There are probably few"*: Pringle, "Hoover: An Enigma Easily Misunderstood."

37 *"Mad Mabel"*: Los Angeles Times, 9/3/28.

37 *an effort to impress Herbert Hoover*: Peretti, *Nightclub City*, p. 86.

37 *"using her office"*: NYT, 7/8/28.

37 *"the center . . . of lawlessness"*: Brown, *Willebrandt*, p. 160; for the quote see *NYT*, 9/8/28.

38 *"no one in authority"*: Brown, *Willebrandt*, p. 166.

38 *"Snarling foes will not"*: For the verse and press conferences, see Lichtman, *Prejudice and the Old Politics*, p. 91.

38 *Colonel Mann operated largely undercover*: For Hoover's Louisiana office, see *NYT*, 8/29/28; for the reaction in Washington, see *NYT*, 8/30/28; for the RNC acknowledgment, see New York World, 9/9/28; for "political viceroy," see, *NYT*, 10/8/28; for more notes on Mann, see Lisio, *Lily-Whites*, pp. 82–92.

39 *Several black advisors:* For black knowledge and endorsement of the Mann policies, see Lisio, *Lily-Whites*, p. 84.

39 *It was a nasty campaign:* Lisio describes the Southern campaign of 1928 in ibid., pp. 85–86.

40 *Slemp had been exposed:* For notes on Slemp and Hoover, see ibid., p. 79; for Slemp's staff position at the RNC, see *NYT*, 7/21/29.

40 *"the mother of ignorance":* Bishop Cannon is quoted in Okrent, *Last Call*, p. 306.

40 *he traveled to Florida:* Dougherty Jr., "Florida and the Presidential Election of 1928."

41 *"progressive economic system":* Hoover campaign speech delivered at Newark, New Jersey, 9/17/28, in Wilbur, ed., *New Day*, p. 78.

42 *"The whole country was":* *NYT*, 3/2/30, quoted in Kennedy, *Freedom from Fear*, p. 43.

42 *"no dangers lie":* Hoover speech at Newark, 9/17/28, in Wilbur, ed., *New Day*, p. 81.

42 *"Today a large amount":* *NYT*, 9/22/28.

FOUR: "HOOVER THE SILENT"

43 *"I should keep entirely":* Hoover to Elihu Root, 11/16/28, quoted in Liebovich, *Bylines in Despair*, p. 83.

44 *"Immediately [when] I picked up":* Hoover to William Allen White, 1/25/38, White Papers, Hoover Institution, Stanford. The fact of Hoover's second meeting with Coolidge, and that it was taken at Hoover's request, was reported in *NYT*, 1/10/29, but the story said then that "not one word of the subject or subjects discussed was forthcoming from the president or the president-elect."

44 *"You could talk":* Ahamed, *Lords of Finance*, p. 310.

44 *"I went to Mr. Coolidge":* Hoover to William Allen White, 1/25/38, White Papers, Hoover Institution.

45 *took Coolidge out of his comfort zone:* For Coolidge's reticence on fiscal matters, see McCoy, *Calvin Coolidge*, pp. 155–56, 318–19.

45 *"He could not believe":* Hoover to William Allen White, 1/25/38, White Papers, Hoover Institution.

45 *"permission"* from Coolidge: Ibid.

45 *"I conferred several times":* Hoover, *Memoirs*, III:16.

45 *Miller tended to alienate:* In brief comments for an oral history, Fed governor Roy Young said Miller was "prone to lecture the board as though he were a professor dealing with his students." See the interview, dated 3/1/54, at Fraser/St. Louis Fed.org.

46 *"Control by rate action":* Miller, "Responsibility for Federal Reserve Policies."

46 *"Checking stock speculation"*: *Wall Street Journal*, quoted in Klingaman, *1929*, p. 117.

46 *Some critics attribute:* For a skeptical assessment of the Fed governors, see Friedman and Schwartz, *Great Contraction*, passim, and especially Chapter 7, "Why Was Monetary Policy So Inept?"

46 *others reject the idea:* One prominent critic of Friedman and Schwartz is Kindleberger, *World in Depression*, pp. 19–20, 136–38, 300. For a concise survey of the debates over the factors leading to the Depression, see, among many others, Temin, "The Great Depression."

47 *"Governor Young contended"*: Hoover, *Memoirs*, III:18.

47 *the record shows:* Fed governor Charles Hamlin records on two separate occasions that Roy Young told him of Hoover congratulating him on the policy of direct pressure, and that on both occasions Young pointed out to Hoover that he did not support the policy. Hamlin Diary, 6/8/29, 8/12/29, LOC.

47 *"Are you as worried"*: Wueschner, *Charting Twentieth Century Monetary Policy*, p. 91.

48 *"the greatest calamities"*: Lenroot to D. R. Crissinger, 11/23/25, quoted in ibid., p. 92.

48 *"had egged on"*: ibid., p. 98, quoting the diary of Charles S. Hamlin, p. 98.

48 *Hoover approached him personally:* Ibid., p. 94.

48 *"Over-optimism can only"*: "Economic Prospects for 1926," Secretary of Commerce press release, 12/31/25, quoted in Ibid., p. 101.

49 *"What Europe needed"*: Hoover, *Memoirs*, III:10.

49 *"The safety of continued prosperity"*: Ibid., p. 11.

49 *"Hoover the Silent"*: *New York Evening Post*, 1/9/29, Clippings File, HHPL.

49 *"the best listener"*: *NYT*, 1/10/29.

50 *"Hoover is very surprised"*: Rickard, Diary, 2/19/29.

50 *"He found himself"*: Lyons, *Herbert Hoover Story*, p. 12; for "fanatic," see p. 30.

50 *"a boy from"*: Hoover acceptance speech, 6/14/28, in Wilbur, ed., *New Day*, p. 9.

51 *"He was one of the most affable"*: Clarence Dill OH.

51 *Thomas Stokes noticed:* See Stokes, *Chip Off My Shoulder*, Chapter 6.

52 *"obviously in need"*: *NYT*, 1/22/29.

52 *"chief undercover Hooverizer"*: *Time*, 2/18/29.

52 *"the busiest man in Florida"*: *NYT*, 1/26/29.

53 *"in charge of all patronage"*: Akerson telegram to Larry Richey, 1/26/29, in Akerson Papers, HH Papers—Campaign and Transition—Correspondence—Fort, Franklin, HHPL.

53 *"retired voluntarily"*: *NYT*, 3/11/29; for notes on Hoover's move against Mann, see Lisio, *Lily-Whites*, pp. 116–17.

53 *"Hoover sun-worshippers"*: Franklin Fort to Hoover, n.d., in HH Papers—Campaign and Transition—Fort, Franklin, Box 23, HHPL.

53 *"Hoover we saw only":* Stokes, *Chip Off My Shoulder*, p. 252.

54 *"atmosphere almost of intimidation":* *Editor & Publisher*, 1/12/29.

54 *"There seems to be some":* Franklin Fort to Hoover, 2/1/29, in HH Papers—Campaign and Transition—Correspondence—Fort, Franklin, HHPL, cited in Lisio, *Lily-Whites*, p. 115, n. 2.

54 *"Observers of Mr. Hoover":* *Editor & Publisher*, 2/16/29.

55 *"somewhat dourly":* For the meeting with Strong, and the quotes, see Paul Leach OH, cited in Liebovich, *Bylines in Despair*, p. 87, n. 16.

55 *"very concerned over the attitude":* Rickard, Diary, 3/3/29.

55 *"a mystery":* NYT, 2/20/29.

56 *"didn't want to come":* Brown, *Last Hero*, pp. 112–13.

56 *"It is impossible":* The meetings with Hoover, Sullivan, and Stone are given in ibid, Mason, *Harlan Fiske Stone*, pp. 112–14; and based on diaries kept by Donovan and by Donovan's friend T. J. McFadden, who sat in on the meeting with Stone.

57 *"vast capacity for intrigue":* Hoover memorandum, "Reasons Donovan was not taken into the Cabinet," HH Papers—Campaign and Transition—Subject File—Cabinet Appointments—Donovan, William, HHPL.

57 *"Daddy said he simply":* LHH to Allan Hoover, 9/1/32, HHPL.

57 *"and you will need":* Mason, *Harlan Fiske Stone*, p. 116.

57 *"I have no dread":* Abbot cited in Burner, *Herbert Hoover*, p. 211.

FIVE: BRIGHT WITH HOPE

59 *"An inauguration as simple":* NYT, 11/8/28.

60 *"Time to go":* For details on inauguration day, see Warren, *Herbert Hoover and the Great Depression*, pp. 51–52; for the Stone visit, see Mason, *Harlan Fiske Stone*, p. 269. See also *Time*, 3/11/29.

60 *Neither Coolidge nor Hoover:* NYT, 3/5/29.

60 *"I would have given":* Hiram Johnson to "Boys," 3/5/29, in Burke, ed. *Diary Letters of Hiram Johnson*.

60 *Lou Hoover and Grace Coolidge:* For Grace Coolidge at the inauguration, see Ross, *Grace Coolidge and Her Era*, pp. 255–56. See also *Time*, 3/11/29.

61 *"a new civilization":* Hoover inaugural speech, 3/3/29.

63 *"The Hoovers came in":* Irwin "Ike" Hoover, *42 Years in the White House*, p. 181.

63 *"as bleak as":* Hoover, *Memoirs*, II:320.

63 *he ordered the tiles painted red:* The journalist James Thomas Williams remarks on Hoover and the roof at Commerce in his interview for the COHC.

64 *"inadequate to his methods":* Rickard, Diary, 1/6/29.

64 *"the big boss":* Roberta Barrows OH, Truman Library.

64 *"We were all scared":* Ruth Durno OH.

64   *"Mr. Richey could be"*: Alonzo Fields OH.

65   *"The new Chief Executive"*: NYT, 3/9/29.

65   *"You have to stand"*: Coolidge quoted by Hoover, in his *Memoirs*, II:55.

65   *"It was a taxing procedure"*: Boone, Memoirs, 111, LOC.

66   *In conformance with tradition:* Bess Furman outlines the White House routine in her *Washington By-line*, p. 46.

66   *"regular form of"*: Boone, OH, 163.

66   *"Mr. Hoover is a man"*: Mason, *Harlan Fiske Stone*, p. 270.

67   *"The President has"*: Hard, "Hoover the President."

67   *"Mrs. Hoover held"*: Ike Hoover quoted in Young, *Lou Henry Hoover*, p. 54.

67   *"They never sat down"*: Lillian Parks OH.

68   *"He ate faster"*: Bascom Timmons OH.

68   *"He did not masticate"*: Boone, Memoirs, p. 217.

69   *"He is a fast"*: Tucker, *Mirrors of 1932*, p. 21.

69   *"Hoover dreaded eating alone"*: Ibid.

69   *"He always wants to have"*: Lyons, *Herbert Hoover Story*, p. 36.

69   *"She protected the president"*: Alonzo Fields OH.

69   *"the instrument by which"*: Quote is from Hoover acceptance speech, 8/11/28, in Wilbur, ed., *New Day*, p. 9.

70   *"The Cabinet is obviously"*: NYT, 3/10/29.

70   *"playing the game"*: NYT, 3/9/29.

71   *Mellon was expected to retire:* For expectations of Mellon, see Cannadine, *Mellon*, p. 380; for reactions in Congress, see *NYT*, 3/6/29.

71   *"a more intimate relationship"*: Hoover press conference, 3/5/29.

72   *"courageous and noble stand"*: Editorial, *Editor & Publisher*, 3/9/29, p. 44.

72   *Remarks at press conferences:* Charles Michelson discusses the press conference rules, and the impact they had, in *The Ghost Talks*, p. 18.

72   *"They have no respect"*: Joslin, Diary, 8/8/32.

73   *"a social war"*: NYT, 4/4/29. See also Longworth, *Crowded Hours*, pp. 330–32; Cordery, *Alice*, pp. 342–45.

73   *"made fashionable Washington gasp"*: Furman, *Washington By-line*, p. 61.

SIX: THE WALL STREET FRANKENSTEIN

75   *Two days after his inauguration:* Myers and Newton, eds., *Hoover Administration*, p. 14.

75   *"heavy liquidations"*: NYT, 2/15/29.

75   *"outrageous interference"*: NYT, 2/18/29.

75   *"violent buying"*: NYT, 3/2/29. This story is one of several that refer to the Hoover Bull Market.

75   *"orgies of speculation"*: NYT, 3/7/29.

76   *"He thinks something"*: Cannadine, *Mellon*, p. 388.

77 *"we should use"*: Hoover, *Memoirs*, III:31.

77 *"a formidable opposition"*: Miller, "Responsibility for Federal Reserve Policies," p. 456.

79 *"to have the market fall"*: Ahamed, *Lords of Finance*, p. 321.

79 *"at odds with one another"*: Ibid., p. 322.

79 *"a Wall Street Frankenstein"*: *NYT*, 3/4/29.

79 *"the most notorious"*: Heflin quoted in Klingaman, *1929*, p. 117.

79 *"Neither the Federal Reserve"*: Plaza Trust Co. president Michael Cahill, quoted in *NYT*, 2/8/29.

80 *"There is a feeling"*: Hiram Johnson to sons, in Burke, ed., *Diary Letters of Hiram Johnson*, 4/13/29.

80 *The Fed chairman grudgingly agreed:* The meeting between Young is recounted in Hamlin, Diary, 8/12/29. Hamlin at that date recorded his conversation with Young, who describes his meeting with Hoover in detail, and recalls the date to be March 18.

81 *"I thought he was all right"*: Eugene Meyer, COHC.

81 *"crazy and dangerous"*: Ibid. See also Pusey, *Eugene Meyer*, p. 201. White House logs show that Meyer and his wife, Agnes, were dinner guests at the White House March 8.

82 *"The present situation"*: *NYT*, 3/15/29.

82 *"frequently unsound"*: Andrew Mellon diary entry, 10/5/28, quoted in Cannadine, *Mellon*, p. 362.

82 *"The fever was"*: Hoover, *Memoirs*, III:16.

82 *"had not exhibited"*: *NYT*, 3/22/29.

83 *the worst declines ever:* Klingaman, *1929*, p. 153. See also Galbraith, *Great Crash*, pp. 35–40.

83 *"a stranglehold on the stock market"*: Hoover, *Memoirs*, III:18.

83 *the week-long crash "evaporated"*: *NYT*, 3/28/29.

84 *"vigorously slaps the board"*: *NYT*, 2/29/29; Hoover quotes Glass, citing the same source, in his *Memoirs*, III:18.

84 *"absurdly low"*: Governor George Norris, Philadelphia Federal Reserve Bank, to Charles Hamlin, 4/25/29, quoted in Chandler, *American Monetary Policy*, p. 66.

84 *"While I have been informed"*: George Harrison to Owen Young, 4/10/29, quoted in ibid., p. 64.

85 *Speaking confidentially with governors:* Charles Hamlin, Diary, 7/31/29, 8/12/29.

85 *"to talk in my name"*: Hoover, *Memoirs* III:17.

85 *"no desire to stretch"*: Ibid.

86 *"fully alive"*: Hoover, *Memoirs* III:16.

86 *"Stock prices have reached"*: The quotes from Irving Fisher and Bernard Baruch are both presented in Galbraith, *Great Crash*, p. 70.

86 *"Hoover thinks we should"*: Rickard, Diary, 4/14/29.

SEVEN: THE SPECIAL SESSION

87 *"to lay the foundations":* Hoover to Congress, 4/16/29.

88 *Borah notified Hoover privately:* For Hoover's meeting with Borah and the genesis of the special session, see Johnson, *Borah of Idaho*, p. 429; see also *NYT*, 10/29/28.

89 *farm foreclosures ran at:* Figures from Irwin, *Peddling Protectionism*, p. 18.

90 *Hoover floated his idea:* For an excellent review of Hoover's thinking on agriculture, see Shideler, "Hoover and the Federal Farm Board Project." For Sapiro's criticism of Hoover, see Koerselman, "Leadership Problems."

91 *"creation of a great instrumentality":* Hoover to Congress, 4/16/29.

91 *Calvin Coolidge made a point:* For Coolidge's approach to Congress, see McCoy, *Calvin Coolidge*, pp. 193–200.

91 *"does not intend to write":* NYT, 3/21/29.

92 *"McKinley was a great":* NYT, 3/26/29.

92 *"The president is so":* Senator Peter Norbeck, quoted in Schwarz, *Interregnum of Despair*, p. 6.

92 *"First Big Victory":* NYT, 6/15/29.

93 *"When Borah speaks":* Ashby, *Spearless Leader*, p. 227.

93 *"They comment sarcastically":* Outlook and Independent, 6/26/29.

94 *"The country was happy":* Michelson, *The Ghost Talks*, p. 17. For more notes on Michelson, see Schlesinger, *Crisis of the Old Order*, p. 274.

95 *"more than any other":* Kent, "Charles Michelson."

95 *"the smear departments":* Hoover, *Memoirs*, III:219.

95 *"Daddy gets overworked":* LHH to Allan Hoover, 4/18/29.

96 *fell to Lou:* Lou Hoover's involvement at the Rapidan is described in Lambert, *Herbert Hoover's Hideaway*; for the quotes, see pp. 48–49.

96 *"Mrs. Hoover was":* Frederic Butler, Miller Center OH.

97 *"If I were not married":* LHH to Allan Hoover, 4/29/29.

97 *"We are beginning to feel":* LHH to Allan Hoover, 5/25/29.

97 *"He was working harder":* Joel Boone, Memoirs, p. 186-k.

98 *"Everything is going":* LHH to Allan Hoover, 5/30/29, underscore in original.

98 *"I am distressed":* LHH to Allan Hoover, 6/11/29.

98 *"condemned to stay here":* NYT, 6/23/29.

EIGHT: THE CRASH

99 *"No causal relationship":* Sobel, *Great Bull Market*, p. 147, cited in Kennedy, *Freedom from Fear*, p. 39.

99 *Various theories ascribe:* A most useful survey of the field is available in Kindleberger, *World in Depression*, pp. 19–30.

101 *a weather analogy:* Bruner and Carr, in their book on *Panic of 1907*, use the sub-
     title *Lessons Learned from the Market's Perfect Storm.* They develop the point in a
     chapter titled "Lessons," pp. 151–63.

102 *"Obviously":* Hoover, *Memoirs*, III:19.

102 *"The fundamental business":* Press conference, 10/25/29.

102 *The bankers . . . pressured Hoover:* Galbraith, *Great Crash*, p. 106, n. 7; see also
     Klingaman, *1929*, p. 272.

102 *"The market situation":* NYT, 10/27/29.

103 *"gone down materially":* NYT, 10/30/29.

103 *"The stock crisis":* Senator Millard Tydings, quoted in *NYT*, 10/30/29.

104 *"Mellon seemed depressed":* Hamlin, Diary Digest. Hamlin's "Digest," a typescript
     summarizing in detail his handwritten diary, is divided by subject. 1929:180.

104 *"Liquidate labor":* Hoover, *Memoirs*, III:30.

104 *"What our people wish":* Hoover address, President's Conference on Unemploy-
     ment, 1921, quoted in Gaddis, *Herbert Hoover*, p. 1.

105 *It was Mills who helped the president:* For Mills's authorship of the Hoover state-
     ment, see Hamlin, Diary, 11/1/29.

106 *"I was possessed":* Time, 7/13/31.

106 *"useful citizen":* Hoover quoted in Rickard, Diary, 12/28/26.

107 *"The ultimate result":* NYT, 11/6/29.

107 *"The great task":* The Nation, 11/27/29, quoted in Romasco, *Poverty of Abundance*,
     p. 26.

108 *"Some reassuring utterance":* William Randolph Hearst, "Open Letter to Presi-
     dent Hoover," 11/14/29.

108 *"persuaded some men":* Morris, *Theodore Rex*, p. 498. See also Bruner and Carr,
     Panic of 1907, p. 109.

108 *"No matter what":* Hoover, *Memoirs*, III:29.

108 *"If any difficult":* Hughes quoted in Lloyd, *Aggressive Introvert*, p. 162.

109 *"viewed the crisis":* There is no transcript of the meeting; the quotes are from
     notes made by Hoover political advisor Walter Newton, reprinted in Hoover,
     Memoirs, III:43.

110 *"doctrine of high wages":* See, in particular, the excellent survey of Hoover's eco-
     nomic thinking in Barber, *From New Era to New Deal*, passim. For notes on high
     wage policy, see pp. 2–30, 65–66.

110 *"We are a long way":* Hoover address, 5/12/26, in Hoover, *Memoirs*, II:108; cited
     in ibid., p. 30.

110 *"The purpose of the tariff":* Hoover campaign speech, 10/6/28, in Wilbur, ed., *New
     Day*, p. 102.

111 *"a serious withdrawal":* NYT, 11/22/29.

111 *"The President of the":* NYT, 11/23/29.

112 *a new bull market:* NYT, 11/22/29.

112 *"The collapse of the"*: Guaranty Survey, quoted in *NYT*, 11/25/29.

112 *"undue pessimism"*: Hoover address to Business Leaders, 12/5/29.

113 *"The great machine"*: *NYT*, 12/6/29.

114 *"A more significant"*: Wesley C. Mitchell, quoted in Barber, *From New Era to New Deal*, p. 87.

114 *"Now, for the first time"*: Foster and Catchings quoted in ibid.

114 *"the fundamental business"*: Hoover press conference, 10/25/29.

114 *"I'm sorry, but"*: Hoover press conference, 10/29/29.

114 *"not from the point"*: Hoover press conference, 11/5/29.

115 *"These are potential difficulties"*. Hoover address to Business Leaders, 12/5/29.

115 *"hysteria"*: Klein quoted in *NYT*, 11/25/29.

115 *"any lack of confidence"*: *NYT*, 11/16/29.

115 *"The president has"*: William Allen White to David Hinshaw, 12/3/29.

116 *"This is not a showman's job"*: Hoover quoted in Joslin, *Hoover Off the Record*, p. 3.

116 *"I got the impression"*: James Thomas Williams COHC.

116 *only a small fraction of the American public:* John Galbraith, among others, addresses this point in *Great Crash*, p. 78. For a Hoover administration comment on the limits of stock holdings, see *NYT*, 10/25/29.

116 *job losses and layoffs:* In late November Labor Secretary Jim Davis reported one million unemployed. See Fausold, *Presidency of Herbert C. Hoover*, p. 77.

NINE: THE PRESIDENT'S HAIR SHIRTS

119 *"This unsatisfactory price level"*: *NYT*, 10/27/29.

119 *"An economic revolution"*: *Philadelphia Record*, quoted in *Literary Digest*, 1/4/30.

119 *"It means that the government"*: *NYT*, 10/28/29.

120 *"He has a rare combination"*: *NYT*, 12/4/33.

120 *"to build up farmer-owned"*: Hoover, "Memorandum on Possible Procedures," 7/13/29, quoted in Lambert, "Hoover and Federal Farm Board Wheat."

120 *"No man presumes"*: *NYT*, 7/13/29.

120 *"I have read"*: Legge quoted in Fausold, "President Hoover's Farm Policies," p. 369.

121 *United Growers named: NYT*, 8/12/29.

121 *"The board is attempting"*: Farm Board Press Service, 8/15/29, in Joseph Stancliffe Davis Papers, Box 1, Hoover Institution.

122 *"I have done more of it"*: Hoover remarks to the Business Man's Conference on Agriculture, 4/15/27, quoted in Wilson, "Hoover's Agricultural Policies."

122 *"I confess I do not"*: Hoover to J. R. Howard, editor of *Homelands Farm*, 7/6/26, quoted in ibid.

123 *"We now determined"*: Hoover, *Memoirs*, III:50.

123 *"not at all pleased"*: Rickard, Diary, 4/3/30.

123 *"The middleman, like Othello"*: St. Louis Post-Dispatch, quoted in *Literary Digest*, 1/4/30.

124 *"the grain trade"*: NYT, 12/5/29.

124 *"discriminatory competition"*: The exchange between Barnes and Legge is reproduced in the *United States Daily*, n.d., HH Papers—Presidential Subject File—Farm Matters Federal Farm Board—Correspondence—1930, May, HHPL.

124 *"As Mr. Hoover had appointed"*: NYT, 12/11/29.

124 *he confessed to being "upset"*: Rickard, Diary, 4/3/30.

125 *"His actions are"*: Ibid., 10/2/29.

125 *"Barnes has some"*: Ibid., 11/30/29.

125 *"We are now putting"*: NYT, 11/24/29.

125 *"About the Barnes committee"*: Lewis Strauss telegram to Larry Richey, 12/13/29, in Lewis Strauss Papers—Early Career Name and Subject Files—Richey, Lawrence, Correspondence, HHPL.

126 *a "most signal victory"*: Senator Furnifold Simmons (D-NC), quoted in *NYT*, 9/8/29.

126 *"one of the worst"*: Ted Clark to Coolidge, 8/19/29, Clark Papers, LOC.

126 *"What sort of chief"*: NYT, 9/14/29.

127 *"We have a complete"*: Johnson, *Borah of Idaho*, p. 439.

127 *Borah allowed the Democrats*: NYT, 9/1/29.

127 *"It goes without saying"*: NYT, 9/2/29.

128 *"the flexible tariff was"*: Hoover, *Memoirs*, II:294.

128 *"gave no indication"*: Hoover notes on Borah, 6/4/33, HH Papers—Post-Presidential Individual Correspondence File—Borah, William, HHPL.

128 *"I haven't thought"*: Hoover press conference, 9/24/29.

128 *"The flexible tariff"*: Ibid.

128 *"It is not my idea"*: Borah's speech is quoted at length in *NYT*, 9/27/29.

130 *stopping by the White House*: Huston's frequent visits are reported in *NYT*, 7/28/29.

130 *"This new figure"*: NYT, 8/2/29.

130 *"This choice of"*: For this and the following quote, see "Psychoanalyzing the New G.O.P. Chief," *Literary Digest*, 9/21/29, p. 13.

130 *"Republican South Expected"*: NYT, 9/9/29.

131 *"warring elements"*: NYT, 9/11/29.

131 *meeting with Huston daily*: In a 10/31/29 letter to Calvin Coolidge, former White House secretary Edward Clark observed that Huston was meeting with the president on a daily basis (Clark Papers, LOC). Three months later, the *Outlook and Independent* reported of Hoover and Huston, "The two confer nearly every afternoon" (2/12/30, p. 262).

131 *The fete turned to ambush*: NYT, 10/24/29.

132 *"sought more freely"*: Ibid.

132 *"Selection of Mr. Kahn"*: NYT, 10/26/29.

132 *"slander," "vague insinuations"*: These epithets and more are catalogued by Nash in *The Engineer*, p. 657 n. 88.

133 *John Hamill approached Hoover's financial advisor:* The following passage is based on several documents on file with the HHPL. They include: FBI field reports, dated 12/19/29 and 12/20/29, with a cover memos from J. Edgar Hoover, filed under Misrepresentations; a lengthy deposition made by John Hamill in August 1930, located in the same file; a White House transcript titled "Conversation with Rickard," in the Edgar Rickard papers; several other documents from the Rickard file, including a memo from Richey to Rickard dated 10/25/28, with attached statements by an attorney and a postal inspector named John Rapelye providing background on O'Brien; a "Memorandum of Isidor J. Kresel," dated 12/24/29; and several communications between Larry Richey and Lewis Strauss, filed in the Strauss papers under Correspondence.

134 *Richey and Strauss had long been friendly:* To track relations between the two Hoover advisors see their many letters in Strauss Papers—Correspondence—HHPL.

135 *"Many years ago"*: Hoover address to the Gridiron Club, 12/14/29.

TEN: "THE PECULIAR WEAKNESS OF MR. HOOVER"

139 *"it was assumed"*: According to the anonymous column "Back Stage in Washington," published in the *Outlook and Independent*, 2/19/30, "there was an almost unanimous belief that Associate Justice Harlan Stone of New York would be made Chief Justice, and that a liberal . . . would be picked to replace Stone."

139 *"Never was there"*: The *NYT* quote, and that from Cardozo, are found in Pusey, *Charles Evans Hughes*, II:654.

140 *"the biggest surprise"*: Baltimore *Sun*, cited in ibid., p. 277.

140 *Hoover made the appointment by mistake:* For this intriguing theory, see Mason, *Harlan Fiske Stone*, pp. 274–80; see also Pringle, "Profile: Chief Justice."

140 *"The president's friends"*: "Back Stage in Washington," *Outlook and Independent*, 2/19/30.

140 *"There is no objection"*: NYT, 2/4/30.

140 *"We have reached a time"*: Norris quoted in Simon, *FDR and Chief Justice Hughes*, p. 180.

141 *"Not in a century"*: NYT, 2/12/30.

141 *as secretary of state:* Hoover reprises Hughes's government service in his *Memoirs*, II:36–37.

142 *"purely political"*: Paul Y. Anderson in *The Nation*, 4/9/30.

143 *"in a condition approximating"*: William Green to Lee Overman, quoted in *NYT*, 4/6/30.

143 *"Judge Parker placed"*: *NYT*, 3/29/30.

143 *"The negro as a class"*: Greensboro, North Carolina, *Daily News*, 4/19/20, read into the record by Walter White. The passage has been widely quoted; my citation is from McCarter, "Confirmation Denied," p. 18.

144 *"Plainly this attitude"*: White, *A Man Called White*, p. 105.

144 *"Parker is seriously"*: *NYT*, 4/12/30.

144 *James Watson . . . made an evening visit:* Ibid.

146 *"The trouble about it is"*: Thomas Walsh statement in Senate Hearings, *Lobby Investigations*, 71st Cong., 2nd Sess., p. 3307.

147 *"We cannot refrain"*: W. E. B. Du Bois, in *The Crisis*, May 1930, p. 62.

147 *"was handicapped"*: Strother quoted in Campbell Hodges, Diary, 5/9/30, cited in Lisio, *Lily-Whites*, p. 225.

149 *"vicious, extortionate, and obnoxious"*: Hoover, quoted in Sobel, Robert, *The Age of Giant Corporations*, p. 87.

149 *"Who is responsible"*: *Congressional Record*, 71st Cong., 2nd Sess., p. 4,594.

149 *"The Republican majority"*: Ibid., 2nd Sess., p. 5,667.

150 *"There was no necessity"*: Michelson, *The Ghost Talks*, p. 32.

150 *Hoover and Lippmann:* James Srodes, in his *On Dupont Circle*, tells the story of Hoover, Roosevelt, Lippmann, and their early days in Washington. See especially pp. 117–19.

150 *This landmark essay:* Lippmann, "The Peculiar Weakness of Mr. Hoover."

152 *"All the press needs"*: Verne Marshall to Hoover, 5/4/30, quoted in Liebovich, *Bylines in Despair*, p. 115.

152 *"I don't believe"*: Henry L. Stoddard to Mark Sullivan, 6/23/30, in ibid., p. 116.

152 *"If I would be helpful"*: Alfred Kirchhofer to Hoover, 7/15/30, in President's Personal File—Newspapers—*Buffalo Evening News*, HHPL.

154 *This prompted a secret meeting:* The story of Howell's espionage is derived from a journal he kept at the time. This remarkable document was unearthed from the National Archives in 1983 by Jeffrey Dorwart, professor of history at Princeton, and used in his *Conflict of Duty*. The relevant journal entries were published verbatim by Barton Bernstein in 1992 under the title "Hoovergate" in *American Heritage* magazine.

155 *"My Navy friends"*: Lewis Strauss to Larry Richey, 6/9/30, in Strauss papers, Correspondence, HHPL.

155 *"Probably some Secret Service"*: *NYT*, 5/6/30.

156 *"I am beastly angry"*: Hiram Johnson to sons, 5/9/30, in Burke, *Letters of Johnson*.

156 *"There was nothing"*: Hiram Johnson to sons, 5/17/30, in Ibid.

158 *the first face Hoover saw:* MacLafferty, Diary, 3/4/29.

158 *"the many perplexities"*: Ibid., 5/28/30.

159 *"the most serious thing":* Ibid., 6/20/30.

160 *"a serious embarrassment":* Hoover press conference, 6/24/30.

160 *"This trait in his":* This quote and those following are taken from the MacLafferty Diary, entries ranging from 5/28 to 7/9/30.

ELEVEN: CHALLENGING FACTS

166 *"business had returned":* NYT, 1/24/30.

166 *"serious danger":* NYT, 3/2/30.

166 *"swamped with appeals":* NYT, 3/19/30.

166 *In Boston:* The story of the woodcutters is from *Congressional Record*, 71st Cong., 2nd Sess., p. 4,597.

167 *a breadline stretching:* NYT, 3/19/30.

167 *the Bureau of Labor Statistics:* For notes on the development of the Bureau of Labor Statistics, see Goldberg and Moye, *First Hundred Years*, p. 128. The "downward bias" was pointed out in 1927 by statisticians from the Federal Reserve. For notes on the U.S. Employment Service, see Duncan and Shelton, *Revolution in United States Government Statistics*, pp. 23–24.

167 *"The tide of employment":* Hoover press conference, 1/21/30.

168 *"the truth":* NYT, 1/23/30.

168 *"a great debt":* NYT, 3/21/30.

168 *"Unfortunately there is developing":* NYT, 1/24/30.

168 *"unnecessary fears":* Hoover address to the American Bankers Association, 10/2/30, quoted in Barber, *From New Era to New Deal*, p. 84.

168 *"huge publicity stunt":* NYT, 1/24/30.

169 *"acute and menacing":* NYT, 3/10/30.

169 *"one of the largest factors":* Hoover telegram to state governors, 11/23/29.

169 *"We cannot fail":* Hoover, State of the Union address, 12/3/29.

169 *"Balanced budgets":* NYT, 2/5/30.

170 *"The whole thing is bunk":* Carter Glass and Pat Harrison are quoted in NYT, 2/25/30.

170 *"a cheap exhibition":* NYT, 2/26/30.

170 *"the different sections":* Hoover press conference, 2/25/30.

171 *"sober consideration":* Congressional Record, 71st Cong., 2nd Sess., p. 4,594.

171 *employment was falling off sharply:* NYT, 3/6/28.

172 *"appreciated the difficulty":* Congressional Record, 71st Cong., 2nd Sess., p. 4,597.

172 *"The low point of business":* Hoover press conference, 3/7/30.

173 *"one of those great economic storms":* Hoover to the Chamber of Commerce, 5/1/30.

173 *"Gentlemen, you have come":* Hoover, quoted in Schesinger, *Crisis of the Old Order*, p. 231.

173 *"an actual increase"*: Chandler, *American Monetary Policy*, p. 97.

173 *Several key industries:* Barber, *From New Era to New Deal*, p. 93.

174 *Federal spending amounted to:* Stein, *Fiscal Revolution in America*, p. 14.

174 *These small gains:* Barber, *From New Era to New Deal*, p. 94.

174 *commodity prices had dropped: Outlook and Independent*, 8/6/30, p. 545.

174 *He dismissed his critics:* For insight into Hoover's state of mind, see MacLafferty, Diary, entries for June 1930.

174 *"speedy recovery": NYT*, 2/14/30.

174 *"the situation is greatly improved": NYT*, 3/5/30.

175 *"A man would have to be": NYT*, 2/5/30.

175 *"Charles Persons":* For the Persons episode, see Goldberg and Moye, *First Hundred Years*, p. 130; see also Persons, "Census Reports on Unemployment," p. 12.

175 *"Everyone here, including":* Clark to Coolidge, 7/1/30, Clark Papers, LOC.

176 *"The only justification":* Clark to Coolidge, 8/2/30, Clark Papers, LOC.

176 *"Somewhere, somehow":* Clark to Coolidge, 7/1/30, Clark Papers, LOC.

TWELVE: FRICTION AT THE FED

177 *"a constant stream of unemployment":* Hoover to Roy Young, Governor, Federal Reserve Board, 3/24/30, in HH Papers—Presidential Subject File—Federal Reserve—Correspondence, 1930, HHPL. This important letter is cited in Barber, *From New Era to New Deal*, p. 96, n. 12.

178 *Studies conducted much later:* See the chart produced in 1971 by Lester Chandler for his *American Monetary Policy*, p. 100. (Chandler cited figures from a 1958 government statistical survey.) See also Clark Warburton, *Depression, Inflation, and Monetary Policy*, pp. 115–16.

179 *"promising field":* E. A. Goldenweiser to Roy Young, 4/11/30, HH Papers—Presidential Subject File—Federal Reserve Board—Correspondence, 1930, HHPL.

180 *"We feel that we should":* Governor George Norris report quoted in minutes of the Open Market Investment Committee of the Federal Reserve, 1/29/30, cited in Chandler, *American Monetary Policy*, p. 136.

180 *"overproduction and excess capacity":* Ibid.

181 *the board in Washington was skeptical:* For notes on the division at the Fed, see Friedman and Schwartz, *Great Contraction*, pp. 43–44, 71.

181 *"at present there is no":* Minutes of the Open Market Investment Committee (predecessor to the Open Market Policy Conference), quoted in ibid., p. 72.

181 *"an abundance of funds":* Ibid., p. 75.

182 *"a very able business man":* Hoover memorandum to Andrew Mellon, 4/29/30, in HH Papers—Presidential Subject File—Federal Reserve Board—Correspondence, 1930, HHPL.

182 *"Hoover considered Young"*: Charles Hamlin Diary Digest, 10/30/30, p. 124.

182 *as Young told the story:* See Young's testimony before a subcommittee of the Senate Committee on Banking and Currency, in *Congressional Record*, 71st Cong., 3rd Sess., "Nomination of Eugene Meyer," p. 71.

183 *"It is clearly evident"*: Young to Hoover, 8/27/30, in HH Papers—Presidential Subject File—Federal Reserve—Correspondence, 1930, HHPL.

183 *vetted by Ogden Mills:* Mills supplied Hoover a draft of Young's resignation on August 27, "in accordance with our understanding of yesterday." Mills to Hoover, 8/27/30, in ibid.

183 *"most able"*: Hoover, *Memoirs*, III:108.

183 *Meyer had been a frequent visitor:* Presidential logs record nine visits by Meyer between January 1930 and his appointment in September 1930.

183 *"There's a vacancy"*: Eugene Meyer, COHC, p. 567.

184 *Platt met in late August:* Testimony of George Rand, president, Marine Trust Co., before Senate Committee on Banking and Currency, *Congressional Record*, 71st Cong., 3rd Sess., p. 65.

184 *"gave him to understand"*: The quotes are from the Charles Hamlin, Diary Digest. Notes on the Meyer appointment appear under headings for Hoover, Mellon, and Meyer, all in the period August–September 1930.

185 *Miller, also taken by surprise:* Ibid., 9/4/30, p. 124.

186 *"ardent crowd of followers"*: Meyer, COHC, p. 347.

187 *"Germany will default"*: Pusey, *Eugene Meyer*, p. 208.

187 *"This would have strengthened"*: Hoover, *Memoirs*, II:177.

187 *Hoover persisted:* For the anecdote, see ibid.; see also Rhodes, "Herbert Hoover and the War Debts," p. 132.

187 *"moral and contractual"*: *NYT*, 10/17/22.

187 *"I don't agree"*: Pusey, *Eugene Meyer*, p. 209.

188 *Hoover came to regard Meyer:* For Hoover's opinion of Meyer, see Joslin, Diary, 8/27/31, 3/16/32.

188 *"A lot of people thought"*: Meyer, COHC, p. 272.

188 *"Governor Meyer takes hold"*: Hamlin, Diary Digest, 9/16/30, p. 158.

188 *"Some newspapers say"*: Ibid., 10/10/30.

188 *Miller is often portrayed:* In *Lords of Finance* (pp. 174–75), Liaquat Ahamed describes Miller as "deeply insecure," who "espouse[d] a series of outmoded beliefs about the way monetary policy was supposed to work." See also Friedman and Schwartz, *Great Contraction*, p. 121, n. 178.

189 *"consider the purchase"*: The quote, and Meyer's reaction, are from Friedman and Schwartz, *Great Contraction*, p. 159.

189 *"raising the price level"*: The proposal came from Representative Will Wood of Indiana. For Hoover's referral to Meyer, and Meyer's response, see the memoranda dated 10/21/30 and 10/22/30 under HH Papers—Presidential Subject

File—Business—Correspondence, 1930 October 16–25, HPPL. The document is cited in Barber, *From New Era to New Deal*, p. 98, n. 17.

189 *monetary easing . . . could have blocked or even reversed:* Milton Friedman was the most influential of the scholars who advocated a policy of aggressive easing. See Friedman and Schwartz, *Great Contraction*, p. 45; see also pp. 71–103.

189 *"any conceivable course":* Meyer memorandum to Hoover, 10/22/30, in HH Papers—Presidential Subject File—Business—Correspondence, 1930 October 16–25, HHPL.

190 *"Money is not really cheap":* Miller statement, 9/25/30, quoted in Friedman and Schwartz, *Great Contraction*, p. 45.

190 *"a mental annex":* Hoover, *Memoirs*, III:9.

190 *his own monetary conundrum:* Hoover discussed both the need for credit at low rates, and the problem of "inflationary booms," in his speech to the American Bankers Association, 10/2/30.

THIRTEEN: THE GROUND GIVES WAY

193 *Twenty-four deaths:* For notes on the July heat wave, see *NYT*, 7/11/30, 8/10/30.

193 *"Most disastrous drought":* *NYT*, 8/5/30.

193 *It came as some relief:* Mark Sullivan recorded later (n.d.) that Hoover responded to the drought "with something like relief, almost of pleasure." The quote appears in Robert Cowley, "The Drought and the Dole."

193 *"a great deal of variation":* Hoover press conference, 8/5/30.

194 *"So that the total amount":* Hoover press conference, 8/8/30.

194 *"It is money we need":* Governor Harry Leslie of Indiana, quoted in *NYT*, 8/15/30.

195 *"great wealth":* For Hoover's pre-conference meeting with Judge Payne, see Hamilton, "Hoover and the Great Drought," p. 857. See also Woodruff, *Rare as Rain*, p. 11; Woodruff says Hoover and Payne agreed that "no Red Cross official" would attend the conference, but Payne did so in the end.

195 *Payne told reporters:* *NYT*, 8/18/30.

195 *both Payne and Hoover:* For Hoover's projection of $17 million, see Hamilton, "Hoover and the Great Drought," p. 857; for Payne's estimate of "extensive" aid work, see Woodruff, *Rare as Rain*, p. 11.

196 *Hoover confessed fears:* MacLafferty, Diary, 8/5/30.

196 *"there will be":* Hoover press conference, 8/5/30.

196 *"stifle" that neighborly impulse:* Hoover spoke frequently on the enterprise-sapping nature of the dole; for a pointed comment on public relief and private charity, see his public statement of 2/3/31, in Hoover, *Memoirs*, III:56.

197 *a three-tiered "cooperative" scheme:* Hoover described his plans for drought relief in a press statement issued 8/14/30.

197   *"The farmer isn't yet"*: Hot Springs *Sentinel Record* quoted in Lambert, "The Arkansas Drought," p. 6.

197   *"It's like old times"*: Rogers quoted in Hamilton, "Hoover and the Great Drought," p. 857.

198   *the slide accelerated*: Friedman and Schwartz, *Great Contraction*, pp. 9–12.

198   *"People felt the ground"*: The quote is from Schumpeter, *Business Cycles*, II:911; it's offered in Kindleberger, *World in Depression*, p. 137.

198   *"We propose to develop"*: Hoover press conference, 10/21/30.

201   *"Mills was particularly"*: Stimson, Diary, 10/21/30.

201   *"The most dangerous"*: Hoover address to the Gridiron Club, 12/14/29.

202   *"all the energy and vigor"*: *NYT*, 10/23/30.

202   *"The spirit of voluntary"*: Hoover press conference, 10/24/30.

202   *Apple growers*: Edward Robb Ellis gives the story of the apple vendors in *Nation in Torment*, pp. 125–26.

202   *"No special session"*: Hoover Statement on the Voluntary Response to the Unemployment problem, 10/24/30.

203   *"We can win this battle"*: Woods radio address, 10/20/30, quoted in Hayes, *Activities of the President's Emergency Committee*, p. 89.

203   *"We are not attacking"*: Hoover quote from MacLafferty, Diary, 9/16/30.

203   *"Hoover under"*: Rickard, Diary, 9/26/30.

204   *"carried the credit system"*: Hoover's October speeches, at Cleveland, Boston, and King's Mountain, North Carolina, are printed in Myers, ed., *State Papers*, I:375–401. The deflation of 1922 was, in fact, sharper at the outset than 1930, but was far less prolonged.

205   *"every part of the United States"*: Bob Lucas quoted by Ted Clark in a letter to Calvin Coolidge, 8/2/30, Clark Papers, LOC.

205   *"It seems to me"*: Hoover to Lamont, 10/1/30, cited in Barber, *From New Era to New Deal*, p. 92.

206   *"Underneath his shyness"*: Stimson, Diary, 10/6/30.

206   *"very forcibly"*: Clark to Coolidge, 11/6/30, Clark Papers, LOC.

FOURTEEN: PLAYING POLITICS WITH HUMAN MISERY

210   *"There was discouragement"*: MacLafferty, Diary, 11/5/30.

210   *"rather sad and depressed"*: Stimson, Diary, 11/5/30.

210   *"the feeling in the White House"*: Clark to Coolidge, 11/29/30, Clark Papers, LOC.

210   *"not only suffering"*: Woodruff, *Rare as Rain*, p. 33.

211   *"If I took this entire"*: *Congressional Record*, 71st Cong., 3rd Sess., p. 398.

211   *"A food program"*: Woodruff, *Rare as Rain*, p. 29.

211   *prices continued to fall*: Agriculture Secretary Arthur Hyde lamented the price

paradox when he reported in December that "demand for farm commodities fell off more than supply did." *NYT*, 12/3/30.

211 *a cascade of bank failures:* Bank failures are one of the distinguishing features of the Depression, and so have been subject to extensive study. One volume I found useful was Elmus Wicker, *The Banking Panics of the Great Depression*; Peter Temin focuses on the failures of 1930 in his *Monetary Forces*, pp. 83–95. See also "Southern Bank Failures," *Outlook and Independent*, 12/5/30.

212 *the number of banks more than doubled:* The figures are given in Hamilton, "The Causes of the Banking Panic of 1930," p. 585. Hamilton is persuasive in arguing that this first banking crisis was brought on by collapsing commodity prices and the drought.

212 *the sudden collapse of Caldwell:* Ibid., pp. 590–94.

212 *"steer legislation in a straight":* *NYT*, 11/8/30.

213 *"Pure political bunk":* MacLafferty, Diary, 11/9/30.

213 *"appeal to the people":* Stimson, Diary, 11/4/30.

213 *"The country would think":* MacLafferty, Diary, 11/9/30.

213 *"very happy":* *NYT*, 11/9/30.

213 *"urging close cooperation":* *NYT*, 11/13/30.

213 *"with a view to":* *NYT*, 11/14/30.

214 *"intended to put":* Stimson, Diary, 11/12/30.

214 *"We need fighters":* The quotes are from MacLafferty, Diary, 11/14/30.

214 *"some astonishment":* *NYT*, 11/14/30.

214 *"sit steady in the boat":* Robinson to Baruch, 11/29/30, quoted in Schwarz, *Interregnum of Despair*, p. 16.

215 *"Hoover and Robinson":* *NYT*, 12/1/30.

215 *"the unusual incident":* *New York Herald Tribune*, 12/1/30.

215 *"The Republican members":* *Congressional Record*, 71st Cong., 3rd Sess., p. 631.

216 *"It seems that":* This episode is described in an important article by Hamilton, "Hoover and the Great Drought." See also Woodruff, *Rare as Rain*, pp. 45–47. For the quote, see Hamilton, p. 866.

217 *"So when the President":* Hyde quoted by Olsen, in Hamilton, "Hoover and the Great Drought," 865, n. 44.

217 *"There are a great many":* *NYT*, 12/8/30.

218 *"Prosperity cannot be":* Hoover press conference, 12/9/30.

218 *"There has not been":* *Congressional Record*, 71st Cong., 3rd Sess., p. 423.

219 *"Irresponsible in Congress":* *NYT*, 12/10/30.

220 *"despair at my personal":* Hoover, *Memoirs*, III:103.

220 *"one of the soundest procedures":* PECE press release, quoted in Hayes, *Activities of the President's Emergency Committee*, p. 42.

221 *"comprehensive plan":* The internal effort to sell Hoover on public works is described by public relations pioneer Ed Bernays, who was a member of the

committee. For the quote, see Bernays's autobiography, *Biography of an Idea*, p. 470.

221 *"certain common-sense limitations"*: Hoover comments, n.d., cited in Hayes, *Activities of the President's Emergency Committee*, p. 44.

221 *"The president's emergency committee"*: Hoover Message to the Senate, 12/16/30.

221 *"The president's failure"*: Bernays, *Biography of an Idea*, p. 473.

FIFTEEN: THE GHOST OF GROVER CLEVELAND

223 *"If there are two"*: For notes on Hoover's New Year's Day reception, see Boone, Memoirs, p. 585; for the quote, see *NYT*, 1/2/31.

224 *"I told the president"*: Boone, Memoir, p. 585.

225 *"We are not going to let"*: The skirmish over Red Cross aid in England, Arkansas, has received extensive coverage. My sources for this account include Lambert, "Hoover and the Red Cross in the Arkansas Drought;" Hamilton, "Hoover and the Great Drought;" and Woodruff, *Rare as Rain.*

225 *"I, with great modesty"*: *NYT*, 1/8/31.

226 *"The president seemed"*: Stimson, Diary, 1/16/31.

226 *"melting down very rapidly"*: *NYT*, 1/11/31.

226 *"a very material increase"*: Hoover press conference, 1/11/31.

227 *"active sympathies"*: Hoover press conference, 1/13/31.

227 *Payne sent telegrams*: *NYT*, 1/13/31.

227 *"The nation's response"*: *NYT*, 1/16/31.

227 *"Hoover apples"*: *NYT*, 2/3/31.

227 *"It is essential"*: Hoover address to the National Red Cross, 5/5/30.

228 *"He sincerely believes"*: Will Rogers in *NYT*, 1/17/31.

228 *distribution of Farm Board wheat*: See Lambert, "Federal Farm Board Wheat," passim.

229 *"It is difficult"*: *NYT*, 1/20/31.

230 *"Let them nail each"*: Hoover quoted in MacLafferty, Diary, 12/16/30.

230 *"It would be foolish"*: Tilson quoted in ibid., 12/16/30.

230 *do away with his aide George Akerson*: For Free's demand, see ibid., 12/16/30 and 12/19/30; see also 11/18/30.

230 *The White House correspondents*: Lewis Strauss told Edgar Rickard that the press corps wanted Akerson out. Rickard, Diary, 12/5/30.

231 *"to enforce the law"*: President's Message to Congress Transmitting Report of the National Commission on Law Enforcement, 1/20/31.

231 *"as bad as it is possible"*: Hoover quoted in MacLafferty, Diary, 1/13/31.

232 *"The attitude of the"*: *NYT*, 1/29/31.

232 *Emaciated bodies were piled in the streets*: For the American Relief Administration

in Russia, see Patenaude, *Big Show in Bololand*, passim. The anecdote of piled corpses is excerpted here: http://news.stanford.edu/news/2011/april/famine -040411.html.

233 *"a period of centralization"*: Hoover address to the Gridiron Club, 12/13/30.

233 *"a centralized despotism"*: Hoover address, 10/22/28, in Wilbur, ed., *New Day*, p. 154.

234 *"I cannot believe"*: Clark to Coolidge, 11/6/30, Clark Papers, LOC.

234 *"You will laugh at"*: Hulda Hoover to her mother, 2/22/1883, quoted in Nash, *The Engineer*, p. 8.

234 *"A condition of hysteria"*: Raymond Clapper, "White House Interview," 2/27/31, in Clapper Papers, LOC.

235 *"He could have"*: Rogers in *NYT*, 2/4/30.

235 *"a mood of insane hysteria"*: Churchill, "The Dole," *Saturday Evening Post*.

236 *"There seems to be"*: *NYT*, 12/8/30.

236 *"There is no new principle"*: Borah's speech is excerpted at length in *NYT*, 2/3/31.

237 *"It is not an easy thing"*: MacLafferty, Diary, 1/19/31.

238 *"I do not wish to add"*: Hoover press statement, "Public Versus Private Financing of Relief," 2/3/31.

241 *"rapidly disgusting"*: *NYT*, 2/4/31.

241 *"We need some"*: Anna Heidler to Dear Sir, 2/25/31, in Lou Henry Hoover Papers, HHPL.

242 *"very quietly"*: Nan Woodruff treats the matter of food aid in the coalfields in *Rare as Rain*, Chapter 9. The quote is from Woods, "Memorandum of Conversation with President Hoover and Judge Payne," 2/11/31, Manuscript Biographies Collection—Woods, Arthur, HHPL, quoted by Woodruff, *Rare as Rain*, p. 162.

243 *"He spoke with a depth"*: Pickett, *For More than Bread*, p. 21.

244 *"If the engineer"*: Charles McNary to John McNary, 12/17/30, quoted in Hamilton, "Hoover and the Great Drought," p. 875.

SIXTEEN: CREDIT CRUNCH

247 *"as an aid to unemployment"*: All the quotes in this passage are from Hoover's State of the Union address, 12/2/30.

248 *the federal government tripled hiring*: Press release, "Number of Governmental Employees," 6/15/31. Construction hires were given at 235,000 in January 1930, 420,000 in October 1930, and 655,000 in June 1931.

248 *spending on public works*: Press release, "Progress on Reads Program," 7/3/31. I:594. See also Barber, *From New Era to New Deal*, p. 107.

248 *"For the first time"*: Hoover address to the Indiana Republican Editorial Association, 6/15/31.

248 *"avoid the opiates"*: Hoover radio address, Lincoln's Birthday, 2/12/31.

249 *"I think the argument"*: Keynes statement, May 1931, quoted in Stein, *Fiscal Revolution*, p. 146.

249 *"Our main trouble"*: Hoover to Raymond Clapper, 2/27/31, Clapper Papers, LOC.

249 *the longest-lasting contraction:* 1873 remains the worst, according to "Business Cycle Expansions and Contractions," National Bureau of Economic Research, cited by Wikipedia.

250 *early signs of economic recovery:* For industrial production, see Friedman and Schwartz, *Great Contraction*, p. 17; for commodity prices, see Kehoe, "The Relation of Herbert Hoover to Congress," p. 92; for breadlines, see Rickard, Diary, 5/9/31; for 120 cities, see Smith, *The Shattered Dream*, p. 60. Friedman and Schwartz find "many of the earmarks of the bottom of a cycle and the beginning of a recovery."

250 *restoration of farm operations:* David Hamilton remarks on the impact of drought loans on rural banks in "Banking Panic of 1930," p. 594, n. 38. See also Rickard, Diary, 5/9/31.

250 *he consented to step out:* NYT, 3/9/30.

251 *"a typical Hoover appointment"*: Clark to Coolidge, 3/28/31.

251 *"This is the hottest"*: Joslin, Diary, 4/30/31.

251 *"intense regret"*: NYT, 3/7/31.

252 *"overshadowing issue"*: For Hoover's engagement in early efforts toward Social Security, see Bornet, "Hoover's Planning for Unemployment." Hoover voices his concern about the Congress, and terms unemployment insurance an "overshadowing issue," in Stimson, Diary, 4/10/31.

253 *"the blighting hand of government"*: Hoover speech to Metropolitan Life managers, 1/27/23, quoted in Bornet, "Hoover's Planning for Unemployment," p. 38.

253 *"The president feels"*: French Strother, 9/6/30, quoted in Bornet, "Hoover's Planning for Unemployment," p. 52.

253 *"The height of the world's"*: Hoover, *Memoirs*, II:314.

254 *"purely social affair"*: NYT, 4/4/31.

254 *"very gloomy situation"*: Ahamed, *Lords of Finance*, p. 383.

254 *"a good long discussion"*: Stimson, Diary, 4/7/31.

255 *"Unless drastic measures"*: Montagu Norman to Clement Moret, quoted in *Time*, 7/27/31.

255 *"Apprehension began to run"*: Hoover, *Memoirs*, III:63.

257 *"Things were about to turn"*: Stimson, Diary, 5/20/31; for "pure indigo," see ibid., 6/2/31.

257 *He would make a bold stroke:* There are many sources for the story of the Hoover moratorium. I attribute several of the quotes that follow, but the text is a composite. As primary sources the Stimson and Joslin diaries are essential; for my

treatment they were complemented by Hoover's statement in his *Memoirs*, Volume III; Stimson and Bundy, *On Active Service*; Morison, *Turmoil and Tradition*; Ahamed, *Lords of Finance*; Kindleberger, *World in Depression*; Joslin, *Hoover Off the Record*; and Eichengreen, *Golden Fetters*. Also helpful were Myers, *Foreign Policies of Herbert Hoover*, and Wilbur and Hyde, eds., *Hoover Policies*.

258   *"Politically it is"*: Ahamed, *Lords of Finance*, p. 407.

258   *"This is perhaps"*: Joslin, *Hoover Off the Record*, p. 91.

259   *"It involved a bold"*: Stimson, Diary, 6/5/31.

259   *"I recognized that"*: Ibid., 7/13/31.

260   *"The situation is"*: Ibid., 6/15/31.

260   *"It reminds me"*: Joslin, Diary, 6/18/31.

261   *"The economic crisis"*: Hindenburg to Hoover, 6/18/31, in Myers and Newton, eds., *Hoover Administration*, p. 90.

262   *"Hoover at his best"*: Joslin, Diary, 6/22/31.

263   *"the most praiseworthy"*: "President Hoover's Great Action," *The Nation*, 7/1/31, p. 4, cited in Schwarz, *Interregnum of Despair*, p. 79.

264   *"clearness and quickness"*: Dawes remarks quoted in Schwarz, *Interregnum of Despair*, p. 106.

266   *"one of the neatest"*: Stimson and Bundy, *On Active Service*, p. 209.

266   *"that Central Europe"*: Hoover, *Memoirs*, III:81.

266   *"The president is dog tired"*: Joslin, Diary, 7/22/31.

266   *"He didn't look to me"*: Byron Price OH.

267   *"We are living this year"*: Keynes, "The Great Slump of 1930," 12/20/30, in Keynes, *Essays in Persuasion*.

SEVENTEEN: THE GIBRALTAR OF WORLD STABILITY

270   *"Our people can take"*: Hoover address to the Indiana Republican Editorial Association, 6/15/31.

270   *"What a strange situation"*: James Mead quoted in Schwarz, *Interregnum of Despair*, p. 31.

270   *"The present economic structure"*: NYT, 8/5/31.

270   *"Economic adjustment is"*: Literary Digest, 7/4/31, p. 9.

271   *"There was more vigor"*: NYT, 6/16/31.

272   *"Never have I seen"*: Joslin, Diary, 6/11/31.

272   *"great inequalities"*: Hoover, *American Individualism*, pp. 3, 36.

272   *"The other idea"*: Hoover address to the Indiana Republican Editorial Association, 6/15/31.

275   *failures jumped in June:* Monthly figures for bank closures are given in Wicker, *Banking Panics*, p. 67.

275   *"suppressed panic"*: Stimson, Diary, 9/12/31.

276 *"our banking system must"*: Hoover to Eugene Meyer, 9/8/32, quoted in Joslin, *Hoover Off the Record*, p. 132.

277 *"living more and more"*: Joslin, Diary, 8/27/31; see also Cannadine, *Mellon*, p. 439.

277 *his views oscillating*: Meyer is credited in some accounts as a consistent advocate for expansion (see Friedman and Schwartz, *Great Contraction*, pp. 82–84; see also Chandler, *American Monetary Policy*, p. 145), but Charles Hamlin's contemporary notes from meetings of the Fed show Meyer to be much more ambivalent.

277 *neither confided much*: For notes on Hoover's view of Meyer, see Joslin, Diary, 8/27/31 (Meyer is termed "very stubborn"); and Rickard, Diary, 2/28/32 (Hoover calls Meyer "difficult to handle").

278 *"He didn't back me up"*: Meyer COHC, p. 616.

278 *"a perfect servant"*: Agnes Meyer, Diary, 2/24/32.

278 *The treasury Secretary hurried back*: The failure of the Bank of Pittsburgh is treated in Cannadine, *Mellon*, pp. 440–43; see also Wicker, *Banking Panics*, p. 82.

279 *Hoover was furious*: Stimson, Diary, 9/22/31.

279 *"Mellon pulled the whistle"*: Cannadine tells the story of Paul Mellon discovering this ditty in *Mellon*, p. 442.

280 *"We were plunged into"*: Hoover speech in Des Moines, Iowa, 10/4/32.

281 *"I cannot make"*: Hoover press conference, 9/22/31.

282 *"that is when"*: J. Bradford DeLong, quoted in Ahamed, *Lords of Finance*, p. 438.

283 *"foreign fears concerning"*: Harrison's and Meyer's comments on interest rates are given in Friedman and Schwartz, *Great Contraction*, pp. 85–86.

283 *"A decidedly wise move"*: Commercial and Financial Chronicle, 10/17/31, quoted in ibid., p. 86, n. 120.

284 *"breathe an atmosphere"*: Agnes Meyer, Diary, 1/29/31.

284 *"a bankers' panic"*: The quote is from notes Hoover prepared for the meeting, in Myers and Newton, eds., *Hoover Administration*, p. 126.

285 *"went after them"*: Hoover gave a thorough account of his address to James MacLafferty, who recorded it in his Diary, 11/8/31.

285 *traveling together from New York*: Meyer gives details of the meeting, and discusses the thinking of the bankers, in his COHC, p. 615.

285 *"they constantly reverted"*: Hoover, *Memoirs*, III:86.

285 *"without visible effect"*: Meyer, "From Laissez Faire with William Graham Sumner to the RFC," p. 24.

286 *"I returned"*: Hoover, *Memoirs*, III:86.

286 *"We want beer!"*: Ibid., III:88.

286 *"dropt egglike"*: Literary Digest, 10/17/31.

286 *"It is a movement"*: Hoover press statement, 10/6/31.

287 *"No one could ask"*: Joslin, Diary, 10/9/31.

287 *"a most constructive and important step"*: Harrison to Hoover, 10/7/31, in George L. Harrison Papers, Columbia University.

288 *"The whole psychology"*: For notes on the positive impact of the National Credit Association, see Wicker, *Banking Panics*, pp. 95–97, 104. Harrison is quoted on p. 96.

288 *"Tens of thousands"*: Hyde to Hoover, 11/14/31, in Egan, *Worst Hard Time*, p. 103.

288 *"In this emergency"*: Joslin, Diary, 8/10/31.

289 *"Rigid economy"*: This phrase was part of Hoover's mantra in dealing with department heads. See Joslin, *Hoover Off the Record*, p. 82.

289 *Hoover opposed raising taxes*: For his explicit declaration against new taxes, see *NYT*, 4/1/31.

289 *"After a long and very"*: Stimson, Diary, 5/26/31.

289 *This was a remarkably flexible view*: For Hoover's conversion from debt finance to budget balance, see Stein, *Fiscal Revolution*, pp. 26–33; see also Barber, *From New Era to New Deal*, pp. 132–35.

290 *experience from the war*: For notes on the tight credit markets during the Great War, see Nash, "Origins of the RFC," p. 456.

290 *"It was the very action"*: Joslin, Diary, 9/23/31.

290 *"The President's anxiety"*: *NYT*, 9/24/31.

   frustrated and disappointed: On the experience of Arthur Woods and his PECE committee members see Bernays, *Biography of an Idea*, pp. 474–75.

291 *Gifford spent the whole time*: Byron Price OH.

291 *"is not merely bewildering"*: Hoover press conference, 8/7/31.

292 *"Smashing at the incubus"*: *Literary Digest*, 10/17/31.

292 *"After a few weeks"*: Hoover, *Memoirs*, III:97.

293 *hoarding had returned*: For notes on the deepening slide in late 1931, see Friedman and Schwartz, *Great Contraction*, pp. 20–23.

293 *"Vast liquidation"*: The quotes are from Hoover's State of the Union address, 12/8/31.

293 *"Certainly the public"*: Hoover to Thomas Lamont, quoted in Burner, *Herbert Hoover*, p. 272.

293 *"seemed shocked"*: Hoover, *Memoirs*, III:90.

EIGHTEEN: RECONSTRUCTION

296 *"Beyond the Potomac"*: Anne O'Hare McKormick in the *NYT*, quoted in Schwarz, *Interregnum of Despair*, p. 74.

296 *The ranks of millionaires*: Figures on the erosion of the upper class are given in Lindsay to John Simon, 12/7/31, in PRO, FO 414/268, p. 42. The report notes further that incomes over $5 million fell from a total $360 million to $122 million, "a loss for the richest class of the country of two-thirds of their net income."

296 *"The indifference towards politics"*: Baltimore *Sun* quoted in Lindsay to John Simon, 11/26/31 in PRO, FO 414/268, p. 38.

296 *"President, politicians, bankers"*: Lindsay to John Simon, 12/31/31, in PRO, FO 414/269, p. 4.

296 *"He exhausts his associates"*: Rickard, Diary, 9/4/31.

297 *"The President of the"*: Keynes, "The End of the Gold Standard," 9/27/31, in *Essays in Persuasion*.

297 *"He is an unpopular"*: Tucker, *Mirrors of 1932*, pp. 6, 20.

297 *talking about being a one-term president*: Bornet, "Hoover's Planning for Unemployment," p. 59. Hoover was discussing timelines for reports from his Recent Social Trends study group with his friend and assistant Edward Eyre Hunt. He wanted results by 1932 at the latest, Hoover said, because "he did not expect to be reelected."

297 *"Three-and-a-half years"*: Hoover quoted in Joslin, *Hoover Off the Record*, p. 246.

297 *"I don't give a damn"*: Joslin, Diary, 11/30/31.

298 *Hoover worried aloud about a "plot"*: Hoover mentioned his fears to Stimson, who recorded them in his Diary, 4/28/31.

298 *encouraging a "draft Coolidge"*: Ted Clark to Coolidge, 8/18/31, Clark Papers, LOC.

298 *"determined to go forward"*: Hoover's concern with the Hamill book is documented in extensive communications between the president, Edgar Rickard, and Larry Richey, with copies on file at the HHPL. In addition, Raymond Clapper followed the story through interviews with *Collier's* editor Tom Beck, who published Train's defense of Hoover. See the note from Clapper's interview with Beck, 3/4/32, in Clapper Papers, LOC; the quote is from Clapper. Ted Joslin also advised Hoover to ignore the "smears"; see Joslin, Diary, 1/4/32. Hoover's engagement in the Train project is reflected in numerous documents; see especially Hoover to Rickard, 12/12/31, filed under Misrepresentations, HHPL. Hoover's interest in exposing the book's sponsors continued well into January; see MacLafferty, Diary, 12/29/31, 1/2/32, 1/13/32.

299 *"They are entirely confident"*: Clark to Coolidge, 9/29/31, Clark Papers, LOC.

299 *"I can win"*: MacLafferty, Diary, 12/5/31.

299 *Hoover wanted the Democrats*: For Hoover's thinking on the parties in Congress, see Joslin, Diary, 10/29/31, 11/4/31. See also Schwarz, *Interregnum of Despair*, p. 53.

299 *"It never occurs to him"*: Clark to Coolidge, 8/17/31, Clark Papers, LOC.

300 *"the Democrats would agree"*: MacLafferty, Diary, 12/5/31.

300 *"The president told me"*: Stimson, Diary, 10/29/31.

301 *"an infamous proposal"*: McFadden's speech is excerpted in *NYT*, 12/16/31.

302 *"If we lift our vision"*: Hoover State of the Union Address, 12/8/31.

304 *"The businesslike quality"*: Editorial, *New York Herald Tribune*, 12/9/31.

304 *"correct but cold"*: *NYT*, 12/9/31.

305 *Hoover did much*: Hoover's sense of urgency, and his meetings December, are recounted in Myers and Newton, eds., *Hoover Administration*, p. 157.

305 *"uppermost in the president's mind"*: NYT, 12/27/31.

306 *"It is a subsidy"*: NYT, 1/12/32.

306 *Glass mounted a dogged resistance:* For notes on compromises imposed on the Reconstruction Finance Corporation, see Olson, *Hoover and the RFC*, pp. 36–38; see also Chamberlain, *President, Congress, and Legislation*, p. 294.

306 *"I am suggesting"*: Glass quoted in NYT, 12/22/31.

307 *"The three Democrats"*: Joslin, Diary, 1/22/32.

308 *Hyde supervised distribution:* The agriculture loans are broken down in Olson, *Hoover and the RFC*, pp. 49–50.

308 *"it is not a battle"*: Hoover message to Congress, 1/4/32.

308 *"Credit is the blood stream"*: Appeal to Citizens to Stop Hoarding, 2/3/32.

308 *"bring relief and hope"*: Meyers and Newton, eds., *Hoover Administration*, p. 164.

309 *"a curiously perverse person"*: Hoover, *Memoirs*, III:112.

310 *"merely a tentative measure"*: Glass statement, 6/17/30, *Congressional Record*, 72nd Cong., 1st Sess., p. 10,973.

310 *"investigate the need"*: Hoover, State of the Union address, 12/8/31. For Glass's opposition to new eligibility requirements, see Hoover, *Memoirs*, III:115.

311 *"seriously impugning our national stability"*: Hoover memorandum, "Senator Glass," typescript, n.d., in HH Papers—Presidential Subject File—Financial Matters—Glass-Steagall Act, HHPL. See also NYT, 1/29/32.

311 *"an assault upon"*: Carter glass radio address, printed in NYT, 11/2/32.

311 *"You have no idea"*: Hoover to Agnes Meyer, in her Diary, 2/13/32.

311 *"densely ignorant"*: Glass quoted by Fed Board member Charles Hamlin in his Diary, 12/16/31.

311 *"a great authority on banking"*: Mills to William Woodward, letter marked "Personal and Confidential," 4/23/32, Mills Papers, LOC.

312 *"sounding like the barking"*: Joslin, Diary, 2/10/32.

312 *"bait" to win votes:* Hoover, *Memoirs*, III:110.

312 *"a club of iron"*: S. Palmer Harman, "Finance," *The Nation*, 12/16/31.

313 *"The emergency measures"*: Hoover press conference, 1/26/32.

313 *"excessive inflation of the currency"*: NYT, 2/12/32.

313 *"It is really"*: Joslin, Diary, 2/10/32.

313 *"the most powerful"*: *Business Week*, 1/27/32, quoted in Kennedy, *Banking Crisis of 1933*, p. 38.

314 *"I frightened him"*: Agnes Meyer, Diary, 2/13/32.

314 *"If the damned hoarders"*: Meyer quoted in Hamlin, Diary, 3/3/32.

315 *"1931 would be remembered"*: This quote and the several reports on bank practices are contained in correspondence forwarded by Hoover to George Harrison in March and April 1932. The letters are collected in the George Harrison Papers, Special Collections, Butler Library, Columbia University. They are filed with a cover letter, Hoover to Harrison, 4/26/32.

315 *"His former optimism"*: Charles Hamlin, Diary, 4/12/32.

315 *"Congress and the administration"*: Mills quoted from committee minutes, cited in Chandler, *American Monetary Policy*, p. 196.

316 *"The poor man"*: Stimson, Diary, 5/16/32.

317 *"Save that bank!"*: The bailout of the Dawes bank is described in Kennedy, *Banking Crisis of 1933*, pp. 40–42; in Timmons, *Portrait of an American*, pp. 316–24; and in Joslin, *Hoover Off the Record*, pp. 249–51. The quote is from Timmons, p. 319.

317 *policymakers at the Federal Reserve*: For the role of gold in the decision to abandon quantitative easing, see Eichengreen, *Golden Fetters*, p. 316; for the vote, see Chandler, *American Monetary Policy*, pp. 200–201.

318 *"one part of the theory"*: Hoover, *Memoirs*, III:118.

318 *"varying the gold content"*: *NYT*, 5/14/32. The quote is from the article, which excerpted Fisher's statement.

318 *Fisher went further*: Fisher's expansionary policies are given in Barber, *From New Era to New Deal*, pp. 160–62.

319 *"the radical and half-baked"*: Barber profiles Kemmerer in ibid., pp. 157–59. The quote is from Kemmerer to Hoover, 11/7/31, and given by Barber at p. 159, n. 38.

319 *"Aggressive monetary policy"*: George W. Bush, *Economic Report of the President*, 2004, p. 40, cited by Paul Krugman in *NYT*, 7/14/14.

319 *adherence to the gold standard*: Barry Eichengreen's *Golden Fetters*, published in 1992, is the bible of this school of thought. There are divisions, however, especially on the question of the utility of an ultimate return to the gold standard. Columbia University economist Charles Calomiris noted the division between Eichengreen and theorist Charles Kindleberger in his "Financial Factors in the Great Depression," p. 72, n. 6.

NINETEEN: ROOSEVELT RISING

323 *"Every morning"*: MacLafferty, Diary, 12/29/31.

323 *"It is surely a test"*: Ibid., 1/28/32.

324 *"I wish I had some way"*: Ibid., 2/23/32.

324 *"Business is fickle"*: Ibid., 3/6/32.

324 *"Hoover is sunk"*: For Vandenberg, see ibid., 1/9/32; for Knutson and his quote, see ibid., 1/13/32.

324 *"Hoover's enemies"*: Ibid., 1/28/32.

325 *a survey in Chicago*: U.S. Senate, 72nd Cong., 1st Sess., Hearings on Unemployment Relief, VII:10. For Dayton and Akron, see *Facts on File* at fofweb.com/History.

325 *Tenino, Washington*: MacLafferty, Diary, 3/10/32. That day, MacLafferty presented Hoover with a wooden nickel from Tenino, sent as a curio by his brother.

326 *"My sober and considered":* Gifford testimony quoted in McElvaine, *Great Depression*, p. 79.

326 *"He's been a sorry":* Hoover quoted in Joslin, Diary, 2/18/32.

326 *"Our first duty":* Hoover press conference, 1/8/32.

327 *"I here give my testimony":* MacLafferty, Diary, 2/1/32.

327 *"would cause the sane people":* Ibid.

328 *"I mean it":* Hoover quoted by Joslin in his Diary, 3/11/32; for the second quote see ibid., 4/2/32.

328 *"drastic economy":* Hoover press conference, 1/8/32.

328 *"Nothing is more":* Statement on efforts to Balance the Budget, 3/8/32.

328 *"Our troubles today":* Lippmann, 11/18/31, in *Interpretations*, p. 8.

329 *"I am now opposed":* Jack Garner quoted in Schwarz, *Interregnum of Despair*, p. 124.

329 *"take a fling":* Joslin, Diary, 3/25/32.

330 *"a liberal-minded man": The New Republic* quoted in Schlesinger, *Crisis of the Old Order*, p. 291.

330 *"too eager to please":* Lippmann, 1/8/32, in *Interpretations*, pp. 259–63.

331 *"the little fellow":* Roosevelt address, "The Forgotten Man," 4/17/32. Roosevelt's speeches are collected at, among other places, the New Deal Network, and available at newdeal.feri.org/texts.

331 *"I protest against": NYT*, 4/14/32.

332 *Roosevelt had for years hewed:* Tugwell, *Brains Trust*, pp. 77–78. After FDR reversed field on the critical question of relief, Tugwell wrote, "Roosevelt could only hope that no one would recall his former views."

332 *"He's a trimmer":* Joslin, Diary, 6/24/32.

332 *"I hope they do nothing":* MacLafferty, Diary, 4/19/32.

332 *"I would prefer Roosevelt":* Joslin, Diary, 2/7/32.

332 *"They are more and more":* MacLafferty, Diary, 3/24/32.

333 *"Their game is to keep":* Joslin, Diary, 5/8/32.

333 *"He shouldn't think":* Joslin, Diary, 4/27/32.

333 *He arrived by train at 1:56:* The president's schedule was published in *NYT*, 4/28/32.

333 *"galvanize the attention":* Joslin, Diary, 4/12/32.

334 *"national impoverishment":* Hoover address to governors, 4/27/32.

334 *"far reaching and liberal":* Roosevelt's speech is excerpted in *NYT*, 4/28/32.

334 *"as though he were":* Eleanor Roosevelt, *This I Remember*, p. 61. The story was disputed even by some of Roosevelt's friends. Alonzo Fields, the White House butler tasked with attending Roosevelt, said in an oral history that he was in constant attendance to the governor, as was Roosevelt's personal valet. Hoover himself never responded to Eleanor Roosevelt's allegation. See Frank Friedel, "Hoover and FDR."

334 *"the next president"*: NYT, 4/29/32.

335 *"They made me look"*: Joslin, Diary, 4/30/32.

335 *"at times more of a warrior"*: Hoover, *Memoirs*, II:366.

336 *"just a proposition"*: Stimson, Diary, 5/24/32; for Hoover's proposal and the reaction in Geneva, see Hoover, *Memoirs*, II:354–57.

336 *"I could see his work"*: Stimson, Diary, 2/10/32; for the second quote see ibid., 5/30/32.

336 *"This has been"*: The quotes from Pat Harrison and Key Pittman are both given in Schwarz, *Interregnum of Despair*, p. 156.

336 *"The effort now"*: Joslin, Diary, 1/5/32.

337 *"political considerations"*: Joslin, Diary, 2/15/32.

337 *"afflict the court"*: The quote is from Leonard Baker, *Back to Back*, p. 121; it is given in Burner, *Herbert Hoover*, p. 396, n. 46.

337 *"the finest act"*: NYT, 3/2/32, cited in Wikipedia.

337 *"I can't afford"*: MacLafferty, Diary, 3/4/32.

338 *So did Attorney General Mitchell:* Ever since Hoover signed the Norris–La Guardia Act his critics—George Norris foremost among them—have asserted that Hoover did so reluctantly and was in truth opposed to the bill. See Norris, *Fighting Liberal*, pp. 314–15. But that interpretation runs at odds with Hoover's long record of promoting labor rights, and with the documents generated at the time he signed the act. For Hoover's decision, see Fausold, *Presidency of Herbert C. Hoover*, pp. 122–23. See also Mitchell's two memoranda, both dated 3/23/32, one marked "Confidential," in HH Papers—Presidential Subject File—Bills—Recommendations, HHPL; and see the memorandum from Walter Newton to Bert Snell, 3/8/32, in HH Papers—Presidential Subject File—Anti-Trust Laws, HHPL. For Doak's intervention, see Ruth O'Brien, *Workers' Paradox*, p. 170. O'Brien accepts the Norris thesis that this intervention was a bid to kill the bill. Perhaps the most compelling statement of Hoover's thinking, because it appears candid and because it comports with the documents cited above, appears in MacLafferty, Diary, 3/8/32. Hoover there expressed concern about the potential for union-led boycotts, but said he expected to sign the bill into law.

339 *"I believe the time has arrived"*: NYT, 5/12/32.

339 *"Nothing is more necessary"*: Hoover to Congress, 5/5/32.

339 *"bitter and savage"*: Baltimore *Sun*, 5/6/32.

339 *"It was a bullseye"*: NYT, 5/6/32.

340 *"It's a complete steal!"*: Joslin, Diary, 5/11/32.

340 *"We have got to"*: Joslin, Diary, 5/12/32.

341 *"The policy steadfastly"*: Hoover Statement on Economic Recovery, 5/12/32.

341 *Meyer resisted the idea:* For Meyer's response, see Olson, *Hoover and the RFC*, p. 61.

341 *"The latest proposals"*: NYT, 5/14/32.

342 *"The most interesting event"*: Hiram Johnson to sons, 5/14/32, in Burke, ed., *Letters of Hiram Johnson*.

TWENTY: THE CONFLICTED CANDIDATE

343 *"Our president is still"*: James Cox's speech is excerpted in Heineman, *A Catholic New Deal*, p. 20.

345 *"We will not see"*: Larry Richey memo quoted in ibid., p. 23.

345 *"I have intense sympathy"*: NYT, 1/8/32.

346 *ponied up the train fare*: NYT, 1/9/32.

346 *"meet the bonus marchers"*: Dawes is quoted by Eugene Meyer in his COHC, p. 643.

348 *"That would almost certainly"*: Joslin, Diary, 6/2/32.

348 *"There seemed no excuse"*: Schlesinger, *Crisis of the Old Order*, p. 265.

348 *a search of records*: Spencer Howard, archivist at the Herbert Hoover Presidential Library in West Branch, Iowa, reviewed phone records and other archives at the author's request.

348 *"would stir the country"*: Bruce Barton to Hoover, 6/6/32, in HH Papers—President's Personal File—Barton, Bruce. Correspondence, HHPL.

348 *"My dear Barton"*: Hoover to Bruce Barton, 6/7/32, in HH Papers—President's Personal File—Barton, Bruce. Correspondence, HHPL.

348 *another important concession*: The order to delay demolition was transmitted to Glassford from Ferry Heath, a close friend of Hoover's and the assistant treasury secretary in charge of the $700 million building program. Most accounts of the Bonus Army cast Hoover as a fearful, vengeful foe of the veterans; Donald Liso gives a compelling, contrary argument in his *President and Protest*, which I rely on here. For Ferry Heath and the demolition project, see p. 78.

349 *"The imperative moment"*: Hoover address to the American Legion, 9/21/31.

349 *"a ten-strike"*: Joslin, Diary, 9/21/31.

350 *"organized raids upon"*: Butler speech to the National Industrial Conference Board, 5/19/32, in George Barr Baker Papers, Correspondence, Box 1, Hoover Institution, Stanford.

350 *Even Franklin Roosevelt*: For Roosevelt's declaration, "I am not in favor of a soldier's bonus," see Davis, *FDR*, II:345.

351 *"I don't give a damn"*: Joslin, Diary, 6/17/32.

351 *"We enormously increased"*: Hoover, *Memoirs*, III:318.

352 *"a great social"*: Hoover Address of Acceptance, 8/11/28, in Wilbur, ed., *New Day*, p. 29.

352 *"in an effort"*: Hoover, *Memoirs*, I:5.

352 *"Mr. Hoover never took"*: Adaline Fuller OH.

353   *"Strong alcoholic drinks":* Hoover, *Memoirs*, II:275.

353   *"sprang up from her chair":* Presidential physician Joel Boone tells the story of the first day of Prohibition in his oral history.

353   *"doubts as to the wisdom":* Stimson, Diary, 12/28/30; for the second quote, see the entry for 1/12/31; for the third, 11/4/30.

354   *"No one can read":* Baker quoted by Edgar Rickard, Diary, 1/21/31.

354   *"we would be the followers":* MacLafferty, Diary, 11/5/30; the second quote is MacLafferty speaking to Hoover, in ibid., 11/22/30.

355   *"special constitutional convention":* Stimson, Diary, 12/28/30; for the second quote, see ibid., 11/4/30.

355   *Respondents . . . endorsed repeal: The Literary Digest* published returns to its poll results over three issues: 2/20, 2/27, and 3/5, 1932.

356   *"If the Democratic platform":* MacLafferty, Diary, 3/6/32; for the Hoover quote, see ibid., 3/4/32.

356   *He changed his mind:* Joslin, "Memoranda: Prohibition," Diary, 4/1/32.

356   *"He was afraid":* Lippmann, 6/16/32, in *Interpretations*, p. 294.

356   *"That convention is dripping wet":* Joslin, Diary, 6/13/32.

356   *the president was on the phone:* Ibid. In his entry for June 14, for example, Joslin reports that Hoover "burned up the wire to Chicago all day and into the night." For the official line that the White House remained "entirely neutral," see *NYT*, 5/25/32, 6/9/32.

357   *"It is wet and dry":* NYT, 6/15/32; for the editorial, see 6/17/32; for Mencken, see Ritchie, *Electing FDR*, p. 98.

357   *"If the convention goes":* Joslin, Diary, 6/14/32.

357   *"We want repeal":* NYT, 6/16/32.

357   *"Well it wasn't exactly":* Joslin, Diary, 6/16/32.

358   *"This convention wants":* NYT, 7/3/32.

358   *"forthright and bold":* NYT, 7/4/32.

359   *"If the president will refrain":* NYT, 5/14/32.

359   *"the most gigantic":* Hoover statement on relief legislation, 7/6/32.

359   *"Well, the administration":* For Glass's commentary, see Hamlin, Diary, "Commentary on Carter Glass," 7/13/32, Vol. 21, p. 71. For coverage of this particular amendment, see *NYT*, 7/12/32, 7/14/32.

360   *"a gigantic centralized":* Hoover Statement About Signing the Emergency Relief and Construction Act of 1932, 7/17/32.

360   *"The president is losing":* Joslin, Diary, 3/16/32.

360   *"It is exasperating":* Ibid., 3/22/32.

361   *Meyer was engaged:* From January through July 1932, Meyer attended seventy-eight of eighty meetings of the Fed Board and those of its executive committee. Butkiewicz, "Eugene Meyer and the Great Contraction," p. 36.

361   *the financier was so "perplexed":* Hamlin, Diary, 7/6/32.

361 *"was not abler"*: Ibid.

361 *"Not a member"*: Ibid., 2/12/32.

361 *"had no time"*: Ibid., 5/31/32, 5/26/32.

362 *"for having set up"*: Jones, *Fifty Billion Dollars*, p. 517.

363 *Adolph Miller said:* Miller's call for committees to stoke credit in each Fed district is recorded in Hamlin, Diary, 5/17/32.

363 *"called together"*: NYT, 5/20/32.

363 *"Something has evidently speeded"*: Hamlin, Diary, 5/20/32.

363 *"I am much"*: Hoover press conference, 5/20/32.

363 *"Hoover has stolen"*: Hamlin, Diary, 5/20/32.

363 *"Hoover is a glutton"*: Ibid., 5/31/32. There are multiple entries in the Hamlin Diary Digest; commentaries on this episode are grouped under the headings "Governor's, Open Market Policy," and "Hoover, President," and then further broken down by date.

364 *"Hoover tries to run"*: Hamlin, Diary, 5/23/32.

364 *"loud, angry tones"*: Agnes Meyer's notes are reproduced in Pusey, *Eugene Meyer*, p. 222.

365 *"The only trouble"*: Mark Sullivan Jr. OH.

TWENTY-ONE: EVIL MAGIC

367 *"I don't want to appear"*: Joslin, Diary, 6/19/32.

368 *Glassford had to assign:* For police protection for departing veterans, see Lisio, *President and Protest*, p. 123. For Hoover's appropriation of transit funds, see Hoover to Speaker of the House, 6/6/32.

369 *Hoover's role went untold:* Lisio, *President and Protest*, pp. 127–32.

370 *"declare war"*: Ibid., p. 148.

370 *Waters told reporters:* NYT, 7/28/32.

371 *"It is high time"*: NYT, 7/29/32.

371 *"mad, seething, howling"*: Grand Jury testimony of D.C. police Lt. Ira Keck, quoted in Lisio, *President and Protest*, p. 182.

372 *Hoover moved with caution:* This account is based largely on the careful exposition of Lisio, *President and Protest*, along with my review of several of the sources he cites, including the communications between Hoover and the District Commissioners, reproduced by the Hoover Library at Hooveronline. See also Joslin, *Hoover Off the Record*, pp. 266–80.

373 *"didn't want to see"*: Hurley quoted in W. L. White, "Story of a Smear," *Reader's Digest* 59 (December 1951), p. 53, cited in Lisio, *President and Protest*, p. 201. See also Joslin, *Hoover Off the Record*, p. 268.

373 *"highly inappropriate"*: Eisenhower, *At Ease*, p. 216, quoted in Lisio, *President and Protest*, p. 193.

373 *"Now here's a general"*: George Drescher OH. Drescher, a Secret Service agent, overheard parts of the conversation—though he did not hear what MacArthur told Hoover. Cited in Lisio, *President and Protest*, pp. 197–98.

374 *"a rotten choice"*: Campbell Hodges, Diary, 8/6/30.

374 *"is to be the signal"*: Report by Conrad Laza, assistant chief of staff, G-2, 2 Corps, 7/5/32, quoted in Lisio, *President and Protest*, p. 192.

374 *"a considerable part"*: Hoover press statement, 7/28/32.

375 *"had orders from the Chief Executive"*: Glassford quoted MacArthur in a newspaper account he authored; the quote is given in Lisio, *President and Protest*, p. 204.

376 *"he did not want"*: Eisenhower tells the story in his autobiography, *At Ease*, p. 217.

376 *"explained the situation"*: The quote is from the memoir of General George Van Horne Moseley, assistant chief of staff, given by Lisio, *President and Protest*, p. 212.

376 *"The rioters lost heart"*: MacArthur to Hoover, n.d., quoted in Joslin, *Hoover Off the Record*, p. 275.

376 *"It was a pitiful scene"*: Eisenhower, *At Ease*, p. 217, quoted in Lisio, *President and Protest*, p. 213.

377 *"There were, in my opinion"*: MacArthur statement to the press 7/28/32, in *Public Papers of the Presidents of the United States: Herbert Hoover, 1932–33*, p. 246.

377 *"a scandal"*: NYT, 7/29/30; the subsequent quotes appear in an Associated Press sampling of editorial comment nationwide, which was "practically unanimous in expressing the opinion that President Hoover was justified in his course." *NYT*, 7/30/32.

378 *"He bawled MacArthur out"*: F. Trubee Davison OH. Davison was an aviator and an assistant secretary of war under Patrick Hurley.

378 *"I know you disobeyed"*: Arthur Curtice OH. Curtice was a petroleum engineer who met and worked with Hoover after his presidency. Donald Lisio quotes Curtice and Davison in *President and Protest*, pp. 226–29.

379 *"A challenge to the authority"*: Hoover press conference, 7/29/32.

379 *"subversive influences"*: Hoover to Luther Reichelderfer, 7/29/32, in Myers, ed., *State Papers*, II:244.

380 he had not, in fact, requested: Glassford's accusation is in *NYT*, 7/30/32.

380 *"those who were responsible"*: NYT, 7/30/32.

380 *"it would be bragging"*: Hurley phone memo, 7/30/32, in Subject File, World War Veterans, Bonus Army—Reports/Depositions—HHPL, cited in Lisio, *President and Protest*, p. 234.

382 *"scenes from a nightmare"*: Tugwell, *Brains Trust*, p. 358.

383 *"Herbert Hoover could have"*: Rosen, *Hoover, Roosevelt, and the Brains Trust*, p. 308.

383 *"The thing to do"*: Joslin, Diary, 7/30/32.

384 *"every possible effort"*: Henry J. Allen to Joslin, 8/24/32. A former Kansas senator

and governor, Allen was then serving as director of publicity for the Republican National Committee.

384 *"This statement is":* Hoover to Eugene Meyer, 7/23/32, printed in full Hamlin, Diary, subject heading "Federal Reserve Discounts," p. 82.

385 *"invading forces":* Hoover address to the Federal Reserve District Banking and Industrial Committees, 8/26/32.

386 *"one might have believed":* NYT, 8/28/32.

386 *"a purely politial conference":* Hamlin, Diary, 8/31/32.

386 *"In 1932":* Tugwell, *Brains Trust*, p. 353.

TWENTY-TWO: PRESIDENT REJECT

387 *"No, not at all":* Joslin, Diary, 5/14/32.

389 *five major speeches:* Ibid., 7/20/32.

389 *"He said the trouble":* Stimson, Diary, 7/19/32.

389 *"What do you mean?":* Joslin, Diary, 9/7/32.

390 *"It is getting to be":* Stimson, Diary, 8/20/32.

390 *"a dreadful shock":* Ibid., 9/6/32.

391 *"The president has the":* Joslin, Diary, 8/21/32.

392 *"the bitter personal hatred":* Ted Clark discussed press relations with the Hoover administration over a series of letters. These quotes derive from Clark to Coolidge, 9/16/32, 11/11/32, 11/14/32, Clark Papers, LOC.

393 *"They have no respect":* Joslin, Diary, 8/8/32.

393 *"There is almost":* Ibid., 7/23/32.

394 *"He was none too hospitable":* Ibid., 8/20/33.

394 *"feeling pretty depressed":* Joel Boone, Memoir. He discusses the Rapidan press day in his oral history, p. 347, and his Memoirs, at pp. 1,220–23.

394 *"We are opposed by":* Joslin, Diary, 10/8/32.

395 *"This means":* Pomerene quoted in Olson, *Hoover and the RFC*, p. 80.

395 *"until we know":* NYT, 8/5/32.

395 *"Our people are not":* Pinchot letter quoted in Bernstein, *Lean Years*, p. 472.

395 *"eminent, patriotic, and sympathetic men":* NYT, 9/21/32.

396 *"in giving help":* Pinchot to Pomerence, 9/24/32, quoted in Olson, *Hoover and the RFC*, p. 84.

397 *"mile upon mile":* Wagner in *The Washington Post*, 10/10/32, quoted in ibid., p. 78.

397 *"To my surprise":* Stimson, Diary, 8/5/32.

398 *"Buying California for Hoover":* The Nation, 10/26/32, quoted in Olson, *Hoover and the RFC*, p. 80.

398 *Hoover fought the provision:* For Hoover's version of the negotiations on the publication clause, see Hoover, *Memoirs*, III:110–11.

398   *"not to save a few"*: Hoover, Acceptance Address, 8/11/32.

399   *"self-interested inexactitude"*: Hoover address in Indianapolis, 10/28/32.

399   *Cassius Clay facing Sonny Liston:* Clay had yet to change his name to Muhammad Ali when he faced Liston in February 1964.

399   *The one time he did:* Donald Ritchie gives the story of Roosevelt writing and discarding his speech in *Electing FDR*, p. 137.

399   *"Bold, persistent experimentation"*: Roosevelt address at Oglethorpe University, 5/22/32.

400   *"revolved around personal attacks"*: Hoover, *Memoirs*, III:234.

400   *"I started this letter"*: LHH to "Herbert and Allan—and their children!," July 1932.

402   *"Nobody disputed"*: Stimson, Diary, 9/25/32.

403   *"mistaken statements"*: For the first quote, see Hoover's speech at Cleveland, 10/15/32; for the second, see his statement at Fort Wayne, 10/5/32.

403   *"which has saved"*: Hoover speech at Des Moines, 10/4/32.

403   *"This is more than"*: Hoover address at Madison Square Garden, 10/31/.

403   *"Our last frontier"*: Roosevelt address at the Commonwealth Club, 9/23/32.

404   *"The grass will grow"*: This unfortunate bit of hyperbole was the result of Hoover for once accepting help in composing a speech. The phrase was proposed by Ted Joslin, as he claimed in his Diary, 11/1/32. He, in turn, borrowed the line from the "Cross of Gold" speech of William Jennings Bryan, who warned, in 1896, "Destroy our farms and the grass will grow in the streets of every city in the country" (Ritchie, *Electing FDR*, p. 147). It is not known if Hoover knew of the Bryan reference.

404   *"At this time"*: Joslin, Diary, memorandum, 9/30–10/1/32. For "wet stones," see the entry of 9/22/32.

404   *"To prevent times"*: *Literary Digest*, 11/5/32.

405   *Hoover asked Ogden Mills:* For Ogden Mills, see Joslin, Diary, 10/17/32; for J. P. Morgan, see ibid., 10/19/32.

405   *"went into action"*: Joslin, Diary, 11/1/32.

405   *"Bert, I have been waiting"*: Lou recounted this conversation to Joel Boone, who recorded it in his Memoirs, p. 1,304. He put her version of her verbatim statements in quotation marks.

406   *"the face of a human"*: Editorial, *Washington Evening Star*, 9/27/32, quoted in ibid., p. 1,247.

406   *"If you don't give me"*: Ritchie, *Electing FDR*, p. 143.

407   *"Why don't they make"*: Edmund Starling, *Starling of the White House*, p. 300. Joel Boone recounts the St. Paul speech in his Memoirs, p. 1,310; see also Ritchie, *Electing FDR*, p. 155.

407   *"I thought I was"*: George Drescher OH.

408   *"All informed observers"*: TRB in *The New Republic*, 11/16/32.

TWENTY-THREE: INTERREGNUM

409 *"Are you up"*: Boone, Memoirs, p. 1,323.

411 *"full of fight"*: Stimson, Diary, 11/10/32.

412 *"The president still has"*: Ibid., 11/12/32.

412 *"It took away"*: Ibid., 11/13/32.

412 *"The political campaign"*: Hoover address, in Glendale California, 11/12/32.

413 *Roosevelt bore little of*: For Roosevelt's thinking at the time, see Schlesinger, *Crisis of the Old Order*, pp. 442–43.

413 *"wholly informal and personal"*: FDR's answer to Hoover, 11/14/32, quoted in Henry, *Presidential Transitions*, p. 287.

413 *Twice he scheduled*: For the canceled press conferences, see Pollard, *Presidents and the Press*, p. 769.

413 *"considerable nervousness"*: Irwin "Ike" Hoover, *42 Years in the White House*, p. 221.

413 *"He has allowed himself"*: Stimson, Diary, 11/22/32.

414 *"It was clear that we"*: Moley, *After Seven Years*, p. 73.

414 *"You must have sat"*: Ibid., p. 77.

415 *"the great causes"*: Hoover statement, Upon the War Debts, 11/23/32.

415 *"existing agencies"*: Hoover quotes the Roosevelt statement in his *Memoirs*, III:183.

415 *"not wholly cooperative"*: Ibid., p. 182.

415 *"It's not my baby"*: NYT, 11/24/32. The remark was widely published (*Detroit Free Press*, Baltimore *Sun*) but sourced only to "dispatches"; it was published as "not his baby" but, if Roosevelt did utter the phrase, it seems likely he referred to "my" baby, and not "his."

416 *"best night's sleep"*: Hiltzik, *Colossus*, p. 302.

416 *"I wonder if you have not"*: Hoover's note is transcribed in Joslin, Diary, 11/19/32.

417 *"great private agencies"*: Hoover, State of Union address, 12/6/32.

418 *"You will expect me"*: Hoover address to the Gridiron Club, 12/10/32.

419 *"I did not want him"*: Stimson, Diary, 12/22/32.

420 *"Governor Roosevelt considers"*: Hoover press statement, 12/22/32.

420 *"addressing complicated notes"*: Lippmann, *New York Herald Tribune*, 12/28/32, quoted in Henry, *Presidential Transitions*, p. 298.

420 *"Why doesn't Harry"*: Stimson, Diary, 12/22/33, quoted in ibid., p. 299.

420 *"He was against it"*: Ibid., 12/23/32.

421 *"a very dangerous and contrary man"*: Ibid., 1/3/33, quoted in Henry, *Presidential Transitions*, p. 145.

421 *he insisted on*: Arrangements for the phone conference were noted by Joslin in his Diary, 1/4/33.

422 *"People stood as he"*: NYT, 1/8/33.

422 *"assume leadership"*: Joslin, Diary, 1/9/33.

422 *"The conferees could not agree"*: NYT, 1/9/33.

423 *"For the first time"*: Timmons, *Garner of Texas*, p. 172.

423 *In Hoover's telling*: Hoover, *Memoirs*, III:192–93.

423 *"I have consistently said"*: Jones, *Fifty Billion Dollars*, p. 83.

423 *"is destroying the usefulness"*: Hoover, Message to Congress, 2/20/33.

424 *"A Republican president"*: Smith, *Carter Glass*, 327–29.

424 *"violent speech in opposition"*: NYT, 1/6/33.

424 *"the most irresponsible"*: Johnson to McClatchy, 1/16/32, quoted in Schwarz, *Interregnum of Despair*, p. 218.

425 *Watson said later*: Watson says it was he who inspired the Long filibuster; see *As I Knew Them*, pp. 304–6.

425 *"The Senate can"*: Joslin, *Hoover Off the Record*, p. 340.

425 *"Our game"*: Joslin, Diary, 1/17/33.

426 *"We are getting"*: Stimson and Bundy, *On Active Service*, p. 293.

426 *"I will never"*: Ibid., 1/19/33.

427 *"close to death"*: Moley quoted in Schlesinger, *Crisis of the Old Order*, p. 448.

427 *"acutely the sense"*: Memorandum by Herbert Feis, 1/24/32, 1/27/32, quoted in Morison, *Turmoil and Tradition*, p. 441.

TWENTY-FOUR: THE SOUND OF CRASHING BANKS

429 *Hoover possessed IRS data*: Joslin, Diary, 2/4/33.

430 *"no safer place"*: Kennedy, *Banking Crisis of 1933*, pp. 75–76.

430 *Commodity prices stopped falling*: Among the many authorities to remark on the mini-recovery of 1932, see Kindleberger, *World in Depression*, p. 194; and Olson, *Hoover and the RFC*, p. 92.

431 *"The sum of all these"*: Hoover, *Memoirs*, III:197.

431 *"The next blow"*: Ibid., p. 199.

432 *"obviously illusory"*: Moley, *After Seven Years*, p. 105.

432 *"They have willed"*: Keynes, "The End of the Gold Standard," 9/27/31, in *Essays in Persuasion*, p. 288.

432 *"There is no doubt"*: Hoover press conference, 1/25/33.

432 *lawmakers began a new push*: For the rising pressure from the farm states, see Eichengreen, *Golden Fetters*, p. 327. See also Wigmore, "Bank Holiday," p. 739.

433 *"The whole question"*: *Commercial and Financial Chronicle*, quoted in Wigmore, "Bank Holiday," p. 740.

433 *"This movement represents"*: George Leslie Harrison, 2/23/33, quoted in Friedman and Schwartz, *Great Contraction*, p. 54, n. 60. For aggregate totals on the January drain on bank deposits, see p. 53.

434 *In July 1932*: Jesse Jones gives details on the Ford interests in Union Guardian, and the initial RFC loans, in *Fifty Billion Dollars*, p. 58.

434 *195 bank failures in Michigan:* Ibid., p. 59; see also Awalt, "Recollections," p. 350.

434 *the president was engaged "unceasingly":* Hoover sketched out his intervention in the Detroit banking crisis in his *Memoirs*, III:206–7. He supplied further detail in an August 1933 telegram to a Wayne County prosecutor looking into the entire episode, filed at the HHPL under Hoover, Bible (a collection of key documents), #2144. Hoover used the term "unceasingly" in the telegram; the document is cited in Barnard, *Independent Man*, p. 225. I also consulted White House telephone logs in piecing together this account.

435 *"I will shout":* Barnard, *Independent Man*, p. 226.

436 *"ranted all over":* The White House conference over the Detroit bank bailout is described in close and often conflicting detail in Kennedy, *Banking Crisis*; Jones, *Fifty Billion Dollars*; Sullivan, *Prelude to Panic*; and Barnard, *Independent Man*; as well as by Hoover himself. The first quote is from *Fifty Billion Dollars*, p. 60; the second is from Hoover's *Memoirs*, III:206.

436 *"Why should the RFC":* Hoover, *Memoirs*, III:207, n. 4. This is not from his own recollection; instead he quotes Malcolm Bingay, editor of the *Detroit Free Press*, who based his account on interviews with Couzens.

436 *"If 800,000 small bank":* Hoover, *Memoirs*, III:207; see also Barnard, *Independent Man*, p. 227.

436 *"Turn them off":* Joslin, Diary, 2/9/33.

436 *Hoover called the automaker:* The phone call is mentioned in Kennedy, *Banking Crisis*, p. 88; and Jones, *Fifty Billion Dollars*, p. 62. White House logs show Hoover made the call at 9 p.m.

437 *"For once in his life":* Jones, *Fifty Billion Dollars*, p. 64.

437 *"inspecting his fields":* Barnard, *Independent Man*, p. 228.

437 *"You say all of these":* Roy Chapin and Arthur Ballantine, "Statement of Interview with Henry Ford," 2/13/33, in Ballantine Papers—Subject File—Banking Crisis of 1933, HHPL.

438 *RFC officials asked Michigan's governor:* There are several versions of how the decision was taken to call for a banking holiday in Michigan, but the most authoritative is given by Francis Gloyd Awalt, serving at the time as acting comptroller of the currency. Awalt was in the meetings and published his account, "Recollections of the Banking Crisis in 1933," in 1969.

439 *"Hello, Mr. Tschirky":* NYT, 2/14/33.

439 *"greatly disturbed":* Rickard, Diary, 2/13/33.

439 *"maintained one Gibraltar":* Hoover, Lincoln Day Address, 2/13/33.

441 *"the step was not taken":* Keynes, "The End of the Gold Standard," 9/27/31, in *Essays in Persuasion*, p. 288.

443 *"We're not going to throw":* Moley, *After Seven Years*, p. 119. Moley gives the quotes from both Roosevelt and Glass.

443 *"controlled reflation": Washington Herald*, 1/30/33, quoted in Myers and Newton, eds., *Hoover Administration*, p. 335.

444 *"were not mutually congenial"*: Jones, *Fifty Billion Dollars*, p. 521.

444 *"A most critical situation"*: Hoover to Roosevelt, 2/17/33, in ibid., p. 338.

445 *Roosevelt took the document*: The curious story of the delivery of Hoover's letter is given in Moley, *After Seven Years*, p. 140.

445 *"I realize that if"*: Hoover to Senator David A. Reed, 2/20/33, in ibid., p. 341.

446 *he later termed it "cheeky"*: Alter, *Defining Moment*, p. 179.

446 *"extraordinary calm"*: Moley, *After Seven Years*, p. 142.

446 *"positively no statement"*: Myers and Newton, eds., *Hoover Administration*, p. 344.

446 *"I wish to leave"*: Hoover to Federal Reserve Board, 2/22/33, in ibid., p. 355.

446 *"not desire to make"*: Eugene Meyer to Hoover, 2/25/33, in ibid., p. 357.

446 *"There is nothing"*: Joslin, Diary, 2/25/33.

447 *"the board is not"*: Hoover to Federal Reserve Board, 2/28/33, in Myers and Newton, eds., *Hoover Administration*, p. 359.

447 *"evidently designed"*: Hamlin, Diary, 3/1/33, p. 131.

447 *"create greater difficulty"*: Eugene Meyer to Hoover, 3/2/33, in Myers and Newton, eds., *Hoover Administration*, p. 362.

448 *"I won't go it alone"*: Joslin, Diary, 3/3/33.

448 *"all stiff, bruised and wounded"*: Cordery, *Alice*, p. 370.

448 *"No one seemed comfortable"*: Irwin "Ike" Hoover, *42 Years in the White House*, p. 227.

449 *"Perhaps it was"*: Moley, *After Seven Years*, p. 146. Moley also recounts the story of Ike Hoover tipping Roosevelt off to Hoover's ambush.

449 *"How horrible it is"*: Joel Boone, OH, p. 253. Boone was in the room and transcribed the conversation verbatim.

449 *"begged him both as"*: Hamlin, Diary, "Bank holiday," 3/3/33.

449 *Hoover rejected the appeal bitterly*: Ibid., Hamlin writes that "Hoover was evidently very angry," and in a separate entry March 8 quotes Adolph Miller describing Hoover as "bitterly angry with Governor Meyer"; see also Pusey, *Eugene Meyer*, p. 234.

450 *"Planning to close them"*: Smith, *Carter Glass*, p. 342.

450 *"They want to jockey"*: Joslin, Diary, 3/3/33.

450 *At 12:30 a.m.*: The midnight delivery and Hoover's response are all detailed in Hamlin, Diary, "Bank Holiday," 3/2–3/4/33. The quote is at 3/4, p. 26.

451 *"He looked like"*: William J. Hopkins OH.

451 *"My husband will come back"*: Lillian Rogers Parks OH.

452 *"I had all the security"*: Smith, *Uncommon Man*, p. 164.

452 *"Hard on Hoover"*: Agnes Meyer Diary, COHC.

EPILOGUE

454   *he never really had the chance:* NYT, 3/8/33.

455   *"just take it easy":* NYT, 3/17/33.

455   *"Let me assert":* FDR, Inaugural Address, 3/4/33.

455   *"Ceaseless effort must be":* Hoover, Lincoln Day address, 2/12/33.

456   *"Nothing is to be":* Thoreau quoted by historian John Buescher in a post at http://
      teachinghistory.org/history-content/ask-a-historian/24468.

456   *"the thing to be feared":* NYT, 2/9/31, quoted in Alter, *Defining Moment*, p. 211.

456   *"Practically everybody feels better already":* New York *Daily News*, 3/5/33, quoted
      in ibid., p. 221.

456   *"transformed . . . into a gay place":* Ibid., p. 221.

457   *"The rulers of":* FDR Inaugural, 3/4/33.

458   *a vague plan to issue scrip:* NYT, 3/7/33, 3/9/33.

458   *like his boss:* Francis Awalt, serving in March 1933 as the acting comptroller of
      the currency, gave an inside account of the critical hours of the banking crisis.
      When at one point he and Woodin stopped by the White House to seek direc-
      tion from Roosevelt, the new president said simply that "he knew nothing about
      the situation and that it was a matter for our determination." It was a distinct
      change in tone from President Hoover, who rarely delegated decisions on such
      core tasks. Awalt tells the story in "Recollections of the Banking Crisis in 1933."
      The anecdote is given at p. 369.

459   *"the wall of hostility":* Ibid., p. 370.

459   *"But I am not working":* Mills to Larry Richey, telephone transcripts, 3/9/33,
      Hoover Papers—Post-Presidential Individual Correspondence File—Mills,
      Ogden; HHPL.

460   *Woodin proclaimed himself "delighted":* NYT, 3/14/33.

460   *federal tax offices were suddenly inundated:* NYT, 3/14/33.

460   *"a gold stampede":* NYT, 3/11/33.

460   *Newspaper advertising rose "decidedly":* NYT, 3/14/33.

460   *commodity prices "shot skyward":* NYT, 3/17/33.

460   *"I have never seen":* NYT, 3/14/33.

461   *"except for the expertness":* Moley quoted in Kennedy, *Banking Crisis*, p. 156.

461   *"lonely beyond measure":* Rickard, Diary, quoted in Smith, *Uncommon Man*,
      p. 173.

462   *Hoover logged ten thousand miles:* Wert, *Fishing President*, p. 221.

462   *"a policy of public silence":* Best, "Herbert Hoover, 1933–1941," in *Herbert Hoover
      Reassessed*, p. 227.

462   *"call to arms":* Hoover public letter, March 1935, quoted in ibid., pp. 231–32.

463   *"the old, everlasting principles":* Lou Hoover to Alice Dickson, 12/28/35, quoted in
      Young, *Lou Henry Hoover*, p. 174.

463 *"the only voice"*: Hoover to A. H. Kirchofer, 4/22/35, quoted in Best, "Herbert Hoover, 1933–1941," in *Herbert Hoover Reassessed*, p. 233.

463 *he would run again:* By October 1935 Edgar Rickard believed Hoover to be "dead set" on the Republican nomination. See ibid., p. 234.

464 *"The great mass of the"*: White to Newton, 6/26/35, quoted in ibid., p. 233.

465 *"You remember the closed banks"*: Roosevelt address to the Teamsters dinner, Washington, 9/23/44.

466 *"In all the history"*: Hoover address on free enterprise, 11/5/38, quoted in Hinshaw, *American Quaker*, p. 445.

466 *Hitler's principal rivalry lay:* Hoover's views are summarized by historian George Nash in his extended introduction to Hoover's magnum opus, *Freedom Betrayed*, pp. lii–liv. See also Hoover's 2/11/46 memorandum, presented in the appendix of that volume as "Document 8," p. 830.

467 *"The president always"*: Smith, *Uncommon Man*, p. 365.

467 *Continuing in residence:* Hoover's days at the Waldorf suite are described in Smith, *Uncommon Man*, pp. 292–93.

468 *Dewey . . . offered to appoint Hoover:* Ibid., p. 380.

BIBLIOGRAPHY

HOOVER WRITINGS AND PAPERS

The public papers of Herbert Hoover, along with those of every president of the modern era, are now available online, in fact from multiple repositories. The source I primarily used for the Hoover papers was the American Presidency Project, an archive maintained free for public use by the University of California at Santa Barbara. The collection makes available and searchable all news conferences and all public statements made during the president's term. Hoover speeches and papers are also collected by the Herbert Hoover Presidential Library and available online at http://www.hoover.archives.gov/; they will be identified here by date.

In addition to these valuable online resources, I made use of several other troves of Hoover statements made before and after his presidency, and his three-volume memoirs.

Below is the roster of Hoover writings and papers I consulted.

Hoover, Herbert.   *American Individualism* (1922).

————.   *The Memoirs of Herbert Hoover*: (1952)

————.   *I: Years of Adventure, 1874–1920*

                                   II: The Cabinet and the Presidency, 1920–1933.

                                   III: The Great Depression, 1929–1941.

————.   *The Ordeal of Woodrow Wilson* (1958)

————.   *Fishing for Fun—And to Wash Your Soul* (1963)

Hoover, Herbert with George H. Nash.   *Freedom Betrayed: Herbert Hoover's Secret History of World War II and Its Aftermath* (2011)

Myers, William Starr, ed. *The State Papers and Other Public Writings of Herbert Hoover*, 2 vols. (1934).

Myers, William S., and Walter H. Newton, eds. *The Hoover Administration: A Documented Narrative* (1936).

Wilbur, Ray Lyman, ed. *The New Day: Campaign Speeches of Herbert Hoover* (1928).

Wilbur, Ray L., and Arthur M. Hyde. *The Hoover Policies* (1937).

OTHER PAPERS CONSULTED

Library of Congress

> Raymond Clapper
> Edward "Ted" Clark
> Ogden Mills

Columbia University

> George Leslie Harrison

Herbert Hoover Presidential Library and Museum

> Lou Henry Hoover
> Lewis Strauss

Huntington Library

> Ralph Arnold

PRINCIPAL DIARIES

Joel Boone (HHPL)

Charles S. Hamlin (Library of Congress)

Campbell Hodges (HHPL)

Ted Joslin (HHPL)

Agnes Meyer (Her diary is filed as an appendix to the oral history interview of her husband, Eugene, at the COHC.)

James MacLafferty (Hoover Institution, Stanford University, Stanford, California)

Edgar Rickard (HHPL)

Henry L. Stimson (Yale University)

ORAL HISTORIES

The oral histories used in this book are collected at the Hoover Presidential Library, unless otherwise noted. Most are also available online from the Miller Center of Public Affairs at the University of Virginia (Millercenter.org).

LETTERS

Burke, Robert E. *The Diary Letters of Hiram Johnson, 1917–1945* (1983).

Johnson, Walter, ed. *Selected Letters of William Allen White, 1899–1943* (1968).

Public Records Office, Foreign Office, "Correspondence," London.

BOOKS

Ahamed, Liaquat. *Lords of Finance: The Bankers Who Broke the World* (2009).

Alter, Jonathan. *The Defining Moment: FDR's Hundred Days and the Triumph of Hope* (2006).

Ashby, LeRoy. *The Spearless Leader: Senator Borah and the Progressive Movement in the 1920s* (1972).

Baker, Leonard. *Back to Back: The Duel Between FDR and the Supreme Court* (1967).

Barber, William J. *From New Era to New Deal: Herbert Hoover, the Economists, and American Economic Policy, 1921 to 1933* (1985).

Barnard, Harry. *Independent Man: The Life of Senator James Couzens* (2002).

Baruch, Bernard. *The Public Years: My Own Story* (1960).

Bernays, Edward. *Biography of an Idea: Memoirs of Public Relations Counsel Edward L. Bernays* (1965).

Bernstein, Irving. *The Lean Years: A History of the American Worker, 1920–1933* (1966).

Brown, Anthony Cave. *The Last Hero: Wild Bill Donovan* (1982).

Brown, Dorothy M. *Mabel Walker Willebrandt: A Study in Power, Loyalty, and Law* (1984).

Bruner, Robert, and Sean Carr. *The Panic of 1907: Lessons Learned from the Market's Perfect Storm* (2007).

Burner, David. *Herbert Hoover: A Public Life* (1979).

Cannadine, David. *Mellon: An American Life* (2006).

Chamberlain, Lawrence H. *The President, Congress, and Legislation* (1946).

Chambers, Clarke A. *Seedtime of Reform: American Social Service and Social Action, 1918–1933* (1963, 1967).

Chandler, Lester. *American Monetary Policy: 1928–1941* (1971).

Clements, Kendrick A. *The Life of Herbert Hoover: Imperfect Visionary, 1918–1928* (2010).

Cordery, Stacy A. *Alice: Alice Roosevelt Longworth, From White House Princess to Washington Power Broker* (2007).

Davis, Kenneth S. *FDR: The New York Years, 1928–1933* (1979).

Dorwart, Jeffrey. *Conflict of Duty: The U.S. Navy's Intelligence Dilemma, 1919–1945* (1983).

Duncan, Joseph W., and William C. Shelton. *Revolution in United States Government Statistics, 1926–1976* (1978).

Dunlop, Richard. *Donovan: America's Master Spy* (1982).

Egan, Timothy. *The Worst Hard Time: The Untold Story of Those Who Survived the Great American Dust Bowl* (2005).

Eichengreen, Barry. *Golden Fetters: The Gold Standard and the Great Depression, 1919–1939* (1992).

Eisenhower, Dwight D. *At Ease: Stories I Tell to Friends* (1967).

Ellis, Edward Robb. *A Nation in Torment: The Great American Depression, 1929–1939* (1970).

Fausold, Martin. *The Presidency of Herbert C. Hoover* (1974).

Friedel, Frank. *1933: Characters in Crisis* (1966).

Friedman, Milton, and Anna Jacobson Schwartz. *The Great Contraction, 1929–1933* (1963).

Furman, Bess. *Washington By-line: The Personal History of a Newspaperwoman* (1949).

Gaddis, Vincent. *Herbert Hoover, Unemployment, and the Public Sphere: A Conceptual History, 1919–1933* (2005).

Galbraith, John Kenneth. *The Great Crash: 1929* (1954).

Goldberg, Joseph P., and William P. Moye. *The First Hundred Years of the Bureau of Labor Statistics* (1985).

Goldman, Ralph Morris. *The National Party Chairmen and Committees: Factionalism at the Top* (1990).

Hayes, Erving Paul. *Activities of the President's Emergency Committee for Employment* (1936).

Heineman, Kenneth J. *A Catholic New Deal: Religion and Reform in Depression Pittsburgh* (2010).

Henry, Darwin L. *Presidential Transitions* (1960).

Hiltzik, Michael. *Colossus: Hoover Dam and the Making of the American Century* (2010).

Himmelberg, Robert F. *Origins of the National Recovery Administration: Business, Government, and the Trade Association Issue, 1921–1933* (1993).

Hinshaw, David. *Herbert Hoover: American Quaker* (1950).

Hoover, Irwin "Ike." *42 Years in the White House* (1934).

Hubbard, Preston J. *Origins of the TVA: The Muscle Shoals Controversy, 1920–1932* (1961).

Irwin, Douglas A. *Peddling Protectionism: Smoot-Hawley and the Great Depression* (2011).

Johnson, Claudius O. *Borah of Idaho* (1936).

Jones, Jesse, with Edward Angly. *Fifty Billion Dollars: My Thirteen Years with the RFC (1932–1945)* (1951).

Joslin, Theodore G. *Hoover Off the Record* (1934).

Kennedy, David M. *Freedom from Fear: The American People in Depression and War, 1929–1945* (1999).

Kennedy, Susan Estabrook. *The Banking Crisis of 1933* (1973).

Keynes, John Maynard. *The Economic Consequences of the Peace* (1920).

———. *Essays in Persuasion* (1931).

Kindleberger, Charles P. *The World in Depression, 1929–1939* (1986).

Klingaman, William A. *1929: The Year of the Crash* (1989).

Lambert, Darwin. *Herbert Hoover's Hideaway: The Story of Camp Hoover on the Rapidan River in Shenandoah National Park* (1971).

Lane, Rose Wilder. *The Making of Herbert Hoover* (1920).

Leuchtenburg, William E. *Herbert Hoover* (2009).

Lichtman, Allan J. *Prejudice and the Old Politics: The Presidential Election of 1928* (1979).

Liebovich, Louis W. *Bylines in Despair: Herbert Hoover, the Great Depression, and the U.S. News Media* (1994).

Lippmann, Walter. *Interpretations, 1931–1932.* Allan Nevins, ed. (1932).

Lisio, Donald J. *The President and Protest: Hoover, MacArthur, and the Bonus Riot* (1974).

———. *Hoover, Blacks, and Lily-Whites: A Study of Southern Strategies* (1985).

Lloyd, Craig. *Aggressive Introvert: Herbert Hoover and Public Relations Management, 1921–1932* (1973).

Longworth, Alice Roosevelt. *Crowded Hours: Reminiscences of Alice Roosevelt Longworth* (1933).

Lower, Richard Coke. *A Bloc of One: The Political Career of Hiram W. Johnson* (1993).

Lyons, Eugene. *The Herbert Hoover Story* (1959).

Mason, Alpheus. *Harlan Fiske Stone: Pillar of the Law* (1956).

McClean, Hulda Hoover. *Hulda's World: A Chronicle of Hulda Minthorn Hoover, 1848–1884* (1989).

McCoy, Donald R. *Calvin Coolidge: The Quiet President* (1967).

McElvaine, Robert S. *The Great Depression: America, 1929–1941* (1984).

Medved, Michael. *The Shadow Presidents: The Secret History of the Chief Executives and Their Top Aides* (1979).

Michelson, Charles. *The Ghost Talks* (1944).

Moley, Ray. *After Seven Years* (1939).

Morison, Elting E. *Turmoil and Tradition: A Study of the Life and Times of Henry L. Stimson* (1960, 2003).

Morris, Edmund. *Theodore Rex* (2001).

Myers, William Starr. *The Foreign Policies of Herbert Hoover, 1929–1933* (1940).

Nash, George H. *The Life of Herbert Hoover: The Engineer, 1874–1914* (1983).

———. *The Life of Herbert Hoover: The Humanitarian, 1914–1917* (1988).

Nash, George H., ed. *Reappraising the Right: The Past and Future of American Conservatism* (2009).

Norris, George. *Fighting Liberal: The Autobiography of George W. Norris* (1945).

O'Brien, Ruth. *Workers' Paradox: The Republican Origins of New Deal Labor Policy, 1886–1935* (1998).

Okrent, Daniel. *Last Call: The Rise and Fall of Prohibition* (2010).

Olson, James Stuart. *Herbert Hoover and the Reconstruction Finance Corporation, 1931–1933* (1977).

Patenaude, Bertrand. *The Big Show in Bololand: The American Relief Expedition to Soviet Russia in the Famine of 1921* (2002).

Pearson, Drew, and Robert S. Allen. *More Merry-Go-Round* (1931).

———. *Washington Merry-Go-Round* (1932).

Peretti, Burton W. *Nightclub City: Politics and Amusement in Manhattan* (2007).

Pickett, Clarence. *For More than Bread: An Autobiographical Account of Twenty-Two Years' Work with the American Friends Service Committee* (1953).

Pollard, James E. *Presidents and the Press* (1947).

Pusey, Merlo J. *Eugene Meyer* (1963).

———. *Charles Evans Hughes* (1974).

Ritchie, Donald A. *Electing FDR: The New Deal Campaign of 1932* (2007).

Romasco, Albert U. *The Poverty of Abundance: Hoover, the Nation, the Depression* (1965).

Roosevelt, Eleanor. *This I Remember* (1949).

Rosen, Elliot. *Hoover, Roosevelt, and the Brains Trust: From Depression to New Deal* (1977).

Ross, Ishbel. *Grace Coolidge and Her Era* (1962).

Schlesinger, Arthur Jr. *The Crisis of the Old Order, 1919–1933* (1957).

Schwarz, Jordan A. *The Interregnum of Despair: Hoover, Congress, and the Depression* (1970).

Simon, James F. *FDR and Chief Justice Hughes: The President, the Supreme Court, and the Epic Battle over the New Deal* (2012).

Smith, Gene. *The Shattered Dream: Herbert Hoover and the Great Depression* (1970).

Smith, Richard Norton. *Uncommon Man: The Triumph of Herbert Hoover* (1984).

Smith, Rixey, and Norman Beasley. *Carter Glass: A Biography* (1939).

Sobel, Robert. *The Great Bull Market: Wall Street in the 1920s* (1968).

———. *The Age of Giant Corporations: A Microeconomic History of American Business, 1914–1970* (1972).

Srodes, James. *On Dupont Circle: Franklin and Eleanor Roosevelt and the Progressives Who Shaped Our World* (2012).

Starling, Edmund. *Starling of the White House: The Story of a Man Whose Secret Service Detail Guarded Five Presidents from Woodrow Wilson to Franklin D. Roosevelt* (1946).

Stein, Herbert. *The Fiscal Revolution in America* (1969).

Stimson, Henry, and McGeorge Bundy. *On Active Service in Peace and War* (1947).

Stokes, Thomas L. *Chip Off My Shoulder* (1940).

Sullivan, Lawrence. *Prelude to Panic: The Story of the Bank Holiday* (1936).

Temin, Peter. *Did Monetary Forces Cause the Great Depression?* (1976).

Timmons, Bascom. *Garner of Texas: A Personal History* (1948).

———. *Portrait of an American: Charles G. Dawes* (1953).

Tucker, Ray Thomas ("Anonymous"). *The Mirrors of 1932* (1931).

Tugwell, Rexford. *The Brains Trust: How Franklin Delano Roosevelt Got Himself Nominated and Elected President* (1968).

Warburton, Clark. *Depression, Inflation, and Monetary Policy: Selected Papers, 1945–1953* (1953).

Warren, Harris Gaylord. *Herbert Hoover and the Great Depression* (1959).

Watson, James E. *As I Knew Them: Memoirs of James E. Watson* (1936).

Wehle, Louis B. *Hidden Threads of History: Wilson Through Roosevelt* (1953).

Wert, Hal Elliott. *Hoover the Fishing President* (2005).

White, Walter E. *A Man Called White* (1948).

Wicker, Elmus. *The Banking Panics of the Great Depression* (1996).

Wilson, Joan Hoff. *Herbert Hoover: Forgotten Progressive* (1975).

Woodruff, Nan Elizabeth. *As Rare as Rain: Federal Relief in the Great Southern Drought of 1930–31* (1985).

Wueschner, Silvano A. *Charting Twentieth Century Monetary Policy: Herbert Hoover and Benjamin Strong, 1919–1927* (1999).

Young, Nancy Beck. *Lou Henry Hoover: Activist First Lady* (2004).

ARTICLES AND ACADEMIC PAPERS

Anari, Ali, James Kolari, and Joseph Mason. "Bank Asset Liquidation and the Propagation of the US Great Depression." *Journal of Money, Credit and Banking* 37 (2005): 753–73.

Arnold, Ralph. "Laying Foundation Stones," in *Southern California Quarterly* 37 (1955): 297–319.

Awalt, Francis Gloyd. "Recollections of the Banking Crisis in 1933." *Business History Review* 43 (1969): 347–71.

Bernanke, Ben. "Non-Monetary Effects of the Financial Crisis in the Propagation of the Great Depression." *The American Economic Review* 73 (1983): 257–76.

Bernstein, Barton. "Hoovergate." *American Heritage* 43 (1992): 106–10.

Bornet, Vaughn Davis. "Hoover's Planning for Unemployment and Old Age Insurance Coverage, 1921 to 1933," in John N. Schacht, ed., *The Quest for Security: Papers on the Origins and Future of the American Social Insurance System* (1982), 35–71.

Best, Gary Dean. "Herbert Hoover, 1933–1941: A Reassessment," in *Herbert Hoover*

Reassessed: Essays Commemorating the Fiftieth Anniversary of the Inauguration of Our Thirty-first President (1981).

Butkiewicz, James L. "Governor Eugene Meyer and the Great Contraction." Working Paper Series, #2005-01, Department of Economics, University of Delaware.

Cahill, James Quinten. "Herbert Hoover's Early Schooling." *Annals of Iowa* 62 (2003): 155–57.

Calomiris, Charles. "Financial Factors in the Great Depression." *Journal of Economic Perspectives* 7 (1993): 61–85.

Churchill, Winston. "The Dole." *The Saturday Evening Post*, 3/29/30, p. 6.

Cowley, Robert. "The Drought and the Dole." *American Heritage* 23 (February 1972).

Degler, Carl N. "The Ordeal of Herbert Hoover." *Yale Review* 52 (1963): 563–83.

Dougherty, Herbert Jr. "Florida and the Presidential Election of 1928." *Florida Historical Quarterly* 26 (1947): 174.

Fausold, Martin L. "President Hoover's Farm Policies." *Agricultural History* 51 (1977): 362–77.

Fisher, Irving. "The Debt-Deflation Theory of Great Depressions." *Econometrica* 1 (1933): 337–57.

Fite, Gilbert C. "The Agricultural Issues in the Presidential Campaign of 1928." *Mississippi Valley Historical Review* 37 (1931): 653–72.

Foster, William Trufant, and Waddill Catchings. "Mr. Hoover's Road to Prosperity." *Review of Reviews*, January 1930.

Friedel, Frank. "Hoover and FDR: Reminiscent Reflections," in Lee Nash, ed., *Understanding Herbert Hoover: Ten Perspectives* (1987).

Hamilton, David. "The Causes of the Banking Panic of 1930: Another View." *The Journal of Southern History* 51 (1985): 581–608.

———. "Herbert Hoover and the Great Drought of 1930." *Journal of American History* 68 (1982): 850–75.

Hard, William. "Hoover the President." *World's Work* (September 1929).

Harman, S. Palmer. "Finance." *The Nation*, 12/16/31.

Kehoe, Loretta. "The Relation of Herbert Hoover to Congress, 1929–1933." Thesis, Loyola University Chicago, 1949.

Kent, Frank. "Charles Michelson." *Scribner's* 88 (September 1930): 290.

Koerselman, Gary H. "Secretary Hoover and National Farm Policy: Problems of Leadership." *Agricultural History* 51 (1977): 393.

Lambert, C. Roger. "Herbert Hoover and Federal Farm Board Wheat." *Heritage of the Great Plains* 10 (1977): 23.

———. "Hoover and the Red Cross in the Arkansas Drought of 1930." *The Arkansas Historical Quarterly* 29 (1970): 3–19.

Lippmann, Walter. "The Peculiar Weakness of Mr. Hoover." *Harper's* 161 (1930): 1.

McCarter, George W. C. "Confirmation Denied: The Senate Rejects John J. Carter." Thesis, Princeton University, 1971.

Meyer, Eugene. "From Laissez Faire with William Graham Sumner to the RFC." *Public Policy* 5 (1954): 5–27.

Miller, Adolph C. "Responsibility for Federal Reserve Policies." *American Economic Review* (25): 456.

Mitchell, Wesley C. "Are There Practical Steps Toward an Industrial Equilibrium?" *Bulletin of the Taylor Society* 15 (1930): 6.

Nash, George H. "The 'Great Enigma' and the 'Great Engineer': The Political Relationship of Calvin Coolidge and Herbert Hoover," in Nash, ed., *Reappraising the Right*, pp. 261–97.

Nash, Gerald D. "Herbert Hoover and the Origins of the RFC." *Mississippi Valley Historical Review* 46 (1959): 455–68.

Persons, Charles. "Census Reports on Unemployment." *Annals of the American Academy of Political and Social Science* 154 (1931): 12.

Pringle, Henry. "Hoover: An Enigma Easily Misunderstood." *World's Work* 56 (1928): 131.

———. "Profile: Chief Justice III." *The New Yorker*, 7/13/35.

Rhodes, Benjamin D. "Herbert Hoover and the War Debts, 1919–1933." *Prologue: The Journal of the National Archives* 6 (1974): 130–34.

Schlesinger, Arthur, Jr. "Hoover Makes a Comeback." *The New York Review of Books* 8 (March 3, 1979): 10.

Shideler, James H. "Hoover and the Federal Farm Board Project." *Mississippi Valley Historical Review* 42 (1956): 710.

Temin, Peter. "The Great Depression." National Bureau of Economic Research Historical Paper #62 (1994).

Villard, Oswald Garrison. "Presidential Possibilities: IV. Herbert C. Hoover." *The Nation* 126 (1928): 235.

Wigmore, Barry A. "Was the Bank Holiday of 1933 Caused by a Run on the Dollar?" *The Journal of Economic History* 47 (1987): 739–55.

Williams, William Appleman. "What This Country Needs." *The New York Review of Books* 15 (November 1970): 7–9.

Wilson, Joan Hoff. "Hoover's Agricultural Policies, 1921–1928." *Agricultural History* 51 (1977): 335–61.

INDEX

Page numbers in *italics* refer to illustrations. Page numbers beginning with 473 refer to endnotes.

ILLUSTRATION CREDITS

CARTOONS

All cartoons by Rollin Kirby. Images courtesy of the Estate of Rollin Kirby Post.

PHOTO INSERT

13. Library of Congress
14. Library of Congress
15. Library of Congress
16. Library of Congress
17. Herbert Hoover Presidential Library
18. Library of Congress
19. White House Collection
20. Herbert Hoover Presidential Library
21. Library of Congress
22. Library of Congress
23. Granger, NYC – All rights reserved
24. Library of Congress
25. Granger, NYC – All rights reserved
26. Library of Congress
27. Library of Congress
28. Granger, NYC – All rights reserved
29. Granger NYC – All rights reserved
30. Library of Congress
31. Library of Congress
32. Library of Congress
33. Library of Congress
34. Library of Congress
35. Library of Congress
36. Library of Congress
37. Library of Congress
38. Library of Congress
39. Herbert Hoover Presidential Library
40. Library of Congress
41. Library of Congress
42. Library of Congress
43. Library of Congress
44. Library of Congress
45. Library of Congress
46. Herbert Hoover Presidential Library
47. Library of Congress

ABOUT THE AUTHOR

CHARLES RAPPLEYE is an award-winning journalist, editor, and author. His previous book, *Sons of Providence: The Brown Brothers, the Slave Trade, and the American Revolution* won the 2006 George Washington Book Prize as the best book on the founding era published that year. He is also cofounder, with his wife, Tulsa Kinney, of *Artillery*, a magazine covering the world of contemporary art. Charles lives in Los Angeles.